EVERYMAN,
I WILL GO WITH THEE,
AND BE THY GUIDE,
IN THY MOST NEED
TO GO BY THY SIDE

DANTE ALIGHIERI

THE
DIVINE
COMEDY

TRANSLATED BY ALLEN MANDELBAUM

WITH AN INTRODUCTION
BY EUGENIO MONTALE
AND NOTES BY PETER ARMOUR

EVERYMAN'S LIBRARY
Alfred A. Knopf New York London Toronto
183

THIS IS A BORZOI BOOK
PUBLISHED BY ALFRED A. KNOPF

First included in Everyman's Library, 1908
This translation first published in Everyman's Library, 1995
Published by arrangement with Bantam Books, a division of
Bantam Doubleday Dell Publishing Group, Inc.

The Divine Comedy of Dante Alighieri: Inferno translated by Allen Mandelbaum.
English translation copyright © 1980 by Allen Mandelbaum.
The Divine Comedy of Dante Alighieri: Purgatorio translated by Allen Mandelbaum.
English translation copyright © 1982 by Allen Mandelbaum.
The Divine Comedy of Dante Alighieri: Paradiso translated by Allen Mandelbaum.
English translation copyright © 1984 by Allen Mandelbaum.

Introduction by Eugenio Montale first published as 'Dante,
Yesterday and Today'. Translation copyright © 1977, 1978, 1979,
1980, 1981, 1982 by Jonathan Galassi. From *The Second Life of Art:
Selected Essays of Eugenio Montale*, edited and translated by Jonathan
Galassi. Published by the Ecco Press.
Bibliography, Chronology and Notes copyright © 1995
by Everyman's Library
Typography by Peter B. Willberg
Twenty-sixth printing (US)

All rights reserved. Published in the United States by Alfred A. Knopf,
a division of Penguin Random House LLC, New York, and in Canada by
Penguin Random House Canada Limited, Toronto. Distributed by
Penguin Random House LLC, New York. Published in the United
Kingdom by Everyman's Library, 50 Albemarle Street, London
W1S 4BD and distributed by Penguin Random House UK,
20 Vauxhall Bridge Road, London SW1V 2SA.

www.randomhouse.com/everymans
www.everymanslibrary.co.uk

ISBN: 978-0-679-43313-2 (US)
978-1-85715-183-1 (UK)

A CIP catalogue reference for this book is available from the
British Library

Book design by Barbara de Wilde and Carol Devine Carson

Typeset in the UK by AccComputing, North Barrow, Somerset

Printed and bound in Germany by GGP Media GmbH, Pössneck

THE DIVINE COMEDY

THE DIVINE COMEDY OF DANTE ALIGHIERI

INFERNO

This translation of the INFERNO
*is inscribed to Elisa Jane Mandelbaum
and her generation:*
A RIVEDER LE STELLE

CONTENTS

The Divine Comedy of Dante Alighieri

Notes

The drawings by Sandro Botticelli
(c. 1445–1510) reproduced in this volume come
from a series produced in the late fifteenth
century for the artist's major patron, Lorenzo
di Pierfrancesco de' Medici. Though hard to
date the series exactly, it is certainly the case
that nineteen of the drawings were engraved
and printed as early as 1481. There are
ninety-two drawings in all of which forty-two
are here reproduced from the collections of the
Vatican and the Staatliche Museum, Berlin.
Previous owners of some of the drawings have
included Queen Christina of Sweden and
William Beckford.

INTRODUCTION

It seems to me that if Dante is a universal patrimony (beyond a certain level of necessary study) — and such he has become, even if he remarked more than once that he was speaking to few who were worthy of hearing him — then his voice can be heard today by everyone as it never was in other ages and as may never again be possible in the future, so that his message can reach the layman no less than the initiate, and in a way that is probably entirely new. After he was crowned with glory in his own lifetime, Dante's readership gradually declined up until the seventeenth century (his dark age), to dawn again with the advent of Romanticism and the simultaneous flowering of an entirely worldly philosophy which sees man as the master and even the creator of himself.

I am not unaware of the differences between these two movements, though I note their convergence. Romanticism looks to the ancient world for inspiration, not because it has renewed and emphasized its myths, but because it is dissatisfied with its own rationalist, enlightened age, and therefore it resolves into a poetic art. Materialism, which appears on the heels of Romanticism, not only accepts its own era but believes that it represents the highest phase in the total evolution of reason. The Gods are dead, even if they had to slake their thirst with human blood in the process, and the divine has come down to earth. Though they differ and are even opposed, these two movements both deserve to be called 'modern', and for different reasons both look to Dante. For the first, Dante is a distant precursor of Romanticism and as such deserves to be rediscovered; for the second, his work is a miraculous product of poetic imagination, but this imagination is not Dante's wisdom, it is only one step and not the last, the *som de l'escalina*, of a Spirit which has not yet become conscious of itself.

Poetry, they have told us, is not reason and only reason can understand it and do it justice, but in the way the strongest does justice to the weakest. It would be unjust to reduce the eighteenth- and nineteenth-century understanding of Dante to this dichotomy. In fact, the nineteenth century saw the birth and early growth – not without some antecedents in the mid-1800s – of research by those who hope to raise the veil which obscures Dante's great creation and fully penetrate the mysteries of his allegory. In the nineteenth century the esoteric Dante is born or reborn, the Dante who even as an historical person (the most absurd hypotheses come to mind) was supposed to have had two faces, one of which remained virtually unknown: the Dante who was a Knight Templar or who enrolled as a Franciscan but then left the order before taking his vows, and above all the Dante who was supposed to have spoken a sectarian tongue that is only decipherable today, and only to the slightest extent, by those who have exhausted themselves in long and deep study. It is easy to criticize this particular aspect of modern Dantology (which in fact has been contested and rejected by a more modern philological and historical approach), but one must admit that apart from its pathological aspects it has the merit at least of having affirmed one great truth: that Dante is *not* a modern poet (a fact also recognized by modern critics and philosophers), and that the instruments of modern culture are not ideally suited to understanding him (a fact denied by the modern philosophers who believe themselves specially authorized to raise the veil). And how? By the extension of modern reasoning.

My conviction, however – and I state it for what it is worth – is that Dante is not a modern in any of these respects: which does not prevent us from understanding him at least partially, nor from feeling that he is strangely close to us. But for this to happen we must also come to another conclusion: that we no longer live in a modern era, but in a new Middle Ages whose characteristics we cannot yet make out. Since this is a personal conviction of mine, I shall refrain from discussing the reasons for it here, where it serves only as an hypothesis. The era which lies before us does not allow for short-term predictions, and to speak of a new Middle Ages is to speak equivocally at best. If the future sees the ultimate triumph of technico-scientific reason, even accompanied by the weak correctives which sociology can devise, the new Middle Ages will be nothing but a new barbarousness. But in such a case it would be wrong to speak of them as 'medieval,' for the Middle Ages were not merely barbarous, nor were they bereft of science or devoid of art. To speak of a new Middle Ages, then, could seem a far from pessimistic hypothesis to the man who does not believe that the thread of reason can unwind *ad infinitum*; and yet an entirely new barbarousness is possible, a stifling and distortion of the very idea of civilization and culture.

But I see that I must return to my argument and ask myself who was Dante, and what he can represent (and this is my theme) for a writer today: I don't say for a poet today, for compared with Dante there are no poets. The literary historians have asked themselves who Dante was and they have succeeded in sketching the outlines – though with many lacunae – of his existence on earth. Shakespeare, more fortunate than he, has so far covered his tracks. It is well known that Sidney Lee, after demonstrating that many of the themes and subjects of Shakespeare's sonnets belong to the *topoi* or commonplaces of the Renaissance sonnet, reached the conclusion that in the sonnets Shakespeare did not 'unlock his heart' as Wordsworth believed but rather disclosed something very different. According to Lee, the only biographical inference which is deducible from them would be 'that at one time in his career Shakespeare ... disdained few weapons of flattery in an endeavour to monopolize the bountiful patronage of a young man of rank': the famous 'onlie begetter' whose identity is disputed.[1]

Whether or not such a conclusion is just, it certainly fails to reveal the great poet of the tragedies. Not that unanswered questions do not hang over his life and part of his work; but modern criticism has managed to set them aside. Only his poetry exists. These are the conclusions of the new 'close reading' which approaches poetry in a totally ahistorical manner. Dante's case is very different; his life and works are so closely associated that we shall never lose interest in the poet's biography. And there are many obscure points in Dante's life and work. The dates of his *rime estravaganti* [miscellaneous poems] have only been partially established; and not only poems, but also letters and until recently a treatise are disputed. Conversely, it may possibly be shown that he wrote the *Fiore*,[2] which until now has been attributed to Ser Durante. We do not know the year in which the first *cantica* of the *Commedia* was bugun, nor do we know (apart from its uncertain beginning) when the poet started the actual drafting of the *Inferno* and the *Purgatorio*. We know only that for something like twenty years (some say fifteen) he dedicated himself, while also writing other works, to the composition of the *poema sacro*. There is also the question whether the *Vita Nuova* is known to us in a later version, which was necessary in order to connect that book to the poem, passing over the compromising second treatise of the *Convivio*. And certainly the questions do not end here. All this demonstrates that a reading of the poem, and naturally of the *rime*, which entirely neglects Dante's life, his background and education, cannot take one very far. And yet an attempt to read him as one reads a modern poet, selecting the most vivid parts and leaving aside the rest – which is judged extraneous to the poetry – has given rise to strange complaints. De Sanctis seems to deplore the fact that too many medieval superstitions overshadowed the poet, impeding him from giving free rein to his characters. The conclusion of his analysis of the *Inferno* in his *History of Italian Literature* is well known: 'these great figures, there on their pedestals, rigid and epic like statues, await the artist who will take them by the hand and toss them into the tumult of life and make them dramatic beings. And that artist was not an Italian: he was Shakespeare.'

Dante, then, is more poet than artist. De Sanctis was very

careful to distinguish between poetry and art, but he was never very sure of his distinction. This gave rise to misunderstandings which have lasted up until today. The truth is that if there was ever an artist in the fullest sense of the word, that artist is certainly Dante. But what was art for this Dante about whom we know so little, the first Dante? It was an art of convention, of tradition, the *ars dictandi* common to him and to those whom we can consider as his correspondents (the *stilnovisti* were not a *tertulia* [conversation club] and their precursor Guinizelli[3] died when Dante was ten). Within the limits of the school, the problem was not originality, but fidelity to one's Dictator. It was an accepted convention inherited from the Provençal troubadours that the poet was dictated to. But the poets of the *Dolce Stil Nuovo* adhere more closely to the Provençal theme and enclose it in a more perfect canon. Their language is the vulgate, but purified and therefore sweet. Guittone[4] can no longer serve as a model, he is considered rough and coarse. Dante starts from Guinizelli but simplifies and strengthens his style; he takes even more from the second Guido [Cavalcanti],[5] and the *Vita Nuova* cannot be understood at all if one does not recognize the presence within it of themes, contrasts, and 'disruptions' from the poetry of his closest friend.

Nevertheless, there is also a new 'style' in Dante, and consciously so. This should not surprise us. Always, at all times, poets have spoken to poets, entering into a real or imaginary correspondence with them. The poets of the new school pose problems, raise questions, expect answers in their poems. Contini has said that 'the *Dolce Stile* is the school which with the greatest consciousness and good grace contains the idea of collaboration in a work of objective poetry'; and after analyzing the sonnet '*Guido i' vorrei*' in which he notes the theme of the flight to an unreal world, he adds: 'The absolute separation from the real which is converted into friendship, this is the definitive emotional element in the *stil nuovo*.' The *donna salutifera*, the lady who heals and redeems, which is the most evident theme of the entire school, is lost in a chorus of friends, and the poet, insofar as he is an empirical individual, recedes. Naturally, the collection of *rime estravaganti* cannot be read as a *canzoniere* [a collection of thematically and/or stylistically related poems], nor as a collection of lyrics in the modern sense of the term. Although there is a great variety of tone in the so-called *canzoniere* and there are signs of an even greater technical restlessness, the fact remains that we cannot read this collection without recognizing it as the first step in a great poetic undertaking which will become conscious of itself in the *Vita Nuova* and which will continue through the doctrinal works to the three *cantiche* which posterity called divine and which Dante defined at two points in the *Inferno* as the *Commedia*.

Beatrice makes her first appearance in the *rime*, and some of the most famous *canzoni* and sonnets are dedicated to her; but it is also possible that the *Donna gentile* whom we shall meet again in the *Vita Nuova* and in the *Convivio* and who has given Dante's hagiographers so much yarn to spin, appears along with her, in a group of poems composed between 1291 and 1293. And there are other ladies, other names which may be *senhals:*[6] the *pargoletta* [little girl] whom several readers identify with the *donna pietra* [lady of stone] and who in this group seems to have been the most dangerous for the poet, and later Fioretta, Violetta, Lisetta, Guido's lady, and still others, and finally the two *donne-schermo* [ladies who stand in for or screen us from Beatrice] whom we shall encounter in the *Vita Nuova*. And since the corpus of the *rime estravaganti* also included the poems inspired by the *donna pietra*, which are almost certainly later than the *Vita Nuova* and which indicate a familiarity with the *miglior fabbro*, Arnaut Daniel,[7] thus we see that the poems which will be fundamental in studying Dante's stylistic development and which will also influence Petrarch, as Ferdinando Neri has exhaustively shown, appear together in a rather unconvincing miscellany. It has been the fate of the *rime pietrose* to have been the source for 'black' nineteenth-century

Pre-Raphaelitism, which goes as far as Gustave Moreau in France; along with an entire school of English painting, the 'white' variety includes considerable poetry, most notably 'The Blessed Damozel' of Rossetti – a poet whom Eliot attacked. Perhaps *donna Pietra* really did exist; insofar as she is a stylistic experiment, however, she will never coincide with a real lady. But if Dante had a precocious intuition of Beatrice's ultimate significance (and the *Vita Nuova* leaves little doubt of it), I would say that both *donna Pietra* and the *donna gentile* would have had to be invented out of thin air if they did not exist; for it is impossible to imagine a process of salvation without the counterpart of error and sin.

After the research of Isidoro Del Lungo, which aroused great interest in 1891, one can no longer doubt the historic existence of a Bice or Beatrice whom Dante could certainly have known and loved, even without her having been aware of it. But what significance can this discovery have? There are two hypotheses: either the meaning which Dante attributed to her has no relation whatsoever to her actual existence; or one can believe, as Pietrobono came to, that the miraculous lady not only lived but was an actual miracle. For those who believe as I do that the miraculous may always be lying in wait at our doorstep, and that our very existence is a miracle, Pietrobono's thesis cannot be refuted by rational argument.

Dante's last years in Florence before his exile saw the composition of the *Vita Nuova*, which narrates in prose and verse the history of his love for Beatrice. We know about her that her short life and her death, as well as her apparition to the poet, took place under the sign of the number nine, and her own name appears nine times in the book. Fate has protected this mysterious girl and prevented many facts of her life from coming down to us: thus she can remain as the image of absolute perfection and the necessary intermediary in Dante's ascent to God. For a modern reader, the realization that the poet has mounted the tiger and can no longer get down begins with the *Vita Nuova*. At this point his destiny is definitively marked. One cannot speak of the *Vita Nuova* without forgetting that it would occupy an intermediate position in the *rime* if it were possible to place the poems in chronological order. Apart from the *rime pietrose*, the *estravaganti* include *canzoni* and *rime* in various forms which were written after the *Vita Nuova* and certainly after the period of inner darkness and distraction which Dante suffered following the death of Beatrice – a period of thirty months during which the poet immersed himself in the study of Boethius and Cicero and completed his reading of the classics (the *litterati poete*, i.e., the great Latin poets) and of Thomist philosophy.

The *Vita Nuova* thus comes at the time of an extraordinarily receptive and digressive poetic experience and gives a preliminary shape, already complete in itself, to what will become Beatrice's process of transhumanization. It does so in a form that would be called narrative today, if the term were appropriate, in which verse compositions alternate with others in prose, according to a scheme that Dante did not invent, narrating from beginning to end the history of Dante's love for the *donna salutifera*. The story, which is better called a vision, also dwells on details which seem realistic today but are included to give form to the conflict between human spirits and transcendent vocation that is defined here as never before in Dante. We shall never know whether the poet, who begins here to reveal himself as protagonist-author (which is apparent from the choice of poems included and even more from the prose commentary), also wished simultaneously both to hide and reveal the names of two ladies well known to his circle of friends in the episodes of the two *donne-schermo*. The problem is to know how deeply the playful spirit of mystification insinuated itself into the texture of his serious poetry. An analogous problem arises with the apparition of the *donna gentile*, who will be a rival here, if such she can be called, of Beatrice, and whom we shall later find transfigured as Philosophy in the *Convivio*, with no apparent reference to the significance which Beatrice assumed in the *Vita Nuova* and which she will take on again in the *poema sacro*. I shall pass over other episodes where the book steps out of its frame of mystical-intellectual adventure and becomes the material for a secular story. Perhaps this great technician of poetry invented these episodes to give greater emphasis to the last pages, with their blood-red color, which will become the color of the entire book in our memories. Certainly one does not err in seeing a distant prefiguration of the *Commedia* in the *Vita Nuova*, which is also indicated by the poet's desire to speak of her – of Beatrice – elsewhere. And the fact that the little book was composed with a great deal of rigor, excluding poems that would have been repetitious and others that would have been extraneous to its general design, only confirms one's sense of the work: that its structure is already determined, but is still in a certain sense preliminary. Perhaps readers who do not see a mystical experience in the *Vita Nuova* are correct. In it wordly experience is recreated as Christian experience; but it is not structured in steps as an ascent, but in a story set entirely within the wordly sphere (as D. De Robertis puts it).

But we have now arrived at the period of the poet's exile, which coincides with the beginning of the two treatises, the serving up of the high rhetoric of the *Convivio* and the *De vulgari eloquentia*, both of them left unfinished; and a similar parallelism will prevent us from creating a sort of psychological itinerary as we follow Dante. It was the opinion of Ferretti, confirmed by numerous internal and external indications, that the first seven *canti* of the *Inferno* were written before Dante's exile, hidden by the poet, and sent to him 'four and more years later', according to events referred to by Boccaccio.[8] If Parodi is correct in his conjecture identifying Henry of Luxembourg as the 515 [DVX] (in which number the Jesuits saw Luther and the Reformation), it seems possible to claim that the composition of the *Inferno* and the *Purgatorio* should be placed between 1307 and 1312: while it is almost certain that the *Paradiso* occupied the poet's last years. Several scholars assign the commencement of the poem to 1313. Others (including

Barbi) propose intermediate dates. The question of dating, however, is not merely academic, as is the problem of the *donne* to which I have alluded above. It involves affirming or denying the possibility that Dante submitted his work to revision and to later re-elaboration. Modern readers are undecided on this issue. On the one hand, we have the impression that many episodes in the *Commedia* were written at a single sitting, with little reworking, thus giving rise to the great prose that is hidden in the texture of the rhythm and rhyme, which, if it had been understood and brought to fulfillment, would have spared us centuries of curial, ceremonious prose. (An impossible hypothesis because the involuntary lofty prose of the poem did not prevent Dante from writing prose in Latin, which was also remarkable.) On the other hand, if we consider all the contributions which the rhetorical, philosophical, and theological culture of the Latin Middle Ages made to the poem and which make it virtually impossible to read its immense theophany in an ingenuous, virginal manner, we are stunned by Dante's encyclopedism and constrained to doubt our initial impression that he could have written at a gallop. That Dante knew and practised the *labor limae*,[9] as Foscolo believed, seems undeniable to those who know the *rime pietrose*, the doctrinal *canzoni*, and the passages in the *Commedia* where he returns to the play of harsh and difficult rhymes. And yet there is no doubt that the conception of his poem, its very structure, had not been predetermined from its first line, but rather modified and enriched itself as it developed, though at the cost of evident contradictions in the course of its elaboration and of its hypothetical revision. Along with Dante the scholar, the learned poet, whom after the studies of Curtius and Auerbach we can no longer ignore, there is Dante the man of letters discovering and exploiting the possibilities of his new language, the man who turns inward and enriches his thought, the exile who hopes to be allowed back into his own country and who later, disillusioned, intensifies the expression of his rancor. Because of this, internal proofs and references are not always decisive in aligning the life and the poetry. The *Convivio*, the treatise which was supposed to have fifteen parts, only four of which were completed, is the work of a theoretician who wants to demonstrate to himself and to his patrons what he had learned in his study of grammar and to derive as far as possible from it the limits of a poetry written in the vernacular. It includes commentaries on three doctrinal *canzoni*, and there are indications that lead us to conjecture which two or three additional *canzoni* would have gone along with the others to make up the fifteen parts the poet planned. His use of the vernacular, on the other hand, is illustrated in the *De vulgari eloquentia*, a treatise planned as a sort of encyclopedia of linguistic science. The *De vulgari* is written in Latin because Dante believed that only Latin, the universal and eternal language, could master an argument which involves the developments of human language up to the 'three-forked tongue' after the fall of man (the tower of Babel) had forever confused and corrupted the primitive language of men.

But my chosen subject, Dante's poetry for a writer of our time, forces me to leave behind his doctrinal works, the two I have mentioned, the *Monarchia*, which should be assigned a later date, and the *Quaestio de aqua e terra*, which is extraneous to my subject. Let me simply say that in respect to *gramatica* [Latin], to the *litterati poete*, Dante always had what today would be called an inferiority complex. He defended his choice to the last, but he made use of Latin as if to underline the exceptional nature of his undertaking; and if after him the vernacular won the field in the areas in which the *sermone umile* was called for, no other great early poet made use of it in approaching the subject matter of the sublime style, the epic.

And now I find myself face to face with the *Commedia*, which in certain respects could be considered an epic poem, but differs substantially in others. Indeed, the *Commedia* does have an heroic protagonist, and sings his adventures, not without the aid and presence of the Muses and the Sacred

Scriptures; but to do this Dante employs a style which is not always tragic but is in fact an extraordinary mixture of styles and manners which certainly do not conform to the dignity and uniformity of the epic style. In the dedicatory epistle of the *Paradiso* addressed to Cangrande della Scala, the Poet explains that his method is poetic, fictive, descriptive, digressive, transumptive, and at the same time definitive, divisive, probative, reprobative, and exemplative. (We can imagine Cangrande's surprise if Dante wished, as we assume, to overwhelm him.)

Furthermore, here too, as previously in the *Vita Nuova*, but with many further complications (and these are poetically the richest of all), the protagonist-hero, protagonist of an undertaking which had up to now been reserved for Aeneas and St Paul, is the writer himself, the Poet, accompanied of course by Virgil. Hence the poem's continual countersong, the possibility of reading it as a narrative which unfolds on only one level, and the temptation – even the necessity – to see it in filigree – not forgetting the significance of the journey beyond the tomb and into the nine heavens, or the reactions of the man either, his feelings and resentments, and the paradox of a double vision which on one side gives on the landscape of eternity and on the other describes earthly events which occupy a few years' time and one fixed place: the life of the city of Florence and what transpired there during the years of the poet's tenure of public office, and the part which the character Dante played in those events. And the fact that the journey into the beyond takes up at most seven days, though the canvas of the poem must extend to 100 cantos (the perfect number), is the reason for the extraordinary diversity of the figures who appear in the three *cantiche* and for the stroke of genius (as Curtius says) of introducing persons still living at the time of Dante's journey, friends and enemies of the poet, next to heroes or villains out of myth or ancient history or the history of the Church, with its blessed, its saints and angels (who are certainly not the last in the exalted hierarchies of the heavens and the general structure of the poem). What unifies material of this sort? First of all, the allegorical sense of the poem, which is extremely clear in its general outlines but vague in many particulars and thus not dense enough to hold together all the episodes of the narrative, in which the allegorical veil is often dropped and only the symbols are allowed to emerge, not all of them transparent. Here our insufficient familiarity with Dante the man and with his ideal library creates obstacles which would seem insurmountable. That Dante was at once a profound theologian and a particularly learned philosopher is not an opinion with which everyone will concur. That he was a mystic – he who was so rational and so taken with the events and concerns of life on earth – has itself been disputed. A great reader and a great observer, he is supposed to have derived his theological ideas not only from St Thomas but from other sources which he often misinterpreted. He even made use of the heretic Siger de Brabant and then reserved a place for him in Paradise. But even if this were true (and I am not competent to decide it), how useful to us can his allegory be? Yet there is a primary unity to the poem – which is sufficient because it has created countless readers of Dante all over the world who are happy with his literal meaning and pass over or are in fact ignorant of the allegorical and anagogical significance of various episodes – an undeniable unity afforded by the concreteness of Dante's images and similes and by the poet's capacity to make the abstract sensible, to make even the immaterial corporeal. It is a quality we encounter also in the English metaphysical poets of the seventeenth century, including mystics who did not read Dante or could not read him in his own language. So that one is permitted to question the opinion that questions the poet's mysticism.

But let us return for a moment to the possibility of sticking close to Dante's merely literal meaning and of reading him in the light of a poetic art that was not his. When I was young and had just begun my reading of Dante, a great Italian philosopher[10] admonished me to be attentive to the letter alone, and to ignore every obscure gloss. In Dante's poem, the philosopher said, there is a structure, a framework, which does not belong to the world of his poetry but has a practical function of its own. This framework is constructed with the materials which Dante found in his time and which permitted prefabricated structures: theological, physical, astronomical, prophetical, legendary materials which no longer resonate for us. These show us the medieval man in Dante, the man ensnared in prejudices which were not always different from the knowledge of his day, but which are certainly toneless, devoid of meaning for modern man. But over the inert scaffolding trails an efflorescence of bluebells or other vegetation which is Dante's poetry, poetry outside time as all true poetry is, and such that it makes us welcome Dante into the pantheon of the greatest poets if not precisely into the heaven of the great seers. This is a view which has found wide acceptance in Italy and will do so in the future as well: but it leaves unexplained the fact that the poem contains an enormous number of correspondences, of references which the literal arouses, while sending us back to its echoes, its mirror-games, its refractions; and that there is hardly a place in the poem – not one episode or line – which is not part of some web, which does not make its presence felt even when its totality appears to us to be more of an attempt at emulating divine wisdom than a universe in which we can dwell without asking for anything else. No poem was ever so crowded with figures, in the literal sense and in the sense of prefiguration or prophecy; in no other poem have actual history and the a-temporal history of myth or theology been so closely fused. Dante is really the end of the world or its anticipation: in historical terms, his prophecy is not of this world, and the symbols of the Cross and Eagle had already fallen into disuse before the *Commedia* was completed. But Dante was summing up, he was bringing an epoch to a close, and he needed many different threads.

Auerbach has shown us that the multiplicity of created things was necessary to Dante because no one of them *in una species* can achieve a total resemblance to God; adding that such multiplicity does not conflict with perfection and is not immobility but movement. He has also asked whether we can read Dante and accept forms and premises which are unrelated to us, as one submits to the rules of a game, and if perhaps there is the possibility in the *Commedia* of metamorphosis without loss of character. 'It seems to me,' Auerbach concluded, that the limit of the poem's power of transformation 'has almost been attained when philosophical commentators begin to praise its so-called poetic beauties as a value in themselves and reject the system, the doctrine, and indeed the entire subject matter as irrelevancies which if anything call for a certain indulgence.'[11] Certainly the limit is reached by philosophical commentators (though not by all of them, thank heaven), but it has proved unreachable for those endowed with a different sort of competence. In fact, anyone who has a feeling for poetry soon realizes that Dante never loses his concreteness even where his structure is least clothed by his so-called efflorescence. Thus one could say that his technical virtuosity reaches the height of its possibilities when plastic, visual representation is no longer sufficient. Look for example at the canto of Folchetto da Marsiglia [*Paradiso*, IX] in which the musical theme of the character is anticipated by a return of rough, difficult rhymes, which remain constant throughout the canto. There is nothing in effects like these to make us think of a formal game, of the skill of a Parnassian of the period. And here only a deaf man could try to distinguish between art and poetry. Dante doesn't write poems to make an impression according to the rules of a literary genre or school. The school is partly our invention, even if the poets of the *Dolce Stile* did in fact belong to an ideal community. Bonagiunta[12] can reprove the first Guido [Guinizelli] for having departed from the style of his predecessors, but Dante's verse would have been little different even if he had had other masters. His voice is entirely his own from the outset, even if he vulgarizes it in a noted *tenzone* or amuses himself in marginal exercises or agrees to write a few poems 'on commission', thus giving future scholiasts something to write about; and there is no doubt that after the allegorical *canzoni* of the *Convivio* the poet's life has been well documented, and it is not the life of a man who aims at rhapsodic lyrical splendors. And if not everyone will accept the hypothesis that the poem's possibilities of transformation (or rather our capacity of understanding it) are virtually exhausted, it will be necessary to see what other literary hypotheses can give us a satisfactory reading.

While the allegorists have kept on desperately marking time – though not in every case – a method of reading which is still acceptable is that suggested by a modern poet, T. S. Eliot, in his essay of 1929. The poet hardly knew Italian when he started reading the *Commedia*. And he found it an easy introduction. He thought that Dante's vernacular was still closely related to medieval Latin and that therefore a reading of the poem aided by a good literal version provided a first and sufficient approach. Further, in his view the allegorical process creates the necessary condition for the growth of that sensuous, bodily imagination which is peculiar to Dante. In short, the metaphorical meanings demand an extremely concrete literal meaning. Thus, from the still-massive figures of the *Inferno* (those figures which to the reluctant Goethe seemed to reek of the stable) to the more modeled figures of the *Purgatorio*, to the luminous, immaterial apparitions of the *Paradiso*, the evidence of the image may change in its colors and forms but remains forever accessible to our senses. The complexity of the embroidery never changes. Words like 'carpet' and 'tapestry' re-occur in this brief essay. In the *Paradiso* even abstraction is visible, and the most abstruse concept is inseparable from its form. And if in the carpet of the third *cantica* the plastic relief is less pronounced, this does not signify a lesser concreteness of imagination, but merely reveals the inexhaustible complexity of the meanings, and at the same time their ineffability. Our world no longer experiences visions, but Dante's world is still that of a visionary. Dante creates objects by naming them, and his syntheses are flashes of lightning. This is the source of his peculiar classicism, which is linked to a creationist and finalist philosophy. Through the narrow channel of the sensible, through the exaltation of forms, Dante negotiates the straits of scholastic thought; but let the experts discuss that. Eliot, however, doesn't mention it; instead he discusses the religious thought, or rather the faith, which the allegory supports. Is it necessary for the reader to share the 'Belief', the faith of the poet? For Eliot it is only necessary for belief to be understood as a function of the poetry which it explains. This is a suspension of judgment which belongs to aesthetic experience, and it is the typical mode of certain Anglo-Saxon culture to grant a certain autonomy to art while denying the distinctions between the aesthetic and the conceptual proposed by idealistic philosophy. No less interesting in Eliot is his rejection of that late falsification of the stilnovistic world which we have already mentioned: Pre-Raphaelitism. Yet even he, as we shall see before we finish, has felt the stilnovistic temptation from time to time.

I am not familiar with all the attempts which undoubtedly have been made to supersede Eliot's theory of Dante's sensible imagination. Setting aside the security that one who can explicate the allegory in its entirety must feel, the most interesting interpreters are those who see the *Commedia* as an immense web of correspondences and who try to follow every strand − or rather certain strands − back to its center. The undertaking cannot be accomplished without an analysis of Dante's metaphors and an examination of the consistency of the situations and characters with the particular psychological-moral and even topical states or levels through which the poet must pass. And, as metaphors are not as frequent in Dante as Eliot would have us believe, and in fact become increasingly rare as the poem progresses, we thus reach a limit or an insufficiency in Eliot's proposed reading of the *Commedia*. Irma Brandeis has devoted herself to an analytic study in the sense I have indicated – though certainly not an exhaustive one, for that would require the labors of a generation of scholars – in her book *The Ladder of Vision* (1961),[13] which is the most suggestive study I have read on the theme of the stairway which leads to God, and which is entrusted for good reason to the patronage of St Bonaventura. 'Since, then, one must climb Jacob's ladder before descending it, let us place the first step of the ascent far down, putting the whole of this sensible world before us as if it were a mirror through which we may pass to reach God.' Ladder or mirror, or mirrored ladder? I confess I don't know, for I have never read St Bonaventura, who sooner or later was certainly part of Dante's library. What is clear is that for this new interpreter Dante is an apprentice who must 'undergo an immense schooling', i.e., complete his initiation into an immense patrimony of universal culture. And the entire poem is didactic, in a certain sense, because his instruction – which was equated with philosophy – was considered an integral part of the poetic work. In this way alone shall we be able to understand passages in Dante like Statius's discourse on the generations of men [*Purgatorio*, XXV, 29–108], for Dante's point of view cannot coincide with the reader's, or rather the reader cannot expect that the poet is going another way, by other means.

And I would say that in general, once he has passed the stage where he is content with an ingenuous reading, the reader's interest grows rather than diminishes as the tangle of symbols becomes more problematic. This does not mean that one should ignore the literal meaning, which is primary in Dante. Precisely by basing her case on the literal, Miss Brandeis makes us feel how vivid and concrete the presence of Beatrice is throughout the poem and how the passages from the *Song of Songs*, St Matthew, and the sixth book of the *Aeneid* are structurally necessary in order to make possible – and, I would add, credible – the apparition of the lady dressed in the three colors of faith, hope, and charity who can arouse the poet who has not forgotten his earthly love, and make him say to Virgil: '*Men che dramma/di sangue me'è rimaso che non tremi:/ conosco i segui dell'antica fiamma*' (*Purgatorio* XXX, 46–48).[14]

It is time now for me to ask: what does the work of Dante mean for a poet today? Is there a lesson, an inheritance which we can take from him? If we consider the *Commedia* as a *summa* and an encyclopedia of wisdom, the temptation to repeat and emulate the prodigy will always be irresistible; but the conditions for success no longer exist.

Dante brought the Middle Ages to a close; after him – once the *Monarchia* was burned in 1329 at Bologna and the wind had changed – the Frezzis and Palmieris[15] will certainly not win our attention. The chivalric poems of the sixteenth century are great works of art, but their encyclopedism does not engage man's deepest thinking. I can also pass over Milton, who is already neoclassic. In the one poem Byron left us which we can still read, his *Don Juan*, the irony and the sense of pastiche produce octaves of a vaguely 'Italian' inspiration. I haven't forgotten *Faust*; but the Enlightenment esoterism that pervades it (to what extent I don't know) makes its protagonist and his pact with the Devil a story of greater interest to the anthropologist and the mythologist than the habitué of Dante's Middle Ages. Shelley and Novalis[16] were certainly among the Romantics who knew Dante, but were more musicians than architects. In our time, I would not think of Daübler's[17] *Das Nordlicht*, which is written in *terza rima* but brings down the light from the North; nor of *Ulysses*, which borrows themes from the *Odyssey* against the background of an infernal, almost symbolic Ireland. But Joyce doesn't look to Dante, nor does he have his monumental formal simplicity: reading him demands philological erudition, but the writer does not create language, he destroys it. On the other hand, the hundred and more *Cantos* of Ezra Pound give evidence of an attempt to 'put one's hand' to a total poem of man's historical experience – but Pound did not try to imitate the symmetry and the rigorous structure of the *Commedia*. The *Cantos* contain all that can be known about a disintegrating world, and in them the sense of the 'carpet' dominates that of a structure, of moving toward a center. (Though if it were true that the ultimate message of Dante's poem was the so-called donation of Constantine, then perhaps we could find a parallel in Pound's usury theme.) To sum up, it does not seem possible, in a world where encyclopedism can no longer create a universe but only an immense amassing of notions of a provisional character, to repeat Dante's itinerary in a highly structured form and with an inexhaustible wealth of both obvious and occult meanings. Even the illusion that a sensual imagination can give life in an acceptable manner to a Pre-Raphaelite tapestry is to be accepted with reservations. To convince ourselves of this, let us reread a few lines from Eliot's 'Ash Wednesday':

> Lady, three white leopards sat under a juniper-tree
> In the cool of the day, having fed to satiety
> On my legs my heart my liver and that which had been contained
> In the hollow round of my skull. And God said
> Shall these bones live? shall these
> Bones live? and that which had been contained
> In the bones (which were already dry) said chirping:
> Because of the goodness of this Lady
> And because of her loveliness, and because
> She honours the Virgin in meditation,
> We shine with brightness.

At moments like these we find ourselves face to face with the work of a poet, a great poet of our times: though if we had to choose, we should prefer the highly concentrated post-symbolist and quasi-cubist Inferno of *The Waste Land*. But it's useless to search for other examples: Dante cannot be repeated. He was considered practically incomprehensible and semi-barbarous a few decades after his death, when the rhetorical and religious invention of a poetry dictated by love had been forgotten. The greatest exemplar of poetic objectivism and rationalism, he remains foreign to our times, to a subjective and fundamentally irrational culture, which bases its meanings on facts and not on ideas. And it is precisely the reason for facts which eludes us today. A concentric poet, Dante cannot furnish models for a world which is progressively distancing itself from the center, and declares itself in perpetual expansion. For this reason the *Commedia* is and will remain the last miracle of world poetry. It was such because it was still possible then for an inspired man, or rather for a particular conjunction of stars in the sky of poetry, or must we consider it a miraculous event, beyond the humanly possible? Around Dante every opinion, indeed every suspicion, revolves. In opposition to those who claim that he really saw the *visibilia* in his poems (and they are few) are others who emphasize the mystificatory nature of his genius. To them, Dante would have been a man who invented himself as *poeta sacro* and at a certain moment, with the help of forces greater than himself, saw his invention become reality. That he was not a true mystic and that he lacked the total absorption in the divine which is characteristic of true mystics is suggested by the fact that the *Commedia* is not the last thing he wrote and that once he had finished the third *cantica*, he was obliged to come out of his labyrinth and rejoin his fellow men. But not for long; and an ageing Dante present at the creation of his controversial legend is unimaginable for us. Still, I can consider Singleton's affirmation that the *poema sacro* was dictated by God and that the poet was only his scribe with equanimity. But I can only cite secondhand and I wonder whether that eminent Dantist meant his judgment literally, or whether here one should recall the inspired and thus received character of all great poetry. But even in the first case I would not object, and I would have no evidence to contest the miraculous nature of the poem, just as I was not frightened by the miraculous character attributed to the historical Beatrice we had thought we could do without.

But I will stop here. That true poetry is always in the nature of a gift, and that it therefore presupposes the dignity of its recipient, is perhaps the greatest lesson Dante has left us. He is not the only one to have taught us this, but he is certainly the greatest of all. And if it is true that he wanted to be a poet and only a poet, the fact remains, almost inexplicable to our modern blindness, that the more distant from us his world becomes, the greater grows our desire to know him and to make him known to those who are blinder than ourselves.

Eugenio Montale

[Final address delivered 24 April, 1965, at the International Congress of Dante Studies held in Florence to mark the 700th anniversary of Dante's birth. Published in the *Atti del Congresso Internazionale di Studi danteschi*, Vol. II., Sansoni, Florence, 1966.]

NOTES

1. Sidney Lee, *A Life of William Shakespeare*, revised edition, Smith, Elder & Co., London, 1915, p. 230.

2. An allegorical poem of 232 sonnets written between 1280 and 1310 in imitation of the *Romance of the Rose*. Ser Durante is the possibly symbolic name (*durante* = persevering, constant) of the author of the *Fiore*. The poem has been attributed to Dante da Maiano, an imitator of the Provençal poets and poetic correspondent of Dante's, and also to Dante Alighieri himself.

3. Guido Guinizelli (1230/40–1276). Bolognese Ghibelline poet and forerunner of Dante, originator of the '*Dolce Stil Nuovo*' [sweet new style]. Originally a follower of Guittone d'Arezzo (see below).

4. Guittone d'Arezzo (1220–1294). Leading poet of the generation preceding Dante's, he wrote in the Provençal-influenced style of the Sicilian school.

5. (1255–1300). Florentine Guelph poet, leader of the *Stilnovisti*, friend of Dante.

6. *Senhal:* Provençal term related to the Italian word *segnale* [signal], used to refer to the fictitious name designating the person to whom the troubadour addressed his poem.

7. (1150–?) Provençal troubadour, inventor of the sestina and leading practitioner of the *trobar ric*, or rich style, which advocated intense condensation of style.

8. Giovanni Boccaccio (1313–1375). The great writer's works included the first biography of Dante, as well as a commentary on the *Inferno*, based on the lectures on Dante he began giving in Florence in 1373.

9. 'Revision'. See Horace, *Ars poetica*, line 291.

10. Croce.

11. Erich Auerbach, *Dante, Poet of the Secular World* [1929], tr. Ralph Manheim, University of Chicago Press, Chicago, 1961. The quotation on transformation appears on p. 159 of Auerbach's text.

12. Bonagiunta Orbicciani, also di Lucca. Thirteenth-century notary, leader of a school of poets influenced by the Sicilian school and Guittone d'Arezzo. Dante criticizes him in the *De vulgari eloquentia*, and he appears in *Purgatorio* XXV.

13. Brandeis, *The Ladder of Vision: A Study of Dante's Comedy* Doubleday and Co., Garden City, NY, 1961.

14. Less than a drop/of my blood remains which does not tremble:/I know the signs of the ancient flame.

15. Federico Frezzi (1346–1416?): Poet from Foligno, author of the allegorical poem *Il Quadriregio*, written in imitation of the *Divine Comedy*. Matteo Palmieri (1406–1475): Florentine politician and writer, author of *La città divina* (1461–1465), poem in tercets imitative of Dante.

16. Pen name of Friedrich Leopold von Hardenberg (1772–1801), great German romantic poet.

17. Theodor Daübler (1876–1934). Expressionist German poet born in Trieste and educated in Italy. His *Das Nordlicht* (1910) is a long religious allegory, showing the author's progress from agnosticism to mystical religion.

SELECT BIBLIOGRAPHY

General introductions to Dante's life, times, and works can be found in K. Vossler, *Medieval Culture: An Introduction to Dante and his Times*, Constable, London, 1929; U. Cosmo, *A Handbook to Dante Studies*, Blackwell, Oxford, 1950; M. Barbi, *Life of Dante*, University of California Press, Berkeley and Los Angeles, 1960; T. G. Bergin, *An Approach to Dante*, Bodley Head, London, 1965; U. Limentani, ed., *The Mind of Dante*, Cambridge University Press, Cambridge, 1965; R. J. Quinones, *Dante Alighieri*, Twayne, Boston, 1979; W. Anderson, *Dante theMaker*, Routledge and Kegan Paul, London, 1980; P. Dronke, *Dante and Medieval Latin Traditions*, Cambridge University Press, Cambridge, 1986; G. Di Scipio and A. Scaglione, eds., *The 'Divine Comedy' and the Encyclopedia of the Arts and Sciences*, Benjamins, Amsterdam, 1988; and R. Jacoff, ed., *The Cambridge Companion to Dante*, Cambridge University Press, Cambridge, 1993.

The *Comedy* is examined in the context of biblical exegesis, allegorical literature, and medieval vision literature by C. S. Singleton, *Dante's 'Commedia: Elements of Structure* and *Journey to Beatrice*, Harvard University Press, Cambridge, Ma., 1954 and 1958; A. C. Charity, *Events and their Afterlife: The Dialectics of Christian Typology in the Bible and Dante*, Cambridge University Press, Cambridge, 1966; R. Hollander, *Allegory in Dante's 'Commedia'*, Princeton University Press, Princeton, 1969; G. Mazzotta, *Dante, Poet of the Desert: History and Allegory in the 'Divine Comedy'*, Princeton University Press, Princeton, 1979; E. Gardiner, *Visions of Heaven and Hell before Dante*, Italica Press, New York, 1989; and A. Morgan, *Dante and the Medieval Other World*, Cambridge University Press, Cambridge, 1990.

Aspects of Dante's intellectual world are covered by E. G. Gardner, *Dante and the Mystics*, Dent, London, 1913; P. H. Wicksteed, *Dante and Aquinas*, Dent, London and Toronto, 1913; A. H. Gilbert, *Dante's Conception of Justice*, Duke University Press, Durham, NC, 1925; G. Holmes, *Dante* (Pastmasters), Oxford University Press, Oxford, 1980; P. Boyde, *Dante Philomythes and*

Philosopher: Man in the Cosmos and *Perception and Passion in Dante's 'Comedy'*, Cambridge University Press, Cambridge, 1981 and 1993; and S. Botterill, *Dante and the Mystical Tradition: Bernard of Clairvaux in the 'Commedia'*, Cambridge University Press, Cambridge, 1994; also of interest are M. Asin, *Islam and the 'Divine Comedy'*, translated and abridged by H. Sunderland, Murray, London, 1926; E. Gilson, *Dante and Philosophy*, Harper and Row, New York, 1963; and M. A. Orr, *Dante and the Early Astronomers*, Allen Wingate, London, 1956.

Dante's political doctrines in relation to the Church and the Empire are discussed in A. P. d'Entrèves, *Dante as a Political Thinker*, Clarendon Press, Oxford, 1952; C. T. Davis, *Dante and the Idea of Rome*, Clarendon Press, Oxford, 1957; and J. M. Ferrante, *The Political Vision of the 'Divine Comedy'*, Princeton University Press, Princeton, 1984; also useful here is C. T. Davis, *Dante's Italy and Other Essays*, University of Pennsylvania Press, Philadelphia, 1984.

Dante's place in the poetic tradition, his aesthetic ideas, and his works other than the *Comedy* are outlined and analysed in T. Barolini, *Dante's Poets: Textuality and Truth in the 'Comedy'*, Princeton University Press, Princeton, 1984; J. Took, *L'Etterno Piacer: Aesthetic Ideas in Dante* and *Dante: Lyric Poet and Philosopher*, Clarendon Press, Oxford, 1984 and 1990; R. Jacoff and J. T. Schnapp, eds., *The Poetry of Allusion: Virgil and Ovid in Dante's 'Commedia'*, Stanford University Press, Stanford, 1991; and M. U. Sowell, ed., *Dante and Ovid: Essays in Intertextuality*, Medieval and Renaissance Texts and Studies, Binghamton, NY, 1991.

Collections of essays and surveys of different aspects of the *Comedy* are provided by E. Moore, *Studies in Dante*, 4 vols., Clarendon Press, Oxford, 1896–1917, reprinted 1968–9); D. L. Sayers, *Introductory Papers on Dante* and *Further Papers on Dante*, Methuen, London, 1954 and 1957; E. Auerbach, *Dante Poet of the Secular World*, Chicago University Press, Chicago, 1961; J. Freccero, ed., *Dante: A Collection of Critical Essays*, Prentice-Hall, Englewood Cliffs, 1965; *Centenary Essays on Dante*, Oxford

University Press, Oxford, 1965; S. B. Chandler and J. A. Molinaro, eds., *The World of Dante*, University of Toronto Press, Toronto, 1966; D. Nolan, ed., *Dante Commentaries* and *Dante Soundings*, Irish Academic Press, Dublin, 1977 and 1981; K. Foster, *The Two Dantes and Other Studies*, Darton, Longman, and Todd, London, 1977; C. Grayson, ed., *The World of Dante: Essays on Dante and his Times*, Clarendon Press, Oxford, 1980; K. Foster and P. Boyde, eds., *Cambridge Readings in Dante's 'Comedy'*, Cambridge University Press, Cambridge, 1981; J. Ahern, 'Singing the Book: Orality in the Reception of Dante's *Comedy*', in *Annals of Scholarship*, vol. 2, no. 4, 1981, pp. 17–40; A. Bartlett Giamatti, *Dante in America: The First Two Centuries*, Medieval and Renaissance Texts and Studies, Binghamton, NY, 1983; U. Limentani, *Dante's 'Comedy': Introductory Readings of Selected Cantos*, Cambridge University Press, Cambridge, 1985; J. Freccero, *Dante: The Poetics of Conversion*, ed. R. Jacoff, Harvard University Press, Cambridge, Ma., 1986; H. Bloom, ed., *Dante*, Chelsea House, New York, 1986; E. Haywood, ed., *Dante Readings*, Irish Academic Press, Dublin, 1987; P. Armour, 'Dante's Virgil', in R. A. Cardwell and J. Hamilton, *Virgil in a Cultural Tradition: Essays to celebrate the Bimillenium*, Nottingham: University of Nottingham Monographs in the Humanities, IV, 1986, pp. 65–76; R. Kirkpatrick, *Dante: The 'Divine Comedy'* (Landmarks of World Literature), Cambridge University Press, Cambridge, 1987; P. Armour, 'Comedy and the Origins of Italian Theatre around the Time of Dante', in J. R. Dashwood and J. E. Everson, *Writers and Performers in Italian Drama from the Time of Dante to Pirandello: Essays in Honour of G. H. McWilliam*, Edwin Mellen Press, Lewiston, Queenston and Lampeter, 1991, pp. 1–31; G. Mazzotta, *Critical Essays on Dante*, Hall, Boston, 1991; T. Barolini, *The Undivine Comedy*, Princeton University Press, Princeton, 1992; J. C. Barnes and J. Petrie, eds., *Word and Drama in Dante*, Irish Academic Press, Dublin, 1993; and G. Mazzotta, *Dante's Vision and the Circle of Knowledge*, Princeton University Press, Princeton, 1993. On particular aspects of the *Inferno*, there is also A. K. Cassell, *Dante's Fearful Art of Justice*, University of

Toronto Press, Toronto, 1984; on the *Purgatorio*, B. Stambler, *Dante's Other World: The 'Purgatorio' as Guide to the 'Divine Comedy'*, New York University Press, New York, 1957; P. Armour, *The Door of Purgatory* and *Dante's Griffin and the History of the World*, Clarendon Press, Oxford, 1983 and 1989; and D. S. Cervigni, *Dante's Poetry of Dreams*, Olschki, Florence, 1986; and, on the *Paradiso*, E. G. Gardner, *Dante's Ten Heavens*, Constable, Westminster, and Scribner, New York, 1900; S. Ralphs, *Etterno Spiro*, Manchester University Press, Manchester, 1959; J. A. Mazzeo, *Structure and Thought in the 'Paradiso'*, Cornell University Press, Ithaca, 1958; R. Kirkpatrick, *Dante's 'Paradiso' and the Limitations of Modern Criticism*, Cambridge University Press, Cambridge, 1978; G. C. Di Scipio, *The Symbolic Rose in Dante's 'Paradiso'*, Longo, Ravenna, 1984; and J. T. Schnapp, *The Transfiguration of History at the Center of Dante's 'Paradiso'*, Princeton University Press, Princeton, 1986.

Commentaries and other annotated translations of the *Comedy* in English include those of D. L. Sayers and B. Reynolds, Penguin Books, Harmondsworth, 1949–62; J. D. Sinclair, Oxford University Press, Oxford, repr. 1971; C. S. Singleton, Princeton University Press, Princeton, 1970–75; M. Musa, Penguin Books, Harmondsworth, 1984–6; C. H. Sisson, ed. D. H. Higgins (World's Classics), Oxford University Press, Oxford, repr. 1993; A. Mandelbaum, Bantam Books, New York, 1982–6; and, of *Hell* only, S. Ellis, Chatto and Windus, London, 1993.

Reference works relating to Dante are E. H. Wilkins and others, *A Concordance to the 'Divine Comedy' of Dante Alighieri*, Belknap Press and Harvard University Press, Cambridge, Ma., 1965; and P. Toynbee (revised C. S. Singleton), *A Dictionary of Proper Names and Notable Matters in the Works of Dante*, Clarendon Press, Oxford, 1968. *The Dante Encyclopedia*, edited by R. Lansing, Garland, New York, is in the course of preparation for publication in 1996. Periodicals devoted to Dante include *Dante Studies* (the Dante Society of America) and *Lectura Dantis* (University of Virginia).

The *history of Dante criticism* is surveyed by M. Caesar, ed., *Dante: The Critical Heritage*, Routledge, London, 1989; his fame by W. P. Friederich, *Dante's Fame Abroad: 1350–1850*, Edizioni di Storia e Letteratura, Rome, 1950; and his presence in English literature by P. Toynbee, *Dante in English Literature from Chaucer to Cary*, 2 vols., Methuen, London, 1909; G. F. Cunningham, *The 'Divine Comedy' in English*, 2 vols., Oliver and Boyd, London and Edinburgh, 1965–6; S. Ellis, *Dante and English Poetry: Shelley to T. S. Eliot*, Cambridge University Press, Cambridge, 1983; S. Y. McDougal, *Dante among the Moderns*, University of North Carolina Press, Chapel Hill and London, 1985; and D. Wallace, 'Dante in English', in *The Cambridge Companion to Dante* (see above), pp. 237–58.

NOTE: The standard modern edition of the *Comedy* in Italian is *La Commedia secondo l'antica vulgata*, ed. G. Petrocchi, 4 vols., Mondadori, Milan, 1966–7; one-volume edition, Einaudi, Turin, 1975. Two excellent annotated editions are those by N. Sapegno, La Nuova Italia, Florence, 1969 and by U. Bosco and G. Reggio, Le Monnier, Florence, 1979. Useful works on background and criticism include N. Zingarelli, *La vita, i tempi e le opere di Dante*, Vallardi, Milan, 1931; B. Nardi, *Saggi di filosofia dantesca*, La Nuova Italia, Florence, 1967; A. Vallone, *Dante*, Vallardi, Milan, 1971; G. Padoan, *Introduzione a Dante*, Sansoni, Florence, 1975; R. Migliorini Fissi, *Dante*, La Nuova Italia, Florence, 1979; B. Andriani, *Aspetti della scienza in Dante*, Le Monnier, Florence, 1981; L. Battaglia Ricci, *Dante e la tradizione letteraria medievale*, Giardini, Pisa, 1983; and C. Paolazzi, *Dante e la 'Commedia' nel Trecento*, Vita e Pensiero, Milan, 1989. Readings of cantos are contained in G. Getto, ed., *Letture dantesche*, Sansoni, Florence, 1955–61, and *Lectura Dantis Scaligera*, Le Monnier, Florence, 1971; continuing series of works on Dante include *Nuove letture dantesche*, Le Monnier, Florence; *Letture classensi*, Longo, Ravenna; and the periodical *Studi danteschi* (of the Società Dantesca Italiana). An indispensable reference work is the *Enciclopedia dantesca*, Istituto della Enciclopedia Italiana, Rome, 1970–78.

CHRONOLOGY

DATE	AUTHOR'S LIFE	CULTURAL CONTEXT
1250		
1260		Birth of Dino Compagni, Florentine chronicler, and (*c.*) of German mystical writer, Meister Eckhart. Pulpit of Baptistry in Pisa by Nicola Pisano, sculptor. (*c.*) Thomas Aquinas: *Summa Theologica*.
1261		
1263		Death of Francesco Accursio, commentator on Roman Law. (*c.*) Balliol College, Oxford, founded.
1264		(*c.*) Death of Vincent of Beauvais, author of encyclopedic *Speculum Majus* ('Great Mirror').
1265	Born in Florence between 12 May and 12 June, son of Alighiero Alighieri (died *c.* 1283) and his first wife Bella (died *c.* 1273); baptized in S. Giovanni.	
1266		(*c.*) Birth of Giotto, painter. Roger Bacon: *Opus Maius*.
1268		
1269		
1270		Births of Cino of Pistoia, jurist and poet, and of Nicholas of Lyra, biblical scholar.
1271		Marco Polo begins his journey to the court of Kublai Khan.
1272		
1273		
1274		Deaths of Thomas Aquinas and Bonaventure, theologians, and of

HISTORICAL EVENTS

Death of Frederick II, Emperor and King of Sicily; the 'Primo Popolo' ('First Republic') in Florence (1250–60).
Defeat of Florence (battle of Montaperti); the Ghibellines take control of the city (1260–66).

Constantinople recaptured by the Greeks.

Simon de Montfort defeats Henry III at the battle of Lewes; 'Mise' of Lewes.

First English Parliament. Death of Simon de Montfort at battle of Evesham.

Charles I of Anjou becomes King of Sicily after the defeat of King Manfred and the Ghibellines (battle of Benevento). The Guelphs return to government in Florence (1266–7); the 'Second Popolo'.
Charles I of Anjou defeats Frederick II's grandson, Conradin (battle of Tagliacozzo). Paper manufacture in Italy (Fabriano).
Dedication of Westminster Abbey.
Death of Louis IX, King of France, during the Eighth Crusade. Succeeded by Philip III.

Prince Henry of Cornwall murdered by Guy de Montfort during Mass at the church of S. Silvestro, Viterbo.
Edward I succeeds Henry III as King of England. Introduces series of legal and administrative reforms (1275–90).
Election of Emperor Rudolph of Habsburg (died 1291).
Second Council of Lyons; the earliest official pronouncements on the doctrine of Purgatory.

DATE	AUTHOR'S LIFE	CULTURAL CONTEXT
1274 *cont.*		Robert de Sorbon, founder of the Paris Sorbonne. Nicola and Giovanni Pisano begin work on the Fontana Maggiore, Perugia.
1275		(*c.*) Births of Giovanni Villani, Florentine chronicler, and of Marsilio of Padua, political writer.
1276		(*c.*) Death of Guido Guinizzelli, poet of Bologna.
1277	Betrothed to Gemma Donati; later married (*c.* 1285?); children: Pietro, Jacopo, Antonia (later Sister Beatrice, a nun in Ravenna), and probably Giovanni.	
1280		Death of Albert of Cologne, theologian. (*c.*) Completion of Jean de Meun's continuation of the *Romance of the Rose*. (*c.*) Angel choir at Lincoln cathedral completed; Strasbourg cathedral completed.
1281		
1282		Restoro of Arezzo: *The Composition of the World*. (*c.*) Giovanni of Genoa (Joannes Balbus): *Prosodia* or *Catholicon*, an encyclopedic reference work for poets and scholars.
1283–90	'A ciascun' alma presa' ('To every captured heart'), a dream poem (1283); other love poems and occasional poetry; perhaps the exchange of comic sonnets with Forese Donati; doubtfully, the *Detto d'Amore* ('Poem of Love') and the *Fiore* ('Flower'), Italian versions of the *Romance of the Rose*.	
1283		(*c.*) Death of Siger of Brabant, philosopher.

Stephen Tempier, Bishop of Paris, condemns 219 prepositions as erroneous; two masters of art – Siger of Brabant and Boethius of Sweden – flee to Italy. In Milan, Visconti ascendancy begins following defeat of the ruling Della Torre family.

Accession of Sultan Osman I and beginning of Ottoman Empire. German Hanseatic League formed.
Rebellion of the Sicilian Vespers; the kingdom of Sicily divided into Naples (the Angevins) and Sicily (the Aragonese). Edward I crushes the revolt of Llewellyn in Wales.

DATE	AUTHOR'S LIFE	CULTURAL CONTEXT
1284		Foundation of Peterhouse, Cambridge. (*c.*) Birth of Sienese painter, Simone Martini.
1285		*On the Government of Princes*, by Egidio Romano (Giles of Rome), also author of *On the Power of the Pope*. (*c.*) Death of Rutebeuf, French *jongleur*. Birth of William of Ockham, philosopher. Duccio's *Rucellai Madonna* commissioned for church of S. Maria Novella.
1286		Death of William of Moerbeke, translator of Aristotle into Latin.
1288		Death of Adam de la Halle, French poet and musician, in Naples. (*c.*) Cimabue's frescoes at the upper church of S. Francisco, Assisi (to *c.* 1290).
1289	Perhaps participates in the battle of Campaldino, in which Guelph Florence defeated Ghibelline Arezzo; witnesses the surrender of the castle of Caprona, near Pisa.	
1290	Death of Beatrice (Bice Portinari, wife of Simone de' Bardi?) (8 June).	(*c.*) Completion of the west front of Rheims cathedral by Bernard de Soissons; Exeter cathedral begun.
1290–96	Poems after the death of Beatrice; the *Vita nuova* ('New Life') (1292–4); poems about another lady (later allegorized as Lady Philosophy); doctrinal poems; poems to the Donna Pietra (the 'Stone Lady').	
1291		
1292		

Death of Alfonso X (the Wise), King of Castile. Genoese fleet destroys the Pisans at Meloria.

Death of Charles I of Anjou, King of Naples; accession of Charles II. Death of Philip III of France; accession of Philip IV.

Election of Nicholas IV, first Franciscan pope.

Guelph ascendancy in Florence established following the battle of Campaldino, but the party soon splits into factions – the Black Guelphs, led by the Donati family, and White Guelphs, led by the Cerchi family.

Expulsion of Jews from England. Death of Eleanor of Castile, wife of Edward I, who raises twelve crosses to mark the stages of her funeral procession from Lincoln to Charing Cross.

Mamluks recapture Acre, the last crusader stronghold in Palestine; Castilian fleet crushes Moors at Marzamosa. Union of three cantons and the start of the Swiss Confederation.
Florentine workers storm the Bargello, seat of the *podestà* (chief magistrate). Giano della Bella's Ordinances of Justice (legal/constitutional reforms). All holders of public office obliged to be members of a guild and of the Guelph party: nobles were thus excluded from the *Signoria*.

DATE	AUTHOR'S LIFE	CULTURAL CONTEXT
1294		Deaths of Guittone of Arezzo, Tuscan poet; of Brunetto Latini, Florentine civic leader, writer of the encyclopedic *Books of the Treasure* in French and of poems in Italian; and of Roger Bacon, English philosopher and scientist.
1295	Enrolled in the Guild of Doctors and Apothecaries; recorded at meeting of the Council of the Twelve Major Guilds and Councillors (14 December) and at its combined meeting with the Council of a Hundred (5 June 1296).	(*c.*) Construction of church of S. Croce in Florence begins.
1296		Start of construction of Florence cathedral by Arnolfo di Cambio.
1297		Palazzo Pubblico at Siena (to 1310).
1298		Start of construction of the new Palace of Government (the Palazzo Vecchio) in Florence. Death of Jacopo of Varazzo, author of the *Golden Legend*. (*c.*) Marco Polo dictates the account of his travels to the Far East.
1300	Florentine ambassador to San Gimignano (May); Prior of Florence (15 June – 15 August); *Inferno* possibly begun.	Death of Guido Cavalcanti, Florentine poet. (*c.*) Birth of Guillaume de Machaut, French poet and musician. (*c.*) Richard of Haldingham paints the Hereford *Mappamundi*.
1301	Appointed to supervise some roadworks (28 April); recorded at Council meetings (14 April; 19 June; 13, 20, 28 September); sent as the White Guelph government's ambassador to Pope Boniface VIII (October); on the arrival of Charles of Valois, the Black Guelphs take control of Florence (1 November).	

Election (5 July) and abdication (13 December) of Pope Celestine V; accession of Pope Boniface VIII.

In England, Edward I summons the 'Model Parliament'. Scots repudiate Edward's nominee, John de Balliol, as king and form an alliance with France. Edward invades Scotland the following year. Matteo Visconti assumes power in Milan.

Boniface VIII excommunicates two Cardinals of the Colonna family and launches a campaign against their supporters. Venetian fleet defeated by Genoese at Curzola. Election of Emperor Albert of Habsburg.

Boniface VIII proclaims a centenary indulgence for pilgrims to Rome (22 February, with effect from 25 December 1299) (the first known Jubilee or Holy Year); his policies towards Florence lead to a skirmish in the city between his supporters (Black Guelphs) and his opponents (White Guelphs) (1 May). Office of *Gonfaloniere*, or standard-bearer of the people, introduced in Florence.

Charles of Valois arrives in Florence, ostensibly as Boniface VIII's peacemaker (1 November).

DATE	AUTHOR'S LIFE	CULTURAL CONTEXT
1302	Summoned back to Florence, with other White Guelphs, to answer charges of corruption while in office (27 January); sentenced to death in his absence for failing to answer the summons (10 March). Details of Dante's travels as an exile are unknown; he certainly spent some time in the Lunigiana (north-western Tuscany), Lucca, Verona (twice), and finally Ravenna.	(*c.*) Deaths of Cimabue and Arnolfo di Cambio. Giovanni Pisano's pulpit for Pisa cathedral (to *c.* 1310).
1303		Foundation of Studium Urbis in Rome.
1304	Breaks with the other White Guelph exiles and goes to Verona; 'Tre donne' ('Three ladies'), a poem about justice and his own unjust exile.	Birth of Petrarch, poet and scholar, the 'father' of Renaissance humanism.
1304–8	*De vulgari eloquentia*, an unfinished treatise in Latin on the vernacular language and poetry (1304–5); *Convivio* ('Banquet'), an unfinished work on philosophy in Italian; the *Inferno* begun or continued.	
1305		
1306	Acts as proxy for the Marquis Franceschino Malaspina in a peace settlement between the Malaspina family and the bishop of Luni (October).	Deaths of Jacopone of Todi, Franciscan mystical poet, and of John of Paris, author of *On Royal and Papal Power*. Pierre Dubois: *On the Recovery of the Holy Land*. (*c.*) Giotto's frescoes in the Arena, or Scrovegni chapel, Padua.
1307		
1308		Death of Duns Scotus, Scottish philosopher. Duccio's *Maestà* (to 1311) for the cathedral at Siena.
1309		

Boniface VIII issues the Bull *Unam sanctam,* claiming supreme universal power in both the spiritual and the temporal spheres.

Between 1302 and 1310, the Friescobaldi, Florentine merchants, having replaced the Riccardi of Lucca as chief financiers to the English Crown, are thought to have loaned £150,000 to Edwards I and II, in return gaining virtual control of revenues including the mint and customs. In 1310 the barons introduce legislation against foreign merchants and the Friescobaldi are forced to flee.

Boniface VIII captured at Anagni (7 September); his death (12 October).

White Guelph exiles fail to recapture Florence (20 July).

Election of Pope Clement V; he establishes the papal court and administration in Avignon (1309). The popes do not return to Rome until 1377.

Robert Bruce crowned king of Scotland.

Death of Edward I; succeeded by Edward II who marries Isabella of France. Piers Gaveston royal favourite.

Assassination of the Emperor Albert of Habsburg; election of Henry VII, count of Luxemburg, as Emperor.

Death of Charles II of Anjou, King of Naples; accession of King Robert.

1310–13	Epistles V–VII (1310–11) on the expedition of the Emperor Henry VII to Italy; Dante's sons excluded from an amnesty offered by the Florentine government to the White Guelph exiles (September 1311); the *Monarchia*, a treatise in Latin on the universal Roman Empire, perhaps begun (Books II–III).	(*c.*) York Minster chapter-house completed.
1311–12		
1312		Gerona cathedral begun.
1313		Births of Boccaccio, writer and scholar, and of Cola di Rienzo, restorer of the Roman Republic. (*c.*) Giotto's *Navicella* mosaic in St Peter's, Rome.
1314	Epistle XI to the Italian Cardinals during the conclave; Epistle XII to a Florentine friend, rejecting the conditions for a pardon; the *Inferno* known to be circulating.	Albertino Mussato: *Ecerinis* ('Ezzelino'), a Latin tragedy, written and performed in Padua. Death of Giovanni Pisano, sculptor.
1315	Further sentence of death and confiscation of property issued by the Florentine government against Dante and his sons as suspected Ghibellines (10 November).	Simone Martini's *Maestà* for the town hall of Siena.
1316	Probably in Verona in the service of Can Grande della Scala; at least some of the *Purgatorio* known to be circulating; first cantos of the *Paradiso* probably written by this time.	Death of Ramon Lull, Catalan scholar, poet, and mystic.
1317		Death of Jean de Joinville, writer of the *History of St Louis*. Simone Martini summoned by Robert of Anjou to paint *St Louis of Toulouse Crowning the King*.
1318–21	In Ravenna in the service of Guido Novello da Polenta;	

The Emperor Henry VII in Italy; crowned king of northern Italy in Milan (6 January 1311), crowned Emperor in Rome (29 June 1312); dies (24 August 1313). Pope Clement V reasserts papal rights over the Empire (1314).

Council of Vienne; Clement V suppresses the Order of the Knights Templar whose Grand Master is burnt at the stake (1314).
Execution of Piers Gaveston in England.
Republican constitution partially abrogated as Florence places herself under the protection of King Robert of Naples (to 1322).

Deaths of Pope Clement V and of Philip IV (the Fair), King of France. Two rival candidates elected Emperor in Germany – Lewis the Bavarian and Frederick of Habsburg. Robert Bruce defeats the English at Bannockburn. Ascendancy of Thomas of Lancaster in England.

The Guelphs defeated by the Ghibellines (battle of Montecatini).

Election of Pope John XXII.

John XXII's first condemnation of the Spiritual Franciscans.

DATE	AUTHOR'S LIFE	CULTURAL CONTEXT
1318–21 cont.	*Monarchia* completed; the *Eclogues*, two poems in Latin written to Giovanni del Virgilio, professor of classics at Bologna University (1319); continues work on the *Paradiso*; delivers the *Questio*, a public lecture on the earth's dry land and seas (20 January 1320).	
1318		(*c.*) Marchetto of Padua: *Lucidarium* and *Pomerium*, two treatises on music. Cambridge receives formal recognition from Pope John XXII as a *studium generale*.
1319		Death of Duccio, Sienese painter.
1321	Ambassador from Ravenna to Venice; is taken ill on his return and dies in Ravenna (14 September, or the evening before).	University of Florence founded. (*c.*) Giotto's frescoes in the Bardi and Peruzzi chapels in S. Croce, Florence.
1322		

John XXII sends army under Cardinal Bertrand du Poujet to defend papal
territories in Italy.
Edward II compelled to banish his current favourites, the Despensers; recalling
them the following year, he defeats the forces of Thomas of Lancaster, who is
executed.

Lewis the Bavarian gains decisive victory over Frederick of Habsburg at the
battle of Mühldorf, securing his position in Germany and making possible a
period of intervention in Italy. Death of Matteo Visconti; succeeded by his son
Galeazzo. Florence releases herself from protection of King Robert of Naples and
reverts to unmixed republican constitution.

CANTO I

The voyager-narrator astray by night in a dark forest. Morning and the sunlit hill. Three beasts that impede his ascent. The encounter with Virgil, who offers his guidance and an alternative path through two of the three realms the voyager must visit.

When I had journeyed half of our life's way,
I found myself within a shadowed forest,
for I had lost the path that does not stray.

Ah, it is hard to speak of what it was, 4
that savage forest, dense and difficult,
which even in recall renews my fear:

so bitter—death is hardly more severe! 7
But to retell the good discovered there,
I'll also tell the other things I saw.

I cannot clearly say how I had entered 10
the wood; I was so full of sleep just at
the point where I abandoned the true path.

But when I'd reached the bottom of a hill— 13
it rose along the boundary of the valley
that had harassed my heart with so much fear—

I looked on high and saw its shoulders clothed 16
already by the rays of that same planet
which serves to lead men straight along all roads.

At this my fear was somewhat quieted; 19
for through the night of sorrow I had spent,
the lake within my heart felt terror present.

And just as he who, with exhausted breath, 22
having escaped from sea to shore, turns back
to watch the dangerous waters he has quit,

so did my spirit, still a fugitive,
turn back to look intently at the pass 25

that never has let any man survive.

    I let my tired body rest awhile.   28
Moving again, I tried the lonely slope—
my firm foot always was the one below.

    And almost where the hillside starts to rise—   31
look there!—A leopard, very quick and lithe,
a leopard covered with a spotted hide.

    He did not disappear from sight, but stayed;   34
indeed, he so impeded my ascent
that I had often to turn back again.

    The time was the beginning of the morning;   37
the sun was rising now in fellowship
with the same stars that had escorted it

    when Divine Love first moved those things of beauty;   40
so that the hour and the gentle season
gave me good cause for hopefulness on seeing

    that beast before me with his speckled skin;   43
but hope was hardly able to prevent
the fear I felt when I beheld a lion.

    His head held high and ravenous with hunger—   46
even the air around him seemed to shudder—
this lion seemed to make his way against me.

    And then a she-wolf showed herself; she seemed   49
to carry every craving in her leanness;
she had already brought despair to many.

    The very sight of her so weighted me   52
with fearfulness that I abandoned hope
of ever climbing up that mountain slope.

    Even as he who glories while he gains   55
will, when the time has come to tally loss,
lament with every thought and turn despondent,

    so was I when I faced that restless beast,   58
which, even as she stalked me, step by step
had thrust me back to where the sun is speechless.

    While I retreated down to lower ground,   61
before my eyes there suddenly appeared
one who seemed faint because of the long silence.

Dante wanders into the Dark Wood.

When I saw him in that vast wilderness,   64
"Have pity on me," were the words I cried,
"Whatever you may be—a shade, a man."

He answered me: "Not man; I once was man.   67
Both of my parents came from Lombardy,
and both claimed Mantua as native city.

And I was born, though late, *sub Julio*,   70
and lived in Rome under the good Augustus—
the season of the false and lying gods.

I was a poet, and I sang the righteous   73
son of Anchises who had come from Troy
when flames destroyed the pride of Ilium.

But why do you return to wretchedness?   76
Why not climb up the mountain of delight,
the origin and cause of every joy?"

"And are you then that Virgil, you the fountain   79
that freely pours so rich a stream of speech?"
I answered him with shame upon my brow.

"O light and honor of all other poets,   82
may my long study and the intense love
that made me search your volume serve me now.

You are my master and my author, you—   85
the only one from whom my writing drew
the noble style for which I have been honored.

You see the beast that made me turn aside;   88
help me, o famous sage, to stand against her,
for she has made my blood and pulses shudder."

"It is another path that you must take,"   91
he answered when he saw my tearfulness,
"if you would leave this savage wilderness;

the beast that is the cause of your outcry   94
allows no man to pass along her track,
but blocks him even to the point of death;

her nature is so squalid, so malicious   97
that she can never sate her greedy will;
when she has fed, she's hungrier than ever.

She mates with many living souls and shall   100

yet mate with many more, until the Greyhound
arrives, inflicting painful death on her.

That Hound will never feed on land or pewter,   103
but find his fare in wisdom, love, and virtue;
his place of birth shall be between two felts.

He will restore low-lying Italy   106
for which the maid Camilla died of wounds,
and Nisus, Turnus, and Euryalus.

And he will hunt that beast through every city   109
until he thrusts her back again to Hell,
from which she was first sent above by envy.

Therefore, I think and judge it best for you   112
to follow me, and I shall guide you, taking
you from this place through an eternal place,

where you shall hear the howls of desperation   115
and see the ancient spirits in their pain,
as each of them laments his second death;

and you shall see those souls who are content   118
within the fire, for they hope to reach—
whenever that may be—the blessed people.

If you would then ascend as high as these,   121
a soul more worthy than I am will guide you;
I'll leave you in her care when I depart,

because that Emperor who reigns above,   124
since I have been rebellious to His law,
will not allow me entry to His city.

He governs everywhere, but rules from there;   127
there is His city, His high capital:
o happy those He chooses to be there!"

And I replied: "O poet—by that God   130
whom you had never come to know—I beg you,
that I may flee this evil and worse evils,

to lead me to the place of which you spoke,   133
that I may see the gateway of Saint Peter
and those whom you describe as sorrowful."

Then he set out, and I moved on behind him.   136

CANTO II

The following evening. Invocation to the Muses. The nar-
rator's questioning of his worthiness to visit the deathless
world. Virgil's comforting explanation that he has been sent
to help Dante by three Ladies of Heaven. The voyager
heartened. Their setting out.

The day was now departing; the dark air
released the living beings of the earth
from work and weariness; and I myself

alone prepared to undergo the battle   4
both of the journeying and of the pity,
which memory, mistaking not, shall show.

O Muses, o high genius, help me now;   7
o memory that set down what I saw,
here shall your excellence reveal itself!

I started: "Poet, you who are my guide,   10
see if the force in me is strong enough
before you let me face that rugged pass.

You say that he who fathered Sylvius,   13
while he was still corruptible, had journeyed
into the deathless world with his live body.

For, if the Enemy of every evil   16
was courteous to him, considering
all he would cause and who and what he was,

that does not seem incomprehensible,   19
since in the empyrean heaven he was chosen
to father honored Rome and her empire;

and if the truth be told, Rome and her realm   22
were destined to become the sacred place,
the seat of the successor of great Peter.

And through the journey you ascribe to him,   25

he came to learn of things that were to bring
his victory and, too, the papal mantle.

Later the Chosen Vessel traveled there,   28
to bring us back assurance of that faith
with which the way to our salvation starts.

But why should I go there? Who sanctions it?   31
For I am not Aeneas, am not Paul;
nor I nor others think myself so worthy.

Therefore, if I consent to start this journey,   34
I fear my venture may be wild and empty.
You're wise; you know far more than what I say."

And just as he who unwills what he wills   37
and shifts what he intends to seek new ends
so that he's drawn from what he had begun,

so was I in the midst of that dark land,   40
because, with all my thinking I annulled
the task I had so quickly undertaken.

"If I have understood what you have said,"   43
replied the shade of that great-hearted one,
"your soul has been assailed by cowardice,

which often weighs so heavily on a man—   46
distracting him from honorable trials—
as phantoms frighten beasts when shadows fall.

That you may be delivered from this fear,   49
I'll tell you why I came and what I heard
when I first felt compassion for your pain.

I was among those souls who are suspended;   52
a lady called to me, so blessed, so lovely
that I implored to serve at her command.

Her eyes surpassed the splendor of the star's;   55
and she began to speak to me—so gently
and softly—with angelic voice. She said:

'O spirit of the courteous Mantuan,   58
whose fame is still a presence in the world
and shall endure as long as the world lasts,

my friend, who has not been the friend of fortune,   61

is hindered in his path along that lonely
hillside; he has been turned aside by terror.

From all that I have heard of him in Heaven,   64
he is, I fear, already so astray
that I have come to help him much too late.

Go now; with your persuasive word, with all   67
that is required to see that he escapes,
bring help to him, that I may be consoled.

For I am Beatrice who send you on;   70
I come from where I most long to return;
Love prompted me, that Love which makes me speak.

When once again I stand before my Lord,   73
then I shall often let Him hear your praises.'
Now Beatrice was silent. I began:

'O Lady of virtue, the sole reason why   76
the human race surpasses all that lies
beneath the heaven with the smallest spheres,

so welcome is your wish, that even if   79
it were already done, it would seem tardy;
all you need do is let me know your will.

But tell me why you have not been more prudent— 82
descending to this center, moving from
that spacious place where you long to return?'

'Because you want to fathom things so deeply,   85
I now shall tell you promptly,' she replied,
'why I am not afraid to enter here.

One ought to be afraid of nothing other   88
than things possessed of power to do us harm,
but things innocuous need not be feared.

God, in His graciousness, has made me so   91
that this, your misery, cannot touch me;
I can withstand the fires flaming here.

In Heaven there's a gentle lady—one   94
who weeps for the distress toward which I send you,
so that stern judgement up above is shattered.

And it was she who called upon Lucia,   97

requesting of her: "Now your faithful one
has need of you, and I commend him to you."

Lucia, enemy of every cruelty,   100
arose and made her way to where I was,
sitting beside the venerable Rachel.

She said: "You, Beatrice, true praise of God,   103
why have you not helped him who loved you so
that—for your sake—he's left the vulgar crowd?

Do you not hear the anguish in his cry?   106
Do you not see the death he wars against
upon that river ruthless as the sea?"

No one within this world has ever been   109
so quick to seek his good or flee his harm
as I—when she had finished speaking thus—

to come below, down from my blessed station;   112
I trusted in your honest utterance,
which honors you and those who've listened to you.'

When she had finished with her words to me,   115
she turned aside her gleaming, tearful eyes,
which only made me hurry all the more.

And, just as she had wished, I came to you: 118
I snatched you from the path of the fierce beast
that barred the shortest way up the fair mountain.

What is it then? Why, why do you resist?   121
Why does your heart host so much cowardice?
Where are your daring and your openness

as long as there are three such blessed women   124
concerned for you within the court of Heaven
and my words promise you so great a good?"

As little flowers, which the chill of night   127
has bent and huddled, when the white sun strikes,
grow straight and open fully on their stems,

so did I, too, with my exhausted force;   130
and such warm daring rushed into my heart
that I—as one who has been freed—began:

"O she, compassionate, who has helped me!   133

And you who, courteous, obeyed so quickly
the true words that she had addressed to you!

    You, with your words, have so disposed my heart   136
to longing for this journey—I return
to what I was at first prepared to do.

    Now go; a single will fills both of us: 139
you are my guide, my governor, my master."
These were my words to him; when he advanced,

    I entered on the steep and savage path.   142

CANTO III

*The inscription above the Gate of Hell. The Ante-Inferno,
where the shades of those who lived without praise and without
blame now intermingle with the neutral angels. He who made
the great refusal. The River Acheron. Charon. Dante's loss
of his senses as the earth trembles.*

THROUGH ME THE WAY INTO THE SUFFERING CITY,
THROUGH ME THE WAY TO THE ETERNAL PAIN,
THROUGH ME THE WAY THAT RUNS AMONG THE LOST.

JUSTICE URGED ON MY HIGH ARTIFICER;   4
MY MAKER WAS DIVINE AUTHORITY,
THE HIGHEST WISDOM, AND THE PRIMAL LOVE.

BEFORE ME NOTHING BUT ETERNAL THINGS   7
WERE MADE, AND I ENDURE ETERNALLY.
ABANDON EVERY HOPE, WHO ENTER HERE.

These words—their aspect was obscure—I read   10
inscribed above a gateway, and I said:
"Master, their meaning is difficult for me."

And he to me, as one who comprehends: 13
"Here one must leave behind all hesitation;
here every cowardice must meet its death.

For we have reached the place of which I spoke,   16
where you will see the miserable people,
those who have lost the good of the intellect."

And when, with gladness in his face, he placed   19
his hand upon my own, to comfort me,
he drew me in among the hidden things.

Here sighs and lamentations and loud cries   22
were echoing across the starless air,
so that, as soon as I set out, I wept.

Strange utterances, horrible pronouncements,   25

accents of anger, words of suffering,
and voices shrill and faint, and beating hands—

all went to make a tumult that will whirl   28
forever through that turbid, timeless air,
like sand that eddies when a whirlwind swirls.

And I—my head oppressed by horror—said: 31
"Master, what is it that I hear? Who are
those people so defeated by their pain?"

And he to me: "This miserable way   34
is taken by the sorry souls of those
who lived without disgrace and without praise.

They now commingle with the coward angels,   37
the company of those who were not rebels
nor faithful to their God, but stood apart.

The heavens, that their beauty not be lessened,   40
have cast them out, nor will deep Hell receive them—
even the wicked cannot glory in them."

And I: "What is it, master, that oppresses   43
these souls, compelling them to wail so loud?"
He answered: "I shall tell you in few words.

Those who are here can place no hope in death,   46
and their blind life is so abject that they
are envious of every other fate.

The world will let no fame of theirs endure;   49
both justice and compassion must disdain them;
let us not talk of them, but look and pass."

And I, looking more closely, saw a banner   52
that, as it wheeled about, raced on—so quick
that any respite seemed unsuited to it.

Behind that banner trailed so long a file   55
of people—I should never have believed
that death could have unmade so many souls.

After I had identified a few,   58
I saw and recognized the shade of him
who made, through cowardice, the great refusal.

At once I understood with certainty: 61
this company contained the cowardly,

hateful to God and to His enemies.

These wretched ones, who never were alive,   64
went naked and were stung again, again
by horseflies and by wasps that circled them.

The insects streaked their faces with their blood,   67
which, mingled with their tears, fell at their feet,
where it was gathered up by sickening worms.

And then, looking beyond them, I could see   70
a crowd along the bank of a great river;
at which I said: "Allow me now to know

who are these people—master—and what law   73
has made them seem so eager for the crossing,
as I can see despite the feeble light."

And he to me: "When we have stopped along   76
the melancholy shore of Acheron,
then all these matters will be plain to you."

At that, with eyes ashamed, downcast, and fearing   79
that what I said had given him offense,
I did not speak until we reached the river.

And here, advancing toward us, in a boat,   82
an aged man—his hair was white with years—
was shouting: "Woe to you, corrupted souls!

Forget your hope of ever seeing Heaven: 85
I come to lead you to the other shore,
to the eternal dark, to fire and frost.

And you approaching there, you living soul,   88
keep well away from these—they are the dead."
But when he saw I made no move to go,

he said: "Another way and other harbors—   91
not here—will bring you passage to your shore:
a lighter craft will have to carry you."

My guide then: "Charon, don't torment yourself: 94
our passage has been willed above, where One
can do what He has willed; and ask no more."

Now silence fell upon the wooly cheeks   97
of Charon, pilot of the livid marsh,
whose eyes were ringed about with wheels of flame.

But all those spirits, naked and exhausted,   100
had lost their color, and they gnashed their teeth
as soon as they heard Charon's cruel words;

they execrated God and their own parents   103
and humankind, and then the place and time
of their conception's seed and of their birth.

Then they forgathered, huddled in one throng,   106
weeping aloud along that wretched shore
which waits for all who have no fear of God.

The demon Charon, with his eyes like embers,   109
by signaling to them, has all embark;
his oar strikes anyone who stretches out.

As, in the autumn, leaves detach themselves,   112
first one and then the other, till the bough
sees all its fallen garments on the ground,

similarly, the evil seed of Adam   115
descended from the shoreline one by one,
when signaled, as a falcon—called—will come.

So do they move across the darkened waters;   118
even before they reach the farther shore,
new ranks already gather on this bank.

"My son," the gracious master said to me,   121
"those who have died beneath the wrath of God,
all these assemble here from every country;

and they are eager for the river crossing   124
because celestial justice spurs them on,
so that their fear is turned into desire.

No good soul ever takes its passage here;   127
therefore, if Charon has complained of you,
by now you can be sure what his words mean."

And after this was said, the darkened plain   130
quaked so tremendously—the memory
of terror then, bathes me in sweat again.

A whirlwind burst out of the tear-drenched earth,   133
a wind that crackled with a bloodred light,
a light that overcame all of my senses;

and like a man whom sleep has seized, I fell.   136

CANTO IV

Dante's awakening to the First Circle, or Limbo, inhabited by those who were worthy but lived before Christianity and/or without baptism. The welcoming of Virgil and Dante by Homer, Horace, Ovid, Lucan. The catalogue of other great-hearted spirits in the noble castle of Limbo.

The heavy sleep within my head was smashed
by an enormous thunderclap, so that
I started up as one whom force awakens;

I stood erect and turned my rested eyes   4
from side to side, and I stared steadily
to learn what place it was surrounding me.

In truth I found myself upon the brink   7
of an abyss, the melancholy valley
containing thundering, unending wailings.

That valley, dark and deep and filled with mist,   10
is such that, though I gazed into its pit,
I was unable to discern a thing.

"Let us descend into the blind world now,"   13
the poet, who was deathly pale, began;
"I shall go first and you will follow me."

But I, who'd seen the change in his complexion,   16
said: "How shall I go on if you are frightened,
you who have always helped dispel my doubts?"

And he to me: "The anguish of the people   19
whose place is here below, has touched my face
with the compassion you mistake for fear.

Let us go on, the way that waits is long."   22
So he set out, and so he had me enter
on that first circle girdling the abyss.

Here, for as much as hearing could discover,   25

there was no outcry louder than the sighs
that caused the everlasting air to tremble.

The sighs arose from sorrow without torments,   28
out of the crowds—the many multitudes—
of infants and of women and of men.

The kindly master said: "Do you not ask   31
who are these spirits whom you see before you?
I'd have you know, before you go ahead,

they did not sin; and yet, though they have merits,   34
that's not enough, because they lacked baptism,
the portal of the faith that you embrace.

And if they lived before Christianity,   37
they did not worship God in fitting ways;
and of such spirits I myself am one.

For these defects, and for no other evil,   40
we now are lost and punished just with this:
we have no hope and yet we live in longing."

Great sorrow seized my heart on hearing him,   43
for I had seen some estimable men
among the souls suspended in that limbo.

"Tell me, my master, tell me, lord," I then   46
began because I wanted to be certain
of that belief which vanquishes all errors,

"did any ever go—by his own merit   49
or others'—from this place toward blessedness?"
And he, who understood my covert speech,

replied: "I was new-entered on this state   52
when I beheld a Great Lord enter here;
the crown he wore, a sign of victory.

He carried off the shade of our first father,   55
of his son Abel, and the shade of Noah,
of Moses, the obedient legislator,

of father Abraham, David the king,   58
of Israel, his father, and his sons,
and Rachel, she for whom he worked so long,

and many others—and He made them blessed;   61

and I should have you know that, before them,
there were no human souls that had been saved."

We did not stay our steps although he spoke;   64
we still continued onward through the wood—
the wood, I say, where many spirits thronged.

Our path had not gone far beyond the point   67
where I had slept, when I beheld a fire
win out against a hemisphere of shadows.

We still were at a little distance from it,   70
but not so far I could not see in part
that honorable men possessed that place.

"O you who honor art and science both,   73
who are these souls whose dignity has kept
their way of being, separate from the rest?"

And he to me: "The honor of their name,   76
which echoes up above within your life,
gains Heaven's grace, and that advances them."

Meanwhile there was a voice that I could hear: 79
"Pay honor to the estimable poet;
his shadow, which had left us, now returns."

After that voice was done, when there was silence,   82
I saw four giant shades approaching us;
in aspect, they were neither sad nor joyous.

My kindly master then began by saying: 85
"Look well at him who holds that sword in hand,
who moves before the other three as lord.

That shade is Homer, the consummate poet;   88
the other one is Horace, satirist;
the third is Ovid, and the last is Lucan.

Because each of these spirits shares with me   91
the name called out before by the lone voice,
they welcome me—and doing that, do well."

And so I saw that splendid school assembled,   94
led by the lord of song incomparable,
who like an eagle soars above the rest.

Soon after they had talked a while together,   97

they turned to me, saluting cordially;
and having witnessed this, my master smiled;
and even greater honor then was mine,   100
for they invited me to join their ranks—
I was the sixth among such intellects.

So did we move along and toward the light,   103
talking of things about which silence here
is just as seemly as our speech was there.

We reached the base of an exalted castle,   106
encircled seven times by towering walls,
defended all around by a fair stream.

We forded this as if upon hard ground;   109
I entered seven portals with these sages;
we reached a meadow of green flowering plants.

The people here had eyes both grave and slow;   112
their features carried great authority;
they spoke infrequently, with gentle voices.

We drew aside to one part of the meadow,   115
an open place both high and filled with light,
and we could see all those who were assembled.

Facing me there, on the enameled green,   118
great-hearted souls were shown to me and I
still glory in my having witnessed them.

I saw Electra with her many comrades,   121
among whom I knew Hector and Aeneas,
and Caesar, in his armor, falcon-eyed.

I saw Camilla and Penthesilea   124
and, on the other side, saw King Latinus,
who sat beside Lavinia, his daughter.

I saw that Brutus who drove Tarquin out,   127
Lucretia, Julia, Marcia, and Cornelia,
and, solitary, set apart, Saladin.

When I had raised my eyes a little higher,   130
I saw the master of the men who know,
seated in philosophic family.

There all look up to him, all do him honor: 133

there I beheld both Socrates and Plato,
closest to him, in front of all the rest;

Democritus, who ascribes the world to chance,   136
Diogenes, Empedocles, and Zeno,
and Thales, Anaxagoras, Heraclitus;

I saw the good collector of medicinals,   139
I mean Dioscorides; and I saw Orpheus,
and Tully, Linus, moral Seneca;

and Euclid the geometer, and Ptolemy,   142
Hippocrates and Galen, Avicenna,
Averroës, of the great Commentary.

I cannot here describe them all in full;   145
my ample theme impels me onward so:
what's told is often less than the event.

The company of six divides in two;   148
my knowing guide leads me another way,
beyond the quiet, into trembling air.

And I have reached a part where no thing gleams.   151

CANTO V

*The Second Circle, where the Lustful are forever buffeted by
violent storm. Minos. The catalogue of carnal sinners.
Francesca da Rimini and her brother-in-law, Paolo Mala-
testa. Francesca's tale of their love and death, at which Dante
faints.*

So I descended from the first enclosure
down to the second circle, that which girdles
less space but grief more great, that goads to weeping.

There dreadful Minos stands, gnashing his teeth: 4
examining the sins of those who enter,
he judges and assigns as his tail twines.

I mean that when the spirit born to evil   7
appears before him, it confesses all;
and he, the connoisseur of sin, can tell

the depth in Hell appropriate to it;   10
as many times as Minos wraps his tail
around himself, that marks the sinner's level.

Always there is a crowd that stands before him: 13
each soul in turn advances toward that judgment;
they speak and hear, then they are cast below.

Arresting his extraordinary task,   16
Minos, as soon as he had seen me, said:
"O you who reach this house of suffering,

be careful how you enter, whom you trust;   19
the gate is wide, but do not be deceived!"
To which my guide replied: "But why protest?

Do not attempt to block his fated path: 22
our passage has been willed above, where One
can do what He has willed; and ask no more."

Now notes of desperation have begun   25

to overtake my hearing; now I come
where mighty lamentation beats against me.

I reached a place where every light is muted,   28
which bellows like the sea beneath a tempest,
when it is battered by opposing winds.

The hellish hurricane, which never rests,   31
drives on the spirits with its violence:
wheeling and pounding, it harasses them.

When they come up against the ruined slope,   34
then there are cries and wailing and lament,
and there they curse the force of the divine.

I learned that those who undergo this torment   37
are damned because they sinned within the flesh,
subjecting reason to the rule of lust.

And as, in the cold season, starlings' wings   40
bear them along in broad and crowded ranks,
so does that blast bear on the guilty spirits:

now here, now there, now down, now up, it drives them. 43
There is no hope that ever comforts them—
no hope for rest and none for lesser pain.

And just as cranes in flight will chant their lays,   46
arraying their long file across the air,
so did the shades I saw approaching, borne

by that assailing wind, lament and moan;   49
so that I asked him: "Master, who are those
who suffer punishment in this dark air?"

"The first of those about whose history   52
you want to know," my master then told me,
"once ruled as empress over many nations.

Her vice of lust became so customary   55
that she made license licit in her laws
to free her from the scandal she had caused.

She is Semíramis, of whom we read   58
that she was Ninus' wife and his successor:
she held the land the Sultan now commands.

That other spirit killed herself for love,   61

and she betrayed the ashes of Sychaeus;
the wanton Cleopatra follows next.

See Helen, for whose sake so many years   64
of evil had to pass; see great Achilles,
who finally met love—in his last battle.

See Paris, Tristan . . ."—and he pointed out   67
and named to me more than a thousand shades
departed from our life because of love.

No sooner had I heard my teacher name   70
the ancient ladies and the knights, than pity
seized me, and I was like a man astray.

My first words: "Poet, I should willingly   73
speak with those two who go together there
and seem so lightly carried by the wind."

And he to me: "You'll see when they draw closer 76
to us, and then you may appeal to them
by that love which impels them. They will come."

No sooner had the wind bent them toward us   79
than I urged on my voice: "O battered souls,
if One does not forbid it, speak with us."

Even as doves when summoned by desire,   82
borne forward by their will, move through the air
with wings uplifted, still, to their sweet nest,

those spirits left the ranks where Dido suffers, 85
approaching us through the malignant air;
so powerful had been my loving cry.

"O living being, gracious and benign,   88
who through the darkened air have come to visit
our souls that stained the world with blood, if He

who rules the universe were friend to us,   91
then we should pray to Him to give you peace,
for you have pitied our atrocious state.

Whatever pleases you to hear and speak   94
will please us, too, to hear and speak with you,
now while the wind is silent, in this place.

The land where I was born lies on that shore   97

to which the Po together with the waters
that follow it descends to final rest.

Love, that can quickly seize the gentle heart,   100
took hold of him because of the fair body
taken from me—how that was done still wounds me.

Love, that releases no beloved from loving,   103
took hold of me so strongly through his beauty
that, as you see, it has not left me yet.

Love led the two of us unto one death.   106
Caïna waits for him who took our life."
These words were borne across from them to us.

When I had listened to those injured souls,   109
I bent my head and held it low until
the poet asked of me: "What are you thinking?"

When I replied, my words began: "Alas,   112
how many gentle thoughts, how deep a longing,
had led them to the agonizing pass!"

Then I addressed my speech again to them,   115
and I began: "Francesca, your afflictions
move me to tears of sorrow and of pity.

But tell me, in the time of gentle sighs,   118
with what and in what way did Love allow you
to recognize your still uncertain longings?"

And she to me: "There is no greater sorrow   121
than thinking back upon a happy time
in misery—and this your teacher knows.

Yet if you long so much to understand   124
the first root of our love, then I shall tell
my tale to you as one who weeps and speaks.

One day, to pass the time away, we read   127
of Lancelot—how love had overcome him.
We were alone, and we suspected nothing.

And time and time again that reading led   130
our eyes to meet, and made our faces pale,
and yet one point alone, defeated us.

When we had read how the desired smile   133

was kissed by one who was so true a lover,
this one, who never shall be parted from me,
    while all his body trembled, kissed my mouth.   136
A Gallehault indeed, that book and he
who wrote it, too; that day we read no more."
    And while one spirit said these words to me,   139
the other wept, so that—because of pity
I fainted, as if I had met my death.
    And then I fell as a dead body falls.   142

CANTO VI

Dante's awakening to the Third Circle, where the Gluttonous, supine, are flailed by cold and filthy rain and tormented by Cerberus. Ciacco and his prophecy concerning Florence. The state of the damned after the Resurrection.

Upon my mind's reviving—it had closed
on hearing the lament of those two kindred,
since sorrow had confounded me completely—

I see new sufferings, new sufferers   4
surrounding me on every side, wherever
I move or turn about or set my eyes.

I am in the third circle, filled with cold,   7
unending, heavy, and accursèd rain;
its measure and its kind are never changed.

Gross hailstones, water gray with filth, and snow   10
come streaking down across the shadowed air;
the earth, as it receives that shower, stinks.

Over the souls of those submerged beneath   13
that mess, is an outlandish, vicious beast,
his three throats barking, doglike: Cerberus.

His eyes are bloodred; greasy, black, his beard;   16
his belly bulges, and his hands are claws;
his talons tear and flay and rend the shades.

That downpour makes the sinners howl like dogs;   19
they use one of their sides to screen the other—
those miserable wretches turn and turn.

When Cerberus, the great worm, noticed us,   22
he opened wide his mouths, showed us his fangs;
there was no part of him that did not twitch.

My guide opened his hands to their full span,   25
plucked up some earth, and with his fists filled full

he hurled it straight into those famished jaws.

Just as a dog that barks with greedy hunger 28
will then fall quiet when he gnaws his food,
intent and straining hard to cram it in,

so were the filthy faces of the demon 31
Cerberus transformed—after he'd stunned
the spirits so, they wished that they were deaf.

We walked across the shades on whom there thuds 34
that heavy rain, and set our soles upon
their empty images that seem like persons.

And all those spirits lay upon the ground, 37
except for one who sat erect as soon
as he caught sight of us in front of him.

"O you who are conducted through this Hell," 40
he said to me, "recall me, if you can;
for you, before I was unmade, were made."

And I to him: "It is perhaps your anguish 43
that snatches you out of my memory,
so that it seems that I have never seen you.

But tell me who you are, you who are set 46
in such a dismal place, such punishment—
if other pains are more, none's more disgusting."

And he to me: "Your city—one so full 49
of envy that its sack has always spilled—
that city held me in the sunlit life.

The name you citizens gave me was Ciacco; 52
and for the damning sin of gluttony,
as you can see, I languish in the rain.

And I, a wretched soul, am not alone, 55
for all of these have this same penalty
for this same sin." And he said nothing more.

I answered him: "Ciacco, your suffering 58
so weighs on me that I am forced to weep;
but tell me, if you know, what end awaits

the citizens of that divided city; 61
is any just man there? Tell me the reason

why it has been assailed by so much schism."

And he to me: "After long controversy,   64
they'll come to blood; the party of the woods
will chase the other out with much offense.

But then, within three suns, they too must fall;   67
at which the other party will prevail,
using the power of one who tacks his sails.

This party will hold high its head for long   70
and heap great weights upon its enemies,
however much they weep indignantly.

Two men are just, but no one listens to them.   73
Three sparks that set on fire every heart
are envy, pride, and avariciousness."

With this, his words, inciting tears, were done;   76
and I to him: "I would learn more from you;
I ask you for a gift of further speech:

Tegghiaio, Farinata, men so worthy,   79
Arrigo, Mosca, Jacopo Rusticucci,
and all the rest whose minds bent toward the good,

do tell me where they are and let me meet them;   82
for my great longing drives me on to learn
if Heaven sweetens or Hell poisons them."

And he: "They are among the blackest souls;   85
a different sin has dragged them to the bottom;
if you descend so low, there you can see them.

But when you have returned to the sweet world,   88
I pray, recall me to men's memory:
I say no more to you, answer no more."

Then his straight gaze grew twisted and awry;   91
he looked at me awhile, then bent his head;
he fell as low as all his blind companions.

And my guide said to me: "He'll rise no more   94
until the blast of the angelic trumpet
upon the coming of the hostile Judge:

each one shall see his sorry tomb again   97
and once again take on his flesh and form,

and hear what shall resound eternally."

So did we pass across that squalid mixture   100
of shadows and of rain, our steps slowed down,
talking awhile about the life to come.

At which I said: "And after the great sentence—   103
o master—will these torments grow, or else
be less, or will they be just as intense?"

And he to me: "Remember now your science,   106
which says that when a thing has more perfection,
so much the greater is its pain or pleasure.

Though these accursed sinners never shall   109
attain the true perfection, yet they can
expect to be more perfect then than now."

We took the circling way traced by that road;   112
we said much more than I can here recount;
we reached the point that marks the downward slope.

Here we found Plutus, the great enemy.   115

CANTO VII

The demon Plutus. The Fourth Circle, where the Avaricious and the Prodigal, in opposite directions, roll weights in semicircles. Fortune and her ways. Descent into the Fifth Circle: the Wrathful and the Sullen, the former besmirched by the muddy Styx, the latter immersed in it.

"Pape Satàn, pape Satàn aleppe!"
so Plutus, with his grating voice, began.
The gentle sage, aware of everything,

said reassuringly, "Don't let your fear   4
defeat you; for whatever power he has,
he cannot stop our climbing down this crag."

Then he turned back to Plutus' swollen face   7
and said to him: "Be quiet, cursed wolf!
Let your vindictiveness feed on yourself.

His is no random journey to the deep: 10
it has been willed on high, where Michael took
revenge upon the arrogant rebellion."

As sails inflated by the wind collapse,   13
entangled in a heap, when the mast cracks,
so that ferocious beast fell to the ground.

Thus we made our way down to the fourth ditch,   16
to take in more of that despondent shore
where all the universe's ill is stored.

Justice of God! Who has amassed as many   19
strange tortures and travails as I have seen?
Why do we let our guilt consume us so?

Even as waves that break above Charybdis,   22
each shattering the other when they meet,
so must the spirits here dance their round dance.

Here, more than elsewhere, I saw multitudes   25

to every side of me; their howls were loud
while, wheeling weights, they used their chests to push.

They struck against each other; at that point,   28
each turned around and, wheeling back those weights,
cried out: "Why do you hoard?" "Why do you squander?"

So did they move around the sorry circle   31
from left and right to the opposing point;
again, again they cried their chant of scorn;

and so, when each of them had changed positions,   34
he circled halfway back to his next joust.
And I, who felt my heart almost pierced through,

requested: "Master, show me now what shades   37
are these and tell me if they all were clerics—
those tonsured ones who circle on our left."

And he to me: "All these, to left and right   40
were so squint-eyed of mind in the first life—
no spending that they did was done with measure.

Their voices bark this out with clarity   43
when they have reached the two points of the circle
where their opposing guilts divide their ranks.

These to the left—their heads bereft of hair—   46
were clergymen, and popes and cardinals,
within whom avarice works its excess."

And I to him: "Master, among this kind   49
I certainly might hope to recognize
some who have been bespattered by these crimes."

And he to me: "That thought of yours is empty: 52
the undiscerning life that made them filthy
now renders them unrecognizable.

For all eternity they'll come to blows: 55
these here will rise up from their sepulchers
with fists clenched tight; and these, with hair cropped close.

Ill giving and ill keeping have robbed both   58
of the fair world and set them to this fracas—
what that is like, my words need not embellish.

Now you can see, my son, how brief's the sport   61

of all those goods that are in Fortune's care,
for which the tribe of men contend and brawl;

for all the gold that is or ever was   64
beneath the moon could never offer rest
to even one of these exhausted spirits."

"Master," I asked of him, "now tell me too: 67
this Fortune whom you've touched upon just now—
what's she, who clutches so all the world's goods?"

And he to me: "O unenlightened creatures,   70
how deep—the ignorance that hampers you!
I want you to digest my word on this.

Who made the heavens and who gave them guides   73
was He whose wisdom transcends everything;
that every part may shine unto the other,

He had the light apportioned equally;   76
similarly, for worldly splendors, He
ordained a general minister and guide

to shift, from time to time, those empty goods   79
from nation unto nation, clan to clan,
in ways that human reason can't prevent;

just so, one people rules, one languishes,   82
obeying the decision she has given,
which, like a serpent in the grass, is hidden.

Your knowledge cannot stand against her force;   85
for she foresees and judges and maintains
her kingdom as the other gods do theirs.

The changes that she brings are without respite: 88
it is necessity that makes her swift;
and for this reason, men change state so often.

She is the one so frequently maligned   91
even by those who should give praise to her—
they blame her wrongfully with words of scorn.

But she is blessed and does not hear these things;   94
for with the other primal beings, happy,
she turns her sphere and glories in her bliss.

But now let us descend to greater sorrow,   97

for every star that rose when I first moved
is setting now; we cannot stay too long."

We crossed the circle to the other shore;   100
we reached a foaming watercourse that spills
into a trench formed by its overflow.

That stream was even darker than deep purple;   103
and we, together with those shadowed waves,
moved downward and along a strange pathway.

When it has reached the foot of those malign   106
gray slopes, that melancholy stream descends,
forming a swamp that bears the name of Styx.

And I, who was intent on watching it,   109
could make out muddied people in that slime,
all naked and their faces furious.

These struck each other not with hands alone,   112
but with their heads and chests and with their feet,
and tore each other piecemeal with their teeth.

The kindly master told me: "Son, now see   115
the souls of those whom anger has defeated;
and I should also have you know for certain

that underneath the water there are souls   118
who sigh and make this plain of water bubble,
as your eye, looking anywhere, can tell.

Wedged in the slime, they say: 'We had been sullen   121
in the sweet air that's gladdened by the sun;
we bore the mist of sluggishness in us;

now we are bitter in the blackened mud.'   124
This hymn they have to gurgle in their gullets,
because they cannot speak it in full words."

And so, between the dry shore and the swamp,   127
we circled much of that disgusting pond,
our eyes upon the swallowers of slime.

We came at last upon a tower's base.   130

CANTO VIII

*Still the Fifth Circle: the Wrathful and the Sullen. The tall
tower. Phlegyas and the crossing of the Styx. Filippo Argenti
and Dante's fury. Approach to Dis, the lower part of Hell:
its moat, its walls, its gate. The demons, fallen angels, and
their obstruction of the poets' entry into Dis.*

I say, continuing, that long before
we two had reached the foot of that tall tower,
our eyes had risen upward, toward its summit,

because of two small flames that flickered there,   4
while still another flame returned their signal,
so far off it was scarcely visible.

And I turned toward the sea of all good sense;   7
I said: "What does this mean? And what reply
comes from that other fire? Who kindled it?"

And he to me: "Above the filthy waters   10
you can already see what waits for us,
if it's not hid by vapors from the marsh."

Bowstring has not thrust from itself an arrow   13
that ever rushed as swiftly through the air
as did the little bark that at that moment

I saw as it skimmed toward us on the water,   16
a solitary boatman at its helm.
I heard him howl: "Now you are caught, foul soul!"

"O Phlegyas, Phlegyas, such a shout is useless   19
this time," my master said; "we're yours no longer
than it will take to cross the muddy sluice."

And just as one who hears some great deception   22
was done to him, and then resents it, so
was Phlegyas when he had to store his anger.

My guide preceded me into the boat.   25

Once he was in, he had me follow him;
there seemed to be no weight until I boarded.

No sooner were my guide and I embarked   28
than off that ancient prow went, cutting water
more deeply than it does when bearing others.

And while we steered across the stagnant channel, 31
before me stood a sinner thick with mud,
saying: "Who are you, come before your time?"

And I to him: "I've come, but I don't stay;   34
but who are you, who have become so ugly?"
He answered: "You can see—I'm one who weeps."

And I to him: "In weeping and in grieving,   37
accursèd spirit, may you long remain;
though you're disguised by filth, I know your name."

Then he stretched both his hands out toward the boat, 40
at which my master quickly shoved him back,
saying: "Be off there with the other dogs!"

That done, he threw his arms around my neck   43
and kissed my face and said: "Indignant soul,
blessèd is she who bore you in her womb!

When in the world, he was presumptuous;   46
there is no good to gild his memory,
and so his shade down here is hot with fury.

How many up above now count themselves   49
great kings, who'll wallow here like pigs in slime,
leaving behind foul memories of their crimes!"

And I: "O master, I am very eager   52
to see that spirit soused within this broth
before we've made our way across the lake."

And he to me: "Before the other shore   55
comes into view, you shall be satisfied;
to gratify so fine a wish is right."

Soon after I had heard these words, I saw   58
the muddy sinners so dismember him
that even now I praise and thank God for it.

They all were shouting: "At Filippo Argenti!"   61

At this, the Florentine, gone wild with spleen,
began to turn his teeth against himself.

We left him there; I tell no more of him.   64
But in my ears so loud a wailing pounded
that I lean forward, all intent to see.

The kindly master said: "My son, the city   67
that bears the name of Dis is drawing near,
with its grave citizens, its great battalions."

I said: "I can already see distinctly—   70
master—the mosques that gleam within the valley,
as crimson as if they had just been drawn

out of the fire." He told me: "The eternal   73
flame burning there appears to make them red,
as you can see, within this lower Hell."

So we arrived inside the deep-cut trenches   76
that are the moats of this despondent land:
the ramparts seemed to me to be of iron.

But not before we'd ranged in a wide circuit   79
did we approach a place where that shrill pilot
shouted: "Get out; the entrance way is here."

About the gates I saw more than a thousand—   82
who once had rained from Heaven—and they cried
in anger: "Who is this who, without death,

can journey through the kingdom of the dead?"   85
And my wise master made a sign that said
he wanted to speak secretly to them.

Then they suppressed—somewhat—their great disdain 88
and said: "You come alone; let him be gone—
for he was reckless, entering this realm.

Let him return alone on his mad road—   91
or try to, if he can, since you, his guide
across so dark a land, you are to stay."

Consider, reader, my dismay before   94
the sound of those abominable words:
returning here seemed so impossible.

"O my dear guide, who more than seven times   97

has given back to me my confidence
and snatched me from deep danger that had menaced,
    do not desert me when I'm so undone;   100
and if they will not let us pass beyond,
let us retrace our steps together, quickly."
    These were my words; the lord who'd led me there   103
replied: "Forget your fear, no one can hinder
our passage; One so great has granted it.
    But you wait here for me, and feed and comfort   106
your tired spirit with good hope, for I
will not abandon you in this low world."
    So he goes on his way; that gentle father   109
has left me there to wait and hesitate,
for *yes* and *no* contend within my head.
    I could not hear what he was telling them;   112
but he had not been long with them when each
ran back into the city, scrambling fast.
    And these, our adversaries, slammed the gates   115
in my lord's face; and he remained outside,
then, with slow steps, turned back again to me.
    His eyes turned to the ground, his brows deprived   118
of every confidence, he said with sighs:
"See who has kept me from the house of sorrow!"
    To me he added: "You—though I am vexed—   121
must not be daunted; I shall win this contest,
whoever tries—within—to block our way.
    This insolence of theirs is nothing new;   124
they used it once before and at a gate
less secret—it is still without its bolts—
    the place where you made out the fatal text;   127
and now, already well within that gate,
across the circles—and alone—descends
    the one who will unlock this realm for us."   130

CANTO IX

*The gate of Dis. Dante's fear. The three Furies, invoking
Medusa. Virgil's warning to Dante lest he look at Gorgon,
Medusa's head. A heavenly messenger. The flight of the demons.
Entry into Dis, where Virgil and Dante reach the Sixth
Circle and its Arch-Heretics, entombed in red-hot sepulchers.*

    The color cowardice displayed in me
when I saw that my guide was driven back,
made him more quickly mask his own new pallor.

    He stood alert, like an attentive listener,   4
because his eye could hardly journey far
across the black air and the heavy fog.

    "We have to win this battle," he began,   7
"if not . . . But one so great had offered aid.
That help seems slow in coming: I must wait!"

    But I saw well enough how he had covered   10
his first words with the words that followed after—
so different from what he had said before;

    nevertheless, his speech made me afraid,   13
because I drew out from his broken phrase
a meaning worse—perhaps—than he'd intended.

    "Does anyone from the first circle, one   16
whose only punishment is crippled hope,
ever descend so deep in this sad hollow?"

    That was my question. And he answered so: 19
"It is quite rare for one of us to go
along the way that I have taken now.

    But I, in truth, have been here once before: 22
that savage witch Erichtho, she who called
the shades back to their bodies, summoned me.

    My flesh had not been long stripped off when she   25

had me descend through all the rings of Hell,
to draw a spirit back from Judas' circle.

That is the deepest and the darkest place, 28
the farthest from the heaven that girds all:
so rest assured, I know the pathway well.

This swamp that breeds and breathes the giant stench 31
surrounds the city of the sorrowing,
which now we cannot enter without anger."

And he said more, but I cannot remember 34
because my eyes had wholly taken me
to that high tower with the glowing summit

where, at one single point, there suddenly 37
stood three infernal Furies flecked with blood,
who had the limbs of women and their ways

but wore, as girdles, snakes of deepest green; 40
small serpents and horned vipers formed their hairs,
and these were used to bind their bestial temples.

And he, who knew these handmaids well—they served 43
the Queen of never-ending lamentation—
said: "Look at the ferocious Erinyes!

That is Megaera on the left, and she 46
who weeps upon the right, that is Allecto;
Tisiphone's between them." He was done.

Each Fury tore her breast with taloned nails; 49
each, with her palms, beat on herself and wailed
so loud that I, in fear, drew near the poet.

"Just let Medusa come; then we shall turn 52
him into stone," they all cried, looking down;
"we should have punished Theseus' assault."

"Turn round and keep your eyes shut fast, for should 55
the Gorgon show herself and you behold her,
never again would you return above,"

my master said; and he himself turned me 58
around and, not content with just my hands,
used his as well to cover up my eyes.

O you possessed of sturdy intellects, 61

observe the teaching that is hidden here
beneath the veil of verses so obscure.

And now, across the turbid waves, there passed   64
a reboantic fracas—horrid sound,
enough to make both of the shorelines quake:

a sound not other than a wind's when, wild   67
because it must contend with warmer currents,
it strikes against the forest without let,

shattering, beating down, bearing off branches,   70
as it moves proudly, clouds of dust before it,
and puts to flight both animals and shepherds.

He freed my eyes and said: "Now let your optic   73
nerve turn directly toward that ancient foam,
there where the mist is thickest and most acrid."

As frogs confronted by their enemy,   76
the snake, will scatter underwater till
each hunches in a heap along the bottom,

so did the thousand ruined souls I saw   79
take flight before a figure crossing Styx
who walked as if on land and with dry soles.

He thrust away the thick air from his face,   82
waving his left hand frequently before him;
that seemed the only task that wearied him.

I knew well he was Heaven's messenger,   85
and I turned toward my master; and he made
a sign that I be still and bow before him.

How full of high disdain he seemed to me!   88
He came up to the gate, and with a wand,
he opened it, for there was no resistance.

"O you cast out of Heaven, hated crowd,"   91
were his first words upon that horrid threshold,
"why do you harbor this presumptuousness?

Why are you so reluctant to endure   94
that Will whose aim can never be cut short,
and which so often added to your hurts?

What good is it to thrust against the fates?   97

Your Cerberus, if you remember well,
for that, had both his throat and chin stripped clean."

At that he turned and took the filthy road,   100
and did not speak to us, but had the look
of one who is obsessed by other cares

than those that press and gnaw at those before him;   103
and we moved forward, on into the city,
in safety, having heard his holy words.

We made our way inside without a struggle;   106
and I, who wanted so much to observe
the state of things that such a fortress guarded,

as soon as I had entered, looked about.   109
I saw, on every side, a spreading plain
of lamentation and atrocious pain.

Just as at Arles, where Rhone becomes a marsh,   112
just as at Pola, near Quarnero's gulf,
that closes Italy and bathes its borders,

the sepulchers make all the plain uneven,   115
so they did here on every side, except
that here the sepulchers were much more harsh;

for flames were scattered through the tombs, and these   118
had kindled all of them to glowing heat;
no artisan could ask for hotter iron.

The lid of every tomb was lifted up,   121
and from each tomb such sorry cries arose
as could come only from the sad and hurt.

And I: "Master, who can these people be   124
who, buried in great chests of stone like these,
must speak by way of sighs in agony?"

And he to me: "Here are arch-heretics   127
and those who followed them, from every sect;
those tombs are much more crowded than you think.

Here, like has been ensepulchered with like;   130
some monuments are heated more, some less."
And then he turned around and to his right;

we passed between the torments and high walls.   133

CANTO X

Still the Sixth Circle: the Heretics. The tombs of the Epicureans. Farinata degli Uberti. Cavalcante dei Cavalcanti. Farinata's prediction of Dante's difficulty in returning to Florence from exile. The inability of the damned to see the present, although they can foresee the future.

Now, by a narrow path that ran between
those torments and the ramparts of the city,
my master moves ahead, I following.

"O highest virtue, you who lead me through   4
these circles of transgression, at your will,
do speak to me, and satisfy my longings.

Can those who lie within the sepulchers   7
be seen? The lids—in fact—have all been lifted;
no guardian is watching over them."

And he to me: "They'll all be shuttered up   10
when they return here from Jehosaphat
together with the flesh they left above.

Within this region is the cemetery   13
of Epicurus and his followers,
all those who say the soul dies with the body.

And so the question you have asked of me   16
will soon find satisfaction while we're here,
as will the longing you have hid from me."

And I: "Good guide, the only reason I   19
have hid my heart was that I might speak briefly,
and you, long since, encouraged me in this."

"O Tuscan, you who pass alive across   22
the fiery city with such seemly words,
be kind enough to stay your journey here.

Your accent makes it clear that you belong   25

among the natives of the noble city
I may have dealt with too vindictively."

This sound had burst so unexpectedly   28
out of one sepulcher that, trembling, I
then drew a little closer to my guide.

But he told me: "Turn round! What are you doing?   31
That's Farinata who has risen there—
you will see all of him from the waist up."

My eyes already were intent on his;   34
and up he rose—his forehead and his chest—
as if he had tremendous scorn for Hell.

My guide—his hands encouraging and quick—   37
thrust me between the sepulchers toward him,
saying: "Your words must be appropriate."

When I'd drawn closer to his sepulcher,   40
he glanced at me, and as if in disdain,
he asked of me: "Who were your ancestors?"

Because I wanted so to be compliant,   43
I hid no thing from him: I told him all.
At this he lifted up his brows a bit,

then said: "They were ferocious enemies   46
of mine and of my parents and my party,
so that I had to scatter them twice over."

"If they were driven out," I answered him,   49
"they still returned both times, from every quarter;
but yours were never quick to learn that art."

At this there rose another shade alongside,   52
uncovered to my sight down to his chin;
I think that he had risen on his knees.

He looked around me, just as if he longed   55
to see if I had come with someone else;
but then, his expectation spent, he said

in tears: "If it is your high intellect   58
that lets you journey here, through this blind prison,
where is my son? Why is he not with you?"

I answered: "My own powers have not brought me;   61
he who awaits me there, leads me through here

perhaps to one your Guido did disdain."

His words, the nature of his punishment—   64
these had already let me read his name;
therefore, my answer was so fully made.

Then suddenly erect, he cried: "What's that: 67
He '*did* disdain'? He is not still alive?
The sweet light does not strike against his eyes?"

And when he noticed how I hesitated   70
a moment in my answer, he fell back—
supine—and did not show himself again.

But that great-hearted one, the other shade   73
at whose request I'd stayed, did not change aspect
or turn aside his head or lean or bend;

and taking up his words where he'd left off,   76
"If they were slow," he said, "to learn that art,
that is more torment to me than this bed.

And yet the Lady who is ruler here   79
will not have her face kindled fifty times
before you learn how heavy is that art.

And so may you return to the sweet world,   82
tell me: why are those citizens so cruel
against my kin in all of their decrees?"

To which I said: "The carnage, the great bloodshed   85
that stained the waters of the Arbia red
have led us to such prayers in our temple."

He sighed and shook his head, then said: "In that,   88
I did not act alone, but certainly
I'd not have joined the others without cause.

But where I was alone was *there* where all   91
the rest would have annihilated Florence,
had I not interceded forcefully."

"Ah, as I hope your seed may yet find peace,"   94
I asked, "so may you help me to undo
the knot that here has snarled my course of thought.

It seems, if I hear right, that you can see   97
beforehand that which time is carrying,
but you're denied the sight of present things."

The Heretics burning in their sepulchres.

"We see, even as men who are farsighted,   100
those things," he said, "that are remote from us;
the Highest Lord allots us that much light.

But when events draw near or are, our minds   103
are useless; were we not informed by others,
we should know nothing of your human state.

So you can understand how our awareness   106
will die completely at the moment when
the portal of the future has been shut."

Then, as if penitent for my omission,   109
I said: "Will you now tell that fallen man
his son is still among the living ones;

and if, a while ago, I held my tongue   112
before his question, let him know it was
because I had in mind the doubt you've answered."

And now my master was recalling me;   115
so that, more hurriedly, I asked the spirit
to name the others who were there with him.

He said: "More than a thousand lie with me: 118
the second Frederick is but one among them,
as is the Cardinal; I name no others."

With that, he hid himself; and pondering   121
the speech that seemed to me so menacing,
I turned my steps to meet the ancient poet.

He moved ahead, and as we made our way,   124
he said to me: "Why are you so dismayed?"
I satisfied him, answering him fully.

And then that sage exhorted me: "Remember   127
the words that have been spoken here against you.
Now pay attention," and he raised his finger;

"when you shall stand before the gentle splendor   130
of one whose gracious eyes see everything,
then you shall learn—from her—your lifetime's journey."

Following that, his steps turned to the left,   133
leaving the wall and moving toward the middle
along a path that strikes into a valley

whose stench, as it rose up, disgusted us.   136

CANTO XI

Still the Sixth Circle. Pope Anastasius' tomb. Virgil on the
parts of Dis they now will visit, where the modes of malice
are punished: violence in the Seventh Circle's Three Rings;
"ordinary" fraud in the Eighth Circle; and treacherous fraud
in the Ninth Circle. Hell's previous circles, Two through
Five, as circles of incontinence. Usury condemned.

    Along the upper rim of a high bank
formed by a ring of massive broken boulders,
we came above a crowd more cruelly pent.

    And here, because of the outrageous stench   4
thrown up in excess by that deep abyss,
we drew back till we were behind the lid

    of a great tomb, on which I made out this,   7
inscribed: "I hold Pope Anastasius,
enticed to leave the true path by Photinus."

    "It would be better to delay descent   10
so that our senses may grow somewhat used
to this foul stench; and then we can ignore it."

    So said my master, and I answered him: 13
"Do find some compensation, lest this time
be lost." And he: "You see, I've thought of that."

    "My son, within this ring of broken rocks,"   16
he then began, "there are three smaller circles;
like those that you are leaving, they range down.

    Those circles are all full of cursed spirits;   19
so that your seeing of them may suffice,
learn now the how and why of their confinement.

    Of every malice that earns hate in Heaven,   22
injustice is the end; and each such end
by force or fraud brings harm to other men.

However, fraud is man's peculiar vice;   25
God finds it more displeasing—and therefore,
the fraudulent are lower, suffering more.

The violent take all of the first circle;   28
but since one uses force against three persons,
that circle's built of three divided rings.

To God and to one's self and to one's neighbor—   31
I mean, to them or what is theirs—one can
do violence, as you shall now hear clearly.

Violent death and painful wounds may be   34
inflicted on one's neighbor; his possessions
may suffer ruin, fire, and extortion;

thus, murderers and those who strike in malice,   37
as well as plunderers and robbers—these,
in separated ranks, the first ring racks.

A man can set violent hands against   40
himself or his belongings; so within
the second ring repents, though uselessly,

whoever would deny himself your world,   43
gambling away, wasting his patrimony,
and weeping where he should instead be happy.

One can be violent against the Godhead,   46
one's heart denying and blaspheming Him
and scorning nature and the good in her;

so, with its sign, the smallest ring has sealed   49
both Sodom and Cahors and all of those
who speak in passionate contempt of God.

Now fraud, that eats away at every conscience,   52
is practiced by a man against another
who trusts in him, or one who has no trust.

This latter way seems only to cut off   55
the bond of love that nature forges; thus,
nestled within the second circle are:

hypocrisy and flattery, sorcerers,   58
and falsifiers, simony, and theft,
and barrators and panders and like trash.

But in the former way of fraud, not only   61
the love that nature forges is forgotten,
but added love that builds a special trust;

   thus, in the tightest circle, where there is   64
the universe's center, seat of Dis,
all traitors are consumed eternally."

   "Master, your reasoning is clear indeed,"   67
I said; "it has made plain for me the nature
of this pit and the population in it.

   But tell me: those the dense marsh holds, or those   70
driven before the wind, or those on whom
rain falls, or those who clash with such harsh tongues,

   why are they not all punished in the city   73
of flaming red if God is angry with them?
And if He's not, why then are they tormented?"

   And then to me, "Why does your reason wander   76
so far from its accustomed course?" he said.
"Or of what other things are you now thinking?

   Have you forgotten, then, the words with which   79
your *Ethics* treats of those three dispositions
that strike at Heaven's will: incontinence

   and malice and mad bestiality?   82
And how the fault that is the least condemned
and least offends God is incontinence?

   If you consider carefully this judgment   85
and call to mind the souls of upper Hell,
who bear their penalties outside this city,

   you'll see why they have been set off from these   88
unrighteous ones, and why, when heaven's vengeance
hammers at them, it carries lesser anger."

   "O sun, that heals all sight that is perplexed,   91
when I ask you, your answer so contents
that doubting pleases me as much as knowing.

   Go back a little to that point," I said,   94
"where you told me that usury offends
divine goodness; unravel now that knot."

"Philosophy, for one who understands,
points out, and not in just one place," he said,
"how nature follows—as she takes her course—

the Divine Intellect and Divine Art;
and if you read your *Physics* carefully,
not many pages from the start, you'll see

that when it can, your art would follow nature,
just as a pupil imitates his master;
so that your art is almost God's grandchild.

From these two, art and nature, it is fitting,
if you recall how *Genesis* begins,
for men to make their way, to gain their living;

and since the usurer prefers another
pathway, he scorns both nature in herself
and art, her follower; his hope is elsewhere.

But follow me, for it is time to move;
the Fishes glitter now on the horizon
and all the Wain is spread out over Caurus;

only beyond, can one climb down the cliff."

CANTO XII

*The Seventh Circle, First Ring: the Violent against their
Neighbors. The Minotaur. The Centaurs, led by Chiron, who
assigns Nessus to guide Dante and Virgil across the boiling
river of blood (Phlegethon). In that river, Tyrants and
Murderers, immersed, watched over by the Centaurs.*

The place that we had reached for our descent
along the bank was alpine; what reclined
upon that bank would, too, repel all eyes.

Just like the toppled mass of rock that struck—   4
because of earthquake or eroded props—
the Adige on its flank, this side of Trent,

where from the mountain top from which it thrust   7
down to the plain, the rock is shattered so
that it permits a path for those above:

such was the passage down to that ravine.   10
And at the edge above the cracked abyss,
there lay outstretched the infamy of Crete,

conceived within the counterfeited cow;   13
and, catching sight of us, he bit himself
like one whom fury devastates within.

Turning to him, my sage cried out: "Perhaps   16
you think this is the Duke of Athens here,
who, in the world above, brought you your death.

Be off, you beast; this man who comes has not   19
been tutored by your sister; all he wants
in coming here is to observe your torments."

Just as the bull that breaks loose from its halter   22
the moment it receives the fatal stroke,
and cannot run but plunges back and forth,

so did I see the Minotaur respond;   25

and my alert guide cried: "Run toward the pass;
it's better to descend while he's berserk."

And so we made our way across that heap   28
of stones, which often moved beneath my feet
because my weight was somewhat strange for them.

While climbing down, I thought. He said: "You wonder,   31
perhaps, about that fallen mass, watched over
by the inhuman rage I have just quenched.

Now I would have you know: the other time   34
that I descended into lower Hell,
this mass of boulders had not yet collapsed;

but if I reason rightly, it was just   37
before the coming of the One who took
from Dis the highest circle's splendid spoils

that, on all sides, the steep and filthy valley   40
had trembled so, I thought the universe
felt love (by which, as some believe, the world

has often been converted into chaos);   43
and at that moment, here as well as elsewhere,
these ancient boulders toppled, in this way.

But fix your eyes below, upon the valley,   46
for now we near the stream of blood, where those
who injure others violently, boil."

O blind cupidity and insane anger,   49
which goad us on so much in our short life,
then steep us in such grief eternally!

I saw a broad ditch bent into an arc   52
so that it could embrace all of that plain,
precisely as my guide had said before;

between it and the base of the embankment   55
raced files of Centaurs who were armed with arrows,
as, in the world above, they used to hunt.

On seeing us descend, they all reined in;   58
and, after they had chosen bows and shafts,
three of their number moved out from their ranks;

and still far off, one cried: "What punishment   61

do you approach as you descend the slope?
But speak from there; if not, I draw my bow."

My master told him: "We shall make reply   64
only to Chiron, when we reach his side;
your hasty will has never served you well."

Then he nudged me and said: "That one is Nessus,   67
who died because of lovely Deianira
and of himself wrought vengeance for himself.

And in the middle, gazing at his chest,   70
is mighty Chiron, tutor of Achilles;
the third is Pholus, he who was so frenzied.

And many thousands wheel around the moat,   73
their arrows aimed at any soul that thrusts
above the blood more than its guilt allots."

By now we had drawn near those agile beasts;   76
Chiron drew out an arrow; with the notch,
he parted his beard back upon his jaws.

When he'd uncovered his enormous mouth,   79
he said to his companions: "Have you noticed
how he who walks behind moves what he touches?

Dead soles are not accustomed to do that."   82
And my good guide—now near the Centaur's chest,
the place where his two natures met—replied:

"He is indeed alive, and so alone   85
it falls to me to show him the dark valley.
Necessity has brought him here, not pleasure.

For she who gave me this new task was one   88
who had just come from singing halleluiah:
he is no robber; I am not a thief.

But by the Power that permits my steps   91
to journey on so wild a path, give us
one of your band, to serve as our companion;

and let him show us where to ford the ditch,   94
and let him bear this man upon his back,
for he's no spirit who can fly through air."

Then Chiron wheeled about and right and said   97

12

Dante and Virgil cross the River of Boiling Blood and enter the Wood of Suicides.

to Nessus: "Then, return and be their guide;
if other troops disturb you, fend them off."

Now, with our faithful escort, we advanced   100
along the bloodred, boiling ditch's banks,
beside the piercing cries of those who boiled.

I saw some who were sunk up to their brows,   103
and that huge Centaur said: "These are the tyrants
who plunged their hands in blood and plundering.

Here they lament their ruthless crimes; here are   106
both Alexander and the fierce Dionysius,
who brought such years of grief to Sicily.

That brow with hair so black is Ezzelino;   109
that other there, the blond one, is Obizzo
of Este, he who was indeed undone,

within the world above, by his fierce son."   112
Then I turned to the poet, and he said:
"Now let him be your first guide, me your second."

A little farther on, the Centaur stopped   115
above a group that seemed to rise above
the boiling blood as far up as their throats.

He pointed out one shade, alone, apart,   118
and said: "Within God's bosom, he impaled
the heart that still drips blood upon the Thames."

Then I caught sight of some who kept their heads   121
and even their full chests above the tide;
among them—many whom I recognized.

And so the blood grew always shallower   124
until it only scorched the feet; and here
we found a place where we could ford the ditch.

"Just as you see that, on this side, the brook   127
continually thins," the Centaur said,
"so I should have you know the rivulet,

along the other side, will slowly deepen   130
its bed, until it reaches once again
the depth where tyranny must make lament.

And there divine justice torments Attila   133

he who was such a scourge upon the earth,
and Pyrrhus, Sextus; to eternity

it milks the tears that boiling brook unlocks   136
from Rinier of Corneto, Rinier Pazzo,
those two who waged such war upon the highroads."

Then he turned round and crossed the ford again.   139

CANTO XIII

The Seventh Circle, Second Ring: the Violent against Themselves (Suicides) or against their Possessions (Squanderers). The dreary wood, with the Suicides transformed into strange trees, and the Squanderers, hounded and rent by bitches. Pier della Vigna. Lano and Jacopo da Santo Andrea. The anonymous Florentine suicide.

Nessus had not yet reached the other bank
when we began to make our way across
a wood on which no path had left its mark.

No green leaves in that forest, only black;   4
no branches straight and smooth, but knotted, gnarled;
no fruits were there, but briers bearing poison.

Even those savage beasts that roam between   7
Cécina and Corneto, beasts that hate
tilled lands, do not have holts so harsh and dense.

This is the nesting place of the foul Harpies,   10
who chased the Trojans from the Strophades
with sad foretelling of their future trials.

Their wings are wide, their necks and faces human;   13
their feet are taloned, their great bellies feathered;
they utter their laments on the strange trees.

And my kind master then instructed me: 16
"Before you enter farther know that now
you are within the second ring and shall

be here until you reach the horrid sand;   19
therefore look carefully; you'll see such things
as would deprive my speech of all belief."

From every side I heard the sound of cries,   22
but I could not see any source for them,
so that, in my bewilderment, I stopped.

I think that he was thinking that I thought   25
so many voices moaned among those trunks
from people who had been concealed from us.

Therefore my master said: "If you would tear   28
a little twig from any of these plants,
the thoughts you have will also be cut off."

Then I stretched out my hand a little way   31
and from a great thornbush snapped off a branch,
at which its trunk cried out: "Why do you tear me?"

And then, when it had grown more dark with blood,   34
it asked again: "Why do you break me off?
Are you without all sentiment of pity?

We once were men and now are arid stumps: 37
your hand might well have shown us greater mercy
had we been nothing more than souls of serpents."

As from a sapling log that catches fire   40
along one of its ends, while at the other
it drips and hisses with escaping vapor,

so from that broken stump issued together   43
both words and blood; at which I let the branch
fall, and I stood like one who is afraid.

My sage said: "Wounded soul, if, earlier,   46
he had been able to believe what he
had only glimpsed within my poetry,

then he would not have set his hand against you;   49
but its incredibility made me
urge him to do a deed that grieves me deeply.

But tell him who you were, so that he may,   52
to make amends, refresh your fame within
the world above, where he can still return."

To which the trunk: "Your sweet speech draws me so   55
that I cannot be still; and may it not
oppress you, if I linger now in talk.

I am the one who guarded both the keys   58
of Frederick's heart and turned them, locking and
unlocking them with such dexterity

that none but I could share his confidence; 61
and I was faithful to my splendid office,
so faithful that I lost both sleep and strength.

The whore who never turned her harlot's eyes 64
away from Caesar's dwelling, she who is
the death of all and vice of every court,

inflamed the minds of everyone against me; 67
and those inflamed, then so inflamed Augustus
that my delighted honors turned to sadness.

My mind, because of its disdainful temper, 70
believing it could flee disdain through death,
made me unjust against my own just self.

I swear to you by the peculiar roots 73
of this thornbush, I never broke my faith
with him who was so worthy—with my lord.

If one of you returns into the world, 76
then let him help my memory, which still
lies prone beneath the battering of envy."

The poet waited briefly, then he said 79
to me: "Since he is silent, do not lose
this chance, but speak and ask what you would know."

And I: "Do you continue; ask of him 82
whatever you believe I should request;
I cannot, so much pity takes my heart."

Then he began again: "Imprisoned spirit, 85
so may this man do freely what you ask,
may it please you to tell us something more

of how the soul is bound into these knots; 88
and tell us, if you can, if any one
can ever find his freedom from these limbs."

At this the trunk breathed violently, then 91
that wind became this voice, "You shall be answered
promptly. When the savage spirit quits

the body from which it has torn itself, 94
then Minos sends it to the seventh maw.
It falls into the wood, and there's no place

to which it is allotted, but wherever
fortune has flung that soul, that is the space
where, even as a grain of spelt, it sprouts.

It rises as a sapling, a wild plant; 100
and then the Harpies, feeding on its leaves,
cause pain and for that pain provide a vent.

Like other souls, we shall seek out the flesh 103
that we have left, but none of us shall wear it;
it is not right for any man to have

what he himself has cast aside. We'll drag 106
our bodies here; they'll hang in this sad wood,
each on the stump of its vindictive shade."

And we were still intent upon the trunk— 109
believing it had wanted to say more—
when we were overtaken by a roar,

just as the hunter is aware of chase 112
and boar as they draw near his post—he hears
the beasts and then the branches as they crack.

And there upon the left were two who, scratched 115
and naked, fled so violently that
they tore away each forest bough they passed.

The one in front: "Now come, death, quickly come!" 118
The other shade, who thought himself too slow,
was shouting after him: "Lano, your legs

were not so nimble at the jousts of Toppo!" 121
And then, perhaps because he'd lost his breath,
he fell into one tangle with a bush.

Behind these two, black bitches filled the wood, 124
and they were just as eager and as swift
as greyhounds that have been let off their leash.

They set their teeth in him where he had crouched; 127
and, piece by piece, those dogs dismembered him
and carried off his miserable limbs.

Then he who was my escort took my hand; 130
he led me to the lacerated thorn
that wept in vain where it was bleeding, broken.

"O Jacopo," it said, "da Santo Andrea,   133
what have you gained by using me as screen?
Am I to blame for your indecent life?"

When my good master stood beside that bush,   136
he said: "Who were you, who through many wounds
must breathe with blood your melancholy words?"

And he to us: "O spirits who have come   139
to witness the outrageous laceration
that leaves so many of my branches torn,

collect them at the foot of this sad thorn.   142
My home was in the city whose first patron
gave way to John the Baptist; for this reason,

he'll always use his art to make it sorrow;   145
and if—along the crossing of the Arno—
some effigy of Mars had not remained,

those citizens who afterward rebuilt   148
their city on the ashes that Attila
had left to them, would have travailed in vain.

I made—of my own house—my gallows place."   151

CANTO XIV

The Seventh Circle, Third Ring: the Violent against God.
The First Zone: Blasphemers, supine on fiery sands. Capa-
neus. Virgil on the Old Man of Crete, whose streaming tears
form the rivers of Hell: Acheron, Phlegethon, Styx, and
Cocytus. The sight of Lethe postponed.

Love of our native city overcame me;
I gathered up the scattered boughs and gave
them back to him whose voice was spent already.

From there we reached the boundary that divides   4
the second from the third ring—and the sight
of a dread work that justice had devised.

To make these strange things clear, I must explain   7
that we had come upon an open plain
that banishes all green things from its bed.

The wood of sorrow is a garland round it,   10
just as that wood is ringed by a sad channel;
here, at the very edge, we stayed our steps.

The ground was made of sand, dry and compact,   13
a sand not different in kind from that
on which the feet of Cato had once tramped.

O vengeance of the Lord, how you should be   16
dreaded by everyone who now can read
whatever was made manifest to me!

I saw so many flocks of naked souls,   19
all weeping miserably, and it seemed
that they were ruled by different decrees.

Some lay upon the ground, flat on their backs;   22
some huddled in a crouch, and there they sat;
and others moved about incessantly.

The largest group was those who walked about,   25

the smallest, those supine in punishment;
but these had looser tongues to tell their torment.

Above that plain of sand, distended flakes 28
of fire showered down; their fall was slow—
as snow descends on alps when no wind blows.

Just like the flames that Alexander saw 31
in India's hot zones, when fires fell,
intact and to the ground, on his battalions,

for which—wisely—he had his soldiers tramp 34
the soil to see that every fire was spent
before new flames were added to the old;

so did the never-ending heat descend; 37
with this, the sand was kindled just as tinder
on meeting flint will flame—doubling the pain.

The dance of wretched hands was never done; 40
now here, now there, they tried to beat aside
the fresh flames as they fell. And I began

to speak: "My master, you who can defeat 43
all things except for those tenacious demons
who tried to block us at the entryway,

who is that giant there, who does not seem 46
to heed the singeing—he who lies and scorns
and scowls, he whom the rains can't seem to soften?"

And he himself, on noticing that I 49
was querying my guide about him, cried:
"That which I was in life, I am in death.

Though Jove wear out the smith from whom he took, 52
in wrath, the keen-edged thunderbolt with which
on my last day I was to be transfixed;

or if he tire the others, one by one, 55
in Mongibello, at the sooty forge,
while bellowing: 'O help, good Vulcan, help!'—

just as he did when there was war at Phlegra— 58
and casts his shafts at me with all his force,
not even then would he have happy vengeance."

Then did my guide speak with such vehemence 61

as I had never heard him use before:
"O Capaneus, for your arrogance

    that is not quenched, you're punished all the more: 64
no torture other than your own madness
could offer pain enough to match your wrath."

    But then, with gentler face he turned to me   67
and said: "That man was one of seven kings
besieging Thebes; he held—and still, it seems,

    holds—God in great disdain, disprizing Him;   70
but as I told him now, his maledictions
sit well as ornaments upon his chest.

    Now follow me and—take care—do not set   73
your feet upon the sand that's burning hot,
but always keep them back, close to the forest."

    In silence we had reached a place where flowed   76
a slender watercourse out of the wood—
a stream whose redness makes me shudder still.

    As from the Bulicame pours a brook   79
whose waters then are shared by prostitutes,
so did this stream run down across the sand.

    Its bed and both its banks were made of stone,   82
together with the slopes along its shores,
so that I saw our passageway lay there.

    "Among all other things that I have shown you   85
since we first made our way across the gate
whose threshold is forbidden to no one,

    no thing has yet been witnessed by your eyes   88
as notable as this red rivulet,
which quenches every flame that burns above it."

    These words were spoken by my guide; at this,   91
I begged him to bestow the food for which
he had already given me the craving.

    "A devastated land lies in midsea,   94
a land that is called Crete," he answered me.
"Under its king the world once lived chastely.

    Within that land there was a mountain blessed   97

with leaves and waters, and they called it Ida;
but it is withered now like some old thing.

It once was chosen as a trusted cradle   100
by Rhea for her son; to hide him better,
when he cried out, she had her servants clamor.

Within the mountain is a huge Old Man,   103
who stands erect—his back turned toward Damietta—
and looks at Rome as if it were his mirror.

The Old Man's head is fashioned of fine gold,   106
the purest silver forms his arms and chest,
but he is made of brass down to the cleft;

below that point he is of choicest iron   109
except for his right foot, made of baked clay;
and he rests more on this than on the left.

Each part of him, except the gold, is cracked;   112
and down that fissure there are tears that drip;
when gathered, they pierce through that cavern's floor

and, crossing rocks into this valley, form   115
the Acheron and Styx and Phlegethon;
and then they make their way down this tight channel,

and at the point past which there's no descent,   118
they form Cocytus; since you are to see
what that pool is, I'll not describe it here."

And I asked him: "But if the rivulet   121
must follow such a course down from our world,
why can we see it only at this boundary?"

And he to me: "You know this place is round;   124
and though the way that you have come is long,
and always toward the left and toward the bottom,

you still have not completed all the circle: 127
so that, if something new appears to us,
it need not bring such wonder to your face."

And I again: "Master, where's Phlegethon   130
and where is Lethe? You omit the second
and say this rain of tears has formed the first."

"I'm pleased indeed," he said, "with all your questions; 133

yet one of them might well have found its answer
already—when you saw the red stream boiling.

You shall see Lethe, but past this abyss,   136
there where the spirits go to cleanse themselves
when their repented guilt is set aside."

Then he declared: "The time has come to quit   139
this wood; see that you follow close behind me;
these margins form a path that does not scorch,

and over them, all flaming vapor is quenched."   142

CANTO XV

*Still the Seventh Circle, Third Ring: the Violent against
God. Second Zone: the Sodomites, endlessly crossing the fiery
sands beneath the rain of fire. Brunetto Latini, whom Dante
treats as mentor. Priscian, Francesco d' Accorso, and Andrea
dei Mozzi, Bishop of Florence.*

Now one of the hard borders bears us forward;
the river mist forms shadows overhead
and shields the shores and water from the fire.

Just as between Wissant and Bruges, the Flemings,   4
in terror of the tide that floods toward them,
have built a wall of dykes to daunt the sea;

and as the Paduans, along the Brenta,   7
build bulwarks to defend their towns and castles
before the dog days fall on Carentana;

just so were these embankments, even though   10
they were not built so high and not so broad,
whoever was the artisan who made them.

By now we were so distant from the wood   13
that I should not have made out where it was—
not even if I'd turned around to look—

when we came on a company of spirits   16
who made their way along the bank; and each
stared steadily at us, as in the dusk,

beneath the new moon, men look at each other.   19
They knit their brows and squinted at us—just
as an old tailor at his needle's eye.

And when that family looked harder, I   22
was recognized by one, who took me by
the hem and cried out: "This is marvelous!"

That spirit having stretched his arm toward me,   25

I fixed my eyes upon his baked, brown features,
so that the scorching of his face could not
    prevent my mind from recognizing him;   28
and lowering my face to meet his face,
I answered him: "Are you here, Ser Brunetto?"

    And he: "My son, do not mind if Brunetto   31
Latino lingers for a while with you
and lets the file he's with pass on ahead."

    I said: "With all my strength, I pray you, stay;   34
and if you'd have me rest awhile with you,
I shall, if that please him with whom I go."

    "O son," he said, "whoever of this flock   37
stops but a moment, stays a hundred years
and cannot shield himself when fire strikes.

    Therefore move on; below—but close—I'll follow;   40
and then I shall rejoin my company,
who go lamenting their eternal sorrows."

    I did not dare to leave my path for his   43
own level; but I walked with head bent low
as does a man who goes in reverence.

    And he began: "What destiny or chance   46
has led you here below before your last
day came, and who is he who shows the way?"

    "There, in the sunlit life above," I answered,   49
"before my years were full, I went astray
within a valley. Only yesterday

    at dawn I turned my back upon it—but   52
when I was newly lost, he here appeared,
to guide me home again along this path."

    And he to me: "If you pursue your star,   55
you cannot fail to reach a splendid harbor,
if in fair life, I judged you properly;

    and if I had not died too soon for this,   58
on seeing Heaven was so kind to you,
I should have helped sustain you in your work.

    But that malicious, that ungrateful people   61

come down, in ancient times, from Fiesole—
still keeping something of the rock and mountain—

for your good deeds, will be your enemy: 64
and there is cause—among the sour sorbs,
the sweet fig is not meant to bear its fruit.

The world has long since called them blind, a people 67
presumptuous, avaricious, envious;
be sure to cleanse yourself of their foul ways.

Your fortune holds in store such honor for you, 70
one party and the other will be hungry
for you—but keep the grass far from the goat.

For let the beasts of Fiesole find forage 73
among themselves, and leave the plant alone—
if still, among their dung, it rises up—

in which there lives again the sacred seed 76
of those few Romans who remained in Florence
when such a nest of wickedness was built."

"If my desire were answered totally," 79
I said to Ser Brunetto, "you'd still be
among, not banished from, humanity.

Within my memory is fixed—and now 82
moves me—your dear, your kind paternal image
when, in the world above, from time to time

you taught me how man makes himself eternal; 85
and while I live, my gratitude for that
must always be apparent in my words.

What you have told me of my course, I write: 88
I keep it with another text, for comment
by one who'll understand, if I may reach her.

One thing alone I'd have you plainly see: 91
so long as I am not rebuked by conscience,
I stand prepared for Fortune, come what may.

My ears find no new pledge in that prediction; 94
therefore, let Fortune turn her wheel as she
may please, and let the peasant turn his mattock."

At this, my master turned his head around 97

and toward the right, and looked at me and said:
"He who takes note of this has listened well."

But nonetheless, my talk with Ser Brunetto   100
continues, and I ask of him who are
his comrades of repute and excellence.

And he to me: "To know of some is good;   103
but for the rest, silence is to be praised;
the time we have is short for so much talk.

In brief, know that my company has clerics   106
and men of letters and of fame—and all
were stained by one same sin upon the earth.

That sorry crowd holds Priscian and Francesco   109
d'Accorso; and among them you can see,
if you have any longing for such scurf,

the one the Servant of His Servants sent   112
from the Arno to the Bacchiglione's banks,
and there he left his tendons strained by sin.

I would say more; but both my walk and words   115
must not be longer, for—beyond—I see
new smoke emerging from the sandy bed.

Now people come with whom I must not be.   118
Let my *Tesoro*, in which I still live,
be precious to you; and I ask no more."

And then he turned and seemed like one of those   121
who race across the fields to win the green
cloth at Verona; of those runners, he

appeared to be the winner, not the loser.   124

CANTO XVI

Still the Seventh Circle, Third Ring, Second Zone: other
Sodomites. Three Florentines, Guido Guerra, Tegghiaio
Aldobrandi, Jacopo Rusticucci. The decadence of Florence.
Phlegethon, cascading into the next zone. The cord of Dante,
used by Virgil to summon a monstrous figure from the waters.

No sooner had I reached the place where one
could hear a murmur, like a beehive's hum,
of waters as they fell to the next circle,

when, setting out together, three shades ran,   4
leaving another company that passed
beneath the rain of bitter punishment.

They came toward us, and each of them cried out: 7
"Stop, you who by your clothing seem to be
someone who comes from our indecent country!"

Ah me, what wounds I saw upon their limbs,   10
wounds new and old, wounds that the flames seared in!
It pains me still as I remember it.

When they cried out, my master paid attention;   13
he turned his face toward me and then he said:
"Now wait: to these one must show courtesy.

And were it not the nature of this place   16
for shafts of fire to fall, I'd say that haste
was seemlier for you than for those three."

As soon as we stood still, they started up   19
their ancient wail again; and when they reached us,
they formed a wheel, all three of them together.

As champions, naked, oiled, will always do,   22
each studying the grip that serves him best
before the blows and wounds begin to fall,

while wheeling so, each one made sure his face   25

was turned to me, so that their necks opposed
their feet in one uninterrupted flow.

And, "If the squalor of this shifting sand,   28
together with our baked and barren features,
makes us and our requests contemptible,"

one said, "then may our fame incline your mind   31
to tell us who you are, whose living feet
can make their way through Hell with such assurance.

He in whose steps you see me tread, although   34
he now must wheel about both peeled and naked,
was higher in degree than you believe:

he was a grandson of the good Gualdrada,   37
and Guido Guerra was his name; in life
his sword and his good sense accomplished much.

The other who, behind me, tramples sand—   40
Tegghiaio Aldobrandi, one whose voice
should have been heeded in the world above.

And I, who share this punishment with them,   43
was Jacopo Rusticucci; certainly,
more than all else, my savage wife destroyed me."

If I'd had shield and shelter from the fire,   46
I should have thrown myself down there among them—
I think my master would have sanctioned that;

but since that would have left me burned and baked,   49
my fear won out against the good intention
that made me so impatient to embrace them.

Then I began: "Your present state had fixed   52
not scorn but sorrow in me—and so deeply
that it will only disappear slowly—

as soon as my lord spoke to me with words   55
that made me understand what kind of men
were coming toward us, men of worth like yours.

For I am of your city; and with fondness,   58
I've always told and heard the others tell
of both your actions and your honored names.

I leave the gall and go for the sweet apples   61
that I was promised by my truthful guide;

but first I must descend into the center."

"So may your soul long lead your limbs and may   64
your fame shine after you," he answered then,
"tell us if courtesy and valor still

abide within our city as they did   67
when we were there, or have they disappeared
completely; for Guiglielmo Borsiere,

who only recently has come to share   70
our torments, and goes there with our companions,
has caused us much affliction with his words."

"Newcomers to the city and quick gains   73
have brought excess and arrogance to you,
o Florence, and you weep for it already!"

So I cried out with face upraised; the three   76
looked at each other when they heard my answer
as men will stare when they have heard the truth.

"If you can always offer a reply   79
so readily to others," said all three,
"then happy you who speak, at will, so clearly.

So, if you can escape these lands of darkness   82
and see the lovely stars on your return,
when you repeat with pleasure, 'I was there,'

be sure that you remember us to men."   85
At this they broke their wheel; and as they fled,
their swift legs seemed to be no less than wings.

The time it took for them to disappear—   88
more brief than time it takes to say "amen";
and so, my master thought it right to leave.

I followed him. We'd only walked a little   91
when roaring water grew so near to us
we hardly could have heard each other speak.

And even as the river that is first   94
to take its own course eastward from Mount Viso,
along the left flank of the Apennines

(which up above is called the Acquacheta,   97
before it spills into its valley bed
and flows without that name beyond Forlì),

reverberates above San Benedetto   100
dell'Alpe as it cascades in one leap,
where there is space enough to house a thousand;

    so did we hear that blackened water roar   103
as it plunged down a steep and craggy bank,
enough to deafen us in a few hours.

    Around my waist I had a cord as girdle,   106
and with it once I thought I should be able
to catch the leopard with the painted hide.

    And after I had loosened it completely,   109
just as my guide commanded me to do,
I handed it to him, knotted and coiled.

    At this, he wheeled around upon his right   112
and cast it, at some distance from the edge,
straight down into the depth of the ravine.

    "And surely something strange must here reply,"   115
I said within myself, "to this strange sign—
the sign my master follows with his eye."

    Ah, how much care men ought to exercise   118
with those whose penetrating intellect
can see our thoughts—not just our outer act!

    He said to me: "Now there will soon emerge   121
what I await and what your thought has conjured:
it soon must be discovered to your sight."

    Faced with that truth which seems a lie, a man   124
should always close his lips as long as he can—
to tell it shames him, even though he's blameless;

    but here I can't be still; and by the lines   127
of this my Comedy, reader, I swear—
and may my verse find favor for long years—

    that through the dense and darkened air I saw   130
a figure swimming, rising up, enough
to bring amazement to the firmest heart,

    like one returning from the waves where he   133
went down to loose an anchor snagged upon
a reef or something else hid in the sea,

    who stretches upward and draws in his feet.   136

CANTO XVII

The monster Geryon. The Seventh Circle, Third Ring, Third Zone: the Violent against Nature and Art (Usurers), each seated beneath the rain of fire with a purse—bearing his family's heraldic emblem—around his neck. Descent to the Eighth Circle on the back of Geryon.

"Behold the beast who bears the pointed tail,
who crosses mountains, shatters weapons, walls!
Behold the one whose stench fills all the world!"

So did my guide begin to speak to me,   4
and then he signaled him to come ashore
close to the end of those stone passageways.

And he came on, that filthy effigy   7
of fraud, and landed with his head and torso
but did not draw his tail onto the bank.

The face he wore was that of a just man,   10
so gracious was his features' outer semblance;
and all his trunk, the body of a serpent;

he had two paws, with hair up to the armpits;   13
his back and chest as well as both his flanks
had been adorned with twining knots and circlets.

No Turks or Tartars ever fashioned fabrics   16
more colorful in background and relief,
nor had Arachne ever loomed such webs.

As boats will sometimes lie along the shore,   19
with part of them on land and part in water,
and just as there, among the guzzling Germans,

the beaver sets himself when he means war,   22
so did that squalid beast lie on the margin
of stone that serves as border for the sand.

And all his tail was quivering in the void   25
while twisting upward its envenomed fork,

which had a tip just like a scorpion's.

My guide said: "Now we'd better bend our path 28
a little, till we reach as far as that
malicious beast which crouches over there."

Thus we descended on the right hand side 31
and moved ten paces on the stony brink
in order to avoid the sand and fire.

When we had reached the sprawling beast, I saw— 34
a little farther on, upon the sand—
some sinners sitting near the fissured rock.

And here my master said to me: "So that 37
you may experience this ring in full,
go now, and see the state in which they are.

But keep your conversation with them brief; 40
till you return, I'll parley with this beast,
to see if he can lend us his strong shoulders."

So I went on alone and even farther 43
along the seventh circle's outer margin,
to where the melancholy people sat.

Despondency was bursting from their eyes; 46
this side, then that, their hands kept fending off,
at times the flames, at times the burning soil:

not otherwise do dogs in summer—now 49
with muzzle, now with paw—when they are bitten
by fleas or gnats or by the sharp gadfly.

When I had set my eyes upon the faces 52
of some on whom that painful fire falls,
I recognized no one; but I did notice

that from the neck of each a purse was hung 55
that had a special color and an emblem,
and their eyes seemed to feast upon these pouches.

Looking about—when I had come among them— 58
I saw a yellow purse with azure on it
that had the face and manner of a lion.

Then, as I let my eyes move farther on, 61
I saw another purse that was bloodred,
and it displayed a goose more white than butter.

*At the rim of the Seventh Circle Dante and Virgil encounter the Beast Geryon and the
burning souls of Usurers.*

And one who had an azure, pregnant sow   64
inscribed as emblem on his white pouch, said
to me: "What are you doing in this pit?

Now you be off; and since you're still alive,   67
remember that my neighbor Vitaliano
shall yet sit here, upon my left-hand side.

Among these Florentines, I'm Paduan;   70
I often hear them thunder in my ears,
shouting, 'Now let the sovereign cavalier,

the one who'll bring the purse with three goats, come!'"   73
At this he slewed his mouth, and then he stuck
his tongue out, like an ox that licks its nose.

And I, afraid that any longer stay   76
might anger him who'd warned me to be brief,
made my way back from those exhausted souls.

I found my guide, who had already climbed   79
upon the back of that brute animal,
and he told me: "Be strong and daring now,

for our descent is by this kind of stairs: 82
your mount in front; I want to be between,
so that the tail can't do you any harm."

As one who feels the quartan fever near   85
and shivers, with his nails already blue,
the sight of shade enough to make him shudder,

so I became when I had heard these words;   88
but then I felt the threat of shame, which makes
a servant—in his kind lord's presence—brave.

I settled down on those enormous shoulders;   91
I wished to say (and yet my voice did not
come as I thought): "See that you hold me tight."

But he who—other times, in other dangers—   94
sustained me, just as soon as I had mounted,
clasped me within his arms and propped me up,

and said: "Now, Geryon, move on; take care   97
to keep your circles wide, your landing slow;
remember the new weight you're carrying."

Just like a boat that, starting from its moorings,   100

CANTO XVII 131

moves backward, backward, so that beast took off;
and when he felt himself completely clear,

he turned his tail to where his chest had been   103
and, having stretched it, moved it like an eel,
and with his paws he gathered in the air.

I do not think that there was greater fear   106
in Phaethon when he let his reins go free—
for which the sky, as one still sees, was scorched—

nor in poor Icarus when he could feel   109
his sides unwinged because the wax was melting,
his father shouting to him, "That way's wrong!"

than was in me when, on all sides, I saw   112
that I was in the air, and everything
had faded from my sight—except the beast.

Slowly, slowly, swimming, he moves on;   115
he wheels and he descends, but I feel only
the wind upon my face and the wind rising.

Already, on our right, I heard the torrent   118
resounding, there beneath us, horribly,
so that I stretched my neck and looked below.

Then I was more afraid of falling off,   121
for I saw fires and I heard laments,
at which I tremble, crouching, and hold fast.

And now I saw what I had missed before: 124
his wheeling and descent—because great torments
were drawing closer to us on all sides.

Just as a falcon long upon the wing—   127
who, seeing neither lure nor bird, compels
the falconer to cry, "Ah me, you fall!"—

descends, exhausted, in a hundred circles,   130
where he had once been swift, and sets himself,
embittered and enraged, far from his master;

such, at the bottom of the jagged rock,   133
was Geryon, when he had set us down.
And once our weight was lifted from his back,

he vanished like an arrow from a bow.   136

CANTO XVIII

*The Eighth Circle, called Malebolge ("Evil-Pouches"),
with its Ten Pouches, where "ordinary" fraud is punished.
The First Pouch, with Panders and Seducers scourged by
horned demons. Venèdico Caccianemico. Jason. The Second
Pouch, with Flatterers immersed in excrement. Alessio
Interminei. Thaïs.*

There is a place in Hell called Malebolge,
made all of stone the color of crude iron,
as is the wall that makes its way around it.

Right in the middle of this evil field   4
is an abyss, a broad and yawning pit,
whose structure I shall tell in its due place.

The belt, then, that extends between the pit   7
and that hard, steep wall's base is circular;
its bottom has been split into ten valleys.

Just as, where moat on moat surrounds a castle   10
in order to keep guard upon the walls,
the ground they occupy will form a pattern,

so did the valleys here form a design;   13
and as such fortresses have bridges running
right from their thresholds toward the outer bank,

so here, across the banks and ditches, ridges   16
ran from the base of that rock wall until
the pit that cuts them short and joins them all.

This was the place in which we found ourselves   19
when Geryon had put us down; the poet
held to the left, and I walked at his back.

Upon the right I saw new misery,   22
I saw new tortures and new torturers,
filling the first of Malebolge's moats.

Along its bottom, naked sinners moved,   25

to our side of the middle, facing us;
beyond that, they moved with us, but more quickly—

as, in the year of Jubilee, the Romans,   28
confronted by great crowds, contrived a plan
that let the people pass across the bridge,

for to one side went all who had their eyes   31
upon the Castle, heading toward St. Peter's,
and to the other, those who faced the Mount.

Both left and right, along the somber rock,   34
I saw horned demons with enormous whips,
who lashed those spirits cruelly from behind.

Ah, how their first strokes made those sinners lift   37
their heels! Indeed no sinner waited for
a second stroke to fall—or for a third.

And as I moved ahead, my eyes met those   40
of someone else, and suddenly I said:
"I was not spared the sight of him before."

And so I stayed my steps, to study him;   43
my gentle guide had stopped together with me
and gave me leave to take a few steps back.

That scourged soul thought that he could hide himself   46
by lowering his face; it helped him little,
for I said: "You, who cast your eyes upon

the ground, if these your features are not false,   49
must be Venèdico Caccianemico;
but what brings you to sauces so piquant?"

And he to me: "I speak unwillingly;   52
but your plain speech, that brings the memory
of the old world to me, is what compels me;

For it was I who led Ghisolabella   55
to do as the Marquis would have her do—
however they retell that filthy tale.

I'm not the only Bolognese who weeps here;   58
indeed, this place is so crammed full of us
that not so many tongues have learned to say

sipa between the Sàvena and Reno;   61
if you want faith and testament of that,

just call to mind our avaricious hearts."

And as he spoke, a demon cudgeled him 64
with his horsewhip and cried: "Be off, you pimp,
there are no women here for you to trick."

I joined my escort once again; and then 67
with but few steps, we came upon a place
where, from the bank, a rocky ridge ran out.

We climbed quite easily along that height; 70
and turning right upon its jagged back,
we took our leave of those eternal circlings.

When we had reached the point where that ridge opens 73
below to leave a passage for the lashed,
my guide said: "Stay, and make sure that the sight

of still more ill-born spirits strikes your eyes, 76
for you have not yet seen their faces, since
they have been moving in our own direction."

From the old bridge we looked down at the ranks 79
of those approaching from the other side;
they too were driven onward by the lash.

And my good master, though I had not asked, 82
urged me: "Look at that mighty one who comes
and does not seem to shed a tear of pain:

how he still keeps the image of a king! 85
That shade is Jason, who with heart and head
deprived the men of Colchis of their ram.

He made a landfall on the isle of Lemnos 88
after its women, bold and pitiless,
had given all their island males to death.

With polished words and love signs he took in 91
Hypsipyle, the girl whose own deception
had earlier deceived the other women.

And he abandoned her, alone and pregnant; 94
such guilt condemns him to such punishment;
and for Medea, too, revenge is taken.

With him go those who cheated so: this is 97
enough for you to know of that first valley
and of the souls it clamps within its jaws."

CANTO XVIII 135

We were already where the narrow path   100
reaches and intersects the second bank
and serves as shoulder for another bridge.

We heard the people whine in the next pouch   103
and heard them as they snorted with their snouts;
we heard them use their palms to beat themselves.

And exhalations, rising from below,   106
stuck to the banks, encrusting them with mold,
and so waged war against both eyes and nose.

The bottom is so deep, we found no spot   109
to see it from, except by climbing up
the arch until the bridge's highest point.

This was the place we reached; the ditch beneath   112
held people plunged in excrement that seemed
as if it had been poured from human privies.

And while my eyes searched that abysmal sight,   115
I saw one with a head so smeared with shit,
one could not see if he were lay or cleric.

He howled: "Why do you stare more greedily   118
at me than at the others who are filthy?"
And I: "Because, if I remember right,

I have seen you before, with your hair dry;   121
and so I eye you more than all: you are
Alessio Interminei of Lucca."

Then he continued, pounding on his pate: 124
"I am plunged here because of flatteries—
of which my tongue had such sufficiency."

At which my guide advised me: "See you thrust   127
your head a little farther to the front,
so that your eyes can clearly glimpse the face

of that besmirched, bedraggled harridan   130
who scratches at herself with shit-filled nails,
and now she crouches, now she stands upright.

That is Thaïs, the harlot who returned   133
her lover's question, 'Are you very grateful
to me?' by saying, 'Yes, enormously.'

And now our sight has had its fill of this."   136

CANTO XIX

The Eighth Circle, Third Pouch, where the Simonists are set, heads down, into holes in the rock, with their protruding feet tormented by flames. Pope Nicholas III. Dante's invective against simoniacal popes.

O Simon Magus! O his sad disciples!
Rapacious ones, who take the things of God,
that ought to be the brides of Righteousness,

and make them fornicate for gold and silver!   4
The time has come to let the trumpet sound
for you; your place is here in this third pouch.

We had already reached the tomb beyond   7
and climbed onto the ridge, where its high point
hangs just above the middle of the ditch.

O Highest Wisdom, how much art you show   10
in heaven, earth, and this sad world below,
how just your power is when it allots!

Along the sides and down along the bottom,   13
I saw that livid rock was perforated:
the openings were all one width and round.

They did not seem to me less broad or more   16
than those that in my handsome San Giovanni
were made to serve as basins for baptizing;

and one of these, not many years ago,   19
I broke for someone who was drowning in it:
and let this be my seal to set men straight.

Out from the mouth of each hole there emerged   22
a sinner's feet and so much of his legs
up to the thigh; the rest remained within.

Both soles of every sinner were on fire;   25
their joints were writhing with such violence,
they would have severed withes and ropes of grass.

As flame on oily things will only stir   28
along the outer surface, so there, too,
that fire made its way from heels to toes.

"Master," I said, "who is that shade who suffers   31
and quivers more than all his other comrades,
that sinner who is licked by redder flames?"

And he to me: "If you would have me lead   34
you down along the steepest of the banks,
from him you'll learn about his self and sins."

And I: "What pleases you will please me too: 37
you are my lord; you know I do not swerve
from what you will; you know what is unspoken."

At this, we came upon the fourth embankment;   40
we turned and, keeping to the left, descended
into the narrow, perforated bottom.

My good lord did not let me leave his side   43
until he'd brought me to the hole that held
that sinner who lamented with his legs.

"Whoever you may be, dejected soul,   46
whose head is downward, planted like a pole,"
my words began, "do speak, if you are able."

I stood as does the friar who confesses   49
the foul assassin who, fixed fast, head down,
calls back the friar, and so delays his death;

and he cried out: "Are you already standing,   52
already standing there, o Boniface?
The book has lied to me by several years.

Are you so quickly sated with the riches   55
for which you did not fear to take by guile
the Lovely Lady, then to violate her?"

And I became like those who stand as if   58
they have been mocked, who cannot understand
what has been said to them and can't respond.

But Virgil said: "Tell this to him at once: 61
'I am not he—not whom you think I am.'"
And I replied as I was told to do.

Dante and Virgil come to the third chasm where the Simoniacs are punished, including Pope Nicholas III.

At this the spirit twisted both his feet, 64
and sighing and with a despairing voice,
he said: "What is it, then, you want of me?

If you have crossed the bank and climbed so far 67
to find out who I am, then know that I
was one of those who wore the mighty mantle,

and surely was a son of the she-bear, 70
so eager to advance the cubs that I
pursed wealth above while here I purse myself.

Below my head there is the place of those 73
who took the way of simony before me;
and they are stuffed within the clefts of stone.

I, too, shall yield my place and fall below 76
when he arrives, the one for whom I had
mistaken you when I was quick to question.

But I have baked my feet a longer time, 79
have stood like this, upon my head, than he
is to stand planted here with scarlet feet:

for after him, one uglier in deeds 82
will come, a lawless shepherd from the west,
worthy to cover him and cover me.

He'll be a second Jason, of whom we read 85
in *Maccabees*; and just as Jason's king
was soft to him, so shall the king of France

be soft to this one." And I do not know 88
if I was too rash here—I answered so:
"Then tell me now, how much gold did our Lord

ask that Saint Peter give to him before 91
he placed the keys within his care? Surely
the only thing he said was: 'Follow me.'

And Peter and the others never asked 94
for gold or silver when they chose Matthias
to take the place of the transgressing soul.

Stay as you are, for you are rightly punished; 97
and guard with care the money got by evil
that made you so audacious against Charles.

And were it not that I am still prevented   100
by reverence for those exalted keys
that you had held within the happy life,

I'd utter words much heavier than these,   103
because your avarice afflicts the world:
it tramples on the good, lifts up the wicked.

You, shepherds, the Evangelist had noticed   106
when he saw her who sits upon the waters,
and realized she fornicates with kings,

she who was born with seven heads and had   109
the power and support of the ten horns,
as long as virtue was her husband's pleasure.

You've made yourselves a god of gold and silver;   112
how are you different from idolaters,
save that they worship one and you a hundred?

Ah, Constantine, what wickedness was born—   115
and not from your conversion—from the dower
that you bestowed upon the first rich father!"

And while I sang such notes to him—whether   118
it was his indignation or his conscience
that bit him—he kicked hard with both his soles.

I do indeed believe it pleased my guide: 121
he listened always with such satisfied
expression to the sound of those true words.

And then he gathered me in both his arms   124
and, when he had me fast against his chest,
where he climbed down before, climbed upward now;

nor did he tire of clasping me until   127
he brought me to the summit of the arch
that crosses from the fourth to the fifth rampart.

And here he gently set his burden down—   130
gently because the ridge was rough and steep,
and would have been a rugged pass for goats.

From there another valley lay before me.   133

CANTO XX

The Eighth Circle, Fourth Pouch, where Diviners, Astrologers, Magicians, all have their heads turned backward. Amphiaraus. Tiresias. Aruns. Manto. Virgil on the origin of Mantua, his native city. Eurypylus. Michael Scot and other moderns adept at fraud.

I must make verses of new punishment
and offer matter now for Canto Twenty
of this first canticle—of the submerged.

I was already well prepared to stare   4
below, into the depth that was disclosed,
where tears of anguished sorrow bathed the ground;

and in the valley's circle I saw souls   7
advancing, mute and weeping, at the pace
that, in our world, holy processions take.

As I inclined my head still more, I saw   10
that each, amazingly, appeared contorted
between the chin and where the chest begins;

they had their faces twisted toward their haunches   13
and found it necessary to walk backward,
because they could not see ahead of them.

Perhaps the force of palsy has so fully   16
distorted some, but that I've yet to see,
and I do not believe that that can be.

May God so let you, reader, gather fruit   19
from what you read; and now think for yourself
how I could ever keep my own face dry

when I beheld our image so nearby   22
and so awry that tears, down from the eyes,
bathed the buttocks, running down the cleft.

Of course I wept, leaning against a rock   25

along that rugged ridge, so that my guide
told me: "Are you as foolish as the rest?

Here pity only lives when it is dead: 28
for who can be more impious than he
who links God's judgment to passivity?

Lift, lift your head and see the one for whom   31
the earth was opened while the Thebans watched,
so that they all cried: 'Amphiaraus,

where are you rushing? Have you quit the fight?'   34
Nor did he interrupt his downward plunge
to Minos, who lays hands on every sinner.

See how he's made a chest out of his shoulders;   37
and since he wanted so to see ahead,
he looks behind and walks a backward path.

And see Tiresias, who changed his mien   40
when from a man he turned into a woman,
so totally transforming all his limbs

that then he had to strike once more upon   43
the two entwining serpents with his wand
before he had his manly plumes again.

And Aruns is the one who backs against   46
the belly of Tiresias—Aruns who,
in Luni's hills, tilled by the Carrarese,

who live below, had as his home, a cave   49
among white marbles, from which he could gaze
at stars and sea with unimpeded view.

And she who covers up her breasts—which you   52
can't see—with her disheveled locks, who keeps
all of her hairy parts to the far side,

was Manto, who had searched through many lands,   55
then settled in the place where I was born;
on this, I'd have you hear me now a while.

When Manto's father took his leave of life,   58
and Bacchus' city found itself enslaved,
she wandered through the world for many years.

High up, in lovely Italy, beneath   61

the Alps that shut in Germany above
Tirolo, lies a lake known as Benaco.

A thousand springs and more, I think, must flow   64
out of the waters of that lake to bathe
Pennino, Garda, Val Camonica.

And at its middle is a place where three—   67
the bishops of Verona, Brescia, Trento—
may bless if they should chance to come that way.

Peschiera, strong and handsome fortress, built   70
to face the Brescians and the Bergamasques
stands where the circling shore is at its lowest.

There, all the waters that cannot be held   73
within the bosom of Benaco fall,
to form a river running through green meadows.

No sooner has that stream begun to flow   76
than it is called the Mincio, not Benaco—
until Govèrnolo, where it joins the Po.

It's not flowed far before it finds flat land;   79
and there it stretches out to form a fen
that in the summer can at times be fetid.

And when she passed that way, the savage virgin   82
saw land along the middle of the swamp,
untilled and stripped of its inhabitants.

And there, to flee all human intercourse,   85
she halted with her slaves to ply her arts;
and there she lived, there left her empty body.

And afterward, the people of those parts   88
collected at that place, because the marsh—
surrounding it on all sides—made it strong.

They built a city over her dead bones;   91
and after her who first had picked that spot,
they called it Mantua—they cast no lots.

There once were far more people in its walls,   94
before the foolishness of Casalodi
was tricked by the deceit of Pinamonte.

Therefore, I charge you, if you ever hear   97

a different tale of my town's origin,
do not let any falsehood gull the truth."

And I: "O master, that which you have spoken   100
convinces me and so compels my trust
that others' words would only be spent coals.

But tell me if among the passing souls   103
you see some spirits worthy of our notice,
because my mind is bent on that alone."

Then he to me: "That shade who spreads his beard   106
down from his cheeks across his swarthy shoulders—
when Greece had been so emptied of its males

that hardly any cradle held a son,   109
he was an augur; and at Aulis, he
and Calchas set the time to cut the cables.

His name's Eurypylus; a certain passage   112
of my high tragedy has sung it so;
you know that well enough, who know the whole.

That other there, his flanks extremely spare,   115
was Michael Scot, a man who certainly
knew how the game of magic fraud was played.

See there Guido Bonatti; see Asdente,   118
who now would wish he had attended to
his cord and leather, but repents too late.

See those sad women who had left their needle,   121
shuttle, and spindle to become diviners;
they cast their spells with herbs and effigies.

But let us go; Cain with his thorns already   124
is at the border of both hemispheres
and there, below Seville, touches the sea.

Last night the moon was at its full; you should   127
be well aware of this, for there were times
when it did you no harm in the deep wood."

These were his words to me; meanwhile we journeyed.   130

CANTO XXI

*The Eighth Circle, Fifth Pouch, with Barrators plunged into
boiling pitch and guarded by demons armed with prongs. A
newly arrived magistrate from Lucca. Ten demons assigned by
Malacoda ("Evil-Tail"), the chief of the Malebranche
("Evil-Claws"), to escort Dante and Virgil. The remark-
able signal for their march.*

We came along from one bridge to another,
talking of things my Comedy is not
concerned to sing. We held fast to the summit,

then stayed our steps to spy the other cleft   4
of Malebolge and other vain laments.
I saw that it was wonderfully dark.

As in the arsenal of the Venetians,   7
all winter long a stew of sticky pitch
boils up to patch their sick and tattered ships

that cannot sail (instead of voyaging,   10
some build new keels, some tow and tar the ribs
of hulls worn out by too much journeying;

some hammer at the prow, some at the stern,   13
and some make oars, and some braid ropes and cords;
one mends the jib, another, the mainsail);

so, not by fire but by the art of God,   16
below there boiled a thick and tarry mass
that covered all the banks with clamminess.

I saw it, but I could not see within it;   19
no thing was visible but boiling bubbles,
the swelling of the pitch; and then it settled.

And while I watched below attentively,   22
my guide called out to me: "Take care! Take care!"
And then, from where I stood, he drew me near.

I turned around as one who is keen to see   25
a sight from which it would be wise to flee,
and then is horror-stricken suddenly—

who does not stop his flight and yet looks back.   28
And then—behind us there—I saw a black
demon as he came racing up the crags.

Ah, he was surely barbarous to see!   31
And how relentless seemed to me his acts!
His wings were open and his feet were lithe;

across his shoulder, which was sharp and high,   34
he had slung a sinner, upward from the thighs;
in front, the demon gripped him by the ankles.

Then from our bridge, he called: "O Malebranche,   37
I've got an elder of Saint Zita for you!
Shove this one under—I'll go back for more—

his city is well furnished with such stores;   40
there, everyone's a grafter but Bonturo;
and there—for cash—they'll change a *no* to *yes*."

He threw the sinner down, then wheeled along   43
the stony cliff: no mastiff's ever been
unleashed with so much haste to chase a thief.

The sinner plunged, then surfaced, black with pitch;   46
but now the demons, from beneath the bridge,
shouted: "The Sacred Face has no place here;

here we swim differently than in the Serchio;   49
if you don't want to feel our grappling hooks,
don't try to lift yourself above that ditch."

They pricked him with a hundred prongs and more,   52
then taunted: "Here one dances under cover,
so try to grab your secret graft below."

The demons did the same as any cook   55
who has his urchins force the meat with hooks
deep down into the pot, that it not float.

Then my good master said to me: "Don't let   58
those demons see that you are here; take care
to crouch behind the cover of a crag.

No matter what offense they offer me,   61
don't be afraid; I know how these things go—
I've had to face such fracases before."

When this was said, he moved beyond the bridgehead.   64
And on the sixth embankment, he had need
to show his imperturbability.

With the same frenzy, with the brouhaha   67
of dogs, when they beset a sorry wretch
who—startled—stops dead in his tracks and begs,

so, from beneath the bridge, the demons rushed   70
against my guide with all their prongs, but he
called out: "Can't you forget your savagery!

Before you try to maul me, just let one   73
of all your troop step forward. Hear me out,
and then decide if I am to be hooked."

At this they howled, "Let Malacoda go!"   76
And one of them moved up—the others stayed—
and as he came, he asked: "How can he win?"

"O Malacoda, do you think I've come,"   79
my master answered him, "already armed—
as you can see—against your obstacles,

without the will of God and helpful fate?   82
Let us move on; it is the will of Heaven
for me to show this wild way to another."

At this the pride of Malacoda fell;   85
his prong dropped to his feet. He told his fellows:
"Since that's the way things stand, let us not wound him."

My guide then spoke to me: "O you, who crouch,   88
bent low among the bridge's splintered rocks,
you can feel safe—and now return to me."

At this I moved and quickly came to him.   91
The devils had edged forward, all of them;
I feared that they might fail to keep their word:

just so, I saw the infantry when they   94
marched out, under safe conduct, from Caprona;
they trembled when they passed their enemies.

My body huddled closer to my guide;
I did not let the demons out of sight;
the looks they cast at us were less than kind.

They bent their hooks and shouted to each other: 100
"And shall I give it to him on the rump?"
And all of them replied, "Yes, let him have it!"

But Malacoda, still in conversation 103
with my good guide, turned quickly to his squadron
and said: "Be still, Scarmiglione, still!"

To us he said: "There is no use in going 106
much farther on this ridge, because the sixth
bridge—at the bottom there—is smashed to bits.

Yet if you two still want to go ahead, 109
move up and walk along this rocky edge;
nearby, another ridge will form a path.

Five hours from this hour yesterday, 112
one thousand and two hundred sixty-six
years passed since that roadway was shattered here.

I'm sending ten of mine out there to see 115
if any sinner lifts his head for air;
go with my men—there is no malice in them."

"Step forward, Alichino and Calcabrina," 118
he then began to say, "and you, Cagnazzo;
and Barbariccia, who can lead the ten.

Let Libicocco go, and Draghignazzo 121
and tusky Ciriatto and Graffiacane
and Farfarello and mad Rubicante.

Search all around the clammy stew of pitch; 124
keep these two safe and sound till the next ridge
that rises without break across the dens."

"Ah me! What is this, master, that I see?" 127
I said. "Can't we do without company?
If you know how to go, I want no escort.

If you are just as keen as usual, 130
can't you see how those demons grind their teeth?
Their brows are menacing, they promise trouble."

And he to me: "I do not want you frightened: 133
just let them gnash away as they may wish;
they do it for the wretches boiled in pitch."

They turned around along the left hand bank: 136
but first each pressed his tongue between his teeth
as signal for their leader, Barbariccia.

And he had made a trumpet of his ass.   139

CANTO XXII

Still the Eighth Circle, Fifth Pouch: the Barrators. The Barrator from Navarre. Fra Gomita and Michele Zanche, two Sardinians. The astuteness of the Navarrese that leads two demons to fall into the pitch.

Before this I've seen horsemen start to march
and open the assault and muster ranks
and seen them, too, at times beat their retreat;

and on your land, o Aretines, I've seen   4
rangers and raiding parties galloping,
the clash of tournaments, the rush of jousts,

now done with trumpets, now with bells, and now   7
with drums, and now with signs from castle walls,
with native things and with imported ware;

but never yet have I seen horsemen or   10
seen infantry or ship that sails by signal
of land or star move to so strange a bugle!

We made our way together with ten demons: 13
ah, what ferocious company! And yet
"in church with saints, with rotters in the tavern."

But I was all intent upon the pitch,   16
to seek out every feature of the pouch
and of the people who were burning in it.

Just as the dolphins do, when with arched back,   19
they signal to the seamen to prepare
for tempest, that their vessel may be spared,

so here from time to time, to ease his torment,   22
some sinner showed his back above the surface,
then hid more quickly than a lightning flash.

And just as on the margin of a ditch,   25
frogs crouch, their snouts alone above the water,

so as to hide their feet and their plump flesh,

so here on every side these sinners crouched;   28
but faster than a flash, when Barbariccia
drew near, they plunged beneath the boiling pitch.

I saw—my heart still shudders in recall—   31
one who delayed, just as at times a frog
is left behind while others dive below;

and Graffiacane, who was closest to him,   34
then hooked him by his pitch-entangled locks
and hauled him up; he seemed to me an otter.

By now I knew the names of all those demons—   37
I'd paid attention when the fiends were chosen;
I'd watched as they stepped forward, one by one.

"O Rubicante, see you set your talons   40
right into him, so you can flay his flesh!"
So did those cursed ones cry out together.

And I: "My master, if you can, find out   43
what is the name of that unfortunate
who's fallen victim to his enemies."

My guide, who then drew near that sinner's side,   46
asked him to tell his birthplace. He replied:
"My homeland was the kingdom of Navarre.

My mother, who had had me by a wastrel,   49
destroyer of himself and his possessions,
had placed me in the service of a lord.

Then I was in the household of the worthy   52
King Thibault; there I started taking graft;
with this heat I pay reckoning for that."

And Ciriatto, from whose mouth there bulged   55
to right and left two tusks like a wild hog's,
then let him feel how one of them could mangle.

The mouse had fallen in with evil cats;   58
but Barbariccia clasped him in his arms
and said: "Stand off there, while I fork him fast."

And turning toward my master then, he said: 61
"Ask on, if you would learn some more from him

before one of the others does him in."

At which my guide: "Now tell: among the sinners   64
who hide beneath the pitch, are any others
Italian?" And he: "I have just left

one who was nearby there; and would I were   67
still covered by the pitch as he is hidden,
for then I'd have no fear of hook or talon."

And Libicocco said, "We've been too patient!"   70
and, with his grapple, grabbed him by the arm
and, ripping, carried off a hunk of flesh.

But Draghignazzo also looked as if   73
to grab his legs; at which, their captain wheeled
and threatened all of them with raging looks.

When they'd grown somewhat less tumultuous,   76
without delay my guide asked of that one
who had his eyes still fixed upon his wound:

"Who was the one you left to come ashore—   79
unluckily—as you just said before?"
He answered: "Fra Gomita of Gallura,

who was a vessel fit for every fraud: 82
he had his master's enemies in hand,
but handled them in ways that pleased them all.

He took their gold and smoothly let them off,   85
as he himself says; and in other matters,
he was a sovereign, not a petty, swindler.

His comrade there is Don Michele Zanche   88
of Logodoro; and their tongues are never
too tired to talk of their Sardinia.

Ah me, see that one there who grinds his teeth!   91
If I were not afraid, I'd speak some more,
but he is getting set to scratch my scurf."

And their great marshal, facing Farfarello—   94
who was so hot to strike he rolled his eyes,
said, "Get away from there, you filthy bird!"

"If you perhaps would like to see or hear,"   97
that sinner, terrified, began again,

"Lombards or Tuscans, I can fetch you some;
  but let the Malebranche stand aside   100
so that my comrades need not fear their vengeance.
Remaining in this very spot, I shall,
  although alone, make seven more appear   103
when I have whistled, as has been our custom
when one of us has managed to get out."

  At that, Cagnazzo lifted up his snout   106
and shook his head, and said: "Just listen to
that trick by which he thinks he can dive back!"

  To this, he who was rich in artifice   109
replied: "Then I must have too many tricks,
if I bring greater torment to my friends."

  This was too much for Alichino and,   112
despite the others, he cried out: "If you
dive back, I shall not gallop after you

  but beat my wings above the pitch; we'll leave   115
this height; with the embankment as a screen,
we'll see if you—alone—can handle us."

  O you who read, hear now of this new sport: 118
each turned his eyes upon the other shore,
he first who'd been most hesitant before.

  The Navarrese, in nick of time, had planted   121
his feet upon the ground; then in an instant
he jumped and freed himself from their commander.

  At this each demon felt the prick of guilt,   124
and most, he who had led his band to blunder;
so he took off and shouted: "You are caught!"

  But this could help him little; wings were not   127
more fast than fear; the sinner plunged right under;
the other, flying up, lifted his chest:

  not otherwise the wild duck when it plunges   130
precipitously, when the falcon nears
and then—exhausted, thwarted—flies back up.

  But Calcabrina, raging at the trick,   133
flew after Alichino; he was keen

to see the sinner free and have a brawl;

    and once the Navarrese had disappeared, 136
he turned his talons on his fellow demon
and tangled with him just above the ditch.

    But Alichino clawed him well—he was 139
indeed a full-grown kestrel; and both fell
into the middle of the boiling pond.

    The heat was quick to disentangle them, 142
but still there was no way they could get out;
their wings were stuck, enmeshed in glue-like pitch.

    And Barbariccia, grieving with the rest, 145
sent four to fly out toward the other shore
with all their forks, and speedily enough

    on this side and on that they took their posts; 148
and toward those two—stuck fast, already cooked
beneath that crust—they stretched their grappling hooks.

    We left them still contending with that mess. 151

CANTO XXIII

Still the Eighth Circle, Fifth Pouch: the Barrators. Pursuit by the demons, with Virgil snatching up Dante and sliding down to the Sixth Pouch, where the Hypocrites file along slowly, clothed in caps of lead. Two Jovial Friars of Bologna, Catalano and Loderingo. Caiaphas. Virgil's distress at Malacoda's deceitfulness.

Silent, alone, no one escorting us,
we made our way—one went before, one after—
as Friars Minor when they walk together.

The present fracas made me think of Aesop—   4
that fable where he tells about the mouse
and frog; for "near" and "nigh" are not more close

than are that fable and this incident,   7
if you compare with care how each begins
and then compare the endings that they share.

And even as one thought springs from another,   10
so out of that was still another born,
which made the fear I felt before redouble.

I thought: "Because of us, they have been mocked,   13
and this inflicted so much hurt and scorn
that I am sure they feel deep indignation.

If anger's to be added to their malice,   16
they'll hunt us down with more ferocity
than any hound whose teeth have trapped a hare."

I could already feel my hair curl up   19
from fear, and I looked back attentively,
while saying: "Master, if you don't conceal

yourself and me at once—they terrify me,   22
those Malebranche; they are after us;
I so imagine them, I hear them now."

And he to me: "Were I a leaded mirror,   25
I could not gather in your outer image
more quickly than I have received your inner.

For even now your thoughts have joined my own;   28
in both our acts and aspects we are kin—
with both our minds I've come to one decision.

If that right bank is not extremely steep,   31
we can descend into the other moat
and so escape from the imagined chase."

He'd hardly finished telling me his plan   34
when I saw them approach with outstretched wings,
not too far off, and keen on taking us.

My guide snatched me up instantly, just as   37
the mother who is wakened by a roar
and catches sight of blazing flames beside her,

will lift her son and run without a stop—   40
she cares more for the child than for herself—
not pausing even to throw on a shift;

and down the hard embankment's edge—his back   43
lay flat along the sloping rock that closes
one side of the adjacent moat—he slid.

No water ever ran so fast along   46
a sluice to turn the wheels of a land mill,
not even when its flow approached the paddles,

as did my master race down that embankment   49
while bearing me with him upon his chest,
just like a son, and not like a companion.

His feet had scarcely reached the bed that lies   52
along the deep below, than those ten demons
were on the edge above us; but there was

nothing to fear; for that High Providence   55
that willed them ministers of the fifth ditch,
denies to all of them the power to leave it.

Below that point we found a painted people,   58
who moved about with lagging steps, in circles,
weeping, with features tired and defeated.

And they were dressed in cloaks with cowls so low   61
they fell before their eyes, of that same cut
that's used to make the clothes for Cluny's monks.

Outside, these cloaks were gilded and they dazzled;   64
but inside they were all of lead, so heavy
that Frederick's capes were straw compared to them.

A tiring mantle for eternity!   67
We turned again, as always, to the left,
along with them, intent on their sad weeping;

but with their weights that weary people paced   70
so slowly that we found ourselves among
new company each time we took a step.

At which I told my guide: "Please try to find   73
someone whose name or deed I recognize;
and while we walk, be watchful with your eyes."

And one who'd taken in my Tuscan speech   76
cried out behind us: "Stay your steps, o you
who hurry so along this darkened air!

Perhaps you'll have from me that which you seek."   79
At which my guide turned to me, saying: "Wait,
and then continue, following his pace."

I stopped, and I saw two whose faces showed   82
their minds were keen to be with me; but both
their load and the tight path forced them to slow.

When they came up, they looked askance at me   85
a long while, and they uttered not a word
until they turned to one another, saying:

"The throbbing of his throat makes this one seem   88
alive; and if they're dead, what privilege
lets them appear without the heavy mantle?"

Then addressed me: "Tuscan, you who come   91
to this assembly of sad hypocrites,
do not disdain to tell us who you are."

I answered: "Where the lovely Arno flows,   94
there I was born and raised, in the great city;
I'm with the body I have always had.

But who are you, upon whose cheeks I see
such tears distilled by grief? And let me know
what punishment it is that glitters so."

And one of them replied: "The yellow cloaks
are of a lead so thick, their heaviness
makes us, the balances beneath them, creak.

We both were Jovial Friars, and Bolognese;
my name was Catalano, Loderingo
was his, and we were chosen by your city

together, for the post that's usually
one man's, to keep the peace; and what we were
is still to be observed around Gardingo."

I then began, "O Friars, your misdeeds . . . "
but said no more, because my eyes had caught
one crucified by three stakes on the ground.

When he saw me, that sinner writhed all over,
and he breathed hard into his beard with sighs;
observing that, Fra Catalano said

to me: "That one impaled there, whom you see,
counseled the Pharisees that it was prudent
to let one man—and not one nation—suffer.

Naked, he has been stretched across the path,
as you can see, and he must feel the weight
of anyone who passes over him.

Like torment, in this ditch, afflicts both his
father-in-law and others in that council,
which for the Jews has seeded so much evil."

Then I saw Virgil stand amazed above
that one who lay stretched out upon a cross
so squalidly in his eternal exile.

And he addressed the friar in this way:
"If it does not displease you—if you may—
tell us if there's some passage on the right

that would allow the two of us to leave
without our having to compel black angels
to travel to this deep, to get us out."

The abyss of the Hypocrites in which Caiaphas and the Sanhedrin are crucified to the floor.

He answered: "Closer than you hope, you'll find   133
a rocky ridge that stretches from the great
round wall and crosses all the savage valleys,

except that here it's broken—not a bridge.   136
But where its ruins slope along the bank
and heap up at the bottom, you can climb."

My leader stood a while with his head bent,   139
then said: "He who hooks sinners over there
gave us a false account of this affair."

At which the Friar: "In Bologna, I   142
once heard about the devil's many vices—
they said he was a liar and father of lies."

And then my guide moved on with giant strides,   145
somewhat disturbed, with anger in his eyes;
at this I left those overburdened spirits,

while following the prints of his dear feet.   148

CANTO XXIV

*Still the Eighth Circle, Sixth Pouch: the Hypocrites. Hard
passage to the Seventh Pouch: the Thieves. Bitten by a serpent,
a thieving sinner who turns to ashes and is then restored:
Vanni Fucci. His prediction of the defeat of the Whites—
Dante's party—at Pistoia.*

In that part of the young year when the sun
begins to warm its locks beneath Aquarius
and nights grow shorter, equaling the days,

    when hoarfrost mimes the image of his white   4
sister upon the ground—but not for long,
because the pen he uses is not sharp—

    the farmer who is short of fodder rises   7
and looks and sees the fields all white, at which
he slaps his thigh, turns back into the house,

    and here and there complains like some poor wretch   10
who doesn't know what can be done, and then
goes out again and gathers up new hope

    on seeing that the world has changed its face   13
in so few hours, and he takes his staff
and hurries out his flock of sheep to pasture.

    So did my master fill me with dismay   16
when I saw how his brow was deeply troubled,
yet then the plaster soothed the sore as quickly:

    for soon as we were on the broken bridge,   19
my guide turned back to me with that sweet manner
I first had seen along the mountain's base.

    And he examined carefully the ruin;   22
then having picked the way we would ascend,
he opened up his arms and thrust me forward.

    And just as he who ponders as he labors,   25

who's always ready for the step ahead,
so, as he lifted me up toward the summit

of one great crag, he'd see another spur,   28
saying: "That is the one you will grip next,
but try it first to see if it is firm."

That was no path for those with cloaks of lead,   31
for he and I—he, light; I, with support—
could hardly make it up from spur to spur.

And were it not that, down from this enclosure,   34
the slope was shorter than the bank before,
I cannot speak for him, but I should surely

have been defeated. But since Malebolge   37
runs right into the mouth of its last well,
the placement of each valley means it must

have one bank high and have the other short;   40
and so we have reached, at length, the jutting where
the last stone of the ruined bridge breaks off.

The breath within my lungs was so exhausted   43
from climbing, I could not go on; in fact,
as soon as I had reached that stone, I sat.

"Now you must cast aside your laziness,"   46
my master said, "for he who rests on down
or under covers cannot come to fame;

and he who spends his life without renown   49
leaves such a vestige of himself on earth
as smoke bequeaths to air or foam to water.

Therefore, get up; defeat your breathlessness   52
with spirit that can win all battles if
the body's heaviness does not deter it.

A longer ladder still is to be climbed;   55
it's not enough to have left them behind;
if you have understood, now profit from it."

Then I arose and showed myself far better   58
equipped with breath than I had been before:
"Go on, for I am strong and confident."

We took our upward way upon the ridge,   61

with crags more jagged, narrow, difficult,
and much more steep than we had crossed before.

I spoke as we went on, not to seem weak;   64
at this, a voice came from the ditch beyond—
a voice that was not suited to form words.

I know not what he said, although I was   67
already at the summit of the bridge
that crosses there; and yet he seemed to move.

I had bent downward, but my living eyes   70
could not see to the bottom through that dark;
at which I said: "O master, can we reach

the other belt? Let us descend the wall,   73
for as I hear and cannot understand,
so I see down but can distinguish nothing."

"The only answer that I give to you   76
is doing it," he said. "A just request
is to be met in silence, by the act."

We then climbed down the bridge, just at the end   79
where it runs right into the eighth embankment,
and now the moat was plain enough to me;

and there within I saw a dreadful swarm   82
of serpents so extravagant in form—
remembering them still drains my blood from me.

Let Libya boast no more about her sands;   85
for if she breeds chelydri, jaculi,
cenchres with amphisbaena, pareae,

she never showed—with all of Ethiopia   88
or all the land that borders the Red Sea—
so many, such malignant, pestilences.

Among this cruel and depressing swarm,   91
ran people who were naked, terrified,
with no hope of a hole or heliotrope.

Their hands were tied behind by serpents; these   94
had thrust their head and tail right through the loins,
and then were knotted on the other side.

And—there!—a serpent sprang with force at one   97

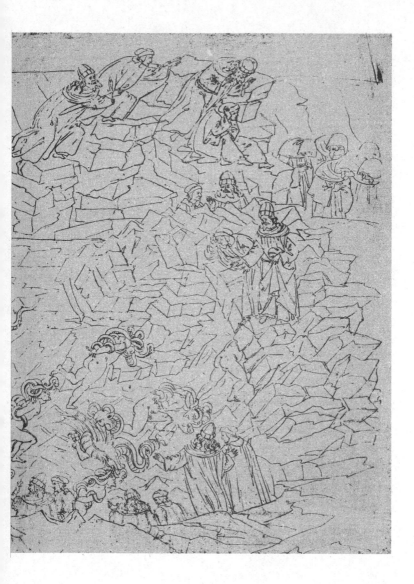

The abyss of Thieves, entwined in reptiles which symbolize their stealth.

who stood upon our shore, transfixing him
just where the neck and shoulders form a knot.

    No *o* or *i* has ever been transcribed 100
so quickly as that soul caught fire and burned
and, as he fell, completely turned to ashes;

    and when he lay, undone, upon the ground, 103
the dust of him collected by itself
and instantly returned to what it was:

    just so, it is asserted by great sages, 106
that, when it reaches its five-hundredth year,
the phoenix dies and then is born again;

    lifelong it never feeds on grass or grain, 109
only on drops of incense and amomum;
its final winding sheets are nard and myrrh.

    And just as he who falls, and knows not how— 112
by demon's force that drags him to the ground
or by some other hindrance that binds man—

    who, when he rises, stares about him, all 115
bewildered by the heavy anguish he
has suffered, sighing as he looks around;

    so did this sinner stare when he arose. 118
Oh, how severe it is, the power of God
that, as its vengeance, showers down such blows!

    My guide then asked that sinner who he was; 121
to this he answered: "Not long since, I rained
from Tuscany into this savage maw.

    Mule that I was, the bestial life pleased me 124
and not the human; I am Vanni Fucci,
beast; and the den that suited me—Pistoia."

    And I to Virgil: "Tell him not to slip 127
away, and ask what sin has thrust him here;
I knew him as a man of blood and anger."

    The sinner heard and did not try to feign 130
but turned his mind and face, intent, toward me;
and coloring with miserable shame,

    he said: "I suffer more because you've caught me 133

in this, the misery you see, than I
suffered when taken from the other life.

    I can't refuse to answer what you ask: 136
I am set down so far because I robbed
the sacristy of its fair ornaments,

    and someone else was falsely blamed for that.   139
But lest this sight give you too much delight,
if you can ever leave these lands of darkness,

    open your ears to my announcement, hear: 142
Pistoia first will strip herself of Blacks,
then Florence will renew her men and manners.

    From Val di Magra, Mars will draw a vapor   145
which turbid clouds will try to wrap; the clash
between them will be fierce, impetuous,

    a tempest, fought upon Campo Piceno,   148
until that vapor, vigorous, shall crack
the mist, and every White be struck by it.

    And I have told you this to make you grieve."   151

CANTO XXV

Still the Eighth Circle, Seventh Pouch: the Thieves. Vanni Fucci and his obscene figs against God. The Centaur Cacus. Five Florentine Thieves, three of them humans and two of them serpents. The astounding metamorphoses undergone by four of them.

When he had finished with his words, the thief
raised high his fists with both figs cocked and cried:
"Take that, o God; I square them off for you!"

From that time on, those serpents were my friends,   4
for one of them coiled then around his neck,
as if to say, "I'll have you speak no more";

another wound about his arms and bound him   7
again and wrapped itself in front so firmly,
he could not even make them budge an inch.

Pistoia, ah, Pistoia, must you last: 10
why not decree your self-incineration,
since you surpass your seed in wickedness?

Throughout the shadowed circles of deep Hell,   13
I saw no soul against God so rebel,
not even he who fell from Theban walls.

He fled and could not say another word;   16
and then I saw a Centaur full of anger,
shouting: "Where is he, where's that bitter one?"

I do not think Maremma has the number   19
of snakes that Centaur carried on his haunch
until the part that takes our human form.

Upon his shoulders and behind his nape   22
there lay a dragon with its wings outstretched;
it sets ablaze all those it intercepts.

My master said: "That Centaur there is Cacus,   25

who often made a lake of blood within
a grotto underneath Mount Aventine.

He does not ride the same road as his brothers   28
because he stole—and most deceitfully—
from the great herd nearby; his crooked deeds

ended beneath the club of Hercules,   31
who may have given him a hundred blows—
but he was not alive to feel the tenth."

While he was talking so, Cacus ran by   34
and, just beneath our ledge, three souls arrived;
but neither I nor my guide noticed them

until they had cried out: "And who are you?"   37
At this the words we shared were interrupted,
and we attended only to those spirits.

I did not recognize them, but it happened,   40
as chance will usually bring about,
that one of them called out the other's name,

exclaiming: "Where was Cianfa left behind?"   43
At this, so that my guide might be alert,
I raised my finger up from chin to nose.

If, reader, you are slow now to believe   46
what I shall tell, that is no cause for wonder,
for I who saw it hardly can accept it.

As I kept my eyes fixed upon those sinners,   49
a serpent with six feet springs out against
one of the three, and clutches him completely.

It gripped his belly with its middle feet,   52
and with its forefeet grappled his two arms;
and then it sank its teeth in both his cheeks;

it stretched its rear feet out along his thighs   55
and ran its tail along between the two,
then straightened it again behind his loins.

No ivy ever gripped a tree so fast   58
as when that horrifying monster clasped
and intertwined the other's limbs with its.

Then just as if their substance were warm wax,   61

they stuck together and they mixed their colors,
so neither seemed what he had been before;

just as, when paper's kindled, where it still   64
has not caught flame in full, its color's dark
though not yet black, while white is dying off.

The other two souls stared, and each one cried: 67
"Ah me, Agnello, how you change! Just see,
you are already neither two nor one!"

Then two heads were already joined in one,   70
when in one face where two had been dissolved,
two intermingled shapes appeared to us.

Two arms came into being from four lengths;   73
the thighs and legs, the belly and the chest
became such limbs as never had been seen.

And every former shape was canceled there: 76
that perverse image seemed to share in both—
and none; and so, and slowly, it moved on.

Just as the lizard, when it darts from hedge   79
to hedge, beneath the dog days' giant lash,
seems, if it cross one's path, a lightning flash,

so seemed a blazing little serpent moving   82
against the bellies of the other two,
as black and livid as a peppercorn.

Attacking one of them, it pierced right through   85
the part where we first take our nourishment;
and then it fell before him at full length.

The one it had transfixed stared but said nothing;   88
in fact he only stood his ground and yawned
as one whom sleep or fever has undone.

The serpent stared at him, he at the serpent;   91
one through his wound, the other through his mouth
were smoking violently; their smoke met.

Let Lucan now be silent, where he sings   94
of sad Sabellus and Nasidius,
and wait to hear what flies off from my bow.

Let Ovid now be silent, where he tells   97

of Cadmus, Arethusa; if his verse
has made of one a serpent, one a fountain,

I do not envy him; he never did   100
transmute two natures, face to face, so that
both forms were ready to exchange their matter.

These were the ways they answered to each other: 103
the serpent split its tail into a fork;
the wounded sinner drew his steps together.

The legs and then the thighs along with them   106
so fastened to each other that the juncture
soon left no sign that was discernible.

Meanwhile the cleft tail took upon itself   109
the form the other gradually lost;
its skin grew soft, the other's skin grew hard.

I saw the arms that drew in at his armpits   112
and also saw the monster's two short feet
grow long for just as much as those were shortened.

The serpent's hind feet, twisted up together,   115
became the member that man hides; just as
the wretch put out two hind paws from his member.

And while the smoke veils each with a new color   118
and now breeds hair upon the skin of one,
just as it strips the hair from off the other,

the one rose up, the other fell; and yet   121
they never turned aside their impious eyelamps,
beneath which each of them transformed his snout:

he who stood up drew his back toward the temples,   124
and from the excess matter growing there
came ears upon the cheeks that had been bare;

whatever had not been pulled back but kept,   127
superfluous, then made his face a nose
and thickened out his lips appropriately.

He who was lying down thrust out his snout;   130
and even as the snail hauls in its horns,
he drew his ears straight back into his head;

his tongue, which had before been whole and fit   133

for speech, now cleaves; the other's tongue, which had
been forked, now closes up; and the smoke stops.

The soul that had become an animal,   136
now hissing, hurried off along the valley;
the other one, behind him, speaks and spits.

And then he turned aside his new-made shoulders   139
and told the third soul: "I'd have Buoso run
on all fours down this road, as I have done."

And so I saw the seventh ballast change   142
and rechange; may the strangeness plead for me
if there's been some confusion in my pen.

And though my eyes were somewhat blurred, my mind 145
bewildered, those three sinners did not flee
so secretly that I could not perceive

Puccio Sciancato clearly, he who was   148
the only soul who'd not been changed among
the three companions we had met at first;

the other one made you, Gaville, grieve.   151

CANTO XXVI

*Still the Eighth Circle, Seventh Pouch: the Thieves. Dante's
invective against Florence. View of the Eighth Pouch, where
Fraudulent Counselors are clothed in the flames that burn
them. Ulysses and Diomedes in one shared flame. Ulysses' tale
of his final voyage.*

Be joyous, Florence, you are great indeed,
for over sea and land you beat your wings;
through every part of Hell your name extends!

Among the thieves I found five citizens   4
of yours—and such, that shame has taken me;
with them, you can ascend to no high honor.

But if the dreams dreamt close to dawn are true,   7
then little time will pass before you feel
what Prato and the others crave for you.

Were that already come, it would not be   10
too soon—and let it come, since it must be!
As I grow older, it will be more heavy.

We left that deep and, by protruding stones   13
that served as stairs for our descent before,
my guide climbed up again and drew me forward;

and as we took our solitary path   16
among the ridge's jagged spurs and rocks,
our feet could not make way without our hands.

It grieved me then and now grieves me again   19
when I direct my mind to what I saw;
and more than usual, I curb my talent,

that it not run where virtue does not guide;   22
so that, if my kind star or something better
has given me that gift, I not abuse it.

As many as the fireflies the peasant   25

(while resting on a hillside in the season
when he who lights the world least hides his face),

just when the fly gives way to the mosquito,   28
sees glimmering below, down in the valley,
there where perhaps he gathers grapes and tills—

so many were the flames that glittered in   31
the eighth abyss; I made this out as soon
as I had come to where one sees the bottom.

Even as he who was avenged by bears   34
saw, as it left, Elijah's chariot—
its horses rearing, rising right to heaven—

when he could not keep track of it except   37
by watching one lone flame in its ascent,
just like a little cloud that climbs on high:

so, through the gullet of that ditch, each flame   40
must make its way; no flame displays its prey,
though every flame has carried off a sinner.

I stood upon the bridge and leaned straight out   43
to see; and if I had not gripped a rock,
I should have fallen off—without a push.

My guide, who noted how intent I was,   46
told me: "Within those fires there are souls;
each one is swathed in that which scorches him."

"My master," I replied, "on hearing you,   49
I am more sure; but I'd already thought
that it was so, and I had meant to ask:

Who is within the flame that comes so twinned   52
above that it would seem to rise out of
the pyre Eteocles shared with his brother?"

He answered me: "Within that flame, Ulysses   55
and Diomedes suffer; they, who went
as one to rage, now share one punishment.

And there, together in their flame, they grieve   58
over the horse's fraud that caused a breach—
the gate that let Rome's noble seed escape.

There they regret the guile that makes the dead   61

Deïdamia still lament Achilles;
and there, for the Palladium, they pay."

"If they can speak within those sparks," I said, 64
"I pray you and repray and, master, may
my prayer be worth a thousand pleas, do not

forbid my waiting here until the flame 67
with horns approaches us; for you can see
how, out of my desire, I bend toward it."

And he to me: "What you have asked is worthy 70
of every praise; therefore, I favor it.
I only ask you this: refrain from talking.

Let me address them—I have understood 73
what you desire of them. Since they were Greek,
perhaps they'd be disdainful of your speech."

And when my guide adjudged the flame had reached 76
a point where time and place were opportune,
this was the form I heard his words assume:

"You two who move as one within the flame, 79
if I deserved of you while I still lived,
if I deserved of you much or a little

when in the world I wrote my noble lines, 82
do not move on; let one of you retell
where, having gone astray, he found his death."

The greater horn within that ancient flame 85
began to sway and tremble, murmuring
just like a fire that struggles in the wind;

and then he waved his flame-tip back and forth 88
as if it were a tongue that tried to speak,
and flung toward us a voice that answered: "When

I sailed away from Circe, who'd beguiled me 91
to stay more than a year there, near Gaeta—
before Aeneas gave that place a name—

neither my fondness for my son nor pity 94
for my old father nor the love I owed
Penelope, which would have gladdened her,

was able to defeat in me the longing 97

I had to gain experience of the world
and of the vices and the worth of men.

Therefore, I set out on the open sea   100
with but one ship and that small company
of those who never had deserted me.

I saw as far as Spain, far as Morocco,   103
along both shores; I saw Sardinia
and saw the other islands that sea bathes.

And I and my companions were already   106
old and slow, when we approached the narrows
where Hercules set up his boundary stones

that men might heed and never reach beyond: 109
upon my right, I had gone past Seville,
and on the left, already passed Ceüta.

'Brothers,' I said, 'o you, who having crossed   112
a hundred thousand dangers, reach the west,
to this brief waking-time that still is left

unto your senses, you must not deny   115
experience of that which lies beyond
the sun, and of the world that is unpeopled.

Consider well the seed that gave you birth: 118
you were not made to live your lives as brutes,
but to be followers of worth and knowledge.'

I spurred my comrades with this brief address   121
to meet the journey with such eagerness
that I could hardly, then, have held them back;

and having turned our stern toward morning, we   124
made wings out of our oars in a wild flight
and always gained upon our left-hand side.

At night I now could see the other pole   127
and all its stars; the star of ours had fallen
and never rose above the plain of the ocean.

Five times the light beneath the moon had been   130
rekindled, and, as many times, was spent,
since that hard passage faced our first attempt,

when there before us rose a mountain, dark   133

because of distance, and it seemed to me
the highest mountain I had ever seen.

And we were glad, but this soon turned to sorrow,   136
for out of that new land a whirlwind rose
and hammered at our ship, against her bow.

Three times it turned her round with all the waters;   139
and at the fourth, it lifted up the stern
so that our prow plunged deep, as pleased an Other,
    until the sea again closed—over us."   142

CANTO XXVII

Still the Eighth Circle, Eighth Pouch: the Fraudulent Counselors. Guido da Montefeltro, for whom Dante provides a panorama of the state of political affairs in Romagna. Guido's tale of the anticipatory—but unavailing—absolution given him by Boniface VIII. The quarrel of a demon and St Francis over Guido's soul.

The flame already was erect and silent—
it had no more to say. Now it had left us
with the permission of the gentle poet,

when, just behind it, came another flame   4
that drew our eyes to watch its tip because
of the perplexing sound that it sent forth.

Even as the Sicilian bull (that first   7
had bellowed with the cry—and this was just—
of him who shaped it with his instruments)

would always bellow with its victim's voice,   10
so that, although that bull was only brass,
it seemed as if it were pierced through by pain;

so were the helpless words that, from the first,   13
had found no path or exit from the flame,
transformed into the language of the fire.

But after they had found their way up toward   16
the tip, and given it that movement which
the tongue had given them along their passage,

we heard: "O you to whom I turn my voice,   19
who only now were talking Lombard, saying,
'Now you may leave—I'll not provoke more speech,'

though I have come perhaps a little late,   22
may it not trouble you to stop and speak
with me; see how I stay—and I am burning!

If you have fallen into this blind world   25

but recently, out of the sweet Italian
country from which I carry all my guilt,

do tell me if the Romagnoles have peace 28
or war; I was from there—the hills between
Urbino and the ridge where Tiber springs."

I still was bent, attentive, over him, 31
when my guide nudged me lightly at the side
and said: "You speak; he is Italian."

And I, who had my answer set already, 34
without delay began to speak to him:
"O soul that is concealed below in flame,

Romagna is not now and never was 37
quite free of war inside its tyrants' hearts;
but when I left her, none had broken out.

Ravenna stands as it has stood for years; 40
the eagle of Polenta shelters it
and also covers Cervia with his wings.

The city that already stood long trial 43
and made a bloody heap out of the French,
now finds itself again beneath green paws.

Both mastiffs of Verrucchio, old and new, 46
who dealt so badly with Montagna, use
their teeth to bore where they have always gnawed.

The cities on Lamone and Santerno 49
are led by the young lion of the white lair;
from summer unto winter, he shifts factions.

That city with its side bathed by the Savio, 52
just as it lies between the plain and mountain,
lives somewhere between tyranny and freedom.

And now, I pray you, tell me who you are: 55
do not be harder than I've been with you,
that in the world your name may still endure."

After the flame, in customary fashion, 58
had roared awhile, it moved its pointed tip
this side and that and then set free this breath:

"If I thought my reply were meant for one 61
who ever could return into the world,

this flame would stir no more; and yet, since none—
    if what I hear is true—ever returned   64
alive from this abyss, then without fear
of facing infamy, I answer you.

    I was a man of arms, then wore the cord,   67
believing that, so girt, I made amends;
and surely what I thought would have been true

    had not the Highest Priest—may he be damned!—   70
made me fall back into my former sins;
and how and why, I'd have you hear from me.

    While I still had the form of bones and flesh   73
my mother gave to me, my deeds were not
those of the lion but those of the fox.

    The wiles and secret ways—I knew them all   76
and so employed their arts that my renown
had reached the very boundaries of earth.

    But when I saw myself come to that part   79
of life when it is fitting for all men
to lower sails and gather in their ropes,

    what once had been my joy was now dejection;   82
repenting and confessing, I became
a friar; and—poor me—it would have helped.

    The prince of the new Pharisees, who then   85
was waging war so near the Lateran—
and not against the Jews or Saracens,

    for every enemy of his was Christian,   88
and none of them had gone to conquer Acre
or been a trader in the Sultan's lands—

    took no care for the highest office or   91
the holy orders that were his, or for
my cord, which used to make its wearers leaner.

    But just as Constantine, on Mount Soracte,   94
to cure his leprosy, sought out Sylvester,
so this one sought me out as his instructor,

    to ease the fever of his arrogance.   97
He asked me to give counsel. I was silent—
his words had seemed to me delirious.

And then he said: 'Your heart must not mistrust: 100
I now absolve you in advance—teach me
to batter Penestrino to the ground.

You surely know that I possess the power   103
to lock and unlock Heaven; for the keys
my predecessor did not prize are two.'

Then his grave arguments compelled me so,   106
my silence seemed a worse offense than speech,
and I said: 'Since you cleanse me of the sin

that I must now fall into, Father, know: 109
long promises and very brief fulfillments
will bring a victory to your high throne.'

Then Francis came, as soon as I was dead,   112
for me; but one of the black cherubim
told him: 'Don't bear him off; do not cheat me.

He must come down among my menials;   115
the counsel that he gave was fraudulent;
since then I've kept close track, to snatch his scalp;

one can't absolve a man who's not repented,   118
and no one can repent and will at once;
the law of contradiction won't allow it.'

O miserable me, for how I started   121
when he took hold of me and said: 'Perhaps
you did not think that I was a logician!'

He carried me to Minos; and that monster   124
twisted his tail eight times around his hide
and then, when he had bit it in great anger,

announced: 'This one is for the thieving fire';   127
for which—and where, you see—I now am lost,
and in this garb I move in bitterness.''

And when, with this, his words were at an end,   130
the flame departed, sorrowing and writhing
and tossing its sharp horn. We moved beyond;

I went together with my guide, along   133
the ridge until the other arch that bridges
the ditch where payment is imposed on those

who, since they brought such discord, bear such loads.   136

CANTO XXVIII

The Eighth Circle, Ninth Pouch, where the Sowers of
Scandal and Schism, perpetually circling, are wounded and—
after each healing—wounded again by a demon with a sword.
Mohammed and Alì. Warning to Fra Dolcino. Curio.
Mosca. Bertran de Born.

Who, even with untrammeled words and many
attempts at telling, ever could recount
in full the blood and wounds that I now saw?

Each tongue that tried would certainly fall short   4
because the shallowness of both our speech
and intellect cannot contain so much.

Were you to reassemble all the men   7
who once, within Apulia's fateful land,
had mourned their blood, shed at the Trojans' hands,

as well as those who fell in the long war   10
where massive mounds of rings were battle spoils—
even as Livy writes, who does not err—

and those who felt the thrust of painful blows   13
when they fought hard against Robert Guiscard;
with all the rest whose bones are still piled up

at Ceperano—each Apulian was   16
a traitor there—and, too, at Tagliacozzo,
where old Alardo conquered without weapons;

and then, were one to show his limb pierced through   19
and one his limb hacked off, that would not match
the hideousness of the ninth abyss.

No barrel, even though it's lost a hoop   22
or end-piece, ever gapes as one whom I
saw ripped right from his chin to where we fart:

his bowels hung between his legs, one saw   25
his vitals and the miserable sack

that makes of what we swallow excrement.

While I was all intent on watching him,   28
he looked at me, and with his hands he spread
his chest and said: "See how I split myself!

See now how maimed Mohammed is! And he   31
who walks and weeps before me is Alì,
whose face is opened wide from chin to forelock.

And all the others here whom you can see   34
were, when alive, the sowers of dissension
and scandal, and for this they now are split.

Behind us here, a devil decks us out   37
so cruelly, re-placing every one
of this throng underneath the sword edge when

we've made our way around the road of pain,   40
because our wounds have closed again before
we have returned to meet his blade once more.

But who are you who dawdle on this ridge,   43
perhaps to slow your going to the verdict
that was pronounced on your self-accusations?"

"Death has not reached him yet," my master answered,   46
"nor is it guilt that summons him to torment;
but that he may gain full experience,

I, who am dead, must guide him here below,   49
to circle after circle, throughout Hell:
this is as true as that I speak to you."

More than a hundred, when they heard him, stopped   52
within the ditch and turned to look at me,
forgetful of their torture, wondering.

"Then you, who will perhaps soon see the sun,   55
tell Fra Dolcino to provide himself
with food, if he has no desire to join me

here quickly, lest when snow besieges him,   58
it bring the Novarese the victory
that otherwise they would not find too easy."

When he had raised his heel, as if to go,   61
Mohammed said these words to me, and then
he set it on the ground and off he went.

Another sinner, with his throat slit through   64
and with his nose hacked off up to his eyebrows,
and no more than a single ear remaining,

had—with the others—stayed his steps in wonder;   67
he was the first, before the rest, to open
his windpipe—on the outside, all bloodred—

and said: "O you whom guilt does not condemn,   70
and whom, unless too close resemblance cheats me,
I've seen above upon Italian soil,

remember Pier da Medicina if   73
you ever see again the gentle plain
that from Vercelli slopes to Marcabò.

And let the two best men of Fano know—   76
I mean both Messer Guido and Angiolello—
that, if the foresight we have here's not vain,

they will be cast out of their ship and drowned,   79
weighed down with stones, near La Cattolica,
because of a foul tyrant's treachery.

Between the isles of Cyprus and Majorca,   82
Neptune has never seen so cruel a crime
committed by the pirates or the Argives.

That traitor who sees only with one eye   85
and rules the land which one who's here with me
would wish his sight had never seen, will call

Guido and Angiolello to a parley,   88
and then will so arrange it that they'll need
no vow or prayer to Focara's wind!"

And I to him: "If you would have me carry   91
some news of you above, then tell and show me
who so detests the sight of Rimini."

And then he set his hand upon the jaw   94
of a companion, opening his mouth
and shouting: "This is he, and he speaks not.

A man cast out, he quenched the doubt in Caesar,   97
insisting that the one who is prepared
can only suffer harm if he delays."

Oh, how dismayed and pained he seemed to me,   100

his tongue slit in his gullet: Curio,
who once was so audacious in his talk!

And one who walked with both his hands hacked off,   103
while lifting up his stumps through the dark air,
so that his face was hideous with blood,

cried out: "You will remember Mosca, too,   106
who said—alas—'What's done is at an end,'
which was the seed of evil for the Tuscans."

I added: "—and brought death to your own kinsmen";   109
then having heard me speak, grief heaped on grief,
he went his way as one gone mad with sadness.

But I stayed there to watch that company   112
and saw a thing that I should be afraid
to tell with no more proof than my own self—

except that I am reassured by conscience,   115
that good companion, heartening a man
beneath the breastplate of its purity.

I surely saw, and it still seems I see,   118
a trunk without a head that walked just like
the others in that melancholy herd;

it carried by the hair its severed head,   121
which swayed within its hand just like a lantern;
and that head looked at us and said: "Ah me!"

Out of itself it made itself a lamp,   124
and they were two in one and one in two;
how that can be, He knows who so decrees.

When it was just below the bridge, it lifted   127
its arm together with its head, so that
its words might be more near us, words that said:

"Now you can see atrocious punishment,   130
you who, still breathing, go to view the dead:
see if there's any pain as great as this.

And so that you may carry news of me,   133
know that I am Bertran de Born, the one
who gave bad counsel to the fledgling king.

I made the son and father enemies: 136

Achitophel with his malicious urgings
did not do worse with Absalom and David.

Because I severed those so joined, I carry— 139
alas—my brain dissevered from its source,
which is within my trunk. And thus, in me
one sees the law of counter-penalty." 142

CANTO XXIX

Still the Eighth Circle, Ninth Pouch: the Sowers of Scandal and Schism. Geri del Bello, an unavenged ancestor of Dante. The Tenth Pouch: the Falsifiers. The First Group, Falsifiers of Metals (Alchemists), plagued by scabs, lying on the earth, scratching furiously. Griffolino. Capocchio.

So many souls and such outlandish wounds
had made my eyes inebriate—they longed
to stay and weep. But Virgil said to me:

"Why are you staring so insistently?   4
Why does your vision linger there below
among the lost and mutilated shadows?

You did not do so at the other moats.   7
If you would count them all, consider: twenty-
two miles make up the circuit of the valley.

The moon already is beneath our feet;   10
the time alloted to us now is short,
and there is more to see than you see here."

"Had you," I answered him without a pause,   13
"been able to consider why I looked,
you might have granted me a longer stay."

Meanwhile my guide had moved ahead; I went   16
behind him, answering as I walked on,
and adding: "In that hollow upon which,

just now, I kept my eyes intent, I think   19
a spirit born of my own blood laments
the guilt which, down below, costs one so much."

At this my master said: "Don't let your thoughts   22
about him interrupt you from here on:
attend to other things, let him stay there;

for I saw him below the little bridge,   25

his finger pointing at you, threatening,
and heard him called by name—Geri del Bello.

But at that moment you were occupied   28
with him who once was lord of Hautefort;
you did not notice Geri—he moved off.''

"My guide, it was his death by violence,   31
for which he still is not avenged," I said,
"by anyone who shares his shame, that made

him so disdainful now; and—I suppose—   34
for this he left without a word to me,
and this has made me pity him the more.''

And so we talked until we found the first   37
point of the ridge that, if there were more light,
would show the other valley to the bottom.

When we had climbed above the final cloister   40
of Malebolge, so that its lay brothers
were able to appear before our eyes,

I felt the force of strange laments, like arrows   43
whose shafts are barbed with pity; and at this,
I had to place my hands across my ears.

Just like the sufferings that all the sick   46
of Val di Chiana's hospitals, Maremma's,
Sardinia's, from July until September

would muster if assembled in one ditch—   49
so was it here, and such a stench rose up
as usually comes from festering limbs.

And keeping always to the left, we climbed   52
down to the final bank of the long ridge,
and then my sight could see more vividly

into the bottom, where unerring Justice,   55
the minister of the High Lord, punishes
the falsifiers she had registered.

I do not think that there was greater grief   58
in seeing all Aegina's people sick
(then, when the air was so infected that

all animals, down to the little worm,   61

collapsed; and afterward, as poets hold
to be the certain truth, those ancient peoples
   received their health again through seed of ants)   64
than I felt when I saw, in that dark valley,
the spirits languishing in scattered heaps.

   Some lay upon their bellies, some upon   67
the shoulders of another spirit, some
crawled on all fours along that squalid road.

   We journeyed step by step without a word,   70
watching and listening to those sick souls,
who had not strength enough to lift themselves.

   I saw two sitting propped against each other—   73
as pan is propped on pan to heat them up—
and each, from head to foot, spotted with scabs;

   and I have never seen a stableboy   76
whose master waits for him, or one who stays
awake reluctantly, so ply a horse

   with currycomb, as they assailed themselves   79
with clawing nails—their itching had such force
and fury, and there was no other help.

   And so their nails kept scraping off the scabs,   82
just as a knife scrapes off the scales of carp
or of another fish with scales more large.

   "O you who use your nails to strip yourself,"   85
my guide began to say to one of them,
"and sometimes have to turn them into pincers,

   tell us if there are some Italians   88
among the sinners in this moat—so may
your nails hold out, eternal, at their work."

   "We two whom you see so disfigured here,   91
we are Italians," one said, in tears.
"But who are you who have inquired of us?"

   My guide replied: "From circle down to circle,   94
together with this living man, I am
one who descends; I mean to show him Hell."

   At this their mutual support broke off;   97

In the ninth and tenth chasms of the Eighth Circle are the Falsifiers, including the alchemists Griffolino and Capocchio (bottom right).

and, quivering, each spirit turned toward me
with others who, by chance, had heard his words.

Then my good master drew more close to me,   100
saying: "Now tell them what it is you want."
And I began to speak, just as he wished:

"So that your memory may never fade   103
within the first world from the minds of men,
but still live on—and under many suns—

do tell me who you are and from what city,   106
and do not let your vile and filthy torment
make you afraid to let me know your names."

One answered me: "My city was Arezzo   109
and Albero of Siena had me burned;
but what I died for does not bring me here.

It's true that I had told him—jestingly—   112
'I'd know enough to fly through air'; and he,
with curiosity, but little sense,

wished me to show that art to him and, just   115
because I had not made him Daedalus,
had one who held him as a son burn me.

But Minos, who cannot mistake, condemned   118
my spirit to the final pouch of ten
for alchemy I practiced in the world."

And then I asked the poet: "Was there ever   121
so vain a people as the Sienese?
Even the French can't match such vanity."

At this, the other leper, who had heard me,   124
replied to what I'd said: "Except for Stricca,
for he knew how to spend most frugally;

and Niccolò, the first to make men see   127
that cloves can serve as luxury (such seed,
in gardens where it suits, can take fast root);

and, too, Caccia d'Asciano's company,   130
with whom he squandered vineyards and tilled fields,
while Abbagliato showed such subtlety.

But if you want to know who joins you so   133

against the Siense, look hard at me—
that way, my face can also answer rightly—
and see that I'm the shade of that Capocchio   136
whose alchemy could counterfeit fine metals.
And you, if I correctly take your measure,
recall how apt I was at aping nature."   139

CANTO XXX

*Still the Eighth Circle, Tenth Pouch: the Falsifiers. Gianni
Schicchi and Myrrha in the Second Group, Counterfeiters of
Others' Persons. Master Adam in the Third Group,
Counterfeiters of Coins. Potiphar's wife and Sinon the Greek
in the Fourth Group, Falsifiers of Words, Liars. The quarrel
between Adam and Sinon.*

When Juno was incensed with Semele
and, thus, against the Theban family
had shown her fury time and time again,

then Athamas was driven so insane   4
that, seeing both his wife and their two sons,
as she bore one upon each arm, he cried:

"Let's spread the nets, to take the lioness   7
together with her cubs along the pass";
and he stretched out his talons, pitiless,

and snatched the son who bore the name Learchus,   10
whirled him around and dashed him on a rock;
she, with her other burden, drowned herself.

And after fortune turned against the pride   13
of Troy, which had dared all, so that the king
together with his kingdom, was destroyed,

then Hecuba was wretched, sad, a captive;   16
and after she had seen Polyxena
dead and, in misery, had recognized

her Polydorus lying on the shore,   19
she barked, out of her senses, like a dog—
her agony had so deformed her mind.

But neither fury—Theban, Trojan—ever   22
was seen to be so cruel against another,
in rending beasts and even human limbs,

as were two shades I saw, both pale and naked,   25
who, biting, ran berserk in just the way
a hog does when it's let loose from its sty.

The one came at Capocchio and sank   28
his tusks into his neck so that, by dragging,
he made the hard ground scrape against his belly.

And he who stayed behind, the Aretine,   31
trembled and said: "That phantom's Gianni Schicchi,
and he goes raging, rending others so."

And, "Oh," I said to him, "so may the other   34
not sink its teeth in you, please tell me who
it is before it hurries off from here."

And he to me: "That is the ancient soul   37
of the indecent Myrrha, she who loved
her father past the limits of just love.

She came to sin with him by falsely taking   40
another's shape upon herself, just as
the other phantom who goes there had done,

that he might gain the lady of the herd,   43
when he disguised himself as Buoso Donati,
making a will as if most properly."

And when the pair of raging ones had passed,   46
those two on whom my eyes were fixed, I turned
around to see the rest of the ill-born.

I saw one who'd be fashioned like a lute   49
if he had only had his groin cut off
from that part of his body where it forks.

The heavy dropsy, which so disproportions   52
the limbs with unassimilated humors
that there's no match between the face and belly,

had made him part his lips like a consumptive,   55
who will, because of thirst, let one lip drop
down to his chin and lift the other up.

"O you exempt from very punishment   58
in this grim world, and I do not know why,"
he said to us, "look now and pay attention

to this, the misery of Master Adam: 61
alive, I had enough of all I wanted;
alas, I now long for one drop of water.

The rivulets that fall into the Arno   64
down from the green hills of the Casentino
with channels cool and moist, are constantly

before me; I am racked by memory—   67
the image of their flow parches me more
than the disease that robs my face of flesh.

The rigid Justice that would torment me   70
uses, as most appropriate, the place
where I had sinned, to draw swift sighs from me.

There is Romena, there I counterfeited   73
the currency that bears the Baptist's seal;
for this I left my body, burned, above.

But could I see the miserable souls   76
of Guido, Alessandro, or their brother,
I'd not give up the sight for Fonte Branda.

And one of them is in this moat already,   79
if what the angry shades report is true.
What use is that to me whose limbs are tied?

Were I so light that, in a hundred years,   82
I could advance an inch, I should already
be well upon the road to search for him

among the mutilated ones, although   85
this circuit measures some eleven miles
and is at least a half a mile across.

Because of them I'm in this family;   88
it was those three who had incited me
to coin the florins with three carats' dross."

And I to him: "Who are those two poor sinners   91
who give off smoke like wet hands in the winter
and lie so close to you upon the right?"

"I found them here," he answered, "when I rained   94
down to this rocky slope; they've not stirred since
and will not move, I think, eternally.

One is the lying woman who blamed Joseph;
the other, lying Sinon, Greek from Troy:
because of raging fever they reek so."

And one of them, who seemed to take offense,   100
perhaps at being named so squalidly,
struck with his fist at Adam's rigid belly.

It sounded as if it had been a drum;   103
and Master Adam struck him in the face,
using his arm, which did not seem less hard,

saying to him: "Although I cannot move   106
my limbs because they are too heavy, I
still have an arm that's free to serve that need."

And he replied: "But when you went to burning,   109
your arm was not as quick as it was now;
though when you coined, it was as quick and more."

To which the dropsied one: "Here you speak true;   112
but you were not so true a witness there,
when you were asked to tell the truth at Troy."

"If I spoke false, you falsified the coin,"   115
said Sinon; "I am here for just one crime—
but you've committed more than any demon."

"Do not forget the horse, you perjurer,"   118
replied the one who had the bloated belly,
"may you be plagued because the whole world knows it."

The Greek: "And you be plagued by thirst that cracks   121
your tongue, and putrid water that has made
your belly such a hedge before your eyes."

And then the coiner: "So, as usual,   124
your mouth, because of racking fever, gapes;
for if I thirst and if my humor bloats me,

you have both dryness and a head that aches;   127
few words would be sufficient invitation
to have you lick the mirror of Narcissus."

I was intent on listening to them   130
when this was what my master said: "If you
insist on looking more, I'll quarrel with you!"

And when I heard him speak so angrily,   133
I turned around to him with shame so great
that it still stirs within my memory.

Even as one who dreams that he is harmed   136
and, dreaming, wishes he were dreaming, thus
desiring that which is, as if it were not,

so I became within my speechlessness: 139
I wanted to excuse myself and did
excuse myself, although I knew it not.

"Less shame would wash away a greater fault   142
than was your fault," my master said to me;
"therefore release yourself from all remorse

and see that I am always at your side,   145
should it so happen—once again—that fortune
brings you where men would quarrel in this fashion:

to want to hear such bickering is base."   148

CANTO XXXI

Passage to the Ninth Circle. The central pit or well of Hell,
where Cocytus, the last river of Hell, freezes. The Giants:
Nimrod, Ephialtes, Briareus, Antaeus. Antaeus' compli-
ance with Virgil's request to lower the two poets into the pit.

The very tongue that first had wounded me,
sending the color up in both my cheeks,
was then to cure me with its medicine—

as did Achilles' and his father's lance,   4
even as I have heard, when it dispensed
a sad stroke first and then a healing one.

We turned our backs upon that dismal valley   7
by climbing up the bank that girdles it;
we made our way across without a word.

Here it was less than night and less than day,   10
so that my sight could only move ahead
slightly, but then I heard a bugle blast

so strong, it would have made a thunder clap   13
seem faint; at this, my eyes—which doubled back
upon their path—turned fully toward one place.

Not even Roland's horn, which followed on   16
the sad defeat when Charlemagne had lost
his holy army, was as dread as this.

I'd only turned my head there briefly when   19
I seemed to make out many high towers; then
I asked him: "Master, tell me, what's this city?"

And he to me: "It is because you try   22
to penetrate from far into these shadows
that you have formed such faulty images.

When you have reached that place, you shall see clearly   25
how much the distance has deceived your sense;

and, therefore, let this spur you on your way."

Then lovingly he took me by the hand   28
and said: "Before we have moved farther on,
so that the fact may seem less strange to you,

I'd have you know they are not towers, but giants,   31
and from the navel downward, all of them
are in the central pit, at the embankment."

Just as, whenever mists begin to thin,   34
when, gradually, vision finds the form
that in the vapor-thickened air was hidden,

so I pierced through the dense and darkened fog;   37
as I drew always nearer to the shore,
my error fled from me, my terror grew;

for as, on its round wall, Montereggioni   40
is crowned with towers, so there towered here,
above the bank that runs around the pit,

with half their bulk, the terrifying giants,   43
who still—whenever Jove hurls bolts from heaven—
remember how his thunder shattered them.

And I could now make out the face of one,   46
his shoulders and his chest, much of his belly,
and both his arms that hung along his sides.

Surely when she gave up the art of making   49
such creatures, Nature acted well indeed,
depriving Mars of instruments like these.

And if she still produces elephants   52
and whales, whoever sees with subtlety
holds her—for this—to be more just and prudent;

for where the mind's acutest reasoning   55
is joined to evil will and evil power,
there human beings can't defend themselves.

His face appeared to me as broad and long   58
as Rome can claim for its St. Peter's pine cone;
his other bones shared in that same proportion;

so that the bank, which served him as an apron   61
down from his middle, showed so much of him

above, that three Frieslanders would in vain
   have boasted of their reaching to his hair;   64
for downward from the place where one would buckle
a mantle, I saw thirty spans of him.

     "*Raphèl maì amècche zabì almi,*"   67
began to bellow that brute mouth, for which
no sweeter psalms would be appropriate.

   And my guide turned to him: "O stupid soul,   70
keep your horn and use that as an outlet
when rage or other passion touches you!

   Look at your neck, and you will find the strap   73
that holds it fast; and see, bewildered spirit,
how it lies straight across your massive chest."

   And then to me: "He is his own accuser;   76
for this is Nimrod, through whose wicked thought
one single language cannot serve the world.

   Leave him alone—let's not waste time in talk;   79
for every language is to him the same
as his to others—no one knows his tongue."

   So, turning to the left, we journeyed on   82
and, at the distance of a bow-shot, found
another giant, far more huge and fierce.

   Who was the master who had tied him so,   85
I cannot say, but his left arm was bent
behind him and his right was bent in front,

   both pinioned by a chain that held him tight   88
down from the neck; and round the part of him
that was exposed, it had been wound five times.

   "This giant in his arrogance had tested   91
his force against the force of highest Jove,"
my guide said, "so he merits this reward.

   His name is Ephialtes; and he showed   94
tremendous power when the giants frightened
the gods; the arms he moved now move no more."

   And I to him: "If it is possible,   97
I'd like my eyes to have experience

Titans in the chasm of Malebolge, including Nimrod (with the horn) and Briareus (foreground).

of the enormous one, Briareus."

At which he answered: "You shall see Antaeus 100
nearby. He is unfettered and can speak;
he'll take us to the bottom of all evil.

The one you wish to see lies far beyond 103
and is bound up and just as huge as this one,
and even more ferocious in his gaze."

No earthquake ever was so violent 106
when called to shake a tower so robust,
as Ephialtes quick to shake himself.

Then I was more afraid of death than ever; 109
that fear would have been quite enough to kill me,
had I not seen how he was held by chains.

And we continued on until we reached 112
Antaeus, who, not reckoning his head,
stood out above the rock wall full five ells.

"O you, who lived within the famous valley 115
(where Scipio became the heir of glory
when Hannibal retreated with his men),

who took a thousand lions as your prey— 118
and had you been together with your brothers
in their high war, it seems some still believe

the sons of earth would have become the victors— 121
do set us down below, where cold shuts in
Cocytus, and do not disdain that task.

Don't send us on to Tityus or Typhon; 124
this man can give you what is longed for here;
therefore bend down and do not curl your lip.

He still can bring you fame within the world, 127
for he's alive and still expects long life,
unless grace summon him before his time."

So said my master; and in haste Antaeus 130
stretched out his hands, whose massive grip had once
been felt by Hercules, and grasped my guide.

And Virgil, when he felt himself caught up, 133
called out to me: "Come here, so I can hold you,"

then made one bundle of himself and me.

Just as the Garisenda seems when seen   136
beneath the leaning side, when clouds run past
and it hangs down as if about to crash,

so did Antaeus seem to me as I   139
watched him bend over me—a moment when
I'd have preferred to take some other road.

But gently—on the deep that swallows up   142
both Lucifer and Judas—he placed us;
nor did he, so bent over, stay there long,

but, like a mast above a ship, he rose.   145

CANTO XXXII

The Ninth Circle, First Ring, called Caïna, where Traitors
to their Kin are immersed in the ice, heads bent down.
Camiscione dei Pazzi. The Second Ring, called Antenora:
the Traitors to their Homeland or Party. Bocca degli Abati's
provocation of Dante. Two traitors, one gnawing at the other's
head.

Had I the crude and scrannel rhymes to suit
the melancholy hole upon which all
the other circling crags converge and rest,

the juice of my conception would be pressed   4
more fully; but because I feel their lack,
I bring myself to speak, yet speak in fear;

for it is not a task to take in jest,   7
to show the base of all the universe—
nor for a tongue that cries out, "mama," "papa."

But may those ladies now sustain my verse   10
who helped Amphion when he walled up Thebes,
so that my tale not differ from the fact.

O rabble, miscreated past all others,   13
there in the place of which it's hard to speak,
better if here you had been goats or sheep!

When we were down below in the dark well,   16
beneath the giant's feet and lower yet,
with my eyes still upon the steep embankment,

I heard this said to me: "Watch how you pass;   19
walk so that you not trample with your soles
the heads of your exhausted, wretched brothers."

At this I turned and saw in front of me,   22
beneath my feet, a lake that, frozen fast,
had lost the look of water and seemed glass.

The Danube where it flows in Austria,   25
the Don beneath its frozen sky, have never
made for their course so thick a veil in winter

as there was here; for had Mount Tambernic   28
or Pietrapana's mountain crashed upon it,
not even at the edge would it have creaked.

And as the croaking frog sits with its muzzle   31
above the water, in the sesaon when
the peasant woman often dreams of gleaning,

so, livid in the ice, up to the place   34
where shame can show itself, were those sad shades,
whose teeth were chattering with notes like storks'.

Each kept his face bent downward steadily;   37
their mouths bore witness to the cold they felt,
just as their eyes proclaimed their sorry hearts.

When I had looked around a while, my eyes   40
turned toward my feet and saw two locked so close,
the hair upon their heads had intermingled.

"Do tell me, you whose chests are pressed so tight,"   43
I said, "who are you?" They bent back their necks,
and when they'd lifted up their faces toward me,

their eyes, which wept upon the ground before,   46
shed tears down on their lips until the cold
held fast the tears and locked their lids still more.

No clamp has ever fastened plank to plank   49
so tightly; and because of this, they butted
each other like two rams, such was their fury.

And one from whom the cold had taken both   52
his ears, who kept his face bent low, then said:
"Why do you keep on staring so at us?

If you would like to know who these two are: 55
that valley where Bisenzio descends,
belonged to them and to their father Alberto.

They came out of one body; and you can   58
search all Caïna, you will never find
a shade more fit to sit within this ice—

not him who, at one blow, had chest and shadow 61
shattered by Arthur's hand; and not Focaccia;
and not this sinner here who so impedes

my vision with his head, I can't see past him; 64
his name was Sassol Mascheroni; if
you're Tuscan, now you know who he has been.

And lest you keep me talking any longer, 67
know that I was Camiscon de' Pazzi;
I'm waiting for Carlino to absolve me."

And after that I saw a thousand faces 70
made doglike by the cold; for which I shudder—
and always will—when I face frozen fords.

And while we were advancing toward the center 73
to which all weight is drawn—I, shivering
in that eternally cold shadow—I

know not if it was will or destiny 76
or chance, but as I walked among the heads,
I struck my foot hard in the face of one.

Weeping, he chided then: "Why trample me? 79
If you've not come to add to the revenge
of Montaperti, why do you molest me?"

And I: "My master, now wait here for me, 82
that I may clear up just one doubt about him;
then you can make me hurry as you will."

My guide stood fast, and I went on to ask 85
of him who still was cursing bitterly:
"Who are you that rebukes another so?"

"And who are you who go through Antenora, 88
striking the cheeks of others," he replied,
"too roughly—even if you were alive?"

"I am alive, and can be precious to you 91
if you want fame," was my reply, "for I
can set your name among my other notes."

And he to me: "I want the contrary; 94
so go away and do not harass me—
your flattery is useless in this valley."

At that I grabbed him by the scruff and said:
"You'll have to name yourself to me or else
you won't have even one hair left up here."

And he to me: "Though you should strip me bald, 100
I shall not tell you who I am or show it,
not if you pound my head a thousand times."

His hairs were wound around my hand already, 103
and I had plucked from him more than one tuft
while he was barking and his eyes stared down,

when someone else cried out: "What is it, Bocca? 106
Isn't the music of your jaws enough
for you without your bark? What devil's at you?"

"And now," I said, "you traitor bent on evil, 109
I do not need your talk, for I shall carry
true news of you, and that will bring you shame."

"Be off," he answered, "tell them what you like, 112
but don't be silent, if you make it back,
about the one whose tongue was now so quick.

Here he laments the silver of the Frenchmen; 115
'I saw,' you then can say, 'him of Duera,
down there, where all the sinners are kept cool.'

And if you're asked who else was there in ice, 118
one of the Beccheria is beside you—
he had his gullet sliced right through by Florence.

Gianni de' Soldanieri, I believe, 121
lies there with Ganelon and Tebaldello,
he who unlocked Faenza while it slept."

We had already taken leave of him, 124
when I saw two shades frozen in one hole,
so that one's head served as the other's cap;

and just as he who's hungry chews his bread, 127
one sinner dug his teeth into the other
right at the place where brain is joined to nape:

no differently had Tydeus gnawed the temples 130
of Menalippus, out of indignation,
than this one chewed the skull and other parts.

"O you who show, with such a bestial sign,   133
your hatred for the one on whom you feed,
tell me the cause," I said; "we can agree

    that if your quarrel with him is justified,   136
then knowing who you are and what's his sin,
I shall repay you yet on earth above,

    if that with which I speak does not dry up."   139

CANTO XXXIII

Still the Ninth Circle, Second Ring. Ugolino's tale of his and his sons' death in a Pisan prison. Dante's invective against Pisa. The Third Ring, Ptolomea, where Traitors against their Guests jut out from ice, their eyes sealed by frozen tears. Fra Alberigo and Branca Doria, still alive on earth but already in Hell.

That sinner raised his mouth from his fierce meal,
then used the head that he had ripped apart
in back: he wiped his lips upon its hair.

Then he began: "You want me to renew   4
despairing pain that presses at my heart
even as I think back, before I speak.

But if my words are seed from which the fruit   7
is infamy for this betrayer whom
I gnaw, you'll see me speak and weep at once.

I don't know who you are or in what way   10
you've come down here; and yet you surely seem—
from what I hear—to be a Florentine.

You are to know I was Count Ugolino,   13
and this one here, Archbishop Ruggieri;
and now I'll tell you why I am his neighbor.

There is no need to tell you that, because   16
of his malicious tricks, I first was taken
and then was killed—since I had trusted him;

however, that which you cannot have heard—   19
that is, the cruel death devised for me—
you now shall hear and know if he has wronged me.

A narrow window in the Eagles' Tower,   22
which now, through me, is called the Hunger Tower,
a cage in which still others will be locked,

had, through its opening, already showed me   25
several moons, when I dreamed that bad dream
which rent the curtain of the future for me.

This man appeared to me as lord and master;   28
he hunted down the wolf and its young whelps
upon the mountain that prevents the Pisans

from seeing Lucca; and with lean and keen   31
and practiced hounds, he'd sent up front, before him,
Gualandi and Sismondi and Lanfranchi.

But after a brief course, it seemed to me   34
that both the father and the sons were weary;
I seemed to see their flanks torn by sharp fangs.

When I awoke at daybreak, I could hear   37
my sons, who were together with me there,
weeping within their sleep, asking for bread.

You would be cruel indeed if, thinking what   40
my heart foresaw, you don't already grieve;
and if you don't weep now, when would you weep?

They were awake by now; the hour drew near   43
at which our food was usually brought,
and each, because of what he'd dreamed, was anxious;

below, I heard them nailing up the door   46
of that appalling tower; without a word,
I looked into the faces of my sons.

I did not weep; within, I turned to stone.   49
They wept; and my poor little Anselm said:
'Father, you look so .... What is wrong with you?'

At that I shed no tears and—all day long   52
and through the night that followed—did not answer
until another sun had touched the world.

As soon as a thin ray had made its way   55
into that sorry prison, and I saw
reflected in four faces, my own gaze,

out of my grief, I bit at both my hands;   58
and they, who thought I'd done that out of hunger,
immediately rose and told me: 'Father,

it would be far less painful for us if   61
you ate of us; for you clothed us in this
sad flesh—it is for you to strip it off.'

Then I grew calm, to keep them from more sadness;   64
through that day and the next, we all were silent;
O hard earth, why did you not open up?

But after we had reached the fourth day, Gaddo,   67
throwing himself, outstretched, down at my feet,
implored me: 'Father, why do you not help me?'

And there he died; and just as you see me,   70
I saw the other three fall one by one
between the fifth day and the sixth; at which,

now blind, I started groping over each;   73
and after they were dead, I called them for
two days; then fasting had more force than grief."

When he had spoken this, with eyes awry,   76
again he gripped the sad skull in his teeth,
which, like a dog's, were strong down to the bone.

Ah, Pisa, you the scandal of the peoples   79
of that fair land where *si* is heard, because
your neighbors are so slow to punish you,

may, then, Caprara and Gorgona move   82
and build a hedge across the Arno's mouth,
so that it may drown every soul in you!

For if Count Ugolino was reputed   85
to have betrayed your fortresses, there was
no need to have his sons endure such torment.

O Thebes renewed, their years were innocent   88
and young—Brigata, Uguiccione, and
the other two my song has named above!

We passed beyond, where frozen water wraps—   91
a rugged covering—still other sinners,
who were not bent, but flat upon their backs.

Their very weeping there won't let them weep,   94
and grief that finds a barrier in their eyes
turns inward to increase their agony;

The four rings of Cocytus where the Treacherous dwell: traitors to their country in the ring of Antenora and betrayers of hospitality in Tolomea.

because their first tears freeze into a cluster,
and, like a crystal visor, fill up all
the hollow that is underneath the eyebrow.

And though, because of cold, my every sense
had left its dwelling in my face, just as
a callus has no feeling, nonetheless,

I seemed to feel some wind now, and I said:
"My master, who has set this gust in motion?
For isn't every vapor quenched down here?"

And he to me: "You soon shall be where your
own eye will answer that, when you shall see
the reason why this wind blasts from above."

And one of those sad sinners in the cold
crust, cried to us: "O souls who are so cruel
that this last place has been assigned to you,

take off the hard veils from my face so that
I can release the suffering that fills
my heart before lament freezes again."

To which I answered: "If you'd have me help you,
then tell me who you are; if I don't free you,
may I go to the bottom of the ice."

He answered then: "I am Fra Alberigo,
the one who tended fruits in a bad garden,
and here my figs have been repaid with dates."

"But then," I said, "are you already dead?"
And he to me: "I have no knowledge of
my body's fate within the world above.

For Ptolomea has this privilege:
quite frequently the soul falls here before
it has been thrust away by Atropos.

And that you may with much more willingness
scrape these glazed tears from off my face, know this:
as soon as any soul becomes a traitor,

as I was, then a demon takes its body
away—and keeps that body in his power
until its years have run their course completely.

The soul falls headlong, down into this cistern;   133
and up above, perhaps, there still appears
the body of the shade that winters here

behind me; you must know him, if you've just   136
come down; he is Ser Branca Doria;
for many years he has been thus pent up."

I said to him: "I think that you deceive me,   139
for Branca Doria is not yet dead;
he eats and drinks and sleeps and puts on clothes."

"There in the Malebranche's ditch above,   142
where sticky pitch boils up, Michele Zanche
had still not come," he said to me, "when this one—

together with a kinsman, who had done   145
the treachery together with him—left
a devil in his stead inside his body.

But now reach out your hand; open my eyes."   148
And yet I did not open them for him;
and it was courtesy to show him rudeness.

Ah, Genoese, a people strange to every   151
constraint of custom, full of all corruption,
why have you not been driven from the world?

For with the foulest spirit of Romagna,   154
I found one of you such that, for his acts,
in soul he bathes already in Cocytus

and up above appears alive, in body.   157

CANTO XXXIV

*The Ninth Circle, Fourth Ring, called Judecca, where
Traitors against their Benefactors are fully covered by ice.
Dis, or Lucifer, emperor of that kingdom, his three mouths
rending Judas, Brutus, and Cassius. Descent of Virgil and
Dante down Lucifer's body to the other, southern hemisphere.
Their vision of the stars.*

"*Vexilla regis prodeunt inferni*
toward us; and therefore keep your eyes ahead,"
my master said, "to see if you can spy him."

Just as, when night falls on our hemisphere   4
or when a heavy fog is blowing thick,
a windmill seems to wheel when seen far off,

so then I seemed to see that sort of structure.   7
And next, because the wind was strong, I shrank
behind my guide; there was no other shelter.

And now—with fear I set it down in meter—   10
I was where all the shades were fully covered
but visible as wisps of straw in glass.

There some lie flat and others stand erect,   13
one on his head, and one upon his soles;
and some bend face to feet, just like a bow.

But after we had made our way ahead,   16
my master felt he now should have me see
that creature who was once a handsome presence;

he stepped aside and made me stop, and said: 19
"Look! Here is Dis, and this the place where you
will have to arm yourself with fortitude."

O reader, do not ask of me how I   22
grew faint and frozen then—I cannot write it:
all words would fall far short of what it was.

I did not die, and I was not alive;   25
think for yourself, if you have any wit,
what I became, deprived of life and death.

The emperor of the despondent kingdom   28
so towered—from midchest—above the ice,
that I match better with a giant's height

than giants match the measure of his arms;   31
now you can gauge the size of all of him
if it is in proportion to such limbs.

If he was once as handsome as he now   34
is ugly and, despite that, raised his brows
against his Maker, one can understand

how every sorrow has its source in him!   37
I marveled when I saw that, on his head,
he had three faces: one—in front—bloodred;

and then another two that, just above   40
the midpoint of each shoulder, joined the first;
and at the crown, all three were reattached;

the right looked somewhat yellow, somewhat white;   43
the left in its appearance was like those
who come from where the Nile, descending, flows.

Beneath each face of his, two wings spread out,   46
as broad as suited so immense a bird:
I've never seen a ship with sails so wide.

They had no feathers, but were fashioned like   49
a bat's; and he was agitating them,
so that three winds made their way out from him—

and all Cocytus froze before those winds.   52
He wept out of six eyes; and down three chins,
tears gushed together with a bloody froth.

Within each mouth—he used it like a grinder—   55
with gnashing teeth he tore to bits a sinner,
so that he brought much pain to three at once.

The forward sinner found that biting nothing   58
when matched against the clawing, for at times
his back was stripped completely of its hide.

Satan, Emperor of the Universe of Pain. Preparing to leave Hell for Purgatory, the two poets approach him.

"That soul up there who has to suffer most," 61
my master said: "Judas Iscariot—
his head inside, he jerks his legs without.

Of those two others, with their heads beneath, 64
the one who hangs from that black snout is Brutus—
see how he writhes and does not say a word!

That other, who seems so robust, is Cassius. 67
But night is come again, and it is time
for us to leave; we have seen everything."

Just as he asked, I clasped him round the neck; 70
and he watched for the chance of time and place,
and when the wings were open wide enough,

he took fast hold upon the shaggy flanks 73
and then descended, down from tuft to tuft,
between the tangled hair and icy crusts.

When we had reached the point at which the thigh 76
revolves, just at the swelling of the hip,
my guide, with heavy strain and rugged work,

reversed his head to where his legs had been 79
and grappled on the hair, as one who climbs—
I thought that we were going back to Hell.

"Hold tight," my master said—he panted like 82
a man exhausted—"it is by such stairs
that we must take our leave of so much evil."

Then he slipped through a crevice in a rock 85
and placed me on the edge of it, to sit;
that done, he climbed toward me with steady steps.

I raised my eyes, believing I should see 88
the half of Lucifer that I had left;
instead I saw him with his legs turned up;

and if I then became perplexed, do let 91
the ignorant be judges—those who can
not understand what point I had just crossed.

"Get up," my master said, "be on your feet: 94
the way is long, the path is difficult;
the sun's already back to middle tierce."

It was no palace hall, the place in which
we found ourselves, but with its rough-hewn floor
and scanty light, a dungeon built by nature.

"Before I free myself from this abyss,
master," I said when I had stood up straight,
"tell me enough to see I don't mistake:

Where is the ice? And how is he so placed
head downward? Tell me, too, how has the sun
in so few hours gone from night to morning?"

And he to me: "You still believe you are
north of the center, where I grasped the hair
of the damned worm who pierces through the world.

And you were there as long as I descended;
but when I turned, that's when you passed the point
to which, from every part, all weights are drawn.

And now you stand beneath the hemisphere
opposing that which cloaks the great dry lands
and underneath whose zenith died the Man

whose birth and life were sinless in this world.
Your feet are placed upon a little sphere
that forms the other face of the Judecca.

Here it is morning when it's evening there;
and he whose hair has served us as a ladder
is still fixed, even as he was before.

This was the side on which he fell from Heaven;
for fear of him, the land that once loomed here
made of the sea a veil and rose into

our hemisphere; and that land which appears
upon this side—perhaps to flee from him—
left here this hollow space and hurried upward."

There is a place below, the limit of
that cave, its farthest point from Beelzebub,
a place one cannot see: it is discovered

by ear—there is a sounding stream that flows
along the hollow of a rock eroded
by winding waters, and the slope is easy.

My guide and I came on that hidden road   133
to make our way back into the bright world;
and with no care for any rest, we climbed—
    he first, I following—until I saw,   136
through a round opening, some of those things
of beauty Heaven bears. It was from there
    that we emerged, to see—once more   the stars.   139

PURGATORIO

This translation of the PURGATORIO
is inscribed to Irma Brandeis and
Helaine Newstead – as l'altro Guido *had it:*
CHÉ 'N TUTTE GUISE VI DEGGIO LAUDARE

CANTO I

Proem and Invocation. The skies of the Southern Pole before dawn. The four stars. Cato of Utica, custodian of the island Mountain of Purgatory. Cato's queries and Virgil's reply. Instructions by Cato. Virgil bathing Dante's face and, on the shore, girding him with a rush.

To course across more kindly waters now
my talent's little vessel lifts her sails,
leaving behind herself a sea so cruel;

and what I sing will be that second kingdom,   4
in which the human soul is cleansed of sin,
becoming worthy of ascent to Heaven.

But here, since I am yours, o holy Muses,   7
may this poem rise again from Hell's dead realm;
and may Calliope rise somewhat here,

accompanying my singing with that music   10
whose power struck the poor Pierides
so forcefully that they despaired of pardon.

The gentle hue of oriental sapphire   13
in which the sky's serenity was steeped—
its aspect pure as far as the horizon—

brought back my joy in seeing just as soon   16
as I had left behind the air of death
that had afflicted both my sight and breast.

The lovely planet that is patroness   19
of love made all the eastern heavens glad,
veiling the Pisces in the train she led.

Then I turned to the right, setting my mind   22
upon the other pole, and saw four stars
not seen before except by the first people.

Heaven appeared to revel in their flames: 25
o northern hemisphere, because you were

denied that sight, you are a widower!

After my eyes took leave of those four stars,   28
turning a little toward the other pole,
from which the Wain had disappeared by now,

I saw a solitary patriarch   31
near me—his aspect worthy of such reverence
that even son to father owes no more.

His beard was long and mixed with white, as were   34
the hairs upon his head; and his hair spread
down to his chest in a divided tress.

The rays of the four holy stars so framed   37
his face with light that in my sight he seemed
like one who is confronted by the sun.

"Who are you—who, against the hidden river,   40
were able to escape the eternal prison?"
he said, moving those venerable plumes.

"Who was your guide? What served you both as lantern 43
when, from the deep night that will always keep
the hellish valley dark, you were set free?

The laws of the abyss—have they been broken?   46
Or has a new, a changed decree in Heaven
let you, though damned, approach my rocky slopes?"

My guide took hold of me decisively;   49
by way of words and hands and other signs,
he made my knees and brow show reverence.

Then he replied: "I do not come through my   52
own self. There was a lady sent from Heaven;
her pleas led me to help and guide this man.

But since your will would have a far more full   55
and accurate account of our condition,
my will cannot withhold what you request.

This man had yet to see his final evening;   58
but, through his folly, little time was left
before he did—he was so close to it.

As I have told you, I was sent to him   61
for his deliverance; the only road
I could have taken was the road I took.

I showed him all the people of perdition;   64
now I intend to show to him those spirits
who, in your care, are bent on expiation.

To tell you how I led him would take long;   67
it is a power descending from above
that helps me guide him here, to see and hear you.

Now may it please you to approve his coming;   70
he goes in search of liberty—so precious,
as he who gives his life for it must know.

You know it—who, in Utica, found death   73
for freedom was not bitter, when you left
the garb that will be bright on the great day.

Eternal edicts are not broken for us;   76
this man's alive, and I'm not bound by Minos;
but I am from the circle where the chaste

eyes of your Marcia are; and she still prays   79
to you, o holy breast, to keep her as
your own: for her love, then, incline to us.

Allow our journey through your seven realms.   82
I shall thank her for kindness you bestow—
if you would let your name be named below."

"While I was there, within the other world,   85
Marcia so pleased my eyes," he then replied,
"each kindness she required, I satisfied.

Now that she dwells beyond the evil river,   88
she has no power to move me any longer,
such was the law decreed when I was freed.

But if a lady come from Heaven speeds   91
and helps you, as you say, there is no need
of flattery; it is enough, indeed,

to ask me for her sake. Go then; but first   94
wind a smooth rush around his waist and bathe
his face, to wash away all of Hell's stains;

for it would not be seemly to approach   97
with eyes still dimmed by any mists, the first
custodian angel, one from Paradise.

This solitary island, all around   100

its very base, there where the breakers pound,
bears rushes on its soft and muddy ground.

There is no other plant that lives below: 103
no plant with leaves or plant that, as it grows,
hardens—and breaks beneath the waves' harsh blows.

That done, do not return by this same pass; 106
the sun, which rises now, will show you how
this hillside can be climbed more easily."

With that he vanished; and without a word, 109
I rose and drew in closer to my guide,
and it was on him that I set my eyes.

And he began: "Son, follow in my steps; 112
let us go back; this is the point at which
the plain slopes down to reach its lowest bounds."

Daybreak was vanquishing the dark's last hour, 115
which fled before it; in the distance, I
could recognize the trembling of the sea.

We made our way across the lonely plain, 118
like one returning to a lost pathway,
who, till he finds it, seems to move in vain.

When we had reached the point where dew contends 121
with sun and, seconded by soft sea-winds,
wins out because it won't evaporate,

my master gently placed both of his hands— 124
outspread—upon the grass; therefore, aware
of what his gesture and intention were,

I reached and offered him my tear-stained cheeks; 127
and on my cheeks, he totally revealed
the color that Inferno had concealed.

Then we arrived at the deserted shore, 130
which never yet had seen its waters coursed
by any man who journeyed back again.

There, just as pleased another, he girt me. 133
O wonder! Where he plucked the humble plant,
that he had chosen, there that plant sprang up

again, identical, immediately. 136

CANTO II

Ante-Purgatory. Dawn on the shore of the island mountain. The sudden light upon the sea. The helmsman angel and the boat full of arriving souls. The encounter with Casella, Dante's friend. Casella's singing. Cato's rebuke. The simile of the doves.

By now the sun was crossing the horizon
of the meridian whose highest point
covers Jerusalem; and from the Ganges,

night, circling opposite the sun, was moving   4
together with the Scales that, when the length
of dark defeats the day, desert night's hands;

so that, above the shore that I had reached,   7
the fair Aurora's white and scarlet cheeks
were, as Aurora aged, becoming orange.

We still were by the sea, like those who think   10
about the journey they will undertake,
who go in heart but in the body stay.

And just as Mars, when it is overcome   13
by the invading mists of dawn, glows red
above the waters' plain, low in the west,

so there appeared to me—and may I see it   16
again—a light that crossed the sea: so swift,
there is no flight of bird to equal it.

When, for a moment, I'd withdrawn my eyes   19
that I might ask a question of my guide,
I saw that light again, larger, more bright.

Then, to each side of it, I saw a whiteness,   22
though I did not know what that whiteness was;
below, another whiteness slowly showed.

My master did not say a word before   25

the whitenesses first seen appeared as wings;
but then, when he had recognized the helmsman,

he cried: "Bend, bend your knees; behold the angel   28
of God, and join your hands; from this point on,
this is the kind of minister you'll meet.

See how much scorn he has for human means;   31
he'd have no other sail than his own wings
and use no oar between such distant shores.

See how he holds his wings, pointing to Heaven,   34
piercing the air with his eternal pinions,
which do not change as mortal plumage does."

Then he—that bird divine—as he drew closer   37
and closer to us, seemed to gain in brightness,
so that my eyes could not endure his nearness

and I was forced to lower them; and he   40
came on to shore with boat so light, so quick
that nowhere did the water swallow it.

The helmsman sent from Heaven, at the stern,   43
seemed to have blessedness inscribed upon him;
more than a hundred spirits sat within.

"*In exitu Isräel de Aegypto*,"   46
with what is written after of that psalm,
all of those spirits sang as with one voice.

Then over them he made the holy cross   49
as sign; they flung themselves down on the shore,
and he moved off as he had come—swiftly.

The crowd that he had left along the beach   52
seemed not to know the place; they looked about
like those whose eyes try out things new to them.

Upon all sides the sun shot forth the day;   55
and from mid-heaven its incisive arrows
already had chased Capricorn away,

when those who'd just arrived lifted their heads   58
toward us and said: "Do show us, if you know,
the way by which we can ascend this slope."

And Virgil answered: "You may be convinced   61

As souls disembark for Purgatory, the Angel Boatman (extreme left) makes the sign of the Cross. Dante kneels in prayer.

that we are quite familiar with this shore;
but we are strangers here, just as you are;

we came but now, a little while before you, 64
though by another path, so difficult
and dense that this ascent seems sport to us."

The souls who, noticing my breathing, sensed 67
that I was still a living being, then,
out of astonishment, turned pale; and just

as people crowd around a messenger 70
who bears an olive branch, to hear his news,
and no one hesitates to join that crush,

so here those happy spirits—all of them— 73
stared hard at my face, just as if they had
forgotten to proceed to their perfection.

I saw one of those spirits moving forward 76
in order to embrace me—his affection
so great that I was moved to mime his welcome.

O shades—in all except appearance—empty! 79
Three times I clasped my hands behind him and
as often brought them back against my chest.

Dismay, I think, was painted on my face; 82
at this, that shadow smiled as he withdrew;
and I, still seeking him, again advanced.

Gently, he said that I could now stand back; 85
then I knew who he was, and I beseeched
him to remain awhile and talk with me.

He answered: "As I loved you when I was 88
within my mortal flesh, so, freed, I love you:
therefore I stay. But you, why do you journey?"

"My own Casella, to return again 91
to where I am, I journey thus; but why,"
I said, "were you deprived of so much time?"

And he: "No injury is done to me 94
if he who takes up whom—and when—he pleases
has kept me from this crossing many times,

for his own will derives from a just will. 97

And yet, for three months now, he has accepted,
most tranquilly, all those who would embark.

Therefore, I, who had turned then to the shore   100
at which the Tiber's waters mix with salt,
was gathered in by his benevolence.

Straight to that river mouth, he set his wings: 103
that always is the place of gathering
for those who do not sink to Acheron."

And I: "If there's no new law that denies   106
you memory or practice of the songs
of love that used to quiet all my longings,

then may it please you with those songs to solace   109
my soul somewhat; for—having journeyed here
together with my body—it is weary."

"*Love that discourses to me in my mind*"   112
he then began to sing—and sang so sweetly
that I still hear that sweetness sound in me.

My master, I, and all that company   115
around the singer seemed so satisfied,
as if no other thing might touch our minds.

We all were motionless and fixed upon   118
the notes, when all at once the grave old man
cried out: "What have we here, you laggard spirits?

What negligence, what lingering is this?   121
Quick, to the mountain to cast off the slough
that will not let you see God show Himself!"

Even as doves, assembled where they feed,   124
quietly gathering their grain or weeds,
forgetful of their customary strut,

will, if some thing appears that makes them fear,   127
immediately leave their food behind
because they are assailed by greater care;

so did I see that new-come company—   130
they left the song behind, turned toward the slope,
like those who go and yet do not know where.

And we were no less hasty in departure.   133

CANTO III

Ante-Purgatory. From the shore to the base of the mountain. Dante's fear when his shadow—and no other—appears. Reassurance by Virgil and explanation of the nature of shades. Consideration of the way to ascend the Mountain of Purgatory. The meeting with the souls of the Late-Repentant who were also Excommunicates. Manfred.

But while their sudden flight was scattering
those souls across the plain and toward the mountain
where we are racked by rightful punishments,
    I drew in closer to my true companion.   4
For how could I have run ahead without him?
Who could have helped me as I climbed the mountain?
    He seemed like one who's stung by self-reproof;   7
o pure and noble conscience, you in whom
each petty fault becomes a harsh rebuke!
    And when his feet had left off hurrying—   10
for haste denies all acts their dignity—
my mind, which was—before—too focused, grew
    more curious and widened its attention;   13
I set my vision toward the slope that rises
most steeply, up to heaven from the sea.
    Behind my back the sun was flaming red;   16
but there, ahead of me, its light was shattered
because its rays were resting on my body.
    And when I saw the ground was dark in front   19
of me and me alone, afraid that I
had been abandoned, I turned to my side;
    and he, my only comfort, as he turned   22
around, began: "Why must you still mistrust?
Don't you believe that I am with—and guide—you?

The body from within which I cast shadows   25
is buried where it now is evening: taken
from Brindisi, it now belongs to Naples.

Thus, if no shadow falls in front of me,   28
do not be more amazed than when you see
the heavens not impede each other's rays.

The Power has disposed such bodiless   31
bodies to suffer torments, heat and cold;
how this is done, He would not have us know.

Foolish is he who hopes our intellect   34
can reach the end of that unending road
only one Substance in three Persons follows.

Confine yourselves, o humans, to the *quia*;   37
had you been able to see all, there would
have been no need for Mary to give birth.

You saw the fruitless longing of those men   40
who would—if reason could—have been content,
those whose desire eternally laments:

I speak of Aristotle and of Plato—   43
and many others." Here he bent his head
and said no more, remaining with his sorrow.

By this time we had reached the mountain's base,   46
discovering a wall of rock so sheer
that even agile legs are useless there.

The loneliest, most jagged promontory   49
that lies between Turbìa and Lerici,
compared with it, provides stairs wide and easy.

"Now who knows where, along this mountainside,"   52
my master, halting, asked, "one finds a rise
where even he who has no wings can climb?"

While he, his eyes upon the ground, consulted   55
his mind, considering what road to take,
and I looked up around the wall of rock,

along the left a band of souls appeared   58
to me to be approaching us—but so
unhurriedly, their movements did not show.

"Lift up your eyes," I told my master; "here   61
are those who can advise us how to go,
if you can find no counsel in yourself."

At this, he looked at them and, less distressed,   64
replied: "Let us go there; their steps are slow;
and you, my gentle son, hold fast to hope."

The distance from that company to us—   67
I mean when we had gone a thousand paces—
was still as far as a fine hurler's toss,

when they all huddled toward the hard rock wall   70
and, once they'd crowded there, refused to budge,
even as men, when apprehensive, halt.

"O chosen souls, you who have ended well,"   73
Virgil began, "by virtue of that peace
which I believe awaits you all, please tell

us where the slope inclines and can be climbed;   76
for he who best discerns the worth of time
is most distressed whenever time is lost."

Even as sheep that move, first one, then two,   79
then three, out of the fold—the others also
stand, eyes and muzzles lowered, timidly;

and what the first sheep does, the others do,   82
and if it halts, they huddle close behind,
simple and quiet and not knowing why:

so, then, I saw those spirits in the front   85
of that flock favored by good fortune move—
their looks were modest; seemly, slow, their walk.

As soon as these souls saw, upon my right,   88
along the ground, a gap in the sun's light,
where shadow stretched from me to the rock wall,

they stopped and then drew back somewhat; and all   91
who came behind them—though they did not know
why those ahead had halted—also slowed.

"Without your asking, I shall tell you plainly   94
that you are looking at a human body;
that's why the sunlight on the ground is broken.

Don't be astonished; rest assured that he
would not attempt to cross this wall without
a force that Heaven sent him as support."
97

These were my master's words. That worthy band
replied: "Come back, and move in our direction,"
and gestured—with backhanded motions—right.
100

And one of them began: "Whoever you
may be, as you move forward, turn and see:
consider if—beyond—you've ever seen me."
103

I turned to look at him attentively:
he was fair-haired and handsome and his aspect
was noble—but one eyebrow had been cleft
106

by a swordstroke. When I had humbly noted
that I had never seen him, he said: "Look
now"—showing me a wound high on his chest.
109

Then, as he smiled, he told me: "I am Manfred,
the grandson of the Empress Constance; thus,
I pray that, when you reach the world again,
112

you may go to my lovely daughter, mother
of kings of Sicily and Aragon—
tell her the truth, lest she's heard something other.
115

After my body had been shattered by
two fatal blows, in tears, I then consigned
myself to Him who willingly forgives.
118

My sins were ghastly, but the Infinite
Goodness has arms so wide that It accepts
who ever would return, imploring It.
121

And if Cosenza's pastor, who was sent
to hunt me down—alive or dead—by Clement,
had understood this facet of God's mercy,
124

my body's bones would still be there—beneath
the custody of the great heap of stones—
near Benevento, at the bridgehead; now
127

rain bathes my bones, the wind has driven them
beyond the Kingdom, near the Verde's banks,
where he transported them with tapers spent.
130

Despite the Church's curse, there is no one 133
so lost that the eternal love cannot
return—as long as hope shows something green.

But it is true that anyone who dies 136
in contumacy of the Holy Church,
though he repented at the end, must wait

along this shore for thirty times the span 139
he spent in his presumptuousness, unless
that edict is abridged through fitting prayers.

Now see if you, by making known to my 142
kind Constance where you saw my soul and why
delay's decreed for me, can make me happy;

those here—through those beyond—advance more 145
  quickly."

CANTO IV

Ante-Purgatory. Still with the Excommunicates; then, on the First Spur, with the Late-Repentant through negligence. Plato's doctrine of the plurality of souls refuted by Dante's experience. The hard climb to the First Spur. Virgil's explanation of the sun's path in the southern hemisphere. Belacqua, Dante's friend. Noon.

When any of our faculties retains
a strong impression of delight or pain,
the soul will wholly concentrate on that,

neglecting any other power it has   4
(and this refutes the error that maintains
that—one above the other—several souls

can flame in us); and thus, when something seen   7
or heard secures the soul in stringent grip,
time moves and yet we do not notice it.

The power that perceives the course of time   10
is not the power that captures all the mind;
the former has no force—the latter binds.

And I confirmed this by experience,   13
hearing that spirit in my wonderment;
for though the sun had fully climbed fifty

degrees, I had not noticed it, when we   16
came to the point at which in unison
those souls cried out to us: "Here's what you want."

The farmer, when the grape is darkening,   19
will often stuff a wider opening
with just a little forkful of his thorns,

than was the gap through which my guide and I,   22
who followed after, climbed, we two alone,
after that company of souls had gone.

San Leo can be climbed, one can descend 25
to Noli and ascend Cacume and
Bismantova with feet alone, but here

I had to fly: I mean with rapid wings 28
and pinions of immense desire, behind
the guide who gave me hope and was my light.

We made our upward way through rifted rock; 31
along each side the edges pressed on us;
the ground beneath required feet and hands.

When we had reached the upper rim of that 34
steep bank, emerging on the open slope,
I said: "My master, what way shall we take?"

And he to me: "Don't squander any steps; 37
keep climbing up the mountain after me
until we find some expert company."

The summit was so high, my sight fell short; 40
the slope was far more steep than the line drawn
from middle-quadrant to the center point.

I was exhausted when I made this plea: 43
"O gentle father, turn around and see—
I will be left alone unless you halt."

"My son," he said, "draw yourself up to there," 46
while pointing to a somewhat higher terrace,
which circles all the slope along that side.

His words incited me; my body tried; 49
on hands and knees I scrambled after him
until the terrace lay beneath my feet.

There we sat down together, facing east, 52
in the direction from which we had come:
what joy—to look back at a path we've climbed!

My eyes were first set on the shores below, 55
and then I raised them toward the sun; I was
amazed to find it fall upon our left.

And when the poet saw that I was struck 58
with wonder as I watched the chariot
of light passing between the north and us,

he said to me: "Suppose Castor and Pollux   61
were in conjunction with that mirror there,
which takes the light and guides it north and south,

then you would see the reddish zodiac   64
still closer to the Bears as it revolves—
unless it has abandoned its old track.

If you would realize how that should be,   67
then concentrate, imagining this mountain
so placed upon this earth that both Mount Zion

and it, although in different hemispheres,   70
share one horizon; therefore, you can see,
putting your mind to it attentively,

how that same path which Phaethon drove so poorly   73
must pass this mountain on the north, whereas
it skirts Mount Zion on the southern side."

I said: "My master, surely I have never—   76
since my intelligence seemed lacking—seen
as clearly as I now can comprehend,

that the mid-circle of the heavens' motion   79
(one of the sciences calls it Equator),
which always lies between the sun and winter,

as you explained, lies as far north of here   82
as it lies southward of the site from which
the Hebrews, looking toward the tropics, saw it.

But if it please you, I should willingly   85
learn just how far it is we still must journey:
the slope climbs higher than my eyes can follow."

And he to me: "This mountain's of such sort   88
that climbing it is hardest at the start;
but as we rise, the slope grows less unkind.

Therefore, when this slope seems to you so gentle   91
that climbing farther up will be as restful
as traveling downstream by boat, you will

be where this pathway ends, and there you can   94
expect to put your weariness to rest.
I say no more, and this I know as truth."

And when his words were done, another voice 97
nearby was heard to say: "Perhaps you will
have need to sit before you reach that point!"

Hearing that voice, both of us turned around, 100
and to the left we saw a massive boulder,
which neither he nor I—before—had noticed.

We made our way toward it and toward the people 103
who lounged behind that boulder in the shade,
as men beset by listlessness will rest.

And one of them, who seemed to me exhausted, 106
was sitting with his arms around his knees;
between his knees, he kept his head bent down.

"O my sweet lord," I said, "look carefully 109
at one who shows himself more languid than
he would have been were laziness his sister!"

Then that shade turned toward us attentively, 112
lifting his eyes, but just above his thigh,
and said: "Climb, then, if you're so vigorous!"

Then I knew who he was, and the distress 115
that still was quickening my breath somewhat,
did not prevent my going to him; and

when I had reached him, scarcely lifting up 118
his head, he said: "And have you fathomed how
the sun can drive his chariot on your left?"

The slowness of his movements, his brief words 121
had stirred my lips a little toward a smile;
then I began: "From this time on, Belacqua,

I need not grieve for you; but tell me, why 124
do you sit here? Do you expect a guide?
Or have you fallen into your old ways?"

And he: "O brother, what's the use of climbing? 127
God's angel, he who guards the gate, would not
let me pass through to meet my punishment.

Outside that gate the skies must circle round 130
as many times as they did when I lived—
since I delayed good sighs until the end—

unless, before then, I am helped by prayer   133
that rises from a heart that lives in grace;
what use are other prayers—ignored by Heaven?"

And now the poet climbed ahead, before me,   136
and said: "It's time; see the meridian
touched by the sun; elsewhere, along the Ocean,
night now has set its foot upon Morocco."   139

CANTO V

Ante-Purgatory. From the First to the Second Spur: the Late-Repentant who died deaths by violence. The shades amazed by Dante's body. Virgil's rebuke. The Second Spur and its new company of shades. Jacopo del Cassero. Buonconte da Montefeltro. La Pia the Sienese.

I had already left those shades behind
and followed in the footsteps of my guide
when, there beneath me, pointing at me, one

    shade shouted: "See the second climber climb: 4
the sun seems not to shine on his left side,
and when he walks, he walks like one alive!"

    When I had heard these words, I turned my eyes   7
and saw the shades astonished as they stared
at me—at me, and at the broken light.

    "Why have you let your mind get so entwined,"   10
my master said, "that you have slowed your walk?
Why should you care about what's whispered here?

    Come, follow me, and let these people talk: 13
stand like a sturdy tower that does not shake
its summit though the winds may blast; always

    the man in whom thought thrusts ahead of thought   16
allows the goal he's set to move far off—
the force of one thought saps the other's force."

    Could my reply be other than "I come"?   19
And—somewhat colored by the hue that makes
one sometimes merit grace—I spoke those words.

    Meanwhile, along the slope, crossing our road   22
slightly ahead of us, people approached
singing the *Miserere* verse by verse.

    When they became aware that I allowed   25
no path for rays of light to cross my body,

they changed their song into a long, hoarse "Oh!"

And two of them, serving as messengers,   28
hurried to meet us, and those two inquired:
"Please tell us something more of what you are."

My master answered them: "You can return   31
and carry this report to those who sent you:
in truth, the body of this man is flesh.

If, as I think, they stopped to see his shadow,   34
that answer is sufficient: let them welcome
him graciously, and that may profit them."

Never did I see kindled vapors rend   37
clear skies at nightfall or the setting sun
cleave August clouds with a rapidity

that matched the time it took those two to speed   40
above; and, there arrived, they with the others
wheeled back, like ranks that run without a rein.

"These people pressing in on us are many;   43
they come beseeching you," the poet said;
"don't stop, but listen as you move ahead."

"O soul who make your way to gladness with   46
the limbs you had at birth, do stay your steps
awhile," they clamored as they came, "to see

if there is any of us whom you knew,   49
that you may carry word of him beyond.
Why do you hurry on? Why don't you stop?

We all were done to death by violence,   52
and we all sinned until our final hour;
then light from Heaven granted understanding,

so that, repenting and forgiving, we   55
came forth from life at peace with God, and He
instilled in us the longing to see Him."

And I: "Although I scrutinize your faces,   58
I recognize no one; but, spirits born
to goodness, if there's anything within

my power that might please you, then—by that   61
same peace which in the steps of such a guide
I seek from world to world—I shall perform it."

Passing a group of spirits who exclaim that they are living beings (bottom left), Dante and Virgil encounter those who died by violence and without the last rites.

And one began: "We all have faith in your   64
good offices without your oath, as long
as lack of power does not curb your will.

Thus I, who speak alone—before the others—   67
beseech you, if you ever see the land
that lies between Romagna and the realm

of Charles, that you be courteous to me,   70
entreating those in Fano to bestow
fair prayers to purge me of my heavy sins.

My home was Fano; but the piercing wounds   73
from which there poured the blood where my life lived—
those I received among Antenor's sons,

there where I thought that I was most secure;   76
for he of Este, hating me far more
than justice warranted, had that deed done.

But I fled instead toward Mira when   79
they overtook me at Oriaco, then
I should still be beyond, where men draw breath.

I hurried to the marsh. The mud, the reeds   82
entangled me; I fell. And there I saw
a pool, poured from my veins, form on the ground."

Another shade then said: "Ah, so may that   85
desire which draws you up the lofty mountain
be granted, with kind pity help my longing!

I was from Montefeltro, I'm Buonconte;   88
Giovanna and the rest—they all neglect me;
therefore, among these shades, I go in sadness."

And I to him: "What violence or chance   91
so dragged you from the field of Campaldino
that we know nothing of your burial place?"

"Oh," he replied, "across the Casentino   94
there runs a stream called Archiano—born
in the Apennines above the Hermitage.

There, at the place where that stream's name is lost,   97
I came—my throat was pierced—fleeing on foot
and bloodying the plain; and there it was

that I lost sight and speech; and there, as I   100

had finished uttering the name of Mary,
I fell; and there my flesh alone remained.

I'll speak the truth—do you, among the living,   103
retell it: I was taken by God's angel,
but he from Hell cried: 'You from Heaven—why

do you deny me him? For just one tear   106
you carry off his deathless part; but I
shall treat his other part in other wise.'

You are aware how, in the air, moist vapor   109
will gather and again revert to rain
as soon as it has climbed where cold enfolds.

His evil will, which only seeks out evil,   112
conjoined with intellect; and with the power
his nature grants, he stirred up wind and vapor.

And then, when day was done, he filled the valley   115
from Pratomagno far as the great ridge
with mist; the sky above was saturated.

The dense air was converted into water;   118
rain fell, and then the gullies had to carry
whatever water earth could not receive;

and when that rain was gathered into torrents,   121
it rushed so swiftly toward the royal river
that nothing could contain its turbulence.

The angry Archiano—at its mouth—   124
had found my frozen body; and it thrust
it in the Arno and set loose the cross

that, on my chest, my arms, in pain, had formed.   127
It rolled me on the banks and river bed,
then covered, girded me with its debris."

"Pray, after your returning to the world,   130
when, after your long journeying, you've rested,"
the third soul, following the second, said,

"may you remember me, who am La Pia;   133
Siena made—Maremma unmade—me:
he who, when we were wed, gave me his pledge

and then, as nuptial ring, his gem, knows that."   136

CANTO VI

Ante-Purgatory. Still the Second Spur. The simile of the gamester. Others who died deaths by violence. The efficacy of prayers for the dead. Virgil and his fellow Mantuan, Sordello. Dante's invective against Italy and Florence.

When dicing's done and players separate,
the loser's left alone, disconsolate—
rehearsing what he'd thrown, he sadly learns;

all of the crowd surrounds the one who won—   4
one goes in front, and one tugs at his back,
and at his side one asks to be remembered;

he does not halt but listens to them all;   7
and when he gives them something, they desist;
and so he can fend off the pressing throng.

And I, in that persistent pack, was such: 10
this way and that, I turned my face to them
and, making promises, escaped their clutch.

There was the Aretine who met his death   13
beneath Ghino di Tacco's bestial hands,
and one who drowned when, in pursuit, he ran.

There, with his outstretched hands, was Federigo   16
Novello, praying, and the Pisan who
made good Marzucco show his fortitude.

I saw Count Orso, and I saw the soul   19
cleft from its body out of spite and envy—
not, so it said, because it had been guilty—

I mean Pier de la Brosse (and may the Lady   22
of Brabant, while she's still in this world, watch
her ways—or end among a sadder flock).

As soon as I was free from all those shades   25
who always pray for others' prayers for them,

so as to reach their blessed state more quickly,

I started: "O my light, it seems to me 28
that in one passage you deny expressly
that prayer can bend the rule of Heaven, yet

these people pray precisely for that end. 31
Is their hope, therefore, only emptiness,
or have I not read clearly what you said?"

And he to me: "My text is plain enough, 34
and yet their hope is not delusive if
one scrutinizes it with sober wit;

the peak of justice is not lowered when 37
the fire of love accomplishes in one
instant the expiation owed by all

who dwell here; for where I asserted this— 40
that prayers could not mend their fault—I spoke
of prayers without a passageway to God.

But in a quandary so deep, do not 43
conclude with me, but wait for word that she,
the light between your mind and truth, will speak—

lest you misunderstand, the *she* I mean 46
is Beatrice; upon this mountain's peak,
there you shall see her smiling joyously."

And I: "Lord, let us move ahead more quickly, 49
for now I am less weary than before;
and—you can see—the slope now casts a shadow."

"As long as it is day, we'll make as much 52
headway as possible," he answered; "but
our climb won't be as rapid as you thought.

You will not reach the peak before you see 55
the sun returning: now he hides behind
the hills—you cannot interrupt his light.

But see—beyond—a soul who is completely 58
apart, and seated, looking toward us; he
will show us where to climb most speedily."

We came to him. O Lombard soul, what pride 61
and what disdain were in your stance! Your eyes

moved with such dignity, such gravity!

He said no thing to us but let us pass, 64
his eyes intent upon us only as
a lion watches when it is at rest.

Yet Virgil made his way to him, appealing 67
to him to show us how we'd best ascend;
and he did not reply to that request,

but asked us what our country was and who 70
we were, at which my gentle guide began
"Mantua"—and that spirit, who had been

so solitary, rose from his position, 73
saying: "O Mantuan, I am Sordello,
from your own land!" And each embraced the other.

Ah, abject Italy, you inn of sorrows, 76
you ship without a helmsman in harsh seas,
no queen of provinces but of bordellos!

That noble soul had such enthusiasm: 79
his city's sweet name was enough for him
to welcome—there—his fellow-citizen;

But those who are alive within you now 82
can't live without their warring—even those
whom one same wall and one same moat enclose

gnaw at each other. Squalid Italy, 85
search round your shores and then look inland—see
if any part of you delight in peace.

What use was there in a Justinian's 88
mending your bridle, when the saddle's empty?
Indeed, were there no reins, your shame were less.

Ah you—who if you understood what God 91
ordained, would then attend to things devout
and in the saddle surely would allow

Caesar to sit—see how this beast turns fierce 94
because there are no spurs that would correct it,
since you have laid your hands upon the bit!

O German Albert, you who have abandoned 97
that steed become recalcitrant and savage,

you who should ride astride its saddlebows—

upon your blood may the just judgment of   100
the stars descend with signs so strange and plain
that your successor has to feel its terror!

For both you and your father, in your greed   103
for lands that lay more close at hand, allowed
the garden of the Empire to be gutted.

Come—you who pay no heed—do come and see   106
Montecchi, Cappelletti, sad already,
and, filled with fear, Monaldi, Filippeschi.

Come, cruel one, come see the tribulation   109
of your nobility and heal their hurts;
see how disconsolate is Santafior!

Come, see your Rome who, widowed and alone,   112
weeps bitterly; both day and night, she moans:
"My Caesar, why are you not at my side?"

Come, see how much your people love each other!   115
And if no pity for us moves you, may
shame for your own repute move you to act.

And if I am allowed, o highest Jove,   118
to ask: You who on earth were crucified
for us—have You turned elsewhere Your just eyes?

Or are You, in Your judgment's depth, devising   121
a good that we cannot foresee, completely
dissevered from our way of understanding?

For all the towns of Italy are full   124
of tyrants, and each townsman who becomes
a partisan is soon a new Marcellus.

My Florence, you indeed may be content   127
that this digression would leave you exempt:
your people's strivings spare you this lament.

Others have justice in their hearts, and thought   130
is slow to let it fly off from their bow;
but your folk keep it ready—on their lips.

Others refuse the weight of public service;   133
whereas your people—eagerly—respond,

even unasked, and shout: "I'll take it on."

You might be happy now, for you have cause!   136
You with your riches, peace, judiciousness!
If I speak truly, facts won't prove me wrong.

Compared to you, Athens and Lacedaemon,   139
though civil cities, with their ancient laws,
had merely sketched the life of righteousness;

for you devise provisions so ingenious—   142
whatever threads October sees you spin,
when mid-November comes, will be unspun.

How often, in the time you can remember,   145
have you changed laws and coinage, offices
and customs, and revised your citizens!

And if your memory has some clarity,   148
then you will see yourself like that sick woman
who finds no rest upon her feather-bed,

but, turning, tossing, tries to ease her pain.   151

CANTO VII

Ante-Purgatory. From the Second Spur to the Valley of the Rulers—they too, through negligence, among the Late-Repentant. Rudolph I of Hapsburg; Ottokar II of Bohemia; Philip III of France; Henry I of Navarre; Peter III of Aragon; Charles I of Anjou; Peter, youngest son of Peter III of Aragon; Henry II of England—all thirteenth-century rulers.

When glad and gracious welcomings had been
repeated three and four times, then Sordello
drew himself back and asked: "But who are you?"

"Before the spirits worthy of ascent   4
to God had been directed to this mountain,
my bones were buried by Octavian.

I am Virgil, and I am deprived of Heaven   7
for no fault other than my lack of faith."
This was the answer given by my guide.

Even like one who, suddenly, has seen   10
something before him and then, marveling,
does and does not believe, saying, "It is . . .

is not," so did Sordello seem, and then   13
he bent his brow, returned to Virgil humbly,
and clasped him where the lesser presence clasps.

He said: "O glory of the Latins, you   16
through whom our tongue revealed its power, you,
eternal honor of my native city,

what merit or what grace shows you to me?   19
If I deserve to hear your word, then answer:
tell me if you're from Hell and from what cloister."

"Through every circle of the sorry kingdom,"   22
he answered him, "I journeyed here; a power

from Heaven moved me, and with that, I come.

   Not for the having—but not having—done,   25
I lost the sight that you desire, the Sun—
that high Sun I was late in recognizing.

   There is a place below that only shadows—   28
not torments—have assigned to sadness; there,
lament is not an outcry, but a sigh.

   There I am with the infant innocents,   31
those whom the teeth of death had seized before
they were set free from human sinfulness;

   there I am with those souls who were not clothed   34
in the three holy virtues—but who knew
and followed after all the other virtues.

   But if you know and you are able to,   37
would you point out the path that leads more quickly
to the true entry point of Purgatory?"

   He answered: "No fixed place has been assigned   40
to us; I'm free to range about and climb;
as far as I may go, I'll be your guide.

   But see now how the day declines; by night   43
we cannot climb; and therefore it is best
to find some pleasant place where we can rest.

   Here to the right are spirits set apart;   46
if you allow me, I shall lead you to them;
and not without delight, you'll come to know them."

   "How is that?" he was asked. "Is it that he   49
who tried to climb by night would be impeded
by others, or by his own lack of power?"

   And good Sordello, as his finger traced   52
along the ground, said: "Once the sun has set,
then—look—even this line cannot be crossed.

   And not that anything except the dark   55
of night prevents your climbing up; it is
the night itself that implicates your will.

   Once darkness falls, one can indeed retreat   58
below and wander aimlessly about

the slopes, while the horizon has enclosed
    the day." At which my lord, as if in wonder,   61
said: "Lead us then to there where, as you say,
we may derive delight from this night's stay."

    We had not gone far off, when I perceived   64
that, just as valleys hollow mountains here
in our world, so that mountain there was hollowed.

    That shade said: "It is there that we shall go—   67
to where the slope forms, of itself, a lap;
at that place we'll await the new day's coming."

    There was a slanting path, now steep, now flat;   70
it led us to a point beside the valley,
just where its bordering edge had dropped by half.

    Gold and fine silver, cochineal, white lead,   73
and Indian lychnite, highly polished, bright,
fresh emerald at the moment it is dampened,

    if placed within that valley, all would be   76
defeated by the grass and flowers' colors,
just as the lesser gives way to the greater.

    And nature there not only was a painter,   79
but from the sweetness of a thousand odors,
she had derived an unknown, mingled scent.

    Upon the green grass and the flowers, I   82
saw seated spirits singing "*Salve Regina*";
they were not visible from the outside.

    "Before the meager sun seeks out its nest,"   85
began the Mantuan who led us here,
"do not ask me to guide you down among them.

    From this bank, you'll be better able to   88
make out the acts and features of them all
than if you were to join them in the hollow.

    He who is seated highest, with the look   91
of one too lax in what he undertook—
whose mouth, although the rest sing, does not move—

    was Emperor Rudolph, one who could have healed   94
the wounds that were the death of Italy,

so that another, later, must restore her.

His neighbor, whose appearance comforts him,   97
governed the land in which are born the waters
the Moldau carries to the Elbe and

the Elbe to the sea: named Ottokar—   100
in swaddling-bands he was more valiant than
his son, the bearded Wenceslaus, who feeds

on wantonness and ease. That small-nosed man,   103
who seems so close in counsel with his kindly
friend, died in flight, deflowering the lily:

see how he beats his breast there! And you see   106
the other shade, who, as he sighs, would rest
his cheek upon his palm as on a bed.

Father and father-in-law of the pest   109
of France, they know his life—its filth, its vice;
out of that knowledge grows the grief that has

pierced them. That other, who seems so robust   112
and sings in time with him who has a nose
so manly, wore the cord of every virtue;

and if the young man seated there behind him   115
had only followed him as king, then valor
might have been poured from vessel unto vessel;

one cannot say this of his other heirs;   118
his kingdoms now belong to James and Frederick—
but they do not possess his best bequest.

How seldom human worth ascends from branch   121
to branch, and this is willed by Him who grants
that gift, that one may pray to him for it!

My words suggest the large-nosed one no less   124
than they refer to Peter, singing with him,
whose heir brings Puglia and Provence distress:

the plant is lesser than its seed, just as   127
the man whom Beatrice and Margaret wed
is lesser than the husband Constance has.

You see the king who led the simple life   130
seated alone: Henry of England—he

has better fortune with his progeny.

He who is seated lowest on the ground,   133
and looking up, is William the Marquis—
for him, both Alexandria and its war
make Monferrato and Canavese mourn."   136

CANTO VIII

Ante-Purgatory. The Valley of the Rulers. Sunset. The two angels. Dante's friend, Nino Visconti. The three stars. The serpent put to flight by the angels. Colloquy with Currado Malaspina.

It was the hour that turns seafarers' longings
homeward—the hour that makes their hearts grow tender
upon the day they bid sweet friends farewell;

the hour that pierces the new traveler   4
with love when he has heard, far off, the bell
that seems to mourn the dying of the day;

when I began to let my hearing fade   7
and watched one of those souls who, having risen,
had signaled with his hand for our attention.

He joined his palms and, lifting them, he fixed   10
all his attention on the east, as if
to say to God: "I care for nothing else."

"*Te lucis ante*" issued from his lips   13
with such devotion and with notes so sweet
that I was moved to move beyond my mind.

And then the other spirits followed him—   16
devoutly, gently—through all of that hymn,
their eyes intent on the supernal spheres.

Here, reader, let your eyes look sharp at truth,   19
for now the veil has grown so very thin—
it is not difficult to pass within.

I saw that company of noble spirits,   22
silent and looking upward, pale and humble,
as if in expectation; and I saw,

emerging and descending from above,   25
two angels bearing flaming swords, of which

the blades were broken off, without their tips.

Their garments, just as green as newborn leaves,   28
were agitated, fanned by their green wings,
and trailed behind them; and one angel came

and stood somewhat above us, while the other   31
descended on the opposite embankment,
flanking that company of souls between them.

My eyes made out their blond heads clearly, but   34
my sight was dazzled by their faces—just
like any sense bewildered by excess.

"Both come from Mary's bosom," said Sordello,   37
"to serve as the custodians of the valley
against the serpent that will soon appear."

At this, not knowing where its path might be,   40
frozen with fear, I turned around, pressing
close to the trusty shoulders. And Sordello

continued: "Let us now descend among   43
the great shades in the valley; we shall speak
with them; and seeing you, they will be pleased."

I think that I had taken but three steps   46
to go below, when I saw one who watched
attentively, trying to recognize me.

The hour had now arrived when air grows dark,   49
but not so dark that it deprived my eyes
and his of what—before—they were denied.

He moved toward me, and I advanced toward him.   52
Noble Judge Nino—what delight was mine
when I saw you were not among the damned!

There was no gracious greeting we neglected   55
before he asked me: "When did you arrive,
across long seas, beneath this mountainside?"

I told him, "Oh, by way of the sad regions,   58
I came this morning; I am still within
the first life—although, by this journeying,

I earn the other." When they heard my answer,   61
Sordello and Judge Nino, just behind him,

drew back like people suddenly astonished.

One turned to Virgil, and the other turned   64
and called to one who sat there: "Up, Currado!
Come see what God, out of His grace, has willed!"

Then, when he turned to me: "By that especial   67
gratitude you owe to Him who hides
his primal aim so that no human mind

may find the ford to it, when you return   70
across the wide waves, ask my own Giovanna—
there where the pleas of innocents are answered—

to pray for me. I do not think her mother   73
still loves me: she gave up her white veils—surely,
poor woman, she will wish them back again.

Through her, one understands so easily   76
how brief, in woman, is love's fire—when not
rekindled frequently by eye or touch.

The serpent that assigns the Milanese   79
their camping place will not provide for her
a tomb as fair as would Gallura's rooster."

So Nino spoke; his bearing bore the seal   82
of that unswerving zeal which, though it flames
within the heart, maintains a sense of measure.

My avid eyes were steadfast, staring at   85
that portion of the sky where stars are slower,
even as spokes when they approach the axle.

And my guide: "Son, what are you staring at?"   88
And I replied: "I'm watching those three torches
with which this southern pole is all aflame."

Then he to me: "The four bright stars you saw   91
this morning now are low, beyond the pole,
and where those four stars were, these three now are."

Even as Virgil spoke, Sordello drew   94
him to himself: "See there—our adversary!"
he said; and then he pointed with his finger.

At the unguarded edge of that small valley,   97
there was a serpent—similar, perhaps,

to that which offered Eve the bitter food.

Through grass and flowers the evil streak advanced;   100
from time to time it turned its head and licked
its back, like any beast that preens and sleeks.

I did not see—and therefore cannot say—   103
just how the hawks of heaven made their move,
but I indeed saw both of them in motion.

Hearing the green wings cleave the air, the serpent   106
fled, and the angels wheeled around as each
of them flew upward, back to his high station.

The shade who, when the judge had called, had drawn   109
closer to him, through all of that attack,
had not removed his eyes from me one moment.

"So may the lantern that leads you on high   112
discover in your will the wax one needs—
enough for reaching the enameled peak,"

that shade began, "if you have heard true tidings   115
of Val di Magra or the lands nearby,
tell them to me—for there I once was mighty.

Currado Malaspina was my name;   118
I'm not the old Currado, but I am
descended from him: to my own I bore

the love that here is purified." I answered: 121
"I never visited your lands; but can
there be a place in all of Europe where

they are not celebrated? Such renown   124
honors your house, acclaims your lords and lands—
even if one has yet to journey there.

And so may I complete my climb, I swear   127
to you: your honored house still claims the prize—
the glory of the purse and of the sword.

Custom and nature privilege it so   130
that, though the evil head contorts the world,
your kin alone walk straight and shun the path

of wickedness." And he: "Be sure of that.   133
The sun will not have rested seven times

within the bed that's covered and held fast
   by all the Ram's four feet before this gracious   136
opinion's squarely nailed into your mind
with stouter nails than others' talk provides—
   if the divine decree has not been stayed."   139

CANTO IX

Ante-Purgatory. The Valley of the Rulers. Aurora in the northern hemisphere and night in Purgatory. The sleep of Dante. His dream of the Eagle. His waking at morning. The guardian angel. The gate of Purgatory. The seven P's. Entry.

Now she who shares the bed of old Tithonus,
abandoning the arms of her sweet lover,
grew white along the eastern balcony;

the heavens facing her were glittering   4
with gems set in the semblance of the chill
animal that assails men with its tail;

while night within the valley where we were   7
had moved across two of the steps it climbs,
and now the third step made night's wings incline;

when I, who bore something of Adam with me,   10
feeling the need for sleep, lay down upon
the grass where now all five of us were seated.

At that hour close to morning when the swallow   13
begins her melancholy songs, perhaps
in memory of her ancient sufferings,

when, free to wander farther from the flesh   16
and less held fast by cares, our intellect's
envisionings become almost divine—

in dream I seemed to see an eagle poised,   19
with golden pinions, in the sky: its wings
were open; it was ready to swoop down.

And I seemed to be there where Ganymede   22
deserted his own family when he
was snatched up for the high consistory.

Within myself I thought: "This eagle may   25
be used to hunting only here; its claws

refuse to carry upward any prey

found elsewhere." Then it seemed to me that, wheeling   28
slightly and terrible as lightning, it
swooped, snatching me up to the fire's orbit.

And there it seemed that he and I were burning;   31
and this imagined conflagration scorched
me so—I was compelled to break my sleep.

Just like the waking of Achilles when   34
he started up, casting his eyes about him,
not knowing where he was (after his mother

had stolen him, asleep, away from Chiron   37
and in her arms had carried him to Skyros,
the isle the Greeks would—later—make him leave);

such was my starting up, as soon as sleep   40
had left my eyes, and I went pale, as will
a man who, terrified, turns cold as ice.

The only one beside me was my comfort;   43
by now the sun was more than two hours high;
it was the sea to which I turned my eyes.

My lord said: "Have no fear; be confident,   46
for we are well along our way; do not
restrain, but give free rein to, all your strength.

You have already come to Purgatory: 49
see there the rampart wall enclosing it;
see, where that wall is breached, the point of entry.

Before, at dawn that ushers in the day,   52
when soul was sleeping in your body, on
the flowers that adorn the ground below,

a lady came; she said: 'I am Lucia;   55
let me take hold of him who is asleep,
that I may help to speed him on his way.'

Sordello and the other noble spirits   58
stayed there; and she took you, and once the day
was bright, she climbed—I following behind.

And here she set you down, but first her lovely   61
eyes showed that open entryway to me;

then she and sleep together took their leave."

Just like a man in doubt who then grows sure,   64
exchanging fear for confidence, once truth
has been revealed to him, so was I changed;

and when my guide had seen that I was free   67
from hesitation, then he moved, with me
behind him, up the rocks and toward the heights.

Reader, you can see clearly how I lift   70
my matter; do not wonder, therefore, if
I have to call on more art to sustain it.

Now we were drawing closer; we had reached   73
the part from which—where first I'd seen a breach,
precisely like a gap that cleaves a wall—

I now made out a gate and, there below it,   76
three steps—their colors different—leading to it,
and a custodian who had not yet spoken.

As I looked more and more directly at him,   79
I saw him seated on the upper step—
his face so radiant, I could not bear it;

and in his hand he held a naked sword,   82
which so reflected rays toward us that I,
time and again, tried to sustain that sight

in vain. "Speak out from there; what are you seeking?"   85
so he began to speak. "Where is your escort?
Take care lest you be harmed by climbing here."

My master answered him: "But just before,   88
a lady came from Heaven and, familiar
with these things told us: 'That's the gate; go there.'"

"And may she speed you on your path of goodness!"   91
the gracious guardian of the gate began
again. "Come forward, therefore, to our stairs."

There we approached, and the first step was white   94
marble, so polished and so clear that I
was mirrored there as I appear in life.

The second step, made out of crumbling rock,   97
rough-textured, scorched, with cracks that ran across

its length and width, was darker than deep purple.

The third, resting above more massively,   100
appeared to me to be of porphyry,
as flaming red as blood that spurts from veins.

And on this upper step, God's angel—seated   103
upon the threshold, which appeared to me
to be of adamant—kept his feet planted.

My guide, with much good will, had me ascend   106
by way of these three steps, enjoining me:
"Do ask him humbly to unbolt the gate."

I threw myself devoutly at his holy   109
feet, asking him to open out of mercy;
but first I beat three times upon my breast.

Upon my forehead, he traced seven *P*'s   112
with his sword's point and said: "When you have entered
within, take care to wash away these wounds."

Ashes, or dry earth that has just been quarried,   115
would share one color with his robe, and from
beneath that robe he drew two keys; the one

was made of gold, the other was of silver;   118
first with the white, then with the yellow key,
he plied the gate so as to satisfy me.

"Whenever one of these keys fails, not turning   121
appropriately in the lock," he said
to us, "this gate of entry does not open.

One is more precious, but the other needs   124
much art and skill before it will unlock—
that is the key that must undo the knot.

These I received from Peter; and he taught me   127
rather to err in opening than in keeping
this portal shut—whenever souls pray humbly."

Then he pushed back the panels of the holy   130
gate, saying: "Enter; but I warn you—he
who would look back, returns—again—outside."

And when the panels of that sacred portal,   133
which are of massive and resounding metal,

turned in their hinges, then even Tarpeia
   (when good Metellus was removed from it,   136
for which that rock was left impoverished)
did not roar so nor show itself so stubborn.

   Hearing that gate resound, I turned, attentive;   139
I seemed to hear, inside, in words that mingled
with gentle music, "*Te Deum laudamus*."

   And what I heard gave me the very same   142
impression one is used to getting when
one hears a song accompanied by organ,

     and now the words are clear and now are lost.   145

CANTO X

The First Terrace: the Prideful. The hard ascent. The sculptured wall with three examples of humility: the Virgin Mary, David, and Trajan. The Prideful punished by bearing the weight of heavy stones.

When I had crossed the threshold of the gate
that—since the souls' aberrant love would make
the crooked way seem straight—is seldom used,

I heard the gate resound and, hearing, knew   4
that it had shut; and if I'd turned toward it,
how could my fault have found a fit excuse?

Our upward pathway ran between cracked rocks;   7
they seemed to sway in one, then the other part,
just like a wave that flees, then doubles back.

"Here we shall need some ingenuity,"   10
my guide warned me, "as both of us draw near
this side or that side where the rock wall veers."

This made our steps so slow and hesitant   13
that the declining moon had reached its bed
to sink back into rest, before we had

made our way through that needle's eye; but when   16
we were released from it, in open space
above, a place at which the slope retreats,

I was exhausted; with the two of us   19
uncertain of our way, we halted on
a plateau lonelier than desert paths.

The distance from its edge, which rims the void,   22
in to the base of the steep slope, which climbs
and climbs, would measure three times one man's body;

and for as far as my sight took its flight,   25
now to the left, now to the right-hand side,

that terrace seemed to me equally wide.

There we had yet to let our feet advance 28
when I discovered that the bordering bank—
less sheer than banks of other terraces—

was of white marble and adorned with carvings 31
so accurate—not only Polycletus
but even Nature, there, would feel defeated.

The angel who reached earth with the decree 34
of that peace, which, for many years, had been
invoked with tears, the peace that opened Heaven

after long interdict, appeared before us, 37
his gracious action carved with such precision—
he did not seem to be a silent image.

One would have sworn that he was saying, "*Ave*"; 40
for in that scene there was the effigy
of one who turned the key that had unlocked

the highest love; and in her stance there were 43
impressed these words, "*Ecce ancilla Dei*,"
precisely like a figure stamped in wax.

"Your mind must not attend to just one part," 46
the gentle master said—he had me on
the side of him where people have their heart.

At this, I turned my face and saw beyond 49
the form of Mary—on the side where stood
the one who guided me—another story

engraved upon the rock; therefore I moved 52
past Virgil and drew close to it, so that
the scene before my eyes was more distinct.

There, carved in that same marble, were the cart 55
and oxen as they drew the sacred ark,
which makes men now fear tasks not in their charge.

People were shown in front; and all that group, 58
divided into seven choirs, made
two of my senses speak—one sense said, "No,"

the other said, "Yes, they do sing"; just so, 61
about the incense smoke shown there, my nose

Within the Gates of Purgatory (bottom centre) Dante and Virgil enter the First Terrace where they find representations of the Annunciation; David dancing before the Ark; and the Emperor Trajan dispensing justice.

and eyes contended, too, with *yes* and *no*.

And there the humble psalmist went before 64
the sacred vessel, dancing, lifting up
his robe—he was both less and more than king.

Facing that scene, and shown as at the window 67
of a great palace, Michal watched as would
a woman full of scorn and suffering.

To look more closely at another carving, 70
which I saw gleaming white beyond Michal,
my feet moved past the point where I had stood.

And there the noble action of a Roman 73
prince was presented—he whose worth had urged
on Gregory to his great victory—

I mean the Emperor Trajan; and a poor 76
widow was near his bridle, and she stood
even as one in tears and sadness would.

Around him, horsemen seemed to press and crowd; 79
above their heads, on golden banners, eagles
were represented, moving in the wind.

Among that crowd, the miserable woman 82
seemed to be saying: "Lord, avenge me for
the slaying of my son—my heart is broken."

And he was answering: "Wait now until 85
I have returned." And she, as one in whom
grief presses urgently: "And, lord, if you

do not return?" And he: "The one who'll be 88
in my place will perform it for you." She:
"What good can others' goodness do for you

if you neglect your own?" He: "Be consoled; 91
my duty shall be done before I go:
so justice asks, so mercy makes me stay."

This was the speech made visible by One 94
within whose sight no thing is new—but we,
who lack its likeness here, find novelty.

While I took much delight in witnessing 97
these effigies of true humility—

dear, too, to see because He was their Maker—
    the poet murmured: "See the multitude   100
advancing, though with slow steps, on this side:
they will direct us to the higher stairs."

    My eyes, which had been satisfied in seeking   103
new sights—a thing for which they long—did not
delay in turning toward him. But I would

    not have you, reader, be deflected from   106
your good resolve by hearing from me now
how God would have us pay the debt we owe.

    Don't dwell upon the form of punishment: 109
consider what comes after that; at worst
it cannot last beyond the final Judgment.

    "Master," I said, "what I see moving toward us   112
does not appear to me like people, but
I can't tell what is there—my sight's bewildered."

    And he to me: "Whatever makes them suffer   115
their heavy torment bends them to the ground;
at first I was unsure of what they were.

    But look intently there, and let your eyes   118
unravel what's beneath those stones: you can
already see what penalty strikes each."

    O Christians, arrogant, exhausted, wretched,   121
whose intellects are sick and cannot see,
who place your confidence in backward steps,

    do you not know that we are worms and born   124
to form the angelic butterfly that soars,
without defenses, to confront His judgment?

    Why does your mind presume to flight when you   127
are still like the imperfect grub, the worm
before it has attained its final form?

    Just as one sees at times—as corbel for   130
support of ceiling or of roof—a figure
with knees drawn up into its chest (and this

    oppressiveness, unreal, gives rise to real   133
distress in him who watches it): such was

the state of those I saw when I looked hard.

They were indeed bent down—some less, some more— 136
according to the weights their backs now bore;
and even he whose aspect showed most patience,

in tears, appeared to say: "I can no more." 139

CANTO XI

Still on the First Terrace: the Prideful, who now pray a
paraphrase of the Lord's Prayer. Omberto Aldobrandeschi.
Oderisi of Gubbio: his discourse on earthly fame; his
presentation of Provenzan Salvani.

"Our Father, You who dwell within the heavens—
but are not circumscribed by them—out of
Your greater love for Your first works above,

    praised be Your name and Your omnipotence,   4
by every creature, just as it is seemly
to offer thanks to Your sweet effluence.

    Your kingdom's peace come unto us, for if   7
it does not come, then though we summon all
our force, we cannot reach it of our selves.

    Just as Your angels, as they sing Hosanna,   10
offer their wills to You as sacrifice,
so may men offer up their wills to You.

    Give unto us this day the daily manna   13
without which he who labors most to move
ahead through this harsh wilderness falls back.

    Even as we forgive all who have done   16
us injury, may You, benevolent,
forgive, and do not judge us by our worth.

    Try not our strength, so easily subdued,   19
against the ancient foe, but set it free
from him who goads it to perversity.

    This last request we now address to You,   22
dear Lord, not for ourselves—who have no need—
but for the ones whom we have left behind."

    Beseeching, thus, good penitence for us   25
and for themselves, those shades moved on beneath

their weights, like those we sometimes bear in dreams—
each in his own degree of suffering   28
but all, exhausted, circling the first terrace,
purging themselves of this world's scoriae.

If there they pray on our behalf, what can   31
be said and done here on this earth for them
by those whose wills are rooted in true worth?

Indeed we should help them to wash away   34
the stains they carried from this world, so that,
made pure and light, they reach the starry wheels.

"Ah, so may justice and compassion soon   37
unburden you, so that your wings may move
as you desire them to, and uplift you,

show us on which hand lies the shortest path   40
to reach the stairs; if there is more than one
passage, then show us that which is less steep;

for he who comes with me, because he wears   43
the weight of Adam's flesh as dress, despite
his ready will, is slow in his ascent."

These words, which had been spoken by my guide,   46
were answered by still other words we heard;
for though it was not clear who had replied,

an answer came: "Come with us to the right   49
along the wall of rock, and you will find
a pass where even one alive can climb.

And were I not impeded by the stone   52
that, since it has subdued my haughty neck,
compels my eyes to look below, then I

should look at this man who is still alive   55
and nameless, to see if I recognize
him—and to move his pity for my burden.

I was Italian, son of a great Tuscan: 58
my father was Guiglielmo Aldobrandesco;
I do not know if you have heard his name.

The ancient blood and splendid deeds of my   61
forefathers made me so presumptuous

that, without thinking on our common mother,

I scorned all men past measure, and that scorn   64
brought me my death—the Sienese know how,
as does each child in Campagnatico.

I am Omberto; and my arrogance   67
has not harmed me alone, for it has drawn
all of my kin into calamity.

Until God has been satisfied, I bear   70
this burden here among the dead because
I did not bear this load among the living."

My face was lowered as I listened; and   73
one of those souls—not he who'd spoken—twisted
himself beneath the weight that burdened them;

he saw and knew me and called out to me,   76
fixing his eyes on me laboriously
as I, completely hunched, walked on with them.

"Oh," I cried out, "are you not Oderisi,   79
glory of Gubbio, glory of that art
they call illumination now in Paris?"

"Brother," he said, "the pages painted by   82
the brush of Franco Bolognese smile
more brightly: all the glory now is his;

mine, but a part. In truth I would have been   85
less gracious when I lived—so great was that
desire for eminence which drove my heart.

For such pride, here one pays the penalty;   88
and I'd not be here yet, had it not been
that, while I still could sin, I turned to Him.

O empty glory of the powers of humans!   91
How briefly green endures upon the peak—
unless an age of dullness follows it.

In painting Cimabue thought he held   94
the field, and now it's Giotto they acclaim—
the former only keeps a shadowed fame.

So did one Guido, from the other, wrest   97
the glory of our tongue—and he perhaps

The poets encounter souls of the Proud, now condemned to creep beneath the burdens of their sin.

is born who will chase both out of the nest.

Worldly renown is nothing other than   100
a breath of wind that blows now here, now there,
and changes name when it has changed its course.

Before a thousand years have passed—a span   103
that, for eternity, is less space than
an eyeblink for the slowest sphere in heaven—

would you find greater glory if you left   106
your flesh when it was old than if your death
had come before your infant words were spent?

All Tuscany acclaimed his name—the man   109
who moves so slowly on the path before me,
and now they scarcely whisper of him even

in Siena, where he lorded it when they   112
destroyed the raging mob of Florence—then
as arrogant as now it's prostitute.

Your glory wears the color of the grass   115
that comes and goes; the sun that makes it wither
first drew it from the ground, still green and tender."

And I to him: "Your truthful speech has filled   118
my soul with sound humility, abating
my overswollen pride; but who is he

of whom you spoke now?" "Provenzan Salvani,"   121
he answered, "here because—presumptuously—
he thought his grip could master all Siena.

So he has gone, and so he goes, with no   124
rest since his death; this is the penalty
exacted from those who—there—overreached."

And I: "But if a spirit who awaits   127
the edge of life before repenting must—
unless good prayers help him—stay below

and not ascend here for as long a time   130
as he had spent alive, do tell me how
Salvani's entry here has been allowed."

"When he was living in his greatest glory,"   133
said he, "then of his own free will he set

aside all shame and took his place upon
the Campo of Siena; there, to free   136
his friend from suffering in Charles's prison,
humbling himself, he trembled in each vein.

I say no more; I know I speak obscurely;   139
but soon enough you'll find your neighbors' acts
are such that what I say can be explained.

This deed delivered him from those confines."   142

CANTO XII

Still on the First Terrace: the Prideful. The sculptured
pavement with thirteen examples of punished pride: Satan,
Briareus, the Giants, Nimrod, Niobe, Saul, Arachne,
Rehoboam, Eriphyle, Sennacherib, Cyrus, Holofernes, Troy.
The angel of humility. Ascent to the Second Terrace. The
First Beatitude. One P erased.

As oxen, yoked, proceed abreast, so I
moved with that burdened soul as long as my
kind pedagogue allowed me to; but when

he said: "Leave him behind, and go ahead;   4
for here it's fitting that with wings and oars
each urge his boat along with all his force,"

I drew my body up again, erect—   7
the stance most suitable to man—and yet
the thoughts I thought were still submissive, bent.

Now I was on my way, and willingly   10
I followed in my teacher's steps, and we
together showed what speed we could command.

He said to me: "Look downward, for the way   13
will offer you some solace if you pay
attention to the pavement at your feet."

As, on the lids of pavement tombs, there are   16
stone effigies of what the buried were
before, so that the dead may be remembered;

and there, when memory—inciting only   19
the pious—has renewed their mourning, men
are often led to shed their tears again;

so did I see, but carved more skillfully,   22
with greater sense of likeness, effigies
on all the path protruding from the mountain.

I saw, to one side of the path, one who   25
had been created nobler than all other

beings, falling lightning-like from Heaven.

I saw, upon the other side, Briareus   28
transfixed by the celestial shaft: he lay,
ponderous, on the ground, in fatal cold.

I saw Thymbraeus, I saw Mars and Pallas,   31
still armed, as they surrounded Jove, their father,
gazing upon the Giants' scattered limbs.

I saw bewildered Nimrod at the foot   34
of his great labor; watching him were those
of Shinar who had shared his arrogance.

O Niobe, what tears afflicted me   37
when, on that path, I saw your effigy
among your slaughtered children, seven and seven!

O Saul, you were portrayed there as one who 40
had died on his own sword, upon Gilboa,
which never after knew the rain, the dew!

O mad Arachne, I saw you already   43
half spider, wretched on the ragged remnants
of work that you had wrought to your own hurt!

O Rehoboam, you whose effigy   46
seems not to menace there, and yet you flee
by chariot, terrified, though none pursues!

It also showed—that pavement of hard stone— 49
how much Alcmaeon made his mother pay:
the cost of the ill-omened ornament.

It showed the children of Sennacherib   52
as they assailed their father in the temple,
then left him, dead, behind them as they fled.

It showed the slaughter and the devastation 55
wrought by Tomyris when she taunted Cyrus:
"You thirsted after blood; with blood I fill you."

It showed the rout of the Assyrians,   58
sent reeling after Holofernes' death,
and also showed his body—what was left.

I saw Troy turned to caverns and to ashes; 61
o Ilium, your effigy in stone—
it showed you there so squalid, so cast down!

Moving from left to right, the two poets encounter Satan, transformed into a monster by pride; the dismembered body of Briareus; the falling Tower of Babel; Saul fallen on his sword; and the besieged Troy.

What master of the brush or of the stylus   64
had there portrayed such masses, such outlines
as would astonish all discerning minds?

The dead seemed dead and the alive, alive: 67
I saw, head bent, treading those effigies,
as well as those who'd seen those scenes directly.

Now, sons of Eve, persist in arrogance,   70
in haughty stance, do not let your eyes bend,
lest you be forced to see your evil path!

We now had circled round more of the mountain   73
and much more of the sun's course had been crossed
than I, my mind absorbed, had gauged, when he

who always looked ahead insistently,   76
as he advanced, began: "Lift up your eyes;
it's time to set these images aside.

See there an angel hurrying to meet us,   79
and also see the sixth of the handmaidens
returning from her service to the day.

Adorn your face and acts with reverence,   82
that he be pleased to send us higher. Remember—
today will never know another dawn."

I was so used to his insistent warnings   85
against the loss of time; concerning that,
his words to me could hardly be obscure.

That handsome creature came toward us; his clothes   88
were white, and in his aspect he seemed like
the trembling star that rises in the morning.

He opened wide his arms, then spread his wings;   91
he said: "Approach: the steps are close at hand;
from this point on one can climb easily.

This invitation's answered by so few: 94
o humankind, born for the upward flight,
why are you driven back by wind so slight?"

He led us to a cleft within the rock,   97
and then he struck my forehead with his wing;
that done, he promised me safe journeying.

As on the right, when one ascends the hill   100

where—over Rubaconte's bridge—there stands
the church that dominates the well-ruled city,

the daring slope of the ascent is broken   103
by steps that were constructed in an age
when record books and measures could be trusted,

so was the slope that plummets there so steeply   106
down from the other ring made easier;
but on this side and that, high rock encroaches.

While we began to move in that direction,   109
"*Beati pauperes spiritu*" was sung
so sweetly—it can not be told in words.

How different were these entryways from those   112
of Hell! For here it is with song one enters;
down there, it is with savage lamentations.

Now we ascended by the sacred stairs,   115
but I seemed to be much more light than I
had been before, along the level terrace.

At this I asked: "Master, tell me, what heavy   118
weight has been lifted from me, so that I,
in going, notice almost no fatigue?"

He answered: "When the *P*'s that still remain   121
upon your brow—now almost all are faint—
have been completely, like this *P*, erased,

your feet will be so mastered by good will   124
that they not only will not feel travail
but will delight when they are urged uphill."

Then I behaved like those who make their way   127
with something on their head of which they're not
aware, till others' signs make them suspicious,

at which, the hand helps them to ascertain;   130
it seeks and finds and touches and provides
the services that sight cannot supply;

so, with my right hand's outspread fingers, I   133
found just six of the letters once inscribed
by him who holds the keys, upon my forehead;

and as he watched me do this, my guide smiled.   136

CANTO XIII

The Second Terrace: the Envious. Virgil's apostrophe to the sun. Voices calling out three incitements to fraternal love: the examples of the Virgin Mary and Orestes, and a dictum of Jesus. The Litany of the Saints. The Envious punished by having their eyelids sewn up with iron wires. Sapia of Siena.

We now had reached the summit of the stairs
where once again the mountain whose ascent
delivers man from sin has been indented.

There, just as in the case of the first terrace,   4
a second terrace runs around the slope,
except that it describes a sharper arc.

No effigy is there and no outline: 7
the bank is visible, the naked path—
only the livid color of raw rock.

"If we wait here in order to inquire   10
of those who pass," the poet said, "I fear
our choice of path may be delayed too long."

And then he fixed his eyes upon the sun;   13
letting his right side serve to guide his movement,
he wheeled his left around and changed direction.

"O gentle light, through trust in which I enter   16
on this new path, may you conduct us here,"
he said, "for men need guidance in this place.

You warm the world and you illumine it;   19
unless a higher Power urge us elsewhere,
your rays must always be the guides that lead."

We had already journeyed there as far   22
as we should reckon here to be a mile,
and done it in brief time—our will was eager—

when we heard spirits as they flew toward us,   25

though they could not be seen—spirits pronouncing
courteous invitations to love's table.

The first voice that flew by called out aloud: 28
"*Vinum non habent*," and behind us that
same voice reiterated its example.

And as that voice drew farther off, before   31
it faded finally, another cried:
"I am Orestes." It, too, did not stop.

"What voices are these, father?" were my words;   34
and as I asked him this, I heard a third
voice say: "Love those by whom you have been hurt."

And my good master said: "The sin of envy   37
is scourged within this circle; thus, the cords
that form the scourging lash are plied by love.

The sounds of punished envy, envy curbed,   40
are different; if I judge right, you'll hear
those sounds before we reach the pass of pardon.

But let your eyes be fixed attentively   43
and, through the air, you will see people seated
before us, all of them on the stone terrace."

I opened—wider than before—my eyes;   46
I looked ahead of me, and I saw shades
with cloaks that shared their color with the rocks.

And once we'd moved a little farther on,   49
I heard the cry of, "Mary, pray for us,"
and then heard, "Michael," "Peter," and "All saints."

I think no man now walks upon the earth   52
who is so hard that he would not have been
pierced by compassion for what I saw next;

for when I had drawn close enough to see   55
clearly the way they paid their penalty,
the force of grief pressed tears out of my eyes.

Those souls, it seemed, were cloaked in coarse haircloth;   58
another's shoulder served each shade as prop,
and all of them were bolstered by the rocks:

so do the blind who have to beg appear   61

12

*On the Second Terrace of Purgatory Dante and Virgil encounter the souls of the Envious,
their weeping eyes stitched closed with wires.*

on pardon days to plead for what they need,
each bending his head back and toward the other,

    that all who watch feel—quickly—pity's touch   64
not only through the words that would entreat
but through the sight, which can—no less—beseech.

    And just as, to the blind, no sun appears,   67
so to the shades—of whom I now speak—here,
the light of heaven would not give itself;

    for iron wire pierces and sews up   70
the lids of all those shades, as untamed hawks
are handled, lest, too restless, they fly off.

    It seemed to me a gross discourtesy   73
for me, going, to see and not be seen;
therefore, I turned to my wise counselor.

    He knew quite well what I, though mute, had meant;   76
and thus he did not wait for my request,
but said: "Speak, and be brief and to the point."

    Virgil was to my right, along the outside,   79
nearer the terrace-edge—no parapet
was there to keep a man from falling off;

    and to my other side were the devout   82
shades; through their eyes, sewn so atrociously,
those spirits forced the tears that bathed their cheeks.

    I turned to them, and "You who can be certain,"   85
I then began, "of seeing that high light
which is the only object of your longing,

    may, in your conscience, all impurity   88
soon be dissolved by grace, so that the stream
of memory flow through it limpidly;

    tell me, for I shall welcome such dear words,   91
if any soul among you is Italian;
if I know that, then I—perhaps—can help him."

    "My brother, each of us is citizen   94
of one true city: what you meant to say
was 'one who lived in Italy as pilgrim.'"

    My hearing placed the point from which this answer   97

had come somewhat ahead of me; therefore,
I made myself heard farther on; moving,

I saw one shade among the rest who looked   100
expectant; and if any should ask how—
its chin was lifted as a blind man's is.

"Spirit," I said, "who have subdued yourself   103
that you may climb, if it is you who answered,
then let me know you by your place or name."

"I was a Sienese," she answered, "and   106
with others here I mend my wicked life,
weeping to Him that He grant us Himself.

I was not sapient, though I was called Sapia;   109
and I rejoiced far more at others' hurts
than at my own good fortune. And lest you

should think I have deceived you, hear and judge   112
if I was not, as I have told you, mad
when my years' arc had reached its downward part.

My fellow citizens were close to Colle,   115
where they'd joined battle with their enemies,
and I prayed God for that which He had willed.

There they were routed, beaten; they were reeling   118
along the bitter paths of flight; and seeing
that chase, I felt incomparable joy,

so that I lifted up my daring face   121
and cried to God: 'Now I fear you no more!'—
as did the blackbird after brief fair weather.

I looked for peace with God at my life's end;   124
the penalty I owe for sin would not
be lessened now by penitence had not

one who was sorrowing for me because   127
of charity in him—Pier Pettinaio—
remembered me in his devout petitions.

But who are you, who question our condition   130
as you move on, whose eyes—if I judge right—
have not been sewn, who uses breath to speak?"

"My eyes," I said, "will be denied me here,   133

but only briefly; the offense of envy
was not committed often by their gaze.

I fear much more the punishment below;   136
my soul is anxious, in suspense; already
I feel the heavy weights of the first terrace."

And she: "Who, then, led you up here among us,   139
if you believe you will return below?"
And I: "He who is with me and is silent.

I am alive; and therefore, chosen spirit,   142
if you would have me move my mortal steps
on your behalf, beyond, ask me for that."

"Oh, this," she answered, "is so strange a thing   145
to hear: the sign is clear—you have God's love.
Thus, help me sometimes with your prayers. I ask

of you, by that which you desire most,   148
if you should ever tread the Tuscan earth,
to see my name restored among my kin.

You will see them among those vain ones who   151
have put their trust in Talamone (their loss
in hope will be more than Diana cost);

but there the admirals will lose the most."   154

CANTO XIV

Still the Second Terrace: the Envious. Two spirits, Guido del Duca and Rinieri da Calboli. Guido's denunciation of the cities in the valley of the Arno, of Rinieri's grandson, Fulcieri da Calboli, and of Romagna. Voices calling out examples of punished envy: Cain and Aglauros.

"Who is this man who, although death has yet
to grant him flight, can circle round our mountain,
and can, at will, open and shut his eyes?"

"I don't know who he is, but I do know   4
he's not alone; you're closer; question him
and greet him gently, so that he replies."

So were two spirits, leaning toward each other,   7
discussing me, along my right-hand side;
then they bent back their heads to speak to me,

and one began: "O soul who—still enclosed   10
within the body—make your way toward Heaven,
may you, through love, console us; tell us who

you are, from where you come; the grace that you've   13
received—a thing that's never come to pass
before—has caused us much astonishment."

And I: "Through central Tuscany there spreads   16
a little stream first born in Falterona;
one hundred miles can't fill the course it needs.

I bring this body from that river's banks;   19
to tell you who I am would be to speak
in vain—my name has not yet gained much fame."

"If, with my understanding, I have seized   22
your meaning properly," replied to me
the one who'd spoken first, "you mean the Arno."

The other said to him: "Why did he hide   25

that river's name, even as one would do
in hiding something horrible from view?"

The shade to whom this question was addressed   28
repaid with this: "I do not know; but it
is right for such a valley's name to perish,

for from its source (at which the rugged chain—   31
from which Pelorus was cut off—surpasses
most other places with its mass of mountains)

until its end point (where it offers back   34
those waters that evaporating skies
drew from the sea, that streams may be supplied),

virtue is seen as serpent, and all flee   37
from it as if it were an enemy,
either because the site is ill-starred or

their evil custom goads them so; therefore,   40
the nature of that squalid valley's people
has changed, as if they were in Circe's pasture.

That river starts its miserable course   43
among foul hogs, more fit for acorns than
for food devised to serve the needs of man.

Then, as that stream descends, it comes on curs   46
that, though their force is feeble, snap and snarl;
scornful of them, it swerves its snout away.

And, downward, it flows on; and when that ditch,   49
ill-fated and accursed, grows wider, it
finds, more and more, the dogs becoming wolves.

Descending then through many dark ravines,   52
it comes on foxes so full of deceit—
there is no trap that they cannot defeat.

Nor will I keep from speech because my comrade   55
hears me (and it will serve you, too, to keep
in mind what prophecy reveals to me).

I see your grandson: he's become a hunter   58
of wolves along the banks of the fierce river,
and he strikes every one of them with terror.

He sells their flesh while they are still alive;   61

then, like an ancient beast, he turns to slaughter,
depriving many of life, himself of honor.

Bloody, he comes out from the wood he's plundered,   64
leaving it such that in a thousand years
it will not be the forest that it was."

Just as the face of one who has heard word   67
of pain and injury becomes perturbed,
no matter from what side that menace stirs,

so did I see that other soul, who'd turned   70
to listen, growing anxious and dejected
when he had taken in his comrade's words.

The speech of one, the aspect of the other   73
had made me need to know their names, and I
both queried and beseeched at the same time,

at which the spirit who had spoken first   76
to me began again: "You'd have me do
for you that which, to me, you have refused.

But since God would, in you, have His grace glow   79
so brightly, I shall not be miserly;
know, therefore, that I was Guido del Duca.

My blood was so afire with envy that,   82
when I had seen a man becoming happy,
the lividness in me was plain to see.

From what I've sown, this is the straw I reap: 85
o humankind, why do you set your hearts
there where our sharing cannot have a part?

This is Rinieri, this is he—the glory,   88
the honor of the house of Calboli;
but no one has inherited his worth.

It's not his kin alone, between the Po   91
and mountains, and the Reno and the coast,
who've lost the truth's grave good and lost the good

of gentle living, too; those lands are full   94
of poisoned stumps; by now, however much
one were to cultivate, it is too late.

Where is good Lizio? Arrigo Mainardi?   97

Still on the Second Terrace, Dante encounters two contemporaries and is astonished (far left) to hear the voice of Cain, the first man guilty of envy.

Pier Traversaro? Guido di Carpigna?
O Romagnoles returned to bastardy!

When will a Fabbro flourish in Bologna?   100
When, in Faenza, a Bernadin di Fosco,
the noble offshoot of a humble plant?

Don't wonder, Tuscan, if I weep when I   103
remember Ugolino d'Azzo, one
who lived among us, and Guido da Prata,

the house of Traversara, of Anastagi   106
(both houses without heirs), and Federigo
Tignoso and his gracious company,

the ladies and the knights, labors and leisure   109
to which we once were urged by courtesy
and love, where hearts now host perversity.

O Bretinoro, why do you not flee—   112
when you've already lost your family
and many men who've fled iniquity?

Bagnacaval does well: it breeds no more—   115
and Castrocaro ill, and Conio worse,
for it insists on breeding counts so cursed.

Once freed of their own demon, the Pagani   118
will do quite well, but not so well that any
will testify that they are pure and worthy.

Your name, o Ugolin de' Fantolini,   121
is safe, since one no longer waits for heirs
to blacken it with their degeneracy.

But, Tuscan, go your way; I am more pleased   124
to weep now than to speak: for that which we
have spoken presses heavily on me!"

We knew those gentle souls had heard us move   127
away; therefore, their silence made us feel
more confident about the path we took.

When we, who'd gone ahead, were left alone,   130
a voice that seemed like lightning as it splits
the air encountered us, a voice that said:

"Whoever captures me will slaughter me";   133

and then it fled like thunder when it fades
after the cloud is suddenly ripped through.

As soon as that first voice had granted us   136
a truce, another voice cried out with such
uproar—like thunder quick to follow thunder:

"I am Aglauros, who was turned to stone";   139
and then, to draw more near the poet, I
moved to my right instead of moving forward.

By now the air on every side was quiet;   142
and he told me: "That is the sturdy bit
that should hold every man within his limits.

But you would take the bait, so that the hook   145
of the old adversary draws you to him;
thus, neither spur nor curb can serve to save you.

Heaven would call—and it encircles—you;   148
it lets you see its never-ending beauties;
and yet your eyes would only see the ground;

thus, He who sees all things would strike you down." 151

CANTO XV

From the Second to the Third Terrace: the Wrathful. Mid-afternoon. The Fifth Beatitude. Virgil on the sharing of heavenly goods. The Third Terrace, where Dante sees, in ecstatic vision, examples of gentleness: the Virgin Mary, Pisistratus, St. Stephen. Virgil on Dante's vision. Black smoke.

As many as the hours in which the sphere
that's always playing like a child appears
from daybreak to the end of the third hour,

so many were the hours of light still left   4
before the course of day would reach sunset;
vespers was there; and where we are, midnight.

When sunlight struck directly at our faces,   7
for we had circled so much of the mountain
that now we headed straight into the west,

then I could feel my vision overcome   10
by radiance greater than I'd sensed before,
and unaccounted things left me amazed;

at which, that they might serve me as a shade,   13
I lifted up my hands above my brow,
to limit some of that excessive splendor.

As when a ray of light, from water or   16
a mirror, leaps in the opposed direction
and rises at an angle equal to

its angle of descent, and to each side   19
the distance from the vertical is equal,
as science and experiment have shown;

so did it seem to me that I had been   22
struck there by light reflected, facing me,
at which my eyes turned elsewhere rapidly.

"Kind father, what is that against which I   25
have tried in vain," I said, "to screen my eyes?
It seems to move toward us." And he replied:

"Don't wonder if you are still dazzled by   28
the family of Heaven: a messenger
has come, and he invites us to ascend.

Soon, in the sight of such things, there will be   31
no difficulty for you, but delight—
as much as nature fashioned you to feel."

No sooner had we reached the blessed angel   34
than with glad voice he told us: "Enter here;
these are less steep than were the other stairs."

We climbed, already past that point; behind us,   37
we heard "*Beati misericordes*" sung
and then "Rejoice, you who have overcome."

I and my master journeyed on alone,   40
we two together, upward; as we walked,
I thought I'd gather profit from his words;

and even as I turned toward him, I asked: 43
"What did the spirit of Romagna mean
when he said, 'Sharing cannot have a part'?"

And his reply: "He knows the harm that lies   46
in his worst vice; if he chastises it,
to ease its expiation—do not wonder.

For when your longings center on things such   49
that sharing them apportions less to each,
then envy stirs the bellows of your sighs.

But if the love within the Highest Sphere   52
should turn your longings heavenward, the fear
inhabiting your breast would disappear;

for there, the more there are who would say 'ours,'   55
so much the greater is the good possessed
by each—so much more love burns in that cloister."

"I am more hungry now for satisfaction,"   58
I said, "than if I'd held my tongue before;
I host a deeper doubt within my mind.

At the foot of the stairs to the Third Terrace stands the Angel of Charity. At the head of the stairway – on the Terrace of the Wrathful – Dante falls into a reverie.

How can a good that's shared by more possessors   61
enable each to be more rich in it
than if that good had been possessed by few?"

  And he to me: "But if you still persist   64
in letting your mind fix on earthly things,
then even from true light you gather darkness.

  That Good, ineffable and infinite,   67
which is above, directs Itself toward love
as light directs Itself to polished bodies.

  Where ardor is, that Good gives of Itself;   70
and where more love is, there that Good confers
a greater measure of eternal worth.

  And when there are more souls above who love,   73
there's more to love well there, and they love more,
and, mirror-like, each soul reflects the other.

  And if my speech has not appeased your hunger,   76
you will see Beatrice—she will fulfill
this and all other longings that you feel.

  Now only strive, so that the other five   79
wounds may be canceled quickly, as the two
already are—the wounds that penance heals."

  But wanting then to say, "You have appeased me,"   82
I saw that I had reached another circle,
and my desiring eyes made me keep still.

  There I seemed, suddenly, to be caught up   85
in an ecstatic vision and to see
some people in a temple; and a woman

  just at the threshold, in the gentle manner   88
that mothers use, was saying: "O my son,
why have you done this to us? You can see

  how we have sought you—sorrowing, your father   91
and I." And at this point, as she fell still,
what had appeared at first now disappeared.

  Then there appeared to me another woman: 94
upon her cheeks—the tears that grief distills
when it is born of much scorn for another.

She said: "If you are ruler of that city
to name which even goddesses once vied—
where every science had its source of light—

revenge yourself on the presumptuous
arms that embraced our daughter, o Pisistratus."
And her lord seemed to me benign and mild,

his aspect temperate, as he replied:
"What shall we do to one who'd injure us
if one who loves us earns our condemnation?"

Next I saw people whom the fire of wrath
had kindled, as they stoned a youth and kept
on shouting loudly to each other: "Kill!"

"Kill!" "Kill!" I saw him now, weighed down by death,
sink to the ground, although his eyes were bent
always on Heaven—they were Heaven's gates—

praying to his high Lord, despite the torture,
to pardon those who were his persecutors;
his look was such that it unlocked compassion.

And when my soul returned outside itself
and met the things outside it that are real,
I then could recognize my not false errors.

My guide, on seeing me behave as if
I were a man who's freed himself from sleep,
said: "What is wrong with you? You can't walk straight;

for more than half a league now you have moved
with clouded eyes and lurching legs, as if
you were a man whom wine or sleep has gripped!"

"Oh, my kind father, if you hear me out,
I'll tell you what appeared to me," I said,
"when I had lost the right use of my legs."

And he: "Although you had a hundred masks
upon your face, that still would not conceal
from me the thoughts you thought, however slight.

What you have seen was shown lest you refuse
to open up your heart unto the waters
of peace that pour from the eternal fountain.

I did not ask 'What's wrong with you?' as one   133
who only sees with earthly eyes, which—once
the body, stripped of soul, lies dead—can't see;
I asked so that your feet might find more force: 136
so must one urge the indolent, too slow
to use their waking time when it returns."
We made our way until the end of vespers,   139
peering, as far ahead as sight could stretch,
at rays of light that, although late, were bright.
But, gradually, smoke as black as night   142
began to overtake us; and there was
no place where we could have avoided it.
This smoke deprived us of pure air and sight.   145

CANTO XVI

Still the Third Terrace: the Wrathful. Their sin punished by dark smoke. Marco Lombardo's discourse on free will, on the causes of corruption, and on three worthy old men, living examples of ancient virtue.

Darkness of Hell and of a night deprived
of every planet, under meager skies,
as overcast by clouds as sky can be,

had never served to veil my eyes so thickly   4
nor covered them with such rough-textured stuff
as smoke that wrapped us there in Purgatory;

my eyes could not endure remaining open;   7
so that my faithful, knowledgeable escort
drew closer as he offered me his shoulder.

Just as a blind man moves behind his guide,   10
that he not stray or strike against some thing
that may do damage to—or even kill—him,

so I moved through the bitter, filthy air,   13
while listening to my guide, who kept repeating:
"Take care that you are not cut off from me."

But I heard voices, and each seemed to pray   16
unto the Lamb of God, who takes away
our sins, for peace and mercy. "*Agnus Dei*"

was sung repeatedly as their exordium,   19
words sung in such a way—in unison—
that fullest concord seemed to be among them.

"Master, are those whom I hear, spirits?" I   22
asked him. "You have grasped rightly," he replied,
"and as they go they loose the knot of anger."

"Then who are you whose body pierces through   25
our smoke, who speak of us exactly like

a man who uses months to measure time?"

A voice said this. On hearing it, my master 28
turned round to me: "Reply to him, then ask
if this way leads us to the upward path."

And I: "O creature who—that you return 31
fair unto Him who made you—cleanse yourself,
you shall hear wonders if you follow me."

"I'll follow you as far as I'm allowed," 34
he answered, "and if smoke won't let us see,
hearing will serve instead to keep us linked."

Then I began: "With those same swaddling-bands 37
that death unwinds I take my upward path:
I have come here by way of Hell's exactions;

since God's so gathered me into His grace 40
that He would have me, in a manner most
unusual for moderns, see His court,

do not conceal from me who you once were, 43
before your death, and tell me if I go
straight to the pass; your words will be our escort."

"I was a Lombard and I was called Marco; 46
I knew the world's ways, and I loved those goods
for which the bows of all men now grow slack.

The way you've taken leads directly upward." 49
So he replied, and then he added: "I
pray you to pray for me when you're above."

And I to him: "I pledge my faith to you 52
to do what you have asked; and yet a doubt
will burst in me if it finds no way out.

Before, my doubt was simple; but your statement 55
has doubled it and made me sure that I
am right to couple your words with another's.

The world indeed has been stripped utterly 58
of every virtue; as you said to me,
it cloaks—and is cloaked by—perversity.

Some place the cause in heaven, some, below; 61
but I beseech you to define the cause,

that, seeing it, I may show it to others."

A sigh, from which his sorrow formed an "Oh," 64
was his beginning; then he answered: "Brother,
the world is blind, and you come from the world.

You living ones continue to assign 67
to heaven every cause, as if it were
the necessary source of every motion.

If this were so, then your free will would be 70
destroyed, and there would be no equity
in joy for doing good, in grief for evil.

The heavens set your appetites in motion— 73
not all your appetites, but even if
that were the case, you have received both light

on good and evil, and free will, which though 76
it struggle in its first wars with the heavens,
then conquers all, if it has been well nurtured.

On greater power and a better nature 79
you, who are free, depend; that Force engenders
the mind in you, outside the heavens' sway.

Thus, if the present world has gone astray, 82
in you is the cause, in you it's to be sought;
and now I'll serve as your true exegete.

Issuing from His hands, the soul—on which 85
He thought with love before creating it—
is like a child who weeps and laughs in sport;

that soul is simple, unaware; but since 88
a joyful Maker gave it motion, it
turns willingly to things that bring delight.

At first it savors trivial goods; these would 91
beguile the soul, and it runs after them,
unless there's guide or rein to rule its love.

Therefore, one needed law to serve as curb; 94
a ruler, too, was needed, one who could
discern at least the tower of the true city.

The laws exist, but who applies them now? 97
No one—the shepherd who precedes his flock

can chew the cud but does not have cleft hooves;
    and thus the people, who can see their guide   100
snatch only at that good for which they feel
some greed, would feed on that and seek no further.

    Misrule, you see, has caused the world to be   103
malevolent; your nature is not corrupt,
not prey to any fatal astral force.

    For Rome, which made the world good, used to have   106
two suns; and they made visible two paths—
the world's path and the pathway that is God's.

    One has eclipsed the other; now the sword   109
has joined the shepherd's crook; the two together
must of necessity result in evil,

    because, so joined, one need not fear the other: 112
and if you doubt me, watch the fruit and flower,
for every plant is known by what it seeds.

    Within the territory watered by   115
the Adige and Po, one used to find
valor and courtesy—that is, before

    Frederick was met by strife; now anyone   118
ashamed of talking with the righteous or
of meeting them can journey there, secure.

    True, three old men are there, in whom old times   121
reprove the new; and they find God is slow
in summoning them to a better life:

    Currado da Palazzo, good Gherardo,   124
and Guido da Castel, whom it is better
to call, as do the French, the candid Lombard.

    You can conclude: the Church of Rome confounds   127
two powers in itself; into the filth,
it falls and fouls itself and its new burden."

    "Good Marco," I replied, "you reason well;   130
and now I understand why Levi's sons
were not allowed to share in legacies.

    But what Gherardo is this whom you mention   133
as an example of the vanished people

whose presence would reproach this savage age?"

"Either your speech deceives me or would tempt me,"   136
he answered then, "for you, whose speech is Tuscan,
seem to know nothing of the good Gherardo.

There is no other name by which I know him,   139
unless I speak of him as Gaia's father.
God be with you; I come with you no farther.

You see the rays that penetrate the smoke   142
already whitening; I must take leave—
the angel has arrived—before he sees me."

So he turned back and would not hear me more.   145

CANTO XVII

From the Third to the Fourth Terrace. Examples of wrath: Procne, Haman, Amata. The angel of gentleness. The Seventh Beatitude. Ascent to the Fourth Terrace. Virgil on love and on Purgatory's seven terraces punishing the seven sins: pride, envy and wrath—resulting from perverted love; sloth—from defective love; avarice, gluttony, and lust—from excessive love of earthly goods.

Remember, reader, if you've ever been
caught in the mountains by a mist through which
you only saw as moles see through their skin,

how, when the thick, damp vapors once begin   4
to thin, the sun's sphere passes feebly through them,
then your imagination will be quick

to reach the point where it can see how I   7
first came to see the sun again—when it
was almost at the point at which it sets.

So, my steps matched my master's trusty steps;   10
out of that cloud I came, reaching the rays
that, on the shores below, by now were spent.

O fantasy, you that at times would snatch   13
us so from outward things—we notice nothing
although a thousand trumpets sound around us—

who moves you when the senses do not spur you?   16
A light that finds its form in Heaven moves you—
directly or led downward by God's will.

Within my fantasy I saw impressed   19
the savagery of one who then, transformed,
became the bird that most delights in song;

at this, my mind withdrew to the within,   22
to what imagining might bring; no thing

that came from the without could enter in.

Then into my deep fantasy there rained   25
one who was crucified; and as he died,
he showed his savagery and his disdain.

Around him were great Ahasuerus and   28
Esther his wife, and the just Mordecai,
whose saying and whose doing were so upright.

And when this image shattered of itself,   31
just like a bubble that has lost the water
beneath which it was formed, there then rose up

in my envisioning a girl who wept   34
most bitterly and said: "O queen, why did
you, in your wrath, desire to be no more?

So as to keep Lavinia, you killed   37
yourself; now you have lost me! I am she,
mother, who mourns your fall before another's."

Even as sleep is shattered when new light   40
strikes suddenly against closed eyes and, once
it's shattered, gleams before it dies completely,

so my imagination fell away   43
as soon as light—more powerful than light
we are accustomed to—beat on my eyes.

I looked about to see where I might be;   46
but when a voice said: "Here one can ascend,"
then I abandoned every other intent.

That voice made my will keen to see the one   49
who'd spoken—with the eagerness that cannot
be still until it faces what it wants.

But even as the sun, become too strong,   52
defeats our vision, veiling its own form,
so there my power of sight was overcome.

"This spirit is divine; and though unasked,   55
he would conduct us to the upward path;
he hides himself with that same light he sheds.

He does with us as men do with themselves;   58
for he who sees a need but waits to be

asked is already set on cruel refusal.

Now let our steps accept his invitation,   61
and let us try to climb before dark falls—
then, until day returns, we'll have to halt."

So said my guide; and toward a stairway, he   64
and I, together, turned; and just as soon
as I was at the first step, I sensed something

much like the motion of a wing, and wind   67
that beat against my face, and words: "*Beati
pacifici*, those free of evil anger!"

Above us now the final rays before   70
the fall of night were raised to such a height
that we could see the stars on every side.

"O why, my strength, do you so melt away?"   73
I said within myself, because I felt
the force within my legs compelled to halt.

We'd reached a point at which the upward stairs   76
no longer climbed, and we were halted there
just like a ship when it has touched the shore.

I listened for a while, hoping to hear   79
whatever there might be in this new circle;
then I turned toward my master, asking him:

"Tell me, my gentle father: what offense   82
is purged within the circle we have reached?
Although our feet must stop, your words need not."

And he to me: "Precisely here, the love   85
of good that is too tepidly pursued
is mended; here the lazy oar plies harder.

But so that you may understand more clearly,   88
now turn your mind to me, and you will gather
some useful fruit from our delaying here.

My son, there's no Creator and no creature   91
who ever was without love—natural
or mental; and you know that," he began.

The natural is always without error,   94
but mental love may choose an evil object

or err through too much or too little vigor.

As long as it's directed toward the First Good   97
and tends toward secondary goods with measure,
it cannot be the cause of evil pleasure;

but when it twists toward evil, or attends   100
to good with more or less care than it should,
those whom He made have worked against their Maker.

From this you see that—of necessity—   103
love is the seed in you of every virtue
and of all acts deserving punishment.

Now, since love never turns aside its eyes   106
from the well-being of its subject, things
are surely free from hatred of themselves;

and since no being can be seen as self-   109
existing and divorced from the First Being,
each creature is cut off from hating Him.

Thus, if I have distinguished properly,   112
ill love must mean to wish one's neighbor ill;
and this love's born in three ways in your clay.

There's he who, through abasement of another,   115
hopes for supremacy; he only longs
to see his neighbor's excellence cast down.

Then there is one who, when he is outdone,   118
fears his own loss of fame, power, honor, favor;
his sadness loves misfortune for his neighbor.

And there is he who, over injury   121
received, resentful, for revenge grows greedy
and, angrily, seeks out another's harm.

This threefold love is expiated here   124
below; now I would have you understand
the love that seeks the good distortedly.

Each apprehends confusedly a Good   127
in which the mind may rest, and longs for It;
and, thus, all strive to reach that Good; but if

the love that urges you to know It or   130
to reach that Good is lax, this terrace, after

a just repentance, punishes for that.

    There is a different good, which does not make   133
men glad; it is not happiness, is not
true essence, fruit and root of every good.

    The love that—profligately—yields to that   136
is wept on in three terraces above us;
but I'll not say what three shapes that love takes—

    may you seek those distinctions for yourself."   139

CANTO XVIII

The Fourth Terrace: the Slothful. Virgil on love, free will, and responsibility. Dante's drowsiness. The Slothful shouting examples of zeal: the Virgin Mary and Caesar. The punishment of the Slothful, made to run without respite. The Abbot of San Zeno. Shouted examples of sloth: the Jews in the desert and the reluctant Trojans in Sicily. Dante overcome by sleep.

The subtle teacher had completed his
discourse to me; attentively he watched
my eyes to see if I seemed satisfied.

And I, still goaded by new thirst, was silent   4
without, although within I said: "Perhaps
I have displeased him with too many questions."

But that true father, who had recognized   7
the timid want I would not tell aloud,
by speaking, gave me courage to speak out.

At which I said: "Master, my sight is so   10
illumined by your light—I recognize
all that your words declare or analyze.

Therefore, I pray you, gentle father dear,   13
to teach me what love is: you have reduced
to love both each good and its opposite."

He said: "Direct your intellect's sharp eyes   16
toward me, and let the error of the blind
who'd serve as guides be evident to you.

The soul, which is created quick to love,   19
responds to everything that pleases, just
as soon as beauty wakens it to act.

Your apprehension draws an image from   22
a real object and expands upon
that object until soul has turned toward it;

and if, so turned, the soul tends steadfastly,   25
then that propensity is love—it's nature
that joins the soul in you, anew, through beauty.

Then, just as flames ascend because the form   28
of fire was fashioned to fly upward, toward
the stuff of its own sphere, where it lasts longest,

so does the soul, when seized, move into longing,   31
a motion of the spirit, never resting
till the beloved thing has made it joyous.

Now you can plainly see how deeply hidden   34
truth is from scrutinists who would insist
that every love is, in itself, praiseworthy;

and they are led to error by the matter   37
of love, because it may seem—always—good;
but not each seal is fine, although the wax is."

"Your speech and my own wit that followed it,"   40
I answered him, "have shown me what love is;
but that has filled me with still greater doubt;

for if love's offered to us from without   43
and is the only foot with which soul walks,
soul—going straight or crooked—has no merit."

And he to me: "What reason can see here,   46
I can impart; past that, for truth of faith,
it's Beatrice alone you must await.

Every substantial form, at once distinct   49
from matter and conjoined to it, ingathers
the force that is distinctively its own,

a force unknown to us until it acts—   52
it's never shown except in its effects,
just as green boughs display the life in plants.

And thus man does not know the source of his   55
intelligence of primal notions and
his tending toward desire's primal objects:

both are in you just as in bees there is   58
the honey-making urge; such primal will
deserves no praise, and it deserves no blame.

Now, that all other longings may conform   61
to this first will, there is in you, inborn,
the power that counsels, keeper of the threshold

of your assent: this is the principle   64
on which your merit may be judged, for it
garners and winnows good and evil longings.

Those reasoners who reached the roots of things   67
learned of this inborn freedom; the bequest
that, thus, they left unto the world is ethics.

Even if we allow necessity   70
as source for every love that flames in you,
the power to curb that love is still your own.

This noble power is what Beatrice   73
means by free will; therefore, remember it,
if she should ever speak of it to you."

The moon, with midnight now behind us, made   76
the stars seem scarcer to us; it was shaped
just like a copper basin, gleaming, new;

and countercourse, it crossed those paths the sun   79
ignites when those in Rome can see it set
between the Corsicans and the Sardinians.

That gracious shade for whom Pietola   82
won more renown than any Mantuan town,
had freed me from the weight of doubt I bore;

so that I, having harvested his clear   85
and open answers to my questions, stood
like one who, nearing sleep, has random visions.

But readiness for sleep was suddenly   88
taken from me by people who, behind
our backs, already turned in our direction.

Just as—of old—Ismenus and Asopus,   91
at night, along their banks, saw crowds and clamor
whenever Thebans had to summon Bacchus,

such was the arching crowd that curved around   94
that circle, driven on, as I made out,
by righteous will as well as by just love.

The Fourth Terrace is occupied by the Slothful who purge their guilt in endless activity.

Soon all that mighty throng drew near us, for   97
they ran and ran; and two, in front of them,
who wept, were crying: "In her journey, Mary

made haste to reach the mountain, and, in order   100
to conquer Lérida, first Caesar thrust
against Marseilles, and then to Spain he rushed."

Following them, the others cried: "Quick, quick,   103
lest time be lost through insufficient love;
where urge for good is keen, grace finds new green."

"O people in whom eager fervor now   106
may compensate for sloth and negligence
you showed in doing good half-heartedly,

he—who's alive, and surely I don't lie   109
to you—would climb above as soon as he
has seen the sun shed light on us again;

then, tell us where the passage lies at hand."   112
My guide said this. One of the souls replied:
"Come, follow us, and you will find the gap.

We are so fully anxious to advance—   115
we cannot halt; and do forgive us, should
you take our penance for discourtesy.

I was St. Zeno's abbot in Verona   118
under the rule of valiant Barbarossa,
of whom Milan still speaks with so much sorrow.

And there is one with one foot in the grave,   121
who soon will weep over that monastery,
lamenting that he once had power there,

because, in place of its true shepherd, he   124
put one who was unsound of body and,
still more, of mind, and born in sin—his son."

I don't know if he said more or was silent—   127
he had already raced so far beyond us;
but I heard this much and was pleased to hear it.

And he who was my help in every need   130
said: "Turn around: see those two coming—they
whose words mock sloth." And I heard those two say

behind all of the rest: "The ones for whom   133
the sea parted were dead before the Jordan
saw those who had inherited its lands;

and those who did not suffer trials until   136
the end together with Anchises' son
gave themselves up to life without renown."

Then, when those shades were so far off from us   139
that seeing them became impossible,
a new thought rose inside of me and, from

that thought, still others—many and diverse—   142
were born: I was so drawn from random thought
to thought that, wandering in mind, I shut

my eyes, transforming thought on thought to dream.   145

CANTO XIX

*From the Fourth to the Fifth Terrace: the Avaricious and the
Prodigal. Dante's dream of the Siren. Waking to the third
morning. The angel of zeal. The Third Beatitude. Ascent to
the Fifth Terrace. Colloquy with Pope Adrian V. The
punishment of the Avaricious: given to earthly goods, they
now, bound hand and foot, lie stretched on the ground, face
down.*

In that hour when the heat of day, defeated
by Earth and, sometimes, Saturn, can no longer
warm up the moon-sent cold, when geomancers

can, in the east, see their *Fortuna major*   4
rising before the dawn along a path
that will be darkened for it only briefly—

a stammering woman came to me in dream: 7
her eyes askew, and crooked on her feet,
her hands were crippled, her complexion sallow.

I looked at her; and just as sun revives   10
cold limbs that night made numb, so did my gaze
loosen her tongue and then, in little time,

set her contorted limbs in perfect order;   13
and, with the coloring that love prefers,
my eyes transformed the wanness of her features.

And when her speech had been set free, then she   16
began to sing so, that it would have been
most difficult for me to turn aside.

"I am," she sang, "I am the pleasing siren,   19
who in midsea leads mariners astray—
there is so much delight in hearing me.

I turned aside Ulysses, although he   22
had longed to journey; who grows used to me

seldom departs—I satisfy him so."

Her lips were not yet done when, there beside me,   25
a woman showed herself, alert and saintly,
to cast the siren into much confusion.

"O Virgil, Virgil, tell me: who is this?"   28
she asked most scornfully; and he came forward,
his eyes intent upon that honest one.

He seized the other, baring her in front,   31
tearing her clothes, and showing me her belly;
the stench that came from there awakened me.

I moved my eyes, and my good master cried: 34
"At least three times I've called you. Rise and come:
let's find the opening where you may enter."

I rose; the daylight had already filled   37
the circles of the sacred mountain—we
were journeying with new sun at our back.

I followed him, bearing my brow like one   40
whose thoughts have weighed him down, who bends as if
he were the semiarch that forms a bridge,

and then I heard: "Draw near; the pass is here,"   43
said in a manner so benign and gentle
as, in our mortal land, one cannot hear.

He who addressed us so had open wings,   46
white as a swan's; and he directed us
upward, between two walls of the hard rock.

And then he moved his plumes and, fanning us,   49
affirmed that those "*Qui lugent*" would be blessed—
their souls would be possessed of consolation.

"What makes you keep your eyes upon the ground?"   52
my guide began to say to me when both
of us had climbed a little, past the angel.

And I: "What makes me move with such misgiving   55
is a new vision: it has so beguiled me
that I cannot relinquish thoughts of it."

"The one you saw," he said, "that ancient witch—   58
for her alone one must atone above;

you saw how man can free himself from her.

Let that suffice, and hurry on your way; 61
fasten your eyes upon the lure that's spun
by the eternal King with His great spheres."

Just like a falcon, who at first looks down, 64
then, when the falconer has called, bends forward,
craving the food that's ready for him there,

so I became—and so remained until, 67
through the cleft rock that lets one climb above,
I reached the point at which the circle starts.

When I was in the clearing, the fifth level, 70
my eyes discovered people there who wept,
lying upon the ground, all turned face down.

"*Adhaesit pavimento anima mea*," 73
I heard them say with sighs so deep that it
was hard to comprehend the words they spoke.

"O God's elect, whose sufferings both hope 76
and justice make less difficult, direct
us to the stairway meant for our ascent."

"If you come here but do not need to be 79
prostrate, and you would find the path most quickly,
then keep your right hand always to the outside."

So did the poet ask, so did reply 82
come from a little way ahead; and I
detected what the speaker had to hide.

I turned my eyes to find my master's eyes; 85
at this, with a glad sign, he ratified
what I had asked for with my eager eyes.

When, free to do as I had wanted to, 88
I moved ahead and bent over that soul
whose words—before—had made me notice him,

saying: "Spirit, within whom weeping ripens 91
that without which there's no return to God,
suspend awhile—for me—your greater care.

Tell me: Who were you? And why are your backs 94
turned up? And there—where I, alive, set out—

would you have me beseech some good for you?"

And he to me: "Why Heaven turns our backs   97
against itself, you are to know; but first
scias quod ego fui successor Petri.

Between Sestri and Chiavari descends   100
a handsome river; and its name is set
upon the upper portion of my crest.

For one month and a little more I learned   103
how the great mantle weighs on him who'd keep it
out of the mire—all other weights seem feathers.

Alas, how tardy my conversion was!   106
But when I had been named the Roman shepherd,
then I discovered the deceit of life.

I saw that there the heart was not at rest,   109
nor could I, in that life, ascend more high;
so that, in me, love for this life was kindled.

Until that point I was a squalid soul,   112
from God divided, wholly avaricious;
now, as you see, I'm punished here for that.

What avarice enacts is here declared   115
in the purgation of converted souls;
the mountain has no punishment more bitter.

Just as we did not lift our eyes on high   118
but set our sight on earthly things instead,
so justice here impels our eyes toward earth.

As avarice annulled in us the love   121
of any other good, and thus we lost
our chance for righteous works, so justice here

fetters our hands and feet and holds us captive;   124
and for as long as it may please our just
Lord, here we'll be outstretched and motionless."

I'd kneeled, wishing to speak: but just as I   127
began—and through my voice alone—he sensed
that I had meant to do him reverence.

"What reason makes you bend your body so?"   130
he said. And I to him: "Your dignity

made conscience sting me as I stood erect."

"Brother, straighten your legs; rise up!" he answered.   133
"Don't be mistaken; I, with you and others,
am but a fellow-servant of one Power.

If you have ever understood the holy   136
sound of the Gospel that says '*Neque nubent*,'
then you will see why I have spoken so.

Now go your way: I'd not have you stop longer;   139
your staying here disturbs my lamentations,
the tears that help me ripen what you mentioned.

Beyond, I have a niece whose name's Alagia;   142
she in herself is good, as long as our
house, by example, brings her not to evil;
and she alone is left to me beyond."   145

CANTO XX

Still the Fifth Terrace, the Avaricious and the Prodigal. Excoriation of avarice. Examples of poverty and generosity: the Virgin Mary, Fabricius, St. Nicholas. Hugh Capet's condemnation of his descendants. Examples of avarice: Pygmalion, Midas, Acan, Sapphira and her husband Ananias, Heliodorus, Polymnestor, Crassus. The mountain's trembling. The shout of the souls on Purgatory.

Against a better will, the will fights weakly;
therefore, to please him, though against my pleasure,
I drew my unquenched sponge out of the water.

I moved on, and my guide moved through the un-   4
encumbered space, hugging the rock, as one
walks on a wall, close to the battlements;

for those whose eyes would melt down, drop by drop,   7
the evil that possesses all the world,
were too close to the edge, on the far side.

May you be damned, o ancient wolf, whose power   10
can claim more prey than all the other beasts—
your hungering is deep and never-ending!

O heavens, through whose revolutions many   13
think things on earth are changed, when will he come—
the one whose works will drive that wolf away?

Our steps were short and slow as we moved on;   16
I was attentive to the shades; I heard
the sorrow in their tears and lamentations.

Then I, by chance, heard one ahead of us   19
crying in his laments, "Sweet Mary," as
a woman would outcry in labor pains.

And he continued: "In that hostel where   22
you had set down your holy burden, there

one can discover just how poor you were."

Following this I heard: "O good Fabricius,   25
you chose, as your possessions, indigence
with virtue rather than much wealth with vice."

These words had been so pleasing to me—I   28
moved forward, so that I might come to know
the spirit from whom they had seemed to come.

He kept on speaking, telling the largesse   31
of Nicholas—the gifts he gave the maidens
so that they might be honorably wed.

"O soul who speaks of so much righteousness,   34
do tell me who you were," I said, "and why
just you alone renew these seemly praises.

Your speaking to me will not go unthanked   37
when I return to finish the short span
of that life which now hurries toward its end."

And he: "I'll tell you—not because I hope   40
for solace from your world, but for such grace
as shines in you before your death's arrived.

I was the root of the obnoxious plant   43
that overshadows all the Christian lands,
so that fine fruit can rarely rise from them.

But if Douai and Lille and Bruges and Ghent   46
had power, they would soon take vengeance on it;
and this I beg of Him who judges all.

The name I bore beyond was Hugh Capet: 49
of me were born the Louises and Philips
by whom France has been ruled most recently.

I was the son of a Parisian butcher.   52
When all the line of ancient kings was done
and only one—a monk in gray—survived,

I found the reins that ruled the kingdom tight   55
within my hands, and I held so much new-
gained power and possessed so many friends

that, to the widowed crown, my own son's head   58
was elevated, and from him began

the consecrated bones of all those kings.

Until the giant dowry of Provence 61
removed all sense of shame within my house,
my line was not worth much, but did no wrong.

There its rapine began with lies and force; 64
and then it seized—that it might make amends—
Ponthieu and Normandy and Gascony.

Charles came to Italy and, for amends, 67
made Conradin a victim, and then thrust
back Thomas into Heaven, for amends.

I see a time—not too far off—in which 70
another Charles advances out of France
to make himself and his descendants famous.

He does not carry weapons when he comes, 73
only the lance that Judas tilted; this
he couches so—he twists the paunch of Florence.

From this he'll gain not land, just shame and sin, 76
which will be all the heavier for him
as he would reckon lightly such disgrace.

The other, who once left his ship as prisoner— 79
I see him sell his daughter, bargaining
as pirates haggle over female slaves.

O avarice, my house is now your captive: 82
it traffics in the flesh of its own children—
what more is left for you to do to us?

That past and future evil may seem less, 85
I see the fleur-de-lis enter Anagni
and, in His vicar, Christ made prisoner.

I see Him mocked a second time; I see 88
the vinegar and gall renewed—and He
is slain between two thieves who're still alive.

And I see the new Pilate, one so cruel 91
that, still not sated, he, without decree,
carries his greedy sails into the Temple.

O You, my Lord, when will You let me be 94
happy on seeing vengeance that, concealed,

The Fifth Terrace of Purgatory is crowded with souls of the Avaricious, who chant the praise of the generous and self-denying.

makes sweet Your anger in Your secrecy?

What I have said about the only bride   97
the Holy Ghost has known, the words that made
you turn to me for commentary—these

words serve as answer to our prayers as long   100
as it is day; but when night falls, then we
recite examples that are contrary.

Then we tell over how Pygmalion,   103
out of his greedy lust for gold, became
a thief and traitor and a parricide;

the wretchedness of avaricious Midas,   106
resulting from his ravenous request,
the consequence that always makes men laugh;

and each of us recalls the foolish Achan—   109
how he had robbed the spoils, so that the anger
of Joshua still seems to sting him here.

Then we accuse Sapphira and her husband;   112
we praise the kicks Heliodorus suffered;
and Polymnestor, who killed Polydorus,

resounds, in infamy, round all this mountain;   115
and finally, what we cry here is: 'Crassus,
tell us, because you know: How does gold taste?'

At times one speaks aloud, another low,   118
according to the sentiment that goads
us now to be more swift and now more slow:

thus, I was not alone in speaking of   121
the good we cite by day, but here nearby
no other spirit raised his voice as high."

We had already taken leave of him   124
and were already struggling to advance
along that road as far as we were able,

when I could feel the mountain tremble like   127
a falling thing; at which a chill seized me
as cold grips one who goes to meet his death.

Delos had surely not been buffeted   130
so hard before Latona planted there

the nest in which to bear the sky's two eyes.

Then such a shout rose up on every side 133
that, drawing near to me, my master said:
"Don't be afraid, as long as I'm your guide."

"*Gloria in excelsis Deo*," they all cried— 136
so did I understand from those nearby,
whose shouted words were able to be heard.

Just like the shepherds who first heard that song, 139
we stood, but did not move, in expectation,
until the trembling stopped, the song was done.

Then we took up again our holy path, 142
watching the shades who lay along the ground,
who had resumed their customary tears.

My ignorance has never struggled so, 145
has never made me long so much to know—
if memory does not mislead me now—

as it seemed then to long within my thoughts; 148
nor did I dare to ask—we were so rushed;
nor, by myself, could I discern the cause.

So, timid, pensive, I pursued my way. 151

CANTO XXI

Still the Fifth Terrace: the Avaricious and the Prodigal. The appearance of Statius. Virgil's explanation of Dante's and his presence in Purgatory. Statius' explanation of the earthquake and the exultation. Statius on himself and on his love for the Aeneid. *Dante's embarrassment, then his introduction of Virgil to Statius. Statius' reverence for Virgil.*

The natural thirst that never can be quenched
except by water that gives grace—the draught
the simple woman of Samaria sought—

tormented me; haste spurred me on the path   4
crowded with souls, behind my guide; and I
felt pity, though their pain was justified.

And here—even as Luke records for us   7
that Christ, new-risen from his burial cave,
appeared to two along his way—a shade

appeared; and he advanced behind our backs   10
while we were careful not to trample on
the outstretched crowd. We did not notice him

until he had addressed us with: "God give   13
you, o my brothers, peace!" We turned at once;
then, after offering suitable response,

Virgil began: "And may that just tribunal   16
which has consigned me to eternal exile
place you in peace within the blessed assembly!"

"What!" he exclaimed, as we moved forward quickly.   19
"If God's not deemed you worthy of ascent,
who's guided you so far along His stairs?"

"If you observe the signs the angel traced   22
upon this man," my teacher said, "you'll see
plainly—he's meant to reign with all the righteous;

but since she who spins night and day had not   25
yet spun the spool that Clotho sets upon

the distaff and adjusts for everyone,

his soul, the sister of your soul and mine,   28
in its ascent, could not—alone—have climbed
here, for it does not see the way we see.

Therefore, I was brought forth from Hell's broad jaws   31
to guide him in his going; I shall lead
him just as far as where I teach can reach.

But tell me, if you can, why, just before,   34
the mountain shook and shouted, all of it—
for so it seemed—down to its sea-bathed shore."

His question threaded so the needle's eye   37
of my desire that just the hope alone
of knowing left my thirst more satisfied.

That other shade began: "The sanctity   40
of these slopes does not suffer anything
that's without order or uncustomary.

This place is free from every perturbation: 43
what heaven from itself and in itself
receives may serve as cause here—no thing else.

Therefore, no rain, no hail, no snow, no dew,   46
no hoarfrost falls here any higher than
the stairs of entry with their three brief steps;

neither thick clouds nor thin appear, nor flash   49
of lightning; Thaumas' daughter, who so often
shifts places in your world, is absent here.

Dry vapor cannot climb up any higher   52
than to the top of the three steps of which
I spoke—where Peter's vicar plants his feet.

Below that point, there may be small or ample   55
tremors; but here above, I know not why,
no wind concealed in earth has ever caused

a tremor; for it only trembles here   58
when some soul feels it's cleansed, so that it rises
or stirs to climb on high; and that shout follows.

The will alone is proof of purity   61
and, fully free, surprises soul into
a change of dwelling place—effectively.

Soul had the will to climb before, but that   64
will was opposed by longing to do penance
(as once, to sin), instilled by divine justice.

And I, who have lain in this suffering   67
five hundred years and more, just now have felt
my free will for a better threshold: thus,

you heard the earthquake and the pious spirits   70
throughout the mountain as they praised the Lord—
and may He send them speedily upward."

So did he speak to us; and just as joy   73
is greater when we quench a greater thirst,
the joy he brought cannot be told in words.

And my wise guide: "I now can see the net   76
impeding you, how one slips through, and why
it quakes here, and what makes you all rejoice.

And now may it please you to tell me who   79
you were, and in your words may I find why
you've lain here for so many centuries."

"In that age when the worthy Titus, with   82
help from the Highest King, avenged the wounds
from which the blood that Judas sold had flowed,

I had sufficient fame beyond," that spirit   85
replied; "I bore the name that lasts the longest
and honors most—but faith was not yet mine.

So gentle was the spirit of my verse   88
that Rome drew me, son of Toulouse, to her,
and there my brow deserved a crown of myrtle.

On earth my name is still remembered—Statius: 91
I sang of Thebes and then of great Achilles;
I fell along the way of that last labor.

The sparks that warmed me, the seeds of my ardor,   94
were from the holy fire—the same that gave
more than a thousand poets light and flame.

I speak of the *Aeneid*; when I wrote   97
verse, it was mother to me, it was nurse;
my work, without it, would not weigh an ounce.

And to have lived on earth when Virgil lived—   100

for that I would extend by one more year
the time I owe before my exile's end."

These words made Virgil turn to me, and as   103
he turned, his face, through silence, said: "Be still"
(and yet the power of will cannot do all,

for tears and smiles are both so faithful to   106
the feelings that have prompted them that true
feeling escapes the will that would subdue).

But I smiled like a man whose eyes would signal;   109
at this, the shade was silent, and he stared
where sentiment is clearest—at my eyes—

and said: "So may your trying labor end   112
successfully, do tell me why—just now—
your face showed me the flashing of a smile."

Now I am held by one side and the other: 115
one keeps me still, the other conjures me
to speak; but when, therefore, I sigh, my master

knows why and tells me: "Do not be afraid   118
to speak, but speak and answer what he has
asked you to tell him with such earnestness."

At this, I answered: "Ancient spirit, you   121
perhaps are wondering at the smile I smiled:
but I would have you feel still more surprise.

He who is guide, who leads my eyes on high,   124
is that same Virgil from whom you derived
the power to sing of men and of the gods.

Do not suppose my smile had any source   127
beyond the speech you spoke; be sure—it was
those words you said of him that were the cause."

Now he had bent to kiss my teacher's feet,   130
but Virgil told him: "Brother, there's no need—
you are a shade, a shade is what you see."

And, rising, he: "Now you can understand   133
how much love burns in me for you, when I
forget our insubstantiality,

treating the shades as one treats solid things."   136

CANTO XXII

From the Fifth to the Sixth Terrace: the Gluttonous. The angel of justice. First part of the Fourth Beatitude. Ascent to the Sixth Terrace. Statius: his true sin, prodigality; his conversion. Virgil on the other souls in Limbo. The Sixth Terrace. The strange tree. Voices citing examples of temperance: the Virgin Mary, the women of ancient Rome, the Golden Age, John the Baptist.

The angel now was left behind us, he
who had directed us to the sixth terrace,
having erased one *P* that scarred my face;

he had declared that those who longed for justice   4
are blessed, and his voice concluded that
message with "*sitiunt,*" without the rest.

And while I climbed behind the two swift spirits,   7
not laboring at all, for I was lighter
than I had been along the other stairs,

Virgil began: "Love that is kindled by   10
virtue, will, in another, find reply,
as long as that love's flame appears without;

so, from the time when Juvenal, descending   13
among us, in Hell's Limbo, had made plain
the fondness that you felt for me, my own

benevolence toward you has been much richer   16
than any ever given to a person
one has not seen; thus, now these stairs seem short.

But tell me (and, as friend, forgive me if   19
excessive candor lets my reins relax,
and, as a friend, exchange your words with me):

how was it that you found within your breast   22
a place for avarice, when you possessed

the wisdom you had nurtured with such care?"

These words at first brought something of a smile   25
to Statius; then he answered: "Every word
you speak, to me is a dear sign of love.

Indeed, because true causes are concealed,   28
we often face deceptive reasoning
and things provoke perplexity in us.

Your question makes me sure that you're convinced—   31
perhaps because my circle was the fifth—
that, in the life I once lived, avarice

had been my sin. Know then that I was far   34
from avarice—it was my lack of measure
thousands of months have punished. And if I

had not corrected my assessment by   37
my understanding what your verses meant
when you, as if enraged by human nature,

exclaimed: 'Why cannot you, o holy hunger   40
for gold, restrain the appetite of mortals?'—
I'd now, while rolling weights, know sorry jousts.

Then I became aware that hands might open   43
too wide, like wings, in spending; and of this,
as of my other sins, I did repent.

How many are to rise again with heads   46
cropped close, whom ignorance prevents from reaching
repentance in—and at the end of—life!

And know that when a sin is countered by   49
another fault—directly opposite
to it—then, here, both sins see their green wither.

Thus, I join those who pay for avarice   52
in my purgation, though what brought me here
was prodigality—its opposite."

"Now, when you sang the savage wars of those   55
twin sorrows of Jocasta," said the singer
of the bucolic poems, "it does not seem—

from those notes struck by you and Clio there—   58
that you had yet turned faithful to the faith

without which righteous works do not suffice.

   If that is so, then what sun or what candles   61
drew you from darkness so that, in their wake,
you set your sails behind the fisherman?"

   And he to him: "You were the first to send me   64
to drink within Parnassus' caves and you,
the first who, after God, enlightened me.

   You did as he who goes by night and carries   67
the lamp behind him—he is of no help
to his own self but teaches those who follow—

   when you declared: 'The ages are renewed;   70
justice and man's first time on earth return;
from Heaven a new progeny descends.'

   Through you I was a poet and, through you,   73
a Christian; but that you may see more plainly,
I'll set my hand to color what I sketch.

   Disseminated by the messengers   76
of the eternal kingdom, the true faith
by then had penetrated all the world,

   and the new preachers preached in such accord   79
with what you'd said (and I have just repeated),
that I was drawn into frequenting them.

   Then they appeared to me to be so saintly   82
that, when Domitian persecuted them,
my own laments accompanied their grief;

   and while I could—as long as I had life—   85
I helped them, and their honest practices
made me disdainful of all other sects.

   Before—within my poem—I'd led the Greeks   88
unto the streams of Thebes, I was baptized;
but out of fear, I was a secret Christian

   and, for a long time, showed myself as pagan;   91
for this halfheartedness, for more than four
centuries, I circled the fourth circle.

   And now may you, who lifted up the lid   94
that hid from me the good of which I speak,

while time is left us as we climb, tell me
    where is our ancient Terence, and Caecilius   97
and Plautus, where is Varius, if you know;
tell me if they are damned, and in what quarter."

    "All these and Persius, I, and many others,"   100
my guide replied, "are with that Greek to whom
the Muses gave their gifts in greatest measure.

    Our place is the blind prison, its first circle;   103
and there we often talk about the mountain
where those who were our nurses always dwell.

    Euripides is with us, Antiphon,   106
Simonides, and Agathon, as well
as many other Greeks who once wore laurel

    upon their brow; and there—of your own people—   109
one sees Antigone, Deiphyle,
Ismene, sad still, Argia as she was.

    There one can see the woman who showed Langia,   112
and there, Tiresias' daughter; there is Thetis;
and, with her sisters, there, Deidamia."

    Both poets now were silent, once again   115
intent on their surroundings—they were free
of stairs and walls; with day's first four handmaidens

    already left behind, and with the fifth   118
guiding the chariot-pole and lifting it,
so that its horn of flame rose always higher,

    my master said: "I think it's time that we   121
turn our right shoulders toward the terrace edge,
circling the mountain in the way we're used to."

    In this way habit served us as a banner;   124
and when we chose that path, our fear was less
because that worthy soul gave his assent.

    Those two were in the lead; I walked alone,   127
behind them, listening to their colloquy,
which taught me much concerning poetry.

    But their delightful conversation soon   130
was interrupted by a tree that blocked

our path; its fruits were fine, their scent was sweet,

    and even as a fir-tree tapers upward   133
from branch to branch, that tree there tapered downward,
so as—I think—to ward off any climber.

    Upon our left, where wall enclosed our path,   136
bright running water fell from the high rock
and spread itself upon the leaves above.

    When the two poets had approached the tree,   139
a voice emerging from within the leaves
cried out: "This food shall be denied to you."

    Then it cried: "Mary's care was for the marriage- 142
feast's being seemly and complete, not for
her mouth (which now would intercede for you).

    And when they drank, of old, the Roman women 145
were satisfied with water; and young Daniel,
through his disdain of food, acquired wisdom.

    The first age was as fair as gold: when hungry, 148
men found the taste of acorns good; when thirsty,
they found that every little stream was nectar.

    When he was in the wilderness, the Baptist   151
had fed on nothing more than honey, locusts:
for this he was made great, as glorious

    as, in the Gospel, is made plain to you."   154

CANTO XXIII

Still the Sixth Terrace: the Gluttonous. Encounter with Forese Donati, Dante's friend, who explains the punishment of the Gluttonous, condemned to emaciating hunger and thirst; praises his widow, Nella; and rebukes the shameless women of Florence. Dante's presentation of Virgil and Statius.

While I was peering so intently through
the green boughs, like a hunter who, so used,
would waste his life in chasing after birds,

my more than father said to me: "Now come,   4
son, for the time our journey can permit
is to be used more fruitfully than this."

I turned my eyes, and I was no less quick   7
to turn my steps; I followed those two sages,
whose talk was such, my going brought no loss.

And—there!—"*Labïa mëa, Domine*"   10
was wept and sung and heard in such a manner
that it gave birth to both delight and sorrow.

"O gentle father, what is this I hear?"   13
I asked. And he: "Perhaps they're shades who go
loosening the knot of what they owe."

Even as pensive pilgrims do, who when   16
they've overtaken folk unknown to them
along the way, will turn but will not stop,

so, overtaking us—they had come from   19
behind but were more swift—a crowd of souls,
devout and silent, looked at us in wonder.

Each shade had dark and hollow eyes; their faces   22
were pale and so emaciated that
their taut skin took its shape from bones beneath.

I don't believe that even Erysichthon   25

had been so dried, down to his very hide,
by hunger, when his fast made him fear most.

Thinking, I told myself: "I see the people 28
who lost Jerusalem, when Mary plunged
her beak into her son." The orbits of

their eyes seemed like a ring that's lost its gems; 31
and he who, in the face of man, would read
OMO would here have recognized the *M*.

Who—if he knew not how—would have believed 34
that longing born from odor of a tree,
odor of water, could reduce souls so?

I was already wondering what had 37
so famished them (for I had not yet learned
the reason for their leanness and sad scurf),

when—there!—a shade, his eyes deep in his head, 40
turned toward me, staring steadily; and then
he cried aloud: "What grace is granted me!"

I never would have recognized him by 43
his face; and yet his voice made plain to me
what his appearance had obliterated.

This spark rekindled in me everything 46
I knew about those altered features; thus,
I realized it was Forese's face.

"Ah, don't reproach me for the dried-out scabs 49
that stain my skin," he begged, "nor for the lack
of flesh on me; but do tell me the truth

about yourself, do tell me who those two 52
souls are there, those who are escorting you;
may you not keep yourself from speaking to me!"

"Your face, which I once wept on when you died," 55
I answered him, "now gives me no less cause
for sad lament, seeing you so deformed.

But tell me, for God's sake, what has unleaved 58
you so; don't make me speak while I'm amazed—
he who's distracted answers clumsily."

And he to me: "From the eternal counsel, 61

the water and the tree you left behind
receive the power that makes me waste away.

    All of these souls who, grieving, sing because   64
their appetite was gluttonous, in thirst
and hunger here resanctify themselves.

    The fragrance of the fruit and of the water   67
that's sprayed through that green tree kindles in us
craving for food and drink; and not once only,

    as we go round this space, our pain's renewed—   70
I speak of pain but I should speak of solace,
for we are guided to those trees by that

    same longing that had guided Christ when He   73
had come to free us through the blood He shed
and, in His joyousness, called out: '*Elì.*'"

    And I to him: "Forese, from that day   76
when you exchanged the world for better life
until now, less than five years have revolved;

    and if you waited for the moment when   79
the power to sin was gone before you found
the hour of the good grief that succors us

    and weds us once again to God, how have   82
you come so quickly here? I thought to find
you down below, where time must pay for time."

    And he to me: "It is my Nella who,   85
with her abundant tears, has guided me
to drink the sweet wormwood of torments: she,

    with sighs and prayers devout has set me free   88
of that slope where one waits and has freed me
from circles underneath this circle. She—

    my gentle widow, whom I loved most dearly—   91
was all the more beloved and prized by God
as she is more alone in her good works.

    For even the Barbagia of Sardinia   94
is far more modest in its women than
is that Barbagia where I left her. O

    sweet brother, what would you have had me say?   97

Dante stares into the Tree of Grace, while Virgil beckons him along the Sixth Terrace where he encounters spirits of the Gluttonous.

A future time's already visible
to me—a time not too far-off from now—
    when, from the pulpit, it shall be forbidden   100
to those immodest ones—Florentine women—
to go displaying bosoms with bare paps.
    What ordinances—spiritual, civil—   103
were ever needed by barbarian or
Saracen women to make them go covered?
    But if those shameless ones had certain knowledge   106
of what swift Heaven's readying for them,
then they would have mouths open now to howl;
    for if our foresight here does not deceive me,   109
they will be sad before the cheeks of those
whom lullabies can now appease grow beards.
    Ah, brother, do not hide things any longer!   112
You see that I am not alone, for all
these people stare at where you veil the sun."
    At this I said to him: "If you should call   115
to mind what you have been with me and I
with you, remembering now will still be heavy.
    He who precedes me turned me from that life   118
some days ago, when she who is the sister
of him"—I pointed to the sun—"was showing
    her roundness to you. It is he who's led   121
me through the deep night of the truly dead
with this true flesh that follows after him.
    His help has drawn me up from there, climbing   124
and circling round this mountain, which makes straight
you whom the world made crooked. And he says
    that he will bear me company until   127
I reach the place where Beatrice is; there
I must remain without him. It is Virgil
    who speaks to me in this way," and I pointed   130
to him; "this other is the shade for whom,
just now, your kingdom caused its every slope
    to tremble as it freed him from itself."   133

CANTO XXIV

*Still the Sixth Terrace: the Gluttonous. Forese on his sister
Piccarda. The poet Bonagiunta da Lucca's praise of Gentucca
and discourse on poetry. Forese on Florence and on the death
of Corso Donati. The second tree. Voices reciting examples of
gluttony: the Centaurs and those Hebrews rejected by Gideon.
The angel of temperance. The last part of the Fourth
Beatitude.*

Our talking did not slow our pace, our pace
not slow our talking; but conversing, we
moved quickly, like a boat a fair wind drives.

And recognizing that I was alive,   4
the shades—they seemed to be things twice dead—drew
amazement from the hollows of their eyes.

And I, continuing my telling, added: 7
"Perhaps he is more slow in his ascent
than he would be had he not met the other.

But tell me, if you can: where is Piccarda?   10
And tell me if, among those staring at me,
I can see any person I should note."

"My sister—and I know not whether she   13
was greater in her goodness or her beauty—
on high Olympus is in triumph; she

rejoices in her crown already," he   16
began, then added: "It is not forbidden
to name each shade here—abstinence has eaten

away our faces." And he pointed: "This   19
is Bonagiunta, Bonagiunta da
Lucca; the one beyond him, even more

emaciated than the rest, had clasped   22
the Holy Church; he was from Tours; his fast

purges Bolsena's eels, Vernaccia's wine."

And he named many others, one by one,　25
and, at their naming, they all seemed content;
so that—for this—no face was overcast.

I saw—their teeth were biting emptiness—　28
both Ubaldin da la Pila and Boniface,
who shepherded so many with his staff.

I saw Messer Marchese, who once had　31
more ease, less dryness, drinking at Forlì
and yet could never satisfy his thirst.

But just as he who looks and then esteems　34
one more than others, so did I prize him
of Lucca, for he seemed to know me better.

He murmured; something like "Gentucca" was　37
what I heard from the place where he could feel
the wound of justice that denudes them so.

"O soul," I said, "who seems so eager to　40
converse with me, do speak so that I hear you,
for speech may satisfy both you and me."

He answered: "Although men condemn my city,　43
there is a woman born—she wears no veil
as yet—because of whom you'll find it pleasing.

You are to journey with this prophecy;　46
and if there's something in my murmuring
you doubt, events themselves will bear me out.

But tell me if the man whom I see here　49
is he who brought the new rhymes forth, beginning:
'Ladies who have intelligence of love.'"

I answered: "I am one who, when Love breathes　52
in me, takes note; what he, within, dictates,
I, in that way, without, would speak and shape."

"O brother, now I see," he said, "the knot　55
that kept the Notary, Guittone, and me
short of the sweet new manner that I hear.

I clearly see how your pens follow closely　58
behind him who dictates, and certainly

that did not happen with our pens; and he
   who wants to probe this matter most profoundly   61
can find no other difference between
the two styles." He fell still, contentedly.

Even as birds that winter on the Nile   64
at times will slow and form a flock in air,
then speed their flight and form a file, so all
   the people who were there moved much more swiftly,   67
turning away their faces, hurrying
their pace because of leanness and desire.

And just as he who's tired of running lets   70
his comrades go ahead and slows his steps
until he's eased the panting of his chest,
   so did Forese let the holy flock   73
pass by and move, behind, with me, saying:
"How long before I shall see you again?"

"I do not know," I said, "how long I'll live;   76
and yet, however quick is my return,
my longing for these shores would have me here
   sooner—because the place where I was set   79
to live is day by day deprived of good
and seems along the way to wretched ruin."

"Do not be vexed," he said, "for I can see   82
the guiltiest of all dragged by a beast's
tail to the valley where no sin is purged.

At every step the beast moves faster, always   85
gaining momentum, till it smashes him
and leaves his body squalidly undone.

Those wheels," and here he looked up at the sky,   88
"do not have long to turn before you see
plainly what I can't tell more openly.

Now you remain behind, for time is costly   91
here in this kingdom; I should lose too much
by moving with you thus, at equal pace."

Just as a horseman sometimes gallops out,   94
leaving behind his troop of riders, so

that he may gain the honor of the first
    clash—so, with longer strides, did he leave us;   97
and I remained along my path with those
two who were such great marshals of the world.

    And when he'd gone so far ahead of us   100
that my eyes strained to follow him, just as
my mind was straining after what he'd said,

    the branches of another tree, heavy   103
with fruit, alive with green, appeared to me
nearby, just past a curve where I had turned.

    Beneath the tree I saw shades lifting hands,   106
crying I know not what up toward the branches,
like little eager, empty-headed children,

    who beg—but he of whom they beg does not   109
reply, but to provoke their longing, he
holds high, and does not hide, the thing they want.

    Then they departed as if disabused;   112
and we—immediately—reached that great tree,
which turns aside so many prayers and tears.

    "Continue on, but don't draw close to it;   115
there is a tree above from which Eve ate,
and from that tree above, this plant was raised."

    Among the boughs, a voice—I know not whose—   118
spoke so; thus, drawing closer, Virgil, Statius,
and I edged on, along the side that rises.

    It said: "Remember those with double chests,   121
the miserable ones, born of the clouds,
whom Theseus battled when they'd gorged themselves;

    and those whom Gideon refused as comrades—   124
those Hebrews who had drunk too avidly—
when he came down the hills to Midian."

    So, keeping close to one of that road's margins,   127
we moved ahead, hearing of gluttony—
its sins repaid by sorry penalties.

    Then, with more space along the lonely path,   130
a thousand steps and more had brought us forward,

each of us meditating wordlessly.

"What are you thinking of, you three who walk   133
alone?" a sudden voice called out; at which
I started—like a scared young animal.

I raised my head to see who it might be;   136
no glass or metal ever seen within
a furnace was so glowing or so red

as one I saw, who said: "If you'd ascend,   139
then you must turn at this point; for whoever
would journey unto peace must pass this way."

But his appearance had deprived me of   142
my sight, so that—as one who uses hearing
as guide—I turned and followed my two teachers.

And like the breeze of May that—heralding   145
the dawning of the day—when it is steeped
in flowers and in grass, stirs fragrantly,

so did I feel the wind that blew against   148
the center of my brow, and clearly sensed
the movement of his wings, the air's ambrosia.

And then I heard: "Blessed are those whom grace   151
illumines so, that, in their breasts, the love
of taste does not awake too much desire—

whose hungering is always in just measure."   154

CANTO XXV

From the Sixth to the Seventh Terrace: the Lustful. Hour and mode of ascent to the Seventh Terrace. Dante's queries about the leanness of bodiless shades. Statius' explanation of generation, souls after death, and aerial bodies. The punishment of the Lustful, purification through fire. The Lustful shouting examples of chastity: the Virgin Mary and Diana.

The hour when climbers cannot pause had come:
the sun had left to Taurus the meridian,
and night had left it to the Scorpion.

Therefore, like one who will not stop but moves   4
along his path, no matter what he sees,
if he is goaded by necessity,

we made our way into the narrow gap   7
and, one behind the other, took the stairs
so strait that climbers there must separate.

And as the fledgling stork will lift its wing   10
because it wants to fly, but dares not try
to leave the nest, and lets its wing drop back,

so I, with my desire to question kindled   13
then spent, arrived as far as making ready
to speak. But my dear father, though our steps

were hurrying, did not stop talking, for   16
he said: "The iron of the arrow's touched
the longbow; let the shaft of speech fly off."

Then I had confidence enough to open   19
my mouth and ask him: "How can one grow lean
where there is never need for nourishment?"

"If you recall how Meleager was   22
consumed," he said, "just when the firebrand
was spent, this won't be hard to understand;

and if you think how, though your body's swift,   25
your image in the mirror captures it,
then what perplexed will seem to you transparent.

But that your will to know may be appeased,   28
here's Statius, and I call on him and ask
that he now be the healer of your doubts."

"If I explain eternal ways to him,"   31
Statius replied, "while you are present here,
let my excuse be: I cannot refuse you."

Then he began: "If, son, your mind receives   34
and keeps my words, then what I say will serve
as light upon the *how* that you have asked.

The thirsty veins drink up the perfect blood—   37
but not all of that blood: a portion's left,
like leavings that are taken from the table.

Within the heart, that part acquires power   40
to form all of another's human limbs,
as blood that flows through veins feeds one's own limbs.

Digested yet again, that part descends   43
to what is best not named; from there it drips
into the natural receptacle,

upon another's blood; the two bloods mix,   46
one ready to be passive and one active
because a perfect place, the heart, prepared them.

The active, having reached the passive, starts   49
to work: first it coagulates—and then
quickens—the matter it has made more dense.

Having become a soul (much like a plant,   52
though with this difference—a plant's complete,
whereas a fetus still is journeying),

the active virtue labors, so the fetus   55
may move and feel, like a sea-sponge; and then
it starts to organize the powers it's seeded.

At this point, son, the power that had come   58
from the begetter's heart unfolds and spreads,
that nature may see every limb perfected.

But how the animal becomes a speaking 61
being, you've not yet seen; this point's so hard,
it led one wiser than you are to err

in separating from the possible 64
intellect the soul, since he could see
no organ for the mind—so did he teach.

Open your heart to truth we now have reached 67
and know that, once the brain's articulation
within the fetus has attained perfection,

then the First Mover turns toward it with joy 70
on seeing so much art in nature and
breathes into it new spirit—vigorous—

which draws all that is active in the fetus 73
into its substance and becomes one soul
that lives and feels and has self-consciousness.

That what I say may leave you less perplexed, 76
consider the sun's heat that, when combined
with sap that flows from vines, is then made wine.

And when Lachesis lacks more thread, then soul's 79
divided from the flesh; potentially,
it bears with it the human and divine;

but with the human powers mute, the rest— 82
intelligence and memory and will—
are more acute in action than they were.

With no delay, the soul falls of itself— 85
astonishingly—on one of two shores;
there it learns—early—what way it will journey.

There, once the soul is circumscribed by space, 88
the power that gives form irradiates
as—and as much as—once it formed live limbs.

And even as the saturated air, 91
since it reflects the rays the sun has sent,
takes rainbow colors as its ornament,

so there, where the soul stopped, the nearby air 94
takes on the form that soul impressed on it,
a shape that is, potentially, real body;

and then, just as a flame will follow after
the fire whenever fire moves, so that
new form becomes the spirit's follower.

Since from that airy body it takes on   100
its semblance, that soul is called 'shade': that shape
forms organs for each sense, even for sight.

This airy body lets us speak and laugh;   103
with it we form the tears and sigh the sighs
that you, perhaps, have heard around this mountain.

Just as we are held fast by longings and   106
by other sentiments, our shade takes form:
this is the cause of your astonishment."

By now we'd reached the final turning we   109
would meet and took the pathway right, at which
we were preoccupied with other cares.

There, from the wall, the mountain hurls its flames;   112
but, from the terrace side, there whirls a wind
that pushes back the fire and limits it;

thus, on the open side, proceeding one   115
by one, we went; I feared the fire on
the left and, on the right, the precipice.

My guide said: "On this terrace, it is best   118
to curb your eyes; the least distraction—left
or right—can mean a step you will regret."

Then, from the heart of that great conflagration, 121
I heard "*Summae Deus clementiae*"
sung—and was not less keen to turn my eyes;

and I saw spirits walking in the flames,   124
so that I looked at them and at my steps,
sharing the time I had to look at each.

After they'd reached that hymn's end, "*Virum non*   127
cognosco" were the words they cried aloud;
then they began the hymn in a low voice

again, and, done again, they cried: "Diana   130
kept to the woods and banished Helice
after she'd felt the force of Venus' poison."

Then they returned to singing; and they praised 133
aloud those wives and husbands who were chaste,
as virtue and as matrimony mandate.

This is—I think—the way these spirits act 136
as long as they are burned by fire: this is
the care and this the nourishment with which

one has to heal the final wound of all. 139

CANTO XXVI

Still the Seventh Terrace: the Lustful. The souls' amazement at Dante's having a body. His explanation to them. Souls coming from the opposite direction: the Lustful who sinned through unnatural acts. Colloquy with the poet Guido Guinizzelli. The poet Arnaut Daniel, who addresses Dante in Provençal.

While we moved at the edge, one first, one after,
and I could often hear my gentle master
saying: "Take care—and do not waste my warning,"

the sun, its rays already altering   4
the coloring of all the west from azure
to white, was striking me on my right shoulder.

And where my shadow fell, it made the flames   7
seem more inflamed; and I saw many shades
walking, intent upon a sight so strange.

This was the reason that first prompted them   10
to speak to me. Among themselves they said:
"He does not seem to have a fictive body."

Then certain of them came as close to me   13
as they were able to while, cautiously,
they never left the boundaries of their burning.

"O you who move behind the others not   16
because of sloth but reverence perhaps,
give me who burn in thirst and fire your answer.

I'm not alone in needing your response;   19
for all these shades thirst so for it—more than
an Indian or Ethiopian

thirsts for cool water. Tell us how you can—   22
as if you're not yet caught within death's net—
make of yourself a wall against the sun."

Thus one of them had spoken to me; I   25
should now have answered clearly, had I not
been fixed on something strangely evident;

for in the middle of the burning path,   28
came people moving opposite to these—
and I, since they moved left, stared in suspense.

There, on all sides, I can see every shade   31
move quickly to embrace another shade,
content—they did not pause—with their brief greeting,

as ants, in their dark company, will touch   34
their muzzles, each to each, perhaps to seek
news of their fortunes and their journeyings.

No sooner is their friendly greeting done   37
than each shade tries to outcry all the rest
even before he starts to move ahead,

the new group shouting: "Sodom and Gomorrah";   40
the other: "That the bull may hurry toward
her lust, Pasiphaë hides in the cow."

Then, just like cranes, of whom a part, to flee   43
the sun, fly north to Riphean mountains, while
the rest, to flee the frost, fly toward the sands,

one group moves with—the other opposite—us;   46
and they return with tears to their first chants
and to the shout appropriate to each.

And those who had entreated me came close   49
again, in the same way they'd done before;
their faces showed how keen they were to listen.

I, seeing their desire once again,   52
began: "O souls who can be sure of gaining
the state of peace, whenever that may be,

my limbs—mature or green—have not been left   55
within the world beyond; they're here with me,
together with their blood and with their bones.

That I be blind no longer, through this place   58
I pass; above, a lady has gained grace
for me; therefore, I bear my mortal body

across your world. So may your deepest longing   61
soon be appeased and you be lodged within
the heaven that's most full of love, most spacious,

please tell me, so that I may yet transcribe it   64
upon my pages, who you are, and what
crowd moves in the direction opposite."

Each shade displayed no less astonishment   67
or less confusion than a mountaineer,
who, even as he stares about, falls silent

when, rough and rustic, he comes to the city;   70
but when they'd set aside astonishment—
that's soon subdued in noble hearts—he who

had questioned me before, began again: 73
"Blessed are you who would, in order to
die better, store experience of our lands!

The people moving opposite us shared   76
the sin for which once, while in triumph, Caesar
heard 'Queen' called out against him; that is why,

as they move off from us, they cry out 'Sodom,'   79
reproaching their own selves, as you have heard,
and through their shame abet the fire's work.

Our sin was with the other sex; but since   82
we did not keep the bounds of human law,
but served our appetites like beasts, when we

part from the other ranks, we then repeat,   85
to our disgrace, the name of one who, in
the bestial planks, became herself a beast.

You now know why we act so, and you know   88
what our sins were; if you would know our names,
time is too short, and I don't know them all.

But with regard to me, I'll satisfy   91
your wish to know: I'm Guido Guinizzelli,
purged here because I grieved before my end."

As, after the sad raging of Lycurgus,   94
two sons, finding their mother, had embraced her,
so I desired to do—but dared not to—

when I heard him declare his name: the father
of me and of the others—those, my betters—
who ever used sweet, gracious rhymes of love.

And without hearing, speaking, pensive, I   100
walked on, still gazing at him, a long time,
prevented by the fire from drawing closer.

When I had fed my sight on him, I offered   103
myself—with such a pledge that others must
believe—completely ready for his service.

And he to me: "Because of what I hear,   106
you leave a trace within me—one so clear,
Lethe itself can't blur or cancel it.

But if your words have now sworn truthfully,   109
do tell me why it is that you have shown
in speech and gaze that I am dear to you."

And I to him: "It's your sweet lines that, for   112
as long as modern usage lasts, will still
make dear their very inks." "Brother," he said,

"he there, whom I point out to you"—he showed   115
us one who walked ahead—"he was a better
artisan of the mother tongue, surpassing

all those who wrote their poems of love or prose   118
romances—let the stupid ones contend,
who think that from Limoges there came the best.

They credit rumor rather than the truth,   121
allowing their opinion to be set
before they hear what art or reason says.

So, many of our fathers once persisted,   124
voice after voice, in giving to Guittone
the prize—but then, with most, the truth prevailed.

Now if you are so amply privileged   127
that you will be admitted to the cloister
where Christ is abbot of the college, then

pray say, for me, to Him, a Paternoster—   130
that is, as much of it as those in this
place need, since we have lost the power to sin."

Then, to make place, perhaps, for those behind him,   133
he disappeared into the fire, just as
a fish, through water, plunges toward the bottom.

Saying that my desire was making ready   136
a place of welcome for his name, I moved
ahead a little, toward the one who had

been pointed out to me. And he spoke freely: 139
"So does your courteous request please me—
I neither could nor would conceal myself

from you. I am Arnaut, who, going, weep   142
and sing; with grief, I see my former folly;
with joy, I see the hoped-for day draw near.

Now, by the Power that conducts you to   145
the summit of the stairway, I pray you:
remember, at time opportune, my pain!"

Then, in the fire that refines, he hid.   148

CANTO XXVII

From the Seventh Terrace to the threshold of the Earthly Paradise. Sunset. The angel of chastity. The Sixth Beatitude. Dante's fear of entering the flames. Virgil's exhortation. The passage through fire. Dante's sleep and dream of Leah, exemplar of the active life, and Rachel, exemplar of the contemplative life. Dante's waking. Virgil's last words to him.

Just as, there where its Maker shed His blood,
the sun shed its first rays, and Ebro lay
beneath high Libra, and the ninth hour's rays

were scorching Ganges' waves; so here, the sun   4
stood at the point of day's departure when
God's angel—happy—showed himself to us.

He stood along the edge, beyond the flames,   7
singing "*Beati mundo corde*" in
a voice that had more life than ours can claim.

Then: "Holy souls, you cannot move ahead   10
unless the fire has stung you first: enter
the flames, and don't be deaf to song you'll hear

beyond," he said when we were close to him;   13
and when I heard him say this, I became
like one who has been laid within the grave.

I joined my hands and stretched them out to fend   16
the flames, watching the fire, imagining
clearly the human bodies I'd once seen

burning. My gentle escorts turned to me,   19
and Virgil said: "My son, though there may be
suffering here, there is no death. Remember,

remember! If I guided you to safety   22
even upon the back of Geryon,
then now, closer to God, what shall I do?

Be sure: although you were to spend a full   25
one thousand years within this fire's center,
your head would not be balder by one hair.

And if you think I am deceiving you,   28
draw closer to the flames, let your own hands
try out, within the fire, your clothing's hem—

put down, by now put down, your every fear;   31
turn toward the fire, and enter, confident!"
But I was stubborn, set against my conscience.

When he saw me still halting, obstinate,   34
he said, somewhat perplexed: "Now see, son: this
wall stands between you and your Beatrice."

As, at the name of Thisbe, Pyramus,   37
about to die, opened his eyes, and saw her
(when then the mulberry became bloodred),

so, when my stubbornness had softened, I,   40
hearing the name that's always flowering
within my mind, turned to my knowing guide.

At which he shook his head and said: "And would   43
you have us stay along this side?"—then smiled
as one smiles at a child fruit has beguiled.

Then he, ahead of me, entered the fire;   46
and he asked Statius, who had walked between us
before, dividing us, to go behind.

No sooner was I in that fire than I'd   49
have thrown myself in molten glass to find
coolness—because those flames were so intense.

My gentle father, who would comfort me,   52
kept talking, as we walked, of Beatrice,
saying: "I seem to see her eyes already."

A voice that sang beyond us was our guide;   55
and we, attentive to that voice, emerged
just at the point where it began to climb.

"*Venite, benedicti Patris mei,*"   58
it sang within a light that overcame me:
I could not look at such intensity.

"The sun departs," it added; "evening comes; 61
don't stay your steps, but hurry on before
the west grows dark." The path we took climbed straight

within the rock, and its direction was 64
such that, in front of me, my body blocked
the rays of sun, already low behind us.

And we had only tried a few steps when 67
I and my sages sensed the sun had set
because the shadow I had cast was spent.

Before one color came to occupy 70
that sky in all of its immensity
and night was free to summon all its darkness,

each of us made one of those stairs his bed: 73
the nature of the mountain had so weakened
our power and desire to climb ahead.

Like goats that, till they grazed, were swift and tameless
among the mountain peaks, but now are sated,
and rest and ruminate—while the sun blazes—

untroubled, in the shadows, silently, 79
watched over by the herdsman as he leans
upon his staff and oversees their peace;

or like the herdsman in the open fields, 82
spending the night beside his quiet flock,
watching to see that no beast drives them off;

such were all three of us at that point—they 85
were like the herdsmen, I was like the goat;
upon each side of us, high rock walls rose.

From there, one saw but little of the sky, 88
but in that little, I could see the stars
brighter and larger than they usually are.

But while I watched the stars, in reverie, 91
sleep overcame me—sleep, which often sees,
before it happens, what is yet to be.

It was the hour, I think, when Cytherea, 94
who always seems aflame with fires of love,
first shines upon the mountains from the east,

that, in my dream, I seemed to see a woman   97
both young and fair; along a plain she gathered
flowers, and even as she sang, she said:

"Whoever asks my name, know that I'm Leah,   100
and I apply my lovely hands to fashion
a garland of the flowers I have gathered.

To find delight within this mirror I   103
adorn myself; whereas my sister Rachel
never deserts her mirror; there she sits

all day; she longs to see her fair eyes gazing,   106
as I, to see my hands adorning, long:
she is content with seeing, I with labor."

And now, with the reflected lights that glow   109
before the dawn and, rising, are most welcome
to pilgrims as, returning, they near home,

the shadows fled upon all sides; my sleep   112
fled with them; and at this, I woke and saw
that the great teachers had already risen.

"Today your hungerings will find their peace   115
through that sweet fruit the care of mortals seeks
among so many branches." This, the speech,

the solemn words, that Virgil spoke to me;   118
and there were never tidings to compare,
in offering delight to me, with these.

My will on will to climb above was such   121
that at each step I took I felt the force
within my wings was growing for the flight.

When all the staircase lay beneath us and   124
we'd reached the highest step, then Virgil set
his eyes insistently on me and said:

"My son, you've seen the temporary fire   127
and the eternal fire; you have reached
the place past which my powers cannot see.

I've brought you here through intellect and art;   130
from now on, let your pleasure be your guide;
you're past the steep and past the narrow paths.

Look at the sun that shines upon your brow;   133
look at the grasses, flowers, and the shrubs
born here, spontaneously, of the earth.

Among them, you can rest or walk until   136
the coming of the glad and lovely eyes—
those eyes that, weeping, sent me to your side.

Await no further word or sign from me: 139
your will is free, erect, and whole—to act
against that will would be to err: therefore

I crown and miter you over yourself."   142

CANTO XXVIII

The Earthly Paradise. The divine forest. Arrival at the
stream of Lethe. Apparition of a woman (Matilda). Her
explanation of the origin of winds and water in the forest. The
ancient poets and the golden age.

Now keen to search within, to search around
that forest—dense, alive with green, divine—
which tempered the new day before my eyes,
    without delay, I left behind the rise   4
and took the plain, advancing slowly, slowly
across the ground where every part was fragrant.
    A gentle breeze, which did not seem to vary   7
within itself, was striking at my brow
but with no greater force than a kind wind's,
    a wind that made the trembling boughs—they all   10
bent eagerly—incline in the direction
of morning shadows from the holy mountain;
    but they were not deflected with such force   13
as to disturb the little birds upon
the branches in the practice of their arts;
    for to the leaves, with song, birds welcomed those   16
first hours of the morning joyously,
and leaves supplied the burden to their rhymes—
    just like the wind that sounds from branch to branch   19
along the shore of Classe, through the pines
when Aeolus has set Sirocco loose.
    Now, though my steps were slow, I'd gone so far   22
into the ancient forest that I could
no longer see where I had made my entry;
    and there I came upon a stream that blocked   25
the path of my advance; its little waves

bent to the left the grass along its banks.

All of the purest waters here on earth,   28
when matched against that stream, would seem to be
touched by impurity; it hides no thing—

that stream—although it moves, dark, dark, beneath   31
the never-ending shadows, which allow
no ray of sun or moon to reach those waters.

I halted, and I set my eyes upon   34
the farther bank, to look at the abundant
variety of newly-flowered boughs;

and there, just like a thing that, in appearing   37
most suddenly, repels all other thoughts,
so great is the astonishment it brings,

I saw a solitary woman moving,   40
singing, and gathering up flower on flower—
the flowers that colored all of her pathway.

"I pray you, lovely lady, you who warm   43
yourself with rays of love, if I may trust
your looks—which often evidence the heart—

may it please you," I asked of her, "to move   46
ahead and closer to this river, so
that I may understand what you are singing.

You have reminded me of where and what—   49
just when her mother was deprived of her
and she deprived of spring—Proserpina was."

As, when she turns, a woman, dancing, keeps   52
her soles close to the ground and to each other
and scarcely lets one foot precede the other,

so did she turn, upon the little red   55
and yellow flowers, to me, no differently
than would a virgin, lowering chaste eyes.

I had beseeched, and I was satisfied,   58
for she approached so close that the sweet sound
that reached me then became intelligible.

No sooner had she reached the point where that   61
fair river's waves could barely bathe the grass,

than she gave me this gift: lifting her eyes.

I do not think a light so bright had shone   64
beneath the lids of Venus when her son
pierced her in extraordinary fashion.

Erect, along the farther bank, she smiled,   67
her hands entwining varicolored flowers,
which that high land, needing no seed, engenders.

The river kept us just three steps apart;   70
but even Hellespont, where Xerxes crossed—
a case that still curbs all men's arrogance—

did not provoke more hatred in Leander   73
when rough seas ran from Abydos to Sestos,
than hatred I bestowed upon that river

when it refused to open. She began: 76
"You are new here and may—because I smile
in this place, chosen to be mankind's nest—

wonder, perplexed, unable to detect   79
the cause; but light to clear your intellect
is in the psalm beginning '*Delectasti*.'

And you, who have stepped forward, who beseeched me,
tell me if you'd hear more; I have come ready
for all your questions till you're satisfied."

I said: "The water and the murmuring forest   85
contend, in me, against the recent credence
I gave to words denying their existence."

At this, she said: "I'll tell you how the source   88
of your amazement has its special cause;
I'll clear the cloud that's left you so distraught.

The Highest Good, whose sole joy is Himself,   91
made man to be—and to enact—good; He
gave man this place as pledge of endless peace.

Man's fault made brief his stay here; and man's fault   94
made him exchange frank laughter and sweet sport
for lamentation and for anxiousness.

Below this mountain, land and water vapors,   97
which follow heat as far as they are able,

From the left, Dante, Virgil and Statius enter the Sacred Wood of the Earthly Paradise where they encounter Matilda, who symbolizes the Soul's Active Life.

produce their perturbations; to prevent
  them from molesting man placed here, this mountain   100
rose up this close to Heaven; from the point
where its gate locks, it's free of such disturbance.

  Now, since all of the atmosphere revolves   103
within a circle, moved by the first circling,
unless its round is broken at some point,

  against this height, which stands completely free   106
within the living air, that motion strikes;
and since these woods are dense, they echo it.

  And when a plant is struck, its power is such   109
that it impregnates air with seeding force;
the air, revolving, casts this seed abroad;

  the other hemisphere, depending on   112
the nature of its land and sky, conceives
and bears, from diverse powers, diverse trees.

  If what I've said were known, you would not need   115
to be amazed on earth when growing things
take root but have no seed that can be seen.

  And you must know: the holy plain on which   118
you find yourself is full of every seed;
and it has fruit that—there—cannot be gathered.

  The water that you see does not spring from   121
a vein that vapor—cold-condensed—restores,
like rivers that acquire or lose their force;

  it issues from a pure and changeless fountain,   124
which by the will of God regains as much
as, on two sides, it pours and it divides.

  On this side it descends with power to end   127
one's memory of sin; and on the other,
it can restore recall of each good deed.

  To one side, it is Lethe; on the other,   130
Eunoe; neither stream is efficacious
unless the other's waters have been tasted:

  their savor is above all other sweetness.   133
Although your thirst might well be satisfied

even if I revealed no more to you,

I'll give you freely, too, a corollary;   136
nor do I think my words will be less welcome
to you if they extend beyond my promise.

Those ancients who in poetry presented   139
the golden age, who sang its happy state,
perhaps, in their Parnassus, dreamt this place.

Here, mankind's root was innocent; and here   142
were every fruit and never-ending spring;
these streams—the nectar of which poets sing."

Then I turned round completely, and I faced   145
my poets; I could see that they had heard
with smiles this final corollary spoken;

that done, my eyes returned to the fair woman.   148

CANTO XXIX

The Earthly Paradise. The banks of the Lethe. Sudden light and melody. Invocation to the Muses. The extraordinary procession. The seven candelabra. The seven pennants. The twenty-four elders. The four animals. The chariot drawn by a griffin. The seven women. Seven more elders. The sudden halt.

Her words were done, but without interruption
she sang—like an enamored woman—thus:
"*Beati quorum tecta sunt peccata!*"

And just as nymphs who used to walk alone   4
among the woodland shadows, some desiring
to see and some to flee the sun, so she

moved countercurrent as she walked along   7
the riverbank; and following her short
footsteps with my own steps, I matched her pace.

Her steps and mine together did not sum   10
one hundred when the banks, still parallel,
so curved about that I was facing east.

Nor had we gone much farther on that path   13
when she turned fully round toward me and said:
"My brother, look and listen"; and I saw

a sudden radiance that swept across   16
the mighty forest on all sides—and I
was wondering if lightning had not struck.

But since, when lightning strikes, it stops at once,   19
while that light, lingering, increased its force,
within my mind I asked: "What thing is this?"

And through the incandescent air there ran   22
sweet melody; at which, just indignation
made me rebuke the arrogance of Eve

because, where earth and heaven were obedient,   25

a solitary woman, just created,
found any veil at all beyond endurance;

if she had been devout beneath her veil,   28
I should have savored those ineffable
delights before, and for a longer time.

While I moved on, completely rapt, among   31
so many first fruits of eternal pleasure,
and longing for still greater joys, the air

before us altered underneath the green   34
branches, becoming like an ardent fire,
and now the sweet sound was distinctly song.

O Virgins, sacrosanct, if I have ever,   37
for your sake, suffered vigils, cold, and hunger,
great need makes me entreat my recompense.

Now Helicon must pour its fountains for me,   40
Urania must help me with her choir
to put in verses things hard to conceive.

Not far beyond, we made out seven trees   43
of gold, though the long stretch of air between
those trees and us had falsified their semblance;

but when I'd drawn so close that things perceived   46
through mingled senses, which delude, did not,
now they were nearer, lose their real features,

the power that offers reason matter judged   49
those trees to be—what they were—candelabra,
and what those voices sang to be "Hosanna."

The upper part of those fair candles flamed   52
more radiantly than the midmonth moon
shines at midnight in an untroubled sky.

Full of astonishment, I turned to my   55
good Virgil; but he only answered me
with eyes that were no less amazed than mine.

Then I looked at the extraordinary   58
things that were moving toward us—but so slowly
that even brides just wed would move more quickly.

The woman chided me: "Why are you only   61

Matilda and the poets walk upstream where they behold the Heavenly Pageant. Seven candlesticks the size of trees stand before twenty-four elders, symbolizing the twenty-four books of the Old Testament. Behind them is Christ's chariot drawn by a Gryphon.

so eager to behold the living lights
and not in seeing what comes after them?"

Then I saw people following those candles,   64
as if behind their guides, and they wore white—
whiteness that, in this world, has never been.

The water, to my left, reflected flames,   67
and it reflected, too, my left-hand side
if I gazed into it, as in a mirror.

When I was at a point along my shore   70
where all that sundered me from them was water,
I stayed my steps in order to see better,

and I could see the candle flames move forward,   73
leaving the air behind them colored like
the strokes a painter's brush might have described,

so that the air above that retinue   76
was streaked with seven bands in every hue
of which the rainbow's made and Delia's girdle.

These pennants stretched far back, beyond my vision; 79
as for the width they filled, I judged the distance
between the outer ones to be ten paces.

Beneath the handsome sky I have described,   82
twenty-four elders moved on, two by two,
and they had wreaths of lilies on their heads.

And all were singing: "You, among the daughters   85
of Adam, *benedicta* are; and may
your beauties blessed be eternally."

After the flowers and the other fresh   88
plants facing me, along the farther shore,
had seen those chosen people disappear,

then—as in heaven, star will follow star—   91
the elders gone, four animals came on;
and each of them had green leaves as his crown;

each had six wings as plumage, and those plumes   94
were full of eyes; they would be very like
the eyes of Argus, were his eyes alive.

Reader, I am not squandering more rhymes   97

in order to describe their forms; since I
must spend elsewhere, I can't be lavish here;

but read Ezekiel, for he has drawn   100
those animals approaching from the north;
with wings and cloud and fire, he painted them.

And just as you will find them in his pages,   103
such were they here, except that John's with me
as to their wings; with him, John disagrees.

The space between the four of them contained   106
a chariot—triumphal—on two wheels,
tied to a griffin's neck and drawn by him.

His wings, stretched upward, framed the middle band   109
with three bands on each outer side, so that,
though he cleaved air, he left the bands intact.

His wings—so high that they were lost to sight;   112
his limbs were gold as far as he was bird;
the rest of him was white mixed with bloodred.

Not only did no chariot so handsome   115
gladden Rome's Africanus or Augustus
himself—even the Sun's own cannot match it;

the Sun's—which, gone astray, was burnt to cinders   118
because Earth offered up her pious prayers,
when Jove, in ways not known to us, was just.

Three circling women, then advancing, danced   121
at the right wheel; the first of them, so red
that even in a flame she'd not be noted;

the second seemed as if her flesh and bone   124
were fashioned out of emerald; the third
seemed to be newly fallen snow. And now

the white one seemed to lead them, now the red;   127
and from the way in which the leader chanted,
the others took their pace, now slow, now rapid.

Upon the left, four other women, dressed   130
in crimson, danced, depending on the cadence
of one of them, with three eyes in her head.

Behind all of the group I have described   133

I saw two elders, different in their dress
but like in manner—grave and decorous.

The first seemed to be one of the disciples   136
of great Hippocrates, whom nature made
for those who are her dearest living beings;

the other showed an opposite concern—   139
his sword was bright and sharp, and even on
this near side of the river, I felt fear.

Then I saw four of humble aspect; and,   142
when all the rest had passed, a lone old man,
his features keen, advanced, as if in sleep.

The clothes these seven wore were like the elders' 145
in the first file, except that these had no
garlands of lilies round their brow; instead,

roses and other red flowers wreathed their heads;   148
one seeing them less closely would have sworn
that all of them had flames above their eyebrows.

And when the chariot stood facing me,   151
I heard a bolt of thunder; and it seemed
to block the path of that good company,

which halted there, its emblems in the lead.   154

CANTO XXX

The Earthly Paradise. The seven candelabra likened to seven stars (as if a Great Bear) of the Empyrean. The disappearance of Virgil. Beatrice's rebuke of Dante. The angels' compassion for Dante. Beatrice's accusations.

When the first heaven's Seven-Stars had halted
(those stars that never rise or set, that are
not veiled except when sin beclouds our vision;

those stars that, there, made everyone aware   4
of what his duty was, just as the Bear
below brings helmsmen home to harbor), then

the truthful band that had come first between   7
the griffin and the Seven-Stars turned toward
that chariot as toward their peace, and one

of them, as if sent down from Heaven, hymned   10
aloud, *"Veni, sponsa, de Libano,"*
three times, and all the others echoed him.

Just as the blessed, at the Final Summons,   13
will rise up—ready—each out of his grave,
singing, with new-clothed voices, Alleluia,

so, from the godly chariot, eternal   16
life's messengers and ministers arose:
one hundred stood *ad vocem tanti senis.*

All of them cried: *"Benedictus qui venis,"*   19
and, scattering flowers upward and around,
"Manibus, oh, *date lilia plenis."*

I have at times seen all the eastern sky   22
becoming rose as day began and seen,
adorned in lovely blue, the rest of heaven;

and seen the sun's face rise so veiled that it   25
was tempered by the mist and could permit

the eye to look at length upon it; so,

within a cloud of flowers that were cast   28
by the angelic hands and then rose up
and then fell back, outside and in the chariot,

a woman showed herself to me; above   31
a white veil, she was crowned with olive boughs;
her cape was green; her dress beneath, flame-red.

Within her presence, I had once been used   34
to feeling—trembling—wonder, dissolution;
but that was long ago. Still, though my soul,

now she was veiled, could not see her directly, 37
by way of hidden force that she could move,
I felt the mighty power of old love.

As soon as that deep force had struck my vision 40
(the power that, when I had not yet left
my boyhood, had already transfixed me),

I turned around and to my left—just as   43
a little child, afraid or in distress,
will hurry to his mother—anxiously,

to say to Virgil: "I am left with less   46
than one drop of my blood that does not tremble:
I recognize the signs of the old flame."

But Virgil had deprived us of himself,   49
Virgil, the gentlest father, Virgil, he
to whom I gave my self for my salvation;

and even all our ancient mother lost   52
was not enough to keep my cheeks, though washed
with dew, from darkening again with tears.

"Dante, though Virgil's leaving you, do not   55
yet weep, do not weep yet; you'll need your tears
for what another sword must yet inflict."

Just like an admiral who goes to stern   58
and prow to see the officers who guide
the other ships, encouraging their tasks;

so, on the left side of the chariot   61
(I'd turned around when I had heard my name—

which, of necessity, I transcribe here),

I saw the lady who had first appeared   64
to me beneath the veils of the angelic
flowers look at me across the stream.

Although the veil she wore—down from her head,   67
which was encircled by Minerva's leaves—
did not allow her to be seen distinctly,

her stance still regal and disdainful, she   70
continued, just as one who speaks but keeps
until the end the fiercest parts of speech:

"Look here! For I am Beatrice, I am!   73
How were you able to ascend the mountain?
Did you not know that man is happy here?"

My lowered eyes caught sight of the clear stream,   76
but when I saw myself reflected there,
such shame weighed on my brow, my eyes drew back

and toward the grass; just as a mother seems   79
harsh to her child, so did she seem to me—
how bitter is the savor of stern pity!

Her words were done. The angels—suddenly—   82
sang, "*In te, Domine, speravi*"; but
their singing did not go past "*pedes meos.*"

Even as snow among the sap-filled trees   85
along the spine of Italy will freeze
when gripped by gusts of the Slavonian winds,

then, as it melts, will trickle through itself—   88
that is, if winds breathe north from shade-less lands—
just as, beneath the flame, the candle melts;

so I, before I'd heard the song of those   91
whose notes always accompany the notes
of the eternal spheres, was without tears

and sighs; but when I heard the sympathy   94
for me within their gentle harmonies,
as if they'd said: "Lady, why shame him so?"—

then did the ice that had restrained my heart   97
become water and breath; and from my breast

and through my lips and eyes they issued—anguished.

    Still standing motionless upon the left   100
side of the chariot, she then addressed
the angels who had been compassionate:

    "You are awake in never-ending day,   103
and neither night nor sleep can steal from you
one step the world would take along its way;

    therefore, I'm more concerned that my reply   106
be understood by him who weeps beyond,
so that his sorrow's measure match his sin.

    Not only through the work of the great spheres—   109
which guide each seed to a determined end,
depending on what stars are its companions—

    but through the bounty of the godly graces,   112
which shower down from clouds so high that we
cannot approach them with our vision, he,

    when young, was such—potentially—that any   115
propensity innate in him would have
prodigiously succeeded, had he acted.

    But where the soil has finer vigor, there   118
precisely—when untilled or badly seeded—
will that terrain grow wilder and more noxious.

    My countenance sustained him for a while;   121
showing my youthful eyes to him, I led
him with me toward the way of righteousness.

    As soon as I, upon the threshold of   124
my second age, had changed my life, he took
himself away from me and followed after

    another; when from flesh to spirit, I   127
had risen, and my goodness and my beauty
had grown, I was less dear to him, less welcome:

    he turned his footsteps toward an untrue path;   130
he followed counterfeits of goodness, which
will never pay in full what they have promised.

    Nor did the inspirations I received—   133
with which, in dream and otherwise, I called

him back—help me; he paid so little heed!

He fell so far there were no other means   136
to lead him to salvation, except this:
to let him see the people who were lost.

For this I visited the gateway of   139
the dead; to him who guided him above
my prayers were offered, even as I wept.

The deep design of God would have been broken   142
if Lethe had been crossed and he had drunk
such waters but had not discharged the debt

of penitence that's paid when tears are shed."   145

CANTO XXXI

The Earthly Paradise. Dante's confession and new rebukes by Beatrice. Dante's repentance and loss of his senses. Matilda's immersion of Dante in Lethe. The four handmaidens of Beatrice. The mystery of the griffin. The other three women beseeching Beatrice. Beatrice unveiled.

"O you upon the holy stream's far shore,"
so she, turning her speech's point against me—
even its edge had seemed too sharp—began

again, without allowing interruption,   4
"tell, tell if this is true; for your confession
must be entwined with such self-accusation."

My power of speech was so confounded that   7
my voice would move and yet was spent before
its organs had released it. She forbore

a moment, then she said: "What are you thinking?   10
Reply to me, the water has not yet
obliterated your sad memories."

Confusion mixed with fear compelled a *Yes*   13
out of my mouth, and yet that *Yes* was such—
one needed eyes to make out what it was.

Just as a crossbow that is drawn too taut   16
snaps both its cord and bow when it is shot,
and arrow meets its mark with feeble force,

so, caught beneath that heavy weight, I burst;   19
and I let tears and sighs pour forth; my voice
had lost its life along its passage out.

At this she said: "In the desire for me   22
that was directing you to love the Good
beyond which there's no thing to draw our longing,

what chains were strung, what ditches dug across   25

your path that, once you'd come upon them, caused
your loss of any hope of moving forward?"

What benefits and what allurements were   28
so evident upon the brow of others
that you had need to promenade before them?"

After I had withheld a bitter sigh,   31
I scarcely had the voice for my reply,
but, laboring, my lips gave my words form.

Weeping, I answered: "Mere appearances   34
turned me aside with their false loveliness,
as soon as I had lost your countenance."

And she: "Had you been silent or denied   37
what you confess, your guilt would not be less
in evidence: it's known by such a Judge!

But when the charge of sinfulness has burst   40
from one's own cheek, then in our court the whet-
stone turns and blunts our blade's own cutting edge.

Nevertheless, that you may feel more shame   43
for your mistake, and that—in time to come—
hearing the Sirens, you may be more strong,

have done with all the tears you sowed, and listen: 46
so shall you hear how, unto other ends,
my buried flesh should have directed you.

Nature or art had never showed you any   49
beauty that matched the lovely limbs in which
I was enclosed—limbs scattered now in dust;

and if the highest beauty failed you through   52
my death, what mortal thing could then induce
you to desire it? For when the first

arrow of things deceptive struck you, then   55
you surely should have lifted up your wings
to follow me, no longer such a thing.

No green young girl or other novelty—   58
such brief delight—should have weighed down your wings,
awaiting further shafts. The fledgling bird

must meet two or three blows before he learns,   61

31

As Beatrice reprimands Dante from her chariot, Matilda immerses him in the waters of Lethe. On the opposite bank dance four maidens representing the Cardinal Virtues.

but any full-fledged bird is proof against
the net that has been spread or arrow, aimed."

As children, when ashamed, will stand, their eyes 64
upon the ground—they listen, silently,
acknowledging their fault repentantly—

so did I stand; and she enjoined me: "Since 67
hearing alone makes you grieve so, lift up
your beard, and sight will bring you greater tears."

There's less resistance in the sturdy oak 70
to its uprooting by a wind from lands
of ours or lands of Iarbas than I showed

in lifting up my chin at her command; 73
I knew quite well—when she said "beard" but meant
my face—the poison in her argument.

When I had raised my face upright, my eyes 76
were able to perceive that the first creatures
had paused and were no longer scattering flowers;

and still uncertain of itself, my vision 79
saw Beatrice turned toward the animal
that is, with its two natures, but one person.

Beneath her veil, beyond the stream, she seemed 82
so to surpass her former self in beauty
as, here on earth, she had surpassed all others.

The nettle of remorse so stung me then, 85
that those—among all other—things that once
most lured my love, became most hateful to me.

Such self-indictment seized my heart that I 88
collapsed, my senses slack; what I became
is known to her who was the cause of it.

Then, when my heart restored my outer sense, 91
I saw the woman whom I'd found alone,
standing above me, saying: "Hold, hold me!"

She'd plunged me, up to my throat, in the river, 94
and, drawing me behind her, she now crossed,
light as a gondola, along the surface.

When I was near the blessed shore, I heard 97

"*Asperges me*" so sweetly sung that I
cannot remember or, much less, transcribe it.

   The lovely woman opened wide her arms;   100
she clasped my head, and then she thrust me under
to that point where I had to swallow water.

   That done, she drew me out and led me, bathed,   103
into the dance of the four lovely women;
and each one placed her arm above my head.

   "Here we are nymphs; in heaven, stars; before   106
she had descended to the world, we were
assigned, as her handmaids, to Beatrice;

   we'll be your guides unto her eyes; but it   109
will be the three beyond, who see more deeply,
who'll help you penetrate her joyous light."

   So, singing, they began; then, leading me   112
together with them to the griffin's breast,
where Beatrice, turned toward us, stood, they said:

   "See that you are not sparing of your gaze: 115
before you we have set those emeralds
from which Love once had aimed his shafts at you."

   A thousand longings burning more than flames   118
compelled my eyes to watch the radiant eyes
that, motionless, were still fixed on the griffin.

   Just like the sun within a mirror, so   121
the double-natured creature gleamed within,
now showing one, and now the other guise.

   Consider, reader, if I did not wonder   124
when I saw something that displayed no movement
though its reflected image kept on changing.

   And while, full of astonishment and gladness,   127
my soul tasted that food which, even as
it quenches hunger, spurs the appetite,

   the other three, whose stance showed them to be   130
the members of a higher troop, advanced—
and, to their chant, they danced angelically.

   "Turn, Beatrice, o turn your holy eyes   133

upon your faithful one," their song beseeched,
"who, that he might see you, has come so far.

Out of your grace, do us this grace; unveil   136
your lips to him, so that he may discern
the second beauty you have kept concealed."

O splendor of eternal living light,   139
who's ever grown so pale beneath Parnassus'
shade or has drunk so deeply from its fountain,

that he'd not seem to have his mind confounded,   142
trying to render you as you appeared
where heaven's harmony was your pale likeness—

your face, seen through the air, unveiled completely?   145

CANTO XXXII

The Earthly Paradise. The eastward path of the procession.
Adam's tree. The griffin, the chariot, and the reflowering tree.
The sleep and waking of Dante. Beatrice's words on Dante's
mission. The eagle, the fox, the dragon, and the transfigured
chariot. The giant and the whore.

My eyes were so insistent, so intent
on finding satisfaction for their ten-
year thirst that every other sense was spent.

And to each side, my eyes were walled in by   4
indifference to all else (with its old net,
the holy smile so drew them to itself),

when I was forced to turn my eyes leftward   7
by those three goddesses because I heard
them warning me: "You stare too fixedly."

And the condition that afflicts the sight   10
when eyes have just been struck by the sun's force
left me without my vision for a time.

But when my sight became accustomed to   13
lesser sensations (that is, lesser than
the mighty force that made my eyes retreat),

I saw the glorious army: it had wheeled   16
around and to the right; it had turned east;
it faced the seven flames and faced the sun.

Just as, protected by its shields, a squadron   19
will wheel, to save itself, around its standard
until all of its men have changed direction;

so here all troops of the celestial kingdom   22
within the vanguard passed in front of us
before the chariot swung around the pole-shaft.

Back to the wheels the ladies then returned;   25

and though the griffin moved the blessed burden,
when he did that, none of his feathers stirred.

The lovely lady who'd helped me ford Lethe,   28
and I and Statius, following the wheel
that turned right, round the inner, smaller arc,

were slowly passing through the tall woods—empty   31
because of one who had believed the serpent;
our pace was measured by angelic song.

The space we covered could be matched perhaps   34
by three flights of an unleashed arrow's shafts,
when Beatrice descended from the chariot.

"Adam," I heard all of them murmuring,   37
and then they drew around a tree whose every
branch had been stripped of flowers and of leaves.

As it grows higher, so its branches spread   40
wider; it reached a height that even in
their forests would amaze the Indians.

"Blessed are you, whose beak does not, o griffin, 43
pluck the sweet-tasting fruit that is forbidden
and then afflicts the belly that has eaten!"

So, round the robust tree, the others shouted;   46
and the two-natured animal: "Thus is
the seed of every righteous man preserved."

And turning to the pole-shaft he had pulled,   49
he drew it to the foot of the stripped tree
and, with a branch of that tree, tied the two.

Just like our plants that, when the great light falls 52
on earth, mixed with the light that shines behind
the stars of the celestial Fishes, swell

with buds—each plant renews its coloring   55
before the sun has yoked its steeds beneath
another constellation: so the tree,

whose boughs—before—had been so solitary,   58
was now renewed, showing a tint that was
less than the rose, more than the violet.

I did not understand the hymn that they   61

then sang—it is not sung here on this earth—
nor, drowsy, did I listen to the end.

Could I describe just how the ruthless eyes   64
(eyes whose long wakefulness cost them so dear),
hearing the tale of Syrinx, fell asleep,

then like a painter painting from a model,   67
I'd draw the way in which I fell asleep;
but I refrain—let one more skillful paint.

I move, therefore, straight to my waking time;   70
I say that radiance rent the veil of sleep,
as did a voice: "Rise up: what are you doing?"

Even as Peter, John and James, when brought   73
to see the blossoms of the apple tree—
whose fruit abets the angels' hungering,

providing endless wedding-feasts in Heaven—   76
were overwhelmed by what they saw, but then,
hearing the word that shattered deeper sleeps,

arose and saw their fellowship was smaller—   79
since Moses and Elijah now had left—
and saw a difference in their Teacher's dress;

so I awoke and saw, standing above me,   82
she who before—compassionate—had guided
my steps along the riverbank. Completely

bewildered, I asked: "Where is Beatrice?"   85
And she: "Beneath the boughs that were renewed,
she's seated on the root of that tree; see

the company surrounding her; the rest   88
have left; behind the griffin they have climbed
on high with song that is more sweet, more deep."

I do not know if she said more than that,   91
because, by now, I had in sight one who
excluded all things other from my view.

She sat alone upon the simple ground,   94
left there as guardian of the chariot
I'd seen the two-form animal tie fast.

The seven nymphs encircled her as garland,   97

32

The tree (right) is the focus of an allegory representing the Vicissitudes of the Church. At its root sits Beatrice as Sapientia, surrounded by the Seven Virtues, instructing Dante in the allegory.

and in their hands they held the lamps that can
not be extinguished by the north or south winds.

"Here you shall be—awhile—a visitor;   100
but you shall be with me—and without end—
Rome's citizen, the Rome in which Christ is

Roman; and thus, to profit that world which   103
lives badly, watch the chariot steadfastly
and, when you have returned beyond, transcribe

what you have seen." Thus, Beatrice; and I,   106
devoutly, at the feet of her commandments,
set mind and eyes where she had wished me to.

Never has lightning fallen with such swift   109
motion from a thick cloud, when it descends
from the most distant limit in the heavens,

as did the bird of Jove that I saw swoop   112
down through the tree, tearing the bark as well
as the new leaves and the new flowering.

It struck the chariot with all its force;   115
the chariot twisted, like a ship that's crossed
by seas that now storm starboard and now port.

I then saw, as it leaped into the body   118
of that triumphal chariot, a fox
that seemed to lack all honest nourishment:

but, as she railed against its squalid sins,   121
my lady forced that fox to flight as quick
as, stripped of flesh, its bones permitted it.

Then I could see the eagle plunge—again   124
down through the tree—into the chariot
and leave it feathered with its plumage; and,

just like a voice from an embittered heart,   127
a voice issued from Heaven, saying this:
"O my small bark, your freight is wickedness!"

Then did the ground between the two wheels seem   130
to me to open; from the earth, a dragon
emerged; it drove its tail up through the chariot;

and like a wasp when it retracts its sting,   133

drawing its venomed tail back to itself,
it dragged part of the bottom off, and went
    its way, undulating. And what was left   136
was covered with the eagle's plumes—perhaps
offered with sound and kind intent—much as
    grass covers fertile ground; and the pole-shaft   139
and both wheels were re-covered in less time
than mouth must be kept open when one sighs.

    Transfigured so, the saintly instrument   142
grew heads, which sprouted from its parts; three grew
upon the pole-shaft, and one at each corner.

    The three were horned like oxen, but the four   145
had just a single horn upon their foreheads:
such monsters never have been seen before.

    Just like a fortress set on a steep slope,   148
securely seated there, ungirt, a whore,
whose eyes were quick to rove, appeared to me;

    and I saw at her side, erect, a giant,   151
who seemed to serve as her custodian;
and they—again, again—embraced each other.

    But when she turned her wandering, wanton eyes   154
to me, then that ferocious amador
beat her from head to foot; then, swollen with

    suspicion, fierce with anger, he untied   157
the chariot-made-monster, dragging it
into the wood, so that I could not see

    either the whore or the amazing beast.   160

CANTO XXXIII

*The Earthly Paradise. The lament of the seven women and the
compassion of Beatrice. Beatrice's prophecy: God's vengeance
against the dragon, the whore, and the giant. Her words on
Adam's tree. Her last rebuke of Dante. Dante led to Eunoe
by Matilda. The sweet draught. Readiness for Paradise.*

    Weeping, the women then began—now three,
now four, alternately—to psalm gently,
"Deus venerunt gentes"; and at this,

    sighing and full of pity, Beatrice   4
was changed; she listened, grieving little less
than Mary when, beneath the Cross, she wept.

    But when the seven virgins had completed   7
their psalm, and she was free to speak, erect,
her coloring like ardent fire, she answered:

    "Modicum, et non videbitis me   10
et iterum, sisters delightful to me,
modicum, et vos videbitis me."

    Then she set all the seven nymphs in front   13
of her and signaled me, the lady, and
the sage who had remained, to move behind her.

    So she advanced; and I do not believe   16
that she had taken her tenth step upon
the ground before her eyes had struck my eyes;

    and gazing tranquilly, "Pray come more quickly,"   19
she said to me, "so that you are more ready
to listen to me should I speak to you."

    As soon as I, responding to my duty,   22
had joined her, she said: "Brother, why not try,
since now you're at my side, to query me?"

    Like those who, speaking to superiors   25

too reverently do not speak distinctly,
not drawing their clear voice up to their teeth—
so did I speak with sound too incomplete   28
when I began: "Lady, you know my need
to know, and know how it can be appeased."

And she to me: "I'd have you disentangle   31
yourself, from this point on, from fear and shame,
that you no longer speak like one who dreams.

Know that the vessel which the serpent broke   34
was and is not; but he whose fault it is
may rest assured—God's vengeance fears no hindrance.

The eagle that had left its plumes within   37
the chariot, which then became a monster
and then a prey, will not forever be

without an heir; for I can plainly see,   40
and thus I tell it: stars already close
at hand, which can't be blocked or checked, will bring

a time in which, dispatched by God, a Five   43
Hundred and Ten and Five will slay the whore
together with that giant who sins with her.

And what I tell, as dark as Sphinx and Themis,   46
may leave you less convinced because—like these—
it tires the intellect with quandaries;

but soon events themselves will be the Naiads   49
that clarify this obstinate enigma—
but without injury to grain or herds.

Take note; and even as I speak these words,   52
do you transmit them in your turn to those
who live the life that is a race to death.

And when you write them, keep in mind that you   55
must not conceal what you've seen of the tree
that now has been despoiled twice over here.

Whoever robs or rends that tree offends,   58
with his blaspheming action, God; for He
created it for His sole use—holy.

For tasting of that tree, the first soul waited   61

On the left Beatrice and the Seven Virtues, seated, weep over the Church's misfortunes. In the centre, she rises and summons Dante to bathe in the river Eunoe, which he does (right) with Matilda's help.

five thousand years and more in grief and longing
for Him who on Himself avenged that taste.

Your intellect's asleep if it can't see 64
how singular's the cause that makes that tree
so tall and makes it grow invertedly.

And if, like waters of the Elsa, your 67
vain thoughts did not encrust your mind; if your
delight in them were not like Pyramus

staining the mulberry, you'd recognize 70
in that tree's form and height the moral sense
God's justice had when He forbade trespass.

But since I see your intellect is made 73
of stone and, petrified, grown so opaque—
the light of what I say has left you dazed—

I'd also have you bear my words within you— 76
if not inscribed, at least outlined—just as
the pilgrim's staff is brought back wreathed with palm."

And I: "Even as wax the seal's impressed, 79
where there's no alteration in the form,
so does my brain now bear what you have stamped.

But why does your desired word ascend 82
so high above my understanding that
the more I try, the more am I denied?"

"That you may recognize," she said, "the school 85
that you have followed and may see if what
it taught can comprehend what I have said—

and see that, as the earth is distant from 88
the highest and the swiftest of the heavens,
so distant is your way from the divine."

And I replied to her: "I don't remember 91
making myself a stranger to you, nor
does conscience gnaw at me because of that."

"And if you can't remember that," she answered, 94
smiling, "then call to mind how you—today—
have drunk of Lethe; and if smoke is proof

of fire, then it is clear: we can conclude 97

from this forgetfulness, that in your will
there was a fault—your will had turned elsewhere.

But from now on the words I speak will be   100
naked; that is appropriate if they
would be laid bare before your still-crude sight."

More incandescent now, with slower steps,   103
the sun was pacing the meridian,
which alters with the place from which it's seen,

when, just as one who serves as escort for   106
a group will halt if he has come upon
things strange or even traces of strangeness,

the seven ladies halted at the edge   109
of a dense shadow such as mountains cast,
beneath green leaves and black boughs, on cold banks.

In front of them I seemed to see Euphrates   112
and Tigris issuing from one same spring
and then, as friends do, separating slowly.

"O light, o glory of the human race,   115
what water is this, flowing from one source
and then, becoming distant from itself?"

Her answer to what I had asked was: "Ask   118
Matilda to explain this"; and the lovely
lady, as one who frees herself from blame,

replied: "He's heard of this and other matters   121
from me; and I am sure that Lethe's waters
have not obscured his memory of this."

And Beatrice: "Perhaps some greater care,   124
which often weakens memory, has made
his mind, in things regarding sight, grow dark.

But see Eunoe as it flows from there: 127
lead him to it and, as you're used to doing,
revive the power that is faint in him."

As would the noble soul, which offers no   130
excuse, but makes another's will its own
as soon as signs reveal that will; just so,

when she had taken me, the lovely lady   133

moved forward; and she said with womanly
courtesy to Statius: "Come with him."

    If, reader, I had ampler space in which   136
to write, I'd sing—though incompletely—that
sweet draught for which my thirst was limitless;

    but since all of the pages pre-disposed   139
for this, the second canticle, are full,
the curb of art will not let me continue.

    From that most holy wave I now returned   142
to Beatrice; remade, as new trees are
renewed when they bring forth new boughs, I was

    pure and prepared to climb unto the stars.   145

PARADISO

This translation of the PARADISO
is inscribed to Toni Burbank and Stanley Holwitz,
whose DOPPIO LUME S'ADDUA

CANTO I

Proem and Invocation to Apollo. Dante's passing beyond the human, beyond the earth, in heavenward ascent with Beatrice. His wonder. Beatrice on the Empyrean and the order of the universe.

The glory of the One who moves all things
permeates the universe and glows
in one part more and in another less.

I was within the heaven that receives   4
more of His light; and I saw things that he
who from that height descends, forgets or can

not speak; for nearing its desired end,   7
our intellect sinks into an abyss
so deep that memory fails to follow it.

Nevertheless, as much as I, within   10
my mind, could treasure of the holy kingdom
shall now become the matter of my song.

O good Apollo, for this final task   13
make me the vessel of your excellence,
what you, to merit your loved laurel, ask.

Until this point, one of Parnassus' peaks   16
sufficed for me; but now I face the test,
the agon that is left; I need both crests.

Enter into my breast; within me breathe   19
the very power you made manifest
when you drew Marsyas out from his limbs' sheath.

O godly force, if you so lend yourself   22
to me, that I might show the shadow of
the blessed realm inscribed within my mind,

then you would see me underneath the tree   25
you love; there I shall take as crown the leaves

of which my theme and you shall make me worthy.

So seldom, father, are those garlands gathered 28
for triumph of a ruler or a poet—
a sign of fault or shame in human wills—

that when Peneian branches can incite 31
someone to long and thirst for them, delight
must fill the happy Delphic deity.

Great fire can follow a small spark: there may 34
be better voices after me to pray
to Cyrrha's god for aid—that he may answer.

The lantern of the world approaches mortals 37
by varied paths; but on that way which links
four circles with three crosses, it emerges

joined to a better constellation and 40
along a better course, and it can temper
and stamp the world's wax more in its own manner.

Its entry from that point of the horizon 43
brought morning there and evening here; almost
all of that hemisphere was white—while ours

was dark—when I saw Beatrice turn round 46
and left, that she might see the sun; no eagle
has ever stared so steadily at it.

And as a second ray will issue from 49
the first and reascend, much like a pilgrim
who seeks his home again, so on her action,

fed by my eyes to my imagination, 52
my action drew, and on the sun I set
my sight more than we usually do.

More is permitted to our powers there 55
than is permitted here, by virtue of
that place, made for mankind as its true home.

I did not bear it long, but not so briefly 58
as not to see it sparkling round about,
like molten iron emerging from the fire;

and suddenly it seemed that day had been 61
added to day, as if the One who can

Leaving the Sacred Wood, Dante begins the ascent to Paradise with Beatrice. He sees the planets and hears their music.

had graced the heavens with a second sun.

The eyes of Beatrice were all intent   64
on the eternal circles; from the sun,
I turned aside; I set my eyes on her.

In watching her, within me I was changed   67
as Glaucus changed, tasting the herb that made
him a companion of the other sea gods.

Passing beyond the human cannot be   70
worded; let Glaucus serve as simile—
until grace grant you the experience.

Whether I only was the part of me   73
that You created last, You—governing
the heavens—know: it was Your light that raised me.

When that wheel which You make eternal through 76
the heavens' longing for You drew me with
the harmony You temper and distinguish,

the fire of the sun then seemed to me   79
to kindle so much of the sky, that rain
or river never formed so broad a lake.

The newness of the sound and the great light   82
incited me to learn their cause—I was
more keen than I had ever been before.

And she who read me as I read myself,   85
to quiet the commotion in my mind,
opened her lips before I opened mine

to ask, and she began: "You make yourself   88
obtuse with false imagining; you can
not see what you would see if you dispelled it.

You are not on the earth as you believe;   91
but lightning, flying from its own abode,
is less swift than you are, returning home."

While I was freed from my first doubt by these 94
brief words she smiled to me, I was yet caught
in new perplexity. I said: "I was

content already; after such great wonder,   97
I rested. But again I wonder how

my body rises past these lighter bodies."

   At which, after a sigh of pity, she   100
settled her eyes on me with the same look
a mother casts upon a raving child,

   and she began: "All things, among themselves,   103
possess an order; and this order is
the form that makes the universe like God.

   Here do the higher beings see the imprint   106
of the Eternal Worth, which is the end
to which the pattern I have mentioned tends.

   Within that order, every nature has   109
its bent, according to a different station,
nearer or less near to its origin.

   Therefore, these natures move to different ports 112
across the mighty sea of being, each
given the impulse that will bear it on.

   This impulse carries fire to the moon;   115
this is the motive force in mortal creatures;
this binds the earth together, makes it one.

   Not only does the shaft shot from this bow   118
strike creatures lacking intellect, but those
who have intelligence, and who can love.

   The Providence that has arrayed all this   121
forever quiets—with Its light—that heaven
in which the swiftest of the spheres revolves;

   to there, as toward a destined place, we now 124
are carried by the power of the bow
that always aims its shaft at a glad mark.

   Yet it is true that, even as a shape   127
may, often, not accord with art's intent,
since matter may be unresponsive, deaf,

   so, from this course, the creature strays at times 130
because he has the power, once impelled,
to swerve elsewhere; as lightning from a cloud

   is seen to fall, so does the first impulse,   133
when man has been diverted by false pleasure,

turn him toward earth. You should—if I am right—
 not feel more marvel at your climbing than   136
you would were you considering a stream
that from a mountain's height falls to its base.
 It would be cause for wonder in you if,   139
no longer hindered, you remained below,
as if, on earth, a living flame stood still."
 Then she again turned her gaze heavenward.   142

CANTO II

Address to the reader. Arrival in the First Heaven, the Sphere of the Moon. Beatrice's vigorous confutation of Dante, who thinks that rarity and density are the causes of the spots we see on the body of the Moon.

O you who are within your little bark,
eager to listen, following behind
my ship that, singing, crosses to deep seas,

turn back to see your shores again: do not   4
attempt to sail the seas I sail; you may,
by losing sight of me, be left astray.

The waves I take were never sailed before;   7
Minerva breathes, Apollo pilots me,
and the nine Muses show to me the Bears.

You other few who turned your minds in time   10
unto the bread of angels, which provides
men here with life—but hungering for more—

you may indeed commit your vessel to   13
the deep salt-sea, keeping your course within
my wake, ahead of where waves smooth again.

Those men of glory, those who crossed to Colchis,   16
when they saw Jason turn into a ploughman
were less amazed than you will be amazed.

The thirst that is innate and everlasting—   19
thirst for the godly realm—bore us away
as swiftly as the heavens that you see.

Beatrice gazed upward. I watched her.   22
But in a span perhaps no longer than
an arrow takes to strike, to fly, to leave

the bow, I reached a place where I could see   25
that something wonderful drew me; and she

from whom my need could not be hidden, turned
to me (her gladness matched her loveliness):   28
"Direct your mind to God in gratefulness,"
she said; "He has brought us to the first star."

It seemed to me that we were covered by   31
a brilliant, solid, dense, and stainless cloud,
much like a diamond that the sun has struck.

Into itself, the everlasting pearl   34
received us, just as water will accept
a ray of light and yet remain intact.

If I was body (and on earth we can   37
not see how things material can share
one space—the case, when body enters body),

then should our longing be still more inflamed   40
to see that Essence in which we discern
how God and human nature were made one.

What we hold here by faith, shall there be seen,   43
not demonstrated but directly known,
even as the first truth that man believes.

I answered: "With the most devotion I   46
can summon, I thank Him who has brought me
far from the mortal world. But now tell me:

what are the dark marks on this planet's body   49
that there below on earth, have made men tell
the tale of Cain?" She smiled somewhat, and then

she said: "If the opinion mortals hold   52
falls into error when the senses' key
cannot unlock the truth, you should not be

struck by the arrows of amazement once   55
you recognize that reason, even when
supported by the senses, has short wings.

But tell me what you think of it yourself."   58
And I: "What seems to us diverse up here
is caused—I think—by matter dense and rare."

And she: "You certainly will see that your   61
belief is deeply sunk in error if

you listen carefully as I rebut it.

The eighth sphere offers many lights to you, 64
and you can tell that they, in quality
and size, are stars with different visages.

If rarity and density alone 67
caused this, then all the stars would share one power
distributed in lesser, greater, or

in equal force. But different powers must 70
be fruits of different formal principles;
were you correct, one only would be left,

the rest, destroyed. And more, were rarity 73
the cause of the dim spots you question, then
in part this planet would lack matter through

and through, or else as, in a body, lean 76
and fat can alternate, so would this planet
alternate the pages in its volume.

To validate the first case, in the sun's 79
eclipse, the light would have to show through, just
as when it crosses matter that is slender.

This is not so; therefore we must consider 82
the latter case—if I annul that too,
then your opinion surely is confuted.

If rarity does not run through and through 85
the moon, then there must be a limit where
thickness does not allow the light to pass;

from there, the rays of sun would be thrown back, 88
just as, from glass that hides lead at its back,
a ray of colored light returns, reflected.

Now you will say that where a ray has been 91
reflected from a section farther back,
that ray will show itself to be more dim.

Yet an experiment, were you to try it, 94
could free you from your cavil—and the source
of your arts' course springs from experiment.

Taking three mirrors, place a pair of them 97
at equal distance from you; set the third

midway between those two, but farther back.

Then, turning toward them, at your back have placed   100
a light that kindles those three mirrors and
returns to you, reflected by them all.

Although the image in the farthest glass   103
will be of lesser size, there you will see
that it must match the brightness of the rest.

Now, just as the sub-matter of the snow,   106
beneath the blows of the warm rays, is stripped
of both its former color and its cold,

so is your mind left bare of error; I   109
would offer now to you a new form, light
so living that it trembles in your sight.

Within the heaven of the godly peace   112
revolves a body in whose power lies
the being of all things that it enfolds.

The sphere that follows, where so much is shown,   115
to varied essences bestows that being,
to stars distinct and yet contained in it.

The other spheres, in ways diverse, direct   118
the diverse powers they possess, so that
these forces can bear fruit, attain their aims.

So do these organs of the universe   121
proceed, as you now see, from stage to stage,
receiving from above and acting downward.

Now do attend to how I pass by way   124
of reason to the truth you want that—then—
you may learn how to cross the ford alone.

The force and motion of the holy spheres   127
must be inspired by the blessed movers,
just as the smith imparts the hammer's art;

and so, from the deep Mind that makes it wheel,   130
the sphere that many lights adorn receives
that stamp of which it then becomes the seal.

And as the soul within your dust is shared   133
by different organs, each most suited to

a different potency, so does that Mind
    unfold and multiply its bounty through   136
the varied heavens, though that Intellect
itself revolves upon its unity.

    With the dear body that it quickens and   139
with which, as life in you, it too is bound,
each different power forms a different compound.

    Because of the glad nature of its source,   142
the power mingled with a sphere shines forth,
as gladness, through the living pupil, shines.

    From this, and not from matter rare or dense,   145
derive the differences from light to light;
this is the forming principle, producing,

    conforming with its worth, the dark, the bright."   148

CANTO III

The First Heaven: the Sphere of the Moon. Dante's first vision of the blessed. Piccarda Donati. Her explanation of the souls' place in the sphere assigned to them by God. The Moon as site of those whose vows gave way before violence. The empress Constance. Disappearance of the souls.

That sun which first had warmed my breast with love
had now revealed to me, confuting, proving,
the gentle face of truth, its loveliness;
and I, in order to declare myself   4
corrected and convinced, lifted my head
as high as my confessional required.
But a new vision showed itself to me;   7
the grip in which it held me was so fast
that I did not remember to confess.
Just as, returning through transparent, clean   10
glass, or through waters calm and crystalline
(so shallow that they scarcely can reflect),
the mirrored image of our faces meets   13
our pupils with no greater force than that
a pearl has when displayed on a white forehead—
so faint, the many faces I saw keen   16
to speak; thus, my mistake was contrary
to that which led the man to love the fountain.
As soon as I had noticed them, thinking   19
that what I saw were merely mirrorings,
I turned around to see who they might be;
and I saw nothing; and I let my sight   22
turn back to meet the light of my dear guide,
who, as she smiled, glowed in her holy eyes.
"There is no need to wonder if I smile,"   25

she said, "because you reason like a child;
your steps do not yet rest upon the truth;

your mind misguides you into emptiness: 28
what you are seeing are true substances,
placed here because their vows were not fulfilled.

Thus, speak and listen; trust what they will say: 31
the truthful light in which they find their peace
will not allow their steps to turn astray."

Then I turned to the shade that seemed most anxious   34
to speak, and I began as would a man
bewildered by desire too intense:

"O spirit born to goodness, you who feel,   37
beneath the rays of the eternal life,
that sweetness which cannot be known unless

it is experienced, it would be gracious   40
of you to let me know your name and fate."
At this, unhesitant, with smiling eyes:

"Our charity will never lock its gates   43
against just will; our love is like the Love
that would have all Its court be like Itself.

Within the world I was a nun, a virgin;   46
and if your mind attends and recollects,
my greater beauty here will not conceal me,

and you will recognize me as Piccarda,   49
who, placed here with the other blessed ones,
am blessed within the slowest of the spheres.

Our sentiments, which only serve the flame   52
that is the pleasure of the Holy Ghost,
delight in their conforming to His order.

And we are to be found within a sphere   55
this low, because we have neglected vows,
so that in some respect we were deficient."

And I to her: "Within your wonderful   58
semblance there is something divine that glows,
transforming the appearance you once showed:

therefore, my recognizing you was slow;   61

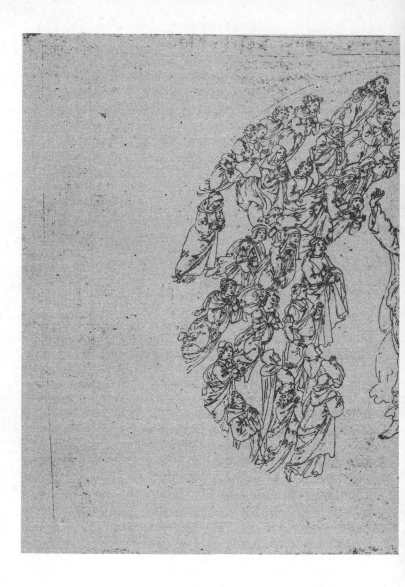

Dante observes a host of Blessed Spirits who remain with the Sphere of the Moon because they were, through no fault of their own, inconstant to their vows.

but what you now have told me is of help;
I can identify you much more clearly.

But tell me: though you're happy here, do you   64
desire a higher place in order to
see more and to be still more close to Him?"

Together with her fellow shades she smiled   67
at first; then she replied to me with such
gladness, like one who burns with love's first flame:

"Brother, the power of love appeases our   70
will so—we only long for what we have;
we do not thirst for greater blessedness.

Should we desire a higher sphere than ours,   73
then our desires would be discordant with
the will of Him who has assigned us here,

but you'll see no such discord in these spheres;   76
to live in love is—here—necessity,
if you think on love's nature carefully.

The essence of this blessed life consists   79
in keeping to the boundaries of God's will,
through which our wills become one single will;

so that, as we are ranged from step to step   82
throughout this kingdom, all this kingdom wills
that which will please the King whose will is rule.

And in His will there is our peace: that sea   85
to which all beings move—the beings He
creates or nature makes—such is His will."

Then it was clear to me how every place   88
in Heaven is in Paradise, though grace
does not rain equally from the High Good.

But just as, when our hunger has been sated   91
with one food, we still long to taste the other—
while thankful for the first, we crave the latter—

so was I in my words and in my gestures,   94
asking to learn from her what was the web
of which her shuttle had not reached the end.

"A perfect life," she said, "and her high merit   97

enheaven, up above, a woman whose
rule governs those who, in your world, would wear
      nun's dress and veil, so that, until their death,   100
they wake and sleep with that Spouse who accepts
all vows that love conforms unto His pleasure.

      Still young, I fled the world to follow her;   103
and, in her order's habit, I enclosed
myself and promised my life to her rule.

      Then men more used to malice than to good   106
took me—violently—from my sweet cloister:
God knows what, after that, my life became.

      This other radiance that shows itself   109
to you at my right hand, a brightness kindled
by all the light that fills our heaven—she

      has understood what I have said: she was   112
a sister, and from her head, too, by force,
the shadow of the sacred veil was taken.

      But though she had been turned back to the world   115
against her will, against all honest practice,
the veil upon her heart was never loosed.

      This is the splendor of the great Costanza,   118
who from the Swabians' second gust engendered
the one who was their third and final power."

      This said, she then began to sing "*Ave*   121
Maria" and, while singing, vanished as
a weighty thing will vanish in deep water.

      My sight, which followed her as long as it   124
was able to, once she was out of view,
returned to where its greater longing lay,

      and it was wholly bent on Beatrice;   127
but she then struck my eyes with so much brightness
that I, at first, could not withstand her force;

      and that made me delay my questioning.   130

CANTO IV

Still the First Heaven: the Sphere of the Moon. Dante's two questions. Beatrice's first answer: the true place of the souls in the Empyrean; how their appearance in lower spheres is suited to Dante's limited apprehension. Her second answer: violence and unfulfilled vows, absolute and relative will. Dante's further query. Beatrice's dazzling gaze.

Before a man bit into one of two
foods equally removed and tempting, he
would die of hunger if his choice were free;

so would a lamb stand motionless between   4
the cravings of two savage wolves, in fear
of both; so would a dog between two deer;

thus, I need neither blame nor praise myself   7
when both my doubts compelled me equally:
what kept me silent was necessity.

I did not speak, but in my face were seen   10
longing and questioning, more ardent than
if spoken words had made them evident.

Then Beatrice did just as Daniel did,   13
when he appeased Nebuchadnezzar's anger,
the rage that made the king unjustly fierce.

She said: "I see how both desires draw you,   16
so that your anxiousness to know is self-
entangled and cannot express itself.

You reason: 'If my will to good persists,   19
why should the violence of others cause
the measure of my merit to be less?'

And you are also led to doubt because   22
the doctrine Plato taught would find support
by souls' appearing to return to the stars.

These are the questions that, within your will,   25
press equally for answers; therefore, I
shall treat the most insidious question first.

Neither the Seraph closest unto God,   28
nor Moses, Samuel, nor either John—
whichever one you will—nor Mary has,

I say, their place in any other heaven   31
than that which houses those souls you just saw,
nor will their blessedness last any longer.

But all those souls grace the Empyrean;   34
and each of them has gentle life—though some
sense the Eternal Spirit more, some less.

They showed themselves to you here not because   37
this is their sphere, but as a sign for you
that in the Empyrean their place is lowest.

Such signs are suited to your mind, since from   40
the senses only can it apprehend
what then becomes fit for the intellect.

And this is why the Bible condescends   43
to human powers, assigning feet and hands
to God, but meaning something else instead.

And Gabriel and Michael and the angel   46
who healed the eyes of Tobit are portrayed
by Holy Church with human visages.

That which Timaeus said in reasoning   49
of souls does not describe what you have seen,
since it would seem that as he speaks he thinks.

He says the soul returns to that same star   52
from which—so he believes—it had been taken
when nature sent that soul as form to body;

but his opinion is, perhaps, to be   55
taken in other guise than his words speak,
intending something not to be derided.

If to these spheres he wanted to attribute   58
honor and blame for what they influence,
perhaps his arrow reaches something true.

Within the Sphere of the Moon, Beatrice explains to Dante how a soul can enjoy bliss even at the lowest level of Heaven.

This principle, ill-understood, misled   61
almost all of the world once, so that Jove
and Mercury and Mars gave names to stars.

The other doubt that agitates you is   64
less poisonous; for its insidiousness
is not such as to lead you far from me.

To mortal eyes our justice seems unjust;   67
that this is so, should serve as evidence
for faith—not heresy's depravity.

But that your intellect may penetrate   70
more carefully into your other query,
I shall—as you desire—explain it clearly.

If violence means that the one who suffers   73
has not abetted force in any way,
then there is no excuse these souls can claim:

for will, if it resists, is never spent,   76
but acts as nature acts when fire ascends,
though force—a thousand times—tries to compel.

So that, when will has yielded much or little,   79
it has abetted force—as these souls did:
they could have fled back to their holy shelter.

Had their will been as whole as that which held   82
tenacious Lawrence to the grate and made
unflinching Mucius punish his own hand,

then, once they had been freed, they'd have gone back   85
to find the path from which they had been dragged;
but seldom can the will be so intact.

And through these words, if you have grasped their bent,   88
you can eliminate the argument
that would have troubled you again—and often.

But now another obstacle obstructs   91
your sight; you cannot overcome it by
yourself—it is too wearying to try.

I've set it in your mind as something certain   94
that souls in blessedness can never lie,
since they are always near the Primal Truth.

But from Piccarda you were also able
to hear how Constance kept her love of the veil:
and here Piccarda seems to contradict me.

Before this—brother—it has often happened
that, to flee menace, men unwillingly
did what should not be done; so did Alcmaeon,

to meet the wishes of his father, kill
his mother—not to fail in filial
piety, he acted ruthlessly.

At that point—I would have you see—the force
to which one yields commingles with one's will;
and no excuse can pardon their joint act.

Absolute will does not concur in wrong;
but the contingent will, through fear that its
resistance might bring greater harm, consents.

Therefore, Piccarda means the absolute
will when she speaks, and I the relative;
so that the two of us have spoken truth."

Such was the rippling of the holy stream
issuing from the fountain from which springs
all truth: it set to rest both of my longings.

Then I said: "O beloved of the First
Lover, o you—divine—whose speech so floods
and warms me that I feel more and more life,

however deep my gratefulness, it can
not match your grace with grace enough; but He
who sees and can—may He grant recompense.

I now see well: we cannot satisfy
our mind unless it is enlightened by
the truth beyond whose boundary no truth lies.

Mind, reaching that truth, rests within it as
a beast within its lair; mind can attain
that truth—if not, all our desires were vain.

Therefore, our doubting blossoms like a shoot
out from the root of truth; this natural
urge spurs us toward the peak, from height to height.

Lady, my knowing why we doubt, invites,   133
sustains, my reverent asking you about
another truth that is obscure to me.

I want to know if, in your eyes, one can   136
amend for unkept vows with other acts—
good works your balance will not find too scant."

Then Beatrice looked at me with eyes so full   139
of sparks of love, eyes so divine that my
own force of sight was overcome, took flight,

and, eyes downcast, I almost lost my senses.   142

CANTO V

Still the First Heaven: the Sphere of the Moon. Beatrice on the cause of her own radiance, and then on the possibility of recompensing for unfulfilled vows. Ascent to the Second Heaven, the Sphere of Mercury. Encounter with the shades there. The nameless holy form whose discourse will constitute the next canto and reveal him to be Justinian.

"If in the fire of love I seem to flame
beyond the measure visible on earth,
so that I overcome your vision's force,

    you need not wonder; I am so because   4
of my perfected vision—as I grasp
the good, so I approach the good in act.

    Indeed I see that in your intellect   7
now shines the never-ending light; once seen,
that light, alone and always, kindles love;

    and if a lesser thing allure your love,   10
it is a vestige of that light which—though
imperfectly—gleams through that lesser thing.

    You wish to know if, through a righteous act,   13
one can repair a promise unfulfilled,
so that the soul and God are reconciled."

    So Beatrice began this canto, and   16
as one who does not interrupt her speech,
so did her holy reasoning proceed:

    "The greatest gift the magnanimity   19
of God, as He created, gave, the gift
most suited to His goodness, gift that He

    most prizes, was the freedom of the will;   22
those beings that have intellect—all these
and none but these—received and do receive

this gift: thus you may draw, as consequence,   25
the high worth of a vow, when what is pledged
with your consent encounters God's consent;

   for when a pact is drawn between a man   28
and God, then through free will, a man gives up
what I have called his treasure, his free will.

   What then, can be a fitting compensation?   31
To use again what you had offered, would
mean seeking to do good with ill-got gains.

   By now you understand the major point;   34
but since the Holy Church gives dispensations—
which seems in contrast with the truth I stated—

   you need to sit at table somewhat longer: 37
the food that you have taken was tough food—
it still needs help, if you are to digest it.

   Open your mind to what I shall disclose,   40
and hold it fast within you; he who hears,
but does not hold what he has heard, learns nothing.

   Two things are of the essence when one vows   43
a sacrifice: the matter of the pledge
and then the formal compact one accepts.

   This last can never be annulled until   46
the compact is fulfilled: it is of this
that I have spoken to you so precisely.

   Therefore, the Hebrews found it necessary   49
to bring their offerings, although—as you
must know—some of their offerings might be altered.

   As for the matter of the vow—discussed   52
above—it may be such that if one shifts
to other matter, one commits no sin.

   But let none shift the burden on his shoulder   55
through his own judgment, without waiting for
the turning of the white and yellow keys;

   and let him see that any change is senseless,   58
unless the thing one sets aside can be
contained in one's new weight, as four in six.

Thus, when the matter of a vow has so   61
much weight and worth that it tips every scale,
no other weight can serve as substitute.

Let mortals never take a vow in jest;   64
be faithful and yet circumspect, not rash
as Jephthah was, in offering his first gift;

he should have said, 'I did amiss,' and not   67
done worse by keeping faith. And you can find
that same stupidity in the Greeks' chief—

when her fair face made Iphigenia grieve   70
and made the wise and made the foolish weep
for her when they heard tell of such a rite.

Christians, proceed with greater gravity: 73
do not be like a feather at each wind,
nor think that all immersions wash you clean.

You have both Testaments, the Old and New,   76
you have the shepherd of the Church to guide you;
you need no more than this for your salvation.

If evil greed would summon you elsewhere,   79
be men, and not like sheep gone mad, so that
the Jew who lives among you not deride you!

Do not act like the foolish, wanton lamb   82
that leaves its mother's milk and, heedless, wants
to war against—and harm—its very self!"

These words of Beatrice I here transcribe;   85
and then she turned—her longing at the full—
to where the world is more alive with light.

Her silence and the change in her appearance   88
imposed a silence on my avid mind,
which now was ready to address new questions;

and even as an arrow that has struck   91
the mark before the bow-cord comes to rest,
so did we race to reach the second realm.

When she had passed into that heaven's light   94
I saw my lady filled with so much gladness
that, at her joy, the planet grew more bright.

Beatrice continues her exposition of divine wisdom as she and Dante ascend from the Sphere of the Moon to the Sphere of Mercury.

And if the planet changed and smiled, what then 97
did I—who by my very nature am
given to every sort of change—become?

As in a fish-pool that is calm and clear, 100
the fish draw close to anything that nears
from outside, if it seems to be their fare,

such were the far more than a thousand splendors 103
I saw approaching us, and each declared:
"Here now is one who will increase our loves."

And even as each shade approached, one saw, 106
because of the bright radiance it sent forth,
the joyousness with which that shade was filled.

Consider, reader, what your misery 109
and need to know still more would be if, at
this point, what I began did not go on;

and you will—unassisted—feel how I 112
longed so to hear those shades narrate their state
as soon as they appeared before my eyes.

"O you born unto gladness, whom God's grace 115
allows to see the thrones of the eternal
triumph before your war of life is ended,

the light that kindles us is that same light 118
which spreads through all of heaven; thus, if you
would know us, sate yourself as you may please."

So did one of those pious spirits speak 121
to me. And Beatrice then urged: "Speak, speak
confidently; trust them as you trust gods."

"I see—plainly—how you have nested in 124
your own light; see—you draw it from your eyes—
because it glistens even as you smile;

but I do not know who you are or why, 127
good soul, your rank is in a sphere concealed
from mortals by another planet's rays."

I said this as I stood turned toward the light 130
that first addressed me; and at this, it glowed
more radiantly than it had before.

Just as the sun, when heat has worn away   133
thick mists that moderate its rays, conceals
itself from sight through an excess of light,

so did that holy form, through excess gladness,   136
conceal himself from me within his rays;
and so concealed, concealed, he answered me

even as the next canto is to sing.   139

CANTO VI

*The Second Heaven: the Sphere of Mercury. Justinian's canto-
long discourse on the destiny and career of the Roman Eagle
and on the souls, in Mercury, of those whose acts were righteous
but motivated by the desire for honor and fame. His praise of
Romeo of Villeneuve.*

"After Constantine had turned the Eagle
counter to heaven's course, the course it took
behind the ancient one who wed Lavinia,

    one hundred and one hundred years and more,   4
the bird of God remained near Europe's borders,
close to the peaks from which it first emerged;

    beneath the shadow of the sacred wings,   7
it ruled the world, from hand to hand, until
that governing—changing—became my task.

    Caesar I was and am Justinian,   10
who, through the will of Primal Love I feel,
removed the vain and needless from the laws.

    Before I grew attentive to this labor,   13
I held that but one nature—and no more—
was Christ's—and in that faith, I was content;

    but then the blessed Agapetus, he   16
who was chief shepherd, with his words turned me
to that faith which has truth and purity.

    I did believe him, and now clearly see   19
his faith, as you with contradictories
can see that one is true and one is false.

    As soon as my steps shared the Church's path,   22
God, of His grace, inspired my high task
as pleased Him. I was fully drawn to that.

    Entrusting to my Belisarius   25

my arms, I found a sign for me to rest
from war: Heaven's right hand so favored him.

My answer to the question you first asked   28
ends here, and yet the nature of this answer
leads me to add a sequel, so that you

may see with how much reason they attack   31
the sacred standard—those who seem to act
on its behalf and those opposing it.

See what great virtue made that Eagle worthy   34
of reverence, beginning from that hour
when Pallas died that it might gain a kingdom.

You know that for three hundred years and more,   37
it lived in Alba, until, at the end,
three still fought three, contending for that standard.

You know how, under seven kings, it conquered   40
its neighbors—in the era reaching from
wronged Sabine women to Lucrece's grief—

and what it did when carried by courageous   43
Romans, who hurried to encounter Brennus,
Pyrrhus, and other principates and cities.

Through this, Torquatus, Quinctius (who is named   46
for his disheveled hair), the Decii,
and Fabii gained the fame I gladly honor.

That standard brought the pride of Arabs low   49
when they had followed Hannibal across
those Alpine rocks from which, Po, you descend.

Beneath that standard, Scipio, Pompey—   52
though young—triumphed; and to that hill beneath
which you were born, that standard seemed most harsh.

Then, near the time when Heaven wished to bring   55
all of the world to Heaven's way—serene—
Caesar, as Rome had willed, took up that standard.

And what it did from Var to Rhine was seen   58
by the Isère, Saône, and Seine and all
the valley-floors whose rivers feed the Rhone.

And what it did, once it had left Ravenna   61

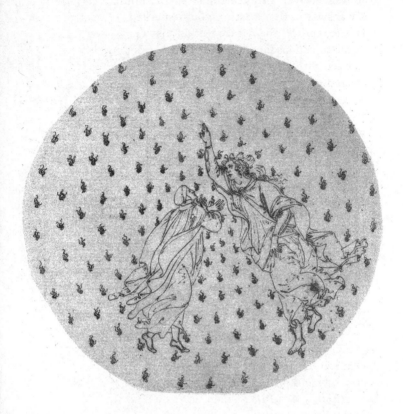

In the Second Sphere of Heaven (Mercury), Dante and Beatrice encounter the souls of those who sought legitimate honour.

and leaped the Rubicon, was such a flight
as neither tongue nor writing can describe.

That standard led the legions on to Spain,   64
then toward Durazzo, and it struck Pharsalia
so hard that the warm Nile could feel that hurt.

It saw again its source, Antandros and   67
Simois, and the place where Hector lies;
then roused itself—the worse for Ptolemy.

From Egypt, lightning-like, it fell on Juba;   70
and then it hurried to the west of you,
where it could hear the trumpet of Pompey.

Because of what that standard did, with him   73
who bore it next, Brutus and Cassius howl
in Hell, and grief seized Modena, Perugia.

Because of it, sad Cleopatra weeps   76
still; as she fled that standard, from the asp
she drew a sudden and atrocious death.

And with that very bearer, it then reached   79
the Red Sea shore: with him, that emblem brought
the world such peace that Janus' shrine was shut.

But what the standard that has made me speak   82
had done before or then was yet to do
throughout the mortal realm where it holds rule,

comes to seem faint and insignificant   85
if one, with clear sight and pure sentiment,
sees what it did in the third Caesar's hand;

for the true Justice that inspires me   88
granted to it—in that next Caesar's hand—
the glory of avenging His own wrath.

Now marvel here at what I show to you: 91
with Titus—afterward—it hurried toward
avenging vengeance for the ancient sin.

And when the Lombard tooth bit Holy Church,   94
then Charlemagne, under the Eagle's wings,
through victories he gained, brought help to her.

Now you can judge those I condemned above,   97

and judge how such men have offended, have
become the origin of all your evils.

For some oppose the universal emblem   100
with yellow lilies; others claim that emblem
for party: it is hard to see who is worse.

Let Ghibellines pursue their undertakings   103
beneath another sign, for those who sever
this sign and justice are bad followers.

And let not this new Charles strike at it with   106
his Guelphs—but let him fear the claws that stripped
a more courageous lion of its hide.

The sons have often wept for a father's fault;   109
and let this son not think that God will change
the emblem of His force for Charles's lilies.

This little planet is adorned with spirits   112
whose acts were righteous, but who acted for
the honor and the fame that they would gain:

and when desires tend toward earthly ends,   115
then, so deflected, rays of the true love
mount toward the life above with lesser force.

But part of our delight is measuring   118
rewards against our merit, and we see
that our rewards are neither less nor more.

Thus does the Living Justice make so sweet   121
the sentiments in us, that we are free
of any turning toward iniquity.

Differing voices join to sound sweet music;   124
so do the different orders in our life
render sweet harmony among these spheres.

And in this very pearl there also shines   127
the light of Romeo, of one whose acts,
though great and noble, met ungratefulness.

And yet those Provençals who schemed against him 130
had little chance to laugh, for he who finds
harm to himself in others' righteous acts

takes the wrong path. Of Raymond Berenger's   133

four daughters, each became a queen—and this,
poor and a stranger, Romeo accomplished.

Then Berenger was moved by vicious tongues 136
to ask this just man for accounting—one
who, given ten, gave Raymond five and seven.

And Romeo, the poor, the old, departed; 139
and were the world to know the heart he had
while begging, crust by crust, for his life-bread,

it—though it praise him now—would praise him more."

CANTO VII

Still the Second Heaven: the Sphere of Mercury. Disappearance of Justinian and his fellow spirits in the wake of hymning and dancing. Beatrice's explanations of Justinian's references to Christ's death as God's just vengeance and the destruction of Jerusalem as vengeance for just vengeance; human corruptibility; the mysteries of Salvation and Resurrection.

"Hosanna, sanctus Deus sabaòth,
superillustrans claritate tua
felices ignes horum malacòth! "

    Thus, even as he wheeled to his own music,   4
I saw that substance sing, that spirit-flame
above whom double lights were twinned; and he

    and his companions moved within their dance,   7
and as if they were swiftest sparks, they sped
out of my sight because of sudden distance.

    I was perplexed, and to myself, I said: 10
"Tell her! Tell her! Tell her, the lady who
can slake my thirst with her sweet drops"; and yet

    the reverence that possesses all of me,   13
even on hearing only *Be* and *ice*,
had bowed my head—I seemed a man asleep.

    But Beatrice soon ended that; for she   16
began to smile at me so brightly that,
even in fire, a man would still feel glad.

    "According to my never-erring judgment,   19
the question that perplexes you is how
just vengeance can deserve just punishment;

    but I shall quickly free your mind from doubt;   22
and listen carefully; the words I speak
will bring the gift of a great truth in reach.

Since he could not endure the helpful curb   25
on his willpower, the man who was not born,
damning himself, damned all his progeny.

For this, mankind lay sick, in the abyss   28
of a great error, for long centuries,
until the Word of God willed to descend

to where the nature that was sundered from   31
its Maker was united to His person
by the sole act of His eternal Love.

Now set your sight on what derives from that.   34
This nature, thus united to its Maker,
was good and pure, even as when created;

but in itself, this nature had been banished   37
from paradise, because it turned aside
from its own path, from truth, from its own life.

Thus, if the penalty the Cross inflicted   40
is measured by the nature He assumed,
no one has ever been so justly stung;

yet none was ever done so great a wrong,   43
if we regard the Person made to suffer,
He who had gathered in Himself that nature.

Thus, from one action, issued differing things: 46
God and the Jews were pleased by one same death;
earth trembled for that death and Heaven opened.

You need no longer find it difficult   49
to understand when it is said that just
vengeance was then avenged by a just court.

But I now see your understanding tangled   52
by thought on thought into a knot, from which,
with much desire, your mind awaits release.

You say: 'What I have heard is clear to me;   55
but this is hidden from me—why God willed
precisely this pathway for our redemption.'

Brother, this ordinance is buried from   58
the eyes of everyone whose intellect
has not matured within the flame of love.

Nevertheless since there is much attempting 61
to find this point, but little understanding,
I shall tell why that way was the most fitting.

The Godly Goodness that has banished every 64
envy from Its own Self, burns in Itself;
and sparkling so, It shows eternal beauties.

All that derives directly from this Goodness 67
is everlasting, since the seal of Goodness
impresses an imprint that never alters.

Whatever rains from It immediately 70
is fully free, for it is not constrained
by any influence of other things.

Even as it conforms to that Goodness, 73
so does it please It more; the Sacred Ardor
that gleams in all things is most bright within

those things most like Itself. The human being 76
has all these gifts, but if it loses one,
then its nobility has been undone.

Only man's sin annuls man's liberty, 79
makes him unlike the Highest Good, so that,
in him, the brightness of Its light is dimmed;

and man cannot regain his dignity 82
unless, where sin left emptiness, man fills
that void with just amends for evil pleasure.

For when your nature sinned so totally 85
within its seed, then, from these dignities,
just as from Paradise, that nature parted;

and they could never be regained—if you 88
consider carefully—by any way
that did not pass across one of these fords:

either through nothing other than His mercy, 91
God had to pardon man, or of himself
man had to proffer payment for his folly.

Now fix your eyes on the profundity 94
of the Eternal Counsel; heed as closely
as you are able to, my reasoning.

The Spirits of Mercury appear as concentric circles of flame as Beatrice explains to Dante the meaning of the Incarnation and Crucifixion.

Man, in his limits, could not recompense;   97
for no obedience, no humility,
he offered later could have been so deep

that it could match the heights he meant to reach   100
through disobedience; man lacked the power
to offer satisfaction by himself.

Thus there was need for God, through His own ways, 103
to bring man back to life intact—I mean
by one way or by both. But since a deed

pleases its doer more, the more it shows   106
the goodness of the heart from which it springs,
the Godly Goodness that imprints the world

was happy to proceed through both Its ways   109
to raise you up again. Nor has there been,
nor will there be, between the final night

and the first day, a chain of actions so   112
lofty and so magnificent as He
enacted when He followed His two ways;

for God showed greater generosity   115
in giving His own self that man might be
able to rise, than if He simply pardoned;

for every other means fell short of justice,   118
except the way whereby the Son of God
humbled Himself when He became incarnate.

Now to give all your wishes full content,   121
I go back to explain one point, so that
you, too, may see it plainly, as I do.

You say: 'I see that water, see that fire   124
and air and earth and all that they compose
come to corruption, and endure so briefly;

and yet these, too, were things created; if   127
what has been said above is true, then these
things never should be subject to corruption.'

Brother, the angels and the pure country   130
where you are now—these may be said to be
created, as they are, in all their being;

whereas the elements that you have mentioned, 133
as well as those things that are made from them,
receive their form from a created power.

The matter they contain had been created, 136
just as within the stars that wheel about them,
the power to give form had been created.

The rays and motion of the holy lights 139
draw forth the soul of every animal
and plant from matter able to take form;

but your life is breathed forth immediately 142
by the Chief Good, who so enamors it
of His own Self that it desires Him always.

So reasoning, you also can deduce 145
your resurrection; you need but remember
the way in which your human flesh was fashioned
when both of the first parents were created." 148

CANTO VIII

Origin of the planet Venus's name. Ascent to the Third
Heaven, the Sphere of Venus. Charles Martel. His discourse
on fathers and sons and the vicissitudes of heredity, and then on
the need to respect men's natural dispositions.

    The world, when still in peril, thought that Cyprus'
fair goddess sent down rays of Frenzied love
as she wheeled round in the third epicycle.

    So that, in ancient error, ancient peoples   4
not only honored her with sacrifices
and votive cries, but honored, too, Diöne

    and Cupid, one as mother, one as son   7
of Venus; and they told how Cupid sat
in Dido's lap; and gave the name of her

    with whom I have begun this canto, to   10
the planet that is courted by the sun,
at times behind her and at times in front.

    I did not notice my ascent to it,   13
yet I was sure I was in Venus when
I saw my lady grow more beautiful.

    And just as, in a flame, a spark is seen,   16
and as, in plainsong, voice in voice is heard—
one holds the note, the other comes and goes—

    I saw in that light other wheeling lamps,   19
some more and some less swift, yet in accord,
I think, with what their inner vision was.

    Winds, seen or unseen, never have descended   22
so swiftly from cold clouds as not to seem
impeded, slow, to any who had seen

    those godly lights approaching us, halting   25
the circling dance those spirits had begun

within the heaven of high Seraphim;

   and a "*Hosanna*" sounded from within 28
their front ranks—such that I have never been
without desire to hear it sound again.

   Then one drew nearer us, and he began 31
alone: "We all are ready at your pleasure,
so that you may receive delight from us.

   One circle and one circling and one thirst 34
are ours as we revolve with the celestial
Princes whom, from the world, you once invoked:

   '*You who, through understanding, move the third* 37
heaven.' Our love is so complete—to bring
you joy, brief respite will not be less sweet."

   After my eyes had turned with reverence 40
to see my lady, after her consent
had brought them reassurance and content,

   they turned back to the light that promised me 43
so much; and, "Tell me, who are you," I asked
in a voice stamped with loving sentiment.

   And how much larger, brighter did I see 46
that spirit grow when, as I spoke, it felt
new gladness added to its gladnesses!

   Thus changed, it then replied: "The world held me 49
briefly below; but had my stay been longer,
much evil that will be, would not have been.

   My happiness, surrounding me with rays, 52
keeps me concealed from you; it hides me like
a creature that is swathed in its own silk.

   You loved me much and had good cause for that; 55
for had I stayed below, I should have showed
you more of my love than the leaves alone.

   The left bank that the Rhone bathes after it 58
has mingled with the waters of the Sorgue,
awaited me in due time as its lord,

   as did Ausonia's horn, which—south of where 61
the Tronto and the Verde reach the sea—

Catona, Bari, and Gaeta border.

Upon my brow a crown already shone— 64
the crown of that land where the Danube flows
when it has left behind its German shores.

And fair Trinacria, whom ashes (these 67
result from surging sulphur, not Typhoeus)
cover between Pachynus and Pelorus,

along the gulf that Eurus vexes most, 70
would still await its rulers born—through me—
from Charles and Rudolph, if ill sovereignty,

which always hurts the heart of subject peoples, 73
had not provoked Palermo to cry out:
'Die! Die!' And if my brother could foresee

what ill-rule brings, he would already flee 76
from Catalonia's grasping poverty,
aware that it may cause him injury;

for truly there is need for either him 79
or others to prevent his loaded boat
from having to take on still greater loads.

His niggard nature is descended from 82
one who was generous; and he needs soldiers
who are not bent on filling up their coffers."

"My lord, since I believe that you perceive 85
completely—where all good begins and ends—
the joy I see within myself on hearing

your words to me, my joy is felt more freely; 88
and I joy, too, in knowing you are blessed,
since you perceived this as you gazed at God.

You made me glad; so may you clear the doubt 91
that rose in me when you—before—described
how from a gentle seed, harsh fruit derives."

These were my words to him, and he replied: 94
"If I can show one certain truth to you,
you will confront what now is at your back.

The Good that moves and makes content the realm 97
through which you now ascend, makes providence

act as a force in these great heavens' bodies;

and in the Mind that, in itself, is perfect,   100
not only are the natures of His creatures
but their well-being, too, provided for;

and thus, whatever this bow shoots must fall   103
according to a providential end,
just like a shaft directed to its target.

Were this not so, the heavens you traverse   106
would bring about effects in such a way
that they would not be things of art but shards.

That cannot be unless the Minds that move   109
these planets are defective, and defective
the First Mind, which had failed to make them perfect.

Would you have this truth still more clear to you?"   112
I: "No. I see it is impossible
for nature to fall short of what is needed."

He added: "Tell me, would a man on earth   115
be worse if he were not a citizen?"
"Yes," I replied, " and here I need no proof."

"Can there be citizens if men below   118
are not diverse, with diverse duties? No,
if what your master writes is accurate."

Until this point that shade went on, deducing;   121
then he concluded: "Thus, the roots from which
your tasks proceed must needs be different:

so, one is born a Solon, one a Xerxes,   124
and one a Melchizedek, and another,
he who flew through the air and lost his son.

Revolving nature, serving as a seal   127
for mortal wax, plies well its art, but it
does not distinguish one house from another.

Thus, even from the seed, Esau takes leave   130
of Jacob; and because he had a father
so base, they said Quirinus was Mars' son.

Engendered natures would forever take   133
the path of those who had engendered them,

did not Divine provision intervene.

Now that which stood behind you, stands in front: 136
but so that you may know the joy you give me,
I now would cloak you with a corollary.

Where Nature comes upon discrepant fortune,   139
like any seed outside its proper region,
Nature will always yield results awry.

But if the world below would set its mind   142
on the foundation Nature lays as base
to follow, it would have its people worthy.

But you twist to religion one whose birth   145
made him more fit to gird a sword, and make
a king of one more fit for sermoning,

so that the track you take is off the road."   148

CANTO IX

*The Third Heaven: the Sphere of Venus. The prophecy of
Charles Martel. Cunizza da Romano and her prophecy.
Folco of Marseille, who points out Rahab, and then denounces
contemporary ecclesiastics and prophesies the regeneration of
the Church.*

Fair Clemence, after I had been enlightened
by your dear Charles, he told me how his seed
would be defrauded, but he said: "Be silent

and let the years revolve." All I can say   4
is this: lament for vengeance well-deserved
will follow on the wrongs you are to suffer.

And now the life-soul of that holy light   7
turned to the Sun that fills it even as
the Goodness that suffices for all things.

Ah, souls seduced and creatures without reverence,   10
who twist your hearts away from such a Good,
who let your brows be bent on emptiness!

And here another of those splendors moved   13
toward me; and by its brightening without,
it showed its wish to please me. Beatrice,

whose eyes were fixed on me, as they had been   16
before, gave me the precious certainty
that she consented to my need to speak.

"Pray, blessed spirit, may you remedy—   19
quickly—my wish to know," I said. "Give me
proof that you can reflect the thoughts I think."

At which that light, one still unknown to me,   22
out of the depth from which it sang before,
continued as if it rejoiced in kindness:

"In that part of indecent Italy   25

that lies between Rialto and the springs
from which the Brenta and the Piave stream,

    rises a hill—of no great height—from which   28
a firebrand descended, and it brought
much injury to all the land about.

    Both he and I were born of one same root: 31
Cunizza was my name, and I shine here
because this planet's radiance conquered me.

    But in myself I pardon happily   34
the reason for my fate; I do not grieve—
and vulgar minds may find this hard to see.

    Of the resplendent, precious jewel that stands   37
most close to me within our heaven, much
fame still remains and will not die away

    before this hundredth year returns five times: 40
see that if man should not seek excellence—
that his first life bequeath another life.

    And this, the rabble that is now enclosed   43
between the Adige and Tagliamento
does not consider, nor does it repent

    despite its scourgings; and since it would shun   46
its duty, at the marsh the Paduans
will stain the river-course that bathes Vicenza;

    and where the Sile and Cagnano flow   49
in company, one lords it, arrogant;
the net to catch him is already set.

    Feltre shall yet lament the treachery   52
of her indecent shepherd—act so filthy
that for the like none ever entered prison.

    The vat to hold the flood of the Ferrarese   55
would be too large indeed, and weary he
who weighs it ounce by ounce—the vat that he,

    generous priest, will offer up to show   58
fidelity to his Guelph party; and
such gifts will suit the customs of that land.

    Above are mirrors—Thrones is what you call them—   61

and from them God in judgment shines on us;
and thus we think it right to say such things."

Here she was silent and appeared to me   64
to turn toward other things, reentering
the wheeling dance where she had been before.

The other joy, already known to me   67
as precious, then appeared before my eyes
like a pure ruby struck by the sun's rays.

On high, joy is made manifest by brightness,   70
as, here on earth, by smiles; but down below,
the shade grows darker when the mind feels sorrow.

"God can see all," I said, "and, blessed spirit, 73
your vision is contained in Him, so that
no wish can ever hide itself from you.

Your voice has always made the heavens glad,   76
as has the singing of the pious fires
that make themselves a cowl of their six wings:

why then do you not satisfy my longings?   79
I would not have to wait for your request
if I could enter you as you do me."

"The widest valley into which the waters   82
spread from the sea that girds the world," his words
began, "between discrepant shores, extends

eastward so far against the sun, that when   85
those waters end at the meridian,
that point—when they began—was the horizon.

I lived along the shoreline of that valley   88
between the Ebro and the Magra, whose
brief course divides the Genoese and Tuscans.

Beneath the same sunset, the same sunrise,   91
lie both Bougie and my own city, which
once warmed its harbor with its very blood.

Those men to whom my name was known, called me   94
Folco; and even as this sphere receives
my imprint, so was I impressed with its;

for even Belus' daughter, wronging both   97

Sychaeus and Creusa, did not burn
more than I did, as long as I was young;

   nor did the Rhodopean woman whom   100
Demophoön deceived, nor did Alcides
when he enclosed Iole in his heart.

   Yet one does not repent here; here one smiles—   103
not for the fault, which we do not recall,
but for the Power that fashioned and foresaw.

   For here we contemplate the art adorned   106
by such great love, and we discern the good
through which the world above forms that below.

   But so that all your longings born within   109
this sphere may be completely satisfied
when you bear them away, I must continue.

   You wish to know what spirit is within   112
the light that here beside me sparkles so,
as would a ray of sun in limpid water.

   Know then that Rahab lives serenely in   115
that light, and since her presence joins our order,
she seals that order in the highest rank.

   This heaven, where the shadow cast by earth   118
comes to a point, had Rahab as the first
soul to be taken up when Christ triumphed.

   And it was right to leave her in this heaven   121
as trophy of the lofty victory
that Christ won, palm on palm, upon the cross,

   for she had favored the initial glory   124
of Joshua within the Holy Land—
which seldom touches the Pope's memory.

   Your city, which was planted by that one   127
who was the first to turn against his Maker,
the one whose envy cost us many tears—

   produces and distributes the damned flower   130
that turns both sheep and lambs from the true course,
for of the shepherd it has made a wolf.

   For this the Gospel and the great Church Fathers   133

are set aside and only the Decretals
are studied—as their margins clearly show.

On these the pope and cardinals are intent.   136
Their thoughts are never bent on Nazareth,
where Gabriel's open wings were reverent.

And yet the hill of Vatican as well   139
as other noble parts of Rome that were
the cemetery for Peter's soldiery

will soon be freed from priests' adultery."   142

CANTO X

Divine wisdom and the harmony of Creation. Ascent to the
Fourth Heaven, the Sphere of the Sun. Thanksgiving to God.
St. Thomas and the other eleven spirits, who form a crown
around Beatrice and Dante.

    Gazing upon His Son with that Love which
One and the Other breathe eternally,
the Power—first and inexpressible—
    made everything that wheels through mind and space   4
so orderly that one who contemplates
that harmony cannot but taste of Him.
    Then, reader, lift your eyes with me to see   7
the high wheels; gaze directly at that part
where the one motion strikes against the other;
    and there begin to look with longing at   10
that Master's art, which in Himself he loves
so much that his eye never parts from it.
    See there the circle branching from that cross-point   13
obliquely: zodiac to bear the planets
that satisfy the world in need of them.
    For if the planets' path were not aslant,   16
much of the heavens' virtue would be wasted
and almost every power on earth be dead;
    and if the zodiac swerved more or less   19
far from the straight course, then earth's harmony
would be defective in both hemispheres.
    Now, reader, do not leave your bench, but stay   22
to think on that of which you have foretaste;
you will have much delight before you tire.
    I have prepared your fare; now feed yourself,   25
because that matter of which I am made

the scribe calls all my care unto itself.

The greatest minister of nature—he 28
who imprints earth with heaven's worth and, with
his light, provides the measurement for time—

since he was in conjunction with the part 31
I noted, now was wheeling through the spirals
where he appears more early every day.

And I was with him, but no more aware 34
of the ascent than one can be aware
of any sudden thought before it starts.

The one who guides me so from good to better 37
is Beatrice, and on our path her acts
have so much swiftness that they span no time.

How bright within themselves must be the lights 40
I saw on entering the Sun, for they
were known to me by splendor, not by color!

Though I should call on talent, craft, and practice, 43
my telling cannot help them be imagined;
but you can trust—and may you long to see it.

And if our fantasies fall short before 46
such heights, there is no need to wonder; for
no eye has seen light brighter than the Sun's.

Such was the sphere of His fourth family, 49
whom the High Father always satisfies,
showing how He engenders and breathes forth.

And Beatrice began: "Give thanks, give thanks 52
to Him, the angels' Sun, who, through His grace,
has lifted you to this embodied sun."

No mortal heart was ever so disposed 55
to worship, or so quick to yield itself
to God with all its gratefulness, as I

was when I heard those words, and all my love 58
was so intent on Him that Beatrice
was then eclipsed within forgetfulness.

But not displeased by this, she smiled, and my 61
rapt mind was split: I watched the sun—and I

Beatrice and Dante ascend to the Sphere of the Sun.

watched, too, the splendor of her smiling eyes.

And I saw many lights, alive, most bright;   64
we formed the center, they became a crown,
their voices even sweeter than their splendor:

just so, at times, we see Latona's daughter   67
circled when saturated air holds fast
the thread that forms the girdle of her halo.

In Heaven's court, from which I have returned,   70
one finds so many fair and precious gems
that are not to be taken from that kingdom:

one of those gems, the song those splendors sang.   73
He who does not take wings to reach that realm,
may wait for tidings of it from the mute.

After those ardent suns, while singing so,   76
had wheeled three times around us, even as
stars that are close to the fixed poles, they seemed

to me like women who, though not released   79
from dancing, pause in silence, listening
until new notes invite to new dancing.

And from within one light I heard begin: 82
"Because the ray of grace, from which true love
is kindled first and then, in loving, grows,

shines with such splendor, multiplied, in you,   85
that it has led you up the stair that none
descends who will not climb that stair again,

whoever would refuse to quench your thirst   88
with wine from his flask, would be no more free
than water that does not flow toward the sea.

You want to know what plants bloom in this garland   91
that, circling, contemplates with love the fair
lady who strengthens your ascent to heaven.

I was a lamb among the holy flock   94
that Dominic leads on the path where one
may fatten well if one does not stray off.

He who is nearest on my right was both   97
my brother and my teacher: from Cologne,

Albert, and I am Thomas of Aquino.

If you would know who all the others are,   100
then even as I speak let your eyes follow,
making their way around the holy wreath.

That next flame issues from the smile of Gratian,   103
who served one and the other court of law
so well that his work pleases Paradise.

That other, who adorns our choir next—   106
he was that Peter who, like the poor widow,
offered his treasure to the Holy Church.

The fifth light, and the fairest light among us,   109
breathes forth such love that all the world below
hungers for tidings of it; in that flame

there is the lofty mind where such profound   112
wisdom was placed that, if the truth be true,
no other ever rose with so much vision.

Next you can see the radiance of that candle   115
which, in the flesh, below, beheld most deeply
the angels' nature and their ministry.

Within the other little light there smiles   118
that champion of the Christian centuries
whose narrative was used by Augustine.

Now, if your mind's eye, following my praising,   121
was drawn from light to light, you must already
be thirsting for the eighth: within that light,

because he saw the Greatest Good, rejoices   124
the blessed soul who makes the world's deceit
most plain to all who hear him carefully.

The flesh from which his soul was banished lies   127
below, within Cieldauro, and he came
from martyrdom and exile to this peace.

Beyond, you see, flaming, the ardent spirits   130
of Isidore and Bede and Richard—he
whose meditation made him more than man.

This light from whom your gaze returns to me   133
contains a spirit whose oppressive thoughts

made him see death as coming much too slowly:

    it is the everlasting light of Siger,   136
who when he lectured in the Street of Straw,
demonstrated truths that earned him envy."

    Then, like a clock that calls us at the hour   139
in which the Bride of God, on waking, sings
matins to her Bridegroom, encouraging

    His love (when each clock-part both drives and draws), 142
chiming the sounds with notes so sweet that those
with spirit well-disposed feel their love grow;

    so did I see the wheel that moved in glory   145
go round and render voice to voice with such
sweetness and such accord that they can not

    be known except where joy is everlasting.   148

CANTO XI

The Fourth Heaven: the Sphere of the Sun. The senseless cares of mortals. The long clarification by St. Thomas of his comment on his own order, the Dominicans. His telling of the life of St. Francis, who wed Poverty and founded the Franciscans.

O senseless cares of mortals, how deceiving
are syllogistic reasonings that bring
your wings to flight so low, to earthly things!

One studied law and one the *Aphorisms*   4
of the physicians; one was set on priesthood
and one, through force or fraud, on rulership;

one meant to plunder, one to politick;   7
one labored, tangled in delights of flesh,
and one was fully bent on indolence;

while I, delivered from our servitude   10
to all these things, was in the height of heaven
with Beatrice, so gloriously welcomed.

After each of those spirits had returned   13
to that place in the ring where it had been,
it halted, like a candle in its stand.

And from within the splendor that had spoken   16
to me before, I heard him, as he smiled—
become more radiant, more pure—begin:

"Even as I grow bright within Its rays,   19
so, as I gaze at the Eternal Light,
I can perceive your thoughts and see their cause.

You are in doubt; you want an explanation   22
in language that is open and expanded,
so clear that it contents your understanding

of two points: where I said, 'They fatten well,'   25
and where I said, 'No other ever rose'—

and here one has to make a clear distinction.

The Providence that rules the world with wisdom 28
so fathomless that creatures' intellects
are vanquished and can never probe its depth,

so that the Bride of Him who, with loud cries, 31
had wed her with His blessed blood, might meet
her Love with more fidelity and more

assurance in herself, on her behalf 34
commanded that there be two princes, one
on this side, one on that side, as her guides.

One prince was all seraphic in his ardor; 37
the other, for his wisdom, had possessed
the splendor of cherubic light on earth.

I shall devote my tale to one, because 40
in praising either prince one praises both:
the labors of the two were toward one goal.

Between Topino's stream and that which flows 43
down from the hill the blessed Ubaldo chose,
from a high peak there hangs a fertile slope;

from there Perugia feels both heat and cold 46
at Porta Sole, while behind it sorrow
Nocera and Gualdo under their hard yoke.

From this hillside, where it abates its rise, 49
a sun was born into the world, much like
this sun when it is climbing from the Ganges.

Therefore let him who names this site not say 52
Ascesi, which would be to say too little,
but *Orient*, if he would name it rightly.

That sun was not yet very distant from 55
his rising, when he caused the earth to take
some comfort from his mighty influence;

for even as a youth, he ran to war 58
against his father, on behalf of her—
the lady unto whom, just as to death,

none willingly unlocks the door; before 61
his spiritual court *et coram patre,*

he wed her; day by day he loved her more.

She was bereft of her first husband; scorned,   64
obscure, for some eleven hundred years,
until that sun came, she had had no suitor.

Nor did it help her when men heard that he   67
who made earth tremble found her unafraid—
serene, with Amyclas—when he addressed her;

nor did her constancy and courage help   70
when she, even when Mary stayed below,
suffered with Christ upon the cross. But so

that I not tell my tale too darkly, you   73
may now take Francis and take Poverty
to be the lovers meant in my recounting.

Their harmony and their glad looks, their love   76
and wonder and their gentle contemplation,
served others as a source of holy thoughts;

so much so, that the venerable Bernard   79
went barefoot first; he hurried toward such peace;
and though he ran, he thought his pace too slow.

O wealth unknown! O good that is so fruitful!   82
Egidius goes barefoot, and Sylvester,
behind the groom—the bride delights them so.

Then Francis—father, master—goes his way   85
with both his lady and his family,
the lowly cord already round their waists.

Nor did he lower his eyes in shame because   88
he was the son of Pietro Bernardone,
nor for the scorn and wonder he aroused;

but like a sovereign, he disclosed in full—   91
to Innocent—the sternness of his rule;
from him he had the first seal of his order.

And after many of the poor had followed   94
Francis, whose wondrous life were better sung
by glory's choir in the Empyrean,

the sacred purpose of this chief of shepherds   97
was then encircled with a second crown

by the Eternal Spirit through Honorius.

And after, in his thirst for martyrdom,   100
within the presence of the haughty Sultan,
he preached of Christ and those who followed Him.

But, finding bearers who were too unripe   103
to be converted, he—not wasting time—
returned to harvest the Italian fields;

there, on the naked crag between the Arno   106
and Tiber, he received the final seal
from Christ; and this, his limbs bore for two years.

When He who destined Francis to such goodness   109
was pleased to draw him up to the reward
that he had won through his humility,

then to his brothers, as to rightful heirs,   112
Francis commended his most precious lady,
and he bade them to love her faithfully;

and when, returning to its kingdom, his   115
bright soul wanted to set forth from her bosom,
it, for its body, asked no other bier.

Consider now that man who was a colleague   118
worthy of Francis; with him, in high seas,
he kept the bark of Peter on true course.

Such was our patriarch; thus you can see   121
that those who follow him as he commands,
as cargo carry worthy merchandise.

But now his flock is grown so greedy for   124
new nourishment that it must wander far,
in search of strange and distant grazing lands;

and as his sheep, remote and vagabond,   127
stray farther from his side, at their return
into the fold, their lack of milk is greater.

Though there are some indeed who, fearing harm,   130
stay near the shepherd, they are few in number—
to cowl them would require little cloth.

Now if my words are not too dim and distant,   133
if you have listened carefully to them,

if you can call to mind what has been said,
  then part of what you wish to know is answered,   136
for you will see the splinters on the plant
and see what my correction meant: 'Where one
  may fatten well, *if one does not stray off.*'"   139

CANTO XII

Still the Fourth Heaven: the Sphere of the Sun. The secondary crown of twelve spirits. St. Bonaventure, a Franciscan. His praise of St. Dominic. The life of St. Dominic. Denunciation of degenerate Franciscans. St. Bonaventure's presentation of the other eleven spirits in his ring.

No sooner had the blessed flame begun
to speak its final word than the millstone
of holy lights began to turn, but it

was not yet done with one full revolution   4
before another ring surrounded it,
and motion matched with motion, song with song—

a song that, sung by those sweet instruments,   7
surpasses so our Muses and our Sirens
as firstlight does the light that is reflected.

Just as, concentric, like in color, two   10
rainbows will curve their way through a thin cloud
when Juno has commanded her handmaid,

the outer rainbow echoing the inner,   13
much like the voice of one—the wandering nymph—
whom love consumed as sun consumes the mist

(and those two bows let people here foretell,   16
by reason of the pact God made with Noah,
that flood will never strike the world again):

so the two garlands of those everlasting   19
roses circled around us, and so did
the outer circle mime the inner ring.

When dance and jubilation, festival   22
of song and flame that answered flame, of light
with light, of gladness and benevolence,

in one same instant, with one will, fell still   25

(just as the eyes, when moved by their desire,
can only close and open in accord),

then from the heart of one of the new lights   28
there came a voice, and as I turned toward it,
I seemed a needle turning to the polestar;

and it began: "The love that makes me fair   31
draws me to speak about the other leader
because of whom my own was so praised here.

Where one is, it is right to introduce   34
the other: side by side, they fought, so may
they share in glory and together gleam.

Christ's army, whose rearming cost so dearly,   37
was slow, uncertain of itself, and scanty
behind its ensign, when the Emperor

who rules forever helped his ranks in danger—   40
only out of His grace and not their merits.
And, as was said, He then sustained His bride,

providing her with two who could revive   43
a straggling people: champions who would
by doing and by preaching bring new life.

In that part of the West where gentle zephyr   46
rises to open those new leaves in which
Europe appears reclothed, not far from where,

behind the waves that beat upon the coast,   49
the sun, grown weary from its lengthy course,
at times conceals itself from all men's eyes—

there, Calaroga, blessed by fortune, sits   52
under the aegis of the mighty shield
on which the lion loses and prevails.

Within its walls was born the loving vassal   55
of Christian faith, the holy athlete, one
kind to his own and harsh to enemies;

no sooner was his mind created than   58
it was so full of living force that it,
still in his mother's womb, made her prophetic.

Then, at the sacred font, where Faith and he   61

brought mutual salvation as their dowry,
the rites of their espousal were complete.

The lady who had given the assent   64
for him saw, in a dream, astonishing
fruit that would spring from him and from his heirs.

And that his name might echo what he was,   67
a spirit moved from here to have him called
by the possessive of the One by whom

he was possessed completely. Dominic   70
became his name; I speak of him as one
whom Christ chose as the worker in His garden.

He seemed the fitting messenger and servant   73
of Christ: the very first love that he showed
was for the first injunction Christ had given.

His nurse would often find him on the ground,   76
alert and silent, in a way that said:
'It is for this that I have come.' Truly,

his father was Felice and his mother   79
Giovanna if her name, interpreted,
is in accord with what has been asserted.

Not for the world, for which men now travail   82
along Taddeo's way or Ostian's,
but through his love of the true manna, he

became, in a brief time, so great a teacher   85
that he began to oversee the vineyard
that withers when neglected by its keeper.

And from the seat that once was kinder to   88
the righteous poor (and now has gone astray,
not in itself, but in its occupant),

he did not ask to offer two or three   91
for six, nor for a vacant benefice,
nor *decimas, quae sunt pauperum Dei*—

but pleaded for the right to fight against   94
the erring world, to serve the seed from which
there grew the four-and-twenty plants that ring you.

Then he, with both his learning and his zeal,   97

and with his apostolic office, like
a torrent hurtled from a mountain source,

    coursed, and his impetus, with greatest force,   100
struck where the thickets of the heretics
offered the most resistance. And from him

    there sprang the streams with which the catholic   103
garden has found abundant watering,
so that its saplings have more life, more green.

    If such was one wheel of the chariot   106
in which the Holy Church, in her defense,
taking the field, defeated enemies

    within, then you must see the excellence   109
of him—the other wheel—whom Thomas praised
so graciously before I made my entry.

    And yet the track traced by the outer rim   112
of that wheel is abandoned now—as in
a cask of wine when crust gives way to mold.

    His family, which once advanced with steps   115
that followed his footprints, has now turned back:
its forward foot now seeks the foot that lags.

    And soon we are to see, at harvest time,   118
the poor grain gathered, when the tares will be
denied a place within the bin—and weep.

    I do admit that, if one were to search   121
our volume leaf by leaf, he might still read
one page with, 'I am as I always was';

    but those of Acquasparta or Casale   124
who read our Rule are either given to
escaping it or making it too strict.

    I am the living light of Bonaventure   127
of Bagnorea; in high offices
I always put the left-hand interests last.

    Illuminato and Augustine are here;   130
they were among the first unshod poor brothers
to wear the cord, becoming friends of God.

    Hugh of St. Victor, too, is here with them;   133

Peter of Spain, who, with his twelve books, glows
on earth below; and Peter Book-Devourer,

    Nathan the prophet, Anselm and Chrysostom   136
the Metropolitan, and that Donatus
who deigned to deal with that art which comes first.

    Rabanus, too, is here; and at my side   139
shines the Calabrian Abbot Joachim,
who had the gift of the prophetic spirit.

    To this—my praise of such a paladin—   142
the glowing courtesy and the discerning
language of Thomas urged me on and stirred,

    with me, the souls that form this company."   145

CANTO XIII

Still the Fourth Heaven: the Sphere of the Sun. Invitation to the reader to exercise his astronomical fantasy. Dance and song of the two rings of spirits. St. Thomas on the wisdom of King Solomon. St. Thomas's warning against hasty judgments.

Let him imagine, who would rightly seize
what I saw now—and let him while I speak
retain that image like a steadfast rock—

in heaven's different parts, those fifteen stars   4
that quicken heaven with such radiance
as to undo the air's opacities;

let him imagine, too, that Wain which stays   7
within our heaven's bosom night and day,
so that its turning never leaves our sight;

let him imagine those two stars that form   10
the mouth of that Horn which begins atop
the axle round which the first wheel revolves;

then see these join to form two signs in heaven—   13
just like the constellation that was shaped
by Minos' daughter when she felt death's chill—

two signs with corresponding radii,   16
revolving so that one sign moves in one
direction, and the other in a second;

and he will have a shadow—as it were—   19
of the true constellation, the double dance
that circled round the point where I was standing:

a shadow—since its truth exceeds our senses,   22
just as the swiftest of all heavens is
more swift than the Chiana's sluggishness.

They sang no Bacchus there, they sang no Paean,   25

but sang three Persons in the divine nature,
and in one Person the divine and human.

The singing and the dance fulfilled their measure; 28
and then those holy lights gave heed to us,
rejoicing as they turned from task to task.

The silence of the blessed fellowship 31
was broken by the very light from which
I heard the wondrous life of God's poor man;

that light said: "Since one stalk is threshed, and since 34
its grain is in the granary already,
sweet love leads me to thresh the other stalk.

You think that any light which human nature 37
can rightfully possess was all infused
by that Force which had shaped both of these two:

the one out of whose chest was drawn the rib 40
from which was formed the lovely cheek whose palate
was then to prove so costly to the world;

and One whose chest was transfixed by the lance, 43
who satisfied all past and future sins,
outweighing them upon the scales of justice.

Therefore you wondered at my words when I— 46
before—said that no other ever vied
with that great soul enclosed in the fifth light.

Now let your eyes hold fast to my reply, 49
and you will see: truth centers both my speech
and your belief, just like a circle's center.

Both that which never dies and that which dies 52
are only the reflected light of that
Idea which our Sire, with Love, begets;

because the living Light that pours out so 55
from Its bright Source that It does not disjoin
from It or from the Love intrined with them,

through Its own goodness gathers up Its rays 58
within nine essences, as in a mirror,
Itself eternally remaining One.

From there, from act to act, light then descends 61

down to the last potentialities,
where it is such that it engenders nothing
but brief contingent things, by which I mean   64
the generated things the moving heavens
bring into being, with or without seed.

The wax of such things and what shapes that wax   67
are not immutable; and thus, beneath
Idea's stamp, light shines through more or less.

Thus it can be that, in the selfsame species,   70
some trees bear better fruit and some bear worse,
and men are born with different temperaments.

For were the wax appropriately readied,   73
and were the heaven's power at its height,
the brightness of the seal would show completely;

but Nature always works defectively—   76
she passes on that light much like an artist
who knows his craft but has a hand that trembles.

Yet where the ardent Love prepares and stamps   79
the lucid Vision of the primal Power,
a being then acquires complete perfection.

In that way, earth was once made worthy of   82
the full perfection of a living being;
thus was the Virgin made to be with child.

So that I do approve of the opinion   85
you hold: that human nature never was
nor shall be what it was in those two persons.

Now if I said no more beyond this point,   88
your words might well begin, 'How is it, then,
with your assertion of his matchless vision?'

But so that the obscure can be made plain,   91
consider who he was, what was the cause
of his request when he was told, 'Do ask.'

My words need not have blocked your seeing clearly 94
that it was as a king that he had asked
for wisdom that would serve his royal task—

and not to know the number of the angels   97

In this unfinished drawing, Beatrice and Dante stand in the Sphere of the Sun where, according to the text, they encounter St Thomas Aquinas.

on high or, if combined with a contingent,
necesse ever can produce *necesse*,

    or *si est dare primum motum esse*,   100
or if, within a semicircle, one
can draw a triangle with no right angle.

    Thus, if you note both what I said and say,   103
by 'matchless vision' it is kingly prudence
my arrow of intention means to strike;

    and if you turn clear eyes to that word 'rose,'   106
you'll see that it referred to kings alone—
kings, who are many, and the good are rare.

    Take what I said with this distinction then;   109
in that way it accords with what you thought
of the first father and of our Beloved.

    And let this weigh as lead to slow your steps,   112
to make you move as would a weary man
to *yes* or *no* when you do not see clearly:

    whether he would affirm or would deny,   115
he who decides without distinguishing
must be among the most obtuse of men;

    opinion—hasty—often can incline   118
to the wrong side, and then affection for
one's own opinion binds, confines the mind.

    Far worse than uselessly he leaves the shore   121
(more full of error than he was before)
who fishes for the truth but lacks the art.

    Of this, Parmenides, Melissus, Bryson,   124
are clear proofs to the world, and many others
who went their way but knew not where it went;

    so did Sabellius and Arius   127
and other fools—like concave blades that mirror—
who rendered crooked the straight face of Scriptures.

    So, too, let men not be too confident   130
in judging—witness those who, in the field,
would count the ears before the corn is ripe;

    for I have seen, all winter through, the brier   133

display itself as stiff and obstinate,
and later, on its summit, bear the rose;

    and once I saw a ship sail straight and swift   136
through all its voyaging across the sea,
then perish at the end, at harbor entry.

    Let not Dame Bertha or Master Martin think   139
that they have shared God's Counsel when they see
one rob and see another who donates:

    the last may fall, the other may be saved."   142

CANTO XIV

Still the Fourth Heaven: the Sphere of the Sun. Beatrice's request to the spirits to resolve Dante's query concerning the radiance of the spirits after the Resurrection. Solomon's reply. Appearance of new spirits. Ascent to the Fifth Heaven, the Sphere of Mars. The vision of a cross and Christ. The rapture of Dante.

From rim to center, center out to rim,
so does the water move in a round vessel,
as it is struck without, or struck within.

What I am saying fell most suddenly   4
into my mind, as soon as Thomas's
glorious living flame fell silent, since

between his speech and that of Beatrice,   7
a similarity was born. And she,
when he was done, was pleased to start with this:

"He does not tell you of it—not with speech   10
nor in his thoughts as yet—but this man needs
to reach the root of still another truth.

Do tell him if that light with which your soul 13
blossoms will stay with you eternally
even as it is now; and if it stays,

do tell him how, when you are once again   16
made visible, it will be possible
for you to see such light and not be harmed."

As dancers in a ring, when drawn and driven   19
by greater gladness, lift at times their voices
and dance their dance with more exuberance,

so, when they heard that prompt, devout request, 22
the blessed circles showed new joyousness
in wheeling dance and in amazing song.

Whoever weeps because on earth we die   25
that we may live on high, has never seen
eternal showers that bring refreshment there.

That One and Two and Three who ever lives   28
and ever reigns in Three and Two and One,
not circumscribed and circumscribing all,

was sung three times by each and all those souls   31
with such a melody that it would be
appropriate reward for every merit.

And I could hear within the smaller circle's   34
divinest light a modest voice (perhaps
much like the angel's voice in speech to Mary)

reply: "As long as the festivity   37
of Paradise shall be, so long shall our
love radiate around us such a garment.

Its brightness takes its measure from our ardor,   40
our ardor from our vision, which is measured
by what grace each receives beyond his merit.

When, glorified and sanctified, the flesh   43
is once again our dress, our persons shall,
in being all complete, please all the more;

therefore, whatever light gratuitous   46
the Highest Good gives us will be enhanced—
the light that will allow us to see Him;

that light will cause our vision to increase,   49
the ardor vision kindles to increase,
the brightness born of ardor to increase.

Yet even as a coal engenders flame,   52
but with intenser glow outshines it, so
that in that flame the coal persists, it shows,

so will the brightness that envelops us   55
be then surpassed in visibility
by reborn flesh, which earth now covers up.

Nor will we tire when faced with such bright light,   58
for then the body's organs will have force
enough for all in which we can delight."

Within the Sphere of Mars, Dante and Beatrice stand reverently before the Cross of Christ (out of picture).

One and the other choir seemed to me   61
so quick and keen to say "Amen" that they
showed clearly how they longed for their dead bodies—

not only for themselves, perhaps, but for   64
their mothers, fathers, and for others dear
to them before they were eternal flames.

And—look!—beyond the light already there,   67
an added luster rose around those rings,
even as a horizon brightening.

And even as, at the approach of evening,   70
new lights begin to show along the sky,
so that the sight seems and does not seem real,

it seemed to me that I began to see   73
new spirits there, forming a ring beyond
the choirs with their two circumferences.

O the true sparkling of the Holy Ghost—   76
how rapid and how radiant before
my eyes that, overcome, could not sustain it!

But, smiling, Beatrice then showed to me   79
such loveliness—it must be left among
the visions that take flight from memory.

From this my eyes regained the strength to look   82
above again; I saw myself translated
to higher blessedness, alone with my

lady; and I was sure that I had risen   85
because the smiling star was red as fire—
beyond the customary red of Mars.

With all my heart and in that language which   88
is one for all, for this new grace I gave
to God my holocaust, appropriate.

Though in my breast that burning sacrifice   91
was not completed yet, I was aware
that it had been accepted and auspicious;

for splendors, in two rays, appeared to me,   94
so radiant and fiery that I said:
"O Helios, you who adorn them thus!"

As, graced with lesser and with larger lights
between the poles of the world, the Galaxy
gleams so that even sages are perplexed;

so, constellated in the depth of Mars,
those rays described the venerable sign
a circle's quadrants form where they are joined.

And here my memory defeats my wit:
Christ's flaming from that cross was such that I
can find no fit similitude for it.

But he who takes his cross and follows Christ
will pardon me again for my omission—
my seeing Christ flash forth undid my force.

Lights moved along that cross from horn to horn
and from the summit to the base, and as
they met and passed, they sparkled, radiant:

so, straight and slant and quick and slow, one sees
on earth the particles of bodies, long
and short, in shifting shapes, that move along

the ray of light that sometimes streaks across
the shade that men devise with skill and art
to serve as their defense against the sun.

And just as harp and viol, whose many chords
are tempered, taut, produce sweet harmony
although each single note is not distinct,

so, from the lights that then appeared to me,
out from that cross there spread a melody
that held me rapt, although I could not tell

what hymn it was. I knew it sang high praise,
since I heard "Rise" and "Conquer," but I was
as one who hears but cannot seize the sense.

Yet I was so enchanted by the sound
that until then no thing had ever bound
me with such gentle bonds. My words may seem

presumptuous, as though I dared to deem
a lesser thing the lovely eyes that bring
to my desire, as it gazes, peace.

But he who notes that, in ascent, her eyes— 133
all beauty's living seals—gain force, and notes
that I had not yet turned to them in Mars,
    can then excuse me—just as I accuse 136
myself, thus to excuse myself—and see
that I speak truly: here her holy beauty
    is not denied—ascent makes it more perfect. 139

CANTO XV

The Fifth Heaven: the Sphere of Mars. The silence of the blessed spirits. Cacciaguida, who reveals himself as Dante's ancestor. Cacciaguida on the Florence of his times and his life there, and on his death in the Holy Land in the Second Crusade, where he served the emperor Conrad.

Generous will—in which is manifest
always the love that breathes toward righteousness,
as in contorted will is greediness—

imposing silence on that gentle lyre,   4
brought quiet to the consecrated chords
that Heaven's right hand slackens and draws taut.

Can souls who prompted me to pray to them,   7
by falling silent all in unison,
be deaf to men's just prayers? Then he may grieve

indeed and endlessly—the man who leaves   10
behind such love and turns instead to seek
things that do not endure eternally.

As, through the pure and tranquil skies of night,   13
at times a sudden fire shoots, and moves
eyes that were motionless—a fire that seems

a star that shifts its place, except that in   16
that portion of the heavens where it flared,
nothing is lost, and its own course is short—

so, from the horn that stretches on the right,   19
down to the foot of that cross, a star ran
out of the constellation glowing there;

nor did that gem desert the cross's track,   22
but coursed along the radii, and seemed
just like a flame that alabaster screens.

With such affection did Anchises' shade   25

reach out (if we may trust our greatest muse)
when in Elysium he saw his son.

"O blood of mine—o the celestial grace 28
bestowed beyond all measure—unto whom
as unto you was Heaven's gate twice opened?"

That light said this; at which, I stared at him. 31
Then, looking back to see my lady, I,
on this side and on that, was stupefied;

for in the smile that glowed within her eyes, 34
I thought that I—with mine—had touched the height
of both my blessedness and paradise.

Then—and he was a joy to hear and see— 37
that spirit added to his first words things
that were too deep to meet my understanding.

Not that he chose to hide his sense from me; 40
necessity compelled him; he conceived
beyond the mark a mortal mind can reach.

And when his bow of burning sympathy 43
was slack enough to let his speech descend
to meet the limit of our intellect,

these were the first words where I caught the sense: 46
"Blessed be you, both Three and One, who show
such favor to my seed." And he continued:

"The long and happy hungering I drew 49
from reading that great volume where both black
and white are never changed, you—son—have now

appeased within this light in which I speak 52
to you; for this, I owe my gratitude
to her who gave you wings for your high flight.

You think your thoughts flow into me from Him 55
who is the First—as from the number one,
the five and six derive, if one is known—

and so you do not ask me who I am 58
and why I seem more joyous to you than
all other spirits in this festive throng.

Your thought is true, for both the small and great 61

of this life gaze into that mirror where,
before you think, your thoughts have been displayed.

But that the sacred love in which I keep   64
my vigil with unending watchfulness,
the love that makes me thirst with sweet desire,

be better satisfied, let your voice—bold,   67
assured, and glad—proclaim your will and longing,
to which my answer is decreed already."

I turned to Beatrice, but she heard me   70
before I spoke; her smile to me was signal
that made the wings of my desire grow.

Then I began: "As soon as you beheld   73
the First Equality, both intellect
and love weighed equally for each of you,

because the Sun that brought you light and heat   76
possesses heat and light so equally
that no thing matches His equality;

whereas in mortals, word and sentiment—   79
to you, the cause of this is evident—
are wings whose featherings are disparate.

I—mortal—feel this inequality;   82
thus, it is only with my heart that I
can offer thanks for your paternal greeting.

Indeed I do beseech you, living topaz,   85
set in this precious jewel as a gem:
fulfill my longing—let me know your name."

"O you, my branch in whom I took delight   88
even awaiting you, I am your root,"
so he, in his reply to me, began,

then said: "The man who gave your family   91
its name, who for a century and more
has circled the first ledge of Purgatory,

was son to me and was your great-grandfather;   94
it is indeed appropriate for you
to shorten his long toil with your good works.

Florence, within her ancient ring of walls—   97

The Sphere of Mars.

that ring from which she still draws tierce and nones—
sober and chaste lived in tranquillity.

No necklace and no coronal were there,   100
and no embroidered gowns; there was no girdle
that caught the eye more than the one who wore it.

No daughter's birth brought fear unto her father,   103
for age and dowry then did not imbalance—
to this side and to that—the proper measure.

There were no families that bore no children;   106
and Sardanapalus was still a stranger—
not come as yet to teach in the bedchamber.

Not yet had your Uccellatoio's rise   109
outdone the rise of Monte Mario,
which, too, will be outdone in its decline.

I saw Bellincione Berti girt   112
with leather and with bone, and saw his wife
come from her mirror with her face unpainted.

I saw dei Nerli and del Vecchio   115
content to wear their suits of unlined skins,
and saw their wives at spindle and at spool.

O happy wives! Each one was sure of her   118
own burial place, and none—for France's sake—
as yet was left deserted in her bed.

One woman watched with loving care the cradle   121
and, as she soothed her infant, used the way
of speech with which fathers and mothers play;

another, as she drew threads from the distaff,   124
would tell, among her household, tales of Trojans,
and tales of Fiesole, and tales of Rome.

A Lapo Salterello, a Cianghella,   127
would then have stirred as much dismay as now
a Cincinnatus and Cornelia would.

To such a life—so tranquil and so lovely—   130
of citizens in true community,
into so sweet a dwelling place did Mary,

invoked in pains of birth, deliver me;   133

and I, within your ancient Baptistery,
at once became Christian and Cacciaguida.

Moronto was my brother, and Eliseo;   136
my wife came from the valley of the Po—
the surname that you bear was brought by her.

In later years I served the Emperor   139
Conrad—and my good works so gained his favor
that he gave me the girdle of his knighthood.

I followed him to war against the evil   142
of that law whose adherents have usurped—
this, through your Pastors' fault—your just possessions.

There, by that execrable race, I was   145
set free from fetters of the erring world,
the love of which defiles so many souls.

From martyrdom I came unto this peace."   148

CANTO XVI

Still the Fifth Heaven: the Sphere of Mars. Pride in birth.
Dante's queries to Cacciaguida. Cacciaguida's replies: the
date of his birth, his ancestors, the population and notable
families of Florence in Cacciaguida's time.

If here below, where sentiment is far
too weak to withstand error, I shou.d see
men glorying in you, nobility

of blood—a meager thing!—I should not wonder, 4
for even where desire is not awry,
I mean in Heaven, I too felt such pride.

You are indeed a cloak that soon wears out, 7
so that if, day by day, we add no patch,
then circling time will trim you with its shears.

My speech began again with *you,* the word 10
that Rome was the first city to allow,
although her people seldom speak it now;

at this word, Beatrice, somewhat apart, 13
smiling, seemed like the woman who had coughed—
so goes the tale—at Guinevere's first fault.

So did my speech begin: "You are my father; 16
you hearten me to speak with confidence;
you raise me so that I am more than I.

So many streams have filled my mind with gladness— 19
so many, and such gladness, that mind must
rejoice that it can bear this and not burst.

Then tell me, founder of my family, 22
who were your ancestors and, in your boyhood,
what were the years the records registered;

and tell me of the sheepfold of St. John— 25
how numerous it was, who in that flock

were worthy of the highest offices."

As at the breathing of the winds, a coal   28
will quicken into flame, so I saw that
light glow at words that were affectionate;

and as, before my eyes, it grew more fair,   31
so, with a voice more gentle and more sweet—
not in our modern speech—it said to me:

"Down from that day when *Ave* was pronounced,   34
until my mother (blessed now), by giving
birth, eased the burden borne in bearing me,

this fire of Mars had come five-hundred-fifty   37
and thirty more times to its Lion—there
to be rekindled underneath its paw.

My ancestors and I were born just where   40
the runner in your yearly games first comes
upon the boundary of the final ward.

That is enough concerning my forebears: 43
what were their names, from where they came—of that,
silence, not speech, is more appropriate.

All those who, at that time, between the Baptist   46
and Mars, were capable of bearing arms,
numbered one fifth of those who live there now.

But then the citizens—now mixed with men   49
from Campi and Certaldo and Figline—
were pure down to the humblest artisan.

Oh, it would be far better if you had   52
those whom I mention as your neighbors (and
your boundaries at Galluzo and Trespiano),

than to have them within, to bear the stench   55
of Aguglione's wretch and Signa's wretch,
whose sharp eyes now on barratry are set.

If those who, in the world, go most astray   58
had not seen Caesar with stepmothers' eyes,
but, like a mother to her son, been kind,

then one who has become a Florentine   61
trader and money changer would have stayed

in Semifonte, where his fathers peddled,

the Counts would still be lords of Montemurlo,   64
the Cerchi would be in Acone's parish,
perhaps the Buondelmonti in Valdigreve.

The mingling of the populations led   67
to evil in the city, even as
food piled on food destroys the body's health;

the blind bull falls more quickly, more headlong,   70
than does the blind lamb; and the one blade can
often cut more and better than five swords.

Consider Luni, Urbisaglia, how   73
they went to ruin (Sinigaglia follows,
and Chiusi, too, will soon have vanished); then,

if you should hear of families undone,   76
you will find nothing strange or difficult
in that—since even cities meet their end.

All things that you possess, possess their death,   79
just as you do; but in some things that last
long, death can hide from you whose lives are short.

And even as the heaven of the moon,   82
revolving, respiteless, conceals and then
reveals the shores, so Fortune does with Florence;

therefore, there is no cause for wonder in   85
what I shall tell of noble Florentines,
of those whose reputations time has hidden.

I saw the Ughi, saw the Catellini,   88
Filippi, Greci, Ormanni, Alberichi,
famed citizens already in decline,

and saw, as great as they were venerable,   91
dell'Arca with della Sannella, and
Ardinghi, Soldanieri, and Bostichi.

Nearby the gate that now is burdened with   94
new treachery that weighs so heavily
that it will bring the vessel to shipwreck,

there were the Ravignani, from whose line   97
Count Guido comes and all who—since—derive

their name from the illustrious Bellincione.

And della Pressa knew already how
to rule; and Galigaio, in his house,
already had the gilded hilt and pommel.   100

The stripe of Vair had mightiness already,   103
as did the Giuochi, Galli, and Barucci,
Fifanti, and Sacchetti, and those who

blush for the bushel; and the stock from which   106
spring the Calfucci was already mighty,
and Sizzi and Arrigucci were already

raised to high office. Oh, how great were those   109
I saw—whom pride laid low! And the gold balls,
in all of her great actions, flowered Florence.

Such were the ancestors of those who now,   112
whenever bishops' sees are vacant, grow
fat as they sit in church consistories.

The breed—so arrogant and dragonlike   115
in chasing him who flees, but lamblike, meek
to him who shows his teeth or else his purse—

was on the rise already, but of stock   118
so mean that Ubertin Donato, when
his father-in-law made him kin to them,

was scarcely pleased. Already Caponsacco   121
had come from Fiesole down to the market;
already citizens of note were Giuda

and Infangato. I shall tell a thing   124
incredible and true: the gateway through
the inner walls was named for the della Pera.

All those whose arms bear part of the fair ensign 127
of the great baron—he whose memory
and worth are honored on the feast of Thomas—

received knighthood and privilege from him,   130
though he whose coat of arms has fringed that ensign
has taken sides now with the populace.

The Gualterotti and the Importuni   133
were there already; were the Borgo spared

new neighbors, it would still be tranquil there.

The house of Amidei, with which your sorrows   136
began—by reason of its just resentment,
which ruined you and ended years of gladness—

was honored then, as were its close companions.   139
O Buondelmonte, through another's counsel,
you fled your wedding pledge, and brought such evil!

Many would now rejoice, who still lament,   142
if when you first approached the city, God
had given you unto the river Ema!

But Florence, in her final peace, was fated   145
to offer up—unto that mutilated
stone guardian upon her bridge—a victim.

These were the families, and others with them: 148
the Florence that I saw—in such repose
that there was nothing to have caused her sorrow.

These were the families: with them I saw   151
her people so acclaimed and just, that on
her staff the lily never was reversed,

nor was it made bloodred by factious hatred."   154

CANTO XVII

Still the Fifth Heaven: the Sphere of Mars. Dante's asking
Cacciaguida for word on what future awaits Dante. Caccia-
guida's prophecy concerning Dante's exile and tribulations.
Words of comfort from Cacciaguida, and his urging of Dante
to fearless fulfillment of his poetic mission.

Like Phaethon (one who still makes fathers wary
of sons) when he had heard insinuations,
and he, to be assured, came to Clymene,

such was I and such was I seen to be   4
by Beatrice and by the holy lamp
that—earlier—had shifted place for me.

Therefore my lady said to me: "Display   7
the flame of your desire, that it may
be seen well-stamped with your internal seal,

not that we need to know what you'd reveal,   10
but that you learn the way that would disclose
your thirst, and you be quenched by what we pour."

"O my dear root, who, since you rise so high,   13
can see the Point in which all times are present—
for just as earthly minds are able to

see that two obtuse angles cannot be   16
contained in a triangle, you can see
contingent things before they come to be—

while I was in the company of Virgil,   19
both on the mountain that heals souls and when
descending to the dead world, what I heard

about my future life were grievous words—   22
although, against the blows of chance I feel
myself as firmly planted as a cube.

Thus my desire would be appeased if I   25

might know what fortune is approaching me:
the arrow one foresees arrives more gently."

So did I speak to the same living light   28
that spoke to me before; as Beatrice
had wished, what was my wish was now confessed.

Not with the maze of words that used to snare   31
the fools upon this earth before the Lamb
of God who takes away our sins was slain,

but with words plain and unambiguous,   34
that loving father, hidden, yet revealed
by his own smile, replied: "Contingency,

while not extending past the book in which   37
your world of matter has been writ, is yet
in the Eternal Vision all depicted

(but this does not imply necessity,   40
just as a ship that sails downstream is not
determined by the eye that watches it).

And from that Vision—just as from an organ   43
the ear receives a gentle harmony—
what time prepares for you appears to me.

Hippolytus was forced to leave his Athens   46
because of his stepmother, faithless, fierce;
and so must you depart from Florence: this

is willed already, sought for, soon to be   49
accomplished by the one who plans and plots
where—every day—Christ is both sold and bought.

The blame, as usual, will be cried out   52
against the injured party; but just vengeance
will serve as witness to the truth that wields it.

You shall leave everything you love most dearly: 55
this is the arrow that the bow of exile
shoots first. You are to know the bitter taste

of others' bread, how salt it is, and know   58
how hard a path it is for one who goes
descending and ascending others' stairs.

And what will be most hard for you to bear   61

will be the scheming, senseless company
that is to share your fall into this valley;

against you they will be insane, completely   64
ungrateful and profane; and yet, soon after,
not you but they will have their brows bloodred.

Of their insensate acts, the proof will be   67
in the effects; and thus, your honor will
be best kept if your party is your self.

Your first refuge and your first inn shall be   70
the courtesy of the great Lombard, he
who on the ladder bears the sacred bird;

and so benign will be his care for you   73
that, with you two, in giving and in asking,
that shall be first which is, with others, last.

You shall—beside him—see one who, at birth,   76
had so received the seal of this strong star
that what he does will be remarkable.

People have yet to notice him because   79
he is a boy—for nine years and no more
have these spheres wheeled around him—but before

the Gascon gulls the noble Henry, some   82
sparks will have marked the virtue of the Lombard:
hard labor and his disregard for silver.

His generosity is yet to be   85
so notable that even enemies
will never hope to treat it silently.

Put trust in him and in his benefits: 88
his gifts will bring much metamorphosis—
rich men and beggars will exchange their states.

What I tell you about him you will bear   91
inscribed within your mind—but hide it there";
and he told things beyond belief even

for those who will yet see them. Then he added: 94
"Son, these are glosses of what you had heard;
these are the snares that hide beneath brief years.

Yet I'd not have you envying your neighbors;   97

your life will long outlast the punishment
that is to fall upon their treacheries."

After that holy soul had, with his silence,   100
showed he was freed from putting in the woof
across the web whose warp I set for him,

I like a man who, doubting, craves for counsel   103
from one who sees and rightly wills and loves,
replied to him: "I clearly see, my father,

how time is hurrying toward me in order   106
to deal me such a blow as would be most
grievous for him who is not set for it;

thus, it is right to arm myself with foresight,   109
that if I lose the place most dear, I may
not lose the rest through what my poems say.

Down in the world of endless bitterness,   112
and on the mountain from whose lovely peak
I was drawn upward by my lady's eyes,

and afterward, from light to light in Heaven,   115
I learned that which, if I retell it, must
for many have a taste too sharp, too harsh;

yet if I am a timid friend of truth,   118
I fear that I may lose my life among
those who will call this present, ancient times."

The light in which there smiled the treasure I   121
had found within it, first began to dazzle,
as would a golden mirror in the sun,

then it replied: "A conscience that is dark—   24
either through its or through another's shame—
indeed will find that what you speak is harsh.

Nevertheless, all falsehood set aside,   127
let all that you have seen be manifest,
and let them scratch wherever it may itch.

For if, at the first taste, your words molest,   130
they will, when they have been digested, end
as living nourishment. As does the wind,

so shall your outcry do—the wind that sends   133

its roughest blows against the highest peaks;
that is no little cause for claiming honor.

Therefore, within these spheres, upon the mountain,   136
and in the dismal valley, you were shown
only those souls that unto fame are known—

because the mind of one who hears will not   139
put doubt to rest, put trust in you, if given
examples with their roots unknown and hidden,

or arguments too dim, too unapparent."   142

CANTO XVIII

Still the Fifth Heaven: the Sphere of Mars. The dazzling gaze of Beatrice, Cacciaguida's presentation of other spirits of the cross. Ascent to the Sixth Heaven, the Sphere of Jupiter. Letters and words formed by the spirits in Jupiter. The shaping of the Eagle. Dante's prayer and his denunciation of evil popes, especially John XXII.

By now that blessed mirror was delighting
in its own inner words; I, tasting mine,
was tempering the bitter with the sweet.

But she, the lady leading me to God,   4
said: "Shift your thoughts: remember—I am close
to Him who lightens every unjust hurt."

Hearing the loving sound my solace spoke,   7
I turned. But here I have to leave untold
what love I saw within her holy eyes,

not just because I do not trust my speech,   10
but, too, because recall cannot retrieve
that much, unless Another is its guide.

This only—of that moment—can I tell: 13
that even as I gazed at her, my soul
was free from any other need as long

as the Eternal Loveliness that shone   16
on Beatrice directly, from her eyes,
contented me with the reflected light.

But, conquering my will with her smile's splendor,   19
she told me: "Turn to him and listen—for
not only in my eyes is Paradise."

As, here on earth, at times our sentiment,   22
if it be passionate enough to take
the soul entirely, shows in the face,

so, in the flaming of the holy fire   25
to which I turned, I saw that he desired

some further words with me. And he began:

"In this fifth resting place, upon the tree   28
that grows down from its crown and endlessly
bears fruit and never loses any leaves,

    are blessed souls that, down below, before   31
they came to heaven, were so notable
that any poem would be enriched by them.

    Therefore look at the cross, along its horns: 34
those whom I name will race as swiftly as,
within a cloud, its rapid lightnings flash."

    Then, just as soon as Joshua was named,   37
I saw a splendor thrust along the cross,
nor did I note the name before the act.

    And at the name of noble Maccabeus,   40
I saw another flame wheel round itself,
and gladness was the whip that spurred that top.

    So, too, for Charlemagne and Roland—my   43
attentive eye held fast to that pair like
a falconer who tracks his falcon's flight.

    The next to draw my eyes along that cross   46
were William and Renouard and, too, Duke Godfrey
and Robert Guiscard. Then, when he had left me

    and mingled with the other lights, the soul   49
who had addressed me showed his artistry,
singing among the singers in that sphere.

    I turned to my right side to see if I   52
might see if Beatrice had signified
by word or gesture what I was to do

    and saw such purity within her eyes,   55
such joy, that her appearance now surpassed
its guise at other times, even the last.

    And as, by feeling greater joyousness   58
in doing good, a man becomes aware
that day by day his virtue is advancing,

    so I became aware that my revolving   61
with heaven had increased its arc—by seeing
that miracle becoming still more brilliant.

And like the rapid change that one can see   64
in a pale woman's face when it has freed
itself from bearing bashful modesty,

such change I, turning, saw: the red of Mars   67
was gone—and now the temperate sixth star's
white heaven welcomed me into itself.

I saw within that torch of Jupiter   70
the sparkling of the love that it contained
design before my eyes the signs we speak.

And just as birds that rise from riverbanks,   73
as if rejoicing after feeding there,
will form a round flock or another shape,

so, in their lights, the saintly beings sang   76
and, in their flight, the figures that they spelled
were now a *D*, now *I*, and now an *L*.

First, they moved to the rhythm of their song;   79
then, after they had finished forming one
letter, they halted for a while, in silence.

O godly Pegasea, you who give   82
to genius glory and long life, as it,
through you, gives these to kingdoms and to cities,

give me your light that I may emphasize   85
these signs as I inscribed them in my mind:
your power—may it appear in these brief lines!

Those blessed spirits took the shape of five   88
times seven vowels and consonants, and I
noted the parts as they were spelled for me.

DILIGITE IUSTITIAM were the verb   91
and noun that first appeared in that depiction;
QUI IUDICATIS TERRAM followed after.

Then, having formed the *M* of the fifth word,   94
those spirits kept their order; Jupiter's
silver, at that point, seemed embossed with gold.

And I saw other lights descending on   97
the apex of the *M* and, settling, singing—
I think—the Good that draws them to Itself.

Then, as innumerable sparks rise up   100

when one strikes burning logs (and in those sparks
fools have a way of reading auguries),

from that *M* seemed to surge more than a thousand 103
lights; and they climbed, some high, some low, just as
the Sun that kindles them assigned positions.

With each light settled quietly in place, 106
I saw that the array of fire had shaped
the image of an eagle's head and neck.

He who paints there has no one as His guide: 109
He guides Himself; in Him we recognize
the shaping force that flows from nest to nest.

The other lights, who were, it seemed, content 112
at first to form a lily on the *M*,
moving a little, formed the eagle's frame.

O gentle star, what—and how many—gems 115
made plain to me that justice here on earth
depends upon the heaven you engem!

Therefore I pray the Mind in which begin 118
your motion and your force, to watch that place
which has produced the smoke that dims your rays,

that once again His anger fall upon 121
those who would buy and sell within that temple
whose walls were built by miracles and martyrs.

O hosts of Heaven whom I contemplate, 124
for all who, led by bad example, stray
within the life they live on earth, do pray!

Men once were used to waging war with swords; 127
now war means seizing here and there the bread
the tender Father would deny to none.

But you who only write to then erase, 130
remember this: Peter and Paul, who died
to save the vines you spoil, are still alive.

Well may you say: "My longing is so bent 133
on him who chose the solitary life
and for a dance was dragged to martyrdom—

I do not know the Fisherman or Paul." 136

CANTO XIX

The Sixth Heaven: the Sphere of Jupiter. The Eagle begins to
speak. Dante's implicit question concerning divine Justice.
The Eagle's voicing of the question and, then, its discourse on
the inscrutability of God's Justice and on salvation. The
Eagle's denunciation of evil Christian rulers.

The handsome image those united souls,
happy within their blessedness, were shaping,
appeared before me now with open wings.

Each soul seemed like a ruby—one in which   4
a ray of sun burned so, that in my eyes,
it was the total sun that seemed reflected.

And what I now must tell has never been   7
reported by a voice, inscribed by ink,
never conceived by the imagination;

for I did see the beak, did hear it speak   10
and utter with its voice both *I* and *mine*
when *we* and *ours* were what, in thought, was meant.

And it began: "Because I was both just   13
and merciful, I am exalted here
to glory no desire can surpass;

the memory I left on earth is such   16
that even the malicious praise it there,
although they do not follow its example."

Thus one sole warmth is felt from many embers, 19
even as from a multitude of loves
one voice alone rose from the Eagle's image.

To which I said: "O everlasting flowers   22
of the eternal gladness, who make all
your fragrances appear to me as one,

do let your breath deliver me from that   25

great fast which kept me hungering so long,
not finding any food for it on earth.

I know indeed that, though God's Justice has   28
another realm in Heaven as Its mirror,
you here do not perceive it through a veil.

You know how keenly I prepare myself   31
to listen, and you know what is that doubt
which caused so old a hungering in me."

Just like a falcon set free from its hood,   34
which moves its head and flaps its wings, displaying
its eagerness and proud appearance, so

I saw that ensign do, that Eagle woven   37
of praises of God's grace, accompanied
by songs whose sense those up above enjoy.

Then it began: "The One who turned His compass   40
to mark the world's confines, and in them set
so many things concealed and things revealed,

could not imprint His Power into all   43
the universe without His word remaining
in infinite excess of such a vessel.

In proof of this, the first proud being, he   46
who was the highest of all creatures, fell—
unripe because he did not wait for light.

Thus it is clear that every lesser nature   49
is—all the more—too meager a container
for endless Good, which is Its own sole measure.

In consequence of this, your vision—which   52
must be a ray of that Intelligence
with which all beings are infused—cannot

of its own nature find sufficient force   55
to see into its origin beyond
what God himself makes manifest to man;

therefore, the vision that your world receives   58
can penetrate into Eternal Justice
no more than eye can penetrate the sea;

for though, near shore, sight reaches the sea floor, 61

you cannot reach it in the open sea;
yet it is there, but hidden by the deep.

Only the light that shines from the clear heaven   64
can never be obscured—all else is darkness
or shadow of the flesh or fleshly poison.

Now is the hiding place of living Justice   67
laid open to you—where it had been hidden
while you addressed it with insistent questions.

For you would say: 'A man is born along   70
the shoreline of the Indus River; none
is there to speak or teach or write of Christ.

And he, as far as human reason sees,   73
in all he seeks and all he does is good;
there is no sin within his life or speech.

And that man dies unbaptized, without faith.   76
Where is this justice then that would condemn him?
Where is his sin if he does not believe?'

Now who are you to sit upon the bench,   79
to judge events a thousand miles away,
when your own vision spans so brief a space?

Of course, for him who would be subtle with me,   82
were there no Scriptures to instruct you, then
there would be place for an array of questions.

O earthly animals, o minds obtuse!   85
The Primal Will, which of Itself is good,
from the Supreme Good—Its Self—never moved.

So much is just as does accord with It;   88
and so, created good can draw It to
itself—but It, rayed forth, causes such goods."

Just as, above the nest, the stork will circle   91
when she has fed her fledglings, and as he
whom she has fed looks up at her, so did

the blessed image do, and so did I,   94
the fledgling, while the Eagle moved its wings,
spurred on by many wills in unison.

Wheeling, the Eagle sang, then said: "Even   97

as are my songs to you—past understanding—
such is Eternal Judgment to you mortals."

After the Holy Ghost's bright flames fell silent   100
while still within the sign that made the Romans
revered throughout the world, again the Eagle

began: "No one without belief in Christ   103
has ever risen to this kingdom—either
before or after He was crucified.

But there are many who now cry 'Christ! Christ!'   106
who at the Final Judgment shall be far
less close to Him than one who knows not Christ;

the Ethiopian will shame such Christians   109
when the two companies are separated,
the one forever rich, the other poor.

What shall the Persians, when they come to see   112
that open volume in which they shall read
the misdeeds of your rulers, say to them?

There one shall see, among the deeds of Albert,   115
that which is soon to set the pen in motion,
his making of a desert of Prague's kingdom.

There one shall see the grief inflicted on   118
the Seine by him who falsifies his coins,
one who shall die beneath a wild boar's blow.

There one shall see the thirst of arrogance   121
that drives the Scot and Englishman insane—
unable to remain within their borders.

That book will show the life of lechery   124
and ease the Spaniard led—and the Bohemian,
who never knew and never wished for valor.

That book will show the Cripple of Jerusalem—   127
his good deeds labeled with an *I* alone,
whereas his evils will be under *M*.

That book will show the greed and cowardice   130
of him who oversees the Isle of Fire,
on which Anchises ended his long life;

and to make plain his paltriness, the letters   133

that register his deeds will be contracted,
to note much pettiness in little space.

And all shall see the filthiness of both   136
his uncle and his brother, who dishonored
a family so famous—and two crowns.

And he of Portugal and he of Norway   139
shall be known in that book, and he of Rascia,
who saw—unluckily—the coin of Venice.

O happy Hungary, if she would let   142
herself be wronged no more! Happy Navarre,
if mountains that surround her served as armor!

And if Navarre needs token of her future,   145
now Nicosia and Famagosta suffer—
as men must see—lament and anger over

their own beast, with his place beside the others."   148

CANTO XX

*Still the Sixth Heaven: the Sphere of Jupiter. The song of the
spirits. The Eagle on the spirits that form its shape. The
Eagle on Dante's amazement at seeing the emperor Trajan
and the Trojan Ripheus redeemed. Predestination.*

When he who graces all the world with light
has sunk so far below our hemisphere
that on all sides the day is spent, the sky,

    which had been lit before by him alone,   4
immediately shows itself again
with many lights reflecting one same source,

    and I remembered this celestial course   7
when, in the blessed beak, the emblem of
the world and of its guardians fell silent;

    for then all of those living lights grew more   10
resplendent, but the songs that they began
were labile—they escape my memory.

    O gentle love that wears a smile as mantle,   13
how ardent was your image in those torches
filled only with the breath of holy thoughts!

    After the precious, gleaming jewels with which   16
the sixth of Heaven's heavens was engemmed
had ended their angelic song in silence,

    I seemed to hear the murmur of a torrent   19
that, limpid, falls from rock to rock, whose flow
shows the abundance of its mountain source.

    Even as sound takes shape at the lute's neck,   22
and even as the wind that penetrates
the blow-hole of the bagpipe, so—with no

    delay—that murmur of the Eagle rose   25
straight up, directly through its neck as if

its neck were hollow; and that murmuring
    became a voice that issued from its beak,   28
taking the shape of words desired by
my heart—and that is where they were transcribed.

    "Now you must watch—and steadily—that part   31
of me that can, in mortal eagles, see
and suffer the sun's force," it then began

    to say to me, "because, of all the flames   34
from which I shape my form, those six with which
the eye in my head glows hold highest rank.

    He who gleams in the center, my eye's pupil—   37
he was the singer of the Holy Spirit,
who bore the ark from one town to another;

    now he has learned the merit of his song—   40
for it had not been spurred by grace alone,
but his own will, in part, had urged him on.

    Of those five flames that, arching, form my brow,   43
he who is nearest to my beak is one
who comforted the widow for her son;

    now he has learned the price one pays for not   46
following Christ, through his experience
of this sweet life and of its opposite.

    And he whose place is next on the circumference 49
of which I speak, along the upward arc,
delayed his death through truthful penitence;

    now he has learned that the eternal judgment   52
remains unchanged, though worthy prayer below
makes what falls due today take place tomorrow.

    The next who follows—one whose good intention   55
bore evil fruit—to give place to the Shepherd,
with both the laws and me, made himself Greek;

    now he has learned that, even though the world   58
be ruined by the evil that derives
from his good act, that evil does not harm him.

    He whom you see—along the downward arc—   61
was William, and the land that mourns his death,

for living Charles and Frederick, now laments;

now he has learned how Heaven loves the just   64
ruler, and he would show this outwardly
as well, so radiantly visible.

Who in the erring world below would hold   67
that he who was the fifth among the lights
that formed this circle was the Trojan Ripheus?

Now he has learned much that the world cannot   70
discern of God's own grace, although his sight
cannot divine, not reach its deepest site."

As if it were a lark at large in air,   73
a lark that sings at first and then falls still,
content with final sweetness that fulfills,

such seemed to me the image of the seal   76
of that Eternal Pleasure through whose will
each thing becomes the being that it is.

And though the doubt within me was as plain   79
as any colored surface cloaked by glass,
it could not wait to voice itself, but with

the thrust and weight of urgency it forced   82
"Can such things be?" out from my lips, at which
I saw lights flash—a vast festivity.

And then the blessed sign—its eye grown still   85
more bright—replied, that I might not be kept
suspended in amazement: "I can see

that, since you speak of them, you do believe   88
these things but cannot see *how* they may be;
and thus, though you believe them, they are hidden.

You act as one who apprehends a thing   91
by name but cannot see its quiddity
unless another set it forth to him.

Regnum celorum suffers violence   94
from ardent love and living hope, for these
can be the conquerors of Heaven's Will;

yet not as man defeats another man: 97
the Will of God is won because It would

be won and, won, wins through benevolence.

You were amazed to see the angels' realm   100
adorned with those who were the first and fifth
among the living souls that form my eyebrow.

When these souls left their bodies, they were not   103
Gentiles—as you believe—but Christians, one
with firm faith in the Feet that suffered, one

in Feet that were to suffer. One, from Hell,   106
where there is no returning to right will,
returned to his own bones, as the reward

bestowed upon a living hope, the hope   109
that gave force to the prayers offered God
to resurrect him and convert his will.

Returning briefly to the flesh, that soul   112
in glory—he of whom I speak—believed
in Him whose power could help him and, believing,

was kindled to such a fire of true love   115
that, when he died a second death, he was
worthy to join in this festivity.

The other, through the grace that surges from   118
a well so deep that no created one
has ever thrust his eye to its first source,

below, set all his love on righteousness,   121
so that, through grace on grace, God granted him
the sight of our redemption in the future;

thus he, believing that, no longer suffered   124
the stench of paganism and rebuked
those who persisted in that perverse way.

More than a thousand years before baptizing,   127
to baptize him there were the same three women
you saw along the chariot's right-hand side.

How distant, o predestination, is   130
your root from those whose vision does not see
the Primal Cause in Its entirety!

And, mortals, do take care—judge prudently: 133
for we, though we see God, do not yet know

all those whom He has chosen; but within
  the incompleteness of our knowledge is   136
a sweetness, for our good is then refined
in this good, since what God wills, we too will."

So, from the image God Himself had drawn,   139
what I received was gentle medicine;
and I saw my shortsightedness plainly.

And as a lutanist accompanies—   142
expert—with trembling strings, the expert singer,
by which the song acquires sweeter savor,

so, while the Eagle spoke—I can remember—   145
I saw the pair of blessed lights together,
like eyes that wink in concord, move their flames

  in ways that were at one with what he said.   148

CANTO XXI

*Ascent to the Seventh Heaven, the Sphere of Saturn. The
golden ladder. Dante's questions to one of the spirits. The
spirit's replies. Another query and a reply concerning
predestination. The spirit's identifying of himself as St. Peter
Damian, and his denunciation of degenerate prelates. The
outcry of the spirits.*

By now my eyes were set again upon
my lady's face, and with my eyes, my mind:
from every other thought, it was withdrawn.

She did not smile. Instead her speech to me   4
began: "Were I to smile, then you would be
like Semele when she was turned to ashes,

because, as you have seen, my loveliness—   7
which, even as we climb the steps of this
eternal palace, blazes with more brightness—

were it not tempered here, would be so brilliant   10
that, as it flashed, your mortal faculty
would seem a branch a lightning bolt has cracked.

We now are in the seventh splendor; this,   13
beneath the burning Lion's breast, transmits
to earth its rays, with which his force is mixed.

Let your mind follow where your eyes have led,   16
and let your eyes be mirrors for the figure
that will appear to you within this mirror."

That man who knows just how my vision pastured   19
upon her blessed face, might recognize
the joy I found when my celestial guide

had asked of me to turn my mind aside,   22
were he to weigh my joy when I obeyed
against my joy in contemplating her.

CANTO XXI · 477

Within the crystal that—as it revolves   25
around the earth—bears as its name the name
of that dear king whose rule undid all evil,

I saw a ladder rising up so high   28
that it could not be followed by my sight:
its color, gold when gold is struck by sunlight.

I also saw so many flames descend   31
those steps that I thought every light displayed
in heaven had been poured out from that place.

And just as jackdaws, at the break of day,   34
together rise—such is their nature's way—
to warm their feathers chilled by night; then some

fly off and never do return, and some   37
wheel back to that point where they started from,
while others, though they wheel, remain at home;

such were the ways I saw those splendors take   40
as soon as they had struck a certain step,
where they had thronged as one in radiance.

The flame that halted nearest us became   43
so bright that in my mind I said: "I see
you clearly signaling to me your love.

But she from whom I wait for word on how   46
and when to speak and to be silent, pauses;
thus, though I would, I do well not to ask."

And she who, seeing Him who sees all things,   49
had seen the reason for my silence, said
to me: "Do satisfy your burning longing."

And I began: "My merit does not make   52
me worthy of reply, but for the sake
of her who gives me leave to question you—

a blessed living soul—who hide within   55
your joy, do let me know the reason why
you drew so near to me. And tell me, too,

why the sweet symphony of Paradise   58
is silent in this heaven, while, below,
it sounds devoutly through the other spheres."

"Your hearing is as mortal as your sight;   61
thus, here there is no singing," he replied,
"and Beatrice, in like wise, did not smile.

When, down the sacred staircase, I descended,   64
I only came to welcome you with gladness—
with words and with the light that mantles me.

The love that prompted me is not supreme;   67
above, is love that equals or exceeds
my own, as spirit-flames will let you see.

But the deep charity, which makes us keen   70
to serve the Providence that rules the world,
allots our actions here, as you perceive."

"O holy lamp," I said, "I do indeed   73
see how, within this court, it is your free
love that fulfills eternal Providence;

but this seems difficult for me to grasp: 76
why you alone, of those who form these ranks,
were he who was predestined to this task."

And I had yet to reach the final word   79
when that light made a pivot of its midpoint
and spun around as would a swift millstone.

Then, from within its light, that love replied: 82
"Light from the Deity descends on me;
it penetrates the light that enwombs me;

its power, as it joins my power of sight,   85
lifts me so far beyond myself that I
see the High Source from which that light derives.

From this there comes the joy with which I am   88
aflame; I match the clearness of my light
with equal measure of my clear insight.

But even Heaven's most enlightened soul,   91
that Seraph with his eye most set on God,
could not provide the *why*, not satisfy

what you have asked; for deep in the abyss   94
of the Eternal Ordinance, it is
cut off from all created beings' vision.

And to the mortal world, when you return,
tell this, lest men continue to trespass
and set their steps toward such a reachless goal.

The mind, bright here, on earth is dulled and smoky.
Think: how, below, can mind see that which hides
even when mind is raised to Heaven's height?"

His words so curbed my query that I left
behind my questioning; and I drew back
and humbly asked that spirit who he was.

"Not far from your homeland, between two shores
of Italy, the stony ridges rise
so high that, far below them, thunder roars.

These ridges form a hump called Catria;
a consecrated hermitage beneath
that peak was once devoted just to worship."

So his third speech to me began; then he
continued: "There, within that monastery,
in serving God, I gained tenacity:

with food that only olive juice had seasoned,
I could sustain with ease both heat and frost,
content within my contemplative thoughts.

That cloister used to offer souls to Heaven,
a fertile harvest, but it now is barren—
as Heaven's punishment will soon make plain.

There I was known as Peter Damian
and, on the Adriatic shore, was Peter
the Sinner when I served Our Lady's House.

Not much of mortal life was left to me
when I was sought for, dragged to take that hat
which always passes down from bad to worse.

Once there were Cephas and the Holy Ghost's
great vessel: they were barefoot, they were lean,
they took their food at any inn they found.

But now the modern pastors are so plump
that they have need of one to prop them up
on this side, one on that, and one in front,

97

100

103

106

109

112

115

118

121

124

127

130

and one to hoist them saddleward. Their cloaks   133
cover their steeds, two beasts beneath one skin:
o patience, you who must endure so much!"

These words, I saw, had summoned many flames,   136
descending step by step; I saw them wheel
and, at each turn, become more beautiful.

They joined around him, and they stopped, and raised   139
a cry so deep that nothing here can be
its likeness; but the words they cried I could

not understand—their thunder overcame me.   142

CANTO XXII

Still the Seventh Heaven: the Sphere of Saturn. Beatrice on the spirits' outcry. St. Benedict and other contemplatives. Dante's desire to see the face of St. Benedict. St. Benedict on the degeneracy of the Benedictines. Ascent to the Eighth Heaven, the Sphere of the Fixed Stars. Invocation to the constellation Gemini. Dante's earthward gaze.

Amazement overwhelming me, I—like
a child who always hurries back to find
that place he trusts the most—turned to my guide;

and like a mother quick to reassure   4
her pale and panting son with the same voice
that she has often used to comfort him,

she said: "Do you not know you are in Heaven,   7
not know how holy all of Heaven is,
how righteous zeal moves every action here?

Now, since this cry has agitated you   10
so much, you can conceive how—had you seen
me smile and heard song here—you would have been

confounded; and if you had understood   13
the prayer within that cry, by now you would
know the revenge you'll see before your death.

The sword that strikes from Heaven's height is neither 16
hasty nor slow, except as it appears
to him who waits for it—who longs or fears.

But turn now toward the other spirits here;   19
for if you set your sight as I suggest,
you will see many who are notable."

As pleased my guide, I turned my eyes and saw   22
a hundred little suns; as these together
cast light, each made the other lovelier.

I stood as one who curbs within himself   25
the goad of longing and, in fear of being
too forward, does not dare to ask a question.

At this, the largest and most radiant   28
among those pearls moved forward that he might
appease my need to hear who he might be.

Then, in that light, I heard: "Were you to see,   31
even as I do see, the charity
that burns in us, your thoughts would have been uttered.

But lest, by waiting, you be slow to reach   34
the high goal of your seeking, I shall answer
what you were thinking when you curbed your speech.

That mountain on whose flank Cassino lies   37
was once frequented on its summit by
those who were still deluded, still awry;

and I am he who was the first to carry   40
up to that peak the name of Him who brought
to earth the truth that lifts us to the heights.

And such abundant grace had brought me light   43
that, from corrupted worship that seduced
the world, I won away the nearby sites.

These other flames were all contemplatives,   46
men who were kindled by that heat which brings
to birth the blessed flowers and blessed fruits.

Here is Macarius, here is Romualdus,   49
here are my brothers, those who stayed their steps
in cloistered walls, who kept their hearts steadfast."

I answered: "The affection that you show   52
in speech to me, and kindness that I see
and note within the flaming of your lights,

have given me so much more confidence,   55
just like the sun that makes the rose expand
and reach the fullest flowering it can.

Therefore I pray you, father—and may you   58
assure me that I can receive such grace—
to let me see, unveiled, your human face."

And he: "Brother, your high desire will be   61
fulfilled within the final sphere, as all
the other souls' and my own longing will.

There, each desire is perfect, ripe, intact;   64
and only there, within that final sphere,
is every part where it has always been.

That sphere is not in space and has no poles;   67
our ladder reaches up to it, and that
is why it now is hidden from your sight.

Up to that sphere, Jacob the patriarch   70
could see that ladder's topmost portion reach,
when it appeared to him so thronged with angels.

But no one now would lift his feet from earth   73
to climb that ladder, and my Rule is left
to waste the paper it was written on.

What once were abbey walls are robbers' dens;   76
what once were cowls are sacks of rotten meal.
But even heavy usury does not

offend the will of God as grievously   79
as the appropriation of that fruit
which makes the hearts of monks go mad with greed;

for all within the keeping of the Church   82
belongs to those who ask it in God's name,
and not to relatives or concubines.

The flesh of mortals yields so easily—   85
on earth a good beginning does not run
from when the oak is born until the acorn.

Peter began with neither gold nor silver,   88
and I with prayer and fasting, and when Francis
began his fellowship, he did it humbly;

if you observe the starting point of each,   91
and look again to see where it has strayed,
then you will see how white has gone to gray.

And yet, the Jordan in retreat, the sea   94
in flight when God had willed it so, were sights
more wonderful than His help here will be."

So did he speak to me, and he drew back   97
to join his company, which closed, compact;
then, like a whirlwind, upward, all were swept.

The gentle lady—simply with a sign—   100
impelled me after them and up that ladder,
so did her power overcome my nature;

and never here below, where our ascent   103
and descent follow nature's law, was there
motion as swift as mine when I took wing.

So, reader, may I once again return   106
to those triumphant ranks—an end for which
I often beat my breast, weep for my sins—

more quickly than your finger can withdraw   109
from flame and be thrust into it, I saw,
and was within, the sign that follows Taurus.

O stars of glory, constellation steeped   112
in mighty force, all of my genius—
whatever be its worth—has you as source:

with you was born and under you was hidden   115
he who is father of all mortal lives,
when I first felt the air of Tuscany;

and then, when grace was granted me to enter   118
the high wheel that impels your revolutions,
your region was my fated point of entry.

To you my soul now sighs devotedly,   121
that it may gain the force for this attempt,
hard trial that now demands its every strength.

"You are so near the final blessedness,"   124
so Beatrice began, "that you have need
of vision clear and keen; and thus, before

you enter farther, do look downward, see   127
what I have set beneath your feet already:
much of the world is there. If you see that,

your heart may then present itself with all   130
the joy it can to the triumphant throng
that comes in gladness through this ether's rounds."

My eyes returned through all the seven spheres   133
and saw this globe in such a way that I
smiled at its scrawny image: I approve

that judgment as the best, which holds this earth   136
to be the least; and he whose thoughts are set
elsewhere, can truly be called virtuous.

I saw Latona's daughter radiant,   139
without the shadow that had made me once
believe that she contained both rare and dense.

And there, Hyperion, I could sustain   142
the vision of your son, and saw Dïone
and Maia as they circled nearby him.

The temperate Jupiter appeared to me   145
between his father and his son; and I
saw clearly how they vary their positions.

And all the seven heavens showed to me   148
their magnitudes, their speeds, the distances
of each from each. The little threshing floor

that so incites our savagery was all—   151
from hills to river mouths—revealed to me
while I wheeled with eternal Gemini.

My eyes then turned again to the fair eyes.   154

CANTO XXIII

The Eighth Heaven: the Sphere of the Fixed Stars. Beatrice's
expectancy. The triumph of Christ. The smile of Beatrice.
The blessed in the radiance of Christ. Triumph and coronation
of Mary. The reascent of Christ and Mary to the Empyrean.
Hymn to Mary. St. Peter.

As does the bird, among beloved branches,
when, through the night that hides things from us, she
has rested near the nest of her sweet fledglings

and, on an open branch, anticipates   4
the time when she can see their longed-for faces
and find the food with which to feed them—chore

that pleases her, however hard her labors—   7
as she awaits the sun with warm affection,
steadfastly watching for the dawn to break:

so did my lady stand, erect, intent,   10
turned toward that part of heaven under which
the sun is given to less haste; so that,

as I saw her in longing and suspense,   13
I grew to be as one who, while he wants
what is not his, is satisfied with hope.

But time between one and the other when   16
was brief—I mean the whens of waiting and
of seeing heaven grow more radiant.

And Beatrice said: "There you see the troops   19
of the triumphant Christ—and all the fruits
ingathered from the turning of these spheres!"

It seemed to me her face was all aflame,   22
and there was so much gladness in her eyes—
I am compelled to leave it undescribed.

Like Trivia—at the full moon in clear skies—   25

smiling among the everlasting nymphs
who decorate all reaches of the sky,

I saw a sun above a thousand lamps;   28
it kindled all of them as does our sun
kindle the sights above us here on earth;

and through its living light the glowing Substance   31
appeared to me with such intensity—
my vision lacked the power to sustain it.

O Beatrice, sweet guide and dear! She said   34
to me: "What overwhelms you is a Power
against which nothing can defend itself.

This is the Wisdom and the Potency   37
that opened roads between the earth and Heaven,
the paths for which desire had long since waited."

Even as lightning breaking from a cloud,   40
expanding so that it cannot be pent,
against its nature, down to earth, descends,

so did my mind, confronted by that feast,   43
expand; and it was carried past itself—
what it became, it cannot recollect.

"Open your eyes and see what I now am;   46
the things you witnessed will have made you strong
enough to bear the power of my smile."

I was as one who, waking from a dream   49
he has forgotten, tries in vain to bring
that vision back into his memory,

when I heard what she offered me, deserving   52
of so much gratitude that it can never
be canceled from the book that tells the past.

If all the tongues that Polyhymnia   55
together with her sisters made most rich
with sweetest milk, should come now to assist

my singing of the holy smile that lit   58
the holy face of Beatrice, the truth
would not be reached—not its one-thousandth part.

And thus, in representing Paradise,   61

the sacred poem has to leap across,
as does a man who finds his path cut off.

But he who thinks upon the weighty theme,   64
and on the mortal shoulder bearing it,
will lay no blame if, burdened so, I tremble:

this is no crossing for a little bark—   67
the sea that my audacious prow now cleaves—
nor for a helmsman who would spare himself.

"Why are you so enraptured by my face   70
as to deny your eyes the sight of that
fair garden blossoming beneath Christ's rays?

The Rose in which the Word of God became   73
flesh grows within that garden; there—the lilies
whose fragrance let men find the righteous way."

Thus Beatrice, and I—completely ready   76
to do what she might counsel—once again
took up the battle of my feeble brows.

Under a ray of sun that, limpid, streams   79
down from a broken cloud, my eyes have seen,
while shade was shielding them, a flowered meadow;

so I saw many troops of splendors here   82
lit from above by burning rays of light,
but where those rays began was not in sight.

O kindly Power that imprints them thus,   85
you rose on high to leave space for my eyes—
for where I was, they were too weak to see You!

The name of that fair flower which I always   88
invoke, at morning and at evening, drew
my mind completely to the greatest flame.

And when, on both my eye-lights, were depicted   91
the force and nature of the living star
that conquers heaven as it conquered earth,

descending through that sky there came a torch, 94
forming a ring that seemed as if a crown:
wheeling around her—a revolving garland.

Whatever melody most sweetly sounds   97

on earth, and to itself most draws the soul,
would seem a cloud that, torn by lightning, thunders,

    if likened to the music of that lyre   100
which sounded from the crown of that fair sapphire,
the brightest light that has ensapphired heaven.

    "I am angelic love who wheel around   103
that high gladness inspired by the womb
that was the dwelling place of our Desire;

    so shall I circle, Lady of Heaven, until   106
you, following your Son, have made that sphere
supreme, still more divine by entering it."

    So did the circulating melody,   109
sealing itself, conclude; and all the other
lights then resounded with the name of Mary.

    The royal cloak of all the wheeling spheres   112
within the universe, the heaven most
intense, alive, most burning in the breath

    of God and in His laws and ordinance,   115
was far above us at its inner shore,
so distant that it still lay out of sight

    from that point where I was; and thus my eyes   118
possessed no power to follow that crowned flame,
which mounted upward, following her Son.

    And like an infant who, when it has taken   121
its milk, extends its arms out to its mother,
its feeling kindling into outward flame,

    each of those blessed splendors stretched its peak 124
upward, so that the deep affection each
possessed for Mary was made plain to me.

    Then they remained within my sight, singing   127
"*Regina coeli*" with such tenderness
that my delight in that has never left me.

    Oh, in those richest coffers, what abundance   130
is garnered up for those who, while below,
on earth, were faithful workers when they sowed!

    Here do they live, delighting in the treasure   133

they earned with tears in Babylonian
exile, where they had no concern for gold.

Here, under the high Son of God and Mary,　　136
together with the ancient and the new
councils, he triumphs in his victory—

he who is keeper of the keys of glory.　　139

CANTO XXIV

Still the Eighth Heaven: the Sphere of the Fixed Stars. Beatrice's request to the spirits, and St. Peter's reply. Her asking of St. Peter to examine Dante on Faith. Dante's preparation and his examination. The approval and blessing of Dante by St. Peter.

"O fellowship that has been chosen for
the Blessed Lamb's great supper, where He feeds
you so as always to fulfill your need,

since by the grace of God, this man receives   4
foretaste of something fallen from your table
before death has assigned his time its limit,

direct your mind to his immense desire,   7
quench him somewhat: you who forever drink
from that Source which his thought and longing seek."

So Beatrice; and these delighted souls   10
formed companies of spheres around fixed poles,
flaming as they revolved, as comets glow.

And just as, in a clock's machinery,   13
to one who watches them, the wheels turn so
that, while the first wheel seems to rest, the last

wheel flies; so did those circling dancers—as   16
they danced to different measures, swift and slow—
make me a judge of what their riches were.

From that sphere which I noted as most precious,   19
I saw a flame come forth with so much gladness
that none it left behind had greater brightness;

and that flame whirled three times round Beatrice   22
while singing so divine a song that my
imagination cannot shape it for me.

My pen leaps over it; I do not write: 25

our fantasy and, all the more so, speech
are far too gross for painting folds so deep.

"O you who pray to us with such devotion—   28
my holy sister—with your warm affection,
you have released me from that lovely sphere."

So, after he had stopped his motion, did   31
the blessed flame breathe forth unto my lady;
and what he said I have reported here.

She answered: "O eternal light of that   34
great man to whom our Lord bequeathed the keys
of this astonishing gladness—the keys

He bore to earth—do test this man concerning   37
the faith by which you walked upon the sea;
ask him points light and grave, just as you please.

That he loves well and hopes well and has faith   40
is not concealed from you: you see that Place
where everything that happens is displayed.

But since this realm has gained its citizens   43
through the true faith, it rightly falls to him
to speak of faith, that he may glorify it."

Just as the bachelor candidate must arm   46
himself and does not speak until the master
submits the question for discussion—not

for settlement—so while she spoke I armed   49
myself with all my arguments, preparing
for such a questioner and such professing.

On hearing that light breathe, "Good Christian, speak,   52
show yourself clearly: what is faith?" I raised
my brow, then turned to Beatrice, whose glance

immediately signaled me to let   55
the waters of my inner source pour forth.
Then I: "So may the Grace that grants to me

to make confession to the Chief Centurion   58
permit my thoughts to find their fit expression";
and followed, "Father, as the truthful pen

of your dear brother wrote—that brother who,   61

with you, set Rome upon the righteous road—
faith is the substance of the things we hope for
    and is the evidence of things not seen;   64
and this I take to be its quiddity."
And then I heard: "You understand precisely,
    if it is fully clear to you why he   67
has first placed faith among the substances
and then defines it as an evidence."

    I next: "The deep things that on me bestow   70
their image here, are hid from sight below,
so that their being lies in faith alone,
    and on that faith the highest hope is founded;   73
and thus it is that faith is called a substance.
And it is from this faith that we must reason,
    deducing what we can from syllogisms   76
without our being able to see more:
thus faith is also called an evidence."

    And then I heard: "If all one learns below   79
as doctrine were so understood, there would
be no place for the sophist's cleverness."

    This speech was breathed from that enkindled love.   82
He added: "Now this coin is well-examined,
and now we know its alloy and its weight.

    But tell me: do you have it in your purse?"   85
And I: "Indeed I do—so bright and round
that nothing in its stamp leads me to doubt."

    Next, from the deep light gleaming there, I heard: 88
"What is the origin of the dear gem
that comes to you, the gem on which all virtues

    are founded?" I: "The Holy Ghost's abundant   91
rain poured upon the parchments old and new;
that is the syllogism that has proved

    with such persuasiveness that faith has truth—   94
when set beside that argument, all other
demonstrations seem to me obtuse."

    I heard: "The premises of old and new   97

Dante and Beatrice observe the circles of stars surrounding Christ the Sun, while Beatrice calls Dante's attention to the Spirit of St Peter hovering over their heads.

impelling your conclusion—why do you
hold these to be the speech of God?" And I:

"The proof revealing truth to me relies   100
on acts that happened; for such miracles,
nature can heat no iron, beat no anvil."

"Say, who assures you that those works were real?"   103
came the reply. "The very thing that needs
proof—no thing else—attests these works to you."

I said: "If without miracles the world   106
was turned to Christianity, that is
so great a miracle that all the rest

are not its hundredth part: for you were poor   109
and hungry when you found the field and sowed
the good plant—once a vine and now a thorn."

This done, the high and holy court resounded   112
throughout its spheres with "*Te Deum laudamus*,"
sung with the melody they use on high.

Then he who had examined me, that baron   115
who led me on from branch to branch so that
we now were drawing close to the last leaves,

began again: "That Grace which—lovingly—   118
directs your mind, until this point has taught
you how to find the seemly words for thought,

so that I do approve what you brought forth;   121
but now you must declare what you believe
and what gave you the faith that you receive."

"O holy father, soul who now can see   124
what you believed with such intensity
that, to His tomb, you outran younger feet,"

I then began, "you would have me tell plainly   127
the form of my unhesitating faith,
and also ask me to declare its source.

I answer: I believe in one God—sole,   130
eternal—He who, motionless, moves all
the heavens with His love and love for Him;

for this belief I have not only proofs   133

both physical and metaphysical;
I also have the truth that here rains down
　　through Moses and the Prophets and the Psalms　　136
and through the Gospels and through you who wrote
words given to you by the Holy Ghost.

　　And I believe in three Eternal Persons,　　139
and these I do believe to be one essence,
so single and threefold as to allow

　　both *is* and *are*. Of this profound condition　　142
of God that I have touched on, Gospel teaching
has often set the imprint on my mind.

　　This is the origin, this is the spark　　145
that then extends into a vivid flame
and, like a star in heaven, glows in me."

　　Just as the lord who listens to his servant's　　148
announcement, then, as soon as he is silent,
embraces him, both glad with the good news,

　　so did the apostolic light at whose　　151
command I had replied, while blessing me
and singing, then encircle me three times:

　　the speech I spoke had brought him such delight.　　154

CANTO XXV

Still the Eighth Heaven: the Sphere of the Fixed Stars. Dante's hope to return to Florence, there to be crowned as poet. The appearance of St. James, who examines Dante on Hope. The appearance of St. John the Evangelist, who dismisses the false belief in his bodily assumption to Heaven. Dante's loss of sight.

If it should happen ... If this sacred poem—
this work so shared by heaven and by earth
that it has made me lean through these long years—
    can ever overcome the cruelty   4
that bars me from the fair fold where I slept,
a lamb opposed to wolves that war on it,
    by then with other voice, with other fleece,   7
I shall return as poet and put on,
at my baptismal font, the laurel crown;
    for there I first found entry to that faith   10
which makes souls welcome unto God, and then,
for that faith, Peter garlanded my brow.
    Then did a light move toward us from that sphere   13
from which emerged the first—the dear, the rare—
of those whom Christ had left to be His vicars;
    and full of happiness, my lady said   16
to me: "Look, look—and see the baron whom,
below on earth, they visit in Galicia."
    As when a dove alights near its companion,   19
and each unto the other, murmuring
and circling, offers its affection, so
    did I see both those great and glorious   22
princes give greeting to each other, praising
the banquet that is offered them on high.

But when their salutations were complete,   25
each stopped in silence *coram me*, and each
was so aflame, my vision felt defeat.

Then Beatrice said, smiling: "Famous life   28
by whom the generosity of our
basilica has been described, do let

matters of hope reecho at this height;   31
you can—for every time that Jesus favored
you three above the rest, you were the figure

of hope." "Lift up your head, and be assured: 34
whatever comes here from the mortal world
has to be ripened in our radiance."

The second fire offered me this comfort;   37
at which my eyes were lifted to the mountains
whose weight of light before had kept me bent.

"Because our Emperor, out of His grace,   40
has willed that you, before your death, may face
His nobles in the inmost of His halls,

so that, when you have seen this court in truth,   43
hope—which, below, spurs love of the true good—
in you and others may be comforted,

do tell what hope is, tell how it has blossomed   46
within your mind, and from what source it came
to you"—so did the second flame continue.

And she, compassionate, who was the guide   49
who led my feathered wings to such high flight,
did thus anticipate my own reply:

"There is no child of the Church Militant   52
who has more hope than he has, as is written
within the Sun whose rays reach all our ranks:

thus it is granted him to come from Egypt   55
into Jerusalem that he have vision
of it, before his term of warring ends.

The other two points of your question, which   58
were not asked so that you may know, but that
he may report how much you prize this virtue,

I leave to him; he will not find them hard   61
or cause for arrogance; as you have asked,
let him reply, and God's grace help his task."

As a disciple answering his master,   64
prepared and willing in what he knows well,
that his proficiency may be revealed,

I said: "Hope is the certain expectation   67
of future glory; it is the result
of God's grace and of merit we have earned.

This light has come to me from many stars;   70
but he who first instilled it in my heart
was the chief singer of the Sovereign Guide.

'May those'—he says within his theody—   73
'who know Your name, put hope in You'; and if
one has my faith, can he not know God's name?

And just as he instilled, you then instilled   76
with your Epistle, so that I am full
and rain again your rain on other souls."

While I was speaking, in the living heart   79
of that soul-flame there came a trembling flash,
sudden, repeated, just as lightning cracks.

Then it breathed forth: "The love with which I still   82
burn for the virtue that was mine until
the palm and my departure from the field,

would have me breathe again to you who take   85
such joy in hope; and I should welcome words
that tell what hope has promised unto you."

And I: "The new and ancient Scriptures set   88
the mark for souls whom God befriends; for me,
that mark means what is promised us by hope.

Isaiah says that all of the elect   91
shall wear a double garment in their land:
and their land is this sweet life of the blessed.

And where your brother treats of those white robes,   94
he has—with words direct and evident—
made clear to us Isaiah's revelation."

At first, as soon as I had finished speaking,
"*Sperent in te*" was heard above us, all
the circling garlands answering this call.

And then, among those souls, one light became
so bright that, if the Crab had one such crystal,
winter would have a month of one long day.

And as a happy maiden rises and
enters the dance to honor the new bride—
and not through vanity or other failing—

so did I see that splendor, brightening,
approach those two flames dancing in a ring
to music suited to their burning love.

And there it joined the singing and the circling,
on which my lady kept her eyes intent,
just like a bride, silent and motionless.

"This soul is he who lay upon the breast
of Christ our Pelican, and he was asked
from on the Cross to serve in the great task."

So spoke my lady; but her gaze was not
to be diverted from its steadfastness,
not after or before her words were said.

Even as he who squints and strains to see
the sun somewhat eclipsed and, as he tries
to see, becomes sightless, just so did I

in my attempt to watch the latest flame,
until these words were said: "Why do you daze
yourself to see what here can have no place?

On earth my body now is earth and shall
be there together with the rest until
our number equals the eternal purpose.

Only those two lights that ascended wear
their double garment in this blessed cloister.
And carry this report back to your world."

When he began to speak, the flaming circle
had stopped its dance; so, too, its song had ceased—
that gentle mingling of their threefold breath—

even as when, avoiding danger or   133
simply to rest, the oars that strike the water,
together halt when rowers hear a whistle.

Ah, how disturbed I was within my mind,   136
when I turned round to look at Beatrice,
on finding that I could not see, though I
    was close to her, and in the world of gladness!   139

CANTO XXVI

Still the Eighth Heaven: the Sphere of the Fixed Stars. St. John's examination of Dante on Charity or Love. Approbation of Dante by the blessed and the restoration of his sight. Adam's answers to Dante's four implicit questions.

While I, with blinded eyes, was apprehensive,
from that bright flame which had consumed my vision,
there breathed a voice that centered my attention,

saying: "Until you have retrieved the power   4
of sight, which you consumed in me, it would
be best to compensate by colloquy.

Then do begin; declare the aim on which   7
your soul is set—and be assured of this:
your vision, though confounded, is not dead,

because the woman who conducts you through   10
this godly region has, within her gaze,
that force the hand of Ananias had."

I said: "As pleases her, may solace—sooner   13
or later—reach these eyes, her gates when she
brought me the fire with which I always burn.

The good with which this court is satisfied   16
is Alpha and Omega of all writings
that Love has—loud or low—read out to me."

It was the very voice that had dispelled   19
the fear I felt at sudden dazzlement,
that now, with further words, made me concerned

to speak again. He said: "You certainly   22
must sift with a still finer sieve, must tell
who led your bow to aim at such a target."

And I: "By philosophic arguments   25
and by authority whose source is here,

that love must be imprinted in me; for

the good, once it is understood as such,   28
enkindles love; and in accord with more
goodness comes greater love. And thus the mind

of anyone who can discern the truth   31
on which this proof is founded must be moved
to love, more than it loves all else, that Essence

which is preeminent (since any good   34
that lies outside of It is nothing but
a ray reflected from Its radiance).

My mind discerns this truth, made plain by him   37
who demonstrates to me that the first love
of the eternal beings is their Maker.

The voice of the true Author states this, too,   40
where He tells Moses, speaking of Himself:
'I shall show you all goodness.' You reveal

this, too, when you begin your high Evangel,   43
which more than any other proclamation
cries out to earth the mystery of Heaven."

I heard: "Through human reasoning and through   46
authorities according with it, you
conclude: your highest love is bent on God.

But tell me, too, if you feel other cords   49
draw you toward Him, so that you voice aloud
all of the teeth by which this love grips you."

The holy intent of Christ's Eagle was   52
not hidden; I indeed was made aware
of what he would most have my words declare.

Thus I began again: "My charity   55
results from all those things whose bite can bring
the heart to turn to God; the world's existence

and mine, the death that He sustained that I   58
might live, and that which is the hope of all
believers, as it is my hope, together

with living knowledge I have spoken of—   61
these drew me from the sea of twisted love

and set me on the shore of the right love.

The leaves enleaving all the garden of   64
the Everlasting Gardener, I love
according to the good He gave to them."

As soon as I was still, a song most sweet   67
resounded through that heaven, and my lady
said with the others: "Holy, holy, holy!"

And just as a sharp light will startle us   70
from sleep because the spirit of eyesight
races to meet the brightness that proceeds

from layer to layer in the eye, and he   73
who wakens is confused by what he sees,
awaking suddenly, and knows no thing

until his judgment helps him; even so   76
did Beatrice dispel, with her eyes' rays,
which shone more than a thousand miles, the chaff

from my eyes: I saw better than I had   79
before; and as if stupefied, I asked
about the fourth light that I saw among us.

My lady answered: "In those rays there gazes   82
with love for his Creator the first soul
ever created by the Primal Force."

As does a tree that bends its crown because   85
of winds that gust, and then springs up, raised by
its own sustaining power, so did I

while she was speaking. I, bewildered, then   88
restored to confidence by that desire
to speak with which I was inflamed, began:

"O fruit that was the only one to be   91
brought forth already ripe, o ancient father
to whom each bride is as a daughter and

daughter-in-law, devoutly as I can,   94
I do beseech you: speak with me. You see
my wish; to hear you sooner, I do not

declare it." And the primal soul—much as   97
an animal beneath a cover stirs,

Blinded by the radiance of St John, Dante shields his eyes. His sight returned, the poet questions the Spirit of Adam (marked 'adamo') concerning life in Eden.

so that its feelings are made evident
  when what enfolds it follows all its movements—   100
showed me, through that which covered him, with what
rejoicing he was coming to delight me.

  Then he breathed forth: "Though you do not declare   103
your wish, I can perceive it better than
you can perceive the things you hold most certain;

  for I can see it in the Truthful Mirror   106
that perfectly reflects all else, while no
thing can reflect that Mirror perfectly.

  You wish to hear how long it is since I   109
was placed by God in that high garden where
this lady readied you to climb a stair

  so long, and just how long it pleased my eyes,   112
and the true cause of the great anger, and
what idiom I used and shaped. My son,

  the cause of my long exile did not lie   115
within the act of tasting of the tree,
but solely in my trespass of the boundary.

  During four thousand three hundred and two   118
re-turnings of the sun, while I was in
that place from which your Lady sent you Virgil,

  I longed for this assembly. While on earth,   121
I saw the sun return to all the lights
along its way, nine hundred thirty times.

  The tongue I spoke was all extinct before   124
the men of Nimrod set their minds upon
the unaccomplishable task; for never

  has any thing produced by human reason   127
been everlasting—following the heavens,
men seek the new, they shift their predilections.

  That man should speak at all is nature's act,   130
but how you speak—in this tongue or in that—
she leaves to you and to your preference.

  Before I was sent down to Hell's sad sighs,   133
on earth, the Highest Good—from which derives

the joy that now enfolds me—was called *I*;
and then He was called *El*. Such change must be: 136
the ways that mortals take are as the leaves
upon a branch—one comes, another goes.

On that peak rising highest from the sea,   139
my life—first pure, then tainted—lasted from
the first hour to the hour that follows on

the sixth, when the sun shifts to a new quadrant."   142

CANTO XXVII

Still the Eighth Heaven: the Sphere of the Fixed Stars. The hymn of the blessed. St. Peter's condemnation of the popes and the corrupt Church. His urging of Dante to fulfill his mission on earth. Dante's earthward gaze. Ascent to the ninth Heaven, the Primum Mobile. Its nature explained by Beatrice. Her discourse on the present straying of the world; her prophecy of its redemption.

"Unto the Father, Son, and Holy Ghost,
glory!"—all Paradise began, so that
the sweetness of the singing held me rapt.

What I saw seemed to me to be a smile   4
the universe had smiled; my rapture had
entered by way of hearing and of sight.

O joy! O gladness words can never speak!   7
O life perfected by both love and peace!
O richness so assured, that knows no longing!

Before my eyes, there stood, aflame, the four   10
torches, and that which had been first to come
began to glow with greater radiance,

and what its image then became was like   13
what Jupiter's would be if Mars and he
were birds and had exchanged their plumages.

After the Providence that there assigns   16
to every office its appointed time
had, to those holy choirs, on every side,

commanded silence, I then heard: "If I   19
change color, do not be amazed, for as
I speak, you will see change in all these flames.

He who on earth usurps my place, my place,   22
my place that in the sight of God's own Son

is vacant now, has made my burial ground
    a sewer of blood, a sewer of stench, so that   25
the perverse one who fell from Heaven, here
above, can find contentment there below."

    Then I saw all the heaven colored by   28
the hue that paints the clouds at morning and
at evening, with the sun confronting them.

    And like a woman who, although secure   31
in her own honesty, will pale on even
hearing about another woman's failing,

    just so did Beatrice change in appearance;   34
and I believe that such eclipse was in
the sky when He, the Highest Power, suffered.

    Then his words followed with a voice so altered   37
from what it was before—even his likeness
did not display a greater change than that.

    "The Bride of Christ was never nurtured by   40
my blood, and blood of Linus and of Cletus,
to be employed in gaining greater riches;

    but to acquire this life of joyousness,   43
Sixtus and Pius, Urban and Calixtus,
after much lamentation, shed their blood.

    We did not want one portion of Christ's people   46
to sit at the right side of our successors,
while, on the left, the other portion sat,

    nor did we want the keys that were consigned   49
to me, to serve as an escutcheon on
a banner that waged war against the baptized;

    nor did we want my form upon a seal   52
for trafficking in lying privileges—
for which I often blush and flash with anger.

    From here on high one sees rapacious wolves   55
clothed in the cloaks of shepherds. You, the vengeance
of God, oh, why do you still lie concealed?

    The Gascons and the Cahorsines—they both   58
prepare to drink our blood: o good beginning,

From the Sphere of the Fixed Stars, Dante and Beatrice look down through the Spheres of Heaven and Beatrice explains the nature of Time.

to what a miserable end you fall!

But that high Providence which once preserved,   61
with Scipio, the glory of the world
for Rome, will soon bring help, as I conceive;

and you, my son, who through your mortal weight   64
will yet return below, speak plainly there,
and do not hide that which I do not hide."

As, when the horn of heaven's Goat abuts   67
the sun, our sky flakes frozen vapors downward,
so did I see that ether there adorned;

for from that sphere, triumphant vapors now   70
were flaking up to the Empyrean—
returning after dwelling here with us.

My sight was following their semblances—   73
until the space between us grew so great
as to deny my eyes all farther reach.

At this, my lady, seeing me set free   76
from gazing upward, told me: "Let your eyes
look down and see how far you have revolved."

I saw that, from the time when I looked down   79
before, I had traversed all of the arc
of the first clime, from its midpoint to end,

so that, beyond Cadiz, I saw Ulysses'   82
mad course and, to the east, could almost see
that shoreline where Europa was sweet burden.

I should have seen more of this threshing floor   85
but for the motion of the sun beneath
my feet: it was a sign and more away.

My mind, enraptured, always longing for   88
my lady gallantly, was burning more
than ever for my eyes' return to her;

and if—by means of human flesh or portraits—   91
nature or art has fashioned lures to draw
the eye so as to grip the mind, all these

would seem nothing if set beside the godly   94
beauty that shone upon me when I turned

to see the smiling face of Beatrice.

The powers that her gaze now granted me   97
drew me out of the lovely nest of Leda
and thrust me into heaven's swiftest sphere.

Its parts were all so equally alive   100
and excellent, that I cannot say which
place Beatrice selected for my entry.

But she, who saw what my desire was—   103
her smile had so much gladness that within
her face there seemed to be God's joy—began:

"The nature of the universe, which holds   106
the center still and moves all else around it,
begins here as if from its turning-post.

This heaven has no other *where* than this: 109
the mind of God, in which are kindled both
the love that turns it and the force it rains.

As in a circle, light and love enclose it,   112
as it surrounds the rest—and that enclosing,
only He who encloses understands.

No other heaven measures this sphere's motion,   115
but it serves as the measure for the rest,
even as half and fifth determine ten;

and now it can be evident to you   118
how time has roots within this vessel and,
within the other vessels, has its leaves.

O greediness, you who—within your depths—   121
cause mortals to sink so, that none is left
able to lift his eyes above your waves!

The will has a good blossoming in men;   124
but then the never-ending downpours turn
the sound plums into rotten, empty skins.

For innocence and trust are to be found   127
only in little children; then they flee
even before a full beard cloaks the cheeks.

One, for as long as he still lisps, will fast,   130
but when his tongue is free at last, he gorges,

devouring any food through any month;

    and one, while he still lisps, will love and heed   133
his mother, but when he acquires speech
more fully, he will long to see her buried.

    Just so, white skin turns black when it is struck   136
by direct light—the lovely daughter of
the one who brings us dawn and leaves us evening.

    That you not be amazed at what I say,   139
consider this: on earth no king holds sway;
therefore, the family of humans strays.

    But well before nine thousand years have passed   142
(and January is unwintered by
day's hundredth part, which they neglect below),

    this high sphere shall shine so, that Providence,   145
long waited for, will turn the sterns to where
the prows now are, so that the fleet runs straight;

    and then fine fruit shall follow on the flower."   148

CANTO XXVIII

The Ninth Heaven: the Primum Mobile. The nine luminous circles of the angelic hierarchies. Their revolutions around a Point. Beatrice's explanation. The celestial hierarchy. The correct angelology of Dionysius and the mistake of St. Gregory.

After the lady who imparadises
my mind disclosed the truth that is unlike
the present life of miserable mortals,
    then, just as one who sees a mirrored flame—   4
its double candle stands behind his back—
even before he thought of it or gazed
    directly at it, and he turns to gauge   7
if that glass tells the truth to him, and sees
that it accords, like voice and instrument,
    so—does my memory recall—I did   10
after I looked into the lovely eyes
of which Love made the noose that holds me tight.
    And when I turned and my own eyes were met   13
by what appears within that sphere whenever
one looks intently at its revolution,
    I saw a point that sent forth so acute   16
a light, that anyone who faced the force
with which it blazed would have to shut his eyes,
    and any star that, seen from earth, would seem   19
to be the smallest, set beside that point,
as star conjoined with star, would seem a moon.
    Around that point a ring of fire wheeled,   22
a ring perhaps as far from that point as
a halo from the star that colors it
    when mist that forms the halo is most thick.   25

It wheeled so quickly that it would outsrip
the motion that most swiftly girds the world.

That ring was circled by a second ring,   28
the second by a third, third by a fourth,
fourth by a fifth, and fifth ring by a sixth.

Beyond, the seventh ring, which followed, was   31
so wide that all of Juno's messenger
would be too narrow to contain that circle.

The eighth and ninth were wider still; and each,   34
even as greater distance lay between
it and the first ring, moved with lesser speed;

and, I believe, the ring with clearest flame   37
was that which lay least far from the pure spark
because it shares most deeply that point's truth.

My lady, who saw my perplexity—   40
I was in such suspense—said: "On that Point
depend the heavens and the whole of nature.

Look at the circle that is nearest It,   43
and know: its revolutions are so swift
because of burning love that urges it."

And I to her: "If earth and the nine spheres   46
were ordered like those rings, then I would be
content with what you have set out before me,

but in the world of sense, what one can see   49
are spheres becoming ever more divine
as they are set more distant from the center.

Thus, if my longing is to gain its end   52
in this amazing and angelic temple
that has, as boundaries, only love and light,

then I still have to hear just how the model   55
and copy do not share in one same plan—
for by myself I think on this in vain."

"You need not wonder if your fingers are   58
unable to undo that knot: no one
has tried, and so that knot is tightened, taut!"

my lady said, and then continued: "If   61

you would be satisfied, take what I tell you—
and let your mind be sharp as I explain.

The size of spheres of matter—large or small—   64
depends upon the power—more and less—
that spreads throughout their parts. More excellence

yields greater blessedness; more blessedness   67
must comprehend a greater body when
that body's parts are equally complete.

And thus this sphere, which sweeps along with it   70
the rest of all the universe, must match
the circle that loves most and knows the most,

so that, if you but draw your measure round   73
the power within—and not the semblance of—
the angels that appear to you as circles,

you will discern a wonderful accord   76
between each sphere and its Intelligence:
greater accords with more, smaller with less."

Just as the hemisphere of air remains   79
splendid, serene, when from his gentler cheek
Boreas blows and clears the scoriae,

dissolves the mist that had defaced the sky,   82
so that the heavens smile with loveliness
in all their regions; even so did I

become after my lady had supplied   85
her clear response to me, and—like a star
in heaven—truth was seen. And when her words

were done, even as incandescent iron   88
will shower sparks, so did those circles sparkle;
and each spark circled with its flaming ring—

sparks that were more in number than the sum   91
one reaches doubling in succession each
square of a chessboard, one to sixty-four.

I heard "*Hosanna*" sung, from choir to choir   94
to that fixed Point which holds and always shall
hold them to where they have forever been.

And she who saw my mind's perplexities   97

said: "The first circles have displayed to you
the Seraphim and Cherubim. They follow
   the ties of love with such rapidity   100
because they are as like the Point as creatures
can be, a power dependent on their vision.

   Those other loves that circle round them are   103
called Thrones of the divine aspect, because
they terminated the first group of three;
   and know that all delight to the degree   106
to which their vision sees—more or less deeply—
that truth in which all intellects find rest.

   From this you see that blessedness depends   109
upon the act of vision, not upon
the act of love—which is a consequence;
   the measure of their vision lies in merit,   112
produced by grace and then by will to goodness:
and this is the progression, step by step.

   The second triad—blossoming in this   115
eternal springtime that the nightly Ram
does not despoil—perpetually sings
   '*Hosanna*' with three melodies that sound   118
in the three ranks of bliss that form this triad;
within this hierarchy there are three
   kinds of divinities: first, the Dominions,   121
and then the Virtues; and the final order
contains the Powers. The two penultimate
   groups of rejoicing ones within the next   124
triad are wheeling Principalities
and the Archangels; last, the playful Angels.

   These orders all direct—ecstatically—   127
their eyes on high; and downward, they exert
such force that all are drawn and draw to God.

   And Dionysius, with much longing, set   130
himself to contemplate these orders: he
named and distinguished them just as I do.

   Though, later, Gregory disputed him,   133

when Gregory came here—when he could see
with opened eyes—he smiled at his mistake.

You need not wonder if a mortal told   136
such secret truth on earth: it was disclosed
to him by one who saw it here above—
both that and other truths about these circles."   139

CANTO XXIX

*Still the Ninth Heaven: the Primum Mobile. The silence of
Beatrice, then her discourse on creation and on rebel and
faithful angels; her digressing diatribe against useless philoso-
phizing and preaching; and her conclusion, on the number of
the angels.*

As long as both Latona's children take
(when, covered by the Ram and Scales, they make
their belt of the horizon at the same

moment) to pass from equilibrium—   4
the zenith held in balance—to that state
where, changing hemispheres, each leaves that belt,

so long did Beatrice, a smile upon   7
her face, keep silent, even as she gazed
intently at the Point that overwhelmed me.

Then she began: "I tell—not ask—what you   10
now want to hear, for I have seen it there
where, in one point, all *whens* and *ubis* end.

Not to acquire new goodness for Himself—   13
which cannot be—but that his splendor might,
as it shines back to Him, declare '*Subsisto*,'

in His eternity outside of time,   16
beyond all other borders, as pleased Him,
Eternal Love opened into new loves.

Nor did he lie, before this, as if languid;   19
there was no *after*, no *before*—they were
not there until God moved upon these waters.

Then form and matter, either separately   22
or in mixed state, emerged as flawless being,
as from a three-stringed bow, three arrows spring.

And as a ray shines into amber, crystal,   25

or glass, so that there is no interval
between its coming and its lighting all,

    so did the three—form, matter, and their union—   28
flash into being from the Lord with no
distinction in beginning: all at once.

    Created with the substances were order   31
and pattern; at the summit of the world
were those in whom pure act had been produced;

    and pure potentiality possessed   34
the lowest part; and in the middle, act
so joined potentiality that they

    never disjoin. For you, Jerome has written   37
that the creation of the angels came
long centuries before all else was made;

    but this, the truth I speak, is written by   40
scribes of the Holy Ghost—as you can find
if you look carefully—on many pages;

    and reason, too, can see in part this truth,   43
for it would not admit that those who move
the heavens could, for so long, be without

    their perfect task. Now you know where and when   46
and how these loving spirits were created:
with this, three flames of your desire are quenched.

    Then, sooner than it takes to count to twenty,   49
a portion of the angels violently
disturbed the lowest of your elements.

    The rest remained; and they, with such rejoicing,   52
began the office you can see, that they
never desert their circling contemplation.

    The fall had its beginning in the cursed   55
pride of the one you saw, held in constraint
by all of the world's weights. Those whom you see

    in Heaven here were modestly aware   58
that they were ready for intelligence
so vast, because of that Good which had made them:

    through this, their vision was exalted with   61

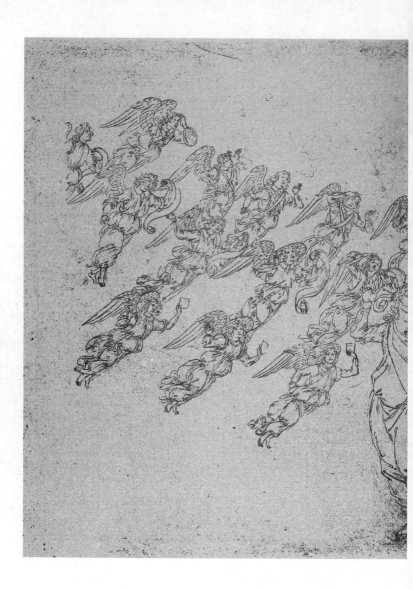

In the Primum Mobile, Beatrice expounds to Dante the various orders of Angels.

illuminating grace and with their merit,
so that their will is constant and intact.

I would not have you doubt, but have you know   64
surely that there is merit in receiving
grace, measured by the longing to receive it.

By now, if you have taken in my words,   67
you need no other aid to contemplate
much in regard to this consistory.

But since on earth, throughout your schools, they teach   70
that it is in the nature of the angels
to understand, to recollect, to will,

I shall say more, so that you may see clearly   73
the truth that, there below, has been confused
by teaching that is so ambiguous.

These beings, since they first were gladdened by   76
the face of God, from which no thing is hidden,
have never turned their vision from that face,

so that their sight is never intercepted   79
by a new object, and they have no need
to recollect an interrupted concept.

So that, below, though not asleep, men dream,   82
speaking in good faith or in bad—the last,
however, merits greater blame and shame.

Below, you do not follow one sole path   85
as you philosophize—your love of show
and thought of it so carry you astray!

Yet even love of show is suffered here   88
with less disdain than the subordination
or the perversion of the Holy Scripture.

There, they devote no thought to how much blood   91
it costs to sow it in the world, to how
pleasing is he who—humbly—holds it fast.

Each one strives for display, elaborates   94
his own inventions; preachers speak at length
of these—meanwhile the Gospels do not speak.

One says that, to prevent the sun from reaching   97

below, the moon—when Christ was crucified—
moved back along the zodiac, so as
    to interpose itself; who says so, lies—   100
for sunlight hid itself; not only Jews,
but Spaniards, Indians, too, saw that eclipse.

    Such fables, shouted through the year from pulpits—   103
some here, some there—outnumber even all
the Lapos and the Bindos Florence has;
    so that the wretched sheep, in ignorance,   106
return from pasture, having fed on wind—
but to be blind to harm does not excuse them.

    Christ did not say to his first company: 109
'Go, and preach idle stories to the world';
but he gave them the teaching that is truth,
    and truth alone was sounded when they spoke;   112
and thus, to battle to enkindle faith,
the Gospels served them as both shield and lance.

    But now men go to preach with jests and jeers,   115
and just as long as they can raise a laugh,
the cowl puffs up, and nothing more is asked.
    But such a bird nests in that cowl, that if   118
the people saw it, they would recognize
as lies the pardons in which they confide—
    pardons through which the world's credulity   121
increases so, that people throng to every
indulgence backed by no authority;
    and this allows the Antonines to fatten   124
their pigs, and others, too, more piggish still,
who pay with counterfeit, illegal tender.

    But since we have digressed enough, turn back   127
your eyes now to the way that is direct;
our time is short—so, too, must be our path.

    The number of these angels is so great   130
that there has never been a mortal speech
or mortal thought that named a sum so steep;
    and if you look at that which is revealed   133

by Daniel, you will see that, while he mentions
thousands, he gives no number with precision.

The First Light reaches them in ways as many   136
as are the angels to which It conjoins
Itself, as It illumines all of them;

and this is why (because affection follows   139
the act of knowledge) the intensity
of love's sweetness appears unequally.

By now you see the height, you see the breadth,   142
of the Eternal Goodness: It has made
so many mirrors, which divide Its light,

but, as before, Its own Self still is One."   145

CANTO XXX

The departure of the spirits. The beauty of Beatrice. Arrival in the Tenth Heaven, the Empyrean. The Celestial Rose. The seat assigned to Henry VII. Beatrice's final words: her condemnation of Boniface VIII.

Perhaps six thousand miles away from us,
the sixth hour burns, and now our world inclines
its shadow to an almost level bed,

 so that the span of heaven high above   4
begins to alter so, that some stars are
no longer to be seen from our deep earth;

 and as the brightest handmaid of the sun   7
advances, heaven shuts off, one by one,
its lights, until the loveliest is gone.

 So did the triumph that forever plays   10
around the Point that overcame me (Point
that seems enclosed by that which It encloses)

 fade gradually from my sight, so that   13
my seeing nothing else—and love—compelled
my eyes to turn again to Beatrice.

 If that which has been said of her so far   16
were all contained within a single praise,
it would be much too scant to serve me now.

 The loveliness I saw surpassed not only   19
our human measure—and I think that, surely,
only its Maker can enjoy it fully.

 I yield: I am defeated at this passage   22
more than a comic or a tragic poet
has ever been by a barrier in his theme;

 for like the sun that strikes the frailest eyes,   25
so does the memory of her sweet smile

deprive me of the use of my own mind.

From that first day when, in this life, I saw   28
her face, until I had this vision, no
thing ever cut the sequence of my song,

but now I must desist from this pursuit,   31
in verses, of her loveliness, just as
each artist who has reached his limit must.

So she, in beauty (as I leave her to   34
a herald that is greater than my trumpet,
which nears the end of its hard theme), with voice

and bearing of a guide whose work is done,   37
began again: "From matter's largest sphere,
we now have reached the heaven of pure light,

light of the intellect, light filled with love,   40
love of true good, love filled with happiness,
a happiness surpassing every sweetness.

Here you will see both ranks of Paradise   43
and see one of them wearing that same aspect
which you will see again at Judgment Day."

Like sudden lightning scattering the spirits   46
of sight so that the eye is then too weak
to act on other things it would perceive,

such was the living light encircling me,   49
leaving me so enveloped by its veil
of radiance that I could see no thing.

"The Love that calms this heaven always welcomes   52
into Itself with such a salutation,
to make the candle ready for its flame."

No sooner had these few words entered me   55
than I became aware that I was rising
beyond the power that was mine; and such

new vision kindled me again, that even   58
the purest light would not have been so bright
as to defeat my eyes, deny my sight;

and I saw light that took a river's form—   61
light flashing, reddish-gold, between two banks

painted with wonderful spring flowerings.

Out of that stream there issued living sparks,   64
which settled on the flowers on all sides,
like rubies set in gold; and then, as if

intoxicated with the odors, they   67
again plunged into the amazing flood:
as one spark sank, another spark emerged.

"The high desire that now inflames, incites,   70
you to grasp mentally the things you see,
pleases me more as it swells more; but first,

that you may satisfy your mighty thirst,   73
you must drink of these waters." So did she
who is the sun of my eyes speak to me.

She added this: "The river and the gems   76
of topaz entering and leaving, and
the grasses' laughter—these are shadowy

prefaces of their truth; not that these things   79
are lacking in themselves; the defect lies
in you, whose sight is not yet that sublime."

No infant who awakes long after his   82
usual hour would turn his face toward milk
as quickly as I hurried toward that stream;

to make still finer mirrors of my eyes,   85
I bent down toward the waters which flow there
that we, in them, may find our betterment.

But as my eyelids' eaves drank of that wave,   88
it seemed to me that it had changed its shape:
no longer straight, that flow now formed a round.

Then, just as maskers, when they set aside   91
the borrowed likenesses in which they hide,
seem to be other than they were before,

so were the flowers and the sparks transformed,   94
changing to such festivity before me
that I saw—clearly—both of Heaven's courts.

O radiance of God, through which I saw   97
the noble triumph of the true realm, give

Surrounded by light, whose river flows beneath them, Dante and Beatrice ascend to the Empyrean.

to me the power to speak of what I saw!

Above, on high, there is a light that makes   100
apparent the Creator to the creature
whose only peace lies in his seeing Him.

The shape which that light takes as it expands   103
is circular, and its circumference
would be too great a girdle for the sun.

All that one sees of it derives from one   106
light-ray reflected from the summit of
the Primum Mobile, which from it draws

power and life. And as a hill is mirrored   109
in waters at its base, as if to see
itself—when rich with grass and flowers—graced,

so in a thousand tiers that towered above   112
the light, encircling it, I saw, mirrored,
all of us who have won return above.

And if the lowest rank ingathers such   115
vast light, then what must be the measure of
this Rose where it has reached its highest leaves!

Within that breadth and height I did not find   118
my vision gone astray, for it took in
that joy in all its quality and kind.

There, near and far do not subtract or add;   121
for where God governs with no mediator,
no thing depends upon the laws of nature.

Into the yellow of the eternal Rose   124
that slopes and stretches and diffuses fragrance
of praise unto the Sun of endless spring,

now Beatrice drew me as one who, though   127
he would speak out, is silent. And she said:
"See how great is this council of white robes!

See how much space our city's circuit spans!   130
See how our seated ranks are now so full
that little room is left for any more!

And in that seat on which your eyes are fixed   133
because a crown already waits above it,

before you join this wedding feast, shall sit
    the soul of noble Henry, he who is,   136
on earth, to be imperial; he shall
show Italy the righteous way—but when
    she is unready. The blind greediness   139
bewitching you, has made you like the child
who dies of hunger and drives off his nurse.
    And in the holy forum such shall be   142
the Prefect then, that either openly
or secretly he will not walk with Henry.
    But God will not endure him long within   145
the holy ministry: he shall be cast
down there, where Simon Magus pays; he shall
    force the Anagnine deeper in his hole."   148

CANTO XXXI

The Tenth Heaven: the Empyrean. The Rose. Dante's
amazement. The appearance of St. Bernard instead of
Beatrice. Dante's vision of—and prayer to—Beatrice. His
response to St. Bernard's urging him to contemplate the Rose
and Mary. Mary's delight in the festive angels.

So, in the shape of that white Rose, the holy
legion was shown to me—the host that Christ,
with His own blood, had taken as His bride.

The other host, which, flying, sees and sings   4
the glory of the One who draws its love,
and that goodness which granted it such glory,

just like a swarm of bees that, at one moment,   7
enters the flowers and, at another, turns
back to that labor which yields such sweet savor,

descended into that vast flower graced   10
with many petals, then again rose up
to the eternal dwelling of its love.

Their faces were all living flame; their wings   13
were gold; and for the rest, their white was so
intense, no snow can match the white they showed.

When they climbed down into that flowering Rose,   16
from rank to rank, they shared that peace and ardor
which they had gained, with wings that fanned their sides.

Nor did so vast a throng in flight, although   19
it interposed between the candid Rose
and light above, obstruct the sight or splendor,

because the light of God so penetrates   22
the universe according to the worth
of every part, that no thing can impede it.

This confident and joyous kingdom, thronged   25

with people of both new and ancient times,
turned all its sight and ardor to one mark.

O threefold Light that, in a single star   28
sparkling into their eyes, contents them so,
look down and see our tempest here below!

If the Barbarians, when they came from   31
a region that is covered every day
by Helice, who wheels with her loved son,

were, seeing Rome and her vast works, struck dumb   34
(when, of all mortal things, the Lateran
was the most eminent), then what amazement

must have filled me when I to the divine   37
came from the human, to eternity
from time, and to a people just and sane

from Florence came! And certainly, between   40
my wonder and my joy—they were complete—
I felt no need to hear, no need to speak.

And as a pilgrim, in the temple he   43
had vowed to reach, renews himself—he looks
and hopes he can describe what it was like—

so did I journey through the living light,   46
guiding my eyes, from rank to rank, along
a path now up, now down, now circling round.

There I saw faces given up to love—   49
graced with Another's light and their own smile—
and movements graced with every dignity.

By now my gaze had taken in the whole   52
of Paradise—its form in general—
but without looking hard at any part;

and I, my will rekindled, turning toward   55
my lady, was prepared to ask about
those matters that inclined my mind to doubt.

Where I expected her, another answered: 58
I thought I should see Beatrice, and saw
an elder dressed like those who are in glory.

His gracious gladness filled his eyes, suffused   61

his cheeks; his manner had that kindliness
which suits a tender father. "Where is she?"

I asked him instantly. And he replied: 64
"That all your longings may be satisfied,
Beatrice urged me from my place. If you

look up and to the circle that is third 67
from that rank which is highest, you will see
her on the throne her merits have assigned her."

I, without answering, then looked on high 70
and saw that round her now a crown took shape
as she reflected the eternal rays.

No mortal eye, not even one that plunged 73
into deep seas, would be so distant from
that region where the highest thunder forms,

as—there—my sight was far from Beatrice; 76
but distance was no hindrance, for her semblance
reached me—undimmed by any thing between.

"O lady, you in whom my hope gains strength, 79
you who, for my salvation, have allowed
your footsteps to be left in Hell, in all

the things that I have seen, I recognize 82
the grace and benefit that I, depending
upon your power and goodness, have received.

You drew me out from slavery to freedom 85
by all those paths, by all those means that were
within your power. Do, in me, preserve

your generosity, so that my soul, 88
which you have healed, when it is set loose from
my body, be a soul that you will welcome."

So did I pray. And she, however far 91
away she seemed, smiled, and she looked at me.
Then she turned back to the eternal fountain.

And he, the holy elder, said: "That you 94
may consummate your journey perfectly—
for this, both prayer and holy love have sent me

to help you—let your sight fly round this garden; 97

by gazing so, your vision will be made
more ready to ascend through God's own ray.

The Queen of Heaven, for whom I am all 100
aflame with love, will grant us every grace:
I am her faithful Bernard." Just as one

who, from Croatia perhaps, has come 103
to visit our Veronica—one whose
old hunger is not sated, who, as long

as it is shown, repeats these words in thought: 106
"O my Lord Jesus Christ, true God, was then
Your image like the image I see now?"—

such was I as I watched the living love 109
of him who, in this world, in contemplation,
tasted that peace. And he said: "Son of grace,

you will not come to know this joyous state 112
if your eyes only look down at the base;
but look upon the circles, look at those

that sit in a position more remote, 115
until you see upon her seat the Queen
to whom this realm is subject and devoted."

I lifted up my eyes; and as, at morning, 118
the eastern side of the horizon shows
more splendor than the side where the sun sets,

so, as if climbing with my eyes from valley 121
to summit, I saw one part of the farthest
rank of the Rose more bright than all the rest.

And as, on earth, the point where we await 124
the shaft that Phaethon had misguided glows
brightest, while, to each side, the light shades off,

so did the peaceful oriflamme appear 127
brightest at its midpoint, so did its flame,
on each side, taper off at equal pace.

I saw, around that midpoint, festive angels— 130
more than a thousand—with their wings outspread;
each was distinct in splendor and in skill.

And there I saw a loveliness that when 133

it smiled at the angelic songs and games
made glad the eyes of all the other saints.

    And even if my speech were rich as my   136
imagination is, I should not try
to tell the very least of her delights.

    Bernard—when he had seen my eyes intent,   139
fixed on the object of his burning fervor—
turned his own eyes to her with such affection

    that he made mine gaze still more ardently.   142

CANTO XXXII

Still the Tenth Heaven: the Empyrean. The placement of the blessed in the Rose. Predestination and the blessed infants. Mary. The angel Gabriel. The great patricians of the Empyrean. Bernard's urging of Dante to beseech Mary.

Though he had been absorbed in his delight,
that contemplator freely undertook
the task of teaching; and his holy words

    began: "The wound that Mary closed and then   4
anointed was the wound that Eve—so lovely
at Mary's feet—had opened and had pierced.

    Below her, in the seats of the third rank,   7
Rachel and Beatrice, as you see, sit.
Sarah, Rebecca, Judith, and the one

    who was the great-grandmother of the singer   10
who, as he sorrowed for his sinfulness,
cried, '*Miserere mei*'—these you can see

    from rank to rank as I, in moving through   13
the Rose, from petal unto petal, give
to each her name. And from the seventh rank,

    just as they did within the ranks above,   16
the Hebrew women follow—ranging downward—
dividing all the tresses of the Rose.

    They are the wall by which the sacred stairs   19
divide, depending on the view of Christ
with which their faith is aligned. Upon one side,

    there where the Rose is ripe, with all its petals, 22
are those whose faith was in the Christ to come;
and on the other side—that semicircle

    whose space is broken up by vacant places—   25
sit those whose sight was set upon the Christ

who had already come. And just as on
  this side, to serve as such a great partition,   28
there is the throne in glory of the Lady
of Heaven and the seats that range below it,

  so, opposite, the seat of the great John—   31
who, always saintly, suffered both the desert
and martyrdom, and then two years of Hell—

  serves to divide; below him sit, assigned   34
to this partition, Francis, Benedict,
and Augustine, and others, rank on rank,

  down to this center of the Rose. Now see   37
how deep is God's foresight: both aspects of
the faith shall fill this garden equally.

  And know that there, below the transverse row   40
that cuts across the two divisions, sit
souls who are there for merits not their own,

  but—with certain conditions—others' merits;   43
for all of these are souls who left their bodies
before they had the power of true choice.

  Indeed, you may perceive this by yourself—   46
their faces, childlike voices, are enough,
if you look well at them and hear them sing.

  But now you doubt and, doubting, do not speak;   49
yet I shall loose that knot; I can release
you from the bonds of subtle reasoning.

  Within the ample breadth of this domain,   52
no point can find its place by chance, just as
there is no place for sorrow, thirst, or hunger;

  whatever you may see has been ordained   55
by everlasting law, so that the fit
of ring and finger here must be exact;

  and thus these souls who have, precociously,   58
reached the true life do not, among themselves,
find places high or low without some cause.

  The King through whom this kingdom finds content   61
in so much love and so much joyousness

that no desire would dare to ask for more,

creating every mind in His glad sight,   64
bestows His grace diversely, at His pleasure—
and here the fact alone must be enough.

And this is clearly and expressly noted   67
for you in Holy Scripture, in those twins
who, in their mother's womb, were moved to anger.

Thus, it is just for the celestial light   70
to grace their heads with a becoming crown,
according to the color of their hair.

Without, then, any merit in their works,   73
these infants are assigned to different ranks—
proclivity at birth, the only difference.

In early centuries, their parents' faith   76
alone, and their own innocence, sufficed
for the salvation of the children; when

those early times had reached completion, then   79
each male child had to find, through circumcision,
the power needed by his innocent

member; but then the age of grace arrived,   82
and without perfect baptism in Christ,
such innocence was kept below, in Limbo.

Look now upon the face that is most like   85
the face of Christ, for only through its brightness
can you prepare your vision to see Him."

I saw such joy rain down upon her, joy   88
carried by holy intellects created
to fly at such a height, that all which I

had seen before did not transfix me with   91
amazement so intense, nor show to me
a semblance that was so akin to God.

And the angelic love who had descended   94
earlier, now spread his wings before her,
singing "*Ave Maria, gratïa plena.*"

On every side, the blessed court replied,   97
singing responses to his godly song,

so that each spirit there grew more serene.

"O holy father—who, for me, endure   100
your being here below, leaving the sweet
place where eternal lot assigns your seat—

who is that angel who with such delight   103
looks into our Queen's eyes—he who is so
enraptured that he seems to be a flame?"

So, once again, I called upon the teaching   106
of him who drew from Mary beauty, as
the morning star draws beauty from the sun.

And he to me: "All of the gallantry   109
and confidence that there can be in angel
or blessed soul are found in him, and we

would have it so, for it was he who carried   112
the palm below to Mary, when God's Son
wanted to bear our flesh as His own burden.

But follow with your eyes even as I   115
proceed to speak, and note the great patricians
of this most just and merciful empire.

Those two who, there above, are seated, most   118
happy to be so near the Empress, may
be likened to the two roots of this Rose:

the one who, on her left, sits closest, is   121
the father whose presumptuous tasting
caused humankind to taste such bitterness;

and on the right, you see that ancient father   124
of Holy Church, into whose care the keys
of this fair flower were consigned by Christ.

And he who saw, before he died, all of   127
the troubled era of the lovely Bride—
whom lance and nails had won—sits at his side;

and at the side of Adam sits that guide   130
under whose rule the people, thankless, fickle,
and stubborn, lived on manna. Facing Peter,

Anna is seated, so content to see   133
her daughter that, as Anna sings hosannas,

she does not move her eyes. And opposite
 the greatest father of a family,   136
Lucia sits, she who urged on your lady
when you bent your brows downward, to your ruin.

 But time, which brings you sleep, takes flight, and now 139
we shall stop here—even as a good tailor
who cuts the garment as his cloth allows—

 and turn our vision to the Primal Love,   142
that, gazing at Him, you may penetrate—
as far as that can be—His radiance.

 But lest you now fall back when, even as   145
you move your wings, you think that you advance,
imploring grace, through prayer you must beseech

 grace from that one who has the power to help you;   148
and do you follow me with your affection—
so may my words and your heart share one way."

 And he began this holy supplication: 151

CANTO XXXIII

Still the Tenth Heaven: the Empyrean. Prayer of St. Bernard
to the Virgin. Her acknowledgment of his prayer. Dante sees
the Eternal Light. The three circles of the Trinity. The
mystery of the Incarnation. The flashing light that fulfills
Dante's vision. His desire and will at one with Love.

"Virgin mother, daughter of your Son,
more humble and sublime than any creature,
fixed goal decreed from all eternity,

   you are the one who gave to human nature   4
so much nobility that its Creator
did not disdain His being made its creature.

   That love whose warmth allowed this flower to bloom   7
within the everlasting peace—was love
rekindled in your womb; for us above,

   you are the noonday torch of charity,   10
and there below, on earth, among the mortals,
you are a living spring of hope. Lady,

   you are so high, you can so intercede,   13
that he who would have grace but does not seek
your aid, may long to fly but has no wings.

   Your loving-kindness does not only answer   16
the one who asks, but it is often ready
to answer freely long before the asking.

   In you compassion is, in you is pity,   19
in you is generosity, in you
is every goodness found in any creature.

   This man—who from the deepest hollow in   22
the universe, up to this height, has seen
the lives of spirits, one by one—now pleads

   with you, through grace, to grant him so much virtue   25

that he may lift his vision higher still—
may lift it toward the ultimate salvation.

And I, who never burned for my own vision   28
more than I burn for his, do offer you
all of my prayers—and pray that they may not

fall short—that, with your prayers, you may disperse   31
all of the clouds of his mortality
so that the Highest Joy be his to see.

This, too, o Queen, who can do what you would,   34
I ask of you: that after such a vision,
his sentiments preserve their perseverance.

May your protection curb his mortal passions.   37
See Beatrice—how many saints with her!
They join my prayers! They clasp their hands to you!"

The eyes that are revered and loved by God,   40
now fixed upon the supplicant, showed us
how welcome such devotions are to her;

then her eyes turned to the Eternal Light—   43
there, do not think that any creature's eye
can find its way as clearly as her sight.

And I, who now was nearing Him who is   46
the end of all desires, as I ought,
lifted my longing to its ardent limit.

Bernard was signaling—he smiled—to me   49
to turn my eyes on high; but I, already
was doing what he wanted me to do,

because my sight, becoming pure, was able   52
to penetrate the ray of Light more deeply—
that Light, sublime, which in Itself is true.

From that point on, what I could see was greater   55
than speech can show: at such a sight, it fails—
and memory fails when faced with such excess.

As one who sees within a dream, and, later,   58
the passion that had been imprinted stays,
but nothing of the rest returns to mind,

such am I, for my vision almost fades   61

completely, yet it still distills within
my heart the sweetness that was born of it.

So is the snow, beneath the sun, unsealed;   64
and so, on the light leaves, beneath the wind,
the oracles the Sibyl wrote were lost.

O Highest Light, You, raised so far above   67
the minds of mortals, to my memory
give back something of Your epiphany,

and make my tongue so powerful that I   70
may leave to people of the future one
gleam of the glory that is Yours, for by

returning somewhat to my memory   73
and echoing awhile within these lines,
Your victory will be more understood.

The living ray that I endured was so   76
acute that I believe I should have gone
astray had my eyes turned away from it.

I can recall that I, because of this,   79
was bolder in sustaining it until
my vision reached the Infinite Goodness.

O grace abounding, through which I presumed   82
to set my eyes on the Eternal Light
so long that I spent all my sight on it!

In its profundity I saw—ingathered   85
and bound by love into one single volume—
what, in the universe, seems separate, scattered:

substances, accidents, and dispositions   88
as if conjoined—in such a way that what
I tell is only rudimentary.

I think I saw the universal shape   91
which that knot takes; for, speaking this, I feel
a joy that is more ample. That one moment

brings more forgetfulness to me than twenty-   94
five centuries have brought to the endeavor
that startled Neptune with the *Argo*'s shadow!

So was my mind—completely rapt, intent,   97

steadfast, and motionless—gazing; and it
grew ever more enkindled as it watched.

Whoever sees that Light is soon made such   100
that it would be impossible for him
to set that Light aside for other sight;

because the good, the object of the will,   103
is fully gathered in that Light; outside
that Light, what there is perfect is defective.

What little I recall is to be told,   106
from this point on, in words more weak than those
of one whose infant tongue still bathes at the breast.

And not because more than one simple semblance   109
was in the Living Light at which I gazed—
for It is always what It was before—

but through my sight, which as I gazed grew stronger, 112
that sole appearance, even as I altered,
seemed to be changing. In the deep and bright

essence of that exalted Light, three circles   115
appeared to me; they had three different colors,
but all of them were of the same dimension;

one circle seemed reflected by the second,   118
as rainbow is by rainbow, and the third
seemed fire breathed equally by those two circles.

How incomplete is speech, how weak, when set   121
against my thought! And this, to what I saw
is such—to call it little is too much.

Eternal Light, You only dwell within   124
Yourself, and only You know You; Self-knowing,
Self-known, You love and smile upon Yourself!

That circle—which, begotten so, appeared   127
in You as light reflected—when my eyes
had watched it with attention for some time,

within itself and colored like itself,   130
to me seemed painted with our effigy,
so that my sight was set on it completely.

As the geometer intently seeks   133

to square the circle, but he cannot reach,
through thought on thought, the principle he needs,

 so I searched that strange sight: I wished to see   136
the way in which our human effigy
suited the circle and found place in it—

 and my own wings were far too weak for that.   139
But then my mind was struck by light that flashed
and, with this light, received what it had asked.

 Here force failed my high fantasy; but my   142
desire and will were moved already—like
a wheel revolving uniformly—by

 the Love that moves the sun and the other stars.   145

NOTES

INFERNO CANTO I

PROLOGUE: The dark forest.

1 *half of our life's way* midway along the road of the human lifespan of seventy years [Psalms].* Dante's journey through the afterlife is set in 1300, his own thirty-fifth year: 'In the middle of my days, I shall go to the gates of Hell' [Isaiah].

2 *a shadowed forest* a realistic image of the darkness and tangle of the world in which Dante has lost the path to truth and goodness.

6 *in recall* in remembering what occurred. In the fiction of the poem, Dante (the 'I') is both the traveller through the afterlife in 1300 and the poet who later, after his return to this life, describes his journey from memory.

11 *sleep* an image of torpor, the loss of intellectual, moral, and spiritual awareness.

17 *that same planet* the Sun, the fourth of the planets revolving round the earth in Ptolemaic astronomy. Often used as a symbol of God and divine light and grace, here it represents guidance from above along the true upward path (the hill).

26 *the pass* the place of mortal danger.

30 *my firm foot* the lower foot, taking Dante's weight in the steep ascent; sometimes interpreted symbolically as his intellect as opposed to his weaker faculty, his will.

32 *a leopard* usually interpreted as a symbol of lust. The three beasts which attack Dante are the same as those sent to punish the sinful leaders of the people [Jeremiah].

39 *the same stars* Aries, the sign of the zodiac in which the Sun rises in springtime, the time of the year in which God had

* Principal sources and parallels, indicated by square brackets, are given in the List of References (p. 792).

created the world in the beginning. The start of the poems, set on a spring morning in 1300, may be dated either to the day before Good Friday (8 April) or to 25 March, the traditional anniversary of the creation of the world, the Incarnation (the conception of Christ as God and man), and the crucifixion of Christ, and also the first day of the centenary year in the Florentine calendar.

45 *a lion* usually interpreted as a symbol of pride.

49 *a she-wolf* a symbol of avarice and particularly avarice in the Church, since a statue of the she-wolf which suckled Rome's founders, Romulus and Remus, then stood outside the papal palace of the Lateran in Rome. For Dante, greed for money, land, power, or authority, was the enemy of love and justice and the main cause of corruption in the Church and in society as a whole: 'For cupidity is the root of all evils' [1 Timothy].

55 *he who glories* the obsessive profiteer and miser, faced by the moment, above all of death, when he must leave all his possessions behind.

63 *one who seemed faint* Virgil, the Roman poet, whose voice is faint because of the many centuries between him and Dante.

66 *a shade* the disembodied soul of a dead person (in Latin, *umbra*, 'shade'). In Dante's afterlife, the immortal human soul has been separated from matter (the body) by death, but it retains its appearance by giving its form to the air around it (*Purg.* XXV, 79–108).

68 *Lombardy* northern Italy, including Mantua near where Virgil was born.

70 *sub Julio* during the lifetime of Julius Caesar (100–44 BC), who for Dante had been the first Roman Emperor.

71 *Augustus* the second Roman Emperor, from 27 BC to AD 14. In Dante's scheme of history, while God's plan for the spiritual salvation of the human race was being fulfilled by the Jews in Israel, He was also working through the Romans to create the Empire – world-government by a single Monarch – which reached its climax during the reign of Augustus when

Christ was born as, in effect, a Roman Jew [Luke; *Convivio*; *Monarchia*]. Virgil (70–19 BC) had therefore lived at the zenith of pre-Christian civilization and Rome's imperial destiny, but he had died just before the era of unassisted human reason, natural ethics, and the worship of the pagan gods (BC), had been superseded by the era of divine revelation, redemption through Christ, and the religion of the one true God (AD). Dante's Virgil is his guide mainly within the sphere of rational enquiry, but he is also, above all, the soul of the master-poet whose epic poem, the *Aeneid*, had celebrated the origin of the Roman Empire and the civic and moral values of Augustan Rome.

74 *son of Anchises* Aeneas. Virgil's *Aeneid* tells how, after the Greeks had captured the city of Troy and set it on fire, the Trojan prince Aeneas escaped and travelled to Latium in central Italy where he established a colony whose descendants founded Rome.

75 *Ilium* Troy, so called from one of its citadels and often presented as a proud city [Virgil] (*Purg.* XII, 61–3).

101 *the Greyhound* a person or movement that will defeat the she-wolf of avarice. Medieval prophecy often encoded its predictions by using animal imagery.

103 *pewter* money.

105 *between two felts* an enigmatic phrase defining the origin or territory of the future deliverer. It has been interpreted as meaning rough clothing (poverty), the region of northern Italy between Feltre and Montefeltro, the whole world from the West to the Mongol Empire in the East, the felt-lined balloting urns used in elections, Dante's birth-sign (Gemini), his reforming poem, and so on. The Greyhound has been identified as a future good Pope, who would fulfil St Francis of Assisi's ideal of poverty in the Church, or more frequently with Dante's future patron, Can Grande della Scala, lord of Verona, or the Emperor Henry VII who was in Italy in 1310–13. More probably, the prophecy, spoken by Virgil and set in a centenary year, should be seen rather as expressing an

indefinite, millenarian desire for the coming of a virtuous Roman Emperor, free from greed, who would re-establish peace, justice, and law in Italy and would reform both world-governments, the temporal (the Empire) and the spiritual (the Church), from Rome.

107–8 *Camilla, Nisus, Turnus, Euryalus* two Italic tribal leaders (Camilla and Turnus) and two Trojan soldiers who were all killed during Aeneas' campaign in Latium. Their names summarize the last Books of Virgil's *Aeneid* and the bloodshed which, providentially, was to lead to the founding of Rome.

114 *an eternal place* Hell.

117 *second death* damnation of the soul.

119 *the fire* the punishments of Purgatory, where the souls accept their temporary sufferings as the necessary way to Heaven.

120 *the blessed people* the souls in Paradise.

122 *a soul more worthy than I am* Beatrice.

124 *the Emperor* God.

125 *rebellious to His law* a pagan.

134 *the gateway of Saint Peter* the entrance to Paradise, guarded by St Peter, the leader of Christ's apostles (see *Purg.* IX, 78, 117–29).

INFERNO CANTO II

THE START OF THE JOURNEY: Virgil's account of Beatrice's visit to Limbo.

7 *Muses* the nine sisters to whom classical poets appealed as if for external inspiration and assistance. This invocation shows Dante's awareness of the epic poetic task ahead of him, for which he will need also the full powers of his own inventive genius.

13 *he who fathered Sylvius* Aeneas. Sylvius, his son and heir by Lavinia, joined together the Trojan and Latin races.

15 *the deathless world* Hades, the eternal underworld, which Aeneas visited while still alive [Virgil].

16 *the Enemy of every evil* God.

18 *all he would cause* the foundation of Rome, the centre both of the Empire (line 21) and the Church (lines 22–4).

20 *in the empyrean heaven* by God, in the infinite heaven beyond the nine spheres known as the 'empyrean', meaning 'filled with fire', that is, with God's light and love.

24 *the successor of great Peter* the Pope, head of the universal Church, whose authority was transmitted from Christ's appointment of St Peter as the Rock or foundation of the Church [Matthew].

28 *the Chosen Vessel* St Paul, one of the first preachers of Christianity and writer of the Epistles, who was chosen by God to be filled with His words and Spirit [Acts]. St Paul tells how he was taken up to a vision of heaven and its mysteries [2 Corinthians]. An apocryphal work, the *Vision of Paul*, which told of a journey by him to Hell also, was a major influence on Christian vision literature before Dante and on the medieval image of Hell and its torments.

35 *wild and empty* rash and presumptuous, unlike the divinely authorized visits to the afterlife of Aeneas and St Paul who had special roles in God's plan to create the Empire and the Church.

44 *that great-hearted one* Virgil, who is 'magnanimous', noble and virtuous in spirit.

52 *those souls who are suspended* the souls in Limbo, the first circle of Hell, who desire without hope (*Inf.* IV, 42).

53 *a lady* Beatrice. Usually identified as the daughter of the Florentine philanthropist, Folco Portinari, she was celebrated in Dante's youthful poems and the *Vita nuova* as the lady through whom he acquired an understanding of Love as a rational, selfless, virtuous, and ultimately redemptive force. She died at the age of twenty-four in June 1290, and Dante's poems after her death present her as a blessed soul in Paradise.

58 *Mantuan* Virgil, born near Mantua in northern Italy.

61 *my friend* Dante, who has loved Beatrice constantly, despite the vicissitudes of fortune, which has also treated him badly through his exile from Florence.

71 *from where* from Paradise.

77 *all that lies* everything on earth, beneath the first of the heavenly spheres, the Moon.

83 *this center* Limbo.

94 *a gentle lady* Mary, mother of Christ and queen of Heaven, who intercedes with God on behalf of all Christians.

96 *stern judgment* God's justice, which should punish Dante, but is mitigated by Mary's intercession.

97 *Lucia* probably St Lucy, the patron of eyesight, whose name means 'light'; hence she represents vision and God's grace.

98 *your faithful one* Dante, who appears to have had a special devotion to St Lucy, perhaps because of an eye illness he once suffered [*Convivio*].

102 *Rachel* Jacob's second wife [Genesis] (*Purg.* XXVII, 104–8; *Par.* XXXII, 8).

108 *that river* symbolically, the river of evil which threatens Dante with spiritual death.

113 *honest utterance* Virgil's ability, as a great poet, to guide Dante with his wise and virtuous words.

INFERNO CANTO III

THE ENTRY INTO HELL: The Gate and the river Acheron.

4 MY HIGH ARTIFICER God, who created Hell as the place of ultimate Justice where all those who die without having repented of serious (mortal) sins will be punished eternally for them. Lines 5–6 allude to the doctrine of the Trinity, that is, of God as three Persons in one: the power of the Father, the wisdom of the Son, and the love of the Holy Spirit.

7 ETERNAL THINGS the angels, the heavens, and prime matter, created by God in the very beginning (*Par.* XXIX,

22–36). Hell was created later, when many angels, led by Lucifer, rebelled against God and were cast down into it from Paradise (*Par.* XXIX, 49–51, 55–7).

18 *the good of the intellect* God as infinite truth, the object of intellectual vision in Paradise, which the souls in Hell have lost for ever.

35 *those* the neutral or cowardly who in life chose neither good nor evil, who have left neither fame nor infamy behind them, and who are rejected not only by Heaven but even by Hell: 'Because you are lukewarm, and neither cold nor hot, I shall begin to vomit you from my mouth' [Revelation]. On his visit to the underworld, Aeneas saw similar crowds of souls, those of the unburied; Dante adapts several elements of this episode from Book VI of the *Aeneid* [Virgil].

37 *coward angels* the angels who remained neutral in Lucifer's rebellion.

55 *Behind that banner* the following of a banner is an eternally ironic expression of the neutrals' lack of any commitment in life.

59–60 *him who made* usually identified as Pope Celestine V, who abdicated after a reign of only five months in 1294, thus making way for the accession of Pope Boniface VIII (1294–1303). Other suggestions are that the soul is Esau, who renounced his birthright to Jacob [Genesis], or Pontius Pilate, who washed his hands of any responsibility for the death of Christ [Matthew].

77 *Acheron* the first river to be crossed when entering the underworld [Virgil].

83 *an aged man* Charon, the boatman who ferries souls across the Acheron [Virgil]. Alongside devils (fallen angels), Dante includes figures from the classical mythology of the underworld as guardians and ministers in Hell, presenting them as grotesque demons. This is a feature of his lower, 'comic' style in contrast to his elevated Latin sources.

93 *A lighter craft* another boat, that of the saved (*Purg.* II, 40–51).

95 *One* God, with the power to achieve whatever He wills.

115 *seed of Adam* human beings, descended from Adam and Eve [Genesis].

117 *called* with the falconer's lure.

INFERNO CANTO IV

THE FIRST CIRCLE: Limbo (the virtuous unbaptized).

8 *an abyss* the conical pit of Hell, leading down to the centre of the earth. Since ancient times, the underworld had been located beneath the surface of the earth; its inhabitants were the *inferi*, the people down below; hence the Italian word *Inferno*, the place below.

24 *that first circle* the first of the nine concentric circles of Dante's Hell is Limbo, from the Latin word *limbus*, 'edge'.

30 *of infants and of women and of men* the souls of all those who died unbaptized and are therefore excluded from going to Paradise. For theologians, the 'Limbo of children' was the place where unbaptized children (the holy innocents) would go after death. Less orthodoxly, Dante includes also the souls of adults who lived well according to human reason and natural ethics but who never achieved complete spiritual fulfilment by being baptized into the Christian faith.

36 *the portal of the faith* baptism, the first of the seven Christian Sacraments, a symbolic washing with water which admits the person into the Church and was regarded as essential for salvation.

42 *we have no hope* the souls in Limbo desire spiritual fulfilment in Paradise but can never hope to achieve it.

50 *blessedness* Paradise. According to the Christian creed (Athanasian version), between His crucifixion and His resurrection Christ 'descended into Hell'. Dante is here enquiring about the belief, based on the apocryphal *Gospel of Nicodemus*, that Christ entered Limbo, where the souls of the patriarchs, holy women, and prophets of the Old Testament were

waiting, and led them out to Paradise.

52 *new-entered* Virgil died in 19 BC, just over fifty years before the traditional date of Christ's death in AD 34.

53 *a Great Lord* Christ.

55 *first father* Adam, the first man, the ancestor of the entire human race [Genesis] (*Par.* XXVI, 82–142).

56 *Abel* son of Adam, killed by his brother Cain [Genesis].

Noah the patriarch who built the Ark and with his family re-founded the human race after the Flood [Genesis].

57 *Moses* the leader of the Israelites in their Exodus from Egypt to the Promised Land, and the founder of the Jewish religion and law [Exodus] (*Par.* XXXII, 130–32).

58 *Abraham* the ancestor of the Israelites with whom God made His special covenant [Genesis].

David the king of Israel and the psalmist (*Par.* XX, 37–42).

59 *Israel, his father, and his sons* Jacob with his father Isaac (Abraham's son) and his own twelve sons, the founders of the twelve tribes of Israel [Genesis].

60 *Rachel* Jacob's second wife, whom he won by working for fourteen years for her father, Laban [Genesis] (*Inf.* II, 102).

68 *a fire* the shining castle of lines 103–8.

72 *honorable men* the bright region of Limbo is reserved for virtuous non-Christians who, through their contributions to human society and civilization, won enduring fame and honour in life (lines 73, 76–7, 80, 100) and are rewarded by God with this special place in the afterlife (line 78). They consist of classical poets, including Virgil himself (lines 82–105); Trojan and Roman heroes (lines 121–8); pagan philosophers, writers, mathematicians, and doctors (lines 130–43); and three Muslims of the post-Christian era (lines 129, 143–4). The apparent injustice of God's exclusion of good non-Christians from Paradise clearly worried Dante, and the poem later contains some exceptions (*Purg.* I, 31–9, 73–90; *Par.* XIX, 70–90; XX, 67–72, 100–138). Here, on the basis of human achievement and fame, he tones down the strict doctrine that all pagans are damned to eternal suffering whilst

preserving the principle that belief in Christ is necessary for salvation.

80 *the estimable poet* Virgil.

88 *Homer* the first Greek poet, writer of two epics: the *Iliad* (on the war of the Greeks against Troy) and the *Odyssey* (on the homeward voyage of the Greek Odysseus).

89 *Horace* the Roman poet (65–8 BC), whose works included satires. In medieval literary theory, satire had a moral purpose in attacking the wicked and was a branch of comedy, like Dante's own poem.

90 *Ovid* the Roman poet (43 BC–AD 8), whose works were Dante's major source for classical myths of love and transformations (metamorphoses).

Lucan the Roman poet (AD 39–65), whose epic *On the Civil War* (also known as the *Pharsalia*) was Dante's main source concerning the civil war between the Roman Republicans and Julius Caesar, the founder of the Empire.

92 *the name* the title of poet, just used by Homer (line 80).

95 *the lord* Homer, the supreme poet (or perhaps Virgil).

102 *the sixth* welcomed among the five pagan poets, Dante expresses his own sense of continuity with and debt to the classical tradition.

104 *things* presumably the secrets of their shared art of poetry, unsuitable for revelation to the lay-person.

106 *an exalted castle* perhaps a symbol of human wisdom or fame, surrounded by the river of eloquence and with seven walls and gates (the seven Liberal Arts of the medieval educational system).

111 *a meadow* this part of Dante's Limbo resembles the Elysian Fields, visited by Aeneas [Virgil].

121 *Electra* the mother of Dardanus, the founder of Troy; her comrades are therefore Trojans.

122 *Hector* the greatest Trojan hero, killed by the Greek Achilles.

Aeneas the Trojan ancestor of the Romans (*Inf.* I, 70–75; II, 13–27).

123 *Caesar* Julius Caesar, the general and founder of the Roman world-Empire.

124 *Camilla* the warrior-queen killed during Aeneas' conquest of Latium (*Inf.* I, 107).

Penthesilea the queen of the Amazons who fought for the Trojans and was killed by Achilles.

125 *Latinus* the king of Latium, who was succeeded by Aeneas.

126 *Lavinia* Aeneas' third wife, from whom the Romans inherited their Empire in Europe [*Monarchia*].

127 *Brutus* Lucius Junius Brutus who in 510 BC expelled Tarquin, the last king of Rome, and became the first consul of the Roman Republic.

128 *Lucretia, Julia, Marcia, Cornelia* four famous women of outstanding virtue from Roman Republican history: after being raped by the son of king Tarquin, Lucretia heroically committed suicide; Julia, the daughter of Julius Caesar, was the wife of Pompey; Marcia was Cato's wife (*Purg.* I, 78–90); and Cornelia was the mother of the Gracchi brothers, two of the greatest tribunes of Rome (though this may be another Cornelia, the second wife of Pompey).

129 *Saladin* Sultan of Egypt 1171–93, he inflicted a series of defeats on the Crusaders but became renowned in the West for his nobility and generosity [*Convivio*].

131 *the master* Aristotle (384–322 BC), the Greek philosopher, here defined as supreme in the field of human knowledge. By Dante's time, his works, translated into Latin, were seen as providing a comprehensive rational system of thought which could be used in the service of theology, the study of the divinely revealed doctrines of the Christian faith. The following impressive list of names – and most were little more than names to Dante and his earliest audience – summarizes the history of human thought from ancient Greece and Rome up to two medieval Muslim scholars, and expresses Dante's belief that all human beings should use their reason in the pursuit of knowledge and fame, even though these can be

perfected only by higher, Christian truths and eternal salvation.

134 *Socrates and Plato* the Greek philosophers, Socrates (469–399 BC) and his pupil Plato (*c.* 429–347 BC), Aristotle's teacher.

136 *Democritus* Greek philosopher (*c.* 460–370 BC), believed to have thought that the universe, composed of tiny bodies (atoms), was the result of mere chance.

137 *Diogenes* the Cynic philosopher (*c.* 400–*c.* 325 BC), famous for having expressed his rejection of material desires by living in a tub.

Empedocles philosopher (fifth century BC), whose doctrine of the universe as based on Love and Strife was known to Dante (*Inf.* XII, 42).

Zeno the founder of Stoicism (*c.* 300 BC), or perhaps Zeno of Elea (fifth century BC).

138 *Thales* the founder of Greek philosophy (*c.* 635–*c.* 545 BC).

Anaxagoras Greek philosopher and astronomer (*c.* 500–*c.* 428 BC).

Heraclitus Greek philosopher (*c.* 500 BC).

140 *Dioscorides* Greek physician and writer of a treatise on the medicinal properties of plants (first century AD).

Orpheus a mythical Greek poet who enchanted the beasts, trees, and stones with his music.

141 *Tully* Marcus Tullius Cicero (106–43 BC), Roman statesman, orator, and philosopher, several of whose works were known to Dante.

Linus a mythical Greek poet, son of the god Apollo and the founder of pastoral poetry [Virgil].

Seneca Roman philosopher and tragedian (4 BC–AD 65), believed to have also written two important moral works, on the four Cardinal Virtues and on Remedies against Fortune.

142 *Euclid* Greek mathematician, famous for his geometry (*c.* 300 BC).

Ptolemy Claudius Ptolemaeus, Greek mathematician and

astronomer from Egypt (second century AD), whose system of the nine heavenly spheres revolving around the stationary earth was the basis of astronomy and cosmology throughout the Middle Ages.

143 *Hippocrates* Greek physician, known as the father of medicine (*c*. 460–370 BC).

Galen a Greek physician from Asia Minor (second century AD), the most important authority on medical matters in the Middle Ages.

Avicenna ibn-Sina (AD 980–1037) from Persia, an Arab philosopher, physician, and commentator on Aristotle and Galen.

144 *Averroës* ibn-Rushd (AD 1126–98), an Arab from Spain who wrote the most important commentary on Aristotle's works.

148 *divides in two* Virgil and Dante leave the other four poets.

INFERNO CANTO V

SECOND CIRCLE: the lustful (sinful lovers and adulterers).

1 *the first enclosure* Limbo.

4 *Minos* a mythical king of Crete and judge in the underworld [Virgil], here a grotesque demon who sentences the damned souls with coils of his tail.

20 *the gate is wide* entry into Hell is easy [Virgil; Matthew].

23 *One* God (*Inf*. III, 95–6).

31 *hellish hurricane* the punishment of the lustful, buffeted by passion during their lives, both expresses and perpetuates the sin in which they died. This matching of sin and punishment is known as the *contrapasso*, the law of the just counter-penalty in Hell (*Inf*. XXVIII, 142).

36 *the divine* God's justice.

39 *subjecting reason* in Dante's ethical system, the two specifically human faculties of reason and will should control the

carnal passions. Instead lust, one of the Seven Deadly Sins, has reversed this by allowing passion to dominate over rationality.

58 *Semíramis* a legendary queen of the Assyrian Empire, successor to her husband, Ninus. She slept with and then killed a succession of lovers and, to conceal her affair with her own son, abolished the laws against incest, thus legalizing all lustful passions (lines 56–7) [Orosius].

60 *the Sultan* the ruler of Egypt in 'Babylon' (old Cairo), confused here with Semiramis' Babylon in Assyria.

61 *That other spirit* Dido who, after the murder of her husband Sychaeus, fled to Carthage in North Africa and became its queen. Forgetting her dead husband, she fell passionately in love with Aeneas and committed suicide when he abandoned her [Virgil].

63 *Cleopatra* queen of Egypt (51–30 BC), the lover of Julius Caesar and then of Mark Antony. After the latter's defeat and suicide, she was unable to win over the victorious Octavian (Augustus) and committed suicide by the poisonous bite of asps.

64 *Helen* the wife of Menelaus, king of Sparta in Greece. Her abduction by the Trojan prince Paris caused the Greek expedition and the ten-year war against Troy.

65 *Achilles* the greatest of the Greek heroes in the Trojan War. In later stories embroidering on Homer's *Iliad*, his love for the Trojan princess Polyxena caused him to be lured into a trap and killed by Paris.

67 *Paris* whose love for Helen (line 64) caused the Trojan War in which he too was killed.

Tristan the lover of Yseult (Isolda), the wife of king Mark, in the Breton cycle of medieval romances. When their love was discovered, king Mark wounded him with a poisoned sword, and as he died, Yseult too died of a broken heart.

71 *pity* both compassion and mental anguish. Dante the traveller's pity used to be seen as a purely emotional response, as if lust were no more than a general human weakness with which he sympathizes. In fact, the presence of these famous

tragic lovers in Hell forces him to realize that in God's eyes they were guilty of serious sin, and to reassess his own moral position regarding love and love stories.

81 *One* God.

82 *doves* models of happy domestic love in medieval books of beasts and birds. The comparison, in contrast with those of the starlings and the cranes, applied to the wind-tossed and lamenting souls (lines 40–41, 46–7), focuses on love as a sweet desire which responds to other loving requests.

97 *The land* Ravenna, on the Adriatic coast of Italy where the river Po and its tributaries flow into the sea. The two souls are Francesca da Polenta, a noblewoman from Ravenna, and her lover, Paolo. In about 1275, Francesca was married to Gianciotto Malatesta, lord of Rimini. Some years later, discovering her adulterous love affair with his brother, Paolo, Gianciotto killed them both.

100 *gentle* noble. In medieval courtly love poetry, true or 'refined' Love was a quality of noble lovers. Francesca's words echo a poem by Dante himself, 'Love and the gentle heart are a single thing' [*Vita nuova*], in which 'gentle' had meant 'noble' in the sense not of rank by birth but of moral goodness, and true Love had been presented as necessarily accompanied by nobility of heart, that is, by virtue. Dante had taken this doctrine from the earlier Bolognese poet, Guido Guinizzelli, and made it the basis of his own 'sweet new style' of poetry praising Beatrice (*Purg.* XXVI, 91–114). Francesca goes on to define Love as an irresistible mutual passion (line 103), thus blaming Love as a universal force personified in the terms of contemporary courtly poetry, masking her own responsibility for her damnation, but at the same time revealing to Dante the moral danger which exists in all such literary conceptions of Love, even perhaps potentially in his own earlier poetry of noble love for Beatrice.

106 *one death* they were both killed, and sent to Hell, by Francesca's husband. The theme of dying for love links her with the other souls in this group, especially Dido (lines 61–9,

85), and with Dante's own death-like swoon at the end of the episode (line 142).

107 *Caïna* a zone of the last circle of Dante's Hell, containing those who betrayed their relatives (*Inf.* XXXII, 59), so named after Cain, who murdered his brother Abel [Genesis]. According to Francesca, Gianciotto, who was still alive in 1300, will go there when he dies.

114 *agonizing pass* the passage from the courtly ideal of noble Love into adultery and so to death and damnation.

123 *your teacher* Virgil [Boethius].

128 *Lancelot* the ideal knight and the lover of queen Guinevere in the Arthurian romances.

132 *one point alone* the moment in the story when the love of Guinevere and Lancelot was first openly expressed with a kiss.

133 *the desired smile* Guinevere's mouth, expressed in a suitably literary metaphor.

135 *this one* Paolo.

137 *Gallehault* Guinevere's steward whom she used as a go-between to arrange the meeting with Lancelot. As Gallehault did in the story, so did the book and its author bring Francesca and Paolo together with the fatal kiss which turned innocent reading into sin. Although in the romance it is Guinevere who takes the initiative in kissing Lancelot, Francesca has throughout cast the blame elsewhere: on Love, on Paolo, and on the book.

INFERNO CANTO VI

THIRD CIRCLE: the gluttons.

2 *kindred* Francesca and her brother-in-law, Paolo.

15 *Cerberus* the three-headed, dog-like monster which guards the entrance to the underworld. The Sibyl, Aeneas' guide, exploited his greed by throwing him a lump of drugged food to silence him [Virgil]; here Dante's guide does the same with a handful of muddy earth (lines 25–32).

36 *empty images* the imitation bodies, composed of air, which the souls inhabit after they have been separated from their physical bodies by death (*Purg.* XXV, 79–108).

42 *was unmade* died. Death is a breaking or 'unmaking' of the union of the immortal soul with the mortal body.

49 *Your city* Florence.

52 *Ciacco* a Florentine about whom nothing else is known beyond Dante's use of him as an example of gluttony, another of the Seven Deadly Sins. The name, perhaps a familiar form of 'Giacomo' (James), may have been one given to pigs and hogs.

61 *that divided city* Florence, torn by the struggle between two factions of the Guelph party in 1300: the White Guelphs who opposed Pope Boniface VIII's attempts to control Florence; and the Black Guelphs who were in favour of a close alliance between Florence and the Pope.

65 *blood* the violent skirmish of 1 May 1300 between Whites and Blacks.

the party of the woods the White Guelphs, led by Vieri de' Cerchi, whose family originated in the countryside.

66 *the other* the Black Guelphs, whose leaders were sent into exile by the White government which Dante served in 1300–1301.

67 *within three suns* in less than three years. This is the first of a series of prophecies inserted into the poem in which souls predict the course of Florentine politics and the circumstances of Dante's exile after the spring of 1300. It refers to the fall of the White Guelph government (1 November 1301), which was followed by the persecution of their leaders by the Blacks (lines 68–72). Dante himself was summoned back to Florence to answer charges of political corruption (27 January 1302) and then sentenced to death in his absence (10 March 1302).

69 *one who tacks his sails* Boniface VIII, already manoeuvring astutely with his Black Guelph allies.

73 *Two men* a vague phrase, emphasizing the almost complete absence of good men in Florence. It answers Dante's

question (line 62), which was itself an echo of Abraham's request to God to spare the wicked cities of Sodom and Gomorrah if any just men could be found there [Genesis].

79–80 *Tegghiaio, Farinata, Arrigo, Mosca, Jacopo Rusticucci* famous Florentines from earlier in the thirteenth century. The list evokes a better and more virtuous city in the past, in contrast with the wicked present. In spite of their relative virtues (line 81), however, they too were sinnners of various sorts and are lower down in Hell; see *Inf.* X, 32 (Farinata), XVI, 41, 44 (Tegghiaio and Jacopo Rusticucci), and XXVIII, 106 (Mosca). Arrigo, perhaps also one of those implicated in the murder of Buondelmonte in 1215, is not mentioned again.

89 *recall me* in the account of the journey. In return for speaking to him, many souls in Hell ask Dante to renew their earthly fame by recording them in the poem.

96 *the coming* the second coming of Christ at the end of the world, when each soul will regain its body, which will rise from the tomb for the universal Judgment (lines 97–9).

107 *perfection* completeness, in this case, when the soul has been rejoined to the body, after which the damned will suffer even greater pain (lines 109–11).

115 *Plutus* the demon guardian of the next circle whose name combines those of Pluto, the god of the underworld, and Plutus, the god of wealth.

INFERNO CANTO VII

FOURTH CIRCLE: the avaricious and the prodigals.

1 *"Pape Satàn, pape Satàn aleppe"* an address to Satan (the Devil, Lucifer), couched in a rudimentary language constructed by Dante as suitable for one of Hell's demons. 'Pape' and 'aleppe' express Plutus' astonishment and anger, perhaps with reference to Satan as his leader and king.

8 *wolf* Plutus, recalling the she-wolf of *Inf.* I, 49. Avarice is another of the Seven Deadly Sins.

10 *His* Dante's.

11 *Michael* the archangel who led the good angels in the defeat of Lucifer and the rebels.

22 *Charybdis* the dangerous whirlpool in the narrow straits between Sicily and mainland Italy [Virgil; Ovid; Lucan].

28 *at that point* where the two groups of souls meet, each having made a half-circle in the opposite direction to the other. One group consists of the avaricious (the hoarders), the other of the prodigals (the spendthrifts). These sins were the two extremes of excess with regard to wealth; the virtue in the middle consisted in prudent house-keeping (the original sense of 'oiconomics') and in generosity to the needy. The punishment of these souls, eternally rolling useless stones, reflects the restless acquisitiveness of misers and the ultimate worthlessness of all earthly possessions.

35 *next joust* next clash, after another half-circle.

39 *tonsured ones* a shaved crown of the head was the sign of those who had entered clerical orders. Dante's question emphasizes the extent of avarice among the clergy.

56 *these here* the avaricious.

will rise up at the resurrection of the body (*Inf.* VI, 94–9).

57 *these* the prodigals.

62 *in Fortune's care* Fortune, an unpredictable goddess in classical times, was personified in the Middle Ages as a woman with a revolving wheel which carried people up and down, redistributing earthly rank and riches in an apparently random way. Virgil here explains that what to humans seems random is, in fact, part of God's ordering of the world through the heavenly spheres.

73 *Who made the heavens* God, the creator of the nine heavens which revolve under the guidance of the nine orders of angels.

78 *general minister and guide* Fortune, like the angelic sphere-movers, fulfils God's will in distributing the goods of this life on earth, beneath the lowest of the heavens, the moon (line 65).

87 *gods* angels.

92 *those* people who should not curse their ill-fortune but rejoice in it, because it leads to their moral and spiritual improvement.

95 *primal beings* angels.

103 *darker than deep purple* perse, almost black.

108 *Styx* another river of Hell [Virgil].

116 *anger* wrath, another of the Seven Deadly Sins, which is punished in the swampy Styx, the fifth circle of Dante's Hell.

122 *in the sweet air* when living on the earth above, where the sun shines.

123 *sluggishness* sullen, rather than violent, anger; or the sin of accidie (sloth), another of the Seven Deadly Sins, which consists in the neglect of spiritual duties, moral apathy, and bitterness of soul.

INFERNO CANTO VIII

FIFTH CIRCLE: the wrathful.

7 *the sea of all good sense* Virgil, the epitome of wisdom.

19 *Phlegyas* a mythical king who took furious vengeance on the god Apollo by setting fire to his temple and was condemned to Tartarus (Hell) for his sacrilege [Virgil]. In Dante he is the fierce demon-ferryman of the circle of the wrathful.

30 *others* the souls, who are light because they have no bodies. Like Aeneas in Charon's boat [Virgil], the living Dante's body weighs the boat down.

33 *time* death.

45 *blessèd is she* words in praise of Christ, the son of Mary [Luke], here confirming the righteousness of Dante's anger against the sinner.

49 *up above* on earth, among the living.

61 *Filippo Argenti* a notoriously arrogant and irascible Florentine known to Dante and here presented as the epitome of uncontrolled, useless, and ultimately self-destructive rage.

68 *Dis* another name for Pluto, the classical god of the

underworld, and for his equivalent, the Devil (*Inf.* XXXIV, 20), here given to the walled city which is the lower part of Hell.

71 *mosques* towers.

80 *pilot* Phlegyas.

83 *rained from Heaven* devils, the fallen angels expelled from Heaven with Lucifer.

96 *here* to this world.

125 *a gate* the first gate of Hell with the inscription (*Inf.* III, 1–12), broken open by Christ when he descended into Limbo (*Inf.* IV, 52–4). Christ's conquest of Hell is the model for the following episode of the Christian Dante's entry through the lower gates with heavenly assistance (line 130).

INFERNO CANTO IX

THE ENTRY INTO THE CITY OF DIS.

1 *color* the pallor of fear.

8 *one* Heaven's assistance for Virgil, confirmed by Beatrice (*Inf.* II, 94–120).

16 *first circle* Limbo, where the souls' hope of Paradise can never be fulfilled (*Inf.* IV, 42).

23 *Erichtho* a witch who knew the secrets of Hell and could summon up the spirits of the dead [Lucan]. Like the Sibyl, Aeneas' guide [Virgil], Virgil reassures Dante by saying that he has already made a journey down through Hell.

25 *stripped off* separated from the soul by death.

27 *Judas' circle* the lowest circle in Hell, where is the soul of the traitor, Judas (*Inf.* XXXIV, 62–3).

29 *the heaven* the highest of the heavenly spheres, which encircles all the others (the Primum Mobile) (*Par.* XXVII, 99–114).

38 *Furies* three horrific female figures of vengeance and remorse [Virgil; Statius], also known as the Erinyes (line 45). Their names are given in lines 46–8.

44 *the Queen* Proserpina or Hecate, wife of Pluto, king of the underworld.

52 *Medusa* one of the three Gorgons (line 56), terrifying women with snakes for hair. The sight of her face turned people into stone [Lucan; Ovid]. Here she is perhaps a symbol of the ultimate sin, despair, which would petrify Dante and so trap him in Hell for ever.

54 *Theseus* the prince of Athens who was captured when he entered the underworld to rescue Proserpina (line 44) and was rescued by Hercules [Virgil; Statius]. The Furies regret not having killed him as a deterrent to other intruders such as Dante.

62 *the teaching* the deeper truth or message concealed within the symbolism of the narrative, namely, that where human powers such as Virgil's are inadequate, God always gives his grace to help the good against the forces of evil (see *Purg.* VIII, 19–21).

80 *a figure* probably an angel (line 85).

98 *Cerberus* the dog-like guardian of Hell (*Inf.* VI, 13–33) who was chained and dragged away by Hercules [Virgil], thus showing the uselessness of Hell's resistance to someone who, like Dante, has heavenly help.

112 *Arles* a town on the river Rhône in southern France, where there is a Roman, and later Christian, cemetery famous for its impressive tombs.

113 *Pola* the site of another famous cemetery, on the Istrian peninsula, once considered part of Italy; now Pula, near the entrance to the gulf of Kvarner (Quarnero), in Croatia.

127 *arch-heretics* founders of heretical movements and sects which denied fundamental doctrines of the Christian Faith.

INFERNO CANTO X

SIXTH CIRCLE: the heretics.

11 *Jehosaphat* the valley near Jerusalem where the souls with

their risen bodies will assemble for the Last Judgment [Joel].

14 *Epicurus* a Greek philosopher (341–270 BC), believed to have held that the supreme goal of human life is pleasure. The word 'Epicurean' described those who lived only for the pleasures of this life, as if there were no afterlife, thus effectively denying the doctrine that the human soul is immortal. For Dante, this heresy, which would deprive the *Comedy* of its entire foundation, was the most foolish and damnable of all, as it contradicted the teachings of the Bible, the Greek and Roman philosophers, and the world's other religions of the Jews, Muslims, and Tartars [*Convivio*]. Eternal imprisonment in tombs is a particularly suitable punishment for those who believed that life ended with the death and burial of the body (line 15).

26 *the noble city* Florence, in Tuscany (line 22).

32 *Farinata* Farinata degli Uberti (died 1264), a leading member of the imperial party, the Ghibellines, in Florence around the middle of the thirteenth century. Their opponents, the Guelphs, were linked politically and financially with the Papacy against the Empire. The first period of Ghibelline government in Florence (1248–50) ended with the death of the Emperor Frederick II (line 119). Between 1250 and 1260 a popular, Guelph-dominated regime expelled many Ghibellines who, led by Farinata, fought alongside the Sienese army which defeated Florence at the battle of Montaperti in 1260 (lines 85–6). The Ghibellines returned to power until 1266, when the defeat of king Manfred (*Purg.* III, 112) allowed the Guelphs to oust them for the second time. Papal and Guelph propaganda presented the Ghibellines as enemies of the Church and heretics, though the main subject of Dante's encounter here is not heresy but Florentine politics, which remain Farinata's major obsession even in the afterlife.

46 *enemies* as traditional Guelphs, Dante's family opposed the Ghibellines.

48 *twice over* in 1248–50 and 1260–66, when Ghibelline governments expelled Guelphs.

50 *both times* in 1251 and 1266–7, when the Guelphs returned.

51 *that art* the ability to make a comeback from exile. After 1266, the exiled Ghibellines never again succeeded in returning to Florence.

52 *another shade* Cavalcante Cavalcanti, a Florentine Guelph who died some time before 1280.

60 *my son* Guido Cavalcanti (*c.* 1255–1300), son of Cavalcante, son-in-law of Farinata, and a major Florentine poet of the 1280s and 1290s. In the *Vita nuova,* which is addressed principally to him, Dante calls him 'the first of my friends', but by 1300 they had gone different ways both as poets (line 63) and as politicians. When Boniface VIII's plans to control Florence led to the splitting of the Guelph party into two factions, the Whites and the Blacks (*Inf.* VI, 61), Guido joined the militant wing of the former and was exiled by his more moderate fellow-Whites in 1300. Recalled to Florence, he died a few days after his return, on 29 August 1300.

62 *he who awaits* Virgil. Cavalcante, obsessed by pride in his son, has mistakenly assumed that Guido's exceptional intellectual powers should have made him too worthy to visit Hell (lines 58–60), whereas Dante owes his unique journey not to his own gifts but to heavenly assistance and Virgil's guidance.

63 *to one* to Beatrice. Guido's poetry, which presents Love as a dark, earthly passion, had amounted to a rejection of Dante's conception of Love as rational, morally ennobling, and the cause of his present journey to Beatrice in Heaven.

69 *the sweet light* of the sun. Guido was still alive in the spring of 1300 (lines 110–11); his father's misunderstanding of the past tense in 'did disdain' underlines Dante's awareness, when he wrote this canto, that his erstwhile friend had only a few months to live and to turn to the path that leads to salvation.

73 *that great-hearted one* Farinata, although a Ghibelline and a heretic, is admired by Dante as a great Florentine.

77 *that art* of returning from exile (lines 51, 81).

79 *the Lady* the moon, personified as Proserpina or Hecate, queen of the underworld (*Inf.* IX, 44). Farinata's prophecy develops that of Ciacco (*Inf.* VI, 64–72), predicting that Dante will be expelled from Florence within fifty full moons (months), a period which covers the sentences passed against him in early 1302 and the failure of an army of White Guelph exiles to break into the city in July 1304.

82 *And so may* a frequent formula in the poem, stating a request in the form of a bargain. In return for wishing Dante the fulfilment of his desire to return to earth, Farinata asks him to answer a question.

83 *those citizens* the Florentine Guelphs. In 1283 Farinata and his wife were posthumously condemned by the Inquisitor in Florence for heresy. Such was the continuing hatred of them that their remains were scattered, and some of their relatives, including two sons, were exiled.

85 *The carnage* the battle of Montaperti (1260), fought near the river Arbia in southern Tuscany, in which the Ghibellines, including Farinata, inflicted a massive defeat on Florence.

87 *prayers in our temple* vindictive decrees by the Florentine government against Farinata's family.

91 *there* at a council, held after the victory of Montaperti, at which Farinata alone defended Florence against the proposal of the other Ghibellines to destroy the city entirely.

94 *seed* descendants. The clause is another wish formula (line 82).

96 *knot* problem. Dante is puzzled because Farinata's prophecy has shown that he can see into the future, whereas Cavalcante is ignorant of the present, not knowing whether his son is alive or dead in the spring of 1300.

107 *the moment* the end of the world, after which there will be no more future, only an eternal present (line 108) which these souls, in their closed tombs (lines 10–12), can never know.

110 *that fallen man* Cavalcante, who fell back into the tomb (line 71).

119 *Frederick* Frederick II (1194–1250), king of Sicily and Roman Emperor, excommunicated several times for his opposition to the Papacy and allegedly an 'Epicurean' heretic (line 14).

120 *the Cardinal* the fiercely pro-Ghibelline Cardinal Ottaviano degli Ubaldini (died 1273).

128 *the words* Farinata's prophecy of Dante's exile.

131 *one* Beatrice in Heaven, where she can see everything, including Dante's future, in the Mind of God. In fact, it will be Dante's ancestor Cacciaguida who will reveal to him the details of his exile (*Par.* XVII, 46–96).

INFERNO CANTO XI

THE STRUCTURE OF HELL.

8 *Anastasius* Anastasius II, Pope from 496–8, at a time when the doctrine of Christ's two natures, as God and man, was the subject of a growing rift between the Western (Latin) and Eastern (Greek) Churches. By showing favour to the Greek cleric Photinus, who had been sent to negotiate with him, Anastasius revealed his support for the heretic Acacius of Constantinople (died 481), who had denied Christ's divinity [Gratian; *The Book of the Popes*].

20 *may suffice* without the need for further explanations from Virgil.

22 *every malice* every evil action which is committed by deliberate choice.

23 *injustice* any infringement or injury of another person's rights. Rather than adopting a standard Christian scheme (such as the ten Commandments or sins of thought, word, and deed), Dante goes back to classical ethical principles and divides the remaining sins into those of violence and those of fraud [Aristotle; Cicero]. As a result, all the sins in the last three circles have a social dimension, and lower Hell (the evil city of Dis) punishes those whose actions during their lives

corrupted human society and destroyed the ideal of true citizenship.

25 *man's peculiar vice* in the hierarchy of living things, animals and humans share physical powers which can be perverted by violence. What distinguishes human beings from animals is the rational soul with its faculties of reason (mind) and will (the freedom to choose to act well or badly). Since only a mind can deceive, fraud is an abuse of what is specifically human and hence a more serious sin than violence.

28 *the first* of the remaining three circles, the seventh in all.

32 *to them or what is theirs* the three concentric rings of the seventh circle contain the souls of those who committed violence against their neighbour or his possessions (lines 34–9), against themselves or their own possessions (lines 40–45), and against God and His 'possession', nature (lines 46–51).

43 *whoever* the suicide.

50 *Sodom* one of the wicked cities destroyed by God for its sins, and particularly because its males lusted after two angels [Genesis]. It gave its name to sodomy, which in Christian moral teaching was a sin against nature.

Cahors a city in southern France whose name had become synonymous with usury, lending money at interest for excessive profit, which is frequently condemned in the Bible. The Greek word for 'interest' was *tokos*, literally 'offspring', so that usury was thought of as the breeding of money from money, and therefore against nature [Aristotle].

56 *the bond* the universal ties of love by which 'we are all friends to each other' [*Convivio*] and which are the basis of a just social order, for 'man is by nature a social animal' [Aristotle]. The following list (lines 58–60) gives some of the sins which Dante will encounter in the eighth circle, of the fraud which breaks this bond (cantos XVIII–XXX).

59 *simony* the sin of selling spiritual goods for money (canto XIX).

60 *barrators* corrupt politicians (see cantos XXI–XXII).

61 *the former way* fraud committed against someone who trusts the deceiver (lines 53–4). This breaks not only the natural bond of human fellowship but the extra bond of trust between individuals. The last circle of Dante's Hell contains the traitors (cantos XXXII–XXXIV).

65 *Dis* Lucifer (Satan) (*Inf.* VIII, 68).

70–72 *those ... tongues* the wrathful (canto VIII), lustful (canto V), gluttonous (canto VI), and avaricious and prodigals (canto VII). Dante wants to know the principle on which these sinners are punished in upper Hell, outside the city of Dis, rather than within it.

80 *Ethics* the *Nicomachean Ethics* [Aristotle].

81 *incontinence* the failure of the will to control the passions. This is punished in upper Hell and is distinguished from the deliberate choice of evil, punished in lower Hell (line 22). The third category, 'mad bestiality' (line 82), does not have a specific section in Dante's Hell but may be linked with violence, as malice could be with fraud.

93 *doubting* questions to which the answers are so satisfying.

96 *divine goodness* Dante is puzzled by the inclusion of usury among the sins of violence against nature and its goodness (line 48).

101 *Physics* Aristotle's *Physics*.

103 *your art* all productive work, including that of artisans and the trade guilds ('arti'). God creates nature, and human art springs from and imitates nature [Aristotle] (lines 103–5). Usury thus offends both nature (God's 'child') and art (His 'grandchild') (lines 110–11).

107 *Genesis* after Adam and Eve committed the first sin, God condemned them and all their descendants to earn their bread by the sweat of their brow, that is, by working [Genesis].

111 *elsewhere* in amassing wealth by exacting interest on loans instead of obeying the natural duty and the biblical command to work productively for a living.

113 *the Fishes* the constellation of Pisces, which in spring is

on the horizon about two hours before the sun rises in the next sign, Aries. At the same time, the Wain (the Great Bear, Ursa Major) is about to set in the north-west, called Caurus from the wind which blew from that direction (line 114). It is about 4 a.m.

INFERNO CANTO XII

SEVENTH CIRCLE: First Ring: the violent against others and their property (tyrants, murderers, robbers).

4 *the toppled mass* the landslip on the banks of the river Adige to the south of the city of Trent in north-east Italy.

12 *the infamy of Crete* the Minotaur, a monster, half man and half bull, conceived by Pasiphaë, wife of king Minos of Crete, who hid herself in a wooden cow in order to consummate her lust for a bull [Virgil; Ovid]. As the guardian of the circle of violence, the Minotaur embodies the bestiality and fury of the sin punished here.

17 *the Duke of Athens* Theseus, who killed the Minotaur at the centre of the labyrinth where it was kept.

20 *your sister* Ariadne, daughter of Minos and Pasiphaë, half-sister of the Minotaur. She assisted Theseus by providing him with a sword and a skein of thread so that he could find his way out of the labyrinth. Dante, though also travelling through a labyrinth (Hell) to the monster in the centre (Lucifer), is not Theseus come again to kill the Minotaur.

30 *strange* because, unlike the souls, Dante still has the weight of his body.

34 *the other time* Virgil's previous descent into lower Hell (*Inf.* IX, 22–7).

38 *the One* Christ, who delivered the souls of the patriarchs and Jews from Limbo, the first circle of Hell (Dis) (*Inf.* IV, 51–61). The landslide in Hell occurred just before this, that is, at the earthquake which marked the moment of Christ's death on the cross [Matthew].

42 *some* the Greek philosopher Empedocles and his fol-
lowers who believed that the universe was held in balance by
the principles of Love and Strife [Aristotle]. Without the
latter, Love would make all things come together, thus bring-
ing disorder and chaos. This pagan and materialistic concep-
tion of Love is contrasted with the supreme Love expressed by
the death of Christ which restored harmony between the
human race and God.

47 *stream* the river Phlegethon (*Inf*. XIV, 116).

56 *Centaurs* creatures, half man and half horse, which, like
the Minotaur, embody a combination of bestial with human
forces. Organized like a roving band of soldiers armed with
bows and arrows, they are the guardians of the river of boiling
blood, the first ring of this circle, for those who committed
acts of violence against others.

65 *Chiron* a son of the god Saturn, born in the form of a
Centaur, tutor to Achilles (line 71).

67 *Nessus* a Centaur who tried to rape Deianira and was
killed by her husband, Hercules. He left his shirt, soaked in his
poisonous blood, to Deianira who later gave it to Hercules,
thus causing his death and giving Nessus his posthumous
revenge (line 69) [Ovid].

72 *Pholus* another Centaur, known for his great strength
[Statius].

81 *what he touches* the stones moved by Dante's weight (line
30).

84 *two natures* of man and of horse.

88 *she* Beatrice, who came down to Limbo from Heaven,
where the souls of the blessed sing their joyful praises of God
(line 89) (*Inf*. II, 52–117).

104 *that huge Centaur* Nessus.

107 *Alexander* Alexander the Great (356–323 BC), who had
a reputation for cruelty [Lucan; Orosius]; or Alexander, the
tyrant of Pherae in Greece (369–358 BC).

Dionysius the tyrant of Syracuse in Sicily (*c*. 430–367 BC).

109 *Ezzelino* Ezzelino III da Romano (1194–1259), the

ruthless Ghibelline lord of the March of Treviso in north-east Italy.

110 *Obizzo* Obizzo II d'Este (1247–93), lord of Ferrara and Ancona, who was reputedly smothered by his son.

119 *God's bosom* a church, the house of God. The soul is Guy de Montfort (died *c.* 1291), son of Simon de Montfort, earl of Leicester. In revenge for the death of his father at the battle of Evesham (1265), he stabbed Edward I's (and his own) cousin, Prince Henry of Cornwall, during Mass in the church of San Silvestro in Viterbo (1271). It was believed that Prince Henry's heart was preserved in a reliquary in London, while his murder went unavenged (line 120). The atrocity and sacrilege of the crime set Guy de Montfort apart from the other men of violence here.

133 *Attila* king of the Huns (died 453), called 'the scourge of God', because his terrifying ravaging of parts of Europe and Italy seemed like divine punishment for sins.

135 *Pyrrhus* the king of Epirus in Greece (319–272 BC), who waged war against the Romans in Italy; or Achilles' son Pyrrhus (Neoptolemus), who butchered king Priam and other members of the Trojan royal household [Virgil].

Sextus (died 35 BC), son of the Roman general Pompey and the leader of a pirate fleet against the Romans [Lucan].

137 *Rinier of Corneto* a highway robber from Corneto, on the coastal route from southern Tuscany to Lazio.

Rinier Pazzo a highway robber from Tuscany (died before 1280); a member of the Pazzi family, his name also means 'mad'.

INFERNO CANTO XIII

SEVENTH CIRCLE: Second Ring: the violent against themselves and their own property (suicides and squanderers).

7–8 *between Cécina and Corneto* in the wild and wooded coastal region of Tuscany, stretching from Cecina (south of Livorno) to Corneto (Tarquinia) in north Lazio.

10 *Harpies* monstrous birds with women's faces and clawed feet (lines 13–14). On their voyage from Troy, Aeneas and his companions landed on the Strophades Islands where their food was attacked and fouled by the Harpies. After the Harpies' leader prophesied a terrible future famine for them, the Trojans set sail and left the islands (lines 11–12) [Virgil].

19 *the horrid sand* the third ring (cantos XIV–XVII).

30 *cut off* proved false. The souls are not hidden among the trees but actually enclosed within them.

48 *within my poetry* in Virgil's own *Aeneid*, where Aeneas plucks saplings growing on a mound; they ooze blood, and the voice of the murdered Trojan prince, Polydorus, speaks from his grave beneath: 'Why do you tear me, Aeneas, wretch that I am? Spare me now in my grave' [Virgil]. In Dante's adaptation of this episode, the soul is literally enclosed within its tree-body. Having deliberately deprived themselves of their bodies, the suicides may never re-inhabit them, even after the resurrection; instead, in Hell, they sprout the 'bodies' of plants, the lowest form of living things (lines 93–108).

54 *the world above* on earth.

58 *the one* Pier delle Vigne (*c.* 1190–1249), lawyer, poet, and chief minister and secretary to the Emperor Frederick II, king of Sicily. Having fallen from favour, he was blinded and cast into prison, where, it was said, he committed suicide by dashing his brains against the wall. His ornate speech to Dante characterizes him as a master of language and rhetoric: the metaphor of the keys indicates his position as Frederick's closest adviser (lines 58–9) [Isaiah]; and he also uses personification (lines 64–6), word-repetition (lines 67–8), and antithesis (lines 69, 72).

64 *The whore* Envy, personified.

65 *Caesar's dwelling* an Emperor's court, always full of envious rivals.

68 *Augustus* the Emperor, Frederick.

72 *unjust* both in the sight of God, by committing suicide, and in the sight of men, by apparently confirming his guilt of

the accusations. The paradox of disdain inspiring escape from disdain and the folly of replacing innocence with eternal guilt underlie the irrationality of suicide, an act of 'me against myself'.

73 *peculiar roots* of his strange tree-body, on which he swears his oath of innocence.

77 *help my memory* clear my name.

86 *so may* the formula for a mutual service (*Inf.* X, 82).

88 *knots* of the twisted trees (line 5).

95 *Minos* the judge who sends the souls to the appropriate circle of Hell (*Inf.* V, 4–15).

103 *seek out the flesh* collect the bodies when they rise from the grave on the Last Day.

118 *The one in front* Lano, from Siena, who was killed at the battle of Pieve del Toppo in Tuscany (1287) (lines 120–21). These running souls are squanderers, who wasted great wealth for entirely trivial purposes, thus committing a surrogate social and financial suicide. Now, naked, they are hunted by hounds, perhaps representing creditors or their own remorse.

119 *The other shade* Jacopo da Santo Andrea (line 133), a notorious spendthrift from Padua (died 1239).

131 *the lacerated thorn* the bush (line 123), torn by Jacopo and the hounds. It contains the soul of an unnamed Florentine, perhaps a disgraced judge or ruined banker, who committed suicide by hanging himself at home (line 151).

143 *first patron* Mars, the god of war, under whose protection Florence was founded by the Romans but who in Christian times was replaced by St John the Baptist as the city's patron saint.

145 *his art* war and civil strife.

146 *the crossing* the main bridge (now the Ponte Vecchio) across the river Arno in Florence. Nearby there stood a mutilated statue, thought to be of Mars, which is here said to be still protecting the city from an annihilation as total as when it was destroyed by Attila and had to be rebuilt (lines 148–50).

SEVENTH CIRCLE: Third Ring: the violent against God (blasphemers).

6 *justice* God's.

11 *a sad channel* the encircling river of blood.

14 *not different* resembling the Libyan desert in north Africa across which Cato led the Roman republican army in 47 BC [Lucan].

22 *Some lay* the blasphemers.

23 *some huddled* the usurers, who are seated (canto XVII).

24 *others moved about* the sodomites (cantos XV–XVI).

29 *fire* the rain of fire recalls God's punishment of the wicked cities of Sodom and Gomorrah [Genesis].

31 *Alexander* Alexander the Great, the subject of a collection of stories circulating in the Middle Ages, including the episode of a rain of fire.

45 *the entryway* the gate of the city of Dis (*Inf.* VIII–IX).

46 *that giant* Capaneus, one of the seven kings who attacked the city of Thebes in Greece (lines 63, 68–9); he impiously taunted the gods and was killed by Jupiter (Jove) with a thunderbolt (lines 52–4) [Statius].

52 *the smith* the god Vulcan who manufactured Jupiter's thunderbolts in his forge in Mongibello (Mount Etna in Sicily). Capaneus, a blasphemer after death as he had been in life (line 51), is challenging Jupiter (God) to make Vulcan and his assistants work to the point of exhaustion to send down the eternal rain of fire; Capaneus himself will never yield to the punishment (line 60).

58 *Phlegra* the site of the battle in which Jupiter hurled his thunderbolts down upon the giants (*Inf.* XXXI, 44–5, 91–6).

65 *madness* foolish defiance of God. Capaneus' greatest torment is not the fire but is within himself, in his eternally futile blasphemy.

79 *Bulicame* a hot spring, near Viterbo in Lazio, whose waters supplied the establishments of prostitutes.

86 *the gate* the upper gate, which has been open since Christ's descent into Hell (*Inf*. III, 1–11; VIII, 125–7).

92 *the food* of knowledge, in this case, the answer which will satisfy Dante's hunger to learn about the red rivulet.

96 *its king* the god Saturn, ancient king of the island of Crete; his reign had been a Golden Age of peace, innocence, and the simple life before greed, lust, and luxury corrupted the human race [Virgil].

98 *Ida* a mountain in central Crete. In the myth of the origin of the gods, Saturn (Time) was devouring his children to avert a prophecy that one of them would depose him. His pregnant wife, Rhea (Cybele), fled to mount Ida, where she gave birth to Jupiter, concealing the baby's crying by ordering her attendants to bang on their shields and helmets with sticks [Ovid].

103 *a huge Old Man* the statue represents the progressive decline of the human race from the innocence of the Golden Age (the head) down to less precious silver, then brass, and finally iron, with one foot of clay [Daniel; Ovid]. From this moral and political degeneration flow the tears of human suffering which form the rivers of eternal punishment in Hell (lines 112–20).

104 *Damietta* a town (Dumyat) near the mouth of the Nile in Egypt. The statue faces away from the East and towards Rome, the city of the Papacy and the Empire, for spiritual and temporal guidance (line 105).

116 *Acheron, Styx, Phlegethon* three of the rivers of Hell [Virgil]. Dante has already seen the Acheron (*Inf*. III, 77), the Styx (*Inf*. VII, 108), and – without knowing its name – the Phlegethon ('fiery'), the river of boiling blood (lines 130, 134–5).

118 *the point* the centre of the earth, from which one can only travel upwards.

119 *Cocytus* another river of the underworld [Virgil]. As a lake of ice, it forms the last circle of Dante's Hell (*Inf*. XXXI, 123).

131 *Lethe* the remaining river of Hell, in which souls

destined for reincarnation are washed free from the memory of their previous lives [Virgil]. Dante rejects this pagan idea and transfers the Lethe from Hell to the summit of Purgatory, where it gives the repentant and purified souls forgetfulness of their past sins (lines 136–8) (*Purg.* XXVIII, 127–30).

INFERNO CANTO XV

SEVENTH CIRCLE: Third Ring: sinners against nature (sodomites).

4 *between Wissant and Bruges* along the coast of Flanders (from the modern Pas-de-Calais into Belgium).

7 *Brenta* the river which flows through Padua and its territories in north-east Italy. When in spring and summer the sun melts the snows in the Carinthian mountains to the north (line 9), its swollen waters bring the danger of floods. The comparison of the river's raised banks to the Flemish dykes and the Paduan embankments exemplifies how humans can defend themselves against and control the forces of nature.

12 *the artisan* God or an agent of His who created the landscapes of Hell.

30 *Ser Brunetto* Brunetto Latini (*c.* 1220–94/95), a Florentine Guelph, addressed here with the respectful title of 'Ser' ('Messer'), given to lawyers and other professional men. After being exiled in France during the period of Ghibelline rule (1260–66), he returned to Florence and was a leading legal adviser and secretary to the Guelph government until his death, which occurred not long before Dante himself entered Florentine political life (lines 58–60). He was also a scholar and poet whose writings include the *Books of the Treasure*, written in French (a compendium of knowledge, with the rules for rhetoric and government as the climax or 'gold' of the treasure) and an unfinished poem in Italian, also called the *Treasure* (now the *Little Treasure*) (line 119). The latter opens by describing how, on hearing of the defeat of Florence and of his

own exile, Brunetto lost his way in a strange wood from which he escaped by making a journey of instruction and repentance. Dante's episode contains a series of parallels and contrasts between Brunetto (a father-figure and teacher who is now in Hell) and Dante himself, making a unique journey from the dark wood to Paradise, with the authority of Beatrice and the guidance of Virgil.

36 *him* Virgil.

47–8 *last day* death.

55 *star* Dante's birth-sign of Gemini, which disposed his natural talents towards intellectual pursuits and poetry by which he could become famous on earth (line 56). Brunetto here attributes Dante's destiny to the stars whereas Dante himself always limited astrological influences within the doctrine of the freedom of the human will, assisted by God's grace (*Purg.* XVI, 67–81).

60 *work* Dante's participation in Florentine politics.

62 *Fiesole* the hill-top town overlooking Florence. After Julius Caesar conquered it, its people came down and mixed with the Roman settlers in newly founded Florence below. For Brunetto here, the modern Florentines have inherited the hard nature and vices of their Fiesolan ancestors instead of the civic and moral values of the noble Romans.

64 *good deeds* Dante's honesty in public affairs and innocence of the charges of corruption for which he was exiled. Dante was to style himself the 'exsul inmeritus', the undeserved exile.

66 *the sweet fig* metaphorically, Dante himself. Since a bad tree cannot bear good fruit [Matthew], Dante will be unable to fulfil his true destiny among corrupt Florentines (the sour sorb-apple trees) and so will have to do so elsewhere, in exile.

71 *one party and the other* both the Black Guelphs, who banished Dante, and his own party, the Whites, who later persecuted him too (*Par.* XVII, 61–8).

72 *keep the grass far from the goat* another metaphor for Dante's escape from his enemies by exile.

74 *the plant* of Florence's true, Roman heritage.

85 *eternal* famous on earth. Dante pays a positive and affectionate tribute to Brunetto as his occasional or unofficial teacher, of philosophy, ethics, and politics and perhaps of rhetoric and poetry too. However, whilst Dante is travelling to his true home, Heaven (line 54), by his damnation Brunetto has lost the only true immortality, salvation.

88 *course* the future course of Dante's life.

89 *another text* Farinata's prophecy (*Inf*. X, 79–81).

90 *one* Beatrice.

93 *prepared* to bear the future cruel blow of exile. It is Fortune's duty to turn her wheel and alter men's lives (*Inf*. VII, 62), just as it is a farmer's job to till the earth (line 96).

108 *one same sin* sodomy. There is no independent evidence that Brunetto Latini or any of the other three named souls in this group of clerics or men of letters were sodomites in a sexual sense. Their sin may therefore have been a connected intellectual error, namely, the denial of the Christian doctrine that nature, created by God, is good (*Inf*. XI, 48).

109 *Priscian* (*c*. AD 500), the writer of the most important book on Latin grammar used in the Middle Ages.

109–10 *Francesco d'Accorso* son of the great jurist Accursius, and professor of law at the University of Bologna (died 1293). He was notorious, above all, for usury.

112 *the one* Andrea de' Mozzi, bishop of Florence (on the river Arno) from 1287 to 1295, when Pope Boniface VIII transferred him to the bishopric of Vicenza (on the river Bacchiglione), where he died in 1296. The 'Servant of the Servants of God' is one of the titles of the Pope.

118 *people* another group of souls.

119 *Tesoro* 'Treasure', the title of two of Brunetto's works, which give him his claim to earthly immortality (see note to line 310).

122–3 *green cloth* the prize given in an annual footrace held in Verona. The simile of Brunetto as the winner of a merely earthly, perishable prize forms the final contrast with Dante's journey to the eternal prize of Heaven [1 Corinthians; *Convivio*].

INFERNO CANTO XVI

SEVENTH CIRCLE: Third Ring: the sodomites (continued).

9 *indecent country* wicked Florence.

26 *opposed* turning their faces towards Dante while continuing to walk in a circle.

31 *one* Jacopo Rusticucci (line 44), a Florentine Guelph politician and diplomat around the middle of the thirteenth century. His reference to his wife (line 45) may indicate that the sin here was of sexual practices regarded as against nature.

38 *Guido Guerra* a Florentine Guelph captain and adviser (died 1272), here identified through his grandmother, Gualdrada, who was famous as a paragon of matriarchal virtues in old Florence.

41 *Tegghiaio Aldobrandi* another Florentine Guelph leader in the 1250s and early 1260s. The three souls, praised for their moral worth (line 57; *Inf.* VI, 79–81), represent the more virtuous civic leadership of Florence in the generation before Dante's, before the decline into the present corruption.

55 *my lord* Virgil.

61 *sweet apples* the joy and fulfilment which are the goal of Dante's journey.

63 *the center* of the earth, the bottom of Hell.

64 *So may* by your wish for a long life and for fame after death (line 65).

66 *courtesy and valor* the old chivalric and moral values of Florentine society in earlier times.

69 *Guiglielmo Borsiere* a Florentine, believed to have been a courtier, who must have died not long before the spring of 1300.

73 *Newcomers* non-Florentines, drawn to the city by greed because of its recent expansion as a centre of banking and trade.

76 *upraised* towards Florence itself, in the world above.

84 *when you repeat* when, after returning to this life, Dante tells in his poem that he really visited Hell.

94 *the river* the Acquacheta, the first river south of the Po to flow directly from the Apennine mountains to the sea and which beyond the town of Forlì in the Romagna was known by another name (the Montone) (lines 98–9). Dante compares the great, roaring cascade of the Phlegethon down into the abyss of Hell to the waterfall formed by this river up in the mountains near the monastery of San Benedetto dell'Alpe.

102 *space enough* enough height to contain a series of smaller cascades rather than a single great waterfall.

108 *the leopard* the first beast to attack Dante (*Inf.* I, 32–6). The symbolism of Dante's cord is uncertain: as a rope to capture the leopard (lust), it has been linked with chastity; however, here it is thrown down into the abyss as a lure or bribe to summon up the monster Geryon from the circle of fraud.

124 *that truth* an incredible fact.

128 *my Comedy* the title of Dante's poem (*Inf.* XXI, 2), alluding to comedy as poetry which starts horribly (in this case, with Hell) and ends happily (in this case, in Heaven) and which is written in a humble style and in Italian, the language of the people [*Epistles* XIII]. Dante's oath, sworn upon the words of his own poem, claims absolute truth for the incredible sight which follows, and thus for the entire amazing journey.

133 *one* a sailor swimming back upwards.

INFERNO CANTO XVII

SEVENTH CIRCLE: Third Ring: sinners against nature and art (the usurers).

1 *the beast* Geryon, a threefold giant, killed by Hercules [Virgil]. In Dante's version, he resembles the mythical beast, the man-eating manticora, and is the embodiment of fraud, with a deceptively honest human face but with a serpent's body and a scorpion's tail. Fraud includes deception in wars

and sieges, and is a universal evil (lines 2–3).

16 *Turks or Tartars* oriental weavers.

18 *Arachne* a woman who, challenging the goddess Minerva, wove a magnificent cloth portraying the loves of the gods [Ovid] (*Purg.* XII, 43–5).

22 *the beaver* believed to catch fish by stirring its tail in the water as a lure.

36 *sinners sitting* the usurers, extortionate moneylenders who lived off interest, not productive work (*Inf.* XI, 94–111).

55 *a purse* a money-bag, the sign of their sin, each marked by a heraldic emblem (line 56). The examples given by Dante, the son of a Florentine moneylender, illustrate the decline of noble families from the courtly ideals of the feudal age into commercial greed and exploitation. The coats of arms described here identify these three usurers as members of the Gianfigliazzi of Florence (lines 59–60), the Obriachi of Florence (lines 62–3), and the Scrovegni of Padua (lines 64–5). The speaker, probably Reginaldo degli Scrovegni (died 1288/89), looks forward to being joined in Hell by a fellow-Paduan usurer, Vitaliano, still living in 1300 (lines 68–9); similarly, the Florentines await the arrival of a supreme usurer from the Becchi family, with their emblem of three goats (lines 72–3).

80 *animal* Geryon.

89 *shame* of showing fear, despite Virgil's assurances.

107 *Phaethon* the son of Apollo, who allowed him to drive the chariot of the Sun; when he lost control of the horses, scorched the Milky Way across the sky (line 108), and almost burnt up the earth, Jupiter struck him down [Ovid].

109 *Icarus* the son of Daedalus who made artificial wings held together with wax so that they could both escape from Crete; despite his father's warning (line 111), Icarus flew too close to the sun, the wax melted, and he plunged to his death in the sea [Ovid]. Dante imagines his own fear of flying on Geryon's back as greater than that of the two greatest classical examples of rashness in flight at the moment when disaster struck them.

INFERNO CANTO XVIII

EIGHTH CIRCLE (the fraudulent): First Ditch: the pro-
curers and seducers of women; Second Ditch: the flatterers.

1 *Malebolge* 'evil pouches', a name (resembling that of a
quarter of a medieval city inhabited by the criminal under-
world) given by Dante to the eighth circle because it consists
of ten concentric ditches (*bolge*, 'pouches') (line 9) in which are
punished souls who committed different sins of deceit (*Inf.* XI,
55–60).

16 *ridges* arches of rock which form bridges over the ditches
down to the central pit.

28 *Jubilee* the centenary year 1300, when Christians who
visited the tombs of St Peter and St Paul in Rome earned a
plenary indulgence from their sins (*Purg.* II, 98–9). So great
were the crowds of pilgrims that regulations were introduced
on the bridge over the river Tiber: those going towards the
Castle of Sant'Angelo and St Peter's had to walk down one
side; those returning towards Monte Giordano, back into the
city, had to keep to the other (lines 31–3). Similarly, here the
procurers (pimps) and the seducers walk in two files, one
coming towards Dante and Virgil, the other moving in the
same direction.

50 *Venèdico Caccianemico* a leading Guelph from Bologna
who was said to have offered his sister, Ghisolabella, for sex as
a favour to his ally, the Marquis of Ferrara (lines 55–6).

51 *sauces so piquant* such sharp torments.

61 "*sipa*" the dialect word for 'yes' in Bologna and its
territory, bordered by the rivers Sàvena and Reno. There are
more Bolognese here in Hell than there are living inhabitants
there.

73 *the point* the top of the arched bridge, from where Dante
can look back and see the faces of the other file, the seducers.

86 *Jason* the Greek hero who sailed in the Argo to Colchis
(on the Black Sea) and, with his bravery and cunning, cap-
tured the precious Golden Fleece (lines 86–7). On his voyage,

he landed on the island of Lemnos where the women were killing all the menfolk, though the princess Hypsipyle had saved her father by a ruse; Jason seduced and then abandoned her, leaving her pregnant with twins (lines 88–94). In Colchis, he promised to marry the princess Medea, but later he abandoned her too for another woman (line 96) [Ovid; Statius].

103 *the next pouch* the second ditch.

117 *lay or cleric* whether he had a cleric's tonsure or not.

123 *Alessio Interminei* from Lucca in Tuscany (died after 1295), known to Dante (line 121), who uses him as an example of the vice of flattery, currying favour with false words of praise and friendship which are here symbolized by the excrement.

133 *Thaïs* the prostitute in *The Eunuch*, a Latin comedy by Terence. Her reply to her lover, as given here, typifies the wild exaggerations of a flatterer [Cicero].

INFERNO CANTO XIX

EIGHTH CIRCLE: Third Ditch: the simoniacs (corrupt churchmen).

1 *Simon Magus* a sorcerer from Samaria who became a Christian and then tried to buy the apostles' power of bestowing the Holy Spirit, at which St Peter told him: 'Take your money with you to damnation, since you thought that the gift of God could be obtained by money' [Acts]. He gave his name to the sin of simony, the trafficking in spiritual goods such as offices and benefices in the Church, indulgences, and other ecclesiastical favours. This, as the sin of churchmen and above all of Popes, was particularly serious in Dante's eyes, as it contaminated the spiritual leadership of the world with greed and amounted to the prostitution of the Church, the Bride of Christ, for money (lines 3–4, 57, 107–8). The intensity of Dante's feelings is conveyed by the series of direct addresses to Simon and his followers, to God's justice in Hell, and to

Constantine (lines 1–6, 10–12, 115–17).

5 *the trumpet* Dante's poem, acting like the trumpet which will summon these souls to Judgment on the Last Day.

17 *San Giovanni* the church of St John the Baptist in Florence where all Florentines are baptized. The fonts used to be set into the floor.

21 *my seal* the true reason for Dante's breaking of the font. The autobiographical reference explains an act which otherwise could have appeared sacrilegious.

50 *the foul assassin* a murderer condemned to execution by being buried head downwards. The simile pointedly reverses the roles, comparing a Pope to a murderer trying to delay the moment of his death, and Dante the layman to a cleric hearing his confession. The punishment of the simoniac Popes, stuck upside down in holes in the rock with flames licking the soles of their feet, is a suitable inversion and eternal parody of their sin: corrupting the inheritance of St Peter, the first Pope (the Rock of the Church), by pocketing wealth (line 72) through selling the gifts of the Holy Spirit, Who descended as flames upon the heads of the apostles at Pentecost [Acts]. This soul is Pope Nicholas III, previously Cardinal Giovanni Gaetano Orsini, who reigned from 1277–80.

54 *The book* of the future. Nicholas mistakes Dante for Pope Boniface VIII, who, in the spring of 1300, still had some three and a half years to live. The error makes it clear where he is destined to go after death.

57 *the Lovely Lady* the Church, the Bride of Christ.

69 *the mighty mantle* the cloak of the Papacy, the highest office in the Church.

70 *son of the she-bear* a member of the Roman family of the Orsini, with a pun on the surname ('orsa' means 'bear', traditionally a greedy animal). The cubs are the Orsini relatives whom Nicholas, as Pope, favoured and enriched (lines 71–2). Alongside simony, nepotism was another major evil associated with papal greed.

77 *the one* Boniface VIII.

79 *a longer time* Nicholas (died 1280) prophesies that Boniface (died 1303) will be topmost in the cleft for a shorter time before being replaced by the next simoniac Pope to die, Clement V, in 1314. Dante either wrote this canto after the latter date or anticipated – correctly, as it turned out – that Clement would not survive Boniface by twenty-three years.

82 *one* Clement V, archbishop of Bordeaux, a native of Gascony in the west of Europe (line 83), elected Pope in 1305. Instead of travelling to Rome (the true seat of the Papacy, for Dante), he stayed in France and in 1309 established the papal residence and administration in Avignon, where it remained for most of the rest of the century.

83 *shepherd* the leader and guide of Christ's flock, the Church (line 106).

85 *Jason* the Jewish high priest, who bought the office by bribing king Antiochus Epiphanes [2 Maccabees]. The prophecy concerns Clement's subservience to king Philip IV (the Fair) of France, who had helped to engineer his election and whose puppet he was considered to be.

92 *the keys* the signs of supreme spiritual and juridical power in the Church, given by Christ to St Peter and passed on to his successors, the Popes (line 101): 'And I shall give to you the keys of the kingdom of Heaven' [Matthew].

95 *Matthias* the apostle elected to take the place of Judas who had hanged himself in remorse at having betrayed Christ [Acts].

99 *Charles* Charles I of Anjou, king of Naples and, until 1282, of Sicily. Nicholas III allegedly received money to foment the rebellion of the Sicilian Vespers which ousted the French from the island (*Par.* VIII, 67–75).

106 *the Evangelist* St John, author of the fourth Gospel and the Book of Revelation. In the latter, he prophesies that, in the time of tribulations before the end of the world, there will appear a prostitute seated on a beast with seven heads and ten horns [Revelation]. Here, fulfilling this prophecy, she stands for the Church prostituted by the avarice of the Popes of

Dante's time (*Purg.* XXXII, 142–60).

111 *her husband* the Pope. The beast's heads (perhaps the seven Sacraments) and ten horns (perhaps the ten Commandments) were sources of good when the Popes were virtuous, before they corrupted the Church.

114 *a hundred* many idols, that is, coins.

115 *Constantine* Roman Emperor (306–37) who became a Christian. According to a document known as the Donation of Constantine, when he transferred the capital of the Empire from Rome to Constantinople (Istanbul), he bequeathed sovereignty over the Western Empire to the then Pope, St Sylvester, and his successors. Only in the century after Dante's death was this document shown to have been written not in the fourth century but around AD 800. Dante accepted its authenticity but denied its validity [*Monarchia*]; for him, Constantine's conversion to Christianity had been good, but his legacy of the Empire to the Popes had led to the fatal corruption of the Church by greed for temporal power and riches (lines 116–17; *Par.* XX, 55–60).

INFERNO CANTO XX

EIGHTH CIRCLE: Fourth Ditch: fraudulent prophets, astrologers, and practitioners of the magic arts.

3 *first canticle* the *Inferno*, of the souls sunk in the pit of Hell. Each of the three parts of the *Comedy* is known as a 'canticle' (*Purg.* XXXIII, 140), a longer song divided into smaller 'songs' or cantos, which would originally have been recited ('sung') before an audience.

13 *twisted* the appropriate punishment for those who claimed to see into the future is that now their faces are completely turned round backwards on their necks.

19 *fruit* moral instruction and the decision to turn from sin to a virtuous life.

22 *our image* the form of the human body.

28 *pity* the paradox forbids Dante to feel pity, which would be equivalent to questioning God's justice in punishing the souls (line 30, alternatively interpreted as referring to the pseudo-prophets' claim to control the future, which belongs only to God).

33 *Amphiaraus* one of the seven kings who waged war on Thebes; he foresaw his own death, which came when the earth opened in front of him and swallowed him up [Statius].

36 *Minos* the judge in Dante's Hell (*Inf.* V, 4–15).

40 *Tiresias* a soothsayer from Thebes who, having separated two mating serpents with his staff, was turned into a woman; seven years later, he struck the serpents again and was changed back into a man [Ovid].

46 *Aruns* an Etruscan soothsayer who foresaw the outcome of the civil war between Julius Caesar and Pompey [Lucan], here presented as a hermit-like astrologer living in the mountains above Carrara, near the abandoned town of Luni in north-west Tuscany (lines 48–51).

55 *Manto* a Theban sorceress, the daughter of Tiresias (lines 40, 58) [Statius]. Mantua, Virgil's birthplace (line 56), was named after her.

59 *Bacchus' city* Thebes, the birthplace of the god Bacchus, which after the death of Oedipus' sons was ruled by the tyrant Creon [Statius].

63 *Benaco* now Lake Garda in northern Italy at the foot of the Alps, south of the region or castle of Tirolo. It is identified by the other rivers which flow from it (lines 64–6), by its island on which three bishops had jurisdiction (lines 67–9), and by the defensive fortress of Peschiera at its southern tip (lines 70–72), near which the river Mincio flows down from the lake, through a marshy region, and into the river Po (lines 73–81).

82 *the savage virgin* Manto.

86 *arts* of prophecy and magic.

87 *empty* dead, deprived of the soul.

93 *cast no lots* practised no divining in choosing the site for the city.

95 *before the foolishness of Casalodi* before 1272, when Alberto da Casalodi, lord of Mantua, was duped by Pinamonte dei Bonaccolsi who then seized power in the city. The coup involved the massacre or expulsion of many noble families.

98 *a different tale* another explanation, namely, that Mantua was founded by Manto's son [Virgil]. Dante's Virgil here rejects the elements of pagan superstition and magic in the legends of the foundation of his birthplace; instead, it was for defensive purposes that rational humans established the social unit of a city on that site, and it was so named only because Manto was buried there.

102 *spent coals* no longer of any use.

106 *That shade* Eurypylus (line 112), a Greek who took part in the expedition against Troy. Dante makes him an associate of the soothsayer Calchas who, when the Greek fleet was unable to set sail from the port of Aulis, advised king Agamemnon to sacrifice his daughter to appease the goddess Diana (lines 110–11). According to the story spun by Sinon (*Inf.* XXX, 98, 113–14), Eurypylus was later sent to consult the oracle of Apollo and brought back a message which Calchas interpreted, that another human sacrifice was necessary if the Trojans were ever to return home [Virgil.]

113 *high tragedy* the *Aeneid*, written in Latin and in an elevated style, and thus contrasted with Dante's more humble *Comedy* in Italian (*Inf.* XVI, 128; XXI, 2).

116 *Michael Scot* (died *c.* 1235), the court astrologer to the Emperor Frederick II. Though a notable scholar, he acquired a more sinister reputation as a sorcerer and prophet.

118 *Guido Bonatti* a famous astrological consultant to several Italian leaders; he died in the late 1290s, and a treatise by him on the stars and horoscopes survives.

Asdente a shoemaker from Parma who abandoned his trade (lines 119–20) and set himself up as an interpreter of prophecies and signs, for which he became notorious in late thirteenth-century Italy [*Convivio*].

121 *sad women* women who now regret having abandoned

their sewing and weaving in order to become witches (lines 121–3).

124 *Cain* the moon, whose spots were seen as the figure of Cain carrying a bundle of thorns, exiled there after he murdered his brother Abel [Genesis].

126 *below Seville* in the Atlantic, beyond Spain. The spring full moon (line 127) would be setting over the western horizon at about dawn (6 a.m.) in Jerusalem, the centre of the northern hemisphere.

INFERNO CANTO XXI

EIGHTH CIRCLE: Fifth Ditch: the barrators (politicians who took bribes).

7 *the arsenal* the shipyard of Venice with the cauldrons of caulking-pitch and the bustle of the workers.

23 *"Take care!"* Virgil's warning and the simile of the man who flees from a fearful danger (lines 25–8) reflect the temptations of political life and the fact that bribe-taking and embezzlement while in office were the crimes for which Dante was sentenced to death. The menacing black devils may be caricatures of his Black Guelph enemies from whom he escaped by exile.

30 *demon* a devil, one of the fallen angels. In cantos XXI–XXII, Dante develops the grotesque image of devils in medieval folklore, art, and popular theatre, choosing a deliberately low, crude, and 'comic' style.

37 *Malebranche* 'evil claws', a family name given by Dante to all the devils here, making them into a violent criminal clan. Each devil also has a harsh personal name (lines 76, 105, 118–23).

38 *an elder*, a member of the city council of Lucca, in Tuscany, where St Zita is buried and venerated as a saint. The unnamed town councillor, who must have just died, exemplifies the extent of political corruption in Lucca, which provides

this ditch of Hell with a constant supply of souls (lines 39–40), and this evil is ironically contrasted with local religious devotions.

41 *Bonturo* a party boss in Lucca in the early fourteenth century who was so notoriously corrupt that the devil is being ironical in making him the sole exception.

42 *a no to yes* the complete reversal of laws and judgments in return for bribes.

48 *The Sacred Face* an ancient wooden crucifix venerated in the cathedral of Lucca; the face of Christ on it was the emblem of the city and was stamped on its coins. The Lucchese grafter cannot escape by praying or buying his way out of Hell.

49 *Serchio* a river near Lucca. Unlike swimmers there, the sinners must stay beneath the surface of the pitch (lines 51, 53).

76 *Malacoda* 'evil tail', the name of one of the devils.

84 *another* Dante.

95 *Caprona* a castle near Pisa, captured by a force of Florentine and other Guelphs in 1289. Dante here records his presence as an eye-witness to the surrender and emergence of the defeated garrison.

105 *Scarmiglione* 'the rougher up', another devil.

111 *another ridge* an arch over the next ditch. It later emerges that Malacoda is telling a lie (*Inf.* XXIII, 140–44).

112 *Five hours from this hour* at midday, five hours after the present time of 7 a.m. The bridges over the next ditch collapsed at noon on the previous day, 1,266 years ago (from 1300), that is, in AD 34, at the moment of Christ's death and the accompanying earthquake (*Inf.* XII, 34–5). The time reference, dating Dante's journey to the anniversaries of the events of the Redemption (*Inf.* I, 39), confirms his position as a follower of Christ in his descent into Hell (*Inf.* IV, 52–4) and as the model Christian traveller in his conversion from sin to salvation.

118–23 *Alichino … Rubicante* the names of the ten devils of the escort, combining harsh surnames and allusions to grotesque physical details, form part of the violent, grating language of Dante's Hell: Alichino (from 'ali', 'wings', perhaps related to the evil sprite who was the forerunner of the trickster Harlequin in later comic theatre), Calcabrina ('frost-trampler'), Cagnazzo ('doggish'), Barbariccia ('curly-beard'), Libicocco (perhaps 'blaster', from the names of two winds, the *libecchio* and the sirocco), Draghignazzo ('dragonish' or 'sneerer'), Ciriatto ('hoggish'), Graffiacane ('dog-scratcher'), Farfarello (perhaps 'moth-winged', also with an echo of names for other evil spirits in popular folklore), and Rubicante ('red', evoking also 'rabid').

137 *between his teeth* as if to 'blow a raspberry', a sign they are ready for their captain's bugle-call.

INFERNO CANTO XXII

EIGHTH CIRCLE: Fifth Ditch: the barrators (continued).

4 *Aretines* the people of Arezzo, in southern Tuscany, a Ghibelline city defeated by a Florentine Guelph army at the battle of Campaldino (1289) at which Dante may have been present (*Purg.* V, 92). Barbariccia's crudely comic bugle-call is stranger than any signal, Italian or foreign (line 9), that Dante has ever heard or seen in the Arezzo campaign, tournaments, military manoeuvres, or navigation (lines 5–12).

15 *'in church ...'* the company one finds will fit the place, so that it is not at all surprising to be with devils in Hell. The phrase has a popular, proverbial tone.

44 *that unfortunate* the sinner, not named by Dante, is traditionally identified as Ciampolo (or Jean-Paul) from the Pyrenean kingdom of Navarre. He exemplifies those corrupt and cunning ministers or courtiers who exploit their position in the service of a virtuous lord – here, king Thibault II of Navarre (1253–70) (lines 52–4). The type would have been known to Dante, the impoverished exile, serving in the house-holds of his patrons.

81 *Fra Gomita* a friar ('Fra' means 'brother'), the chief minister of Nino Visconti, governor of the province of

Gallura in Sardinia (*Purg.* VIII, 53), who had him hanged in *c.* 1290, when it was discovered that he had taken a bribe in return for releasing some prisoners (lines 83–5).

88 *Don Michele Zanche* the governor or a minister in the province of Logodoro, also in Sardinia, who was murdered by his son-in-law, Branca Doria (*Inf.* XXXIII, 137–43).

94 *marshal* Barbariccia, the captain of the escort.

100 *Malebranche* the devils (*Inf.* XXI, 37).

109 *he* the wily Ciampolo.

116 *this height* the edge of the ditch, giving Ciampolo a head start.

118 *new sport* a race so extraordinary that no one before Dante has ever seen or described one like it.

120 *he first* Cagnazzo, already suspicious (line 108).

125 *he* Alichino, who had challenged Ciampolo (lines 112–17). What follows – the outwitting of the devils and the fall of two of them into the same torment as the barrators – brings the episode to a grimly farcical but morally satisfying conclusion, which allows Dante to escape, as he did in reality from his condemnation for the same crime.

INFERNO CANTO XXIII

EIGHT CIRCLE: Sixth Ditch: the hypocrites.

3 *Friars Minor* Franciscans, members of the order of friars founded by St Francis of Assisi in the early thirteenth century.

4 *Aesop* an ancient Greek, the supposed author of a collection of fables widely used as school texts and moral lessons, including one, attributed to him, about a treacherous frog which fell into its own trap. Having tied itself to a mouse, which it had promised to ferry across a river, it then tried to drown its companion by diving, but a hawk seized up the mouse and caught the frog attached to it too. Similarly, the two devils, fighting together, have both ended up in the boiling pitch.

27 *your inner* Dante's thoughts, which Virgil can read as instantly as a mirror would reflect back Dante's outward appearance.

58 *a painted people* the hypocrites in their gilded cloaks and cowls (line 64). Hypocrisy is the sin of appearing to be what one is not, in particular of hiding interior wickedness beneath a virtuous exterior [Cicero; St Thomas]. As with the evil friar, False-Seeming, in *The Romance of the Rose*, it was the typical sin of corrupt clergy, deceitfully pretending to be pious and saintly; hence the references to religious orders in the canto (lines 3, 63, 103). The word 'hypocrisy' was thought to mean 'gold on the outside', and the punishment here, which consists of outward show (the gold) and inner weight (the lead), echoes Christ's condemnation of the hypocritical scribes and Pharisees (line 116) as whitened sepulchres, fair on the outside but full of corruption within [Matthew].

63 *Cluny* a famous Benedictine abbey in Burgundy.

66 *were straw* seemed light. The Emperor Frederick II reputedly executed traitors by putting them inside cloaks of lead, which were then melted over a fire.

88 *this one* Dante, whose breathing shows he is still alive.

95 *the great city* Florence, on the Arno.

103 *Jovial Friars* members of a brotherhood of religious and laymen, officially called the Knights of Saint Mary but popularly known as the *Frati Godenti* ('pleasure-loving friars') because of their often easy and worldly lifestyles. Among those who founded the order in 1261, with the aim of reconciling the warring factions and families in the Italian cities, were the two sinners here: Catalano, a Guelph (died 1285), and Loderingo degli Andalò, a Ghibelline (died 1293), both from Bologna. In 1266 they were appointed jointly to the office of *podestà*, the chief executive and magistrate of Florence (lines 106–7); but instead of being impartial, they hypocritically favoured the Guelphs, who in revenge against the Ghibellines destroyed the house and tower of the Uberti family (*Inf.* X, 32, 83–4). The site – in the Gardingo area of Florence (near the

present Piazza della Signoria) – was left abandoned as a sign of continuing hatred (lines 107–8).

111 *one crucified* the soul is Caiaphas, the Jewish high priest who told the council of priests and Pharisees that it was expedient to put one man to death in order to save the whole people (lines 115–17), thus persuading them to deliver an innocent man, Christ, to the Romans for crucifixion [John].

114 *Fra* Brother, the title given to a friar.

116 *Pharisees* Jews of strict observance who, in the New Testament, frequently interrogated and argued against Christ and whose name became synonymous with religious hypocrisy.

122 *father-in-law* Annas, joint high priest with Caiaphas.

124 *amazed* because Virgil's previous visit to Hell (*Inf.* IX, 22–30) had been before Christ's crucifixion.

131 *black angels* devils.

140 *He* the devil Malacoda, who had told them there was still one bridge intact over this ditch (*Inf.* XXI, 111).

142 *Bologna* the two friars' native city (line 103), noted above all for its University.

INFERNO CANTO XXIV

EIGHTH CIRCLE: Seventh Ditch: the thieves.

1 *that part* in January and early February when the sun is in the sign of Aquarius, and the days begin to lengthen as the spring equinox approaches (line 3). In Dante's day, the sun entered each new sign of the zodiac on about the 12th of each month (*Par.* XXVII, 142–4).

4–5 *his white sister* snow, which would deprive the poor farmer of grazing for his flocks, whereas the ground-frost soon melts. His despair replaced by joy illustrates Dante's reaction to Virgil's anger which then gives way to reassuring calm and care (lines 16–21).

21 *the mountain's base* the foot of the hill (*Inf.* I, 13–136).

25 *he who ponders* someone who plans ahead at each stage of a task.

31 *those* the hypocrites, weighed down and unable to climb out of their ditch.

32 *he, light* Virgil, a soul, unlike Dante who still has his body.

38 *last well* the central pit down towards which the eighth circle slopes.

47 *he who rests* a lazy person, always in bed, who never makes any effort towards permanent achievement and will leave no lasting trace of his life to posterity (lines 50–51). Virgil's lesson indicates fame as the spur for Dante to be ceaselessly active on his journey and in writing the poem he will leave behind him.

55 *longer ladder* the climb up the mountain of Purgatory.

73 *the other belt* the lower bank of the ditch.

85 *Libya* the North African desert, which teems with exotic and poisonous snakes (lines 86–7; *Inf.* XXV, 94–5) [Lucan] but which, alongside other snake-infested regions in Africa and Arabia (lines 88–9), is surpassed by this ditch. The thieves have their freedom and even their human forms stolen from them by snakes, symbols of deceit, which bind their hands (lines 94–6) and incinerate or transform them (lines 100–105; *Inf.* XXV, 46–144).

93 *a hole or heliotrope* escape by hiding or by becoming invisible (a power which the heliotrope, a precious stone, was believed to give to its bearer).

100 *o or i* the two letters of the alphabet which are the quickest to write.

108 *the phoenix* the fabulous Oriental bird which builds its nest of perfumes and every five hundred years is burnt to ashes from which it rises to life again [Ovid].

112 *he who falls* someone who falls unconscious, either through possession by a demon (line 113) or from some natural physical blockage (line 114).

125 *Vanni Fucci* the bastard son ('mule', line 124) of a

nobleman of Pistoia in Tuscany; he died in early 1300. Though notorious for his violence, in Hell he is not among the robbers (*Inf.* XII) but lower down, among the deceitful thieves (lines 127–35). In 1293, he had raided the chapel in Pistoia cathedral where the precious church treasures were kept, a crime for which the authorities had at first arrested someone else (lines 137–9).

142 *announcement* prophecy. Lest Dante gloat at finding him here, Vanni Fucci, a Black Guelph, foretells the downfall of Dante's own party, the Whites, between 1301 and 6: though they would expel the Blacks from Pistoia (line 143), in Florence it would be the Whites, including Dante, who would be ousted and replaced by the Blacks (line 144; *Inf.* VI, 64–72; X 79–81; XV, 71–2), and then White Pistoia too would be defeated by Black Guelph forces led by Moroello Malaspina (lines 145–50).

145 *a vapor* Moroello Malaspina, marquis of the Lunigiana (in the valley of the Magra in Tuscany), captain of the Black Guelphs who captured Pistoia in 1306. The prophecy is encoded in meteorological images: he is a lightning-flash summoned up by the god of war, and the battle for Pistoia is the storm in which he will strike and destroy the opposing clouds (the Whites). The 'Campo Piceno' ('Field of Picenum') is the territory of Pistoia, so called from a misinterpretation of the Roman historian, Sallust.

INFERNO CANTO XXV

EIGHTH CIRCLE: Seventh Ditch: the thieves (continued).

2 *both figs* both thumbs stuck out between the first and second fingers in an obscene sexual gesture by which Vanni Fucci tells God what he thinks of Him (line 3).

4 *friends* allies, in punishing Vanni Fucci's blasphemy.

12 *your seed* the founders of Pistoia, the soldiers who had fought for the Roman traitor, Catiline (died 62 BC).

15 *he* Capaneus, the blasphemer (*Inf.* XIV, 46–72).

17 *Centaur* for the other Centaurs, see *Inf.* XII, 56.

19 *Maremma* the coastal region of southern Tuscany, a wild and lonely area in Dante's day.

21 *the part* where the two forms of horse and man join.

25 *Cacus* a fire-breathing monster, half human and half beast, who lived in a cave beneath the Aventine (one of the seven hills on which Rome was later built) where the ground was soaked with the blood of the humans on whom he preyed. When Hercules drove Geryon's herd of cattle through Italy, Cacus stole some of them, pulling them backwards into his cave to reverse their hoof-prints and put Hercules off the trail; but he discovered the hiding-place, entered the cave, and killed Cacus [Virgil; Livy]. Dante makes Cacus a Centaur who has been condemned to this lower circle of Hell because, unlike the other Centaurs who are creatures of violence, his was the worse sin of deceit (lines 28–9; *Inf.* XI, 25–7).

43 *Cianfa* a Florentine burglar who died in the 1280s. The other three thieves, also Florentines, miss him because he has been changed into the serpent which then attacks one of them, Agnello (line 68), fusing with him into a monstrous hybrid – an incredible but true sight (lines 46–8) which Dante proceeds to describe in loathsome anatomical detail (lines 50–78).

45 *raised my finger* as a sign to Virgil not to speak.

73 *four lengths* Cianfa the serpent's two forelegs and Agnello's two arms.

77 *perverse image* the monstrous form, both snake and man, but neither snake nor man.

82 *serpent* another Florentine thief (identified in line 151) who has been changed into a serpent. He attacks one of the two remaining souls, a thief called Buoso (line 140), in the navel (line 86).

94 *Lucan* the Roman poet (*Inf.* IV, 90), writer of the *Pharsalia* (*On the Civil War*), in which he describes the gruesome transformation of two soldiers who, during their march across the Libyan desert (*Inf.* XXIV, 85), were bitten by

snakes: one, Sabellus, rotted away and fell to pieces; the other, Nasidius, swelled up and burst [Lucan].

97 *Ovid* the Roman poet (*Inf*. IV, 90) whose *Metamorphoses* include the stories of the transformation of Cadmus into a serpent and of Arethusa into a spring [Ovid]. In asking Lucan and Ovid to withdraw from competition with what comes next in the narrative (line 96) – namely, the double and simultaneous metamorphosis of man into snake and snake into man (lines 100–102) – Dante is elevating the virtuosity of his own poetry, the amazing account of God's Justice in the afterlife, above that of two of his main classical predecessors. The high-flown challenge is concluded by an ironically humble apology to the reader for any defects he has shown in meeting it (lines 143–4).

105 *steps* legs.

116 *the member* the genitals.

124 *his* his snout, changing from a snake's into a man's.

142 *the seventh ballast* the thieves, the worthless dregs in the seventh ditch.

148 *Puccio Sciancato* a Florentine thief, nicknamed 'Sciancato', 'the lame', who died some time after 1280.

151 *the other one* the thief just turned back into human form is Francesco de' Cavalcanti, whose killing by men from Gaville near Florence led to a bloody reprisal raid on the village by his relatives.

INFERNO CANTO XXVI

EIGHTH CIRCLE: Eighth Ditch: the deceitful advisers.

1 *Be joyous* the address is ironical, since Florence's fame in Hell is really infamy and disgrace (lines 5–6).

7 *close to dawn* at the end of the night, when dreams are frequently true visions of future events (*Purg*. IX, 13–18). Dante predicts the certain punishment of Florence which, though it has not yet occurred (line 12), will be welcome to her

enemies, such as the neighbouring city of Prato (or perhaps Cardinal Niccolò of Prato) (line 9).

19 *again* in remembering and recording it in the poem.

23 *kind star* Dante's birth-sign, Gemini, which gave him his natural predisposition and talents for his life as an intellectual and poet but whose influence would be insufficient, even dangerous, without the supernatural assistance of God's grace (*Inf*. XV, 55; *Purg*. XVI, 67–81). The punishment of the deceitful advisers, especially Ulysses, is presented as a warning of particular relevance to Dante himself as a thinker, an adviser to patrons, and the daring poet who explores and describes God's scheme of the afterlife. This is a sin into which he too could easily have fallen (lines 43–5), and the lesson to him is that he must rein his powers within the bounds of virtue and the limits set by God on the questing and questioning human mind.

27 *he* the sun when the days are longest, that is, in summer. The simile of the peasant looking down at the fireflies on a summer evening (lines 27–8) is unusually idyllic in the context of Hell and hints at the ambiguity in Dante's presentation of the human intellect, the light of the soul, both a supreme gift from God and a potential source of evil.

34 *he* the prophet Elisha who cursed some children who had teased him for his baldness, whereupon two bears came out of the forest and killed them. The comparison refers to when Elisha watched his master, Elijah, being taken up towards heaven in a chariot of fire until he was out of sight within the flame [2(4) Kings]. In the same way, each flame here envelops a sinner (lines 42, 47–8).

52 *twinned* forked, like the flames on the funeral pyre of Eteocles and his brother Polynices (line 54). Cursed to eternal enmity by their father, Oedipus, they killed each other; when their bodies were burnt on the pyre, the flames parted as a sign of their continuing hatred [Statius].

55 *Ulysses* Odysseus (in Latin, Ulysses), one of the greatest Greek heroes in the Trojan War. In the tradition stemming

from Homer's *Iliad*, which describes the war, he is notably intelligent and cunning; in Homer's other epic, the *Odyssey*, he sails on a great voyage round the Mediterranean from Troy back to his home on the island of Ithaca. Dante's Ulysses combines these two aspects of the use and abuse of the intellect: his Ulysses is both the deceitful adviser (lines 58–63) and the intrepid, but presumptuous, explorer (lines 90–142).

56 *Diomedes* a fellow-Greek. The three acts of deception which Ulysses and Diomedes committed and for which they are punished together in Hell (lines 56–7) are: the trick of introducing Greek soldiers into Troy hidden in the wooden horse, thus breaking the siege, an event which was followed by the escape of Aeneas and his companions, the ancestors of the Romans (lines 58–60); persuading the Greek hero Achilles to take part in the war, abandoning his wife Deidamia, who died of grief (lines 61–2); and the theft of the Palladium, the sacred statue of the goddess Pallas, which was believed to protect Troy (line 63) [Virgil; Statius].

75 *your speech* Italian, Dante's language, descended from 'vulgar' Latin. Virgil, the classical Latin poet, acts as Dante's intermediary with the two illustrious Greeks.

82 *my noble lines* the *Aeneid*, in which Virgil had celebrated the two Greeks.

85 *greater horn* the larger fork of the flame, containing Ulysses.

91 *Circe* the beautiful sorceress who lived on an island or promontory on the west coast of Italy; having transformed Ulysses' crew into swine, she kept them in her power for a year before releasing them [Ovid]. Aeneas later founded the town of Gaeta on this coast, naming it after his nurse, Caieta (line 92) [Virgil]. Homer's *Odyssey* ends with Ulysses' return home and reunion with his family: his father Laertes, his son Telemachus, and his wife Penelope. Dante was either unaware of this or chose to invent an alternative, and fatal, voyage in which, after leaving Circe, Ulysses turns his back on his family ties (lines 94–6) and, driven by the desire to know, sails away

in the opposite direction across the western Mediterranean (lines 103–105).

107 *the narrows* the Straits of Gibraltar, with a mountain on each side, known since ancient times as the Pillars of Hercules, set there to mark the boundary of the world for navigators. To sail beyond them out into the great uncrossable sea, Oceanus, was to overstep a limit set by God.

110 *Seville* the Spanish coast, on Ulysses' right as he sails westwards through the Straits, the town of Ceuta on the Moroccan coast being on his left (line 111).

114 *brief waking-time* this short life on earth, when the human senses are open to all their perceptions and experiences before they are closed by death.

116 *beyond* westwards, following the course of the sun to beyond where it sets.

117 *the world* the southern hemisphere. Medieval writers debated whether it contained any land or inhabitants (antipodeans), but in Dante's cosmography it is covered by the waters of Oceanus, except for the island-mountain of Purgatory.

120 *worth* virtue. Virtue and knowledge perfect the two faculties – the will and the intellect – which distinguish human beings from brute animals. Ulysses' speech to his crew presents the proposed voyage as the ultimate moral and intellectual goal in life for all true men. Dante would have accepted this, not least in his own journey of discovery, the poem, but not at the expense of overstepping divine limits, as Ulysses did.

124 *morning* the east, where the sun rises.

125 *wild flight* the rash and presumptuous voyage. The image of the ship's oars as wings reverses that of Daedalus' wings of wax with which he and his over-daring son Icarus 'rowed' themselves through the air [Virgil] (*Inf.* XVII, 109–11).

126 *left-hand side* in a southerly direction.

127 *the other pole* the celestial pole and stars of the southern hemisphere, those of the north being now invisible beyond the horizon (lines 128–9).

130 *the light* of the full moon; five months had passed since the perilous crossing through the Straits (line 132).

133 *a mountain* Purgatory.

141 *as pleased an Other* as God decreed, because Ulysses had travelled beyond the limits set by Him on human nature and its potentially limitless, but theologically and morally dangerous, desire always to know more and more. Since Ulysses was a pagan who lived many centuries before Christ, he could not be allowed to use his natural powers to discover and explore the supernatural realm of Purgatory, reserved for the future era of Christian salvation. Ulysses' voyage stands as both a parallel and a warning in relation to Dante's audacious enterprise, the journey-poem, which is his own epic voyage of exploration but which, unlike that of Ulysses, is being made by a Christian who has the authorization and assistance of Heaven.

INFERNO CANTO XXVII

EIGHT CIRCLE: the deceitful advisers (continued).

7 *Sicilian bull* a brass bull used as an ingenious method of execution by the tyrant of Agrigentum in Sicily (sixth century BC), who tried it out first on its inventor, Perillus (lines 8–9). The cries of the victims being roasted alive inside it came out of its mouth as if it were bellowing.

17 *that movement* the flickering of the flame, matching that of the sinner's tongue within. In this episode, Dante emphasizes the torment of the sinners burning within the flames and illustrates the function of the tongue, of speech and language, in the giving of deceitful advice: 'The tongue is a fire, a world of wickedness, [...] kindled by Hell' [James].

20 *Lombard* Italian, the language of Virgil's last words to Ulysses (line 21).

24 *burning* both literally, in the flame, and metaphorically, with desire for news from Italy.

28 *Romagnoles* the people of the Romagna, the region of Italy around the lower Po valley and the adjacent Adriatic coast.

29 *there* Montefeltro, in the Romagna, between the city of Urbino and the Apennine mountains, where the river Tiber has its source. The soul is Guido, count of Montefeltro (died 1298), the greatest Ghibelline captain of the time.

40 *Ravenna* on the Adriatic coast, with territory stretching south to Cervia, governed since 1275 by the da Polenta family whose coat of arms bore an eagle. Dante's report to Guido on the political situation in the Romagna in 1300 illustrates the process by which some self-governing Italian cities were being taken over by local lords or 'tyrants' and becoming small hereditary principalities. The heraldic beasts of the families illustrate these tyrants' cruel and predatory rule.

43 *The city* Forlì, which had successfully repelled an attack by French Angevin and other Guelph troops in 1282 and in 1300 was ruled by the Ordelaffi family, whose emblem was a green lion.

46 *Both mastiffs* Malatesta and his son Malatestino da Verrucchio, lords of Rimini, who killed the Ghibelline leader Montagna and who now, like dogs, are cruelly tearing Rimini to pieces.

49 *The cities* Faenza, on the river Lamone, and Imola, on the Santerno, were ruled by Maghinardo Pagani da Susinana, whose emblem was a blue lion on a white field.

52 *That city* Cesena, on the river Savio, still a free city in 1300 but in danger of being taken over by a tyrant. Its precarious political condition resembles its in-between geographical location (lines 53–4).

66 *infamy* the shame of the news getting back to the living that he is in Hell. In 1296, when he was in his mid-seventies, Guido abandoned his military and political career and entered the religious order of the Franciscan friars. The living could therefore legitimately assume that he had died a holy death and been saved, and indeed Dante himself had used Guido's

conversion as an example of how in old age a man should prepare for death by repenting and turning to God [*Convivio*]. Ironically, Guido is here unwittingly revealing his identity to the one person, Dante, who will take the news of his relapse and damnation back to the world.

67 *cord* the simple girdle of the Franciscans.

70 *Highest Priest* the Pope, Boniface VIII (*Inf.* XIX, 52–7, 76–81).

75 *fox* an animal associated with cunning and deception, as opposed to the physical strength and bravery of the lion.

79 *that part* old age, the time for a tranquil approach into the harbour of death.

85 *The prince* Boniface VIII, the leader of modern deceivers and religious hypocrites, like the Pharisees who tried to trick Christ (*Inf.* XXIII, 116).

86 *the Lateran* the papal palace in Rome. The war near Rome is the crusade launched by Boniface VIII against two Cardinals of the Colonna family and their supporters who were hostile to his policies and had declared him deposed from office. In proclaiming this campaign to be a holy war, Boniface was abusing his spiritual powers, directing them against members of his own Church instead of against the enemies of Christianity: the Jews, the Saracens (who had recaptured Acre, the last crusader stronghold in Palestine, in 1291) (line 89), and merchants who broke the Church's ban on trading with the Saracens (line 90).

93 *leaner* by fasting, in accordance with the austere rules of the Franciscan Order.

94 *Constantine* the Roman Emperor who, afflicted by leprosy, went to Pope Sylvester, then in hiding on a mountain near Rome, and was cured (*Inf.* XIX, 115).

101 *absolve you in advance* pronounce your sin forgiven before you commit it. Boniface's claim to this power, by which he persuades the foxy Guido to relapse into his sin, is fraudulent (lines 118–20). In Christian theology, only God can forgive a sin, and then only when the sinner repents of it; thus, not even

a Pope can declare an unrepentant sinner absolved [*Monarchia*].

102 *Penestrino* Palestrina, a hill-town near Rome, in which in 1297 the Colonnas and their supporters were besieged by Boniface's troops.

104 *the keys* of supreme papal power, including that of absolving sins (*Inf*. XIX, 92, 101).

105 *my predecessor* Pope Celestine V, who had abdicated in 1294 (*Inf*. III, 59–60).

110 *long promises* long-term pledges to be broken immediately – the essence of the sin of political and military deceit. In fact, having persuaded Palestrina to surrender with the promise of an amnesty, Boniface then had the town destroyed.

112 *Francis* St Francis of Assisi, come to collect the soul of the friar Guido at his death. The scene of a contest between a saint and a devil for a soul dramatizes the moment of death as the final, crucial choice between damnation and salvation.

120 *law of contradiction* a contradiction in terms and in theology, since it is impossible to be sorry for a sin and deliberately to commit it at the same time (line 101).

124 *Minos* the judge of Hell who sentences the damned with his tail (*Inf*. V, 4–15).

135 *the ditch* the ninth, containing sinners who caused schisms and divisions in society.

INFERNO CANTO XXVIII

EIGHTH CIRCLE: Ninth Ditch: the sowers of discord.

8 *Apulia* southern Italy. The scene of mutilations here is worse than the combined carnage of wars and battlefields throughout the history of the south: in its conquest by the Romans, descendants of Aeneas' Trojans (line 9); in the Second Punic War (219–202 BC), in which Hannibal took back to Carthage a pile of rings taken from the Romans killed in battle [Livy] (lines 10–12); in its conquest from the Greeks and Arabs by the Norman adventurer, Robert Guiscard, in the

eleventh century (lines 13–14); in the war of 1265–6, when the southern barons' treachery in allowing Charles of Anjou to pass the bridge at Ceperano led to the defeat and death of king Manfred in the battle of Benevento (*Purg.* III, 112–32) (lines 16–17); and at the battle of Tagliacozzo in 1268 in which, through the strategy of the general, Alardo (Erard de Valéry), Charles of Anjou defeated Manfred's nephew Conradin (lines 17–18).

31 *Mohammed* the founder of Islam (*c.* 570–632), who in the Middle Ages was believed to have been a renegade Christian and a schismatic. The complementary nature of the wounds of Mohammed and of Alì, his nephew, son-in-law, and successor (line 32), reflects the major political and religious rift in human society in Dante's time.

38 *re-placing* renewing the wounds.

44 *the verdict* of damnation. Mohammed mistakes Dante for a damned soul.

48 *experience* knowledge of the eternal results of evil.

56 *Fra Dolcino* leader of the heretical sect of the Apostolic Brothers and still alive in 1300. Condemned by the Pope, he and his followers took refuge in the mountains of Piedmont, near Novara, from where a crusade was launched against them; in 1307, reduced by winter starvation, they were captured (lines 58–9), and Dolcino and his mistress were burnt at the stake. Mohammed's prophecy points to the continuation of heresies, schisms, and violent religious discord in early fourteenth-century Italy.

73 *Pier da Medicina* a political trouble-maker, known to Dante (lines 70–72).

74 *gentle plain* the valley of the river Po.

76 *the two best men* two leading noblemen of Fano, Guido del Cassero and Angiolello (lines 77, 88), who, according to Pier da Medicina's prophecy, would be treacherously assassinated by being thrown overboard into the sea near Cattolica, on the instructions of the one-eyed lord of Rimini, Malatestino (line 85; *Inf.* XXVII, 46).

82 *Between the isles* in the entire Mediterranean, from east to west.

83 *Neptune* the god of the sea.

84 *Argives* Greeks, and sailors in general from the Argonauts onwards.

86 *the land* Rimini, where Curio committed his sin (lines 94–102).

90 *Focara's wind* a dangerous wind along the Adriatic coast. It will be no threat to the two men because they will be drowned not by it but deliberately.

95 *a companion* Gaius Curio, the Roman tribune, who is here in Hell for advising Julius Caesar to cross the river Rubicon, near Rimini, thus starting the Civil War (47 BC) [Lucan].

106 *Mosca* Mosca de' Lamberti who in 1215 advised the Amidei family to put a swift and certain end to their vendetta against Buondelmonte de' Buondelmonti by killing him (line 107). The murder was seen as the cause of the division of Florence into Ghibellines and Guelphs and thus of all subsequent strife and bloodshed in the city (line 108; *Par*. XVI, 136–47). In 1258, Mosca's own family was punished by exile (line 109).

115 *conscience* the certainty of speaking the truth in describing an otherwise incredible sight.

125 *two in one and one in two* the separated trunk and head, acting as one in seeing and speaking.

134 *Bertran de Born* (died *c*. 1215), lord of Hautefort in south-western France (*Inf*. XXIX, 29) and a troubadour noted for his poetry on war [*De vulgari eloquentia*]. He is here in Hell for inciting Henry the Young of England (1155–83) to rebel against his father, Henry II, just as Achitophel encouraged Absalom to rebel against his father, king David [2 Samuel/Kings] (lines 137–8).

142 *counter-penalty* the *contrapasso*, from the Latin word 'contrapassum', meaning the proportionate reciprocity which is the basis of justice in society, namely, that a wrong-doer should be punished according to what he has done to others

[Aristotle]. The biblical law of retaliation also states that revenge should be in exact proportion to the crime [Exodus]. Bertran de Born's punishment (with head split from body) precisely matches his sin (splitting a father from a son). The law of the just *contrapasso* can be applied throughout Dante's Hell, in which the torments are frequently both images and eternal expressions of the sins (see note to *Inf.* V, 31).

INFERNO CANTO XXIX

EIGHTH CIRCLE: Ninth Ditch (continued); Tenth Ditch: the falsifiers (alchemists).

10 *beneath our feet* in the southern hemisphere; in the northern hemisphere above, the sun is high in the sky. It is early afternoon on the day after the evening when Dante started his journey (*Inf.* II, 1–5).

20 *a spirit* Dante's cousin, Geri del Bello Alighieri, whose killing laid on his relatives the duty to take vengeance in blood (lines 31–3). Here Dante both recognizes and implicitly rejects the socially divisive custom of the vendetta and the blood-feuds between families in his time.

21 *down below* in the ditch.

29 *him* Bertran de Born.

40 *final cloister* the last ditch, ironically expressed as a religious community of lay-brothers (line 41).

46 *all the sick* all the sick people who, in summer, could be found in the hospitals of the unhealthy and malarial regions of Tuscany (the Chiana valley and the Maremma coastline) and Sardinia. As in the list of scenes of carnage in *Inf.* XXVIII, 7–21, the hypothetical assembly of all of them in one place conveys a heightened sense of the sight and stench of the diseased souls here. This ditch contains various sorts of falsifiers: of metals (the alchemists, afflicted with leprosy), their appearance (the impostors, who are mad), coinage (a forger, swollen by dropsy), and words (liars and perjurers,

punished by fever). The total image is of the corruption which results when truth, the basis of social relations and exchange, is abandoned in all these ways.

55 *Justice* personified as God's servant.

59 *Aegina* a Greek island struck by a universal pestilence sent by the goddess Juno; its king prayed to Jupiter who restored the population by changing ants into men (lines 63–4) [Ovid].

89 *so may* the formula making a wish as part of a bargain (*Inf*. X, 82).

104 *within the first world* among the living.

105 *suns* years.

109 *One* the unnamed soul from Arezzo in Tuscany is traditionally identified as Griffolino, an alchemist burnt at the stake some time before 1272. Alchemy, which claimed to be able to transmute base metals into gold, is here judged by Dante to be a fraudulent science, though the soul explains that he was executed for an entirely different foolish claim – that he could fly – for which his gullible patron, Albero of Siena, handed him over to a protector (perhaps the bishop or the Inquisitor) for execution (lines 110, 117).

116 *Daedalus* the inventor of flying (*Inf*. XVII, 109–11).

118 *Minos* the judge of Hell (*Inf*. V, 4–15).

122 *vain* foolish and wasteful.

125 *Stricca* a notorious profligate of Siena. The list of exceptions, of sensible Sienese, is ironical as it consists of well-known squanderers, such as Niccolò, an expert on an expensive spice (lines 127–9), and members of the 'Spendthrift Gang' of wealthy wastrels, including Caccia d'Asciano and Abbagliato (a nickname meaning 'the Dazed') (lines 130–2).

136 *Capocchio* an alchemist burnt at the stake in Siena in 1293. Dante must have known him as very good at imitating nature, as either a mimic or an artist (line 139).

INFERNO CANTO XXX

EIGHTH CIRCLE: Tenth Ditch (continued) (impersonators, forgers, and liars).

4 *Athamas* the brother-in-law of the Theban princess Semele. In revenge for Semele's love affair with her husband Jupiter, the goddess Juno made him go mad; in his delusion, he mistook his wife Ino and their two sons for a lioness with her cubs, and killed one son, Learchus, whereupon Ino threw herself into the sea with the other [Ovid].

16 *Hecuba* the queen of Troy. When the Greeks sacked Troy, they killed king Priam and took her prisoner, but when she saw the bodies of her daughter Polyxena, who had been sacrificed, and of her murdered son Polydorus, she went mad and, barking like a dog, tore out the eyes of his murderer [Ovid].

22 *Theban, Trojan* of Athamas or of Hecuba. The frenzy of the two impostors surpasses both these examples of extreme madness from classical literature.

31 *the Aretine* Griffolino.

32 *Gianni Schicchi* a Florentine (died *c.* 1280), who impersonated Buoso Donati so that he could dictate a false will, making himself the heir to a valuable mare (line 43).

38 *Myrrha* the princess of Cyprus who disguised herself as another woman so that she could commit incest with her father [Ovid].

42 *other phantom* Gianni Schicchi.

45 *most properly* in full legal form.

48 *ill-born* the damned.

51 *that part* the top of the legs. Without legs, the sinner would have been shaped like a lute, with a belly swollen by fluids but tapering towards a normal-sized head (line 54). The dropsy is presented, according to medieval medical beliefs, as the result of an imbalance between the body's four humours (blood, phlegm, yellow bile, and black bile) (line 53).

61 *Master Adam* perhaps an Englishman who in 1281 was

burnt at the stake for forging debased Florentine gold florins for his masters, the counts of Romena, in the Casentino region of Tuscany. His torment of eternal thirst is justly increased by the memory or mental image of the streams there (lines 64–72).

74 *the currency* the gold florin, stamped on one face with the image of Florence's patron saint, John the Baptist.

75 *above* on earth.

77 *Guido* count Guido of Romena (died 1292) (line 79) and his two brothers, who had employed Master Adam as a forger. To see them too in Hell, he would sacrifice quenching his thirst at the Fonte Branda, a fountain in Siena (or a stream in the Casentino) (line 78).

90 *dross* base metal. The genuine florin was made of pure 24-carat gold.

97 *the lying woman* the wife of Potiphar, Joseph's Egyptian master. When Joseph rejected her amorous advances, she falsely accused him, using a piece of his clothing to prove that he had slept with her, and had him thrown into prison [Genesis].

98 *Sinon* a Greek who, pretending he had changed sides, persuaded the Trojans to admit the wooden horse into the city and then released the soldiers hidden within it (line 118; *Inf.* XXVI, 58–60) [Virgil].

110 *quick* free to move, because at his execution his arms were bound.

129 *mirror of Narcissus* a pool of water (*Par.* III, 17–18).

136 *one who dreams* a person who, during a bad dream, wishes it were only a dream (which it is). The phenomenon of an entirely interior reality illustrates how Dante's very inability to express his inner guilt in words is itself an apology for having become engrossed in the quarrel.

The Giants.

1 *The very tongue* the same speaker, Virgil, who has just rebuked and now comforts Dante, like the spear of Peleus and his son Achilles which inflicted wounds and then healed them [Ovid (in medieval readings)] (lines 4–6).

16 *Roland's horn* the ivory horn, called Olivant, of the knight Roland, the hero of the romance, *The Song of Roland*. In this, Roland was attacked by the Saracens as he led part of Charlemagne's army through the pass of Roncesvalles in the Pyrenees; with a mighty horn-blast which burst the veins in his temples, he summoned Charlemagne who heard it from several miles away but arrived too late to save Roland and his troops from destruction.

31 *giants* a race of huge men who lived on the earth before the Flood [Genesis]. In classical mythology, they tried to storm mount Olympus, the home of the gods, but were repelled by the gods and Jupiter's thunderbolts (lines 44–5; *Purg.* XII, 28–33) [Virgil: Ovid]. Their challenge to the divine parallels the sin of Lucifer whose inner guard they are, standing like the towers of his citadel (lines 40–42, 136), the last circle of Hell.

40 *Montereggioni* a hill-fortress near Siena, ringed by walls bearing a circle of towers.

44 *Jove* Jupiter, whose thunderbolts remain a salutary reminder of how he punished the giants' rebellion.

51 *Mars* war. Though Nature continues to produce elephants and whales, which are huge but irrational, she has wisely eliminated the giants whose enormous strength combined with the power of reason and an evil will would have made them invincible in any war against humans (lines 52–7).

59 *St. Peter's pine cone* a pine cone made of bronze, about four metres high, which Dante would have seen at the entrance to the basilica of St Peter's in Rome. It is now in a courtyard within the Vatican Palaces.

63 *Frieslanders* north Europeans (from a region now in Holland and Germany) who were famous for their height.

65 *from the place* from the throat down to the waist.

66 *thirty spans* about seven metres. The measurements, including the head and the rest of the body, hidden below the rim of the well, make the giant over twenty metres tall.

67 *"Raphèl maì amècche zabì almi"* a string of words which sounds like a primitive, pre-Hebraic language, now lost and no longer intelligible to anyone (line 81). This giant is Nimrod ('rebel'), the mighty hunter, who organized the building of the tower of Babel ('confusion') so that men could reach Heaven and challenge God; in punishment, God destroyed it and scattered the people, condemning them to speak different languages, whereas before there had been one language throughout the world [Genesis]. Dante presents him as a giant whose sin parallels that of the other giants who tried to storm Olympus; and his incomprehensible pseudo-language is part of the punishment of the sinner who brought linguistic disunity and confusion into the world [*De vulgari eloquentia*].

69 *psalms* words or sounds.

77 *thought* the plan to build the tower of Babel.

94 *Ephialtes* the giant who, with his brother, piled up two mountains, Pelion and Ossa, in order to reach Olympus but was cast down by Jupiter.

99 *Briareus* another giant who attacked Olympus and was struck down by Jupiter's thunderbolt (*Purg*. XII, 28–30). He was particularly huge [Statius], with a hundred arms and fifty heads [Virgil].

100 *Antaeus* a giant who lived in Libya and was a great slayer of lions (lines 115–18); he was defeated by Hercules who lifted him up from the earth, from which he drew his strength, and squeezed him to death [Lucan; Ovid] (lines 131–2). Since he was born after the battle with the gods (lines 119–21), he is not chained in punishment for rebellion.

103 *The one* Briareus.

114 *five ells* about seven metres (line 66).

115 *the famous valley* near Zama in Libya where in 202 BC the Roman general Scipio defeated the Carthaginians under Hannibal.

120 *high war* the battle against the gods.

121 *the sons of earth* the giants, whose mother was the Earth. Virgil is flattering Antaeus with the idea that, had he fought with the other giants, they would have won.

123 *Cocytus* a river of Hell [Virgil], here a lake of ice which is the ninth and last circle of Dante's Hell.

124 *Tityus or Typhon* two other rebellious giants hurled down by Jupiter [Virgil; Ovid; Lucan].

125 *here* in Hell, where sinners want their fame to be renewed on earth by being mentioned in Dante's poem (line 127).

129 *grace* God, if He should decree an earlier death for Dante.

136 *the Garisenda* a leaning tower in Bologna which, when seen from the overhanging side against moving clouds in the sky, seems to lean even more.

142 *the deep* the lowest circle of Hell, containing Lucifer and Judas (*Inf.* XXXIV, 28–63).

INFERNO CANTO XXXII

NINTH CIRCLE: First Zone: Caïna (traitors to their relatives); Second Zone: Antenora (traitors to their cities and parties).

1 *crude and scrannel rhymes* the harshest possible poetic language. Human language, which at one extreme includes childish terms of endearment (line 9), has no words to describe the opposite, the most horrible and hateful place in the world, the bottom of Hell, and Dante, conscious that he cannot express his theme fully, is intimidated by the challenge which he must now confront (line 6). In fact, he goes on to introduce a series of rare and harsh-sounding words and rhymes which

pushes Italian towards the limits of expression of the horrific.

10 *those ladies* the nine Muses who inspire poets (*Inf.* II, 7) and who gave Amphion the power to move stones with his music to build the city of Thebes [Horace; Statius]. Dante's appeal to them for the power to match his verses to the reality (line 12) again underlines his awareness of the uniquely difficult poetic task ahead of him.

15 *goats or sheep* animals, unconscious of the full horror of their fate.

27 *veil* of ice, thicker than that formed in winter on two great rivers of the north, and capable of resisting the weight of mountains, such as Tambura or Pietrapana in the Tuscan Apennines. (Alternatively, Tambernic is a mountain in the Balkans).

32 *the season* early summer, when harvest-time is approaching.

34 *the place* the face which, by blushing, reveals when someone is ashamed.

38 *bore witness* by their chattering teeth.

39 *proclaimed* by weeping.

55 *these two* the brothers Napoleone and Alessandro degli Alberti who, some time before 1286, killed each other in a dispute over their inheritance from their father Alberto who owned estates by the river Bisenzio, near Florence.

59 *Caïna* the name given by Dante to the first zone of this circle, for those who betrayed their relatives; so called after Cain, who murdered his brother Abel [Genesis].

61 *him* the traitor Mordred who tried to kill his uncle, king Arthur, but was himself pierced right through by Arthur's lance so that light shone through the wound.

62 *Focaccia* the nickname of Vanni de' Cancellieri of Pistoia who, during an outbreak of violence between members of his family, murdered his cousin who was innocently visiting a tailor's shop.

65 *Sassol Mascheroni* a Florentine who killed a young relative so that he would succeed to an inheritance instead.

68 *Camiscion de' Pazzi* a Tuscan who murdered a kinsman. In 1302, a relative of his, Carlino de' Pazzi, betrayed his party by handing over a castle to the Black Guelphs – an act of treachery more heinous than Camiscione's for which, when he dies, Carlino will be punished in the next zone of this circle (line 69).

73 *the center* of the earth towards which, according to Aristotelian physics, all heavy matter and falling bodies are attracted (*Inf.* XXXIV, 111).

80 *add to the revenge* punish the sinner even more for the crushing defeat of the Florentine Guelphs at the battle of Montaperti in 1260 (*Inf.* X, 85–6). The speaker is the most notorious of all Florentine traitors, Bocca degli Abati (line 106), who during the battle cut off the hand of the Florentines' standard-bearer, throwing the army into disarray and bringing about its defeat.

88 *Antenora* the name of the second zone of this circle, for traitors to their city, country, or party; so called after Antenor, a Trojan who was believed to have betrayed Troy to the Greeks.

93 *notes* of Dante's 'song', that is, the poem.

94 *the contrary* to be forgotten on earth. Hence he resists Dante's torturing of him to make him reveal his name until another soul betrays it (lines 106, 114).

107 *the music* the chattering teeth.

116 *him of Duera* Buoso da Duera, a Ghibelline leader in Cremona who in 1265 accepted a bribe from the French Guelphs (line 115) and allowed the army of Charles of Anjou to pass through Lombardy on its expedition against king Manfred and the Ghibellines in the south.

119 *one of the Beccheria* Tesauro dei Beccheria, the papal legate in Tuscany, whom the Guelph government of Florence accused of conspiracy with the Ghibellines and executed in 1258.

121 *Gianni de' Soldanieri* (died after 1285) a Florentine Ghibelline who in 1266 joined a rebellion against his own party then

in power, thus assisting the return of the Guelphs.

122 *Ganelon* the traitor who, by persuading Charlemagne to withdraw across the Pyrenees, caused Roland and his army to be massacred by the Saracens (*Inf.* XXXI, 16–18).

Tebaldello a Ghibelline from Faenza (died 1282) who in 1280, because of a petty quarrel, betrayed his party by opening the city gates of Bologna to the Guelphs.

130 *Tydeus* one of the seven kings who made war on Thebes. He slew the Theban Menalippus (Melanippus) but not before being mortally wounded by him; as he lay dying, he had Menalippus' head brought to him and began to devour it, smearing his mouth with blood and brains [Statius].

139 *that with which I speak* Dante's tongue. With this strange oath, expressing a virtual impossibility, Dante promises, in his poem, to justify the sinner's eternal meal of revenge upon his enemy.

INFERNO CANTO XXXIII

NINTH CIRCLE: Second Zone (continued); Third Zone: Ptolomea (traitors to their guests).

13 *Count Ugolino* a powerful nobleman who, though of Ghibelline family, became the leader of the Guelph government of Pisa in the 1280s. To avert war, he ceded some castles to Florence and Lucca, an act for which he was later accused of treason (lines 85–6). In 1288, the Ghibelline archbishop of Pisa, Ruggieri (died 1295) (line 14), took over the government; breaking earlier understandings, he imprisoned Ugolino with two sons and two grandsons in a tower where they were kept for eight months until the door was nailed up, and they were left to starve to death (1289).

22 *the Eagles' Tower* so called because it was used as a mew where the municipal eagles were kept during the moulting season.

26 *moons* months.

bad dream the precognitive dream (line 27) in which Ugolino foresaw his own and his children's deaths in the form of a huntsman (Ruggieri) and his hounds (the Ghibelline families named in line 33) hunting down and killing a wolf and its cubs.

30 *the mountain* the range of hills between Pisa and Lucca.

38 *sons* in fact, two sons, Gaddo and Uguiccione (lines 67, 89), and two grandsons, Anselmo and Nino (nicknamed Brigata) (lines 50, 89), three of whom were adults at the time. In Ugolino's speech, however, aimed at convincing Dante of the inhuman cruelty of the archbishop, all four are portrayed as innocent and uncomprehending children in what is an extreme example of the custom of condemning sons together with their fathers.

57 *gaze* expression, with the signs of approaching death.

62 *you clothed us* Ugolino, as the father, gave the children life. The children's offer of their own bodies is a supreme example of self-sacrifice, and Gaddo's dying words (line 69) echo Christ's words on the cross, asking why God, His Father, had forsaken Him [Matthew].

66 *open up* to swallow Ugolino and put an end to his suffering.

75 *fasting* starvation, not the extremity of grief, killed him. As the promised description of Ugolino's death (lines 19–21), this is unlikely to mean, as some critics have argued, that he began to eat the children's flesh.

80 *fair land* Italy, the language area in which the word for 'yes' is 'sì' [*De vulgari eloquentia*].

82 *Caprara and Gorgona* two islands off the coast of Tuscany. Dante's exaggerated apocalyptic wish is that they should move to block the mouth of the river Arno, causing a flood which would annihilate the entire population of the wicked city of Pisa.

88 *Thebes renewed* Pisa, addressed as the modern equivalent of Thebes, the scene of many atrocities.

90 *other two* Anselmo and Gaddo (lines 50, 67).

99 *the hollow* the eye-socket.

105 *every vapor* winds produced by temperature variations which cannot exist in sunless, icy Hell. Hence Dante is puzzled by the cause of the wind he can feel.

110 *O souls* Dante and Virgil, here mistaken for the souls of even worse traitors condemned to the last zone of this circle.

112 *veils* of ice, the frozen tears which prevent further weeping (lines 97–9).

117 *may I go* Dante's oath is equivocal: the soul, believing him damned (line 111), takes it as a certainty and so reveals his identity, whereas Dante knows he will go there but not to stay, for he will return to earth and record this traitor in his poem.

118 *Fra Alberigo* a leading Guelph of Faenza in the Romagna who became a Jovial Friar (*Inf.* XXIII, 103). In 1285, under the pretence of reconciliation in a family dispute, he invited two relatives to dinner during which, at a pre-arranged signal when he ordered the fruit to be served, his men attacked and killed them. The fruit, the sign of his treachery, is here a metaphor applied to Alberigo himself, an evil citizen of an evil city (line 119), and to his crime (the figs) for which he is now paying with a rarer and costlier variety of fruit (dates) – the eternal torments of Hell (line 120).

124 *Ptolomea* the third zone of this circle, for those who betrayed their guests; so called from Ptolemy, the governor of Jericho, who killed his father-in-law Simon Maccabeus and two of the latter's sons at a dinner [1 Maccabees], or from Ptolemy XIII, Cleopatra's brother, king of Egypt, who murdered the refugee Roman general, Pompey (*Par.* VI, 69). The 'privilege' of Ptolomea is, in fact, a more terrible sentence from God: some souls are cast down into Hell immediately after committing the sin: 'Living, they shall descend into Hell' [Psalms]; meanwhile, on earth, their bodies are taken over by demons until their death, the moment when Atropos, one of the three Fates, snips the thread of life spun by the others (line 126; *Purg.* XXI, 25–7). This instant damnation, which seems to go against the orthodox Christian doctrine that God will

accept a sinner's repentance right up to the moment of death, conveys Dante's utter condemnation of those who break the laws of hospitality, in which shared meals are a major sign of the love and trust which should bind society together.

137 *Ser Branca Doria* from Genoa, who with a relative slew his father-in-law, Michele Zanche, at a banquet. Dante knew he was still alive in 1300 (lines 139–41) and is told that his soul arrived here in Hell even before that of his victim reached the ditch of the barrators (*Inf.* XXII, 88) (lines 142–7), and that the living Branca Doria is a devil in human form (line 157).

150 *courtesy* by breaking his ambiguous oath (line 117), Dante is behaving correctly towards a traitor justly condemned by God.

151 *Genoese* as in the address to Pisa (lines 79–90), Dante (speaking as the poet rather than the traveller) condemns a specific Italian city and expresses a wish for the destruction of its wicked citizens.

154 *foulest spirit* Fra Alberigo.

INFERNO CANTO XXXIV

NINTH CIRCLE: Fourth Zone: Judecca (traitors to their benefactors).

1 "*Vexilla regis prodeunt inferni*" 'The banners of the king of Hell approach'. The first three words are the opening of a Latin hymn, sung during Passiontide, in which the king is Christ and his banners are the sign of his victory, the cross. Here, in a shocking parody of a religious text, they are applied to the king of Hell and his wings, presenting Lucifer (Satan) as the antithesis of Christ and the greatest enemy of humanity redeemed by the cross.

4 *our hemisphere* the northern hemisphere, inhabited by the human race.

10 *meter* verse.

11 *covered* beneath the ice.

18 *handsome presence* Lucifer, one of the greatest of the archangels before he rebelled against God (lines 34–6), now punished by being reduced to a monstrous, silent brutishness (lines 28–54), the terrifying but ultimately contemptible source of universal evil and suffering.

20 *Dis* Satan (*Inf.* VIII, 68).

30 *match better* in the ratio of Dante's size to a giant's (*Inf.* XXXI, 58–66).

39 *three faces* Lucifer is a blasphemous parody of the Trinity, of God as three in one.

44 *like those* black, like the inhabitants of Africa, denoted by its main river, the Nile.

62 *Judas Iscariot* the apostle who for thirty pieces of silver betrayed Christ to capture and death [Matthew], an act of betrayal against the Son of God, the greatest benefactor of the human race.

64 *beneath* hanging head downwards outside Lucifer's jaws and so punished less severely than Judas. Brutus and Cassius were the leaders in the assassination of their patron and leader, Julius Caesar, in 44 BC. For Dante, the worst traitor is Judas, who betrayed the founder of the Church, the spiritual power; the next worst are the two men who betrayed the founder of the supreme temporal power, the Roman Empire.

92 *the ignorant* those who, like Dante himself here, cannot understand that he has just passed through the centre of the earth.

96 *middle tierce* about 7.30 a.m., halfway between the first hour and the third in the Church's division of the day.

105 *from night to morning* within a short time Virgil has said that it is night-time (line 68) and morning (line 96).

110 *the point* the centre of the earth (*Inf.* XXXII, 73–4).

112 *hemisphere* the southern hemisphere, on the other side of the world from the northern which, for Dante, contained all the dry land inhabited by the human race, extending for 180° from India to Spain; at its centre stood Jerusalem [Ezekiel],

where the sinless Christ, both God and Man, was crucified (lines 113–15).

117 *Judecca* the last zone of the ice, named after Judas (line 62).

122 *the land* the southern land, which was replaced by sea when it fled to the northern hemisphere. Lucifer's passage through to the centre of the earth also threw up the only land which remains in the south (mount Purgatory), leaving a hollow cavern which is as long as Hell is deep (lines 124–8) and up which Dante and Virgil climb back to the surface of the earth (lines 133–9). This explanation of the division of the earth's land and waters is not scientific [*Questio*] but theological: at the moment of Lucifer's cataclysmic fall, the world was prepared both for the future Redemption of the human race in Jerusalem and for the purification of souls after death in Purgatory.

128 *Beelzebub* Lucifer, the 'prince of devils' [Matthew].

137 *those things* the heavenly spheres.

NOTES

PURGATORIO CANTO I

The shore of Purgatory.

2 *my talent* Dante's intellect and poetic skills. With the metaphor of the journey-poem as a voyage, he leaves Hell and the description of God's just punishments behind him (line 3) and embarks upon a new and positive stage in his journey: the exploration of the realm of God's mercy where the souls of the dead travel to salvation. This journey, though presented as having really taken place in the spring of 1300, is also the poem which, as a fiction, now poses a different and more exalted challenge to his inventive, narrative, and technical powers.

4 *second kingdom* Purgatory, the second realm in Dante's afterlife. The traditional doctrine of Purgatory, which was later rejected by the Protestant reformers, was developed by theologians in the later Middle Ages and defined as an article of faith in the early thirteenth century. It is based on the principle that every sin, as an offence against God, carries with it the obligation to make amends to Him by undergoing some penance or punishment. Sins, moreover, could be divided into the serious (mortal sins, carrying a potential 'death sentence') and the less serious (the venial or easily pardoned). Whilst those who die without having repented of mortal sins are condemned to the eternal fires of Hell, those who die with the stain merely of venial sins on their souls or who, more generally, have not performed acts of penance for all their sins during their lives, have first to undergo the 'temporal fire' or punishments of Purgatory before they can go to Heaven. Before Dante, Purgatory was thought of as close to Hell and as literally a place of fire, from which each soul would be released after a required period of torment. Dante's concep-

tion of it as the arduous ascent of a mountain, in which the souls perform a variety of penances for their sins, paying off their debt to God and becoming worthy to go to Paradise, is his own invention. His Purgatory is a realm of temporary punishment, a description of a process (not, like Hell, of an unchanging state), and a place where all the souls have hope in the certainty that they will eventually go to Heaven (*Inf.* I, 118–20). It is divided into three main sections: the lower slopes (often known as Antepurgatory), where the souls wait for admission to Purgatory proper (Day 1: *Purg.* III–VIII); the seven terraces of the punishments of Purgatory (Days 2–3: *Purg.* X–XXVII); and, on the summit of the mountain, the earthly Paradise, that is, the Garden of Eden, where Adam and Eve lived in innocence and earthly happiness until, after committing the first sin, they were expelled [Genesis] (morning of Day 4: *Purg.* XXVIII–XXXIII).

7 *Muses* the nine sisters who inspired classical poets (*Inf.* II, 7; XXXII, 10–12). At the moment when his poetry must rise from Hell and death to a new life (line 8), Dante appeals in particular for assistance from Calliope, the muse of epic poetry, to elevate his poem too to the epic level (line 9), and he praises the great power of the Muses by referring to their defeat of the Pierides, the nine daughters of king Pierus who challenged them to a singing contest and were punished by being changed into magpies (lines 10–12) [Ovid]. The image of the resurrection of his poetry matches the actual moment in Dante's journey, since he emerges from Hell on the anniversary of the day when Christ too, after descending into Hell, rose from the dead.

13 *gentle hue* the blue with yellow of the eastern sky just before sunrise. After the elevated exordium (lines 1–12), the narrative of the *Purgatorio* begins with a description of the dawn, tranquillity, and space, with Dante's own inner transformation from grief to joy (lines 16–18). Thus he establishes a new tone and poetic voice for the second canticle in which hope, the sight of the eternally revolving heavenly spheres,

and the passage of time will mark a distinct contrast with the fixed and starless eternity of Hell.

19 *planet* Venus, the morning star, which transmits the power of love down to humans on earth (*Par.* VIII, 1–12); here it outshines the stars of Pisces (the sign immediately before Aries, in which the springtime sun rises) (line 21). Love will be the key concept in Dante's theology of Purgatory (*Purg.* XVII, 91–139).

23 *other pole* the southern celestial pole, with four stars which have never been seen by humans since Adam and Eve were cast out of the Garden of Eden and banished to the northern hemisphere (lines 24, 26–7). These stars also have a symbolic function as the four principal or Cardinal Virtues – Prudence, Justice, Fortitude, and Temperance (Moderation) – which were known to pre-Christian moral philosophers and are the basis of natural ethics (*Purg.* VII, 34–6; VIII, 89).

29 *other pole* the northern, with the Great Bear (the Wain) now invisible over the horizon.

31 *patriarch* the bearded, authoritative figure, whose face is illuminated by the four stars, initially recalls Moses, whose face shone with light when he came down from mount Sinai [Exodus] (lines 37–9). Astonishingly, however, he is Cato the Younger (95–46 BC), who during the Civil War supported Pompey and the Roman Republic against Julius Caesar, even letting his grey hair and beard grow uncut as a sign of his grief at the fall of the Republic (lines 34–6). After the defeat of Pompey, he went to Africa and led an army across the Libyan desert to Utica, where he committed suicide so as not to fall into Caesar's hands. Devoted to divine laws and a lover of virtue, he believed that he had been born to serve not merely his own country, Rome, but the whole world [Lucan]; in the underworld he is a lawgiver to the spirits of the good [Virgil]. Dante regarded him as a supreme example of stern virtue and Stoicism, and interpreted his suicide as an inexpressible sacrifice by which, 'in order to kindle the love of liberty in the world, he showed how precious liberty is when he chose to

depart from life a free man rather than to remain in it without freedom', showing firm constancy in preferring to die rather than to look upon the face of a tyrant [*Convivio; Monarchia*]. In Dante's scheme, Cato has been led out of Limbo with the Jewish patriarchs (line 90; *Inf.* IV, 46–63) and is now the guardian of Purgatory until the Last Day, when he will go to Heaven (lines 74–5). His presence here seems to subvert some of the basic principles of the *Comedy*: as a virtuous pagan, he should still be in Limbo, never to be saved; as a suicide, he might have been placed in Hell proper (*Inferno* XIII); and as an opponent of Julius Caesar, he could have been regarded as an enemy of the Roman Empire, like Brutus and Cassius, whom Dante has just seen in Hell (*Inf.* XXXIV, 64–7). The anomaly is never solved directly, except in the general doctrine that God in His infinite and inscrutable wisdom can save whoever He wants (*Par.* XX, 100–138). Cato stands here at the beginning of Purgatory as the greatest example of self-sacrifice for liberty, both moral (in the individual's pursuit of good) and civic (in his devotion to the public good, the freedom of the Roman people). Dante's ascent of Purgatory is a journey to acquire freedom from the effects of sin and thus to regain true freedom of the will. With love, freedom is the other key concept in Dante's Purgatory (line 71; *Purg.* XVIII, 49–75).

40 *river* the stream which flows down into Hell and whose sound has guided Dante and Virgil up to Purgatory (*Inf.* XXXIV, 129–32).

41 *eternal prison* Hell.

51 *knees and brow* the former by kneeling, the latter by bowing his head.

53 *a lady* Beatrice (*Inf.* II, 52–120).

58 *final evening* death and, if Virgil had not rescued Dante, the damnation of his soul.

75 *garb* Cato's body, which will rise and clothe his soul again on the Last Day and will be glorified in Heaven.

77 *Minos* the judge who sends souls to the second and lower

circles of Dante's Hell (*Inf.* V, 4–15). Virgil, in the first circle, Limbo, has not been sentenced by him.

79 *Marcia* Cato's second wife, now in Limbo (*Inf.* IV, 128), whom he allowed to marry his friend Hortensius, after whose death she remarried Cato [*Convivio*]. Because of his salvation Cato can no longer be moved by his earthly love for his wife who is in Hell, beyond the river Acheron (*Inf.* III, 70–129), but only by Virgil's mission from Heaven (lines 88–94).

99 *angel* the angel-doorkeeper (*Purg.* IX, 78).

102 *rushes* simple and pliant plants (lines 103–5). Dante's girding with one of them (line 133) symbolizes the humility and pliability of the will which are needed in those who embark on the process of purification from sins.

107 *the sun* symbol of God's light and grace which show the way up Purgatory.

119 *one returning* a traveller who has found the true path again. In contrast with the lost path and failure to climb the sunlit hill (*Inf.* I, 1–60), this is the ascent of another mountain with the guidance of the sun.

121 *dew* symbol of grace and hope, with which Virgil cleanses Dante's face from the grime and tears of Hell (lines 127–9).

132 *any man* principally Ulysses, the pagan explorer, who did not return from seeing Purgatory (*Inf.* XXVI, 141).

134 *humble plant* the reed. Like the golden bough which the Sibyl plucked at the start of Aeneas' visit to the underworld [Virgil], it miraculously grows again. Purgatory will be a realm of supernatural renewal.

PURGATORIO CANTO II

The shore of Purgatory (continued).

1 *crossing the horizon* setting over the western horizon of the inhabited northern hemisphere at whose centre stands Jerusalem (*Inf.* XXXIV, 112–15). The time is sunset in Jerusalem

(lines 1–3), midnight in the far east (over the river Ganges, in India) (lines 3–5), and thus sunrise in Purgatory, which is at the centre of the southern hemisphere, diametrically opposite Jerusalem (lines 7–9; *Purg*. IV, 67–84).

5 *the Scales* Libra, the constellation which in springtime (when the sun is in the opposite sign of Aries) dominates the night sky; after the autumn equinox it is the sun, not the night, which is in Libra (lines 5–6).

8 *Aurora* the goddess of dawn, changing to the golden colour of the sun's light.

12 *in heart* in intention, but not physically.

13 *Mars* the planet, which has reddish light.

17 *again* for the second time, after death. Dante's journey illustrates his personal conversion, in life, from evil to good so that he will die in a state of grace and go to Purgatory again on his way to Heaven (lines 91–2).

28 *the angel* the ferryman of the souls of the saved to Purgatory, the first of a series of angels who administer the rituals of Dante's Purgatory on God's behalf. According to theologians, angels (God's 'messengers') are pure Intelligences, without material bodies, but they were traditionally shown in human form with wings and robes. As immortal creatures belonging to Heaven, shining with the light of their vision of God, they dazzle Dante's merely human eyes (lines 39–40).

46 *"In exitu Isräel de Aegypto"* 'When Israel went forth from Egypt', the opening words of Psalm 113 (114), which praises God for delivering the Israelites and ends: 'The dead will not praise you, Lord; nor will all they who go down into Hell. But we who live bless the Lord, from now and for all eternity.' The Exodus of the Israelites from slavery in Egypt to the Promised Land was interpreted in three ways: as prefiguring the Redemption of the human race by Christ; as representing the moral conversion of Christians from sin to grace during their lives; and as foreshadowing the final journey of the souls of the saved, after death, from this world to Heaven. In his

journey, the living Dante, following Christ by descending into Hell and rising again, is making his moral Exodus; the souls of the saved are making their final journey of Exodus from earth to Paradise [*Convivio*; *Epistles*].

56 *arrows* rays. Rising in Aries, the sun makes the constellation of Capricorn disappear from the sky (line 57).

71 *olive branch* the symbol of peace. The simile defines Dante's unique position as a living man travelling through the afterlife.

75 *perfection* purification, and ultimately Paradise.

79 *empty* made of air (*Purg.* XXV, 88–108). In the underworld, Aeneas had similarly tried three times in vain to embrace the shade of his father, Anchises [Virgil].

91 *Casella* a friend of Dante (lines 88–9), a singer and composer of musical settings for poems. Dante's question (lines 92–3) indicates that he must have died some unspecified time before the day of Dante's arrival in Purgatory.

92 *where I am* Purgatory (lines 16–17).

95 *he* the angel-boatman. The reason why he refused to allow Casella to embark is not explained, but it is clearly a just decree of God Himself (line 97).

98 *for three months now* since Christmas 1299. The reference is to the Great Pardon of the centenary year 1300, which was authorized by Pope Boniface VIII on 22 February, with retrospective effect from the previous Christmas Day. This granted a plenary pardon or indulgence (the remission of all the temporal punishment due to sins) to pilgrims who visited the shrines of St Peter and St Paul in Rome; it came to be known as the Jubilee (*Inf.* XVIII, 28). The indulgence is here seen as valid also for the dead, such as Casella, lifting their sentence of delay and admitting them to Purgatory, the realm of full and final pardon.

100 *the shore* where the river Tiber flows into the sea. Whilst the damned plunge down to the river Acheron (line 105), the saved assemble at the mouth of the river on which Rome stands.

106 *no new law* no divinely decreed obstacle which would prevent the soul of a dead person from singing.

112 *"Love that discourses to me in my mind"* the first line of a poem by Dante, written in the 1290s, in which he praises the divine and heavenly beauties and virtues of a lady whom he loves. He later provided an allegorical reading of the poem, in which the lady is Philosophy, his new beloved [*Convivio*].

119 *grave old man* Cato. His rebuke shows that all earthly attractions, including poetry and music, are impediments on the way to God and must be cast off like a snake's old skin (lines 122–3).

129 *greater care* the fear which overcomes their hunger.

PURGATORIO CANTO III

The lower slopes: the excommunicates.

3 *rightful punishments* the just penances of Purgatory.

20 *afraid* because Virgil, as a soul, has no shadow.

26 *where* in Naples, where Virgil's body was taken for burial after his death in Brindisi in 19 BC. As the sun rises in Purgatory, evening approaches in Italy, situated 45° west of Jerusalem.

30 *heavens* the heavenly spheres, made of an eternal transparent substance, on which the planets revolve.

31 *The Power* of God in decreeing the mysterious process by which the souls' aerial bodies can suffer physical punishments.

35 *unending road* the infinite and eternal works of God, whose own Being as three Persons in One (the Trinity) is the ultimate mystery beyond human comprehension (line 36).

37 *quia* the fact, not the reason why it is so. The Latin word is taken from philosophical terminology. If the human mind had been able to fathom God's mysteries, it would not have been necessary for Christ, the son of Mary, to come to earth to reveal them (lines 38–9); and, in any case, the greatest pagan thinkers would have come to know them and would now be

saved, not condemned to an eternity of hopeless desire in Limbo (*Inf.* IV, 31–45, 130–35) (lines 40–44).

50 *between Turbia and Lerici* along the coastline of north-western Italy (from La Turbie, near modern Monaco, to Lerici near La Spezia), with its many inlets and mountains which fall sheer into the sea.

73 *ended* died.

74 *peace* of Heaven.

105 *beyond* on earth.

112 *Manfred* the illegitimate son of the Emperor Frederick II (*Inf.* X, 119) and thus the grandson of the Empress Constance (*Par.* III, 118). After his father's death in 1250, Manfred took over the government of Sicily and the South, and was proclaimed King in 1258. As a Ghibelline and suspected heretic, he was twice excommunicated (expelled from the Church) by papal decree, in 1258 and 1261. The Popes offered the kingdom to Charles of Anjou who defeated Manfred and the Ghibellines at the battle of Benevento in which Manfred himself was killed (1266). Dante introduces Manfred, a great sinner who died excommunicated and suddenly but who here appears among the saved, as a striking example of God's mercy which will accept a sinner's repentance right up to the moment of death (lines 121–3). The world should not suppose that such a man has gone to Hell (line 117), nor should churchmen believe that their sentences of excommunication can override a final act of repentance and God's forgiveness (lines 124–6, 133–5).

115 *daughter* Manfred's daughter, Constance, the wife of king Peter III of Aragon (north-eastern Spain). In 1300, she was the Queen Mother, one of her sons having succeeded to the kingdom of Sicily (the island, occupied by the Aragonese in 1282), the other to Aragon itself (*Purg.* VII, 119, 129). Manfred's request is the first example of an important theme in the *Purgatorio*: since Dante will return to earth, he will be able to tell the souls' living relatives to pray for them and so speed their way to Heaven (lines 141–4).

124 *Cosenza's pastor* the bishop of the southern city of Cosenza, who was ordered by Pope Clement IV to exhume Manfred's body from beneath the cairn where his soldiers had buried it, and to cast it out of the kingdom as an unholy object. The fate of Manfred's body, abandoned to the elements by a mistaken judgment of the Church, is contrasted with the fate of his soul, saved by God.

131 *Verde* the river Liri or Garigliano, between Naples and Rome, marking the border between the kingdom of Sicily and the territories of the Pope.

137 *in contumacy* excommunicated. The lower slopes of Dante's Purgatory contain souls who for different reasons did not perform acts of penance for their sins while they were alive; unless this defect is made good by the prayers of the living, they must wait below for specified periods of time before they are allowed to enter Purgatory proper (lines 141–4; *Purg.* IV, 130–35). These groups are: the excommunicates (*Purg.* III); those who delayed their repentance until the end of their lives, namely, the lazy (*Purg.* IV) and those who died violently (*Purg.* V–VI); and the negligent rulers (*Purg.* VII–VIII).

PURGATORIO CANTO IV

A ledge of the mountain: the lazy.

5 *the error* Plato's alleged belief that the human soul consists of several levels, each with separate functions. The three types of soul (the immaterial form of living things) are the vegetative (plants), the sensitive (animals), and the rational (humans). For Dante, the human soul is not added to the others but absorbs their powers in a single, indivisible soul [*Convivio*] (*Purg.* XXV, 52–78). This underlying unity of both mind and senses (including the perception of time) is proved by the fact that his own mind's total concentration on Manfred overpowered his awareness of the passage of time (lines 7–12).

22 *the gap* its extreme narrowness recalls Christ's words: 'Enter through a narrow gate, for the gate is wide and the path is broad that leads to damnation, and there are many who enter through it. How narrow is the door and tight the path that leads to life, and how few are those who find it!' [Matthew].

25 *San Leo* a town near Urbino which could be reached only by climbing the steep mountain on which it stands. Noli on the Ligurian coast was accessible on foot only by a precipitous descent, and Cacume and Bismantova are mountains in the Apennines (lines 26–7). To climb the even steeper mountain of Purgatory, Dante needs the strongest inner motivation (lines 28–9).

42 *middle-quadrant* the midpoint of the circumference of a quarter-circle. The slope is steeper than 45°.

59 *the chariot* the sun. North of the Tropic of Cancer, someone facing east will see the sun rise and move across the sky to his right, towards the south; Dante is astonished that it is now to his left, between him and the north. The explanation is that Purgatory, in the southern hemisphere, is at the antipodes of Jerusalem (lines 67–71) (*Purg.* II, 1–3).

61 *Castor and Pollux* the constellation of Gemini, the Twins, which the sun enters in summer. If it were now not spring but summer in the northern hemisphere, the sun, moving between the two Tropics (lines 61–3), would be shining even further to the north (the hemisphere distinguished by the Great Bear and the Little Bear) (lines 64–5) – assuming it had not changed its orbit entirely (line 66).

69 *Mount Zion* one of the hills of Jerusalem, frequently used as another name for Jerusalem itself.

73 *that same path* the course of the sun. Phaethon drove the chariot of the sun astray (*Inf.* XVII, 107).

80 *Equator* the celestial equator which the sun crosses at each equinox; it therefore always lies between the sun and whichever hemisphere is in winter. It is the same distance north of Purgatory as it is south of Jerusalem (lines 82–4).

Mount Purgatory (the way to salvation after death) is situated at the antipodes of mount Zion (Jerusalem, where Christ the Saviour died).

93 *downstream* naturally, without any effort.

94 *this pathway* the ascent of Purgatory, which, like all journeys of moral and spiritual conversion, is more difficult at first but becomes progressively easier.

123 *Belacqua* traditionally identified as a Florentine maker of musical instruments, personally known to Dante who here shows affection for him, whilst also indicating that in life he had been habitually lazy (lines 111, 124–6) and had delayed his repentance to the very end of his life (line 132). Dante's exhaustion, and his use of a breathing-space for scientific discussion and explanation, is superseded by an example of unproductive indolence in which – unless the time is reduced by the prayers of the living – Belacqua must remain in Antepurgatory for the equivalent of his lifetime of laziness (lines 130–35).

128 *God's angel* the angel-doorkeeper (*Purg.* IX, 76–132).

131 *as many times* for as many years.

137 *time* mid-day in Purgatory, and night, which has just fallen in the west, in the whole northern hemisphere (lines 137–9).

PURGATORIO CANTO V

The next slope: the fatally wounded who repented at the moment of death.

5 *not to shine* to cast a shadow – evidence that Dante is a living man, with his body.

14 *sturdy tower* an image of steadfastness and singleness of purpose, contrasted with the person who is easily distracted (lines 15–18).

20 *the hue* blushing; someone who is ashamed can be forgiven.

24 *Miserere* the opening of one of the penitential psalms: 'Have mercy on me, O God, in your great mercy, and in the multitude of your mercies wipe out my wickedness. Wash me further from my wickedness, and cleanse me from my sin, for I recognize my wickedness, and my sin is always before me [. . .]' [Psalms].

36 *profit* by prayers from the living, to whom Dante will return.

37 *kindled vapors* shooting-stars, an image – with that of the shafts of sunlight – of virtually instantaneous motion.

42 *without a rein* freely.

50 *beyond* to the world of the living.

62 *peace* of Heaven.

66 *lack of power* some obstacle which might prevent Dante from fulfilling his promise.

68 *the land* the March of Ancona, the region of central Italy along the Adriatic coast between the Romagna to the north and the kingdom of Naples (ruled in 1300 by Charles II of Anjou) to the south. The soul is Jacopo del Cassero, a Guelph politician and soldier from the town of Fano. In 1298, while travelling through the territory of Padua on his way to Milan, he was set upon by assassins hired by his enemy, Azzo VIII, lord of Ferrara; the attack took place near the castle of Oriaco on the river Brenta, not far from the town of La Mira (lines 73–80).

75 *Antenor's sons* the Paduans, whose city was reputedly founded by the Trojan Antenor (*Inf.* XXXII, 88).

85 *so may* the mutual wish formula (*Inf.* X, 82). The soul wishes Dante success in his ascent in return for help from him (namely, prayers to reduce his time in Antepurgatory).

88 *Buonconte* son of Guido da Montefeltro (*Inf.* XXVII, 29), he was a Ghibelline captain in the war between Florence and Arezzo, and was killed at the battle of Campaldino in 1289; his body was never found.

89 *Giovanna* Buonconte's widow; his surviving family do not remember him in their prayers.

94 *Casentino* the region of Tuscany where the battle was fought and through which the river Archiano, which has its source in the mountains above the monastery of Camaldoli, flows to the place where its waters join the Arno (lines 95–7).

101 *Mary* the mother of Christ. The invocation of her name marks the moment of Buonconte's repentance.

105 *he from Hell* a devil. The contest for Buonconte's soul recalls that for his father's, with the opposite outcome (*Inf.* XXVII, 112–23): the apparently repentant Guido relapsed and is in Hell; his son repented at the last minute and, like Manfred, was saved by God's infinite mercy (*Purg.* III, 118–23).

107 *deathless part* immortal soul.

108 *other part* the body.

109 *moist vapor* water-bearing vapours which turn to rain when they reach the cold region of the upper air.

115 *valley* the battlefield, between mount Pratomagno and the Apennines.

122 *royal river* the Arno.

133 *La Pia* a lady from Siena who was murdered by her husband in the Maremma, in Tuscany (line 134). Though traditionally identified as Pia de' Tolomei, she may be another Pia, a widow whose kidnapping, with her daughters, in 1285 led to a campaign by the Sienese to rescue them. The unnamed husband, who alone knows the secret of her death (lines 135–6), was probably Nello dei Pannocchieschi who – according to later accounts – had Pia thrown out of a window of his castle so that he could be free to marry the great heiress, Margherita Aldobrandeschi.

PURGATORIO CANTO VI

Those who died violently (continued); Dante's 'digression' on the state of Italy.

1 *dicing* the game of *zara*, in which gamblers bet on the

result of the throws of three dice. Like the winner, Dante has favours to bestow on the souls who besiege him, by promising to have prayers said for them (line 12).

13 *the Aretine* Benincasa da Laterina, from Arezzo, who was murdered by the Sienese robber Ghin di Tacco because in 1285, while serving as a judge in Siena, he had condemned the latter's brother to death.

15 *one* usually identified as Guccio de' Tarlati, a Ghibelline from Arezzo who, while in pursuit of a group of Guelph exiles, was drowned in the Arno.

16–17 *Federigo Novello* son of Count Guido Novello, he was killed in about 1290, perhaps by a Guelph from Arezzo.

17 *the Pisan* probably Gano degli Scornigiani, who was murdered by Count Ugolino's faction in Pisa in 1287. His father, Marzucco, who is here praised for reacting to the event with fortitude, became a Franciscan friar and ended his days in Florence, where Dante could have known him.

19 *Count Orso* a member of the feuding family of the Alberti (*Inf.* XXXII, 55), murdered by his cousin in *c.* 1286.

the soul Pier de la Brosse, the chamberlain to king Philip III of France; he accused Marie of Brabant, Philip's second wife, of complicity in the mysterious death of the Dauphin so that her own son, Philip the Fair, would become heir to the throne; in 1278 he was executed for treason. Perhaps implying that Philip the Fair had become king only as a result of a crime, Dante here judges Pier to have been the innocent victim of malicious accusations made by Marie who, as the Queen Mother of France, still living in 1300, is exhorted to repent in order to escape going to Hell (lines 22–4).

29 *in one passage* Virgil's *Aeneid* contains the line: 'Abandon any hope of changing the decrees of the gods by prayers' [Virgil]. Dante is in a dilemma: either these souls' request for prayers is useless, or he has misinterpreted Virgil (lines 32–3). Virgil's reply denies both alternatives: God's justice is not changed, but the souls' debt of expiation is commuted and paid in another way, by the charitable prayers of their loved

ones (lines 37–40); and Virgil's own words referred to prayers to the pagan gods, not those of Christians to the true God (lines 40–42).

57 *interrupt his light* cast a shadow.

61 *Lombard* north Italian. The soul is Sordello (died *c.* 1270), born in Goito, a village near Mantua; he spent much of his life outside Italy serving in various courts, especially that of Raymond IV, Count of Provence, and his son-in-law and successor, Charles of Anjou, with whom he returned to Italy in 1265–6. He was the most important Italian troubadour in the Occitan (Provençal) language, noted especially for upholding the moral and courtly ideals of the feudal ethos and for his attacks on those rulers who did not live up to them. His most famous poem is a lament on the death of a Provençal baron which takes the form of a series of fierce rebukes against the Emperor and the kings of Europe for cowardice and neglecting their princely duties. His main functions here are as an Italian and fellow-citizen of Virgil (lines 74–5), as a poet (*Purg.* VII, 16–17), and as a political moralist in his review of European rulers (*Purg.* VII, 91–136).

76 *Italy* the imperial territories in Italy, principally the north and – for Dante – temporal authority in Tuscany, central Italy, and Rome. In Dante's day, the elected king of Germany was also king of northern Italy and king of the Romans (Emperor), but between 1250 and 1310 no Emperor came to Italy to claim the two latter crowns. The following diatribe, inserted by Dante into the poem as a 'digression' from the narrative (line 128), contains the first explicit statement in the *Comedy* of his doctrine that the Roman Emperor, the supreme temporal ruler, should be independent of the Popes whose universal authority should be exclusively spiritual [*Convivio*; *Monarchia*]. It consists of a series of apostrophes or direct addresses: to Italy, torn by wars between and within its cities (lines 76–8, 82–90); to church leaders who have usurped powers which rightfully belong to the Emperors (lines 91–6); to Albert of Habsburg, the absentee Emperor-elect in 1300

(lines 97–117); to God, in an appeal for justice in Italy (lines 118–26); and to Florence (lines 127–51).

78 *queen of provinces* a title given to Rome as once the mistress or ruler of the provinces of her world-Empire.

83 *those* inhabitants of the same city.

88 *Justinian* Eastern Roman Emperor (527–65), whose reform and codification of Roman Law was the basis and model for laws and legislation in Italy and many other countries of medieval Europe (*Par*. VI). Dante's image of temporal government is that of a rider (the Emperor) of a horse (Italy) which he controls with the bridle and the bit (Roman Law, the written corpus of civil law transmitted by Justinian) [*Convivio*]. Without an Emperor, the horse runs wild (lines 94–9).

92 *things devout* spiritual matters, which should be kept separate from authority in secular affairs: 'Give to Caesar the things which are Caesar's, and to God the things which are God's' [Matthew]. In Dante's view, the fundamental cause of the wars and injustices in Italy was the fact that, on the basis of the Donation of Constantine (*Inf*. XIX, 115), the Popes claimed powers, territory, and legal rights which legitimately and by God's will belonged to the Empire (*Purg*. XVI, 94–114).

94 *Caesar* the Emperor.

97 *Albert* of Habsburg, Duke of Austria, son of Rudolph (*Purg*. VII, 94); elected Emperor in 1298, he never came to Italy and was never crowned; he was assassinated in 1308. Dante accuses him of having ignored his imperial duties in Italy (lines 97–9), calls down heavenly justice upon him and his family (lines 100–102), attributes his and his father's absenteeism to their greed for territories north of the Alps (lines 103–5), and invites him to come to see the effects of his neglect in Italy and Rome (lines 106–15).

105 *garden of the Empire* Italy.

107 *Montecchi, Cappelletti* two families, respectively of Verona and Cremona. With two rival families of Orvieto (line 108), they epitomize the strife and bloodshed in Italy through-

out the thirteenth century in the conflict between the Ghibellines (supporters of the Emperors) and the Guelphs (backed by the Popes).

111 *Santafior* the town and estates of the counts of Santafiora, much of which had, by 1300, been seized by forces from neighbouring Siena.

112 *Rome* the city which was willed by God to be the seat of the Empire (*Inf.* II, 16–21).

118 *Jove* God, here specifically God the Son (Christ).

122 *a good* the punishment of the wicked, the reform of both Empire and Church, and the re-establishment of Roman justice and law in Italy.

125 *tyrants* the absolutist lords who in 1300 were seizing power and effectively abolishing civil government in the Italian city-states (*Inf.* XXVII, 40–54).

126 *Marcellus* a verbose demagogue, so called after a Roman consul, one of three of that name who, between 51 and 49 BC, opposed Julius Caesar.

128 *exempt* not mentioned. The whole passage is ironical, pretending to praise Florence but in fact accusing her citizens of paying mere lip-service to justice (lines 130–32) and of a selfish scramble for public office (lines 133–5). The real state of the city is the opposite of happiness, peace, and justice (lines 136–8).

139 *Athens and Lacedaemon* the ancient Greek city-states of Athens and Sparta which invented the first codes of law from which all later civil law derived [Justinian]. Again ironically, their permanent contribution to civilized life under the law is compared unfavourably to that of Florence where laws and decisions are changed every six weeks or so (lines 142–4).

147 *revised* by alternately exiling or recalling members of the different factions.

149 *sick woman* an image of Florence's instability, a sign of a deep sickness in the body politic.

The valley of the European rulers.

4 *the spirits* the souls of the saved. Virgil died in 19 BC, during the reign of Augustus (Octavian), before Christ redeemed the human race, so opening Purgatory as the way to Heaven for Christians who die a good death.

15 *where* perhaps Virgil's feet, in a sign of homage from the lesser poet to the supreme master-poet.

17 *tongue* the language of poetry: Virgil's Latin and its descendants, the Romance vernaculars, such as Sordello's Occitan and Dante's Italian.

18 *native city* Mantua.

25 *Not for the having ... done* not for having committed evil but for having lacked the true faith. As a pagan, Virgil can never go to see God in Heaven but must remain in Limbo, with the unbaptized infants and the other virtuous pagans (lines 26–36) (*Inf.* I, 70–72, 124–9; IV, 28–42).

35 *the three holy virtues* the Theological Virtues specific to Christianity: Faith, Hope, and Charity (*Purg.* VIII, 89–93).

57 *implicates* impedes. Without the sun, symbol of God's light and grace, the souls cannot proceed upwards.

72 *had dropped* was only half as high. The valley, with its grass and flowers whose natural colours surpass the brightest known on earth, and with its other-worldly fragrance (lines 73–81), is the setting for the rulers who, living among the luxuries of their palaces, neglected their spiritual duties and also, in various ways, their duties as rulers (lines 91–136).

83 *"Salve, Regina"* 'Hail, O Queen [of mercy]', the first words of a hymn, sung in the evening, addressed to Mary, the mother of Christ: 'We, the exiled children of Eve, cry to you; to you we sigh, groaning and weeping in this valley of tears.'

85 *seeks out its nest* sets over the horizon.

86 *the Mantuan* Sordello.

94 *Rudolph* of Habsburg, Duke of Austria, elected Emperor in 1273, died 1291. Like his son Albert (*Purg.* VI, 97–105), he

did not cross the Alps to restore imperial rule in Italy and Rome, and as a result he allowed Italy to degenerate into a state of perhaps terminal disorder (line 96). He sits higher than the rulers of kingdoms, which, for Dante, were the units of social organization immediately beneath the universal Empire. The ideal medieval king would possess all the Christian and feudal virtues; he would be wise, brave, just, generous, and so on; and he had a duty to leave a worthy heir. These negligent kings in the valley summarize the defective government of Europe in the previous generation, contrasted with the even worse situation in 1300, under their successors.

98 *the land* Bohemia, the central European kingdom with its capital in Prague, here identified by its principal river, the Moldau (Vltava). Ottokar II, king of Bohemia 1253–78, was a bitter rival of Rudolph and died in battle against him; they are now reconciled in Purgatory. Even as a baby, he was better than his grown-up son and successor, Wenceslaus II (1278–1305) (lines 100–103).

103 *that small-nosed man* Philip III (the Bold), king of France 1270–85; defeated by the Aragonese, he withdrew and died on his journey back through France – an event here presented as an act of cowardice which brought shame upon his kingdom (symbolized by the emblem of the fleur-de-lys) (line 105).

104–5 *his kindly friend* Henry I (the Fat), king of Navarre 1270–74; his daughter married Philip III's son, Philip IV (the Fair), king of France 1285–1314, whose vices are the cause of remorse and grief to both these kings (lines 109–12) (*Inf.* XIX, 85–8; *Purg.* XX, 91).

112 *That other* Peter III, king of Aragon 1276–85.

113 *him* Charles I of Anjou (died 1285), king of Sicily until 1282 when the island was occupied by the Aragonese. These two kings, bitter enemies in life, also exemplify reconciliation in the afterlife.

115 *the young man* probably Peter III's youngest son, who predeceased his father. But for his death, he would have been a worthy heir to his father's virtues (lines 116–17), unlike the

two sons actually reigning in 1300: James II of Aragon (1291–1327) and Frederick II of Sicily (1296–1337). The lesson is that virtue is not hereditary but a gift of God (lines 121–3).

124 *the large-nosed one* Charles I (lines 113–14), who was succeeded by his son Charles II (1285–1309), here accused of worse crimes both as king of southern Italy (Puglia) and as Count of Anjou and Provence (line 126).

127 *the plant* Charles II, who is inferior to his father, Charles I, in the same degree as the latter is inferior to Peter of Aragon. Charles I is indicated by his two wives, Beatrice of Provence and Margaret of Burgundy; Peter by his wife, Constance (*Purg.* III, 115–17, 142–3).

131 *Henry* Henry III, king of England 1216–72, here set apart from the other negligent kings because of his own simple life and because he left a worthier heir, Edward I (1272–1307).

134 *William* William VII, Marquis of Monferrato and the Canavese, in north-western Italy; a Ghibelline leader, he attacked the town of Alessandria but was captured, imprisoned in a cage, and left to die (1292). In revenge, his son declared war against the Alessandrians who invaded and seized parts of the marquisate (lines 135–6).

PURGATORIO CANTO VIII

The valley of the rulers (continued).

1 *the hour* evening, when the church bell is rung for the last prayers of the day (lines 5–6).

13 "*Te lucis ante*" the first words of a hymn sung during the Church's office of Compline each evening: 'Before the end of the light, O creator of all things, we beg you of your mercy to be our leader and our guard. May dreams and the phantasms of the night flee far from us; and crush our enemy lest our bodies be defiled [...].'

20 *the veil* of symbolism (*Inf.* IX, 61–3). The particular

message which lies beneath the surface here (the episode of the angels and the serpent) is that God's help is always given to humans against the attacks and temptations of the Devil.

26 *two angels* sent from Heaven, where Mary is queen (line 37). Their colour, green, represents hope; their blunted swords evoke God's justice tempered by mercy.

51 *what* being able to see and recognize each other.

53 *Nino* Nino Visconti (died 1296), governor of Gallura, one of the Judicatures or provinces of Sardinia. With his maternal grandfather, Count Ugolino (*Inf.* XXXIII, 1–90), he was a leading Guelph in the government of Pisa; when the Ghibellines seized power, he went into exile and was in Florence on several occasions between 1288–93, when Dante must have met him.

61 *the other* eternal life after death.

64 *One* Sordello.

the other Nino, who calls to another Italian, Currado Malaspina (lines 118–20). Since in the dark Dante has no shadow, the souls have not so far realized that he is a living man, his journey being an extraordinary example of God's will, which is incomprehensible to humans (lines 66–70).

71 *Giovanna* Nino's daughter, who in 1300 was nine years old.

73 *her mother* Beatrice d'Este, Nino's widow, who married Galeazzo Visconti of Milan in 1300. In remarrying, she put aside the white veils which widows were required to wear, but to her cost, since in 1302 she was expelled from Milan with her new husband (lines 73–5). Nino regrets that her tomb will bear a serpent, the emblem of the Visconti of Milan, which flies over that city's encampments when it is at war, rather than his own much worthier arms, the cockerel ('gallo') of the Visconti of Pisa and of Gallura (lines 79–81).

86 *that portion* the southern celestial pole, around which the nearest stars revolve more slowly.

89 *three torches* three stars, which have replaced the four which were there at dawn (*Purg.* I, 23). Symbolically, the four

natural virtues, known also to pagans, have given way to the three supernatural virtues of the Christian era: Faith, Hope, and Charity.

98 *serpent* a beast associated with deceit; the Devil took the form of a snake when he persuaded Eve to eat the fruit of the forbidden tree, with fatal consequences for the human race [Genesis] (line 99). The following scene dramatizes the defeat of the Tempter by the agents of God's grace, the two guardian angels (lines 103–8).

112 *So may* the bargain formula (*Inf*. X, 82), expressed in the metaphor of the lantern of God's light and guidance, which Dante will need to feed with the candle-wax of his own will-power and perseverance for a successful ascent of the mountain (lines 112–14, 127–8).

116 *the lands* the Lunigiana, around the Magra valley in north-west Tuscany, where the Malaspina family had titles and estates. The soul is Currado Malaspina the younger (died 1294), the grandson of Currado I; here he is being purified of an earthly and selfish love for his family and caste (lines 118–21). Although in 1300 Dante had not been to the Lunigiana (lines 122, 126), here he pays tribute to the Malaspina as famous for their generosity and valour (line 129); virtuous both by nature and in practice, they are unique in a world led astray by the corrupt leadership of the Church (lines 130–33).

134 *rested seven times* entered the spring sign of Aries, the Ram, seven times. The prophecy, set in the springtime of 1300, concerns Dante's future exile and the hospitality he would receive in the Lunigiana from two of Currado's cousins: Franceschino Malaspina, in 1306, and Moroello Malaspina later. Within seven years, according to God's plan for Dante's life (line 139), he will know the Malaspina family's generosity not just by their reputation, but from personal experience.

The dream of the eagle; the door of Purgatory.

1 *she* Aurora, the goddess of the dawn, wife of Tithonus, from whose bed she rises each day in the east to herald the coming of the sun [Ovid]; in spring, the constellation of Scorpio shines on the opposite horizon (lines 4–6). It is dawn in Italy; in Purgatory it is night-time, about 9 p.m. (when, of the twelve hours into which the night was officially divided, two had passed, and the third was coming to an end) (lines 7–9).

10 *something of Adam* the body.

15 *ancient sufferings* the rape and mutilation of the princess Philomela, who (in this version of the myth) was transformed into a swallow [Ovid].

18 *divine* able to perceive truths hidden in dreams, those inner images of reality which are perceived during sleep, when the mind is free of conscious thought and the senses are closed to external reality. Dreams experienced just before dawn were believed to be the most likely to be true, even to be prophetic visions of the future (*Inf.* XXVI, 7). At the end of each of the three nights which Dante spends in Purgatory, he has a symbolic and implicitly heaven-sent dream which gives him an insight into the meaning of his journey (*Purg.* XIX, 1–33; XXVII, 91–108).

19 *an eagle* symbol of Jupiter (God), Rome, justice, and renewal: 'Your youth shall be renewed as an eagle's' [Psalms]. Just as Jupiter in the form of an eagle seized the beautiful youth, Ganymede, from a mountain near Troy and bore him away to Olympus, the home of the gods [Ovid] (lines 22–4), this eagle takes Dante upwards to burn in the sphere of fire, between the earth and the moon (line 30). Symbolically, the dream defines Dante's journey through Purgatory as an ascent through refining fire to renewed love and, like Ganymede, to Heaven. Later, it emerges that the dream was caused by a parallel external reality: while Dante dreamt of being borne

upwards, Lucia carried him up the mountain (lines 52–63).

34 *Achilles* the Greek hero whose mother took him away in his sleep from Thessaly – where his tutor was Chiron (line 37; *Inf.* XII, 65, 71) – to the island of Skyros, where he woke up astonished to find himself in an entirely new place [Statius]. He left Skyros when Ulysses and Diomedes persuaded him to join the expedition against Troy (line 39; *Inf.* XXVI, 61–2).

43 *my comfort* Virgil.

54 *flowers* in the valley of the rulers.

55 *Lucia* the second of the three ladies of Heaven who saw Dante's plight and helped to rescue him from the dark wood (*Inf.* II, 97–108). Here she represents the illumination ('luce'), grace, and assistance given by Heaven to Dante in his ascent of Purgatory.

71 *my matter* the subject and themes of Dante's narrative, here raised to a higher level (the description of Purgatory above the door) and thus requiring a more elevated poetic language (line 72). The rest of this canto is usually interpreted as an allegory of the Christian Sacrament of Penance: the three steps represent contrition (sorrow for sins), confession (telling the sins to a priest), and satisfaction (performing penances to make amends for the sins); the angel symbolizes the priest with the powers of justice (the sword) and of absolution and discernment (the two keys); the seven P's stand for Dante's sins, and the opening of the door for his absolution. The following notes give an alternative explanation which clarifies Dante's moral thinking and polemical attitude towards the Church in the *Purgatorio*.

78 *a custodian* the angel-doorkeeper of Purgatory. Holding St Peter's keys to a door which leads eventually to Heaven (line 127; *Inf.* I, 134; *Purg.* XXI, 54), he is the Pope of the new Church which Dante is about to enter – the community of the saved in Purgatory (the Church Suffering). Thus he is also an ideal model for the reform of the evil earthly Papacy of Dante's time.

82 *sword* the sign of spiritual authority, illuminated from

above; it recalls the fiery sword of the angel who, after the expulsion of Adam and Eve, was set at the entrance to the Garden of Eden to guard the way to the tree of life [Genesis]. With the angel who has only one sword, Dante is attacking the claims made by medieval Popes, including Boniface VIII in 1302, that they possessed two: not only supreme spiritual power but also supreme temporal power over the Emperor and all the kings and rulers of the world – a claim which, for Dante, was the main cause of the corruption of the Church by secular ambitions, power, and wealth (*Purg.* XVI, 106–12, 127–9).

94 *the first step* the first stage in the ascent to a higher moral state – the mirror of self-knowledge.

97 *The second step* the next stage – the sinner's recognition of the darkness and scars of sin upon his soul.

100 *The third* the final stage, more precious (like porphyry), the colour of blood shed from veins – the sinner's desire to expiate his sins in Purgatory, following the example of Christ's sacrifice on the cross.

104 *threshold* the precious diamond rock of Christ's infinite merits upon which the Church of Purgatory is based, recalling the words of Christ to St Peter, the first Pope: 'You are Peter, and upon this rock I shall build my Church' [Matthew].

112 *seven P's* the signs of the Seven Deadly Sins, wounds (line 114) which are healed on the journey through the seven terraces above the door. The letter P stands for 'Peccatum' (sin) and 'Poena' (the debt of punishment which remains after repentance and must be paid off in Purgatory after death).

115 *Ashes* symbol of penance and, in the liturgy of Ash Wednesday (the first day of the penitential season of Lent), of the humble condition of mortal humans: 'Remember, man, that you are dust, and into dust you shall return'. The angel's greyish or brownish robe, resembling the habits of Franciscan friars, makes a pointed contrast with the costly vestments of Popes and prelates in the earthly Church.

117 *two keys* given to the angel by St Peter (line 127), just as

Christ gave to St Peter the two keys of authority in the earthly Church (*Inf.* XIX, 90–92). Here the gold key, representing the Church's supernatural powers to administer God's grace, is therefore more precious (line 124). The silver key refers to jurisdiction in the Church which belongs in the highest degree to the Pope; since the Popes' main juridical powers – to excommunicate and to grant indulgences – were often abused for political or financial gain, this key requires greater prudence and care in its application (lines 124–5). Here, in line with Christ's metaphor of the keys which bind and loose [Matthew], it unties the bonds of temporal punishment in Purgatory (line 126), giving admission to the realm of final pardon or indulgence from the seven sins.

120 *plied* opened.

135 *Tarpeia* the treasury of ancient Rome, situated on the Tarpeian hill. In 49 BC, overcoming the opposition of the tribune Metellus, Julius Caesar opened its doors and brought out the vast treasures amassed by Rome over many centuries [Lucan]. The door of Purgatory leads to treasures which are even greater and can never be stolen – the infinite merits of Christ through which the souls can finally pay off their debts to God.

141 *"Te Deum laudamus"* 'We praise you, God', the opening words of a great hymn of praise and thanksgiving, which here accompanies Dante's entry upon a new stage of his journey, into the penitential Church of Purgatory which is the path to Heaven.

PURGATORIO CANTO X

FIRST TERRACE: Pride.

2 *aberrant love* sin, the misdirection or misuse of the power of love, which is cured in Purgatory (*Purg.* XVII, 91–139).

6 *fault* disobeying the angel's warning to anyone who relapses (*Purg.* IX, 131–3).

16 *needle's eye* the narrow and difficult path to moral purifi-
cation: 'It is easier for a camel to pass through the eye of a
needle than for a rich man to enter the kingdom of heaven'
[Matthew].

31 *carvings* relief sculptures, more realistic than the works of
one of the most famous sculptors of ancient Greece, Polycletus
(fifth century BC), and more real even than nature, the model
which human art tries to imitate (lines 32–3; *Inf.* XI, 103).
They are the creations of God's supernatural artistry which,
miraculously, makes Dante not only see but also hear and even
smell the scenes (lines 39–40, 43–5, 58–63, 82–93, 94–6).

34 *The angel* Gabriel who came down from Heaven to
announce to the Virgin Mary that she was to be the mother of
Christ, thus beginning the long-awaited redemption of hu-
mans from the sin of Adam and Eve (lines 34–7). Each terrace
of Purgatory contains positive examples of the virtue which
corrects the sin (*Purg.* XIII, 39), always beginning with an
episode taken from the life of Mary. This sculpture, the first of
three examples of humility which are part of the purification
from pride, shows the Annunciation, when the angel
addressed Mary with the words, '*Ave gratia plena*' ('Hail, full of
grace'), and she – humbly accepting her role in the revelation
of God's love for mankind – replied, 'Behold the handmaiden
of the Lord' (lines 40–44) [Luke].

56 *sacred ark* the wooden chest in which the Israelites kept
the tablets of the Law; when Uzzah touched it, God struck
him down as a warning to others not to take on duties which
belong only to priests (line 57). The scene portrays the
psalmist, king David, dancing before the ark as it was taken to
the temple in Jerusalem, in an act of self-humiliation before
God which showed his true greatness as a king, but which
his proud wife, Michal, viewed with scorn (lines 66–9)
[2 Samuel/Kings].

73–4 *a Roman prince* the Emperor Trajan (AD 98–117),
whose soul was saved by God in answer to the prayers of Pope
Gregory (lines 74–5) (*Par.* XX, 106–17). In the third scene of

humility, a poor widow persuades the Emperor to administer justice on her behalf before he leaves for war.

94 *One* God, Who knows everything in eternity, whereas humans can never see such miraculous art on earth (lines 95–6).

108 *the debt* of punishment for sin in Purgatory.

111 *final Judgment* when Christ will send souls to Heaven or Hell for eternity, and Purgatory will cease to be necessary.

124 *worms* lowly creatures (grubs) who have no cause for pride because, like butterflies, their true destiny is in their next life (lines 124–9).

131 *a figure* a carved support in the form of a crouching human figure. The souls' punishment of being bowed down by weights is an appropriate corrective for the sin of pride.

PURGATORIO CANTO XI

FIRST TERRACE: Pride (continued).

1 "*Our Father* ..." the Lord's Prayer, which Christ taught to his disciples [Matthew]. Each tercet cites and then amplifies a phrase: 'Our Father, which art in Heaven' (not literally 'inside' heaven, for God is infinite, but because He loves the heavens, which he created first) (lines 1–3): 'hallowed be thy name' (and power and spirit) (lines 4–6); 'thy kingdom come' (for human powers alone cannot bring God's peace) (lines 7–9); 'thy will be done on earth as it is in Heaven' (by men as by the angels) (lines 10–12); 'Give us this day our daily bread' (necessary for life's journey, like the manna which fed the Israelites in the desert [Exodus]) (lines 13–15); 'and forgive us our trespasses as we forgive those who trespass against us' (lines 16–18); 'and lead us not into temptation, but deliver us from evil' (the work of the Devil) (lines 19–21). Since they can no longer be tempted or sin, the souls recite the last part on behalf of the living (lines 22–4); in return, good people on earth should pray for them (lines 31–6).

27 *dreams* nightmares from which one wakes up under the weight of an incubus.

30 *scoriae* the remains of sin.

58 *son* Omberto, son of Guiglielmo of the Aldobrandeschi family, lords in the Tuscan Maremma; he was killed in 1259, probably while defending his fortress of Campagnatico (line 66). He exemplifies the overweening family pride of the nobility, which made him forget that ultimately all men are equal, all descended from Eve and born of woman (line 63).

70 *satisfied* by payment of the debt of penance. The punishments of Purgatory make up, after death, for the failure to do penance for sin during life (lines 70–71).

79 *Oderisi* a manuscript illuminator from Gubbio, in Umbria, who died in the late 1290s. He exemplifies the pride of a famous artist. In Purgatory, he shows he has learnt humility: first, he praises the work of another miniaturist, Franco of Bologna, above his own (lines 82–4); and then he delivers a homily to Dante on the emptiness and transience of earthly fame, including that of artists (lines 94–6) and poets (lines 97–9).

92 *green* an image of fame which passes away like a leaf on a tree, lasting a little longer only if the next age produces no famous people.

94 *Cimabue* the Florentine painter and mosaicist, still living in 1300, although his fame had already been eclipsed by his pupil, Giotto (*c.* 1266–1337).

97 *one Guido* Guido Cavalcanti (*Inf.* X, 63), whose fame as a poet has eclipsed that of the earlier Guido, Guinizzelli (*Purg.* XXVI, 92). The poet who might surpass them both could be Dante himself; at the end, he accepts the homily on the vanity of fame as a corrective to his own pride (lines 118–20).

101 *wind* an image of the insubstantiality and variability of fame, like the wind which, changing direction, is the same except for its name (line 102).

105 *the slowest sphere* the sphere of the Fixed Stars, which revolves by only one degree a century. Compared to eternity, a

human millennium is shorter than the blink of an eye compared to the 36,000 years of a complete revolution of the stars. Even so, by then Dante's fame will have been surpassed; even if he dies in old age (as a celebrated poet), it will be the same as if he had died in childhood (still talking baby language) (lines 106–8).

109 *the man* Provenzan Salvani (line 121), a leading Sienese Ghibelline at the time of the crushing defeat of Florence at Montaperti (1260) (lines 112–14); he was captured and killed at the battle of Colle in 1269 (*Purg.* XIII, 115).

115 *grass* an image of fame, which is born and dies under the same force, the sun (time).

129 *below* on the lower slopes, where a late repentant must wait for the length of his lifetime (*Purg.* IV, 130–32); this time has been shortened for Provenzan Salvani because of a great act of humility, when he publicly begged for money with which to ransom a friend captured by king Charles of Sicily (lines 133–8). Penances performed in life can reduce those required after death (lines 70–72).

140 *your neighbors* Dante's fellow-Florentines who would force him into exile in 1301–2. Oderisi's prophecy obliquely implies that, in exile, Dante will have to beg for his living but that if he accepts this humiliation, it will be for him, as for Provenzan Salvani, a positive penance for his pride and will reduce his own punishment in Purgatory after death (*Purg.* XIII, 136–8).

PURGATORIO CANTO XII

FIRST TERRACE: Pride (continued).

5 *wings and oars* metaphorically, the efforts needed to drive the will on its moral journey.

17 *effigies* relief carvings of the deceased to which devout relatives come to remember and mourn them. The following scenes are sculpted on the rock floor of the terrace. In addition

to examples of the virtue which corrects the sin (the 'whips'), each terrace contains examples of the sin punished (the 'bridles') (*Purg.* XIII, 38–41). The thirteen examples of pride are listed in thirteen tercets which in Italian contain an acrostic, spelling VOM ('uomo', 'man'): pride is the human race's fundamental sin.

25 *one* Lucifer, the archangel, whose rebellion against God was the first and greatest act of pride, punished when he was cast down into Hell at the centre of the earth (*Inf.* XXXIV, 34–7, 121): 'I saw Satan falling from the sky like lightning' [Luke].

28 *Briareus* one of the Giants who tried to storm Olympus, the home of the gods, and was struck down by Jupiter's thunderbolt (*Inf.* XXXI, 99).

31 *Thymbraeus* Apollo, with the other gods who repelled the attack of the Giants [Ovid; Statius].

34 *Nimrod* the builder of the tower of Babel in the land of Shinar, portrayed at the moment when God destroyed it and brought confusion of language among the people as a punishment for their pride (*Inf.* XXXI, 67–81).

37 *Niobe* the queen of Thebes, whose seven sons and seven daughters were killed by Apollo and Diana because she had boasted that she was superior to their mother, Latona; turned into stone, she continued to weep for them [Ovid].

40 *Saul* the first king of Israel; he disobeyed God and, defeated by the Philistines on mount Gilboa, committed suicide by falling on his sword. Afterwards, David cursed the battlefield with perpetual sterility: 'O mountains of Gilboa, neither dew nor rain shall fall on you' [1–2 Samuel/Kings].

43 *Arachne* a woman who challenged Minerva to a contest of weaving; the goddess destroyed her tapestry and, as she tried to hang herself, transformed her into a spider [Ovid].

46 *Rehoboam* Solomon's son and successor as king of Israel whose threats to rule even more oppressively than his father led to a rebellion, and he was forced to flee in his chariot to Jerusalem [1(3) Kings].

50 *Alcmaeon* who killed his mother, Eriphyle, making her pay the price of death for having accepted a goddess's necklace as a bribe for betraying her husband Amphiaraus (*Inf.* XX, 33); the necklace brought misfortune upon all the women who owned it [Virgil; Ovid; Statius].

52 *Sennacherib* king of the Assyrians whose army was wiped out in his invasion of Israel and who was later killed by his sons as he was praying in his temple [2(4) Kings].

56 *Tomyris* queen of the Scythians who, in revenge for the death of her son, captured and killed the Persian king Cyrus, decapitated him, and, with mocking words (line 57), plunged the head into a flask of blood [Orosius].

59 *Holofernes* the Assyrian general whose head was cut off and taken away by Judith; hearing of this and finding the headless body, the Assyrian army fled in panic [Judith].

61 *Troy* 'proud Ilium' (line 62), the city which the Greeks captured and destroyed by fire (*Inf.* I, 74-5).

64 *master* artist. Like the examples of humility (*Purg.* X, 31-99), these carvings are the supernaturally realistic works of God.

70 *sons of Eve* all human beings.

79 *an angel* the first of a series of angels who mark Dante's passage from one terrace to the next. Each, with his wing, erases one of the seven P's from Dante's forehead (lines 98, 118-35) and sings or pronounces a Beatitude (line 110).

80 *the sixth* hour of the day. It is just after midday.

90 *star* the morning-star, Venus.

100 *the hill* overlooking Florence, with a steep flight of steps which leads up from Rubaconte's bridge (named after a governor of Florence in the 1230s, now the Ponte alle Grazie) to the church of San Miniato al Monte. The description of Florence as well ruled is ironical (line 102), as is clear also from the contrast between a past, more honest age and two recent scandals involving some falsified legal records and the trial of a merchant for using crooked scales (line 105).

110 *"Beati pauperes spiritu"* 'Blessed are the poor in spirit

[for theirs is the kingdom of heaven]', the first of the Beatitudes (blessings pronounced by Christ during His sermon on the mount) [Matthew]. As he leaves the terrace of pride, Dante hears words which promise the eternal rewards for humility.

121 *the P's* carved by the angel-doorkeeper (line 135) (*Purg.* IX, 112–14). Their progressive removal as Dante leaves each terrace makes him lighter in weight, and his uphill journey for moral freedom less difficult.

PURGATORIO CANTO XIII

SECOND TERRACE: Envy.

25 *spirits* invisible voices, which pronounce the examples of the virtue opposite to envy – love for others (line 27).

29 "*Vinum non habent*" 'They have no wine', the words of Mary's touching appeal to Christ when the wine ran out at the wedding-feast in Cana, which he answered by turning water into wine [John].

33 "*I am Orestes*" the words with which, in a Roman play, Pylades pretended to be his friend Orestes so that he would be killed instead, while the real Orestes said the same in order to save his friend [Cicero].

36 "*Love those ...*" words spoken by Christ during the sermon on the mount: 'Love your enemies, do good to those who hate you, and pray for those who persecute and slander you' [Matthew].

39 *the scourging lash* the examples of love. The moral life – the control of passions and sinful desires by the will – is expressed in the metaphor of a rider controlling a horse [*Convivio*]. On each terrace, the examples of the virtue opposite to the sin are the 'whips' to urge the souls (and Dante and the reader) towards good; the examples of the sin punished are the 'bridles' to rein them in and turn them away from sinful inclinations and habits (lines 40–41; *Purg.* XIV, 142–3). Purgatory is a place not merely of punishments but of positive moral

education and the training of the will away from sin and towards good.

42 *pass of pardon* the place where Dante will leave this terrace and the second P will be cancelled as the sign of pardon from the debt of punishment for envy.

50 *the cry* the souls' prayer is the litany of the saints: 'Holy Mary, pray for us', 'St Michael, pray for us', and so on.

62 *pardon days* when religious feasts and indulgences would attract large congregations and hence more beggars outside the churches. The word 'envy' ('invidia') was connected with the idea of seeing ('videre'), and the corrective penance of the envious, who in life cast their eyes on what belonged to others, is to be blinded and reduced to the state of beggars.

71 *hawks* whose eyelids were sewn up by the falconers to keep them under control until they were properly trained.

88 *impurity* the remains, and even the memory, of sin.

95 *one true city* the community of the saved in the afterlife, where a soul's nationality during its earthly pilgrimage through life is no longer relevant (line 96).

109 *Sapia* a woman from the Salvani family of Siena (died before 1289), a bitter opponent of the Ghibellines in her city. Her sin represents another aspect of envy, not the desire for what other people have, but extreme *Schadenfreude*, an over-powering delight in their downfall. With the pun on her own name, she now acknowledges her foolishness, despite her mature years (line 114).

115 *Colle* near Siena, where the Ghibellines – including her own nephew, Provenzan Salvani (*Purg.* XI, 109–38) – were defeated in battle in 1269. Sapia now recognizes that this was by God's will and not in answer to her prayers (line 117).

123 *the blackbird* which, according to a fable, thinks that a little good weather in January means that winter is over and comes out to sing defiantly: 'Lord, I am not afraid of you any more, as I have survived the winter'.

128 *Pier Pettinaio* a venerable and saintly man who lived in Siena (died 1289); from his name, he appears to have been a

humble tradesman of combs used in textile manufacture ('pettini'). Since Sapia repented only at the end of her life, without his prayers she would still be on the lower slopes (*Purg.* IV, 130–35), not already doing penance for envy (lines 124–6).

136 *below* on the terrace of pride, where Dante expects to be severely punished beneath the stones after he dies (lines 137–8).

144 *on your behalf* with prayers (line 147).

151 *those vain ones* the Sienese, notoriously wasteful (*Inf.* XXIX, 121–2), whose civic projects included two very expensive failures: the search for a non-existent underground stream called the Diana for the city's water supply; and the attempt, begun in 1303, to develop a port at silted up and malarial Talamone on the coast (lines 152–4).

PURGATORIO CANTO XIV

SECOND TERRACE: Envy (continued).

2 *flight* of the soul from the body.

7 *two spirits* Guido del Duca, an active political and legal administrator in the Romagna in the first half of the thirteenth century (died after 1249); and Rinieri da Calboli, a leading Guelph politician in the Romagna in the second half of the century, who was killed when the Ghibellines recaptured Forlì in 1296 (lines 81, 88–9).

10 *one* Guido del Duca, the main speaker in the canto (line 28). Though full of envy in life (lines 82–4), in Purgatory he shows a stern moral attitude in his condemnation of wickedness in Tuscany (lines 28–54), his prophecy (lines 55–66), and his lament on the degeneration of the Romagna (lines 91–123).

17 *little stream* the river Arno (line 24), which has its source at mount Falterona in the Apennines and flows through Tuscany. It passes through Florence, Dante's birthplace (line 19).

31 *rugged chain* the Apennine range, which extends down to

the toe of Italy, where it was broken off from cape Pelorus in Sicily when the Straits of Messina were formed (line 32). Guido del Duca traces the course of the Arno – from among the highest mountains down to the sea (lines 34–6) – in terms of the wickedness of those who live on its banks, shunning all virtue (lines 37–9), as if Circe had changed them into beasts (line 42; *Inf.* XXVI, 91): pigs in the Casentino (lines 43–5), dogs in Arezzo, where the Arno changes direction (lines 46–8), wolves in Florence (lines 49–51), and finally foxes in Pisa (lines 52–4).

55 *my comrade* Rinieri da Calboli. Using imagery of hunting and butchery, Guido del Duca prophesies that Rinieri's grandson, Fulcieri da Calboli, would launch cruel reprisals against the remaining White Guelphs in Florence, leaving the city devastated (lines 64–6). Fulcieri was the Black Guelph *podestà* of Florence in 1303, the year after Dante was exiled.

78 *refused* Dante has not revealed his name (lines 20–21).

85 *straw* metaphorically, the punishment for the sin.

87 *there* on earthly goods (*Purg.* XV, 44–78).

91 *between the Po* ... in the Romagna, the region whose borders are the rivers Po and Reno, the Apennines, and the Adriatic Sea.

97 *Lizio* a Guelph politician from the Romagna (died after 1279). Starting with the motif of '*Ubi sunt?*' ('Where have all the good men gone?'), Guido del Duca evokes older, better times in the Romagna with his list of famous and worthy men, all dead: his own friend and ally, Arrigo Mainardi (died after 1228); Pier Traversaro, a Ghibelline leader in Ravenna (died 1225); Guido di Carpigna (died *c.* 1280); Fabbro dei Lambertazzi, a powerful Ghibelline in Bologna (died 1259); the humbly born Bernardin di Fosco, in Faenza (died after 1249); Ugolino d'Azzo, a Tuscan who lived in the Romagna (died 1293); Guido da Prata from near Faenza (died after 1228); Federigo Tignoso from Rimini. With the decline of the Romagna into moral bastardy (line 99), great families, representing a past age of courtly ideals and chivalry (lines 109–11),

have also become extinct: the Traversari and Anastagi of Ravenna (lines 106–7); the Counts of Bretinoro, Guido del Duca's own town, which might as well disappear too, as most of its good citizens have left (lines 112–14); the Counts of Bagnacavallo (line 115). Conversely, some families would have done better to die out, since they continue to produce wicked men who besmirch the family name: the Counts of Castrocaro and Conio (lines 116–17); and the Pagani of Faenza, who will become extinct (but too late to improve their reputation) on the death of the evil Maghinardo in 1302 (lines 118–20). Finally, since both the sons of Ugolino de' Fantolini (died *c.* 1278) were dead by 1300, his family's reputation is safe: it can produce no evil heirs (lines 121–3).

131 *a voice* words which, from no visible source (*Purg.* XIII, 25–36), pronounce the examples of envy punished.

133 *"Whoever ..."* the words of Cain who, having killed his brother Abel out of envy, thought his sin so great that any man would have the right to kill him in revenge [Genesis].

139 *Aglauros* an Athenian princess who envied her sister, with whom the god Mercury was in love, and was turned by him into a stone [Ovid].

143 *bit* a metaphor for moral control by means of these warning examples, the 'bridles' (*Purg.* XIII, 40–42).

146 *old adversary* the Devil.

PURGATORIO CANTO XV

SECOND TERRACE: Envy (concluded); THIRD TERRACE: Wrath.

1 *the sphere* the sun, with its constantly changing motion, here indicating the first three hours of the day. In Purgatory, it is the same period of time before sunset, and thus it is midnight in Italy (lines 4–6).

18 *angle* of reflection, which is equal to the angle of incidence, on the opposite side of the perpendicular. Dante mis-

takenly thinks that the sudden dazzling light is being reflected back at him from another source.

29 *family of Heaven* angels.

38 *"Beati misericordes"* 'Blessed are the merciful [for they shall obtain mercy]' [Matthew], the Beatitude which marks Dante's departure from the terrace of envy.

44 *spirit of Romagna* Guido del Duca, who had bewailed the fact that humans always desire earthly goods which are finite: the more they are shared, therefore, the smaller the share each individual receives (*Purg*. XIV, 86–7). This is the cause of envy (lines 49–51).

52 *the love* God and the supernatural good of Heaven which is infinite: the more souls there are to share it (saying 'ours', rather than 'my'), the more each one receives (lines 55–7).

67 *That Good* God, supreme and infinite Good, the eternal cause and goal of love which He reflects throughout Heaven. Upon each soul which loves Him, He bestows more of His goodness; thus there is more to love, and more love to be shared without being diminished. Therefore, the more souls there are in Heaven, the more love each receives and reflects to the others throughout the ideal, loving community of the blessed (lines 67–75).

77 *Beatrice* who will reveal such supernatural truths to Dante in a way that Virgil himself, arguing from purely rational principles, cannot.

81 *wounds* the P's carved on Dante's forehead (*Purg*. IX, 112–14; XII, 121–35).

86 *an ecstatic vision* the three examples of meekness and peace, and later the examples of wrath punished (*Purg*. XVII, 13–45), take the form of visions which miraculously spring up in Dante's imagination.

87 *a woman* Mary. When she and her husband Joseph lost the child Jesus in the Temple at Jerusalem and then found him debating with the scholars, Mary meekly asked him: 'My son, why have you done this to us? Your father and I were full of grief looking for you' [Luke].

97 *that city* Athens, whose naming caused a quarrel between Athena and Neptune but which was the first great intellectual centre of the ancient world (lines 98–9). The woman is the wife of Pisistratus, tyrant of Athens (sixth century BC). When she asked him to execute a young man who had kissed their daughter in public, he replied: 'If we kill those who love us, what shall we do to those who hate us?' [Valerius Maximus].

107 *a youth* St Stephen, the first Christian martyr, who scandalized the Jews when he said, 'I can see the heavens opened, and the Son of Man standing at the right hand of God', and was taken out to be executed by stoning; during his martyrdom, he prayed to Jesus to receive his soul and, at the moment of death, cried out: 'Lord, do not charge this sin to them' [Acts].

117 *not false errors* the visions which, though imaginary, both seem real and express real truths.

132 *eternal fountain* God.

134 *earthly eyes* which see only what is literally visible. Virgil can read Dante's thoughts (lines 127–9).

142 *smoke* the punishment of the terrace of wrath.

PURGATORIO CANTO XVI

THIRD TERRACE: Wrath.

18 *"Agnus Dei"* 'Lamb of God, [who takes away the sins of the world, have mercy on us, . . . have mercy on us, . . . give us peace]', a prayer used during the Christian rite of the Mass. The wrathful pray to the Lamb of God, Christ, the innocent victim sacrificed to redeem the human race from sin [John; Revelation].

24 *knot* the debt of punishment, which holds them back from going to Heaven (*Purg.* IX, 126).

27 *months* earthly time, as opposed to time in Purgatory, which is measured by the interior purification of the will (*Purg.* XXI, 61–6).

37 *swaddling-bands* Dante's body, which clothes his soul.

46 *Marco* a north Italian courtier who lived earlier in the thirteenth century, the representative of an older, better world before its degeneration into the wicked present.

47 *those goods* the moral standards and values of the old days, at which the world no longer aims (lines 48, 115–20).

57 *another's* Guido del Duca's (*Purg.* XIV, 91–123).

61 *heaven* the heavenly spheres. Dante wants to know whether the evil of the world is caused by the planets and stars whose conjunctions and influences, according to astrologers, determine events on earth; or by human beings themselves living on the earth below.

69 *motion* not only external events but also movements of the soul (inner choices, desires, and appetites). To hold that these are caused by the stars is to deny the freedom of the human will to choose between good and evil, upon which depends the whole Christian doctrine of just rewards (Heaven) and just punishments (Hell) (lines 70–72). The position of the stars influences the process of the natural generation of the body in the womb, and contributes to forming a person's physical temperament, natural talents, and propensities towards certain desires and pursuits, good or evil (line 73). However, the stars have no power over the soul, which is created directly by God and has the intellect to distinguish and the will freely to choose between good and evil; indeed, the moral life consists in the will's gradual conquest of the natural appetites (lines 74–81). Thus evil is caused not by the stars but by humans themselves (lines 82–3).

85 *Issuing* at the moment of its creation. The soul, created in a moment of happiness by a loving God, has an innate, unconscious desire to find that happiness again (lines 85–90). However, as it grows to experience earthly pleasures, it begins to seek that happiness in them (lines 91–2), and not where it can truly be found, with God.

94 *law* at the universal level, the bridle of Roman Law with which the Emperor should guide the human race on earth in

the light of the higher spiritual laws which lead it to Heaven (line 96). In 1300, however, there was no effective Emperor (line 97; *Purg.* VI, 88–96).

98 *shepherd* the Pope, who may know the Scriptures and Church Law but does not distinguish correctly, separating the spiritual from the temporal (line 99; the imagery is taken from the Jewish law on animals fit for consumption [Leviticus]).

101 *that good* earthly goods and pleasures, for which the Popes are greedy, and the people follow. Hence evil is due not to any fundamental wickedness in human nature but to the bad government of the Church (lines 103–5).

107 *two suns* the Empire and the Church, both centred in Rome, and both receiving their authority directly from God in, respectively, the temporal and spiritual spheres (line 108) [*Monarchia*]. The image of both powers as suns is an attack on the papal argument that the Emperor, like the moon which shines only with light reflected from the sun, derives his power from the Pope.

109 *sword* the symbol of temporal power.

110 *shepherd's crook* the symbol of spiritual power, the crozier. The image is an attack on the Popes' claim to possess the two swords of supreme power in both spheres (*Purg.* IX, 82).

113 *fruit and flower* the visible effects which prove the case, namely, that the illicit appropriation of temporal power by the Papacy is the cause of the evil in the world (lines 127–9).

115 *territory* northern Italy, defined by two principal rivers.

117 *valor and courtesy* the moral and feudal values of the early thirteenth century, before the conflict between the Papacy and the Emperor Frederick II (died 1250).

120 *secure* certain that he will not find any virtuous inhabitants there (lines 118–20).

121 *three old men* representatives, still alive in 1300, of the earlier, more virtuous age, and living rebukes to the wicked present (lines 134–5). They are Currado da Palazzo, a Guelph leader from Brescia; Gherardo da Camino, lord of Treviso (died 1306); and Guido da Castel (died 1315), an honest Italian

even in the opinion of the mistrustful French (lines 124–6).

131 *Levi's sons* the Jewish tribe descended from Jacob's son, Levi. As ministers to the priests and the Temple rites, they were banned from inheriting worldly goods; thus they illustrate the need to separate spiritual offices from earthly wealth [Numbers; *Monarchia*].

140 *Gaia* Gherardo's daughter (died 1311) who, it seems, was notorious for her sexual promiscuity; thus she summarizes the rapid moral decline from her father's generation to the present.

PURGATORIO CANTO XVII

THIRD TERRACE: Wrath (concluded);
FOURTH TERRACE: Sloth (spiritual negligence).

3 *moles* animals thought to be able to see only dimly through membranes covering their eyes.

13 *fantasy* the imagination. Like the examples of meekness (*Purg.* XV, 86, 115–23), those of wrath punished are engrossing interior visions, caused by a heavenly illumination within and not by sense perception of the external world (lines 16–18, 22–4).

20 *one* Procne who, in revenge for the rape of her sister, killed her own son and served him up as food for his father; she was transformed into a nightingale (*Purg.* IX, 15).

26 *one who was crucified* Haman, a Persian official who, enraged that Mordecai, a Jew, would not pay reverence to him, ordered all the Jews to be killed; after the Jewish queen Esther interceded with king Ahasuerus, Haman was hanged on the gallows or cross prepared for Mordecai [Esther].

34 *a girl* the Latin princess Lavinia, whose mother Amata hated Aeneas so much that, believing her daughter was to be married to him, she hanged herself [Virgil].

47 *a voice* that of the angel, whose heavenly light dazzles Dante (lines 52–4, 57). His unsolicited kindness echoes

Christ's command, 'Love your neighbour as yourself' [Matthew] (line 58).

68–9 *"Beati pacifici"* 'Blessed are the peacemakers, [for they shall be called the children of God]' [Matthew], the Beatitude which marks the passage from the terrace of evil wrath, as opposed to righteous anger directed against the wicked.

86 *too tepidly pursued* neglected. The sin of sloth – more accurately, accidie, that is, slackness in pursuing the love of God – is punished on this terrace by haste (line 87).

92 *love* the desire for good, which is the essence of God Himself and the principle upon which all His creatures pursue the goals of their existence. The following passage expounds Dante's doctrine that, in the case of human beings, love, the function of the will, is the cause not only of virtue but also of sin (lines 103–5). Purgatory is structured as the sevenfold process by which the repentant soul's errant desires and choices are corrected after death; as such, it is also the model for the training of the will in this life.

natural the universal principle which, in humans, is the soul's natural and instinctive response to love what is good and beautiful, and ultimately its innate desire to return to God (*Purg.* XVI, 85–90; XVIII, 19–33). This cannot be sinful (line 94).

93 *mental* pertaining to the human will's freedom to choose what and how to love something. This love can be sinful in three ways: *a*) when the object is evil; *b*) when the object is good (God), but the love is defective; *c*) when the object is not God, supreme Good, but secondary, earthly goods which may be loved in moderation but not to excess (lines 95–102).

107 *its subject* the self. The first sort of sinful love cannot be hatred of oneself (lines 106–8) or of God, the source of one's being (lines 109–11); it must therefore be to want evil for one's fellow human being (lines 112–14). It has three forms: pride, envy, and wrath (the desire for revenge), the sins of the three lower terraces (lines 115–25).

114 *clay* the human condition, inherited from Adam whom God fashioned out of clay [Genesis].

126 *distortedly* to the wrong degree. The other two sorts of sinful love are the defective love of God – sloth, the sin punished on this terrace (lines 127–32) – and the excessive love of earthly goods which cannot bring true happiness, namely, as Dante will discover, of money, food and drink, and sex, the subjects of the remaining three terraces (lines 133–9). In Dante's Purgatory, the human will is progressively purified of antisocial desires, spiritual apathy, and material obsessions and is restored to the love of God Himself, Who alone brings the complete, eternal happiness which each soul naturally desires.

PURGATORIO CANTO XVIII

FOURTH TERRACE: Sloth.

4 *thirst* for knowledge.

15 *opposite* sin.

17 *the blind* false teachers, like the blind who offer to guide the blind with the result that they both fall into the ditch [Matthew]. The error is to believe that love is always good (lines 34–9).

21 *beauty* a pleasing object which is first perceived through the senses, then becomes an internal image in the mind, and finally arouses in the will the desire to possess and enjoy it (lines 22–33). This process is as natural as it is for fire to burn upwards, towards its permanent home in the sphere of fire between the earth and the moon (lines 28–30; *Purg.* IX, 30).

39 *each seal* a specific love, which may be sinful, even though the power of love in general is good.

43 *from without* from the external object which causes the soul to respond in the only way it can – with love (lines 22–33). It would therefore seem to be the object of the love, not the soul's freedom of choice, which determines whether that love is virtuous or sinful.

46 *reason* rational argument, the basis of human philosophy. The freedom of the will can, however, be fully known only

through theology, which is based on the revealed truths of Christianity (lines 73–5; *Par*. V, 19–25).

49 *Every substantial form* each human soul, which in life is joined to the body, has two specific faculties, the intellect and the will, whose existence and nature can be defined not directly but by their effects and operations. As if by instinct, the intellect possesses those basic ideas without which no further reasoning is possible (such as the awareness of its own and the world's existence), whilst the will naturally and without sin desires happiness (lines 55–60).

63 *the power* the mind, and specifically the conscience, which judges between good and evil desires. Even if a desire springs up naturally, the will can always control it (lines 70–72).

67 *Those reasoners* the ancient philosophers for whom the freedom of the will was the basis of natural ethics.

79 *those paths* the sun's course from east to west (where, seen from Rome, it sets in the straits between Corsica and Sardinia).

82 *gracious shade* Virgil, whose birth in the village of Pietola, near Mantua, has made it famous.

91 *Ismenus and Asopus* two rivers in ancient Greece where the citizens of Thebes assembled, shouting invocations to the god Bacchus [Statius]. The penance of the spiritually slothful is to run at great speed with loud cries, driven by the will to love God (line 96).

99 *Mary* who, when told of her cousin Elizabeth's pregnancy, immediately hurried to the mountains to visit her [Luke]. This is the first of the examples of zealous haste, the virtue opposite to sloth.

101 *Caesar* Julius Caesar, the founder of the Roman Empire. In 49 BC he besieged Marseilles and then marched rapidly into Spain, where he defeated a republican army at Lérida [Lucan].

104 *insufficient love* sloth, the defective love of God (*Purg*. XVII, 85–7, 127–32).

118 *St. Zeno's abbot* probably Gherardo (died 1187), the abbot of the monastery of San Zeno in Verona during the reign of the Emperor Frederick I (Barbarossa, 'Redbeard') (1152–90), who captured and destroyed Milan in 1162 (lines 119–20). Sloth (accidie) was the besetting sin of monks and other religious who became apathetic or embittered in their spiritual lives.

121 *one* Alberto della Scala, lord of Verona. The prophecy concerns his imminent death, which occurred in September 1301, and his punishment in the afterlife for having bestowed the office of abbot of San Zeno on his disabled and morally corrupt illegitimate son, Giuseppe (died 1314).

133 *The ones* the Israelites who passed through the Red Sea with Moses; because they constantly complained against his leadership, God decreed that, with two exceptions, they would all die before reaching the river Jordan and the Promised Land [Numbers]. This is the first of the examples of spiritual negligence punished.

136 *those* the Trojans who, instead of accompanying Aeneas to Latium to found the Roman Empire, stayed behind in Sicily and so lost the opportunity to become famous [Virgil].

PURGATORIO CANTO XIX

FOURTH TERRACE: Sloth (concluded);
FIFTH TERRACE: Avarice.

1 *that hour* the end of the night, when the heat left by the sun has been diminished by the cold influences of the earth, the moon, and Saturn (when it shines).

3 *geomancers* fortune-tellers who drew random shapes on the ground and matched them to the stars. The *Fortuna major* ('Greater Fortune') was a pattern formed by stars of Pisces and Aquarius which in springtime appear briefly on the horizon just before sunrise. Dreams which occur at this time are the most likely to be true (*Purg.* IX, 13–18).

19 *siren* a beautiful sea-nymph who with her singing lured sailors to destruction on the rocks.

22 *Ulysses* the Greek hero who, however, in Homer's *Odyssey*, was led astray not by the sirens but by Circe (*Inf.* XXVI, 91–2).

26 *a woman* symbol of a higher truth who urges Virgil to reveal that earthly goods, however alluring (the siren), are essentially ugly and subject to corruption and decay (the hag) (lines 31–3). In his second morning-dream, Dante is made aware of the false glamour of earthly goods and pleasures, the source of the three sins of excessive love which are purged on the remaining three terraces (lines 58–60).

45 *mortal land* on earth.

50 *"Qui lugent"* '[Blessed are] those who mourn, [for they shall be consoled]' [Matthew], the Beatitude which marks the passage from the terrace of sloth, linked with spiritual anguish, towards the eternal joy of Heaven.

62 *lure* the bait which the falconer swings in circles to call the bird to him; an image for the revolving heavenly spheres with which God attracts humans towards Heaven.

73 *"Adhaesit ..."* 'My soul has adhered to the ground' [Psalms]. The verse illustrates both the punishment of the prostrate souls (line 72) and the nature of the sin of avarice, the excessive clinging to an earthly object – money (lines 118–20).

81 *the outside* the edge of the terrace.

92 *that* the debt of punishment. The avaricious, lying inert like pledges at a pawnbroker's, are suffering in order to mature their spiritual money, pay off their debt, and go to Heaven.

96 *good* prayers from the living.

99 *"scias ..."* 'I would have you know that I was a successor of Peter', that is, a Pope. The soul is Pope Hadrian V, a member of the Fieschi family who took their title of counts of Lavagna from the river of that name in Liguria (lines 100–102); he died in 1276, having reigned as Pope for just over five weeks (line 103). Here he exemplifies avarice in the

Church, although, unlike the simoniac Popes (*Inf.* XIX), he repented before he died (lines 106–13).

104 *great mantle* of the Papacy.

107 *Roman shepherd* Pope.

111 *this life* the afterlife.

115 *declared* revealed, in the matching of the sin to the punishment (lines 118 26).

131 *dignity* the high office of Pope, which has made Dante kneel out of respect.

137 *"Neque nubent"* 'Nor shall they marry', words with which Christ explained that marriage would no longer apply among the blessed in Heaven [Matthew], here extended to mean that in the afterlife all earthly distinctions, such as that between a Pope and a layman, are abolished.

141 *what you mentioned* the debt (lines 91–2).

142 *Beyond* in the world of the living.

Alagia the wife of Moroello Malaspina, who was probably one of Dante's patrons during his exile (*Purg.* VIII, 134–9).

PURGATORIO CANTO XX

FIFTH TERRACE: Avarice (continued).

3 *sponge* the thirst for further knowledge (the water).

7 *melt down* by weeping for having committed the sin of avarice, which corrupts the whole world (line 8).

10 *ancient wolf* avarice. The image, followed by the appeal for a deliverer, recalls the she-wolf and the prophecy of the Greyhound (*Inf.* I, 49–51, 88–111).

20 *Mary* who gave birth to Christ in a poor stable at Bethlehem [Luke] (lines 22–4). This is the first of the examples of voluntary poverty, the virtue opposite to avarice.

25 *Fabricius* the Roman republican leader (third century BC) who refused to accept gifts from Rome's enemies and died so poor that the State had to pay for his funeral [Virgil; *Convivio*; *Monarchia*].

32 *Nicholas* St Nicholas (fourth century AD), who gave three bags of gold to an impoverished man as dowries for his daughters [*Golden Legend*], an example of generosity to the poor, the only virtuous use of money [*Convivio*].

43 *obnoxious plant* the Capetian dynasty of the kings of France (987–1328) and, through Charles of Anjou, of Naples (1266–1343). The soul is Hugh Capet, its founder, who is presented here as a man of humble origin who, upon the extinction of the male line of Charlemagne's successors (except for one, a monk), rose to govern France and was able to promote his son to the throne (lines 49–60). He exemplifies avarice in the temporal sphere, as illustrated particularly by his condemnation of his wicked descendants, the kings of France and Naples in Dante's time, and by his calls for God to punish them (lines 48, 94–6).

46 *Douai* ... cities in Flanders which the French king Philip IV (the Fair) conquered in 1297–9 but which rebelled and inflicted a major defeat on him in 1302.

50 *Louises and Philips* the most common names of the kings of France.

61 *Until* up to 1245, when Charles of Anjou, the brother of Louis IX, married Beatrice of Provence and annexed her lands to the French royal house.

65 *amends* ironically: to make amends for one crime, the Capetian kings committed a worse one (lines 67, 69).

66 *Ponthieu* ... regions occupied by the French in opposition to the claims of the kings of England.

67 *Charles* of Anjou, who invaded Italy and, after defeating Manfred, became the first Capetian king of Sicily (1266–82) and Naples (1266–85) (*Purg.* III, 112; VII, 113).

68 *Conradin* Manfred's nephew, who tried to recapture the kingdom but was defeated by Charles and executed in 1268.

69 *Thomas* the theologian, St Thomas Aquinas, who died in 1274, allegedly poisoned on Charles's orders.

70 *see* foresee. Hugh Capet begins a series of prophecies of crimes which would be committed by his descendants after the springtime of 1300.

71 *another Charles* Charles of Valois (1270–1325), brother of Philip the Fair. Invited into Italy by Pope Boniface VIII, he entered Florence on 1 November 1301 and, instead of acting as a peacemaker, allowed the Black Guelphs to seize power in a coup which resulted in the exile of leading White Guelphs, including Dante (*Inf.* VI, 67–9).

74 *the lance* treachery, the crime of Judas (*Inf.* XXXIV, 62).

77 *heavier* even more inglorious, in that he cares little for his own good reputation anyway (line 78).

79 *The other* Charles II of Anjou, king of Naples (1285–1309), who during a naval battle in 1284 had been taken prisoner by the Aragonese; in 1305, for his own political and financial advantage, he married off his youngest daughter to the lord of Ferrara.

82 *house* dynasty.

86 *fleur-de-lis* the lily, the emblem of the French kings.

Anagni a town in Lazio, where for three days in 1303 agents of Philip the Fair held Pope Boniface VIII hostage. Although Dante constantly condemns Boniface (*Inf.* XIX, 52–7; XXVII, 85–92), here the outrage against the man who bore the title of Christ's vicar on earth is presented as a repetition of the Passion of Christ Himself, Who was captured, mocked, given vinegar and gall to drink, and crucified between two thieves [Matthew]. Philip is therefore the modern equivalent of Pontius Pilate, the Roman governor responsible for Christ's death (line 91).

93 *the Temple* the order of the Knights Templar. In 1307, in order to seize their wealth, Philip the Fair began a campaign of arrest and torture against them, and in 1312–13 he had the order suppressed and its Grand Master burnt at the stake.

95 *vengeance* the punishment of the wicked, which is still hidden in God's secret plan for the future.

97 *the only bride* Mary, the virgin who conceived Christ by the power of the Holy Spirit [Matthew; Luke], the first example of poverty (lines 20–24).

102 *examples* of avarice punished.

103 *Pygmalion* the king of Tyre who murdered his uncle and

brother-in-law Sychaeus in order to acquire his wealth [Virgil].

106 *Midas* the greedy king of Phrygia who asked Bacchus for the power to turn into gold everything he touched; since even his food became gold, he had to ask the god to revoke the gift; he then offended Apollo who punished him by changing his ears into those of an ass [Ovid].

109 *Achan* an Israelite who stole some of the booty captured at Jericho and, on the orders of Joshua, was executed by stoning [Joshua].

112 *Sapphira* an early Christian who, with her husband Ananias, embezzled some of the money belonging to the Church; they were both struck down dead by God [Acts].

113 *Heliodorus* a Syrian official who, when sent to seize the treasures of the Temple in Jerusalem, was driven away by kicks from a horse mounted by a terrifying rider [2 Maccabees].

114 *Polymnestor* the king of Thrace who treacherously murdered the Trojan prince Polydorus in order to steal the treasure he was carrying [Virgil; Ovid].

116 *Crassus* a wealthy Roman political leader (died 53 BC) whose greed was so notorious that, when his severed head was sent to the king of Parthia, he poured molten gold into the mouth, saying, 'You were thirsty for gold; now drink it' [Florus; Cicero].

122 *the good* the examples of poverty and generosity (lines 19–33).

130 *Delos* a floating island which was not fixed to the sea-bed until Jupiter's mistress Latona took refuge there and gave birth to his twin children, Apollo (the Sun) and Diana (the Moon) (line 132) [Ovid].

136 *"Gloria ..."* 'Glory to God in the highest', the words sung by the angels when they announced the birth of Christ to the shepherds watching their flocks near Bethlehem (line 139) [Luke].

145 *ignorance* Dante's intense desire to know the reason for the earthquake and the shouting of the *Gloria*.

PURGATORIO CANTO XXI

FIFTH TERRACE: Avarice (continued) and Prodigality.

1 *natural thirst* the innate human desire to know, which cannot be fully satisfied except by the supernatural truths of Christianity – the eternally quenching water which the Samaritan woman asked Christ to give her at the well [John].

9 *two* the two disciples who, fleeing from Jerusalem after Christ's death, were travelling along the road to Emmaus when they were joined by the risen Christ, though they did not at first recognize Him [Luke].

16 *just tribunal* God's justice, which has sentenced Virgil to Limbo.

22 *the signs* the three remaining P's carved on Dante's brow by the angel-doorkeeper (*Purg.* IX, 112–14).

25 *she* the Fate Lachesis who spins the thread of a person's life which her sister Clotho prepares and which the third Fate, Atropos, cuts off at the time appointed for death. Dante is not yet dead, and his soul, still in the body, needed a guide through the afterlife (lines 28–30).

37 *needle's eye* an image of the precision with which Virgil asks the question to which Dante so intensely desires the answer.

43 *This place* the upper part of Purgatory, which can be affected only by influences coming from the heavens above (lines 44–5). All natural forms of weather are confined to the lower slopes, up to the three steps leading to the door guarded by the angel (lines 46–54; *Purg.* IX, 76–132).

50 *Thaumas' daughter* Iris, the rainbow.

52 *Dry vapor* the cause of winds and of natural earthquakes, which were thought to be the effects of winds imprisoned in the earth (lines 57–8). The quaking of the mountain has therefore a supernatural origin: it marks the moment of a soul's release from its purification (lines 58–60).

60 *that shout* the *Gloria* (*Purg.* XX, 136).

63 *a change* the ascent from one terrace to the next. Each

soul desires both to ascend and to stay on the terrace to be purified; when the purification is completed, the will feels within itself its freedom to ascend (lines 64–6, 68–9).

76 *net* the obstacle to the soul's ascent, namely, its simultaneous desire to undergo the penances.

82 *In that age* around AD 70 when Jerusalem was captured and sacked by the Romans under Titus – an event which Christian writers saw as God's punishment of the Jews for their part in having Christ, betrayed by Judas, put to death (*Par.* VI, 92–3).

86 *the name* the title of poet, which brings enduring fame.

87 *faith* Christianity. The soul is the Roman poet Statius (*c.* AD 45–96), born (it was once thought) in Toulouse in France, and the prize-winning author of two epics: the *Thebaid* (on the war of the seven kings against Thebes); and the *Achilleid* (on Achilles and the Trojan War), which was left unfinished at his death (line 93). Dante apparently invented the story that he was converted to Christianity. As a pagan poet who is saved, he acts as a link between Virgil – to whom he pays a series of tributes – and Dante himself, the Christian poet who was also the heir to the classical poetic tradition (*Purg.* XXII, 127–9).

94 *sparks* the poetic inspiration which Statius derived from Virgil's *Aeneid* (line 97). Statius' first tribute is to Virgil as the master of poetry and the model for the poets who followed him.

102 *exile* in Purgatory. Despite Virgil's glance, Dante is unable to suppress a spontaneous smile at the fact that Statius is unaware that Virgil is present (lines 103–9).

112 *So may* the bargain formula (*Inf.* X, 82), wishing Dante success in his ascent of Purgatory.

132 *shade* a disembodied soul, which cannot be embraced (*Purg.* II, 79–81).

Ascent to the Sixth Terrace (Gluttony).

6 *"sitiunt"* 'are thirsty', a partial quotation of the Beatitude, 'Blessed are those who are [. . .] thirsty for justice' [Matthew], not for riches. For Dante, greed was the principal enemy of justice in the world.

12 *appears without* is expressed externally, thus creating a reciprocal love, based on virtue, between two friends.

13 *Juvenal* the Roman satirist (died *c.* AD 130).

18 *stairs* the ascent of Purgatory.

20 *reins* restraint.

35 *lack of measure* prodigality. Not only avarice (excessive hoarding) but the opposite sin, prodigality (excessive spending), is punished on the fifth terrace (lines 49–54; *Inf.* VII, 28–60).

38 *verses* the lines in the *Aeneid* in which Virgil curses the greed for gold which drives men to terrible crimes [Virgil]; they are cited, in an adapted form, in lines 40–42. Statius' second tribute to Virgil is to the moral teacher whose words saved him from going to Hell (where the avaricious and prodigals circle and clash eternally) by inducing him to recognize and repent of his prodigality (lines 42–5; *Inf.* VII, 25–35).

47 *cropped close* the mark of the prodigals at the resurrection of the body (*Inf.* VII, 57).

51 *their green* like dying plants, both sins gradually wither away in Purgatory.

55 *savage wars* the fratricidal enmity, described in Statius' *Thebaid*, between Oedipus' two sons by his mother, Jocasta (*Inf.* XXVI, 54).

56 *the singer* Virgil, writer of the *Eclogues* (poems which generally have a rustic or pastoral setting).

58 *notes* the poems written by Statius, inspired by Clio, the Muse of history.

59 *the faith* belief in Christ, without which no pagan, however virtuous, can be saved. Since Statius' poetry is

entirely pagan, Virgil wants to know what enlightened him to become a Christian, a follower of St Peter, the ex-fisherman and apostle who established the Church in Rome (lines 61–3).

65 *to drink* to become a poet. Poetic inspiration was expressed as the drinking of the waters of a spring at the foot of Parnassus, the mountain sacred to Apollo, the god of poetry, and the Muses.

67 *by night* in the simile, in the darkness of paganism.

70–72 *"The ages ..."* lines from Virgil's fourth Eclogue: 'The great order of the centuries is born anew. Now the virgin returns; now Saturn is king again. Now a new offspring descends from heaven on high' [Virgil]. Originally referring to a Golden Age under the Emperor Augustus, with the return of the virgin Astraea (Justice) and the birth of a wonder-child, the words came to be seen by Christians as perhaps an unconscious prophecy of the new era which began when the Virgin Mary gave birth to Christ, the Son of God. Statius' third tribute to Virgil is to the pagan precursor of Christianity to whom he himself, matching Virgil's words to the new religion, owes his conversion and salvation (lines 73–4, 94–5).

76 *messengers* the apostles and disciples who spread Christianity throughout the Roman Empire and in Rome itself.

83 *Domitian* the Roman Emperor (AD 81–96).

88 *my poem* the *Thebaid*.

93 *fourth circle* the terrace of sloth.

95 *the good* Christianity.

97–8 *Terence, Caecilius, Plautus* Roman writers of comedies in the second century BC. The list of great Greek and Roman authors in Limbo evokes the long and glorious history of classical literature.

98 *Varius* a Roman poet who edited the *Aeneid* after Virgil's death in 19 BC.

100 *Persius* a Roman poet (AD 34–62).

101 *that Greek* Homer, the supreme poet (*Inf.* IV, 88).

103 *the first circle* Limbo (*Inf.* IV).

104 *the mountain* Parnassus (line 65).

105 *our nurses* the Muses.

106 *Euripides* the Greek writer of tragedies (died 406 BC).

Antiphon a Greek orator (died 411 BC).

107 *Simonides* a Greek lyric poet (died 467 BC).

Agathon a Greek writer of tragedies (died *c.* 400 BC).

108 *laurel* the crowns of laurel leaves awarded to great poets.

109 *your own people* protagonists in Statius' own two poems. Those listed are all women.

110–11 *Antigone, Ismene* the daughters of Oedipus (*Thebaid*).

Deiphyle, Argia the wife of king Tydeus and her sister (*Thebaid*).

112 *the woman* Hypsipyle, who took the seven kings to the fountain of Langia (*Thebaid*).

113 *Tiresias' daughter* Manto (*Thebaid*), whom, however, Dante has seen not in Limbo but among the sorcerers (*Inf.* XX, 52–87).

Thetis the mother of Achilles (*Achilleid*).

114 *her sisters* the other women.

Deidamia the princess abandoned by Achilles when he joined the Greek expedition against Troy (*Achilleid*) (*Inf.* XXVI, 61–2).

117 *handmaidens* the hours of daylight, numbered as twelve (as at an equinox), starting at 6 a.m. Since the sun is in the fifth hour (lines 118–20), the time is between 10 and 11 a.m.

141 *"This food ..."* words recalling God's forbidding of Adam and Eve to eat the fruit of the tree in the Garden of Eden [Genesis].

142 *Mary's care* when the wine ran out at the wedding-feast at Cana (*Purg.* XIII, 28–30). This is the first example of temperance, the virtue opposed to gluttony.

145 *Roman women* the women of ancient Rome who, according to some sources, did not drink wine.

146 *Daniel* the prophet who refused king Nebuchadnezzar's

food and wine and chose to live frugally on pulse-vegetables and water; in reward, God gave him wisdom and the power to interpret dreams and visions [Daniel].

148 *first age* the primeval Golden Age of human innocence and the simple life, when people lived on acorns and water (*Purg.* XXVIII, 139–44).

151 *the Baptist* John the Baptist, Christ's cousin, and one of the greatest of the saints, who lived in the wilderness on locusts (the fruit of the carob-tree) and wild honey [Matthew].

PURGATORIO CANTO XXIII

SIXTH TERRACE: Gluttony.

2 *hunter* a bird-catcher.

4 *more than father* Virgil.

9 *my going* the resumption of the journey, made pleasant by the two poets' conversation.

10 *"Labïa mea, Domine"* '[Open] my lips, O Lord [and my mouth will proclaim your praise]', a verse from the *Miserere* [Psalms] (*Purg.* V, 24), recited by the gluttons whose mouths were the cause of their sin.

15 *knot* the debt of punishment.

25 *Erysichthon* a Greek prince who offended the goddess Ceres and was punished with such a terrible hunger that he ate his own flesh and died [Ovid].

28 *people* the starving citizens of Jerusalem during the siege by the Romans (AD 70), when hunger drove a woman called Mary to eat her own baby son [Josephus].

33 *OMO* 'man'. The word could be seen as if written on the human face in the two O's of the eye-sockets and in the M of the cheekbones, eyebrows, and nose, which here stand out sharply because of the souls' emaciation.

48 *Forese* Forese Donati (died 1296), a Florentine friend of Dante.

58 *unleaved* stripped of flesh, through starvation.

61 *eternal counsel* God's just decree.

73 *longing* the souls' desire to do penance, modelled on Christ's self-sacrifice on the cross, when He called out, 'Eli, Eli – my God, my God, why have you forsaken me?' [Matthew].

76 *that day* of Forese's death in 1296. Since he repented only at the end of his life (lines 79–82), he should still be on the lower slopes where the lazy must wait for the equivalent of another lifetime (line 84), unless helped by the prayers of the living (*Purg.* IV, 130–35).

85 *Nella* Forese's widow, whose prayers have released him from the lower slopes and the first five terraces (lines 88–90). Forese's loving tribute to his widow and her unique virtue in Florence (lines 91–3) stands in contrast with a series of comic sonnets of insults which he had exchanged with Dante, in which Dante accused Forese (among other things) of neglecting his wife and leaving her cold and alone in her bed.

87 *sweet wormwood* the punishments which are joyfully accepted (line 71).

94 *Barbagia* a region of Sardinia notorious for its rough and primitive inhabitants; the other Barbagia is, sarcastically, Florence (line 96).

103 *ordinances* religious and secular laws, which are not needed by women with natural modesty, such as those in primitive societies or the Arab world (lines 104–5).

107 *swift Heaven* God's punishment, prepared in the stars, is imminent (line 108) and will be achieved before today's baby boys reach puberty (lines 110–11).

114 *veil the sun* cast a shadow.

117 *heavy* painful. The reference seems to be to a period of dissipation in Dante's life in which Forese, now among the gluttons, had participated.

118 *He* Virgil, who rescued Dante from the dark forest (*Inf.* I) on a night when the moon was full (lines 119–21).

122 *truly dead* the damned.

126 *crooked* by sin.

131 *this other* Statius.

SIXTH TERRACE: Gluttony (continued).

7 *telling* Dante's words about Statius (*Purg.* XXIII, 131–3).

10 *Piccarda* Forese's sister. Dante will meet her in Paradise (*Par.* III, 49).

15 *Olympus* Paradise, the Christian equivalent of the mountain which was the home of the gods.

20 *Bonagiunta* a Tuscan poet from Lucca who died in the late 1290s.

21 *the one* Martin IV, a Frenchman who had held office in Tours cathedral and reigned as Pope 1281–5. His starvation in Purgatory is his penance for gluttony, epitomized by his fondness for eels (from lake Bolsena in Lazio) and white *vernaccia* wine (lines 23–4).

29 *Ubaldin da la Pila* a Tuscan nobleman (died 1291).

Boniface Bonifazio dei Fieschi, archbishop of Ravenna 1274–94, the pastor of a large flock (his diocese and his court) (line 30).

31 *Messer* a title of respect ('Sir').

Marchese a political leader from Forlì in the Romagna who died in the late 1290s. His insatiable drinking is punished in Purgatory by a drier thirst than he ever knew in life (lines 31–3).

37 *Gentucca* probably the name of the woman of lines 44–5.

38 *the place* Bonagiunta's mouth, which is being starved in punishment for his gluttony.

43 *my city* Lucca. Bonagiunta prophesies that a woman, not yet married in 1300, would give the exiled Dante hospitality in Lucca.

44 *veil* the sign of a married woman.

51 "*Ladies who have intelligence of love*" the first line of a poem, written by Dante in the mid-1280s, which marked a watershed in his development as a poet. The line came to him as if by miraculous inspiration, and the poem was the first in which, having abandoned the theme of love as the cause of

intense interior suffering, he took up a new and loftier theme – the praise of Beatrice – addressed to her companions, ladies capable of understanding his new and more subtle doctrine of noble, virtuous love [*Vita nuova*]. Dante's reply to Bonagiunta defines the essential feature of this new style as fidelity to the inner dictates of Love himself, personified: Love is the true poet, Dante merely his scribe or copyist (lines 52–4).

55 *knot* the obstacle which made earlier Italian poets unable to understand the new style.

56 *the Notary* Giacomo da Lentini, the leading poet of the Sicilian School at the court of the Emperor Frederick II in the 1230s and 1240s.

Guittone from Arezzo (died 1294), the most famous Tuscan poet of the time (*Purg.* XXVI, 125).

me Bonagiunta himself had introduced Sicilian poetry into Tuscany and, in a sonnet, had criticized Guido Guinizzelli, the poet who was the major influence on Dante's new style (*Purg.* XXVI, 92).

57 *sweet new manner* the 'dolce stil novo', the term which defines Dante's own innovatory position in the evolution of late thirteenth-century Italian love poetry, and which has since been extended to cover the new themes of love and virtue and the sweeter, more musical style both of Guinizzelli (the precursor) and of other poets in the small circle to which Dante belonged up to and around the year 1300.

59 *him* Love (line 53).

79 *the place* Florence.

83 *the guiltiest* Forese's brother, Corso Donati, the violent leader of the Black Guelphs who seized power in Florence in 1301. In 1308, he fled from the city but was captured; falling from his horse, he was killed and dragged along behind it – an event which, in the prophecy, becomes a journey straight to Hell (line 84).

88 *wheels* the heavenly spheres.

111 *holds high* to tease the children.

116 *a tree above* the forbidden tree in the Garden of Eden, on

the summit of mount Purgatory (*Purg.* XXXII, 37–9).

121 *those* the Centaurs, the first example of gluttony punished. Binary creatures (*Inf.* XII, 56) born of a cloud shaped in the form of Juno, they attended a wedding banquet during which, overcome by food, drink, and lust, they tried to kidnap the women but were defeated in battle by Theseus and his companions [Ovid].

125 *those Hebrews* the Israelite soldiers who drank some water too greedily and, on God's instructions, were excluded by Gideon from taking part in the glorious victory over the Midianites [Judges].

142 *deprived* by dazzling Dante, as do the other angels.

151–4 "*Blessed* ..." a paraphrase of the Beatitude, 'Blessed are those who are hungry and thirsty for justice, for they shall have their fill' [Matthew]. The desire for food and drink should be controlled by the virtue of temperance, or replaced by the love of justice (line 154; *Purg.* XXII, 4–6).

PURGATORIO CANTO XXV

Ascent from the Sixth Terrace to the Seventh (Lust).

1 *The hour* about 2 p.m. Two hours after the sun in Aries has crossed it, the celestial meridian is in the following sign, Taurus, and – on the other side of the world – Scorpio (it is about 2 a.m. in Jerusalem).

17 *the iron* the arrow-head on a fully drawn bow. Dante's desire to ask a question is stretched to the limit.

21 *where* in the afterlife. The dead do not need to eat or drink; yet Dante has just seen the gluttons starving.

22 *Meleager* a prince at whose birth the Fates put a log on a fire and decreed that he would live only for as long as it continued to burn; it was removed for a time, but as soon as it was thrown back in the fire and consumed, he died [Ovid]. With the image of the mirror which reflects every movement exactly (lines 25–6), the myth illustrates how an external,

material object can have a precisely corresponding effect upon something which is immaterial – in the case in point, the soul.

37 *blood* one of the four humours which, in medieval physiology, is formed in the heart and fills the veins. In a male, some is converted into semen which has the active power to generate other human bodies when it is joined in the womb with the passive blood of the mother (lines 40–48). This power creates the organs first for the vegetative functions of life (nourishment, growth, reproduction) and then for the sensitive (the five senses, locomotion) (lines 52–60), thus preparing the foetus to receive the soul. Before entering the terrace of lust, Dante learns that natural generation, from the father's seed, is the prelude to the direct creation of the immortal, rational soul by God and that its effect continues after death in the formation of the souls' bodies composed of air.

54 *journeying* on the way to becoming a higher form of life.

61–2 *a speaking being* a human, the powers of speech and laughter (line 103) being distinguishing features of the rational soul.

63 *one* the Arab philosopher Averroes (*Inf.* IV, 144), who had argued that, since the possible intellect (which abstracts the universal forms from sense perceptions) has no visible organ through which it acts, it must therefore be separate from the soul and shared collectively by all living humans. Christian theologians condemned this proposition as incompatible with the doctrine of the indivisibility of every human soul.

70 *First Mover* God.

74 *one soul* the single soul which combines the powers of all three levels of life – vegetative, sensitive, and self-aware (rational) (line 75; *Purg.* IV, 5–7) – in the new entity of a human being, just as the immaterial (heat) and the material (grapejuice) combine to create wine (lines 76–8).

79 *Lachesis* the Fate who spins the thread of a person's life (*Purg.* XXI, 25). Released from the material body by death, the soul's immaterial faculties operate more perfectly (lines 79–84).

If damned, it goes to the bank of the river Acheron; if saved, to the mouth of the Tiber (lines 85–7; *Inf*. III, 70–127; *Purg*. II, 100–101). There its generative power gives to the surrounding air the form of a body, the 'shade', which matches the original body in appearance and in its reactions to the soul's inner operations, such as the punishments of Purgatory (lines 88–105). This is how the gluttons are starved by their desire to do penance (lines 106–8).

122 *"Summae Deus clementiae"* 'O God of supreme clemency', the opening words of a hymn which contains a prayer for purification by fire from the sin of lust.

127–8 *"Virum non cognosco"* 'I have never known a man', the reply which the Virgin Mary made to the angel when he told her that she would conceive Jesus [Luke]. This is the first of the examples of chastity, the virtue opposite to lust.

130 *Diana* the chaste goddess who lived in the forests with her company of nymphs, one of whom, Callisto (Helice), was driven away after she was seduced by Jupiter [Ovid].

132 *Venus' poison* illicit love.

134 *wives and husbands* examples of how sexual love should be restrained by virtue and within marriage.

138 *care* the punishment by fire. The flames are an image both of lust and of the spiritual love by which it is corrected.

nourishment the moral examples of chastity.

139 *final wound* lust, represented by the last of the seven P's (*Purg*. IX, 112).

PURGATORIO CANTO XXVI

SEVENTH TERRACE: Lust.

12 *fictive* made of air (*Purg*. XXV, 88–103).

16 *the others* Virgil and Statius.

21 *Indian or Ethiopian* an inhabitant of the hottest regions of Asia or Africa.

24 *a wall* by casting a shadow (lines 7–8).

40 *Sodom and Gomorrah* two cities destroyed by God for their wickedness, and particularly for sodomy (*Inf.* XI, 50). The first example of lust punished is shouted by the homosexuals, who circle the terrace in the opposite direction to the heterosexuals (lines 76–81).

42 *Pasiphaë* the greatest classical example of lust, she concealed herself inside a wooden cow in order to have sex with a bull (*Inf.* XII, 12).

44 *Riphean mountains* situated, according to ancient geographers, in the cold northern regions of Europe.

45 *sands* the hot deserts of Africa.

55 *limbs* body. Dante has not yet died, either in old age or in youth.

58 *blind* ignorant and sinful.

68 *mountaineer* a peasant or shepherd who lives in the mountains and is amazed when he visits a city.

72 *noble* virtuous and capable of restraining emotions.

77 *the sin* homosexual lust, sodomy (lines 40, 79). Some of Julius Caesar's soldiers ironically called him 'Queen' because of his suspected sexual intimacy with Nicomedes, king of Bithynia.

86 *one* Pasiphaë (lines 41–2).

92 *Guido Guinizzelli* a poet from Bologna (died before 1276) (*Purg.* XI, 97).

93 *grieved* repented.

94 *Lycurgus* a king who, in revenge for the death of his son, condemned Hypsipyle to death; just before her execution, her two sons arrived and, recognizing her, rushed to embrace and rescue her [Statius].

97 *father* the predecessor and model for later Italian love poets, including Dante himself. Guinizzelli's poems – especially 'Love always takes refuge in a noble heart' and the sonnet, 'I wish truly to praise my lady' – were the principal influence on Dante's poetry in the 1280s, when he adopted the 'sweet new style' of praising Beatrice as the supreme example on earth of

moral nobility and the virtuous power of Love (*Inf.* V, 100; *Purg.* XXIV, 49–57).

108 *Lethe* the river of forgetfulness (*Inf.* XIV, 131; *Purg.* XXVIII, 130). Guinizzelli will never forget Dante's tribute to him.

113 *modern usage* the sweet new style of Dante and his contemporaries.

115 *he there* Arnaut Daniel (line 142), a late twelfth-century troubadour in the Occitan (Provençal) language whose often technically complex poetry is at times explicitly erotic.

117 *mother tongue* Occitan, the language of the earliest poems composed in a Romance vernacular. Guinizzelli's tribute, setting Arnaut above the other troubadours and the authors of the prose romances (mainly in French), makes him also the greatest forerunner of the love lyric in the third of the Romance literary languages – Italian.

120 *Limoges* a town in the region of the Limousin in central France, not far from the birthplace of Giraut de Borneil (early thirteenth century), regarded by some as the greatest of the troubadours.

123 *art or reason* the proper tools for assessing poetry, as opposed to mere rumour and fame.

125 *Guittone* from Arezzo (died 1294) (*Purg.* XXIV, 56), the most famous and influential Tuscan poet of the late thirteenth century. Dante condemned his language and style, and called those who praised it ignorant [*De vulgari eloquentia*]. In life, Guinizzelli had paid tribute to Guittone as his poetic 'father'; here, he effectively excludes him from the poetic family tree which descends from Guinizzelli himself, Dante's 'father' (lines 97–8), to Dante's own sweet new style.

130 *Paternoster* the Lord's Prayer, omitting the last request, since the souls cannot now be tempted to sin (*Purg.* XI, 1–24).

136 *desire* to know the soul's identity. In the original, Arnaut Daniel's reply (lines 140–47) is not in Italian but in Occitan.

PURGATORIO CANTO XXVII

SEVENTH TERRACE: Lust (concluded).

1 *there* in Jerusalem, where Christ was crucified, and where it is now dawn. Thus it is midnight in the extreme west (over the river Ebro in Spain), midday in the extreme east (over the river Ganges in India), and approaching sunset in Purgatory (lines 4–5).

8 "*Beati mundo corde*" 'Blessed are the pure of heart [for they shall see God]' [Matthew], the Beatitude appropriate to those who have been purified of lust.

23 *Geryon* the flying monster (*Inf.* XVII, 1, 79–136).

37 *Thisbe* the Babylonian girl whose lover Pyramus, thinking she was dead, stabbed himself with his own sword; finding him dying, bleeding, beneath a mulberry tree, she spoke to him, 'Pyramus, answer me; your dearest Thisbe is calling you', at which he opened his eyes to see her once more before he died. Ever since, the mulberry tree has borne red fruits [Ovid].

58 "*Venite* ..." 'Come, O blessed of my Father, [take possession of the kingdom prepared for you since the creation of the world]' the words with which, on the day of Judgment, Christ will invite the souls of the saved to enter Heaven [Matthew].

59 *light* of an angel.

92 *sleep* in which dreams just before dawn may be visions of the future (*Purg.* IX, 13–18), as indeed is this one, the last of Dante's three miraculously significant morning-dreams in Purgatory (*Purg.* XXVIII, 40–42).

94 *Cytherea* Venus, the planet of the goddess of love.

100 *Leah* Jacob's first wife, the sister of his second wife, Rachel [Genesis]. She symbolizes the Active Life on earth, in which the soul must work to adorn itself with virtues and honour; Rachel represents the Contemplative Life, the study of heavenly truths which leads to the eternal vision of God's beauty, as in a mirror, in Paradise (lines 103–8).

114 *teachers* Virgil and Statius.

116 *sweet fruit* the perfect happiness which all human beings desire and try to find in many different ways.

123 *flight* the ascent which has now become easy (*Purg.* IV, 91–4; XII, 121–6).

127 *temporary fire* Purgatory.

eternal fire Hell.

131 *pleasure* will. Healed of the effects of sin, Dante's will cannot now choose anything but that which is good, and he must now follow its guidance, instead of Virgil's, until Beatrice comes (lines 136–41).

142 *crown and miter* bestow the symbols of temporal and spiritual power, signifying that Dante has now acquired complete freedom and autonomy over his actions in both spheres.

PURGATORIO CANTO XXVIII

The Earthly Paradise (the Garden of Eden).

2 *forest* the paradise or garden of pleasure, planted by God in the beginning, and containing all kinds of beautiful trees and fruit. God placed Adam and Eve in the garden to tend it, forbidding them, on pain of death, to eat the fruit of the tree of the knowledge of good and evil. When they disobeyed Him, they were cast out and, with their descendants, the whole human race, were condemned to labour and toil for a living and to die [Genesis]. In contrast to the terrifying dark forest of *Inferno* I, Dante's Garden of Eden is a primeval living forest of perpetual spring and perfect natural beauty, situated on the summit of Purgatory. The paradise lost by sin is the goal of the journey by which the soul, purified of the effects of sin, is restored to humanity's original condition of innocence and earthly happiness before ascending to eternal happiness in the Heavenly Paradise.

11 *direction* westwards.

18 *burden* their rustling, which provides a musical accompaniment to the birdsong.

20 *Classe* a region with pine-trees, once the site of a Roman port, on the Adriatic coast near Ravenna.

21 *Aeolus* the god who controls the winds, imprisoning and releasing them.

Sirocco the hot, dry wind which blows into Italy from north Africa.

40 *a solitary woman* later named Matilda (*Purg.* XXXIII, 119). Of the many theories concerning her identity and meaning, the one preferred here is that she is the beautiful lady Wisdom who was the joyful companion of God at the creation of the world [Proverbs; Ecclesiasticus]. As true Wisdom, which perfects the human mind, she is a new version of Dante's lady Philosophy ('love of wisdom') whom he had come to love after the death of Beatrice [*Convivio*]. Fulfilling his dream of Leah (Active Life), she is his guide to the garden of earthly happiness and leads him to the lady who is the companion of Rachel in Heaven – Beatrice (*Inf.* II, 101–2; *Purg.* XXVII, 97–108).

51 *Proserpina* a beautiful girl who, while picking flowers, was taken away from her mother, Ceres, by Pluto to be his wife and queen of the underworld [Ovid].

65 *Venus* the goddess of love who, accidentally pierced by one of her son Cupid's arrows, fell passionately in love with Adonis [Ovid]. The light in Matilda's eyes expresses an even greater and higher love.

69 *needing no seed* because their growth has a heavenly cause (lines 103–11).

71 *Hellespont* the narrow straits (now the Dardanelles in Turkey), across which in 480 BC Xerxes, king of Persia, invaded Europe with a great army, but after his defeat by the Greeks he was forced back again in humiliating retreat (line 72).

73 *Leander* a young man who used to swim across the straits from Abydos in Asia to visit his lover Hero at Sestos on the opposite shore [Ovid]. Dante hates the stream which separates him from Matilda more than Leander when storms prevented him crossing to his beloved.

76 *open* divide, leaving a dry path across, like the Red Sea or the Jordan for the Israelites [Exodus; Joshua].

81 *"Delectasti"* 'You have given me joy, [O Lord, in Your creation, and I shall exult in the works of our hands]' [Psalms]. Matilda rejoices in the beauties of the paradise created by God to be the home of the human race.

85 *water* the stream. The presence of water and wind seems to contradict the fact that there is no weather in Purgatory above the door (lines 97–102; *Purg.* XXI, 43–54).

91 *Highest Good* God, Whose essence is goodness and joy.

93 *endless peace* in Heaven.

104 *first circling* the revolution of the first of the heavenly spheres, the moon. The air which circles with it, broken by the mountain-top, causes the ceaseless breeze and seeds the plants (lines 106–11).

112 *other* the northern hemisphere, to which the seeds are carried, though the paradise contains some which are unknown there (line 120).

122 *vein* a natural water-source, from which clouds take water up to the cold regions of the air and return it to earth as rain, forming rivers which, depending on the weather, run fast or slow (line 123; *Purg.* V, 109–23). The source of this water is supernatural, unchangingly replenished by God's will (lines 124–6). This stream is the Lethe, the river of forgetfulness; its twin is the Eünoè ('memory of good') (lines 130–31; *Inf.* XIV, 136–8; *Purg.* XXXIII, 112–45).

140 *golden age* the primeval age of human innocence, an eternal springtime when the earth bore fruits without ploughing, and the rivers ran with milk and nectar [Ovid] (*Purg.* XXII, 148–50). The pagan myth, created by classical poets inspired by the Muses on mount Parnassus, was perhaps an intuition of the Christian truth of the Garden of Eden. Hence the pleasure of Virgil and Statius on hearing Matilda's words (lines 146–7).

The Earthly Paradise (continued): The procession.

3 *"Beati ..."* 'Blessed are those whose sins have been covered up' [Psalms], that is, by repentance in life and purification in Purgatory.

4 *nymphs* beautiful young women who, in classical mythology, lived in the woods and forests.

27 *veil* limitation. If Eve had not disobeyed God, all humans, including Dante, would have been born and lived in the Earthly Paradise (lines 28–30).

37 *Virgins* the Muses, who live on mount Helicon – the same as Parnassus, in some sources – with its springs of water (*Inf.* II, 7; XXXII, 10–12; *Purg.* I, 7–12; XXII, 64–5, 104–5). To them – and especially to Urania, the Muse of heavenly poetry – Dante appeals for help in meeting the arduous poetic and intellectual challenge of the next section of his poem (line 42).

47 *mingled senses* both Dante's sight and his hearing, through which his mind receives knowledge (line 49); their first perceptions are corrected as the lights and singing draw near.

50 *candelabra* traditionally interpreted as the Seven Gifts of the Holy Spirit [Isaiah]. Dante bases the first part of the procession on St John's vision of Heaven, with seven lights, twenty-four elders, and four animals surrounding the throne of God and the Lamb (Christ) [Revelation], in order to create what is both a pageant of sacred history and a millenarian vision of the ideal state of the Christian world.

51 *"Hosanna"* the Hebrew word of praise addressed to Christ at His entry into Jerusalem [Matthew], and used in the *Sanctus* of the Mass: 'Holy, holy, holy Lord God of hosts, [...] Hosanna in the highest'.

61 *woman* Matilda.

77 *bands* seven streamers of light, the effects of the Seven Gifts.

78 *Delia's girdle* the halo round the moon, which also

contains the seven colours of the spectrum. Diana, goddess of the moon, was born on Delos (*Purg.* XX, 130–32).

83 *twenty-four elders* personifications of the books of the Old Testament [St Jerome].

86 *"benedicta"* 'blessed'. The elders' song is a paraphrase of the angel's words to Mary: 'Blessed are you among women' [Luke].

92 *four animals* a man, a lion, an ox, and an eagle, which appear in the visions of both Ezekiel (where they each have four wings) and St John (where they have six, as here) (lines 100–105) [Ezekiel; Revelation]. They symbolize the writers of the four Gospels (Matthew, Mark, Luke, and John).

96 *Argus* a monster whose hundred eyes were set in the tail of the peacock [Ovid] (*Purg.* XXXII, 64–6).

107 *triumphal* like that in which a victorious general or Emperor rode in the great processions held in ancient Rome, but more splendid (lines 115–17).

108 *griffin* a fierce beast with a head, beak, and wings like an eagle's, the rest of its body like a lion (lines 109–14). It is usually interpreted as a symbol of Christ, both God and man, Who founded the Church (the chariot) and joined it to God's justice (*Purg.* XXXII, 43–51). Alternatively, it symbolizes the Roman Empire, the union of the world-monarch (the eagle) and the people (the lion), leading human society (the chariot). Appearing among the books of the Bible, it is the Empire at the time of universal peace during the reign of Augustus when Christ was born [Luke]; and it is Dante's ideal of the Empire in his own day, with the Emperor as the temporal leader chosen by God to lead the whole human race to peace, freedom, justice, and happiness on earth, which is symbolized by the Earthly Paradise [*Convivio*; *Monarchia*].

109 *band* of light (line 77).

116 *Africanus* Scipio, the Roman republican general who defeated Hannibal and the Carthaginians in north Africa (202 BC), for which he was awarded a great triumphal procession on his return to Rome.

Augustus the Roman Emperor (27 BC–AD 14), in whose honour three splendid triumphal processions were held in Rome [Virgil].

117 *the Sun's* the chariot of the Sun which was driven astray by Phaethon until, to save the Earth from being burnt up, Jupiter cast him down (*Inf.* XVII, 106–8).

121 *Three ... women* the Theological Virtues personified: Charity (lines 122–3), Hope (lines 124–5), and Faith (lines 125–6).

130 *four ... women* the Cardinal Virtues, led by Prudence, who has three eyes for considering the past, the present, and the future (*Purg.* I, 23; VIII, 89–93).

134 *two elders* the books of the New Testament which follow the Gospels: the Acts of the Apostles, written by St Luke, a doctor (a follower of Hippocrates, who founded medicine for the benefit of humans) (lines 136–8); and the Epistles of St Paul, who was traditionally portrayed holding a sword (lines 139–41).

142 *four* the Epistles of Sts James, Peter, John, and Jude.

143 *old man* the last book of the Bible, the Book of Revelation (the Apocalypse), St John's account of his visions which he wrote down in his old age.

154 *emblems* the seven candlesticks.

PURGATORIO CANTO XXX

The Earthly Paradise (continued): The appearance of Beatrice.

1 *Seven-Stars* the seven lights, which belong to the infinite Heaven beyond the spheres and are eternal guides to virtue, just as the seven stars of the Great Bear (Ursa Major) guide sailors (lines 2–6).

7 *band* the twenty-four elders.

11 *"Veni, ..."* 'Come, bride, from Lebanon', king Solomon's words to his beautiful bride [Song of Songs], applied in

the liturgy to Mary, the virgin mother of Christ, and by theologians to the Church, the Bride of Christ.

13 *Final Summons* the resurrection of the dead for the Last Judgment.

15 *Alleluia* a Hebrew word, used in the Christian liturgy, meaning 'praise God'.

17 *messengers and ministers* angels (line 29).

18 *ad vocem ...* 'at the voice of such a noble old man', namely, the elder who has just intoned the hymn (lines 9–12).

19 *"Benedictus ..."* 'Blessed are you who come', a slight adaptation of the words addressed to Christ at His entry into Jerusalem: 'Blessed is he who comes [in the name of the Lord]' [Matthew].

21 *"Manibus ..."* 'Strew lilies with full hands', words taken from the lament for the death of Augustus' young nephew, Marcellus [Virgil].

31 *a woman* Beatrice (*Inf.* II, 53), who died in 1290 at the age of twenty-four, when her soul was taken by God to eternal light and glory with Mary and the angels in Heaven [*Vita nuova*]. Here, recalling both Christ's Bride and Christ Himself (lines 11, 19), she reappears among angels; her garments have the same colours as Faith, Hope, and Charity (*Purg.* XXIX, 121–9); her garland of olive leaves represents peace and heavenly wisdom (line 68).

48 *old flame* love. The line is a quotation from the *Aeneid* [Virgil].

52 *all* the beauties of the Earthly Paradise, lost by Eve.

53 *washed* on the shore of Purgatory (*Purg.* I, 121–9).

57 *sword* Beatrice's later accusations.

68 *Minerva* the goddess of wisdom, to whom the olive-tree was sacred.

83–4 *"In te, ... pedes meos"* 'In you, O Lord, I have placed my hope ... [in a wide place you have set] my feet' [Psalms]. On Dante's behalf, the angels sing the first verses of a psalm on God's deliverance of the person who trusts in Him.

86 *spine of Italy* the Apennine mountains, when cold north-east winds blow into Italy (line 87).

89 *shade-less lands* the African desert from which hot winds blow into Italy, melting the ice.

91 *those* the angels, whose music is that of the heavenly spheres which they revolve (*Par.* XXVIII, 64–78).

103 *never-ending day* the eternal vision of God, in Whose Mind the angels can see everything that happens on earth.

109 *spheres* the heavens whose position and conjunction influence a person's natural disposition – in Dante's case, his birth-sign of Gemini which gave him his intellectual and poetic talents (*Inf.* XV, 55; *Purg.* XVI, 73; *Par.* XXII, 112–17).

112 *graces* supernatural help from God in Heaven.

125 *second age* life after death.

127 *another* another object of his love. After Beatrice's death, Dante loved another lady, whom he later called lady Philosophy [*Vita nuova*; *Convivio*]; more generally, he strayed from Beatrice by loving the false goods of this world which cannot bring perfect happiness (lines 131–2).

134 *dream* Dante's visions of Beatrice after her death [*Vita nuova*].

138 *lost* damned.

139 *gateway* Limbo, the first circle of Hell, where Beatrice asked Virgil to rescue Dante (*Inf.* II, 52–117).

PURGATORIO CANTO XXXI

The Earthly Paradise (continued): Dante's confession and crossing of the Lethe.

11 *water* the Lethe.

23 *Good* God.

25 *chains . . . ditches* obstacles.

29 *others* other ladies and objects of Dante's love, the empty attractions of this life (lines 34–5, 54–60).

42 *our blade* heavenly justice which is more merciful when the guilty person confesses.

45 *Sirens* seductive earthly beauties (*Purg.* XIX, 19–21).

51 *dust* in the grave. The death of Beatrice should have turned Dante away from love of mortal to love of eternal beauty (lines 52–4).

69 *beard* a sign of Dante's adulthood, in pungent contrast to the immaturity of his actions (lines 74–5).

71–2 *from lands* ... from Europe, to the north, or from Africa, where Iarbas was king in Aeneas' time.

77 *first creatures* the angels, created first by God.

80 *animal* the griffin which unites the forms of eagle and lion and so resembles Christ, Who is one Person with two natures (God and man) (line 81). For Dante, the Roman Empire too was both divine and human, and the Emperor should be as another Christ in his leadership of the people.

92 *the woman* Matilda.

98 "*Asperges me*" 'You will sprinkle me [with hyssop, and I shall be cleansed; you will wash me, and I shall be whiter than snow]' [Psalms].

104 *four ... women* the Cardinal Virtues, also represented as stars (*Purg.* I, 23).

110 *three* the Theological Virtues, who are superior (lines 130–31).

116 *emeralds* Beatrice's eyes, in which Dante sees the griffin reflected, its two forms – of eagle and lion – miraculously alternating (lines 118–26). Ideal earthly government has two powers, of the Emperor and the people, whose origin is in Heaven.

128 *food* of truth.

138 *second beauty* Beatrice's smile. In Dante's earlier poetry, Beatrice has two beauties: her eyes, which bear Love (line 117); and her mouth whose smile enraptures him with a sweetness which cannot be described in words [*Vita nuova*]. Hence not even the most experienced poet, inspired by the Muses on Parnassus, could convey the vision of that smile now, for it expresses heavenly joy (lines 139–45).

The Earthly Paradise (continued): The dramas of the tree and the chariot.

3 *thirst* the desire to see Beatrice, who died in 1290, ten years before the date of Dante's journey.

26 *blessed burden* Beatrice in the triumphal chariot.

32 *one* Eve, tempted by the Devil in the form of a serpent.

38 *a tree* the tree whose fruit Adam and Eve ate. Its bareness signifies the effect of the first sin.

42 *Indians* who, it was believed, lived where there were immensely tall trees.

52 *when* in spring, when the sun is in Aries (the constellation which follows Pisces) and before it passes into the next sign (Taurus) (lines 56–7). According to theologians, the tree of the Fall prefigured the tree of the cross, and Dante's scene, in which the griffin (the justice of Rome) joins the chariot (human society) to the bare tree, renewing it with leaves and flowers the colour of venous blood (lines 59–60), is a symbolic dramatization of the crucifixion when Christ, the new Adam, shed His blood to redeem the whole human race from Adam's sin [*Monarchia*] (*Par.* VI, 82–90). It is also a millenarian vision of a future time when God's Justice would again be renewed in the world (*Purg.* XXXIII, 70–2).

64 *ruthless eyes* the hundred eyes of the monster Argus, whom Mercury lulled to sleep with the story of the nymph Syrinx and then killed [Ovid] (*Purg.* XXIX, 96). Dante's enraptured slumber is impossible to describe in words.

73 *Peter, John and James* the three apostles who were overcome by the vision of Christ transfigured, His face shining with light and His garments as white as snow, between Moses and the prophet Elijah; when Christ told them, 'Arise; do not be afraid', they looked up and found Him alone again and with his normal appearance [Matthew] (lines 79–81). In the same way, Dante awakes to see a different scene.

74 *blossoms* the glory of the transfigured Christ, which gave

the three apostles a preliminary sight of the future, eternal vision of Him as the food of the angels in Heaven.

78 *the word* the same word, 'Arise', with which Christ raised the dead to life again.

83 *she* Matilda.

92 *one* Beatrice.

98 *lamps* the seven candlesticks, whose light is eternal (*Purg*. XXX, 1–2).

102 *the Rome* Heaven, the true Eternal City, ruled by Christ.

103 *to profit* to reform the wicked world of the living. The following episode is Dante's version of the Book of Revelation, St John's vision of the terrible tribulations which will afflict the world before the end.

112 *bird of Jove* an eagle, symbol of the Roman Empire. Its attack represents the persecution of the early Christians by Nero and other pagan Emperors, and in general the violence which accompanied the disputes between Emperors and Popes in the Middle Ages.

119 *fox* symbol of the heresies which threatened to contaminate the Church from the fourth century to Dante's own time.

126 *its plumage* symbolizing the power of the Empire which Constantine bequeathed to the Church and which the medieval Popes claimed to possess (*Inf*. XIX, 115–17).

129 *bark* the Church, the 'boat of Peter', corrupted by the Popes' usurpation of temporal power. The voice is probably that of St Peter himself, the first Pope.

131 *dragon* a symbol taken from St John [Revelation], probably representing Mohammedanism, which in the seventh century had separated a large part of the human race from the Church (*Inf*. XXVIII, 31), and which in 1291 finally reconquered the whole of the Holy Land from the crusaders.

137 *eagle's plumes* the imperial power, conceded to the Papacy first by Constantine and then, in 1303, by the Emperor Albert (lines 137–8). It now rapidly corrupts the whole Church, transforming it into the seven-headed, ten-horned

beast which is one of St John's signs of the future rule of
Antichrist, the ally of Satan, before the end of the world
[Revelation] (lines 139–47).

149 *whore* the prostitute riding the beast, another of St
John's signs of the time of Antichrist [Revelation], here
representing the Papacy corrupted by greed and temporal
power (*Inf.* XIX, 106–11).

151 *a giant* one of the kings who whore with the prostitute,
an ally of Antichrist [Revelation]. Here he represents Philip
the Fair, king of France, whose alliance with Pope Clement V
led, in 1309, to the transfer of the Papacy from Rome to
Avignon (lines 157–60; *Inf.* XIX, 82–8). Dante presents the
state of the Church and the world in the early fourteenth
century as if the reign of Antichrist had already begun.

PURGATORIO CANTO XXXIII

The Earthly Paradise (continued).

3 "*Deus, venerunt gentes*" 'O God, the unbelieving nations
have come [into Your inheritance; they have defiled Your holy
temple]' [Psalms], a psalm asking God to help His people by
punishing their cruel and sacrilegious persecutors.

6 *Mary* the supreme example of grief when she saw her son,
Christ, dying on the cross.

10–12 "*Modicum . . . et vos videbitis me*" 'A little while, and
you shall not see me, and again a little while, and you shall see
me', words spoken by Christ to His disciples foretelling His
coming death and resurrection [John], here used as a prophecy
that the evil will soon be punished, just as Christ will come
again in Judgment on the Last Day.

14 *lady* Matilda.

15 *sage* Statius.

34 *vessel* the chariot attacked by the dragon (*Purg.* XXXII,
130–36). St John too was told: 'the beast which you have seen
was and is not' [Revelation].

43–4 *a Five Hundred and Ten and Five* a saviour, God's avenger, who will be an heir of the eagle (the Empire) (lines 37–40). As in Virgil's prophecy of the coming reform of Italy by a 'Greyhound' (*Inf.* I, 100–111), this prophecy also is deliberately enigmatic. The identity of the deliverer is encoded in number symbolism: he will be a 515 (in Roman numerals DXV, an anagram of DUX, 'leader'), the enemy of 666, the number of the beast [Revelation]. No theory has managed to match this number convincingly to a specific person, and it is most probably an expression of Dante's continuing hopes – after the failure of the Emperor Henry VII's expedition into Italy (1310–13) – that a virtuous Emperor would soon come to bring peace and restore Roman justice and law in Italy and throughout the world. The identity of the 515 will thus be revealed only by the event itself (lines 49–50). Reversing the apocalyptic events described in the preceding scene, this future messianic figure, whoever he will be, will also prefigure the Second Coming of Christ in Judgment.

46 *Sphinx and Themis* the riddle of the Sphinx (a Theban monster which killed everyone who could not answer it) and the obscure oracle of the prophetess Themis [Ovid].

49 *Naiads* nymphs who will solve the prophecy. In medieval manuscripts of Ovid, the Sphinx's riddle was solved by the 'Naiades' – a mistaken reading for 'Laiades' (Oedipus, the son of Laius).

51 *grain or herds* the fields and flocks of the Thebans which were plundered by a monster sent by Themis after the Sphinx's riddle had been solved. The 515 will wreak God's vengeance in a different way.

54 *life* mortal life. Beatrice again instructs Dante to reveal these prophetic words and scenes in his reforming poem (*Purg.* XXXII, 103–6).

57 *twice* by the eagle and the giant.

61 *first soul* Adam.

63 *Him* Christ, Who redeemed humanity from Adam's sin

and led Adam himself out of Limbo to Paradise (*Inf.* IV, 55) (*Par.* XXVI, 118–23).

67 *Elsa* a river in Tuscany whose waters formed calcifying encrustations on anything in them. Similarly, false, earthly ideas and pleasures have encrusted Dante's mind and made it dark, just as the white mulberry was darkened by Pyramus' blood (lines 69–70, 73–4; *Purg.* XXVII, 37–9).

71 *moral sense* as a moral example, the tree symbolizes divine Justice, first expressed in the ban placed on it by God, and thus a lesson to humans not to violate God's Law (lines 58–60).

78 *palm* the sign that a person had made a pilgrimage to the Holy Land. Beatrice's heavenly knowledge, recorded in the poem, will prove that Dante has visited the afterlife.

85 *the school* earthly knowledge, which is as far beneath God's Wisdom as the earth itself is distant from the Primum Mobile (the ninth Heaven, beyond the stars) (lines 88–90). The fact that Dante has forgotten his pursuit of merely earthly wisdom proves that his memory has been cleansed of it in the Lethe, and therefore that it was sinful (lines 91–9).

104 *meridian* the celestial meridian, whose position is different to observers in different places. It is midday.

112–13 *Euphrates … Tigris* two rivers in the East, believed to flow from the Earthly Paradise [Genesis].

119 *Matilda* the lady's name, now given by Beatrice, has been linked principally with that of the Countess Matilda of Tuscany (1046–1115), daughter of the Countess Beatrice. Here it may mean that perfect earthly Wisdom is the daughter of God's.

124 *greater care* the important events which Dante has witnessed since Matilda explained the function of the streams (*Purg.* XXVIII, 127–32).

127 *Eunoe* the stream whose waters will restore Dante's memory of good (line 129). Their sweetness is inexpressible in words (lines 137–8).

131 *its own* by obeying the request.

141 *curb of art* the structure of the *Comedy*, which limits the *Purgatorio* to thirty-three cantos.

145 *the stars* Paradise. Each of the poem's three canticles ends with the word 'stars', the highest of the heavenly spheres which humans can see in their aspiration to God.

NOTES

PARADISO CANTO I

The ascent of Beatrice and Dante from the Earthly Paradise.

4 *the heaven* the infinite Heaven (the Empyrean) beyond the spheres. The *Paradiso* is structured on ancient Greek astronomy, as systematized by Ptolemy (second century AD) (*Inf.* IV, 142). The earth is stationary in the centre of the universe; around it revolve nine transparent circular spheres, bearing the visible heavenly bodies – the Moon, Mercury, Venus, the Sun, Mars, Jupiter, Saturn, and the Fixed Stars – beyond which is the Primum Mobile (the First Moved Heaven or Crystalline Heaven), which exists in the Empyrean. Through these and their light, God's creative power and providence in the natural order are transmitted down to the earth; through these, Dante has ascended to the infinite source of light: the Power, Wisdom, and Love of God (Father, Son, and Holy Spirit). Having returned to earth, he must now describe that ascent in its crescendo of experiences, above all, of light. This will be the supreme poetic challenge, since the supernatural knowledge, love, and ecstatic happiness of Paradise are beyond the powers of the human mind to grasp, of human language to express, even of his memory to retain (lines 5–9). Throughout the *Paradiso* Dante restates this fundamental motif: the reality of Heaven infinitely exceeds his powers to describe it in his poem.

13 *Apollo* the god of poetry. In the *Inferno* and the *Purgatorio*, Dante had appealed for poetic inspiration to the nine Muses, who live on one peak of mount Parnassus; now, for the last and greatest test of his ability to find the words to match his theme (however inadequately), he needs the help of the divinity himself, who lives on Cyrrha, the other peak (lines 16–18, 36; *Purg.* XXIX, 37–42).

21 *Marsyas* a satyr who challenged Apollo to a musical contest, lost, and was punished by being skinned alive, during which he asked the god, 'Why are you drawing me out of myself?' [Ovid]. Recalling Apollo's victory, Dante wants to be emptied of himself so that he may be filled with divine, poetic power (lines 14, 19).

25 *the tree* the laurel. Apollo loved the nymph Daphne, but she escaped from him by being changed into a laurel-tree [Ovid]. The myth symbolizes a poet's pursuit of fame, the laurel-leaves with which, in ancient Greece and Rome, great poets were crowned and which Dante too desires to win (lines 15, 26–7; *Par.* XXV, 9).

28 *seldom* in Dante's own decadent times, with its dearth of men who desire to be great leaders or poets.

31 *Peneian* of the laurel (Daphne, daughter of Peneus).

33 *Delphic deity* Apollo (from Delphi, the site of his principal temple in ancient Greece).

34 *small spark* Dante's poetry, which may inspire greater poets to request and receive Apollo's help (lines 35–6).

37 *lantern* the sun. Resuming the narrative of his journey, Dante describes his ascent from the earth with the astronomical and theological symbolism of circles, crosses, springtime renewal, and the light of the sun. At the spring equinox, at the point where the equator, the ecliptic, and the equinoctial colure form a triple intersection on the fourth circle (the horizon), the sun rises in Aries, and its warming and life-giving power is increasing (lines 38–42). From sunrise in the Earthly Paradise (when it had been evening in Jerusalem), it is now midday (and night-time over the whole northern hemisphere) (lines 43–6).

47 *eagle* a bird which, it was thought, could look directly into the light of the sun, unlike humans (lines 53–4).

49 *second ray* of reflected light, which is the incident ray redirected upwards (*Purg.* XV, 16–21).

57 *that place* the Earthly Paradise.

65 *circles* the heavenly spheres.

68 *Glaucus* a fisherman who tasted a magic herb and was changed into a sea-god [Ovid]. Dante is raised above the merely human to a state which cannot be described in words; hence the example can only imperfectly illustrate the reality which those who receive God's grace and go to Heaven will experience for themselves (lines 70–72). Throughout the *Paradiso*, it is Dante's sight of the increased light and joy in Beatrice's eyes and smile which marks his instantaneous ascent from one heaven to the next. He has already left the earth (line 91).

73 *the part* the soul, which God creates after the body (the foetus) has been prepared to receive it (*Purg.* XXV, 67–75). St Paul too said that he was taken up to a vision of Heaven, 'whether in the body, I know not; whether out of the body, I know not; God knows' [2 Corinthians] (*Par.* II, 37).

76 *wheel* the circular motion of the heavenly spheres, caused by their eternal desire to be united with God.

78 *harmony* the perfect order and proportion of the heavens from which earthly harmonies, including music, are derived.

92 *abode* the sphere of fire, between the earth and the moon. From it lightning strikes downwards, whereas other fires naturally tend up towards it (lines 115, 132–3, 141; *Purg.* IX, 30; XVIII, 28–30).

105 *form* the specifying principle of existence, by which everything is what it is.

106 *higher beings* creatures with intelligence, namely, angels and humans. In the Middle Ages, the hierarchy of being consisted of: God (infinite Being, Mind, and Love), angels (pure Intelligences), human beings (who have immortal souls, with the powers of reason and will), animals, plants, and the four elements of the sublunar world (earth, air, fire, and water). According to the principle of teleology, which defines things according to the purposes for which they were made, all created beings have natural goals towards which they move or are drawn: for fire, the sphere of fire; for animals (with mortal souls), movement from one place to another; for earth,

the centre of the earth (*Inf.* XXXII, 73–4; XXXIV, 110–11) (lines 109–17). The goal of creatures who have intellect and will is God Himself and the appeasement of all their desires in the Empyrean Heaven beyond the Primum Mobile; hence Beatrice and Dante are now being drawn naturally to the goal of happiness for which they were created (lines 119–26).

127 *a shape* a work of art in which the imperfections and limitations of his material prevent the artist from fully realizing his intentions. Similarly, humans, with their free will, may refuse to respond to their natural goal and, instead, turn their love towards earthly pleasures (lines 130–35). Now that Dante's will has been purified, it is as natural for him to go to Heaven as it is for water to run downhill or for fire to strive upwards (lines 135–41).

PARADISO CANTO II

THE MOON.

3 *my ship* Dante's intellect and poetic skills (*Purg.* I, 2). The *Paradiso* will be too arduous and profound for unprepared listeners to follow (lines 1–6).

8 *Minerva* the goddess of wisdom. In the metaphor of the voyage, wisdom is the wind, the motive force of the *Paradiso*; and Apollo and the Muses (poetry and inspiration) are, respectively, the helmsman and the guiding stars.

11 *bread of angels* knowledge and wisdom which, on earth, perfect the human mind and instil the desire for the full vision of God's Wisdom in Heaven. The principal audience to whom the *Paradiso* is addressed is the small group of scholars, theologians, and philosophers ('lovers of wisdom') who, like Dante, have dedicated their lives to the pursuit of knowledge: 'O, happy are those few who sit at the table where the bread of the angels is eaten!' [*Convivio*].

16 *men* the Argonauts who sailed with Jason to Colchis, where they saw him harness two fire-breathing oxen, plough a

field, and sow dragon's teeth, from which armed men sprang up [Ovid] (*Inf.* XVIII, 86).

30 *first star* the Moon.

38 *things material* physical objects, which on earth cannot exist in the same space at the same time. If Dante still has his body (*Par.* I, 73–4), it interpenetrates the substance of the Moon. This miracle should make humans even more eager to see the supreme mystery of the Incarnation, of Christ as both God and man – an article of faith on earth but the object of direct, intuitive vision in Heaven (lines 40–45).

51 *Cain* the first murderer who, according to popular belief, was banished to the moon by God and can be seen there in its spots (*Inf.* XX, 124). Since the heavenly spheres were thought to be composed of a fifth, eternal and unchanging element, it was difficult to account both for the apparent imperfection in the moon's reflection of the sun's light and for the multiplicity and variety of lights in the heaven of the stars. The solution proposed was that the fifth element was distributed unevenly in these heavens, more densely in some parts, more thinly in others (line 60).

57 *short wings* a limited capacity for understanding heavenly truths.

64 *eighth sphere* of the fixed stars. Since the many differing stars all have different powers to influence the world below, the essential principle of this heaven must be, not the uneven distribution of the same light, but multiplicity (lines 67–73).

73 *rarity* a thinner distribution of the moon's light-reflecting substance in its dark areas. In this case, either the rarefied areas stretch right through the body of the moon; or there are alternating layers of rarer and more dense material (as of lean flesh and fat in a body) (lines 75–8). The first explanation is disproved by the fact that, when the sun is eclipsed by the moon, its light does not shine right through the moon's darker parts (lines 79–81). In the second hypothesis, what makes the sun's light darker must be that it is reflected to the earth from the first dense layer it meets beneath

the moon's surface, and thus from further away; however, the experiment of the three mirrors proves that the light reflected from the furthest is smaller but no less bright than that reflected from the others (lines 82–105).

89 *glass* a mirror.

96 *your arts' course* human knowledge and science.

106 *sub-matter* water.

112 *the heaven* the Empyrean, where the Primum Mobile revolves, containing in itself the power to bring into existence all the natural things below it. The next heaven (the stars) receives this power and multiplies it into many different powers, which it transmits downwards and which each sphere in succession receives and varies, producing a diversity of influences and effects, down to the earth below (lines 113–23).

128 *movers* the nine orders of angels who move the nine spheres; they are the true causes, the heavens are the means by which they achieve their effects (line 129). The doctrine of angels derives from the Bible, combined with the Aristotelian concept of intelligent, immaterial creatures who, in the chain of being, occupy the position between rational humans and God. From the neo-Platonists of the third century AD, the Christian (and Arab) Aristotelian tradition inherited the doctrine that their specific function and purpose was to move the heavenly spheres on God's behalf (*Par.* XXVIII, 46–78).

131 *sphere* the stars, which receive and transmit the power of the One God, Who is Mind.

133 *dust* the human body, in which the soul carries out its different operations through the various organs of life, the senses, and perception. Similarly, the One God differentiates His creative power through heavens whose substance is joined to intelligences (angels) – as a body is to a soul – in differing degrees, each shining according to the angels' joy in their vision of God (lines 139–44). This, not rarity and density, is the cause of the moonspots (lines 145–8). Beatrice's theological explanation of a cosmological phenomenon establishes fundamental points for the whole of the *Paradiso*: the Oneness

of God as the source of multiplicity in His creation; the heavens and their angel-movers as His intermediaries in the ordered process of differentiation, change, and generation in nature; and the physical, metaphysical, and theological function of light, through which God's creative power is distributed down through the heavens to the earth, and which Dante explores, in increasingly intense and supernatural degrees, in his ascent from the earth back through the heavens to its Source.

PARADISO CANTO III

THE MOON: Souls who in life were forced to abandon vows made to God.

1 *That sun* Beatrice who, when alive, had been the origin of all Dante's experiences and poetry of Love.

6 *confessional* the declaration (lines 4–5).

17 *mistake* Dante's belief that the souls are behind him and that the faces are reflections. Narcissus made the opposite mistake when he took his own reflection in the pool as a beautiful reality and fell in love with it [Ovid] (lines 17–18).

44 *just will* a desire which conforms with the divine Love to which and in which the souls of all the blessed are united (lines 79–84).

49 *Piccarda* a Florentine, the sister both of Dante's friend, Forese Donati, and of his political opponent, Corso Donati (*Purg.* XXIV, 10–16, 83–7). At some time (apparently) between 1283–93, Corso had her abducted from the convent, where she had taken vows as a nun, and forced her to marry one of his political friends (lines 103–8).

52 *the flame* Love, the principal attribute of the Holy Spirit, one of the three Persons of God.

85 *peace* the perfect contentment of all desires in loving God. God is the goal of everything He continues to create, both directly (the human soul) or indirectly (by natural processes transmitted through the heavens) (*Par.* I, 112–20).

89 *grace* God's illumination and love, distributed to all the souls in Heaven according to the merits and capacity of each.

95 *web* the vow which she did not fulfil (lines 55–7).

98 *a woman* St Clare (1194–1253), who in 1212, with the assistance of St Francis of Assisi, founded an order of Franciscan nuns (the Poor Clares). As brides of Christ, the nuns took strict vows, including that of perpetual chastity (lines 101–2).

117 *the veil* her inner faithfulness to her religious vows (*Par.* IV, 98).

118 *Costanza* the Empress Constance (1152–98), queen of Sicily, wife of the Emperor Henry VI (died 1197) and mother of Frederick II (*Inf.* X, 119) (respectively, the second and third Emperors of the powerful Hohenstaufen dynasty, dukes of Swabia) (lines 119–20). It was rumoured that she was forcibly removed from a convent so that she could be married off to Henry.

121–2 *"Ave Maria"* 'Hail, Mary', the first words of a prayer to the mother of Christ, based on the angel's greeting to her: 'Hail, full of grace, the Lord is with you; blessed are you among women' [Luke].

PARADISO CANTO IV

THE MOON (continued).

2 *equally removed* equidistant and equally desirable. With no basis on which to distinguish between them, the man would be unable to choose either, any more than the lamb could decide from which wolf to flee, or the dog which deer to attack (lines 4–6). Dante, torn between two equal problems to which he wants the answers, is forced to silence (lines 8–9, 16–18). (The dilemma formed part of discussions on whether the human will is truly free; the most famous example, attributed to the fourteenth-century philosopher, Jean Buridan, is that of a hungry ass which would starve to death between two haystacks.)

13 *Daniel* the prophet who in a heaven-sent vision was given the power to see and interpret the secret dream of king Nebuchadnezzar, so calming his rage against dream-diviners [Daniel]. Beatrice sees Dante's two unspoken problems in God's Mind.

19 *will to good* constancy in virtue; in the case in point, remaining faithful to their vows in their hearts (*Par.* III, 117). Dante's first problem is why these souls, though inwardly constant, are in the lowest heaven as a result of external violence, over which they had no control.

23 *Plato* the Greek philosopher (*Inf.* IV, 134). His dialogue, the *Timaeus*, contains the proposition that each human soul has its own planet or star to which it returns between its different reincarnations until finally, having lived a perfect life on earth, it returns to live there happily for ever (lines 52–4). Dante's second problem is that the presence of souls in the Moon apparently proves a doctrine of the soul and of heaven which is fundamentally opposed to Christian beliefs (lines 26–7).

28 *the Seraph* the highest angel in the highest order of angels, the Seraphim, who are closest to God (*Par.* XXVIII, 99). The souls whom Dante has seen in the Moon live eternally in the same Heaven (the Empyrean) as the angels, the greatest Jewish prophets, and the greatest Christian saints (including both St Johns, the Baptist and the Evangelist). They are in the Moon now only for the benefit of the living Dante, so that his human senses can perceive that theirs is the lowest degree of bliss. Each soul in Paradise is perfectly happy, according to its individual capacity to receive and enjoy the vision of God.

40 *signs* images which can be perceived by the senses, which – according to the fundamental principle of Aristotelian epistemology – are the only means by which humans can know the external world: 'There is nothing in the intellect which was not formerly in the senses.' Hence, the Bible presents God's powers in human terms, as if He had limbs, and angels are portrayed in human form (lines 43–8).

46 *Gabriel* the angel of the Annunciation to the Virgin Mary [Luke].

Michael the angel who defeated Lucifer (*Inf.* VII, 11).

the angel Raphael whom God sent to cure Tobit (Tobias) of blindness [Tobit].

49 *Timaeus* the chief speaker in the *Timaeus* (lines 23–4). Plato's doctrine, which he presents as literally true, is not the reason why Dante has seen souls in the Moon; interpreted symbolically, it may contain some truth, in that the heavens do exercise some influence on humans' natural inclinations towards certain virtues or sins (*Purg.* XVI, 73), and may therefore deserve praise or blame accordingly. Even this truth, however, was misinterpreted by pagans in ancient times and led them to worship the planets as gods (lines 58–63; *Par.* VIII, 1–12).

64 *other doubt* the problem of violence and vows (lines 19–21). The solution reveals the mystery of God's justice which to mere humans might seem unjust but is, in fact, a doctrine of true faith which should dispel Dante's doubts (lines 67–9, 88–90).

73 *violence* external violence to which the victim, though unwilling, nevertheless submits. Merit is diminished because the human will has the absolute power to resist force, however great; indeed, this is its very nature, as it is fire's nature to rise upwards (lines 76–8; *Par.* I, 115).

81 *holy shelter* the convent (lines 85–6).

83 *Lawrence* the Christian saint who was martyred by being roasted over a fire on a gridiron (AD 258).

84 *Mucius* Mucius Scaevola, a hero of ancient Rome who, when sentenced to be burnt, thrust his right hand in a fire and held it there.

98 *love of the veil* her inner will to keep her vows (*Par.* III, 117). If Constance had the steadfastness just described, the problem of her lower degree of blessedness remains (lines 19–21).

102 *Alcmaeon* who obeyed his father by killing his mother

[Ovid] (*Purg.* XII, 50–51). His action, which he saw as a filial duty but which was really a terrible crime, exemplifies the difference between the absolute will, which can always refuse to yield to external force, and the relative will which, in the circumstances of a given case, chooses what is perceived to be the lesser of two evils (lines 109–14).

115 *stream* Beatrice's knowledge, whose source is God, infinite Truth. The human mind naturally desires contentment in this perfect Truth, towards which it progresses by the process of resolving doubts and questions (lines 126–32).

137 *other acts* other vows which God will accept as equal to the first (*Par.* V, 13–15).

PARADISO CANTO V

THE MOON (continued); MERCURY.

5 *vision* of God, the Truth Who, when known by the mind, is seen also as Good and draws the will to love Him (lines 5–9). All objects of love reflect His Goodness in some way (lines 10–12).

23 *beings* angels and human beings. Hence a vow is the gift of a person's most precious treasure, free will, to God; thereafter, it belongs to Him (lines 25–33).

38 *the food* of knowledge.

44 *the matter* the thing which is promised to God; this may be varied (lines 52–4).

45 *compact* the actual promise to God; this must be kept. God required all the Jews to make offerings and sacrifices to Him, but the priests were authorized to assess and change the thing offered in individual cases [Leviticus] (lines 49–51).

55 *burden* the vow.

57 *keys* the spiritual and juridical powers of the Pope and prelates of the Church (*Purg.* IX, 117–29). The material of a vow can never be changed except with the permission of the Church authorities; the content of the new vow must be

greater than that of the first; and if there is nothing greater, the first vow cannot be commuted (lines 58–63).

66 *Jephthah* the Israelite judge who made a vow to God that, if he won a coming battle, he would sacrifice the first of his possessions to meet him on his return, and then kept his vow by sacrificing his only daughter [Judges].

69 *Greeks' chief* king Agamemnon who sacrificed his daughter, Iphigenia, in order to keep his vow to sacrifice his fairest possession to the goddess Diana (*Inf.* XX, 106–12).

75 *all immersions* any easy way of cancelling vows or other obligations to God.

77 *shepherd* the Pope.

81 *deride* mock Christians for their greed and folly: 'the Jews, Saracens, and unbelieving nations laugh at our sabbaths, and [...] cry out "Where is their God?"' [*Epistles*] (line 81).

93 *second realm* the heaven of Mercury.

105 *one* Dante, whose questions increase the souls' joy in answering them (lines 131–2).

111 *did not go on* leaving the reader in suspense.

128 *sphere* Mercury, which often cannot be seen because of the sun's light.

PARADISO CANTO VI

MERCURY: Souls who in life were motivated by the desire for fame.

1 *the Eagle* the sign of the Roman Empire (*Par.* XIX, 16–18, 101–2; XX, 8–9). Its founder, Aeneas, came from the East ('Troy) to the West (Italy), where his marriage to Lavinia joined together the Trojan and Latin races from which the Romans were descended (lines 2–3; *Inf.* II, 13–27; IV, 122, 126). In AD 330, the Emperor Constantine moved its capital back from the West (Rome) to the East (lines 1–2) – to Byzantium (Constantinople, now Istanbul), on the edge of Europe and not far from Troy itself; there, some two centuries later, Justinian succeeded to the Empire (lines 4–9).

10 *Justinian* the Eastern Emperor (527–65), who commissioned a complete reform of Roman Law; the *Corpus of Civil Law*, which was issued under his name, was the basis of law in Italy and much of Europe throughout the Middle Ages (*Purg.* VI, 88–9). This reform is presented here as a mighty enterprise inspired by the love of God (lines 11–12, 22–4). For Dante, the Emperor's principal, God-given duty was to administer justice [*Monarchia*].

15 *that faith* the monophysite heresy which held that Christ had only one nature, of God and not of man.

16 *Agapetus* the Pope (535–6) who converted Justinian from heresy to true Christian belief [*The Book of the Popes*].

25 *Belisarius* (*c.* 505–65), Justinian's general who won many victories for him, including the reconquest of Italy from the Goths.

28 *question* on the soul's identity (*Par.* V, 127).

32 *sacred standard* the eagle, the true ideal of the Empire, misused by the Ghibellines (the imperial party) and opposed by the Guelphs. In his younger days, Dante, a Guelph, had held that the Romans had created their Empire by violence alone. During his exile, he came to believe that it was necessary for the world to have an Emperor as the supreme temporal authority and minister of universal justice; and he developed an idealizing and theological interpretation of Roman history: the Romans won their Empire (their legitimate right to world-jurisdiction) because God was working through them to prepare the world for the birth of Christ during the reign of Augustus and for His death during that of Tiberius [*Convivio*; *Monarchia*]. Justinian's history of the Roman eagle both confirms Dante's doctrine that the Emperor's authority comes directly from God (and not from the Pope), and is an attack on the two warring factions of his day for acting against God's will (lines 32–3, 97–111).

36 *Pallas* a brave Trojan prince, slain in battle by king Turnus; in revenge, Aeneas killed Turnus, so winning the right to marry Lavinia, and to found what would become the Roman Empire [Virgil].

38 *Alba* Alba Longa, a town founded by Aeneas' son, which was the capital of the Latin state until its three champions (the Curiatii brothers) were killed by the three Horatii on a bridge across the Tiber, and Rome (founded by Romulus and Remus in 753 BC) became the dominant city in Latium.

41 *the era* from Romulus, the first king of Rome, to the seventh and last, Tarquinius Superbus. The former, needing to populate the city, invited the neighbouring Sabine people to a festival, during which the Romans abducted their women. The latter was expelled in 510 BC after his son had raped Lucretia; as a result, Rome became a Republic (*Inf.* IV, 127–8).

43 *what it did* the extraordinary, noble, and self-sacrificing actions of the heroes of the Roman Republic which prove that its acquisition of its world-Empire was willed and assisted by God.

44 *Brennus* the leader of the Gauls who captured Rome (390 BC) but were driven away by Camillus who then, in obedience to the Senate, returned into exile [*Convivio*; *Monarchia*].

45 *Pyrrhus* the king of Epirus whose invasions of Italy were repelled by the Romans (275 BC) (*Inf.* XII, 135).

principates and cities kingdoms and republics.

46 *Torquatus* the consul and general who defeated the Gauls and the Latins, and who sentenced his own son to death 'out of his love for the public good' (fourth century BC) [*Convivio*].

Quinctius known as Cincinnatus ('curly'), who left his farm to defeat the Aequians and then returned to his plough and a simple, frugal life (fifth century BC) [*Convivio*; *Monarchia*].

47 *Decii* a father, son, and grandson who died fighting for Rome against her enemies (fourth–third centuries BC): 'sacred victims [...] who devotedly laid down their lives for the public good' [*Monarchia*; *Convivio*].

48 *Fabii* a leading Roman family which provided a line of heroes, consuls, and generals, of whom the most famous earned the title 'Cunctator', the 'Delayer', because of the tactics he employed against Hannibal.

49 *Arabs* the Carthaginians, from north Africa (occupied by the Arabs in Dante's day). Led by Hannibal, they invaded Italy across the Alps (where the river Po has its source) and inflicted major defeats on the Romans until they withdrew back to Africa (203 BC).

52 *Scipio* the general who, while still only in his early thirties, fought for Rome's freedom and finally defeated Hannibal in Africa (202 BC) [*Convivio*; *Monarchia*] (*Inf.* XXXI, 116–17; *Purg.* XXIX, 116; *Par.* XXVII, 61–3).

Pompey (106–48 BC), the Roman general who in his youth had fought against the rebel, Marius, and who later commanded the Republican army against Julius Caesar (line 72).

53 *that hill* Fiesole, situated on a hill overlooking Florence and destroyed by the Romans in the war against the conspirator, Catiline (died 62 BC) (*Inf.* XV, 62).

55 *the time* when God willed that the earth should be brought to a state of temporal happiness and universal peace in preparation for the birth of Christ, His Son.

57 *Caesar* Julius Caesar (100–44 BC) who, for Dante, was the first Emperor (*Inf.* IV, 123). In his hands, the eagle won its world-Empire.

58–60 *Var ... Rhone* rivers of Gaul, which he conquered (58–49 BC).

62 *Rubicon* the river, south of Ravenna, across which he invaded the territory of the Republic (49 BC) (*Inf.* XXVIII, 95–102).

64 *Spain* where he defeated supporters of Pompey at Léri[da] (*Purg.* XVIII, 100–102).

65 *Durazzo* now Durrës, in Albania, where he landed in pursuit of Pompey.

Pharsalia in north-eastern Greece, where he defeated P[om]pey at the battle of Pharsalus (48 BC), after which Pompey t[ook] refuge in Egypt where he was killed (line 66).

67 *its source* Troy where the Roman eagle had origin[ated] (lines 2–3) and where Caesar landed in order to visit the [site] of the city [Lucan]. The region of Troy (in modern Turk[ey]

identified by Antandros, the port from which Aeneas set sail; the river Simois; and the tomb of the Trojan hero, Hector [Virgil].

69 *Ptolemy* king of Egypt (51–47 BC), who had Pompey murdered (line 66; *Inf.* XXXIII, 124); he was deposed in favour of his sister, Cleopatra, and defeated by Julius Caesar (48–47 BC).

70 *Juba* king of Numidia, an ally of Pompey and the Republicans in north Africa; after their defeat by Julius Caesar (46 BC), he committed suicide.

71 *the west of you* Spain, where Caesar defeated Pompey's sons (45 BC).

73 *him* Octavian (Augustus), Julius Caesar's great-nephew and adopted son and heir, the second Roman Emperor (27 BC–AD 14).

74 *Brutus and Cassius* Julius Caesar's assassins, defeated by Mark Antony and Octavian at the battle of Philippi (north-eastern Greece) (42 BC); Brutus committed suicide, Cassius was killed. In Dante's eyes, both were traitors to their benefactor and to the divinely founded Empire and are now in Hell (*Inf.* XXXIV, 64–7).

75 *Modena* in northern Italy where Octavian defeated his rival, Mark Antony (43 BC).

Perugia in central Italy where Octavian defeated Mark Antony's brother (40 BC).

76 *Cleopatra* queen of Egypt, mistress of Julius Caesar and later of Mark Antony. After the latter's defeat by Octavian at the battle of Actium (31 BC), she committed suicide, poisoned by the venom of an asp. She is now in Hell (*Inf.* V, 63).

80 *Red Sea shore* Octavian's conquest of Egypt (30 BC).

81 *Janus' shrine* the temple of the god Janus in the Roman forum; its doors were left open during times of war and closed in times of peace. In 27 BC Octavian, newly titled Augustus, closed them as a sign that the Empire was at peace. For Dante, this marked the climax of God's plan to bring the whole world to its most perfect condition of earthly peace, happiness, and

justice in preparation for the birth of Christ, Who was enrolled in human society (*Inf.* I, 71) at the time of Augustus' census of the Empire [Luke; *Convivio*; *Monarchia*].

87 *third Caesar* Tiberius, the third Roman Emperor (AD 14–37). Because he possessed universal jurisdiction (represented in Palestine by his governor, Pontius Pilate), Christ's death, which satisfied God's Justice, redeemed the entire human race from Adam's sin [*Monarchia*].

92 *Titus* the Roman general, and later Emperor, who captured Jerusalem (AD 70) (*Purg.* XXI, 82–4). The paradox of line 93 is explained in *Par.* VII, 19–51.

95 *Charlemagne* king of the Franks (776–814), who invaded Italy in 771 in support of the Church against the Lombards, and whose coronation as Emperor in Rome in 800 marked the revival of the Roman Empire in the West.

97 *those* the Ghibellines and the Guelphs (lines 32–3). The former have appropriated the eagle for their own faction, so divorcing the Empire from its true purpose: justice (lines 101–5). The latter have fought against it under the banner of the golden fleur-de-lys (the French kings of Sicily and Naples) (lines 100-101, 106–11).

106 *Charles* Charles II of Anjou, king of Naples 1285–1309. The eagle has defeated more powerful enemies than him (lines 107–8).

112 *planet* Mercury. Justinian answers Dante's second question (*Par.* V, 127–9).

128 *Romeo* Romieu de Villeneuve (*c.* 1170–1250), a pilgrim (it was believed) who entered the service of Raymond Berenger, count of Provence, and became his chief minister, arranging royal marriages for all his daughters. He exemplifies the faithful steward who returned more than he received in his service of his lord (line 138) but who – like Dante himself – was unjustly driven away into a life of exile and poverty.

MERCURY (continued).

1–3 *"Hosanna, . . ."* 'Hosanna, holy God of hosts, Who with Your brightness pour down Your light upon the happy flames of these kingdoms'. The Latin hymn, with its three Hebrew words – 'Hosanna' (an exclamation of praise), 'sabaoth' ('armies'), and 'ma[m]lacoth' ('kingdoms') – is Dante's invention, based on the *Sanctus* of the Christian Mass: 'Holy, holy, holy Lord God of hosts [. . .] Hosanna in the highest' (*Purg.* XXIX, 51).

5 *that substance* Justinian, whose doubled light perhaps refers to his additional glory, in Heaven, as a great Emperor and legislator.

12 *thirst* for knowledge.

14 *'Be' and 'ice'* the first and last syllables of her name. Dante extended the Florentine name, Bice, into its full form, Beatrice, 'the lady who bestows bliss' [*Vita nuova*].

18 *fire* the most intense pain.

21 *vengeance* the punishment of Adam's sin by Christ's death, an act of God's Justice.

punishment of the Jews by the destruction of Jerusalem, also an act of God's Justice (*Par.* VI, 90, 93).

26 *the man* Adam, who was created directly by God. By eating the fruit of the forbidden tree, he rejected the limit set by God upon his human powers; this was the original sin which separated him, his descendants, and human nature as such from God (*Par.* XXVI, 115–17).

30 *Word of God* God the Son, the second Person of the Trinity, Who joined human nature in its original sinlessness to His divinity (lines 31–6). The crucifixion of Christ as man was an act of divine Justice, for the punishment of fallen human nature; His crucifixion as God was a supreme act of injustice, and the earth quaked [Matthew] (lines 40–48).

57 *this pathway* the Incarnation and death of Christ, both God and man, one of the greatest mysteries of the Christian

Faith. It is explained as follows: God is infinite Goodness and Love; everything created directly by Him is, like Him, eternal and is most perfect when it most resembles Him (lines 64–76). Having lost this perfection, human nature could not be restored to it unless the defect caused by sin was remedied in one of two ways: either by a free pardon from God, or by humans themselves making amends (lines 76–93). The human race, however, could never make full satisfaction for its offence against the Deity (lines 97–102). This only God Himself could do, and, since a true act of amendment must be an expression of sincere love by the offender, He chose both ways: by becoming man, He freely made humanity capable of making satisfaction to Him (lines 103–20): 'Christ, ... being in the form of God, ... humbled Himself, becoming obedient unto death, even the death of the cross' [Philippians].

124–5 *water ... fire and air and earth* the four elements of which all material things on earth are composed. Since God created them, they too should be eternal, not transient (lines 67–9, 127–9).

130 *pure country* the heavens. The eternal things created by God in the beginning were the angels, the heavenly spheres, and prime (undifferentiated) matter (lines 130–32, 136; *Par.* XXIX, 22–37). Everything made of the elements and the souls of animals and plants are created indirectly, by the power He gave to the heavens to influence prime matter, generating its many forms on earth (lines 133–41); hence these change and pass away. God creates each human soul directly so that it may love and return to Him, and it is therefore eternal; and, since He created the bodies of Adam and Eve directly, the body too will rise again on the Last Day to live for ever (lines 142–8).

PARADISO CANTO VIII

VENUS: Souls influenced by love.

1 *peril* the age of false, pagan religion, when the planets

were thought to have such a determining influence on human life that they were worshipped as gods. For Dante, the stars affect only a person's natural disposition, which can always be controlled by the will assisted by God's grace (*Purg.* XVI, 67–81), and it is these which determine whether Venus' influence leads to a sinful or a virtuous love (*Purg.* I, 19–20; *Par.* IX, 31–2, 95–6).

2 *goddess* Venus, the goddess of passionate and often adulterous love in classical times, who was born from the sea and landed on the island of Cyprus.

3 *epicycle* the smaller sphere on which, in Ptolemaic astronomy, a planet revolves and is carried along the circumference of its main sphere.

6 *Diöne* a sea-goddess, Venus' mother.

7 *Cupid* Venus' son, the boy-god of love (*Purg.* XXVIII, 65–6). Disguised as Aeneas' son, he went to queen Dido and, as she hugged and embraced him in her lap, made her fall passionately in love with Aeneas [Virgil] (*Inf.* V, 61–2).

11 *planet* Venus, the morning-star just before sunrise, the evening-star after sunset.

18 *the note* the fixed line of the chant (the *cantus firmus*) which, in early polyphonic music, the other voice embellished with more freely moving melodies. Within the light of the planet, the lights in which the souls are cocooned (lines 52–4) stand out distinctly.

22 *Winds* lightning (an ignited vapour, which is visible) or whirlwinds.

27 *the heaven* the Empyrean, from which the souls come down to the different heavens to meet Dante (*Par.* IV, 28–39).

28 *"Hosanna"* see *Par.* VII, 1.

36 *Princes* the Principalities (*Par.* XXVIII, 125), the order of angels who, while contemplating God eternally in Heaven, move the sphere of Venus on His behalf.

37–8 *"You who ... heaven"* the first line of a poem addressed to the angels of Venus, written by Dante in the 1290s, when his soul was divided between his love for Beatrice in Heaven and his love for the 'noble lady' who had taken pity on him [*Vita nuova*; *Convivio*].

47 *spirit* Charles Martel (1271–95), the eldest son of Charles II, king of Naples, and Mary of Hungary. In 1292, he was crowned king of Hungary (lines 64–6); in 1294, he visited Florence where Dante must have met him and seen him as a future king of exceptional promise (lines 55–7); but he died too young to succeed to his father's dominions (Provence and Naples) (lines 49–51, 58–63). Here he illustrates the theme of love applied to society, to ideal kingship and the integration of human nature into the social order, contrasted with the examples of misrule by his grandfather (lines 72–5) and brother (lines 75–84).

58 *left bank* the County of Provence, east of the river Rhône, south of its confluence with the Sorgue.

61 *Ausonia's horn* . . . the kingdom of Naples, southern Italy, defined by its borders: two rivers to the north; and three ports in, respectively, Calabria, Puglia, and southern Lazio.

65 *that land* Hungary.

67 *Trinacria* Sicily, the triangular island, identified by the volcanic ash which falls from mount Etna along its eastern coast. The myth that the eruptions were caused by Typhoeus, a giant imprisoned beneath Etna [Ovid], is dismissed in favour of a natural explanation (lines 67–8). Pachynus and Pelorus are the ancient names for the island's south-eastern and north-eastern promontories; Eurus is the south-east wind which is prevalent along that coast (lines 69–70).

72 *Charles and Rudolph* respectively, Charles Martel's father (Charles II) and his wife's father, the Emperor Rudolph (*Purg.* VII, 94). Their children and descendants would have succeeded also to the kingdom of Sicily, if misgovernment had not provoked the rebellion of 1282 (the Sicilian Vespers), when the people of Palermo, crying 'Death to the French!', launched a massacre of the occupying troops which led to the expulsion of the French from the island and its annexation by the Aragonese.

75 *brother* Robert of Anjou, king of Naples 1309–43. The prophetic warning concerns his over-reliance on greedy Catalan advisers and protégés, the extortion and oppression which his people will have to bear, and his personal meanness (lines 77–84).

86 *where* in God (line 90).

93 *harsh fruit* king Robert's meanness, despite his ancestors' generosity (lines 82–3). Dante wants to know why virtues are not inherited (*Purg.* VII, 121–3).

96 *confront* see plainly what is now hidden (line 136).

98 *providence* God's purposeful design, transmitted through the heavenly spheres to His creatures on the earth below, directing each towards its own natural goal (lines 98–105). Without this, the world would be entirely disordered, and thus the angels who move the spheres and their Creator, God Himself, would have produced a deliberately flawed universe (which is an impossibility) (lines 106–11). Nature, so organized by God, must therefore always achieve its goals: 'God and nature are never defective in what is necessary' [*Monarchia*] (lines 113–14).

116 *citizen* a member of organized human society, which, for Dante, consisted of units of increasing size: the family, the neighbourhood, the city, the kingdom, and the universal Empire [*Convivio*; *Monarchia*].

120 *your master* Aristotle, who stated that human beings are by nature social animals, and social organization requires different people to perform different tasks [Aristotle; *Convivio*]. Hence nature must predispose people from birth towards specific roles in society (lines 122–3).

124 *Solon* a lawyer and political leader; from the Athenian legislator (sixth century BC).

Xerxes a king and soldier; from the Persian king (fifth century BC) (*Purg.* XXVIII, 71–2).

125 *Melchizedek* a priest [Genesis].

126 *he* a craftsman and inventor, another Daedalus (*Inf.* XVII, 109–11; XXIX, 116).

127 *Revolving nature* the heavenly spheres, through which nature predisposes humans as individuals, not as members of a particular family (line 129). Hence, twins can differ, and so can fathers and sons (lines 130–32). Without this providential variation, children would always have the same natures as their fathers (lines 133–5).

130 *Esau* Isaac's elder son, who even in the womb had an entirely different nature and destiny from his twin brother, Jacob [Genesis] (*Par.* XXXII, 68–9).

132 *Quirinus* Romulus, the founder of Rome, the heroic son of a father so obscure and low-born that the Romans claimed his real father must have been a god, Mars.

139 *discrepant fortune* external circumstances which distort the natural order, the basis of a good social order (lines 142–4). Society is disordered when the link between a man's nature and his social role is broken, such as when a natural soldier is forced to become a priest, a natural priest to become a king (lines 145–8).

PARADISO CANTO IX

VENUS (continued).

1 *Clemence* either Charles Martel's widow, who died not long after her husband in 1295; or his daughter of the same name, the wife of Louis X (king of France 1314–16).

2 *seed* Charles Martel's son, Charles Robert (king of Hungary 1308–42), who was allegedly defrauded of the throne of Naples by his uncle, king Robert.

5 *vengeance* God's punishment of king Robert for his crimes against Clemence's family.

8 *Sun* God, infinite Goodness.

21 *reflect* see mirrored in God's mind.

25 *that part* the March of Treviso, in north-east Italy, between Venice (identified by its principal island) and the Alps where the rivers Brenta and Piave have their sources.

28 *a hill* Romano, the site of the castle from which the family took its name.

29 *firebrand* the tyrant Ezzelino III da Romano (1194–1259) (*Inf.* XII, 109).

32 *Cunizza* da Romano (*c.* 1189–*c.* 1279), Ezzelino's sister (line 31). In the 1220s, she left her husband and eloped with the troubadour, Sordello (*Purg.* VI, 61); after another love-affair and two more marriages, she moved to Florence where the young Dante probably knew her as a woman with a scandalous past who turned to God in her old age and died a holy death. Here he presents her as someone who, under the influence of Venus, turned her natural disposition to love from sexual love to love of God.

35 *the reason* excessive dominance by love, which has earned her one of the lower degrees of blessedness.

37 *jewel* another soul whose fame will last more than five centuries from the present centenary year (1300). The lesson is that those who achieve great deeds in life earn fame which lives on after them (lines 38–42).

43 *rabble* the inhabitants of the March of Treviso, bordered by the two rivers. Cunizza prophesies their punishment in a series of events which would occur after 1300: the bloody defeat of the Paduan Guelphs at the river Bacchiglione near Vicenza (1314) (lines 47–8); the assassination of the Ghibelline lord of Treviso (identified by its two rivers) (1312) (lines 49–51); and the treachery of the pro-Guelph bishop of Feltre who handed over some refugees from Ferrara for execution (1314) (lines 52–60).

61 *mirrors* angels who reflect God's Justice (*Par.* XXVIII, 103–5).

67 *other joy* the other soul (line 37).

71 *smiles* the outer sign of inner joy: 'And what is a smile but a coruscation of the delight of the soul, that is, a light which appears outside, expressing what is within?' [*Convivio*]. On earth, however, there are also sad expressions which reveal inner grief (lines 71–2).

77 *pious fires* the highest angels, the Seraphim, who enfold themselves in their six wings [Isaiah].

81 *enter you* see the soul's thoughts, as he can see Dante's, reflected in God's knowledge of everything (lines 73–5). In Italian, pushing the language beyond its normal structure in his attempt to express the inexpressible, Dante conveys this supernatural process in words invented around pronouns: 'en-Him' (line 74), 'en-you', and 'en-me' (line 81).

82 *valley* the Mediterranean, the largest sea filled by Oceanus, which encircles the inhabited world (*Inf.* XXVI, 107). It was thought to extend for 90°, dividing Europe from Africa (line 84); thus, the celestial meridian over its eastern shore (where Jerusalem is) has its horizon at the westernmost end (the Straits of Gibraltar) (lines 85–7).

88 *along the shoreline* at Marseilles, which was believed to be situated halfway between the rivers Ebro (in Spain) and Magra (the border between Liguria and Tuscany), and on the same meridian as Bougie (Bejaia, in modern Algeria) (lines 91–2).

93 *blood* shed in the slaughter which accompanied the Romans' capture of Marseilles in 49 BC.

95 *Folco* or Folchetto (Folquet) of Marseilles (died 1231), a celebrated troubadour who abandoned the life of a courtier and love poet to become a monk and eventually bishop of Toulouse. He is in Venus because in life its influence had disposed him to love – indeed, in his youth, to the fire of earthly love at its most passionate (lines 97–102).

97 *Belus' daughter* Dido who, by falling in love with Aeneas, betrayed both her husband's memory and Aeneas' wife (*Inf.* V, 61–2; *Par.* VIII, 8–9).

100 *Rhodopean woman* Phyllis, who killed herself when she thought her lover Demophoön had broken his promise to marry her [Ovid].

101 *Alcides* Hercules, whose passion for Iole made his wife jealous and unwittingly caused his own death [Ovid] (*Inf.* XII, 67–9).

104 *fault* the sin of lust, whose memory has been washed

away in the Lethe (*Purg.* XXVIII, 127–8).

105 *Power* God's loving providence which works through the heavens to achieve good on earth (line 108). Like Cunizza, Folco illustrates how Venus' power transforms earthly love into love of God.

115 *Rahab* the prostitute who, by protecting Joshua's spies, helped him to capture Jericho and so conquer the Promised Land [Joshua] (lines 124–5). An ancestress of Christ, she was saved because of her role in God's plan for the Redemption [Matthew; Hebrews; James].

118 *heaven* Venus, the last planet which the earth's conical shadow can reach.

120 *taken up* from Limbo (*Inf.* IV, 52–61; XII, 38–9).

123 *palm on palm* with both hands, nailed to the cross.

125 *Holy Land* Palestine, Christ's homeland. Folco, who, as bishop of Toulouse, had played a leading role in the crusade launched in 1208 against the heretics of southern France, here condemns Pope Boniface VIII for neglecting his spiritual duty to proclaim a crusade to reconquer the Holy Land from the Saracens.

127 *Your city* Florence, founded by the Devil (lines 128–9).

130 *flower* the Florentine florin, stamped with a lily, which has corrupted the Pope and the Church with greed.

134 *Decretals* the books of Canon Law, the collections of laws and papal decrees by which the Church was governed and administered. In 1314, Dante accused the Italian Cardinals of neglecting the great Doctors of the Church and reading only the Decretals, which deal with revenues and benefices [*Epistles*] (*Par.* XII, 82–3, 91–3).

135 *margins* well thumbed and heavily annotated.

137 *Nazareth* the village in Palestine where the angel Gabriel announced to Mary that she would be Christ's mother [Luke]; one of the holiest Christian places to be won back by a crusade.

139 *Vatican* the hill in Rome where St Peter, the first Pope, was martyred and buried.

141 *soldiery* the early Christian martyrs, buried in Rome's churches and catacombs.

142 *adultery* the prostitution of the Church by the greed for money (*Inf.* XIX, 3–4, 106–12). Folco is prophesying the punishment of the Popes and the reform of Rome.

PARADISO CANTO X

THE SUN: Souls of the wise.

3 *Power* God the Father, Who contemplates His own infinite Idea (God the Son) in the Love that proceeds from both (God the Holy Spirit) (lines 50–51), so bringing the rest of creation into being in all its perfect order through the angels and the heavenly spheres. The theological definition of the ultimately incomprehensible mystery of the Trinity opens the episode of the heaven of the wise men and theologians.

8 *that part* the intersection between the celestial equator (the median line of the heavens' daily rotation from east to west) and the ecliptic (the path of the planets' annual rotation through the signs of the zodiac from west to east) (lines 13–15). Upon the angle of inclination between them (just over 23°) depends the entire universal order by which the heavens govern the cycle of nature on earth (lines 16–21).

28 *greatest minister* the sun, at the equinoctial point in Aries; it is spring (lines 31–3).

42 *splendor* by being brighter than the sun itself; hence, in human terms, it is an unimaginable miracle that Dante can look at them (lines 43–8).

49 *fourth family* the souls in the sun, content in their vision and love of the Trinity, the heavenly Sun Who has allowed Dante to ascend to His image, the real sun (lines 50–54).

67 *Latona's daughter* the moon (*Purg.* XXIX, 78).

74 *take wings* strive to go to Heaven and hear the music Dante heard, which no one could describe in words (line 75).

81 *new notes* the resumption of the singing. The simile refers

to the choreographed ballads of Dante's time.

88 *thirst* for knowledge. Because Dante has God's grace to ascend through the heavens (lines 83–7), to answer his questions is as natural for the souls as it is for water to flow downwards (line 90).

91 *plants* the souls forming the circle around Beatrice and Dante (line 102).

94 *flock* the Dominican order. Line 96 is explained in *Par.* XI, 124–39.

99 *Albert* a Dominican friar (1193–1280; later canonized), who taught at Cologne; one of the greatest scholars and thinkers of his time, he wrote important works of theology, commentaries on the Scriptures and Aristotle, and treatises on other religious and scientific subjects.

Thomas also a Dominican friar, born in Aquino (Campania) (1226–74; canonized in 1323), the pupil of Albert, a lecturer in Cologne, Paris, and elsewhere, and the greatest theologian, philosopher, and commentator on Aristotle of the thirteenth century. He was the major formative influence on the intellectual environment in which Dante lived and, to a large extent, on the poet's own theology, philosophy, and methods of argument in the *Comedy*.

103 *Gratian* an Italian monk who, in about 1139–50, compiled the *Decretum*, a collection of ecclesiastical laws and decrees which became the basis of Canon Law in the Middle Ages (*Par.* IX, 134). The two courts are the Church's spiritual jurisdiction in matters of conscience (the internal forum) and its official adjudications and sentences (the public forum); or perhaps ecclesiastical and civil law.

107 *Peter* Peter Lombard (died 1160), a major theologian, author of the *Sentences*, which, in the prologue, he humbly calls a poor contribution to God's treasury, like the small coin given to God by the widow [Luke].

109 *fifth light* Solomon, the king of Israel and author of the wisdom books of the Bible: Proverbs, Ecclesiastes, Song of Songs (interpreted as a song of mystical love), and Wisdom.

Theologians debated whether he was saved because of his wisdom or damned for the sins of lust and idolatry he committed in his old age [1(3) Kings]. Line 114 is explained in *Par.* XIII, 88–108.

115 *candle* the shining soul of Dionysius the Areopagite (first century AD), who was converted to Christianity by St Paul [Acts] and was believed to have written *On the celestial hierarchy*, the most authoritative work on angels (*Par.* XXVIII, 130–32).

119 *champion* probably Paulus Orosius (early fifth century AD) whose *Histories against the Pagans*, written for St Augustine, set out to prove that the world had not declined in the centuries since Christianity had been founded.

125 *soul* Boethius (*c.* 480–524), a Roman statesman and philosopher who was accused of treason against Theodoric, the Gothic king of Italy, and imprisoned and executed; he was buried in the church of San Pietro in Ciel d'Oro in Pavia and came to be regarded as a Christian martyr (lines 127–9). *On the Consolation of Philosophy*, which he wrote in prison, was widely known as a fundamental work of Christian philosophy and morality; it was one of the consoling books which Dante read after the death of Beatrice, and a major influence on his portrayal of Philosophy as a beautiful lady [*Convivio*].

131 *Isidore* St Isidore, bishop of Seville (*c.* AD 570–636), theologian and author of the *Etymologies*, an encyclopedia of information about the world, drawn from classical and Christian sources.

Bede the Venerable (*c.* 673–735), an Anglo-Saxon monk at Jarrow, theologian, natural philosopher, and historian of the Christian Church in England.

Richard (died 1173) prior of the monastery of St Victor near Paris, biblical commentator and one of the most important writers on mystical theology, which investigated the process by which the soul, contemplating God, ascends to a state of supernatural ecstasy in His love (line 132).

136 *Siger* from Brabant (died *c.* 1283), teacher in the school

of philosophy, located in the Rue du Fouarre, at Paris University (line 137). His doctrines, strongly influenced by Averroes (*Inf.* IV, 144; *Purg.* XXV, 63–6), were contested by St Thomas himself, among others, and condemned by the bishop of Paris in 1277. Siger appealed to Rome and died while in papal custody, apparently assassinated by a deranged cleric. In presenting him as a victimized seeker of the truth, St Thomas, his opponent in life, is reconciled to him as his companion in Heaven. In Dante's scheme, the tendency of Averroists, such as Siger, to divorce the truths of reason from those of faith is superseded in the higher Wisdom of Heaven, which is above both.

140 *Bride of God* the Church, represented by the monks who rise to sing the early morning office of matins. The simile of the escapement alarm-clock, with its wheels and sound, expresses the precision of the souls' circular movement and inexpressible heavenly song (lines 145–8).

PARADISO CANTO XI

THE SUN (continued).

1 *senseless cares* the foolish earthly preoccupations and false reasoning of humans in their various pursuits in life.

4 *Aphorisms* the medical textbook by Hippocrates, with the commentary of Galen (*Inf.* IV, 143).

25 *two points* those in *Par.* X, 96, 114.

31 *Bride* the Church, founded by Christ when He died on the cross.

35 *two princes* St Francis, from the east (Italy), and St Dominic, from the west (Spain); the former is associated with love (the chief characteristic of the Seraphim, the highest order of angels), the latter with intellectual illumination (the chief function of the next order, the Cherubim) (lines 37–9; *Par.* XXVIII, 98–9).

40 *one* St Francis of Assisi (1182–1226; canonized 1228), the

founder of the Franciscan order of mendicant friars, dedicated to a life of poverty. St Thomas, a Dominican, delivers a fervent eulogy on the life of the founder of the order which was then often considered the rival of his own.

45 *high peak* mount Subasio in Umbria, on whose lower slopes stands the town of Assisi. It rises between the two river-valleys (the second, the Chiascio, flows from the mountain where Ubaldo, a twelfth-century bishop of Gubbio, had lived as a hermit) and faces Perugia in the direction of that city's eastern gate, the Sun Gate, so affecting the temperature there, and has two other towns in less favourable positions on its opposite side (lines 46–8).

50 *a sun* St Francis, rising like the sun in the east (line 51). Assisi (which in its Tuscan form, 'Ascesi', perhaps evokes also the idea of ascent) should therefore be called the true, spiritual East (lines 52–4).

59 *her* Poverty, personified as a lady (lines 74–5), shunned like death itself by everybody else (lines 60–61).

62 *spiritual court* of the bishop of Assisi.

et coram patre 'and in the presence of his father', a legal phrase appropriate to the image of a spiritual wedding with Poverty. In 1207, when his father, a rich merchant (line 89), summoned him before the bishop, St Francis stripped off his clothes as a sign of his dedication to a life of total poverty.

64 *first husband* Christ, the supreme example of Poverty, the lady who was even closer to Him than Mary when He died on the cross (lines 70–72).

69 *Amyclas* a poor fisherman who let Julius Caesar (lines 67–8) into his house, knowing that his poverty made him safe from the ravages and plundering of war [Lucan; *Convivio*].

79 *Bernard* of Quintavalle, St Francis' first follower, who also renounced his wealth in favour of poverty and a life of hardship and penance.

82 *wealth* the spiritual riches of poverty.

83 *Egidius, Sylvester* two other early followers of St Francis and lady Poverty.

87 *cord* of the Franciscan friars.

92 *Innocent* Pope Innocent III, who in 1209 approved the Rule of the new Franciscan order, which was definitively confirmed by Honorius III in 1223 (lines 97–9).

101 *Sultan* the ruler of Egypt and Palestine. In 1219, during the fifth crusade, St Francis with some of his friars went on a mission to try to convert him and his subjects.

106 *crag* mount Verna in the Apennines, where Christ appeared to St Francis and pierced him with the stigmata, His own five wounds, on his hands, feet, and side.

117 *no other bier* only Poverty. As his death approached, St Francis expressed his love of poverty by asking his friars to lay him naked on the bare ground to die.

118 *that man* St Dominic. Having praised St Francis, St Thomas condemns the corruption of his own order, explaining his earlier words (lines 138–9; *Par.* X, 95–6).

120 *bark of Peter* the Church.

123 *worthy merchandise* of virtues and grace.

124 *flock* the Dominicans, most of whom now neglect his Rule in favour of other, worldly pursuits. Good Dominicans are few (lines 130–32), and the order is fragmented (line 137).

PARADISO CANTO XII

THE SUN (continued).

8 *Muses ... Sirens* the most beautiful human poetry and music (*Purg.* XIX, 19; XXIX, 37).

9 *firstlight* a light source, which is brighter than its reflection.

12 *handmaid* Iris, Juno's messenger, who travels down to earth on the rainbow [Virgil].

14 *voice* an echo, which repeats the original voice exactly. Because of her unrequited love for Narcissus, the nymph Echo pined away until all that was left of her was her voice [Ovid] (line 15).

17 *pact* God's promise to Noah, when He put a rainbow in the clouds as a sign that He would never again send a universal Flood to destroy the human race [Genesis].

26 *the eyes* both eyes, which react simultaneously at the sight of something which arouses desire or pleasure; another simile for the precise correspondence between the two circles of souls.

30 *needle* the magnetized needle of the compass.

32 *other leader* St Dominic. The speaker is a Franciscan, St Bonaventure (lines 33, 127–8). Like St Thomas in canto XI, he here delivers a fervent eulogy of the founder of the rival order, followed by an attack upon the corruption of his own.

37 *Christ's army* the Church, Christ's Bride, for which He died (line 42; *Par.* XI, 31–2).

46 *that part* in Spain (from where the west wind blows, bringing spring to the rest of Europe), near the westernmost coast of the northern hemisphere, where the sun sets after the year's longest day (the summer solstice) (lines 49–51).

52 *Calaroga* Calaruega, a village in Castile, the birthplace of St Dominic (1170–1221; canonized 1234). The coat of arms of the kingdom of Castile and León bore a lion and a castle quartered (the lion above in one half, below on the other) (lines 53–4).

60 *prophetic* by causing her to dream that she would give birth to a black and white dog with a torch in its mouth which sets fire to the whole world. The Dominicans (sometimes represented as *Domini canes*, 'the dogs of the Lord') wear white habits and black cloaks.

61 *font* at his baptism. As St Francis was the bridegroom of lady Poverty, St Dominic married the Faith.

64 *lady* St Dominic's godmother who, in a dream, saw the boy with a star on his brow, the sign that he would guide the world to salvation.

68 *spirit* a heavenly inspiration to christen the child with the name which would reveal and epitomize his future life of total dedication to God – 'Dominic' ('belonging to the Lord'). Medieval lives of the saints often noted a remarkable

correspondence between the saint's name and his or her particular brand of virtue and holiness. Similarly, the names of St Dominic's father and mother – Felice ('happy') and Giovanna ('grace of God') – match the reality of their position as parents of the future saint (lines 78–81).

72 *garden* the Church, Christ's vineyard [Matthew] (lines 86–7, 103–5).

75 *first injunction* the precept of poverty and humility, with reference either to the first Beatitude ('Blessed are the poor in spirit') or to Christ's command to a rich young man first to give all his wealth to the poor and then to follow Him [Matthew]. By leaving his bed to lie on the ground, the child showed his dedication, from an early age, to a life of austerity and penance (lines 76–8).

83 *Taddeo* probably Taddeo d'Alderotto (died 1295), a famous doctor and writer of medical treatises.

Ostian Henry of Susa, cardinal-bishop of Ostia near Rome (died 1271), author of a celebrated commentary on the *Decretals* (*Par.* IX, 133–5). St Dominic did not study in order to become a wealthy doctor or canon lawyer but to acquire true, heavenly knowledge (line 84; *Par.* XI, 4–5).

88 *seat* the Papacy.

91 *to offer* to give to the poor only a third or a half of the money collected for them, keeping the rest.

93 *decimas* ... 'the tithes, which belong to God's poor'. St Dominic did not seek a profitable position in the Church but permission to combat heresy and falsehood on behalf of the true Faith (lines 94–6). In 1205 the Pope sent him to preach and try to convert the Albigensian heretics in southern France (lines 97–102, 108–9); the Dominican order (the Order of Preachers) received full papal approval in 1216.

96 *plants* the souls in the two circles.

103 *streams* the members of the Dominican order.

106 *chariot* the leadership of the earthly Church (the Church Militant), to which, in the early thirteenth century, the founders of the two mendicant orders gave new direction and guidance.

110 *other wheel* St Francis, whose order has strayed from his path, become corrupted, and is now walking backwards (lines 112–17).

118 *harvest time* the Day of Judgment, when the weeds (the damned) will be set aside for burning, and the good wheat (the saved) will be gathered into the grainstore [Matthew].

122 *our volume* the Rule of the Franciscan order, to which very few friars are still faithful (line 123). By 1300, the Franciscan order was deeply split between two rival wings: those who had relaxed the Rule and lived in settled communities, sometimes rising to high office in the Church; and the Spirituals, who continued to preach absolute poverty and attacked the wealth and corruption of the Church, for which they were condemned by a series of Popes. Both extremes are condemned here (lines 124–6).

124 *Acquasparta* Cardinal Matteo d'Acquasparta who, as General of the Franciscan Order 1287–1302, effectively supported the relaxation of St Francis' Rule.

Casale Ubertino da Casale (c. 1259 – after 1329), one of the leaders of the excessively strict Spiritual Franciscans.

127 *Bonaventure* (1221–74; later canonized), a leading theologian, General of the Franciscan Order from 1257; he was made a Cardinal just before his death.

129 *left-hand interests* worldly affairs and positions.

130 *Illuminato ... Augustine* two of St Francis' earliest followers and members of his order.

133 *Hugh of St Victor* (c. 1097–1141), abbot of St Victor, near Paris, commentator on the Bible, theologian, and writer on mysticism (*Par.* X, 131–2).

134 *Peter of Spain* (c. 1226–77), author of an important treatise on logic, divided into twelve parts. He became Pope John XXI (1276–7).

135 *Peter Book-Devourer* Petrus Comestor ('Eater', so called because of his voracious appetite for reading), writer of a compendium of biblical and Church history, and chancellor of the University of Paris (died 1179).

136 *Nathan* a Jewish prophet at the time of king David [Kings].

Anselm (died 1109; later canonized), a theologian, archbishop of Canterbury 1093–1109.

Chrysostom St John Chrysostom ('Golden Mouth') (*c.* AD 345–407), one of the greatest theologians of the Greek Church.

137 *Donatus* a Roman scholar (fourth century AD), writer of the standard treatise on Grammar, which was the first of the seven Liberal Arts taught and studied in medieval schools.

139 *Rabanus* (*c.* 776–856), theologian, biblical commentator, and scholar; archbishop of Mainz.

140 *Joachim* (*c.* 1132–1202), a Cistercian abbot who founded a religious community at Fiore in Calabria. His writings envisaged the imminent reform of the Church in a new age just begun, the age of the Spirit, which would last to the end of the world. Throughout the thirteenth century (and for long afterwards), his name was linked with a tradition of apocalyptic prophecies and pseudo-prophecies predicting the punishment of evil rulers, especially Popes, and the restoration of the Church to spiritual purity. Dante too used the technique of encoded prophecy as part of his call for urgent world-reform (*Inf.* I, 100–111; *Purg.* XXXIII, 34–54). Joachimite doctrines, with those of the extremist Spiritual Franciscans, were opposed by St Bonaventure; but here, like St Thomas and Siger, the two are side by side, reconciled in the higher truth of Heaven.

142 *paladin* St Dominic, champion of the Church.

144 *stirred* to show their joy by circling and singing (lines 1–21).

PARADISO CANTO XIII

THE SUN (continued).

4 *fifteen stars* the stars of first magnitude.

7 *Wain* the seven stars of Ursa Major, the constellation which never sets below the horizon of the northern hemisphere.

11 *Horn* Ursa Minor, imagined as shaped like a drinking-horn or horn of plenty, with two bright stars at its 'mouth' and with its point at the Pole Star (Polaris), the axis around which the Primum Mobile and all the heavenly spheres revolve (line 12).

15 *Minos' daughter* Ariadne (*Inf.* XII, 20). On her death her garland (or, in other versions, she herself) was changed by the god Bacchus into the constellation of Corona (the Crown) [Ovid]. Dante's instructions to the reader to imagine twenty-four bright stars rearranged in two concentric circles, revolving in opposite directions, is his imperfect attempt to describe, in visualized human terms, the vastly superior heavenly reality of the double constellation of the twenty-four souls in the Sun (lines 19–24).

23 *the swiftest* the Primum Mobile.

24 *Chiana* a river in Tuscany which then flowed extremely slowly through marshy terrain.

25 *Paean* Apollo. The souls celebrate not pagan gods but the two greatest mysteries of the Christian Faith: the Trinity and the Incarnation of Christ as God and man (lines 26–7).

32 *light* St Thomas.

33 *God's poor man* St Francis (*Par.* XI, 43–117).

34 *one stalk* one of Dante's difficulties; the second concerns St Thomas' earlier words on Solomon, the fifth soul in his circle (line 48; *Par.* X, 114; XI, 26).

39 *these two* Adam, from whose rib God created Eve, who was tempted to the first sin [Genesis] (lines 40–42); and Christ, Whose side was pierced by a lance when He died on the cross to make infinite atonement for all sins (lines 43–5). Dante's belief that these were the wisest of all men and St Thomas' words on the unparalleled wisdom of Solomon are both equally correct (lines 50–51).

54 *Idea* God the Son Whose reflection from the Father in

the love of the Holy Spirit is the source of all created things, both immortal and mortal (*Par*. X, 1–6). Through the nine orders of angels who move the nine spheres, the One eternal, infinite Light of the Trinity is transmitted down to the sublunar world of prime matter, the transient things made of the elements, the human body, and the mortal souls of animals and plants (lines 55–66). According to the disposition both of the heavens and of the matter, nature varies the reception of this light, producing differences in, for instance, plants and humans (lines 67–72). When the heavens and the matter are perfect, the creation will be perfect; otherwise, not (lines 73–8). Only twice has the Trinity disposed nature perfectly and created two perfect human beings: Adam and Christ (the son of the Virgin Mary) (lines 79–87).

90 *vision* wisdom.

93 *"Do ask"* God's words to Solomon, 'Ask what you want, and I shall give it to you'; when Solomon asked to be a just and discerning king, God was pleased and said: 'I have given you a heart so wise and intelligent that no man like you has ever lived before you or will rise up after you' [1 (3) Kings]. Hence, Solomon's wisdom pertained only to his request to be a good king; it was not given to him so that he could solve difficult – and for him irrelevant – questions of theology, logic, physics, and geometry (lines 94–102).

97 *the number* an abstruse and ultimately insoluble problem for human minds (*Par*. XXVIII, 91–3; XXIX, 130–35).

98 *contingent* a non-necessary premiss in Aristotelian logic, for instance, that A may be B; even if the other premiss states that A is necessarily C, it is impossible to conclude that B must necessarily be C. To debate this question is fruitless.

100 *si est . . .* 'if it can be granted that a first motion exists', that is, whether there exists something which, though not moved by anything else, produces motion. Since the strict application of Aristotelian principles of motion would entail a potentially infinite search for movers which move other movers, the argument underlies one of the medieval proofs of

the existence of God, the ultimate Unmoved Mover [St Thomas].

101 *semicircle* in which every triangle drawn between the diameter and the circumference must be right-angled. To dispute or try to disprove this fundamental principle is useless.

106 *"rose"* to the rank of king. By making this distinction in interpreting God's words in the Bible, St Thomas reconciles his statement on Solomon's supreme wisdom as a king with the doctrine of the perfect wisdom, in the absolute sense, of Adam and Christ (lines 109–11). The method of argument is a lesson for all thinkers and scholars, warning them of the dangers of drawing over-hasty conclusions without careful consideration, proper distinctions, and skill (lines 112–23).

124 *Parmenides, Melissus* Greek philosophers (fifth century BC), who made false assumptions and did not reason according to logic [*Monarchia*].

Bryson a Greek mathematician (fourth century BC) who tried to devise ways of squaring the circle, an insoluble problem (*Par.* XXXIII, 133–5).

127 *Sabellius* a heretic who disputed the doctrine of the Trinity (third century AD).

Arius (died AD 336), the founder of the heresy which denied that God the Son was an equal Person of the Trinity.

139 *Dame Bertha or Master Martin* stock names, standing for any town gossip or self-appointed sage. No one should presume to see into God's mind and know whether a thief has gone to Hell or a charitable alms-giver has been saved, for the opposite may be true (lines 140–42).

PARADISO CANTO XIV

THE SUN (continued); MARS.

8 *similarity* precise correspondence, as in the simile of the movement of water (lines 1–3).

17 *made visible* reunited with the body after it rises from the grave on the Last Day (lines 43–5, 57, 63–6).

28 *One and Two and Three* the Trinity, infinite and all-containing (line 30).

35 *divinest light* Solomon, speaking reverently like Gabriel to Mary [Luke].

39 *garment* of enveloping light. This is proportionate to each soul's love, vision, and grace; when joined again to the body, the human being will be complete once more (*Inf.* VI, 103–11); the blessed will receive more grace, vision, love, and therefore light, and their eyes will be made strong enough to bear it (lines 40–60).

71 *lights* stars, appearing faintly. The third circle, associated with the Holy Spirit (line 76), concludes the episode with a final reference to the Trinity.

81 *take flight* cannot even be remembered (*Par.* I, 5–9).

84 *higher blessedness* in the next Heaven, Mars.

88 *language* the inner thoughts and feelings which are common to all human beings, whatever language they speak. Dante makes an interior, wordless sacrifice of himself to God (lines 90–93).

96 *Helios* God; from the Greek name for the Sun, connected with the Hebrew 'Eli' ('God').

98 *Galaxy* the Milky Way, stretching across the Heaven of the Stars between the celestial poles. Its uneven distribution of light posed problems for philosophers and astronomers [*Convivio*] (*Par.* II, 64–73).

101 *sign* a cross.

106 *he* a good Christian, as Christ said: 'If anyone wishes to come after me, let him deny himself and take up his cross and follow me' [Matthew].

113 *particles* specks of material seen in a shaft of light in a shaded place (lines 115–17).

125 *"Rise"* and *"Conquer"* words from the Church's Easter liturgy, celebrating Christ's conquest of death by His resurrection.

130 *presumptuous* in apparently raising this experience above the vision of Beatrice's eyes. Dante's apologetic self-accusation reaffirms the parallel between her increase of beauty and his own ascent through the heavens (lines 133–9).

PARADISO CANTO XV

MARS: Soldiers who fought for religion.

1 *Generous will* the souls' united response to God's will, contrasted with human beings' misdirected desire for transient earthly things (lines 3, 10–12). They all cease singing to allow Dante to address them (lines 4–9).

14 *fire* a shooting-star.

19 *horn* the arm of the cross of lights formed by the souls.

24 *a flame* shining through semi-transparent alabaster.

25 *Anchises* the shade of Aeneas' dead father who, seeing his son approaching in the Elysian fields, stretched out his hands and wept, saying: 'Have you come here at last? Has your duty to your father, as expected, overcome the hard journey? Am I now to see your face, my son, and hear and exchange words with you as before? I knew it for sure in my mind; counting the time, I thought of the future [...]' [Virgil]. The soul is Cacciaguida, Dante's great-great-grandfather, who, according to the account given here, was born in 1091, was knighted, and died as a crusader in the Holy Land during the Second Crusade (1147–8). Just as Anchises revealed to Aeneas his destiny as the ancestor of the Romans, so will Cacciaguida foretell his descendant's destiny as an exile and poet (*Par.* XVII).

26 *muse* poet, that is, Virgil.

28 *blood* descendant, seed (line 48). The tercet, which is in Latin in the original, has a solemn Virgilian and biblical tone [Virgil].

30 *twice* on the journey and again, eventually, after death. Only St Paul has preceded Dante in visiting Heaven as a living man (*Inf.* II, 28–30, 32; *Par.* I, 73–5).

41 *necessity* the fact that Cacciaguida sees, in God's Mind, things which Dante's merely human mind cannot comprehend (line 39).

43 *sympathy* love for his descendant.

50 *volume* God's certain knowledge of future events, in which Cacciaguida has long foreseen Dante's arrival.

56 *First* the Unity from Whom the multiplicity of Creation derives, just as all numbers are multiples of one.

67 *better satisfied* increased by hearing Dante express his thoughts in words.

74 *First Equality* God, in Whom Mind and Love – like the light and heat of the sun – are coextensive and identical. Cacciaguida sees and loves God equally and together, whereas mere humans such as Dante cannot match great love with words (lines 79–82).

89 *root* the founder of Dante's family.

91 *The man* Alighiero, from whom the family took the surname Alighieri; Dante believed he had died before 1200 (line 92).

93 *first ledge* the terrace of the proud, where Alighiero is still doing penance, presumably for pride in his father's ennoblement (*Purg.* XI, 58–72).

96 *good works* particularly, prayers for his great-grandfather's soul.

97 *Florence* the city of Cacciaguida's time, enclosed within its smallest and oldest circle of walls, before the great expansion which led to the building of a much bigger outer circle (1173), and then an even larger one (from 1284). The following passage contrasts the small, idealized civic community of about 1100 with the large, commercialized, and morally corrupt Florence of Dante's own time.

98 *tierce and nones* two of the Church's daily hours for prayers, rung on the bells of the Badia (the 'Abbey' church) close to the old walls of Florence.

100 *No necklace* ... no ostentatious display of wealth. In the old days, the Florentine women dressed simply.

104 *then* in old Florence, when fathers did not arrange marriages for their daughters at too young an age or for an excessively large dowry.

107 *Sardanapalus* sexual promiscuity and self-indulgence; from the legendary Assyrian king who neglected his royal duties and shut himself away in his room with his wives and concubines.

109 *Uccellatoio* a hill a few miles outside Florence, from where the city and its splendid buildings could be seen.

110 *Monte Mario* a hill from which travellers and pilgrims from the north would catch their first view of Rome. Florence had not yet come to surpass Rome in size, wealth, and magnificence; but its fall will be faster than Rome's (line 111).

112 *Bellincione Berti* a Florentine of the twelfth century, the father of Gualdrada (*Inf.* XVI, 37; *Par.* XVI, 98–9); he, his wife, and two other couples (lines 115–17) exemplify the plain dress and frugal, industrious lives of the citizens of Florence in the old days.

118 *sure* of dying and being buried in Florence. Since then, the political conflicts have sent many women into exile with their husbands, and the growth in commerce has caused men to leave their wives in order to trade in France (lines 119–20).

123 *speech* baby-language.

125 *tales* the oral tradition, which transmitted the stories of ancient heroes: the Trojan ancestors of the Romans; and the civic origins of Florence itself at the time of the Romans' conquest of Fiesole (line 126; *Inf.* XV, 62).

127 *Lapo Saltarello, Cianghella* respectively, a corrupt Florentine politician of Dante's own party around 1300; and a Florentine woman notorious for her sexual promiscuity. Such types would have shocked old Florence.

129 *Cincinnatus and Cornelia* respectively, the honest, frugal Roman leader (*Par.* VI, 46–7); and the virtuous Roman matriarch (*Inf.* IV, 128). Such types would shock guilty modern Florence.

132 *Mary* Christ's mother, to whom Cacciaguida's mother prayed in childbirth.

134 *Baptistery* where all Florentines, including Dante, were baptized into the Church and named (*Inf.* XIX, 17; *Par.* XXV, 9).

137 *wife* probably from the Aldighieri family of Ferrara, whose name Dante inherited through their son Alighiero (lines 91–4). Nothing is known for certain of the brothers (line 136).

140 *Conrad* Conrad III (Emperor 1138–52), one of the leaders of the Second Crusade (1147–8).

142 *war* the crusade to win back the Holy Land from its Saracen occupiers.

144 *Pastors* the Popes of Dante's time who ignored their duty, as spiritual leaders of Christendom, to proclaim a new crusade (*Par.* IX, 136–8).

PARADISO CANTO XVI

MARS (continued).

1 *here below* on earth, where pride in nobility of birth can be sinful (*Purg.* XI, 58–69). For Dante, a family can be called noble only when its members possess true, inner nobility of soul which is expressed in a virtuous life; without such members, in time the family will become morally degenerate and base (lines 7–9) [*Convivio*] (*Purg.* VII, 121–3; XIV, 115–23). Here it is legitimate, though still a human weakness, for him to be proud of his great-great-grandfather, a knight who died for Christ and is now in Heaven.

10 *you* the plural pronoun 'voi' in Italian, expressing respect; the usage was believed to have originated in ancient Rome to honour Julius Caesar, though it has since died out there (lines 11–12). In the *Comedy*, Dante uses this mode of address with Beatrice and a few souls presented as particularly worthy of deference; normally, he addresses the souls, and

they address him, with the more familiar singular form 'tu'.

14 *woman* a lady who, in the romance of Lancelot, gave a cough to show she had overheard queen Guinevere's first declaration of love for him (*Inf.* V, 127–38). Beatrice's smile reveals she is aware of Dante's pride in his ancestor.

24 *years* the dates of Cacciaguida's early life.

25 *sheepfold* the population of Florence, whose cathedral church was then the Baptistery, dedicated to the city's patron saint, John the Baptist (*Par.* XV, 134).

33 *modern speech* the Florentine language of Dante's day. Cacciaguida presumably speaks in archaic, twelfth-century Florentine.

34 *Ave* 'Hail, [full of grace]', the words of the angel Gabriel to Mary [Luke]. After the day of Christ's Incarnation, Mars (whose revolution was calculated at 687 days) entered the sign of Leo 580 times until Cacciaguida was born (AD 1091). The reference to Mars and Leo alludes to the heavenly influences upon his destiny as a brave soldier.

40 *where* the place in Florence where the riders in the annual horse-race (run on the feast of St John the Baptist) entered the last of the quarters into which the old city was divided – that of the Porta San Piero (near the present Old Market). The house of the Alighieri in Dante's time was not there but in the parish of San Martino.

46 *All those* the adult male population of old Florence, between the Baptistery (line 25) and the bridge (now the Ponte Vecchio) where a statue of Mars then stood (lines 146–7).

49–50 *Campi ... Certaldo... Figline* areas of Florentine territory in the neighbouring countryside (the *contado*) from where families had migrated and established themselves in the city. Florence would be a happier place now if they had stayed there, and if it had limited its territory to just a few miles around the city (lines 52–4).

56 *Aguglione's wretch* Baldo d'Aguglione, so called from the country castle where his family had originated. Involved in a legal fraud in 1299 (*Purg.* XII, 105), he was a member of the

Black Guelph party which in 1302 exiled Dante on charges of political corruption (barratry); in 1311 he issued the decree excluding Dante, among others, from the amnesty offered to the White Guelph exiles.

Signa's wretch Fazio da Signa, whose family had come from the village of that name near Florence. Also a Black Guelph, he was a leader in Florence's opposition to the Emperor Henry VII in 1310–13.

58 *those* the Popes. Their opposition to the Emperors of the late twelfth and the thirteenth centuries – with the resulting struggles between Guelphs and Ghibellines – is presented as the cause of Florence's territorial expansion and growth into a commercial centre which attracted countryfolk to the city.

63 *Semifonte* a fortress near Florence, from where the Velluti family had migrated to the city.

64 *Counts* the Counts Guidi, who in 1254 had ceded their fortress of Montemurlo to Florence.

65 *Acone* a village near Florence, the original home of the Cerchi family.

66 *Valdigreve* a river valley south of Florence, where the Buondelmonti family had once possessed a castle (lines 140–44).

70–72 *the blind bull ... five swords* proverbial expressions applied to Florence, now disastrously enlarged to five times its previous size (line 48).

73 *Luni, Urbisaglia* two once powerful Roman towns (in northern Tuscany and the March of Ancona) which had vanished by Dante's day.

74–5 *Sinigaglia ... Chiusi* two towns (near Ancona and in southern Tuscany) which were apparently in terminal decline in Dante's day. The examples illustrate the transience of cities, as of families, over the course of several human lifetimes (lines 76–81).

83–4 *conceals ... reveals* by causing tides. In the list of old Florentine families which follows, some were already in decline in Cacciaguida's day, and extinct or reduced to insignificance by Dante's (lines 88–99, 109–16, 121–6); others were already powerful and destined to remain so (lines 100–109).

95 *new treachery* by the Cerchi family (line 65), especially Vieri, leader of the White Guelphs in the crisis of 1300–1301 which led to Dante's exile (*Inf.* VI, 65). Their house, which stood near the city gate of San Piero, had been bought from the Counts Guidi, descendants of the Ravignani and Bellincione Berti (lines 97–9; *Par.* XV, 112–14).

102 *hilt and pommel* the emblems of knighthood.

103 *Vair* fur, the symbol of the Pigli family.

105 *those* the Chiaramontesi, one of whom had been found guilty of selling false measures of salt in 1283 (*Purg.* XII, 105).

106 *stock* the Donati.

109 *those* the Uberti family on whom the Guelphs took revenge after the death of the Ghibelline leader, Farinata (*Inf.* X, 83–7; XXIII, 107–8).

110 *gold balls* emblem of the powerful Lamberti clan, allies of the Uberti (*Inf.* XXVIII, 106–9).

112 *those* the Visdomini and Tosinghi families who had lucrative rights to administer the diocese of Florence during an interregnum between bishops.

115 *breed* the Adimari, cruel to those who try to escape from them, meek to those who threaten or bribe them. Then they were so inferior that Ubertin Donato, Bellincione Berti's son-in-law, opposed the marriage of his wife's sister to one of them (lines 118–21).

121 *Caponsacco* the Caponsacchi who lived near the Old Market.

126 *della Pera* a family which had become extinct or obscure by Dante's time; or perhaps the wealthy Peruzzi.

128 *great baron* Hugh, Marquis of Tuscany (died 1001); the anniversary of his death, the feast of St Thomas (21 December), was commemorated each year in the church of the Badia where he is buried. Several noble Florentine families had the right to bear variations on his coat of arms.

131 *he* Giano della Bella, whose family bore Hugh's arms

bordered in gold. In 1293 he was the principal author of the Ordinances of Justice, which excluded the great nobility from holding political office in Florence.

133 *Gualterotti ... Importuni* families who lived in a ward of the city (the Borgo Santi Apostoli), where the Buondelmonti – the cause of all the subsequent strife – later came to live (lines 66, 140–44).

136 *Amidei* the family who later brought Florence's time of peace and happiness to an end.

140 *Buondelmonte* who in 1215 was persuaded to break his promise to marry a woman of the Amidei family, and they and their associates killed him in revenge (*Inf.* XXVIII, 106–9). The murder split the city between the Guelph and the Ghibelline factions and was regarded as the origin of the violence and conflict which continued throughout the rest of the century.

144 *Ema* a stream between Florence and the Buondelmonti family's country estate (line 66). If Buondelmonte had been drowned in it before reaching the city, the catastrophe would have been averted.

147 *guardian* the statue of Mars, near which Buondelmonte was murdered (line 47; *Inf.* XIII, 146–7).

153 *lily* the emblem of Florence.

reversed carried upside down as a sign of contempt after a humiliating victory.

154 *hatred* the wars between the Guelphs and Ghibellines which in 1251 led the Guelphs to change Florence's original white lily on a red field to a red lily on white.

PARADISO CANTO XVII

MARS (continued).

1 *Phaethon* the son of Apollo and Clymene. Told that he was not really Apollo's son, he first asked his mother for the truth; his father then allowed him to drive the chariot of the Sun,

with fatal consequences [Ovid] (*Inf.* XVII, 106–8; *Purg.* IV, 73; XXIX, 118–20).

5 *lamp* Cacciaguida.

8 *desire* for knowledge, which must be expressed externally in corresponding words. Though both Beatrice and Cacciaguida know the question in Dante's mind, he must ask it so that they may answer (lines 9–12). The question itself concerns the most deeply personal, even autobiographical, theme in the *Comedy*: the accusations of corruption while in office made against Dante and other White Guelph leaders (27 January 1302), his effective banishment from Florence under sentence of death (10 March 1302), and his subsequent life as an exile and poet in the service of various Italian lords on whom he relied for shelter, hospitality, and support.

14 *Point* God's Mind, in which Cacciaguida can see – as certainly as humans understand a basic principle of geometry – the circumstances of Dante's future life, which have been obscurely prophesied by several souls in Hell and Purgatory (lines 15–22; *Inf.* VI, 67–72; X, 79–81; XV, 61–72, 88–96; XXIV, 140–51; *Purg.* VIII, 134–9; XI, 139–41).

24 *as a cube* foursquare, firmly prepared to face and bear the cruel blows of adverse fortune (*Inf.* XV, 91–6).

31 *maze* the enigmatic oracles of pagan times, before the death of Christ (lines 32–3; *Purg.* XVI, 18).

36 *Contingency* apparently fortuitous events and chains of events which occur only on the sublunar, material earth (lines 37–8). God's foreknowledge does not in itself make them inevitable, any more than an observer causes a ship to follow its natural, unimpeded course (lines 40–42). Dante's future life is here presented as God's mysterious providential plan for the man who, in exile, would also be the poet.

46 *Hippolytus* prince of Athens, son of Theseus. When his stepmother, Phaedra, falsely accused him of being in love with her, he was forced to flee from the city [Ovid].

50 *the one* Pope Boniface VIII, to whom the Florentine Black Guelphs appealed for help; his ally, Charles of Valois,

was the agent of the coup of November 1301 which led to the collapse of the White Guelph government and the exile of its leaders (*Purg.* XX, 70–78).

51 *where* in Rome, the city of simony (line 51; *Inf.* XIX).

53 *vengeance* God's punishment, which will reveal who was really guilty.

57 *bitter taste* the humiliation of poverty which would force Dante to live off the hospitality of others and in their homes, not his own (lines 59–60).

62 *company* the other White Guelph exiles, who in 1302–3 made several unsuccessful attempts to fight their way back to power in Florence; in 1304, after Dante had left them, their army suffered a particularly serious defeat (line 66). Having broken with his old party, the Guelphs, Dante began to evolve his own, independent solution to the problems of government in Italy (line 69) and, through his study of the classics and meditation on Roman history, came to take up a moderate and idealizing Ghibelline position, which looked to the restoration of the Roman Empire to bring peace, justice, and true freedom to the faction-ridden and warring Italian city-states. Hence his ardent support for the expedition of Henry VII into Italy (1310–13), and his hope that the wicked Florentines would submit to his imperial jurisdiction [*Epistles*].

71 *great Lombard* probably Bartolomeo della Scala, lord of Verona 1301–4, whose family's emblem was a ladder ('scala'); the addition of an eagle represented their allegiance, as Ghibellines, to the Empire (line 72). He will be generous to Dante before being asked (lines 73–5).

76 *one* Can Grande della Scala, Bartolomeo's younger brother (1291–1329); appointed imperial vicar by Henry VII, he became sole lord of Verona in 1312. Perhaps shortly after Henry's death in 1313, Dante moved to Verona where he was accepted into Can Grande's service, presumably as an adviser, poet, and courtier; in about 1316, Dante gratefully and affectionately offered him some cantos of the *Paradiso* in return [*Epistles*]. Here, through Cacciaguida's prophecy, Dante pays

tribute to his dedicated and generous patronage of the poor (lines 81–90).

77 *star* Mars, whose natal influence predisposes men to military skills and bravery.

82 *Gascon* Pope Clement V who, almost immediately after Henry VII's coronation in Rome in 1312, withdrew his support for the new Emperor.

95 *glosses* the specific details which explain the earlier prophecies (*Inf.* XV, 89–90).

101 *putting in the woof* answering Dante's question, so completing his knowledge of his destiny.

110 *place* Florence. The exile's dilemma is that the truths, messages, and invectives contained in his poem's three parts may be unpalatable to potential hosts and patrons, so making him permanently homeless (lines 111–17); on the other hand, if he does not bravely write the truth, his poem will not win him fame among posterity (lines 118–20). Cacciaguida's answer defines the moral and reformist purpose of the *Comedy*: to prick the consciences of the guilty and to correct society, particularly by chastising its leaders (lines 124–35), through giving notable and clear examples of how human actions in this life will be justly punished, purified, or rewarded in the next (lines 136–42).

PARADISO CANTO XVIII

MARS (concluded); JUPITER: Lovers of justice.

1 *mirror* Cacciaguida, who sees and reflects God's light.

28 *resting place* Mars, the fifth heaven.

tree Paradise.

29 *crown* God in the Empyrean above.

37 *Joshua* the leader of the Israelites, Moses' successor, who conquered the Promised Land (*Par.* IX, 124–5).

40 *Maccabeus* Judas Maccabeus (died 160 BC), the heroic leader of the Jews in their fight to defend their religion against

the tyrannical and sacrilegious king of Syria [1 Maccabees].

43 *Charlemagne* (died 814) the king of the Franks, later Emperor, who fought on behalf of the Church in Lombardy (*Par*. VI, 94–6) and against the Saracens in Spain and France.

Roland the greatest Christian knight in the medieval poems and legends about Charlemagne's war against the Saracens (*Inf*. XXXI, 16–18).

47 *William* Duke of Orange, who became a monk (died 812). He is the hero of a cycle of medieval epics in which he is one of Charlemagne's generals.

Renouard a character in the epics of William of Orange, a Saracen giant who becomes a Christian, fights alongside William, and eventually, like him, enters a monastery.

Godfrey de Bouillon, Duke of Lorraine (died 1100), one of the leaders of the First Crusade which captured Jerusalem in 1099.

48 *Robert* nicknamed 'Guiscard' ('cunning') (died 1085), the Norman conqueror of southern Italy; he too was thought to have fought against the Saracens of Sicily and Calabria.

64 *change* from red to white again. Dante has ascended from Mars to Jupiter (lines 67–9).

72 *signs we speak* words.

82 *Pegasea* Poetry, personified as a Muse who brings enduring fame both to the poet and to the nations and states which he immortalizes in his works. The Muses' sacred spring of water gushed forth when the winged horse, Pegasus, struck the ground of mount Helicon with his hoof (*Purg*. XXIX, 37–40).

91–3 DILIGITE IUSTITIAM ... QUI IUDICATIS TERRAM 'Love justice, O you who judge the earth' [Wisdom]. All earthly government and law must be based on the love of justice.

94 *M* perhaps referring to the Monarchy, the Roman world-jurisdiction, and thus to the Emperor as the supreme minister of justice over all the other kingdoms and cities on earth.

102 *fools* superstitious people who count the sparks.

105 *Sun* God, the Artist Who creates the designs formed by the souls in Heaven and the natures of all creatures, such as birds, in their different places on earth (lines 109–11).

113 *lily* the *M* which in medieval script resembled a lily. The eagle formed by the souls in Jupiter represents heavenly Justice, the source of the universal earthly justice once entrusted to the Roman Empire (lines 115–17; *Purg.* X, 80–81; XXIX, 108; *Par.* VI, 1–9, 28–111; XIX, 16–18, 101–2; XX, 8–9).

119 *that place* the papal Curia (in Rome in 1300, in Avignon after 1309), the Church's leadership which, by its bad example, has led the whole world into evil (lines 124–6; *Purg.* XVI, 98–114, 127–9); like the merchants and money-changers whom Christ drove out of the Temple in Jerusalem [Matthew], the Popes have defiled the Church with their simony (lines 122–3).

128 *bread* grace, the spiritual benefits which God wants the Church to administer impartially to everyone. Instead, the Popes abuse their spiritual powers, using excommunication and interdict as weapons against their military or political enemies.

130 *you* Pope John XXII (1316–34), here accused of issuing decrees (such as excommunications) only to revoke them later, solely for his own advantage.

132 *vines* the Church (*Par.* XII, 72).
alive in Heaven.

134 *him* St John the Baptist, who lived in the wilderness and was executed by king Herod as a reward to Salome for her dancing [Matthew]. His image was stamped on the coinage of Florence, the gold and silver florins which are, in Dante's sarcastic attack, the true object of John XXII's devotion (*Par.* IX, 127–32).

136 *Fisherman* St Peter (*Purg.* XXII, 63).

11 *I and mine* the first person singular, instead of the plural. The souls in the eagle speak as one, in the perfect concord of a society united by justice and love (line 24).

16 *memory* the eagle of the Roman Empire, once glorious but now neglected on earth (lines 101–2; *Par.* XVIII, 94–117).

26 *fast* the desire to know the answer to a problem which cannot be solved by human reasoning, only by the supernatural truths revealed in the Scriptures (lines 27, 82–4).

29 *realm* the Thrones, the angels who reflect God's Justice directly to all the blessed (*Par.* IX, 61–2).

44 *His Word* God the Son [John], through Whom the world was brought into being (*Par.* X, 1–6; XIII, 52–4).

46 *first proud being* Lucifer, who was punished because he rebelled against the limitations placed on even the highest order of beings, the angels (*Inf.* XXXIV, 34–6). Hence God's infinite Power exceeds that of lesser beings to an even greater extent, and the deep mystery of His Justice cannot be penetrated by the minds of humans living on the material, sinful earth (lines 49–66).

70 *A man* a person born in, for instance, the Far East. One of Dante's deepest intellectual problems was the apparent injustice of God's exclusion of virtuous non-Christians from the possibility of going to Heaven (*Inf.* I, 124–6; IV, 31–45, 72; *Purg.* III, 34–45; VII, 25–36).

86 *Primal Will* God, Whose love of Himself as supreme Good is the model and source of all justice, heavenly and earthly (lines 88–90).

104 *this kingdom* Paradise, which consists of Old Testament figures who believed in Christ to come and Christians who believed in Him after the Redemption (*Inf.* IV, 46–63; *Par.* XXXII, 19–27).

106 *many* self-professed Christians: 'Not everyone who says to me, "Lord, Lord", will enter into the kingdom of Heaven'

[Matthew]. The innocence of virtuous non-Christians (African or Asian), projected forward in time to the end of the world, is contrasted with the crimes of the so-called Christian rulers of early fourteenth-century Europe: 'The men of Nineveh will rise for judgment with this generation and will condemn it' [Matthew].

110 *two companies* the saved and the damned.

113 *volume* the book in which are written the deeds by which the risen dead will be judged on the Last Day (line 116) [Revelation].

115 *Albert* the Emperor-Elect in 1300 (died 1308) (*Purg.* VI, 97–117); in 1304 he invaded Bohemia (line 117).

119 *him* Philip IV, king of France 1285–1314; to increase his revenues, he reduced the content of precious metal in his currency (a crime against justice); he died when he fell off his horse during a boar-hunt (*Inf.* XIX, 87; *Purg.* VII, 109–12; XX, 91–3; XXXII, 151).

122 *Scot and Englishman* the dispute over the succession to the throne of Scotland from 1291; the English invasions by Edward I and Edward II, and the Scots' retaliation under Robert the Bruce.

125 *the Spaniard* Ferdinand IV, king of Castile and León 1295–1312.

the Bohemian Wenceslaus II, king of Bohemia 1278–1305 (*Purg.* VII, 101–3).

127 *the Cripple* the lame Charles II of Anjou, king of Naples 1285–1309, titular king of Jerusalem (*Purg.* VII, 127; XX, 79–81).

128 *I* one, as opposed to *M* (a thousand) in Roman numerals.

131 *him* Frederick II of Aragon, king of Sicily 1296–1337 (*Purg.* VII, 118–20). Sicily is indicated by its volcano, mount Etna, and by the fact that Aeneas' father died there.

134 *contracted* written small.

137 *uncle* James of Aragon, king of Majorca 1276–1311.

brother James II, king of Aragon 1291–1327 (*Purg.* VII, 118–20).

139 *he of Portugal* king Diniz 1279–1325.

he of Norway Haakon V 1299–1319.

140 *he of Rascia* Stephen Uroš II, king of Serbia 1275–1321, who forged imitation Venetian coins.

142 *Hungary* ruled in 1300 by Andrew III (1290–1301); he had occupied the throne instead of Charles Martel (*Par.* VIII, 64–6) whose son, Charles Robert, was king 1308–42.

143 *Navarre* the Pyrenean kingdom annexed to France through the marriage of Philip IV and Jeanne of Navarre; their son (Louis X) was king of Navarre 1305–16 and of France 1314–16.

146 *Nicosia and Famagosta* Cyprus, also governed in 1300 by a French king, Henry II of Lusignan 1285–1324 (line 148).

PARADISO CANTO XX

JUPITER (continued).

1 *he* the sun whose light, at nightfall, is replaced by its reflection from many stars (line 6).

8 *emblem* the eagle of the Romans and their Emperors.

31 *that part* the eye (*Par.* I, 47–8).

38 *the singer* David, king of Israel, who composed the Psalms and had the Ark of the Covenant taken to Jerusalem (*Inf.* IV, 58; *Purg.* X, 55–69). As author of the Psalms, he received, and freely chose to accept, divine inspiration (lines 40–52).

44 *one* Trajan, Roman Emperor AD 98–117 (*Purg.* X, 73–93). He spent some four centuries among the virtuous pagans in Limbo before coming to Heaven (lines 46–8, 106–17).

49 *he* Hezekiah, king of Judah; during an illness, he prayed to God and was given fifteen more years of life [2(4) Kings; Isaiah]. God does not cancel but may delay His Justice in answer to the prayers of the good (lines 52–4; *Purg.* VI, 28–42).

55 *The next* Constantine, Roman Emperor 306–37, a convert to Christianity who transferred the capital of the Empire

to the Greek city of Byzantium (Constantinople), leaving the Western Empire in the care of the Papacy. This donation of temporal power to the Church has corrupted the world (*Inf.* XIX, 115–17; XXVII, 94–5; *Purg.* XXXII, 126–9, 136–8; *Par.* VI, 1–6).

62 *William* II (the Good), king of Naples and Sicily 1166–89, the ideal of the just king, contrasted with the evil rulers of the two kingdoms in 1300 (line 63; *Par.* XIX, 127–35).

69 *Ripheus* a Trojan killed while defending Troy against the Greeks: 'Ripheus also fell, uniquely the most just of all the Trojans, the most faithful preserver of equity; but the gods decided otherwise' [Virgil]. In reward for his love of justice, God, in His unfathomable Will and infinite grace, has made him an astonishing exception to the law that, in pagan times, no one could be saved (lines 70–72, 118–32).

76 *image* the eagle. Justice has its source in God, the supreme Good and Creator of everything (*Par.* XIX, 86–90).

79 *plain* transparent, for the souls can already see Dante's question clearly in God's Mind.

92 *quiddity* essence, the intellectual understanding of what the thing perceived and named actually is.

94 *Regnum celorum* 'the kingdom of heaven [suffers force, and the violent seize it]' [Matthew] – not by coercing God but by their great love and hope to which He willingly responds (lines 95–9).

101 *first and fifth* Trajan and Ripheus. They both died not as pagans but as Christians: the former believing in Christ after the Redemption, the latter in Christ to come (lines 103–6; *Par.* XIX, 103–5).

106 *One* Trajan. In answer to the fervent prayers of St Gregory (Pope 590–604), God brought Trajan's soul out of Limbo and reunited it with his body; converted, he died a Christian and came to Heaven [*Golden Legend*] (*Purg.* X, 74–5).

118 *other* Ripheus. In His mysterious Providence, God revealed the future Redemption to him, and he became a Christian, baptized not in water but spiritually, by the Virtues of Faith, Hope, and Charity (lines 127–9; *Purg.* XXIX, 121–9).

SATURN: Contemplatives.

6 *Semele* the Theban princess who rashly asked to look upon the full majesty of Jupiter, which so overwhelmed her that she burst into flames and was burnt to ashes [Ovid; Statius].

11 *mortal faculty* Dante's eyesight which, like his hearing, is merely human (lines 61–3; *Par.* XXII, 10–13).

13 *seventh splendor* Saturn whose influence, joined with that of the sign of Leo (lines 14–15), illustrates the two themes in this heaven: the contemplative life, directed towards God, and the angry denunciation of corruption on earth.

17 *figure* the ladder (lines 28–30; *Par.* XXII, 70–71).

18 *this mirror* Saturn, whose light reflects God's.

27 *king* the god Saturn, who reigned during the Golden Age (*Inf.* XIV, 96; *Purg.* XXII, 148–50; XXVIII, 139–44).

67 *not supreme* no greater than that of other souls. Like all the blessed in their various degrees, this soul too is acting in free obedience to God's Love and Will (lines 67–75, 83–90). However, not even the greatest saint or highest angel (*Par.* IV, 28–30) can know why God chose him in particular to speak to Dante; and since no creature, even in Heaven, can fully understand God's Will, humans on earth must acknowledge their even greater limitations in trying to understand His mysteries (lines 91–102).

107 *ridges* the Apennines, which run down the centre of the Italian peninsula, in a region not far from Florence where their peaks rise high above the thunderclouds (lines 106, 108).

109 *Catria* a mountain on the borders of Umbria and the Marches, the site of a monastery of the Camaldolese (reformed Benedictine) order. The soul is St Peter Damian (1007–72), a monk and later the abbot there, who contrasts his own frugal and austere life, dedicated to contemplation, with the present monks' neglect of their Rule (lines 113–20). He was commonly identified with another Peter ('Peter the Sinner') who founded the monastery of St Mary on the coast near Ravenna (lines

122–3). In 1057 he reluctantly accepted appointment as a Cardinal (an office which was later symbolized by the conferment of a red hat) (lines 124–6).

127–8 *Cephas . . . vessel* Sts Peter and Paul (*Inf.* II, 28), whose poverty is contrasted with the rich lifestyle of modern prelates, with their retinues and extravagant robes (lines 130–34). God is too tolerant in delaying their punishment (line 135).

PARADISO CANTO XXII

SATURN (continued); Ascent to the Stars.

3 *that place* his mother's side.

13 *confounded* overwhelmed (*Par.* XXI, 4–12, 61–3).

16 *sword* God's punishment which will come in His time, not in relative human time (in which the good want it soon, the wicked to defer it).

35 *high goal* the final vision of God.

37 *Cassino* Montecassino, in the hills of Campania (southern Italy). The speaker is St Benedict (480–543) who converted the pagan inhabitants of the region to Christianity (lines 40–45) and in *c.* 529 founded a monastery there, the parent-house of the Benedictine order. His Rule (line 74) became the model, in the Western Church, for the ideal monastic life of strict vows, prayer, contemplation, manual work, and spiritual education.

47 *heat* the love of God.

49 *Macarius* St Macarius (fourth century AD). Of the two Egyptian saints of that name, one was a hermit in the desert, the other a founder of the monastic tradition in the East.

Romualdus (*c.* 956–1027), who founded an order of hermits who followed a strict, reformed version of St Benedict's Rule; its parent-monastery was at Camaldoli (*Purg.* V, 96; *Par.* XXI, 109).

50 *brothers* Benedictine monks.

60 *unveiled* directly. At present the human forms of the blessed are hidden from Dante by their enveloping light.

62 *final sphere* the Empyrean Heaven, beyond time and place (lines 65–7).

70 *Jacob* the Jewish patriarch who, in a vision, saw angels going up and down a ladder which stretched from earth to heaven; from the top, God spoke to him [Genesis]. Here it represents the degrees of contemplation and love in the ascent to God.

76 *robbers' dens* 'My house shall be called a house of prayer; you have made it a den of thieves' [Matthew].

78 *usury* a serious sin (*Inf.* XI, 50, 109–11; XVII, 43–78).

80 *fruit* the monasteries' revenues, which should be distributed to the poor (lines 82–3).

86 *does not run* lasts no longer than the time from the planting of an oak-tree to the appearance of its first acorns. Hence the rapid decline of the Church, the Benedictine order, and the Franciscans from the ideals of their founders into wickedness (lines 88–93).

94 *Jordan . . . the sea* the river Jordan and the Red Sea, whose waters parted to allow the Israelites to cross [Joshua; Exodus]. The God Who can work such miracles can easily punish the wicked and restore good religion in the world (line 96).

106 *may I* the wish formula (*Inf.* X, 82). By his desire to die repentant and go to Heaven again for ever, Dante swears that his ascent to the sphere of the Fixed Stars was instantaneous, even quicker than the reader would withdraw his finger from a fire (lines 109–10, 118–19).

111 *the sign* Gemini, the Twins, the constellation of the zodiac in which the sun was rising and setting when Dante was born in Florence (May–June 1265) (lines 115–17). He invokes the stars which gave him his natural intellectual and poetic talents, to help him in the supreme poetic task ahead, the description of the upper heights of Paradise (lines 121–3; *Inf.* XV, 55; *Purg.* XXX, 109).

134 *globe* the earth, stationary at the centre of the universe.

138 *elsewhere* away from earth and towards Heaven. The episode and its moral are based on Cicero's *Dream of Scipio*.

139 *Latona's daughter* the Moon (*Purg.* XX, 130–32; *Par.* X, 67) which has no dark spots on the side seen from the stars (*Par.* II, 59–148).

143 *your son* the Sun, whose father (in some myths) was Hyperion [Ovid].

Dïöne Venus, the daughter of Dione (*Par.* VIII, 6–7).

144 *Maia* Mercury, the son of Maia [Virgil].

146 *his father* Saturn.

his son Mars.

150 *threshing floor* a plot of earth used by a farmer for threshing grain; an image for the dry land of the northern hemisphere, tiny but the cause of wars and strife between the humans who live on it (line 151).

PARADISO CANTO XXIII

THE STARS: Dante's vision of Christ, Mary, and the blessed.

11 *that part* the zenith where, seen from the earth, the sun seems to hover at midday. Dante's hopeful expectation is fulfilled almost immediately (lines 14–18).

19 *troops* Christ's Church Triumphant, all the blessed who have been saved by their responses, in life, to the good influences of the heavenly spheres (lines 20–21).

25 *Trivia* the moon, personified as Diana with a retinue of nymphs (the stars).

30 *sights* the other heavens.

31 *Substance* Christ, 'the Power of God and the Wisdom of God' [1 Corinthians]. Awaited throughout the Old Testament period, by coming down to earth He made it possible for humans to ascend from earth to Heaven (lines 37–9).

42 *against its nature* unlike other fires which naturally strive upwards (*Par.* I, 115, 132–3).

43 *feast* the vision of Christ, an experience so ecstatic that it exceeds Dante's power to recall it (lines 45, 49–51; *Par.* I, 5–9).

54 *the book* memory.

55 *tongues* poets who have received the fullest inspiration from Polyhymnia (whose name means 'many hymns') and the other Muses. Beatrice's smile far exceeds the power of the greatest human poetry to describe (lines 59–60; *Purg.* XXXI, 139–45).

62 *sacred poem* the *Paradiso*, with its heavenly themes and moral objectives, the work of a man assisted by God (*Par.* XXV, 1–2). The term may also be taken as a new internal title for the whole poem, replacing or extending that of *Comedy* which, in the *Paradiso* in particular, goes far beyond both styles of human poetry, comedy and tragedy (*Par.* XXX, 22–4).

68 *sea* the poetry of Paradise, the supreme test of Dante's intellectual and poetic powers (*Purg.* I, 1–3; *Par.* II, 1–15).

72 *garden* of the blessed (lines 79–83).

73 *Rose* Mary, the mother of God's Word made flesh [John] (lines 104–5). One of her titles was the 'Mystic Rose'.

74 *lilies* the apostles who first preached Christianity.

78 *brows* Dante's eyes, which cannot bear the light until Christ has ascended out of sight (lines 84–7).

88 *flower* Mary (line 73), also called the 'Morning Star' and 'Star of the Sea'; her light in Heaven surpasses that of the other saints just as her holiness on earth was greater than that of all other human beings (lines 92–3, 101–2).

94 *torch* an angel, later identified as Gabriel (*Par.* XXXII, 94–114), who here acts as the crown of Mary, Queen of Heaven.

99 *cloud* a tuneless clap of thunder.

107–8 *sphere supreme* the Empyrean, to which Mary too ascends (lines 118–20).

112 *royal cloak* the Primum Mobile, the ninth and outermost of the heavenly spheres (*Par.* XXVII, 106–14).

123 *outward flame* external expressions of love.

128 *"Regina coeli"* the first words of an antiphon to Mary, sung during the Church's Easter liturgy: 'O Queen of Heaven, [rejoice, alleluia!, for He Whom you deserved to bear in your womb, alleluia!, has risen, as He promised, alleluia!; pray to

God for us, alleluia!]'.

131 *those* the saved who, during their lives, won the true treasure of Heaven through virtue and suffering, not through greed for gold (lines 133–5). Earthly life, like the captivity of the Jews in Babylon, is an exile from the human race's true home, Heaven.

138 *councils* the saints of the Old Testament and the Christian eras.

he St Peter (*Par.* XXIV, 35–7).

PARADISO CANTO XXIV

THE STARS (continued): Dante's examination in Faith by St Peter.

2 *supper* the eternally satisfying vision and love of Christ in Heaven: 'Blessed are those who are called to the wedding-supper of the Lamb' [Revelation] (*Purg.* XVI, 18).

15 *rest* hardly to move at all. The groups' different speeds of rotation express their degrees of joy (line 18).

20 *flame* St Peter.

27 *painting folds* conceiving and describing the experiences of Paradise in all their depth and subtlety.

35 *the keys* to the kingdom of heaven which Christ gave to St Peter [Matthew] (*Purg.* IX, 117). St Peter proved his total faith in Christ when he stepped out of his fishing-boat and walked upon the water [Matthew] (line 38).

41 *Place* God's Mind.

46 *bachelor* a student during one of the public debates and disputations held in medieval Universities, in which he would have to expound and defend a theological or philosophical point proposed by the master; a few days later, the master would deliver his own judgment on the question (lines 48–9).

56 *waters* of intellectual knowledge.

58 *Chief Centurion* St Peter, leader of the apostles and the first Pope.

61 *brother* St Paul, St Peter's colleague in preaching the Christian gospel in Rome. According to his double definition, faith is both a substance (something which exists) and evidence (the grounds for argument and enquiry) [Hebrews] (lines 63–4). This is explained: the truths of Heaven, which Dante now sees directly, are real; on earth, where they cannot be seen, belief in them is the basis both of the hope of salvation and of the rational, logical investigation of them by theologians (lines 70–78).

81 *sophist's cleverness* theologians who use false logic or over-subtle methods of argument.

83 *coin* faith, a precious treasure and the first of the Christian virtues (lines 89–91).

92 *rain* inspiration.

parchments the Scriptures, both the Old and the New Testaments (line 97), containing the divinely revealed truths which are the certain foundation of faith. That the Bible is God's word is proved by the miracles, which could not have occurred by merely natural processes (lines 100–102). However, since this argument relies on evidence for which the Bible itself is the only source, it needs a final, independent proof, the greatest miracle of all: the fact that the whole world was converted to Christianity, and the Church was founded, by poor men such as St Peter himself (lines 103–11).

113 *"Te Deum laudamus"* 'We praise You, God', the first words of a hymn of praise and thanksgiving (*Purg.* IX, 141).

116 *from branch to branch* through the stages of the examination to its concluding points: the actual doctrines which Dante believes and the source of his belief (lines 122–3).

126 *younger feet* St John with whom St Peter raced to see the empty tomb of the risen Christ [John].

130 *I believe* ... the opening of the Christian Creed: 'I believe in one God, the Father almighty, Creator of heaven and earth. And in one Lord, Jesus Christ, the only-begotten Son of God. [...] And in the Holy Spirit, the Lord and giver of life, Who proceeds from the Father and the Son, Who is

adored and glorified together with the Father and the Son, Who spoke through the prophets [. . .].' Dante's version states the essential doctrine: that there is One God, the Unmoved Mover (which can be proved by philosophical arguments as well as the Scriptures), and that He is Three-in-One (the mystery of the Trinity, revealed in the Gospels) (lines 130–44).

PARADISO CANTO XXV

THE STARS (continued): Dante's examination in Hope by St James.

4 *cruelty* the sentence of exile from Florence.

7 *with other voice* a greater poet, but now with grey hair. Dante hopes that his poem might earn him a pardon so that he may return to his native city to be crowned with the poet's laurels in the church where he was baptized (San Giovanni) (lines 9–11): 'Would it not be better for me to comb my hair for my triumph and, on the banks of the Arno where I was born – if I ever return there – cover my once bright, now grey, locks with the garland of leaves?' [*Eclogues*].

13 *sphere* the same circle of souls.

14 *the first* St Peter, the first Pope. One of the papal titles is 'vicar of Christ', that is, Christ's deputy on earth.

17 *baron* St James the Great, the apostle whose tomb at Santiago de Compostela in Galicia (Spain) was a major shrine for pilgrims from all over Europe during the Middle Ages.

26 *coram me* 'in front of me' (*Par.* XI, 62).

30 *basilica* God in Heaven. In his Epistle (now ascribed to St James the Less), St James tells of God's generosity and the eternal reward promised to those who suffer for love of Him [James] (lines 76–8).

33 *three* Sts Peter, James, and John, Christ's chosen inner group of apostles (*Purg.* XXXII, 73–81), symbols also of, respectively, Faith, Hope, and Charity (Love).

38 *mountains* the two apostles, with their dazzling light.

45 *others* the hearers and readers of the poem (line 78).

52 *Church Militant* the Church on earth.

54 *Sun* God's Mind.

55 *Egypt* the world of the living. Dante's journey is his moral Exodus from enslavement in this sinful and corrupt world to the freedom of the heavenly Jerusalem (*Purg.* II, 46).

57 *term* earthly life, which is a campaign for the victory of good over evil (lines 52, 84).

58 *two points* the definition and the source of hope (lines 46–8). The definition given (lines 67–9) is that of the twelfth-century theologian, Peter Lombard (*Par.* X, 107–8).

70 *stars* biblical texts and the writings of the Fathers of the Church.

72 *singer* king David (*Par.* XX, 37–42).

73 *theody* 'divine song', the Psalms, one of which is cited [Psalms].

78 *your rain* the refreshing virtue of hope, inspired by St James' Epistle and loved by him up to his martyrdom (lines 83–4).

89 *mark* the goal of hope, Heaven.

92 *double garment* the two possessions which the saved will have in Heaven [Isaiah]; they were interpreted as the soul and the body (line 128).

94 *brother* St John, in his vision of Heaven and the blessed, robed in white [Revelation].

98 "*Sperent in te*" 'May those [...] put hope in You' (lines 73–4).

101 *Crab* the constellation which, in December–January, rises on the eastern horizon when the sun is setting in the opposite sign of Capricorn; hence, if it had a star as bright as another sun, there would be no night-time for a whole month.

112 *he* St John the Evangelist, Christ's beloved disciple, who leant his head on Christ's breast during the Last Supper, and to whom Christ committed the care of His mother (line 114) [John].

113 *Pelican* a bird which was believed to tear its own breast

and feed its young on its blood; a symbol of Christ who shed His blood to redeem the human race.

123 *what* St John's body. The legend that St John did not die but was taken up bodily into Heaven is here rejected: he left his body on earth, and it will not rise until the Last Day, when God's plan for the number of the saved will be complete (line 126). Only Christ and Mary (the latter according to the doctrine of the Assumption) are present in Heaven with their human bodies (lines 127–8).

PARADISO CANTO XXVI

THE STARS (continued): Dante's examination in Love by St John; Adam.

12 *force* the power to restore Dante's eyesight, as Ananias cured St Paul's blindness [Acts].

15 *the fire* Love which first came to Dante from Beatrice, passing through his eyes into his heart (*Purg.* XXXI, 116–17; *Par.* XXVIII, 11–12).

16 *The good* God, supreme Good.

17 *Alpha and Omega* the beginning and the end [Revelation].

23 *sift* provide more details and distinctions in accounting for the source of Love.

26 *authority* of the Scriptures, God's word (lines 40–45).

28 *good* anything which, once apprehended, becomes the object of the will and thus of love (*Purg.* XV, 67–75; XVII, 91–2, 97–9; XVIII, 19–33). Whoever understands that God is supreme Good and the source of all lesser goods must of necessity love Him (lines 30–36).

39 *eternal beings* the angels. Dante's direct source for this argument (line 37) is not known.

40 *Author* God, in His words to Moses [Exodus].

43 *Evangel* St John's Gospel, whose first words define the mystery of Christ as God's Word made flesh [John].

49 *cords* other motives for loving God (lines 51, 55–63).

52 *Eagle* St John, whose symbol was an eagle (*Purg.* XXIX, 92).

59 *that which* Heaven (lines 64–6).

62 *twisted love* the false love of earthly goods.

69 "*Holy, holy, holy!*" the words with which Heaven praises God [Isaiah; Revelation] (see note to *Par.* VII, 1–3).

71 *spirit* the minute intermediary which moves to the pupil of the eye, from where it conveys the image of an object to the brain [*Convivio*]. In medieval physiology, the vital spirits link the body's physical organs with the operations of the immaterial soul.

78 *shone* would have been visible even from a vast distance away.

83 *first soul* Adam, created fully formed by God, the ancestor of the whole human race, not only of all wives but also of their husbands (lines 91–4). Like the other souls, he sees Dante's unspoken questions in God's Mind (lines 95–7, 103–8).

101 *that* the light enveloping his soul.

110 *high garden* the Earthly Paradise, on the summit of mount Purgatory (*Purg.* XXVIII–XXXIII). Dante wants to know four things: the date of Adam's creation (lines 109–12, 118–23); the length of time he spent in the Garden of Eden between his creation and his expulsion (lines 112, 139–42); the nature of the first sin (lines 113, 115–17); and the language which he spoke (lines 114, 124–38).

115 *exile* the exclusion of Adam and Eve and all their descendants from the Earthly Paradise. The first sin lay not in eating the fruit but in presumptuous disobedience, the overstepping of a limit which God had forbidden human beings to cross (line 117).

119 *re-turnings* revolutions, years.

120 *that place* Limbo (line 133; *Inf.* II, 52–120; IV, 55; *Purg.* XXXIII, 61–3). Adam lived for 930 years [Genesis] (lines 121–3); 4,302 years passed between his death and Christ's (AD 34) (the calculations are those of St Eusebius' world-

chronology); hence in 1300 it is 6,498 years since he was
created.

125 *Nimrod* builder of the Tower of Babel, the reason why
humans no longer speak one language but many (*Inf.* XXXI,
67–81). Dante had earlier written that Adam's language was
created by God, that his first spoken word was 'El' ('God'),
and that, after Babel, this language survived in Hebrew [*De
vulgari eloquentia*]. Here, instead, he presents language as a
human creation, and as therefore subject to human choice and
variation. Hence 'I', the original name for God (perhaps
expressing the essential simplicity of His Oneness), was
changed after Adam's death to 'El' (lines 126–38). Dante's
interest in the medieval debate on Adam's language reflects his
preoccupation with his own language and its varieties, and
with his need, as a poet, to select the most suitable words in
which to express his themes.

139 *that peak* the Garden of Eden (line 110), where Adam
lived from dawn to after midday (when the sun enters the
third quarter of the twelve-hour day) (lines 140–42). Dante's
source for this information was Petrus Comestor (*Par.* XII,
135).

PARADISO CANTO XXVII

THE STARS (continued); Ascent to the Primum Mobile.

1–2 *"Unto the Father ... glory!"* the prayer in praise of the
Trinity, used frequently in the Church's liturgy: 'Glory be to
the Father, and to the Son, and to the Holy Spirit, [as it was in
the beginning, is now, and ever shall be, world without end.
Amen.]'

11 *that* St Peter, whose light changes from white (the
colour of Jupiter) to red (that of Mars), expressing his anger
and shame (lines 14–15, 19–21, 54).

22 *He* Boniface VIII, the Pope reigning in 1300 (*Inf.* XIX,
52–7; XXVII, 70, 85–111).

my place the office of Pope, successor of St Peter.

24 *burial ground* Rome (*Par.* IX, 139–41).

26 *perverse one* Lucifer in Hell.

29 *hue* red.

35 *eclipse* the darkness which obscured the sun and covered the whole earth at the moment of Christ's death [Luke]. Beatrice too changes colour (probably also to red), as if blushing for shame at hearing of Boniface's crimes (lines 31–3).

40 *Bride of Christ* the Church.

41 *Linus, Cletus* the second and third Popes, saints and martyrs, like St Peter himself.

42 *riches* earthly wealth.

43 *this life* Heaven.

44 *Sixtus and Pius, Urban and Calixtus* Popes of the second and third centuries, also saints and martyrs.

46 *Christ's people* the Church whose unity has been destroyed by Popes such as Boniface VIII who have divided it into their favourites and their enemies, Guelphs and Ghibellines, Black Guelphs and Whites.

49 *the keys* of St Peter, the emblem of the Papacy.

51 *war* false crusades proclaimed against fellow-Christians (such as the Colonnas) (*Inf.* XXVII, 85–90, 103–5).

52 *form* St Peter's image, portrayed on the papal seal.

53 *privileges* offices, benefices, or other ecclesiastical favours which the Popes authorized in return for money.

55 *wolves* greedy Popes and prelates: 'Attend to yourselves and to the universal flock over which the Holy Spirit has set you as bishops to rule the Church of God which He won with His own blood. I know that after my departure rapacious wolves will enter among you, not sparing the flock' (St Paul's sermon to the Ephesians); 'Beware of false prophets, who come to you in sheep's clothing, but within they are ravenous wolves' [Acts; Matthew].

57 *concealed* in the future.

58 *Gascons* Clement V, Pope 1305–14 (*Inf.* XIX, 82–8; *Purg.* XXXII, 148–60; *Par.* XVII, 82; XXX, 142–8).

Cahorsines John XXII, Pope 1316–34, from Cahors, the city of usurers (*Inf.* XI, 50; *Par.* XVIII, 130–36).

59 *beginning* the Church's origins.

62 *Scipio* the Roman general who defeated Hannibal (*Par.* VI, 49–52). The prophecy, which Dante is ordered to reveal in his poem (lines 64–6), probably predicts the imminent coming of a Roman Emperor who will be God's agent in punishing the wicked and reforming the Church and the world (*Inf.* I, 101–11; *Purg.* XXXIII, 37–45, 52 4).

67 *when* in winter, when the sun is in Capricorn.

68 *frozen vapors* snow.

81 *clime* the first climatic zone of land north of the equator, with Jerusalem at its centre. Since Dante's previous look down to the earth (*Par.* XXII, 133–53), he has revolved with the Heaven of the Stars 90° westwards, from above Jerusalem to above Spain.

83 *course* the Ocean, beyond the Straits, across which Ulysses rashly sailed (*Inf.* XXVI, 106–42).

84 *shoreline* the eastern coast of the Mediterranean, from where Jupiter, disguised as a bull, carried off the Phoenician princess, Europa [Ovid].

85 *threshing floor* the inhabited dry land (*Par.* XXII, 150). The rest is in darkness because the sun has also moved westwards. It is in Aries, more than one sign ahead of Gemini, where Dante is (Taurus comes between) (line 87).

92 *lures* examples of earthly beauty (physical or in paintings), which attract the will to love.

98 *nest of Leda* Gemini, the twins. Leda gave birth to them in an egg, after Jupiter in the form of a swan made love to her [Ovid].

99 *swiftest sphere* the Primum Mobile, the First Moved Heaven, the ninth sphere in Ptolemy's system of the universe (*Inf.* IV, 142). It is the source of the motion of all the lower heavens which transmit natural influences down to the stationary earth (lines 106–8, 111); it is moved directly by God, beyond all space and place, in the infinite, all-encompassing

Empyrean (lines 109–114); its speed of revolution determines that of the others with arithmetical exactitude (just as $10 = \frac{10}{2} \times \frac{10}{5}$) (lines 115–17); and hence it is the invisible source of time (the measurement of motion), which is made visible and measured by the revolutions of the other spheres (lines 118–20). Without the Primum Mobile, there would be no natural generation on earth, and 'no night or day, no weeks or months or years, but the whole universe would be disordered, and the movement of the other spheres would have no purpose' [*Convivio*].

121 *greediness* 'the root of all evils', the chief enemy of love and justice in society [1 Timothy; *Monarchia*]. It corrupts the whole human race (lines 121–3), turning initial virtue into sinfulness (lines 124–6), making innocent children grow up to abandon virtues, break the Church's fasts, and even hate their mothers (lines 127–35).

136 *white skin* original goodness, destroyed by greed (lines 59–60). The obscure tercet perhaps refers specifically to the corrupting love of earthly pleasures, symbolized by the enchantress Circe, daughter of the Sun [Virgil; Ovid] (lines 137–8; *Inf.* XXVI, 91; *Purg.* XIV, 42).

140 *no king* no Emperor to administer the law and guide human society in the temporal sphere (*Purg.* VI, 88–105; XVI, 94–114).

144 *hundredth part* the $\frac{1}{100}$ part of a day (approximately) by which the solar year falls short of 365 days 6 hours. Since the Julian Calendar took no account of this discrepancy, by Dante's time the sun was entering each new sign of the zodiac not on the 21st of each month but on about the 12th; eventually (after at least 7,100 and in fact over 9,000 years), it would have entered Aries on 1 January, which would therefore have become the first month of spring. Using the rhetorical device of litotes, Beatrice means that the reform of the world, prepared in the heavens, will occur well before then, in fact, very soon (line 63).

147 *fleet* human society, which will be turned away from

evil and back towards its true harbour, happiness, first on earth and then in Heaven.

148 *the flower* of the human will, which will be restored to virtue and the path to salvation (line 124).

PARADISO CANTO XXVIII

THE PRIMUM MOBILE: God, the angels, and the universe.

8 *glass* the mirror. From its reflection in Beatrice's eyes – the source of Love for Dante (*Par.* XXVI, 14–15) – he turns to the vision itself.

14 *sphere* the Primum Mobile.

16 *a point* God, represented as an infinitesimal point of pure light, surrounded by nine revolving circles (the nine orders of the angels), their speed and light decreasing from the innermost to the outermost (lines 16–39, 41–5).

24 *halo* round the sun or moon.

32 *all of Juno's messenger* a rainbow extended to form a complete circle (*Par.* XII, 12).

49 *world of sense* the visible universe in which the earth is at the centre, and the powers of the nine spheres increase from the innermost (the Moon) to the outermost (the Primum Mobile) (lines 46–51). The model (the vision) is the exact reverse of the copy (the universe) (lines 55–6).

59 *knot* problem. The solution lies in the correspondence between the size of each sphere and the power it contains, which is in proportion to the blessedness of the angels, the pure Intelligences, who move it; and this in turn is in proportion to the grace which each angelic order receives from God in response to its vision and, therefore, love of Him (lines 64–9, 98–114). Hence the Primum Mobile is the widest sphere because it receives the power of the angels closest to God (lines 43–5, 70–72, 99); the lower spheres are progressively smaller because their powers come from the angels of the

circles which are progressively wider and more distant from God (lines 73–8).

81 *Boreas* the north wind, shown on medieval charts as a face which, from its right cheek, blows the milder north-west wind.

91 *the sum* the immense number of grains of corn which, in a legend, the inventor of chess asked the king of Persia to give him, starting with one and then doubling the number on each square of the board; the sum ($2^{64} - 1$) exceeded all the grain in the kingdom. The number of angels is uncountable (*Par.* XXIX, 130–32).

94 *"Hosanna"* the song of the angels (line 118; *Par.* VII, 1).

99 *Seraphim* the angels closest to God, associated particularly with love (*Par.* IV, 28; VIII, 27; XI, 37; XXI, 92); the next, the Cherubim, were linked with knowledge (*Par.* XI, 39), and the third, the Thrones, with justice (*Par.* IX, 61–2). The division of the nine circling orders into three groups of three reflects the perfect number, the Trinity. The names of the angelic orders derive from various references in the Bible, as systematized by Dionysius (line 130).

116 *nightly Ram* Aries, which can be seen in the night sky in all the seasons except spring (when the sun rises and sets in it). Heaven has no change of seasons.

126 *Angels* the name of the lowest order, as well as the generic word for all these heavenly beings.

130 *Dionysius* the disciple of St Paul and, reputedly, the author of *On the celestial hierarchy* (*Par.* X, 115–17). Whereas in the *Convivio*, Book II, Dante had followed an alternative classification of the angelic orders proposed by St Gregory, he here follows that of Dionysius and presents St Gregory's as mistaken (lines 131–5). By changing his mind, he again puts himself in line with his predecessor in visiting Paradise, Dionysius' stated source for his knowledge about angels – St Paul, who was taken up to Heaven and learnt mysteries beyond the knowledge of mortal men [2 Corinthians] (lines 136–9; *Par.* I, 73–5; II, 37; XV, 29–30).

PARADISO CANTO XXIX

THE PRIMUM MOBILE (continued): Angels.

1 *Latona's children* the sun (in Aries) and the moon (in Libra) in the brief period when they are as if in balance on opposite sides of the horizon, before one sets below it and the other rises above it (lines 2–6; *Purg.* XX, 130–32).

11 *there* in God's Mind, the eternal, transcendent source of all points in time and place (*'ubis'*, 'wheres').

14 *splendor* reflected light, namely, those beings whom God created to be conscious of their own existence (*'Subsisto'*, 'I exist') (line 15; *Par.* XIII, 52–60).

18 *new loves* the angels. In eternity, God's Spirit 'moved over the waters' [Genesis] (line 21) and simultaneously created form, matter, and the combination of both (lines 22–30): the angels (pure form) (line 33); prime matter (primordial, undifferentiated matter, containing the potentialities of all material things) (line 34); and the heavens (the eternal union of form and matter) (lines 35–7).

37 *Jerome* St Jerome, one of the greatest Doctors of the Church (*c.* 340–420) [St Jerome]. His doctrine (lines 38–9) is incompatible with several inspired biblical texts, such as 'He who lives in eternity created all things together' [Ecclesiasticus] (lines 40–42); it is also contrary to philosophical reasoning, for it is inconceivable that God would have created the angels long before creating the heavens which it is their essential function to move (lines 43–6). Aristotle had similarly argued that Intelligences without a heaven to move would be eternally without purpose [*Convivio*].

48 *flames* facts about angels which Dante wanted to know.

50 *a portion* the rebel angels, who were cast down to the earth, at whose centre Dante has seen Lucifer (lines 51, 55–7; *Inf.* XXXIV, 28–111).

52 *the rest* the good angels who humbly acknowledged their Creator and so deserved to receive the grace to contemplate Him eternally (lines 53–4, 57–66). For Aristotle too, the main

function of the non-material beings was the contemplative life [*Convivio*].

69 *consistory* the angels.

72 *recollect* to possess the faculty of memory (in addition to those of intellect and will). However, since their vision of God is eternal and continuous, the angels do not need memories (lines 76–81).

82 *below* on earth, where some philosophers think up doctrines which are vainglorious delusions (lines 82–7).

88 *here* in Heaven.

91 *they* the false preachers who ignore the Scriptures for which the apostles and martyrs died, and who mislead the faithful with showy sermons on invented subjects, not found in the Gospels (lines 94–6, 115–17). Thus it is false to preach that the darkness at Christ's death was caused by the moon moving to eclipse the sun, for the sun's light was hidden not just in Jerusalem but 'over the whole earth' [Luke], that is, from west to east (lines 97–102).

105 *Lapos, Bindos* very common names in Florence.

106 *sheep* the people who hear these empty sermons and, by their own fault, are ignorant enough to believe them (line 108).

109 *company* the apostles and disciples.

117 *cowl* of the vain monk or friar who is preaching.

118 *bird* the Devil.

120 *pardons* false indulgences which the preacher offers in order to draw crowds (lines 121–3).

124 *Antonines* the monks of the order of St Anthony, the Egyptian hermit, who was often shown with a pig (representing the devil who tempted him). The monks used to breed pigs which the gullible people regarded as sacred and gave money to maintain.

126 *tender* fraudulent indulgences and empty doctrines, given to the people in return for real money.

134 *Daniel* the prophet who wrote of the angels: 'Thousands of thousands ministered to Him, and ten thousand times

a hundred thousand attended upon Him' [Daniel]. Although
the number of angels is inconceivable to human minds, each
angel receives the grace to see and love God in an individual
degree (lines 130–32, 136–41; *Par.* XXVIII, 91–3).

144 *mirrors* the innumerable angels, in which the One Light
of the infinite God is multiplied and reflected.

PARADISO CANTO XXX

THE EMPYREAN HEAVEN.

1 *six thousand miles* more than a quarter of the earth's
circumference, then calculated at 20,400 miles. The sun is at
midday that distance away, and the conical shadow cast by the
earth is declining towards the horizon (lines 2–3; *Par.* IX,
118–19). The simile describes the sky about an hour before
sunrise, when the dawn is extinguishing the lights of the stars
one by one (lines 7–9).

10 *triumph* the angelic orders which, circling around the
point of light, apparently encompass Him Who in reality
encompasses them (line 12).

16 *that which* all Dante's poetry in praise of Beatrice, from
his first sight of her to now (lines 28–30) [*Vita nuova*].

23 *comic or ... tragic* any poet. In Dante's day, comedy and
tragedy were considered to be styles of poetry, rather than of
theatre; comedy was poetry in the humble style (and, in
practice, in the vernacular); tragedy was in the sublime style
(in Latin or the vernacular) [*De vulgari eloquentia*; *Epistles*] (*Inf.*
XVI, 128; XX, 113; XXI, 2). The ecstatic memory of Bea-
trice's beauty and smile is beyond the powers of any poet to
describe, beyond all Dante's poetry of her, beyond the linguis-
tic and expressive possibilities of the *Comedy* itself, and can be
communicated only by preterition (lines 25–33).

35 *herald* a poet with greater skills.

38 *sphere* the Primum Mobile.

39 *heaven* the Empyrean, the Heaven of infinite light,

wisdom, love, goodness, and bliss: 'Christians say that beyond all the heavenly spheres, there exists the Empyrean Heaven, that is, the fiery or luminous heaven; and they say that it is motionless because in its every part it possesses all that its substance needs. [...] The place of the supreme Godhead, Who alone has complete vision of Himself, is still and at peace. [...] This is the uppermost palace of the world, in which the whole world is enclosed, and outside it there is nothing, and it does not exist in any place but is formed solely in the First Mind' [*Convivio*].

43 *both ranks* the angels and the blessed, the latter with the human forms which they will have again when their bodies rise on the Last Day (lines 44–5; *Par.* XXII, 58–63).

46 *spirits* the tiny corpuscles which link the eye and the brain (*Par.* XXVI, 71).

54 *candle* the eyes of the newcomer. Dante's sight must be made capable of sustaining the superhuman visions of the Empyrean (lines 55–7, 80–81).

79 *prefaces* prefigurations, hidden in symbols, of the reality of Heaven. First, Dante's eyes must acquire more perfect vision by eagerly drinking in the light of the symbolic river; only then can he look upon Heaven as it really is: a great circle in which the flowers come to be seen as the blessed, the sparks as the angels (lines 84–96). Invoking no longer the Muses or Apollo, he appeals to God Himself to give him the poetic powers to describe it (lines 97–9).

100 *a light* the light of God which shines down and, expanding to form an immense circle, is reflected from the upper surface of the Primum Mobile (lines 103–9).

109 *a hill* in springtime, when its natural beauties are reflected in a lake.

114 *all of us* the blessed, all the human beings whose good lives and deaths have made them worthy of Heaven.

117 *leaves* petals. The vast celestial Rose of the blessed represents the fertile results of God's grace given to them; its scent is the praise which they return to Him (lines 125–6).

121 *near and far* distance which in Heaven, unlike in the natural world, makes no difference. Dante can see the entire Rose with perfect clarity.

129 *council* the blessed (*Par.* XXV, 94).

131 *so full* nearly complete. Hence the end of the world may be nigh: 'We are already in the last age of the world, and truly we await the consummation of the movements of the heavens' [*Convivio*].

135 *wedding feast* Heaven (*Par.* XXIV, 2).

136 *Henry* Henry VII, Emperor 1308–13; crowned in Rome 1312; died near Siena, August 1313. When he came to Italy in 1310, Dante welcomed him as a messianic, even Christ-like, figure who would restore the Roman Empire and bring back peace, justice, and law, if only the Guelphs, and especially Florence, would accept his rule [*Epistles*].

143 *Prefect* Pope Clement V, who had approved Henry's expedition to Italy but who then began to reassert papal claims to rights over the Empire (*Par.* XVII, 81–2). The prophecy predicts his death not long afterwards (in 1314) and his eternal damnation for simony (lines 145–7).

148 *Anagnine* Pope Boniface VIII (died 1303), from Anagni (Lazio), who will be Clement's predecessor among the simoniac Popes in Hell (*Inf.* XIX, 79–88).

PARADISO CANTO XXXI

THE EMPYREAN: The Rose.

2 *host* the Church Triumphant, the ideal eternal fulfilment of the earthly Church, Christ's Bride.

4 *other host* the angels.

30 *tempest* human wickedness and sufferings on earth.

32 *a region* northern Europe, where Ursa Major and Boötes are visible throughout the year. The nymph Callisto (Helice) was transformed into the former constellation, her son Arcas into the latter [Ovid] (*Purg.* XXV, 130–32).

34 *works* the magnificent buildings, especially the Lateran Palace which the Emperor Constantine donated to the Popes (lines 35–6). Dante's even greater astonishment expresses the infinitely more wonderful splendour of Heavenly Rome, the true Eternal City (in contrast to corrupt Florence), the goal of his pilgrimage which he will have to describe, when he returns to earth, in his poem (lines 36–45, 102–8).

60 *dressed* in a white robe (*Par.* XXX, 129). The old man, the last of Dante's guides in the afterlife, is St Bernard (1091– 1153), abbot of Clairvaux in Burgundy, a theologian particularly associated with devotion to Mary and the ascent, through contemplation, to mystical union with God (lines 100–102, 109–11; *Par.* XXXII, 2).

75 *that region* the upper air. Despite the even greater distance, Dante can see Beatrice clearly (*Par.* XXX, 121–3).

81 *Hell* Limbo (*Inf.* II, 52–117).

85 *from slavery to freedom* Dante's moral Exodus from the evil of the world to Paradise (*Purg.* II, 46; *Par.* XXV, 55–6).

89 *set loose* by death.

93 *fountain* God, the infinite source of grace and happiness.

102 *one* a pilgrim from a distant part of Europe.

104 *Veronica* the piece of cloth bearing a miraculous image of Christ's features, imprinted on it when the holy woman Veronica wiped His face as He carried His cross to Calvary. Kept in St Peter's in Rome, where it was displayed for public veneration on Fridays and feast-days, it was the principal goal of pilgrims, for to look upon Christ's earthly image was an anticipation of the eternal vision of Him in glory in Heaven [*Vita nuova*].

125 *shaft* the sun, with reference to the myth of Phaethon (*Inf.* XVII, 106–8; *Purg.* IV, 73; XXIX, 118–20; *Par.* XVII, 1–2).

127 *oriflamme* 'golden flame', the red and gold war-standard of the French kings but here, in contrast, signifying heavenly peace; an image for the brighter part of the Rose's upper rim where Mary Queen of Heaven is enthroned (lines 116–17, 133–5).

THE EMPYREAN: The Rose (continued).

4 *wound* the first sin, committed by Eve and healed by Christ, the son of the new Eve, Mary.

8 *Rachel* Jacob's second wife (*Inf.* II, 101–2; IV, 60; *Purg.* XXVII, 104–8; *Par.* XXXI, 66–9.

9 *Sarah* Abraham's wife [Genesis].

Rebecca Isaac's wife [Genesis].

Judith who saved the Israelites from the Assyrians (*Purg.* XII, 58–60).

the one Ruth, the great-grandmother of king David, composer of the penitential psalm, 'Have mercy on me' [Psalms] (line 12).

22 *ripe* full. The line of holy Hebrew women, from Mary downwards, divides the Rose vertically into two halves: one full, because it contains the souls of the Old Testament men and women who believed in Christ, the Messiah, to come (*Inf.* IV, 52–63); the other, which still has some empty places, consists of saved Christians, who believed in Christ after His coming (lines 19–27). After the end of time, the numbers in each half will be equal (lines 38–9).

31 *John* St John the Baptist, who lived in the wilderness and was executed two years before Christ delivered him from Limbo (*Purg.* XXII, 151–4; *Par.* XVIII, 134–5). The line of souls beneath him divides the Rose's two halves on the opposite side (line 34).

35 *Francis* St Francis of Assisi (*Par.* XI, 40–117).

Benedict St Benedict (*Par.* XXII, 28–99).

36 *Augustine* St Augustine (354–430), one of the greatest theologians and Doctors of the Church.

40 *transverse row* the row which divides the Rose horizontally into an upper and a lower half. Below it are the innocent children who died too young to earn salvation of their own free choice and have been saved through the merits of their parents (lines 42–8, 73–84).

56 *law* God's justice, which bestows a precisely matching degree of happiness to each of the children too (lines 57–60).

68 *twins* Jacob and Esau, who clashed in Rebecca's womb; in loving Jacob and rejecting Esau, God revealed the deep mystery of His justice and providential choice [Genesis; Romans].

72 *the color of their hair* the distinct degree of merit which has been earned for each child. Esau was distinguished from Jacob by the colour of his hair [Genesis].

75 *proclivity* the potentiality to receive God's grace.

76 *early centuries* between Adam and Abraham, when the parents' belief in the future Messiah was sufficient to save their innocent children who died. After Abraham, male circumcision was required for the children to receive God's saving grace (lines 78–82); and in the Christian era, baptism is necessary, and unbaptized children who die go to Limbo (*Inf.* IV, 30–36) (lines 82–4).

85 *the face* of Mary, Christ's mother.

89 *intellects* angels.

94 *angelic love* the angel of *Par.* XXIII, 94–110.

96 "*Ave* ..." 'Hail, Mary, full of grace' (*Par.* III, 121–2).

107 *beauty* Mary's light by which St Bernard is illuminated, as Venus is by the sun (line 108).

112 *he* the angel Gabriel. Artists often showed him carrying a palm-branch, the sign of Heaven's victory over sin, when he announced to Mary that she was to be the mother of God the Son made man [Luke].

116 *patricians* saints. On either side of Mary sit the two leaders of, respectively, the Old and New Testament saints (lines 118–20).

122 *father* Adam (*Inf.* IV, 55; *Purg.* XXXII, 37; XXXIII, 61–3; *Par.* XXVI, 82–142).

124 *ancient father* St Peter (*Par.* XXIII, 136–9; XXIV, 34–6).

127 *he* St John the Evangelist, who in his old age wrote the Book of Revelation, recounting his prophetic vision of the

tribulations which the Church would suffer in the Last Days before the end of the world. Christ founded the Church, His Bride, when He died nailed to the cross and was pierced by the centurion's lance (*Par.* XI, 31–2; XXXI, 2–3).

130 *guide* Moses, who led the often complaining and unwilling Israelites through the desert, where they were fed on manna from heaven [Exodus].

133 *Anna* St Anne, the mother of Mary.

136 *greatest father* Adam.

137 *Lucia* who told Beatrice of Dante's danger in the dark wood (*Inf.* II, 97–108; *Purg.* IX, 55–63, 88–91).

140 *a good tailor* someone who makes the best use of what he has, in this case, the time remaining to Dante on his journey.

146 *wings* of the desire to ascend to the vision of God.

148 *that one* Mary who will obtain God's grace for Dante (*Inf.* II, 94–6).

PARADISO CANTO XXXIII

THE EMPYREAN: St Bernard's prayer to Mary; Dante's final visions.

1 *Virgin mother* ... the first of the miraculous paradoxes of Mary, the mother of her own Creator, the supreme example of both humility and perfection (lines 1–2), the human who, in God's plan for the Redemption, was so perfect that her Creator became a human creature in her (lines 3–6). St Bernard's prayer is in two parts: the praise of Mary (lines 1–21) and the request for her help for Dante that he may be given, first, the superhuman power to see God (lines 22–33) and then, when he returns to earth, the grace to remain good for the rest of his life (lines 34–7).

7 *this flower* the Rose of all those saved by God's Love through Christ, Mary's son.

9 *above* in Heaven.

10 *torch* sun.

15 *may long ... no wings* is seeking the impossible. God's grace is given only through Mary's intercession.

55 *greater* beyond words and even recall (*Par.* I, 4–12). Dante is like someone who wakes up from a dream, still feeling its effects but unable to remember it; his sense of supreme joy remains, but the memory itself has been dissolved and dispersed (lines 58–66, 93–6; *Par.* XXIII, 49–51). Dante's description of his final visions opens with his invocation to God Himself to assist his memory and poetic skills (lines 67–75), and is permeated with the language of mystical ecstasy (lines 82–4, 92–3, 97–9, 124–6, 140–45) and with his consciousness of the impossibility of putting into adequate words what is inexpressible, inconceivable, and even unimaginable (lines 89–90, 106–8, 121–3, 142).

66 *Sibyl* the prophetess who wrote down her verses and predictions on leaves; but when the wind blew into her cave, it scattered and separated them so that their meaning could no longer be reconstructed and was lost [Virgil].

78 *astray* unable to look again. The fear gives Dante the power to look even more deeply into the divine Light (lines 79–81).

86 *one single volume* the essential unity of the universe created by the loving God. Within God's Oneness Dante sees those metaphysical principles of existence which, on earth, appear as multiplicity: substances (beings which have independent existence), accidents (qualities which exist only in substances, differentiating them within their species), and the interrelationships between the two (line 88).

92 *knot* the binding together of all being in God's Being.

96 *Neptune* the sea, first crossed by the Argonauts 2,500 years before (*Par.* II, 16–18). Even the innumerable and largely forgotten exploits of sailors over that vast span of time have left a greater trace in human memory than this single moment, immeasurable in human time, has left in Dante's.

100 *Light* God as Supreme Good, the love of Whom is the supreme goal of the human will, infinitely above even the

most beautiful of earthly goods (lines 103–5; *Purg.* XVI, 85–90; XVII, 97, 127–9; XVIII, 19–33).

107 *more weak* less adequate than a baby's.

109 *simple semblance* God's Light, which remains eternally One (lines 111, 113).

115 *three circles* both distinct and coextensive (an impossibility in human terms) (lines 116–17). Dante sees the mystery of the Trinity, the perfect union of three Persons in One God: the Father, the Son (His self-reflection, Whom He knows and Who knows Him), and the Holy Spirit (the Love Who proceeds from both) (lines 118–20, 124–6; *Par.* X, 1–3; XIII, 52–7). This supernatural reality is not only beyond words but far beyond even Dante's remembered idea of it (lines 121–3).

127 *That circle* God the Son Who became man as Christ, the Word made flesh (*Par.* VII, 94–120). Dante's final vision is of the mystery of the Incarnation. The perfect union of the divine and human natures in the one Person of Christ is revealed to him as the human form identical and coextensive with the circle of divine Light – a union which it is impossible for the human mind and merely human powers to visualize, conceive, or understand (lines 130–39).

134 *square the circle* to draw a square which has the same area as a circle; a problem which, since the time of the ancient Greeks, had proved beyond the powers of the human mind to solve.

141 *what it had asked* the understanding of the mystery of Christ.

142 *fantasy* Dante's imagination, both as man and as poet, overwhelmed by the vision and by the utter impossibility of putting it into thoughts, poetic images, or words.

143 *desire and will* both Dante's intellect (his desire to know) and his will (his faculty of love). He receives the understanding of God made man only after his whole soul has transcended its human condition to perfect union with God, the Divine Love Who created and sustains the revolving heavens and, through them, the world (*Par.* I, 1–2).

LIST OF REFERENCES

Note: Biblical quotations are translated from the Latin Vulgate, with references as in the Douai English Bible. The principal works of Latin poets are abbreviated as follows: *Aen.* (Virgil, *Aeneid*), *Metam.* (Ovid, *Metamorphoses*), *Phars.* (Lucan, *Pharsalia* [*De bello civili*]), *Theb.* and *Achill.* (Statius, *Thebaid* and *Achilleid*); references are as in F. A. Hirtzel's edition of Virgil's works and in the Loeb Classics editions of the other authors. Dante's works are abbreviated as follows: *VN* (*Vita nuova*), *Conv.* (*Convivio*), *DVE* (*De vulgari eloquentia*), *Mon.* (*Monarchia*), *Ep.* (*Epistles*), *Ecl.* (*Eclogues*).

INFERNO

I, 1 Ps. 89: 10; Isa. 38: 10; **32** Jer. 5: 6; **49** 1 Tim. 6: 10; **71** Luke 2: 1; *Conv.* IV. v. 8; *Mon.* I. xvi. 1–2; II. x. 6–8; **75** *Aen.* III, 2–3.

II, 15 *Aen.* VI, 102–899; **24** Matt. 16: 18; **28** Acts 9: 15; 2 Cor. 12: 2–4; **98** *Conv.* III. ix. 15–16; **102** Gen. 29: 16 ff.

III, 35 Rev. 3: 15–16; *Aen.* VI, 298–304, 305–12, 557–8; **59–60** Gen. 25: 29–34; Matt. 27: 24; **77** *Aen.* VI, 295; **83** *Aen.* VI, 298–301; **115** Gen. 1: 26–8; 2: 20–24.

IV, 55 Gen. 1: 26 ff.; **56** Gen. 4: 2–8; 6: 11 ff.; **57** Exod. 13: 18 ff.; **58** Gen. 12: 1 ff.; **59** Gen. 25: 19 ff.; 29: 31–5; 30: 1–24; 35: 16–18; **60** Gen. 29: 16–30; **111** *Aen.* VI, 637–41, 656–9, 673–5; **126** *Mon.* II. iii. 16–17; **129** *Conv.* IV. xi. 14; **141** *Eclogue* IV, 55–7.

V, 4 *Aen.* VI, 432–3; **20** *Aen.* VI, 126–9; Matt. 7: 13–14; **58** *Historarum libri VII*, I. iv.; **61** *Aen.* IV, 552, 642–705; **100** *VN* XX; **107** Gen. 4: 1–16; **123** *De consolatione philosophiae*, II. iv (lines 4–6).

VI, 15 *Aen.* VI, 417–23; **73** Gen. 18: 23 ff.

VII, 22 *Aen.* III, 420–23; *Metam.* VII, 62–4; *Phars.* IV, 459–61; **108** *Aen.* VI, 134, 323, 369.

VIII, 19 *Aen.* VI, 618–20; **30** *Aen.* VI, 412–14; **45** Luke 11: 27.

IX, 23 *Phars.* VI, 507–830; *Aen.* VI, 564–5; **38** *Aen.* VI, 554–5;

Theb. I, 103–16;   **52** *Phars.* IX, 624–99; *Metam.* IV, 614–20; **54** *Aen.* VI, 392–7; *Theb.* VIII, 52–6;   **98** *Aen.* VI, 395–6.

X, 11 Joel 3: 2;   **14** *Conv.* II. viii. 8–9.

XI, 8 *Decretum*, I. xix. 9; *Liber pontificalis*, LII;   **23** *Nicomachean Ethics*, V. ii. 13; *De officiis*, I, xiii (41);   **50** Gen. 19: 4–5; *Politics*, I. 10. 5;   **56** *Conv.* III. xi. 7; *Politics*, I. 2. 9;   **80** *Nicomachean Ethics*, VII. i. 1;   **103** *Physics*, II. ii (194a–b); viii (199a);   **107** Gen. 3: 17–19.

XII, 12 *Aen.* VI, 24–6; *Metam.* VIII, 131–7, 152–82;   **38** Matt. 27: 51;   **42** *Metaphysics*, I. iv. 3; II. i. 1; III. i. 13; iv. 15, 26; XII. vi. 9; x. 7;   **67** *Metam.* IX, 101–272;   **72** *Theb.* II, 563–4;   **107** *Phars.* X, 20–46; *Historiarum libri VII*, III. vii; xviii; xx;   **135** *Aen.* II, 469–558; *Phars.* VI, 419–22.

XIII, 10 *Aen.* III, 209–69;   **48** *Aen.* III, 22–47;   **58** Isa. 22: 22.

XIV, 14 *Phars.* IX, 371–949;   **29** Gen. 19: 24–5;   **46** *Theb.* X, 897–939; XI, 1–17;   **96** *Aen.* III, 104–5; VIII, 314–27;   **98** *Fasti*, IV, 197–214;   **103** Dan. 2: 31–45; *Metam.* I, 89–150;   **116** *Aen.* VI, 134, 295, 323, 369, 550–51;   **119** *Aen.* VI, 297, 323;   **131** *Aen.* VI, 703–51.

XV, 66 Matt. 7: 16–20;   **122–3** 1 Cor. 9: 24; *Conv.* IV. xxii. 6.

XVI, 128 *Ep.* XIII, 10.

XVII, 1 *Aen.* VI, 289; VIII, 201–4;   **18** *Metam.* VI, 5–145; **107** *Metam.* I, 750–79; II, 1–328;   **109** *Metam.* VIII, 183–235.

XVIII, 86 *Metam.* VII, 1–158, 396–7; *Heroides*, VI, XII; *Theb.* V, 28–39, 236–325, 403–85;   **133** *De amicitia*, xxvi (98).

XIX, 1 Acts 8: 9–24;   **50** Acts 2: 1–4;   **85** 2 Macc. 4: 7–26; **92** Matt. 16: 19;   **95** Acts 1: 24–6;   **106** Rev. 17: 1–3; **115** *Mon.* III. x. 1–17.

XX, 33 *Theb.* VII, 690–823; VIII, 1–20, 84–9;   **40** *Metam.* III, 322–31;   **46** *Phars.* I, 584–638;   **55** *Theb.* IV, 463–8;   **59** *Theb.* XI, 648–756;   **98** *Aen.* X, 198–201;   **106** *Aen.* II, 114–19; **118** *Conv.* IV. xvi. 6;   **124** Gen. 4: 11–16.

XXIII, 58 *De officiis*, I. xiii (41); *Summa theologica*, IIa–IIae, Q. 111; Matt. 23: 27–8;   **111** John 11: 49–52; 18: 14.

XXIV, 85 *Phars.* IX, 700–726;   **108** *Metam.* XV, 392–400.

XXV, 25 *Aen.* VIII, 193–305; *Ab urbe condita*, I. vii. 3–7;   **94** *Phars.* IX, 762–804;   **97** *Metam.* IV, 563–603; V, 572–641.

XXVI, 34 2 [4] Kgs. 2: 11–12, 23–4;   **52** *Theb.* XII, 429–32; **56** *Aen.* II, 6–8, 44, 90, 97–9, 122–9, 163–8; *Achill.* I, 538–960;

91 *Metam.* XIV, 241–308; *Aen.* VII, 1–4;   **125** *Aen.* VI, 14–19.

XXVII, 17 Jas. 3: 6;   **66** *Conv.* IV. xxviii. 8;   **101** *Mon.* III. viii. 7.

XXVIII, 8 *Ab urbe condita*, XXIII. xii. 1;   **95** *Phars.* I, 261–95; **134** *DVE* II. ii. 9; 2 Sam. [Kgs.] 15: 31; 16: 21–3; 17: 1–23; **142** *Nicomachean Ethics*, V. v. 1–6; Exod. 21: 24–5.

XXIX, 59 *Metam.* VII, 523–657.

XXX, 4 *Metam.* IV, 512–30;   **16** *Metam.* XIII, 404–7, 488–575; **38** *Metam.* X, 298–502;   **97** Gen. 39: 7–20;   **98** *Aen.* II, 57–198.

XXXI, 1 *Metam.* XIII, 171–2; *Remedia Amoris*, 47–8;   **31** Gen. 6: 4; *Aen.* VI, 580–84; *Metam.* I, 151–62; X, 150–51;   **67** Gen. 10: 8–9; 11: 1–9; *DVE* I. vii. 4;   **99** *Theb.* II, 595–601; *Aen.* X, 565–8;   **100** *Phars.* IV, 593–653; *Metam.* IX, 183–4;   **123** *Aen.* VI, 297, 323;   **124** *Aen.* VI, 595–600; IX, 715–16; *Metam.* III, 303; V, 319–26; *Phars.* IV, 595–6.

XXXII, 10 *Ars poetica*, 394–6; *Theb.* X, 873–7;   **59** Gen. 4: 8; **130** *Theb.* VIII, 733–66.

XXXIII, 62 Matt. 27: 46;   **80** *DVE* I. viii. 6;   **124** 1 Macc. 16: 11–17; Ps. 54: 16.

XXXIV, 62 Matt. 26: 14–16, 21–5, 46–50; 27: 3–10;   **112** Ezek. 5: 5; **122** *Questio de aqua et terra*, XX–XXI;   **128** Matt. 12: 24, 27.

PURGATORIO

I, 4 Gen. 2: 8 to 3: 24;   **7** *Metam.* V, 293–340, 662–78;   **31** Exod. 34: 29–30; *Phars.* II, 372–6, 380–83, 389–90; IX, 554–7; *Aen.* VIII, 670; *Conv.* IV. v. 16; vi. 10; xxvii. 3; xxviii. 15; *Mon.* II. v. 15; **79** *Conv.* IV. xxviii. 13–19;   **134** *Aen.* VI, 143–4.

II, 46 *Conv.* II. i. 2–7;   *Ep.* XIII, 7;   **79** *Aen.* VI, 700–701; **112** *Conv.* III.

IV, 5 *Conv.* III. ii. 11–14;   **22** Matt. 7: 13–14.

V, 24 Ps. 50.

VI, 29 *Aen.* VI, 376;   **76** *Conv.* IV. iv–v; *Mon.* III;   **88** *Conv.* IV. ix. 8–10;   **92** Matt. 22: 21;   **139** *Institutes*, I. ii. 10.

VIII, 98 Gen. 3: 1–5.

IX, 1 *Metam.* IX, 421–2; *Heroides*, XVIII, 111–12;   **15** *Metam.* VI, 424–674;   **19** Ps. 102: 5; *Metam.* X, 155–61;   **34** *Achill.* I, 247–50;   **82** Gen. 3: 24;   **104** Matt. 16: 18;   **117** Matt. 16: 19; **135** *Phars.* III, 112–68.

PARADISO

VIII, 7 *Aen.* I, 657–722; **37–8** *VN* XXXV–XXXVIII; *Conv.*
II. ii. 1–5; **67** *Metam.* V, 346–58; XIV, 1; **98** *Mon.* I. x. 1;
116 *Conv.* IV. iv. 1–4; *Mon.* I. iii. 2–4; v. 4–10; **120** *Politics*, I. 2.
8–16; VII. 8. 8–9; 9. 1–10; *Conv.* IV. iv. 5–6; **125** Gen. 14: 18;
130 Gen. 25: 22–5.

IX, 71 *Conv.* III. viii. 11; **77** Isa. 6: 2; **100** *Heroides*, II;
101 *Metam.* IX, 136–46; *Heroides*, IX; **116** Josh. 2: 1–21; 6:
22–5; Matt. 1: 5; Heb. 11: 31; Jas. 2: 25; **134** *Ep.* XI, 7;
137 Luke 1: 26.

X, 107 Luke 21: 2–4; **109** 1 [3] Kgs. 11: 1–10; **115** Acts 17: 34;
125 *Conv.* II. xii. 2.

XI, 69 *Phars.* V, 515–31; *Conv.* IV. xiii. 12.

XII, 12 *Aen.* IV, 693–702; V, 605–10, 657–8; **14** *Metam.* III,
356–401; **17** Gen. 9: 12–17; **72** Matt. 20: 1–16; **75** Matt. 5:
3; 19: 21; **118** Matt. 13: 24–30; **136** 2 Sam. [Kgs.] 12: 1 ff.;
1 [3] Kgs. 1: 10 ff.

XIII, 15 *Metam.* VIII, 176–82; **39** Gen. 2: 21 to 3: 6; **93** 1 [3]
Kgs. 3: 5–12; **100** *Summa theologica*, I, Q. 2, a. 3, resp.;
124 *Mon.* III. iv. 4.

XIV, 35 Luke 1: 26–38; **98** *Conv.* II, xiv. 5–8; **106** Matt. 16: 24.

XV, 25 *Aen.* VI, 684–91; **28** *Aen.* VI, 835.

XVI, 1 *Conv.* IV. xxix. 8–11; **34** Luke 1: 28.

XVII, 1 *Metam.* I, 748–72; II, 1–328; **46** *Metam.* XV, 492–505;
62 *Ep.* V–VI; **76** *Ep.* XIII, 1–3.

XVIII, 40 1 Macc. 3: 1 to 9: 22; **91–3** Wisd. 1: 1; **119** Matt. 21:
12–13; **134** Matt. 3: 1–3; 14: 1–12.

XIX, 44 John 1: 1–3; **106** Matt. 7: 21–3; 12: 41; **113** Rev. 20: 12.

XX, 49 2 [4] Kgs. 20: 1–7; Isa. 38: 1–9; **69** *Aen.* II, 426–8;
94 Matt. 11: 12; **106** *Jacobi a Voragine Legenda aurea* (ed.
T. Grässe), XLVI. 10.

XXI, 6 *Metam.* III, 287–309; *Theb.* X, 903.

XXII, 70 Gen. 28: 12–15; **76** Matt. 21: 13; **94** Josh. 3: 15–17;
Exod. 14: 21–2; **143** *Metam.* IV, 192, 241; **144** *Aen.* VIII,
138–9.

XXIII, 31 1 Cor. 1: 24; **73** John 1: 14.

XXIV, 2 Rev. 19: 9; **35** Matt. 16: 19; 14: 28–9; **61** Heb. 11: 1;
126 John 20: 3–8.

XXV, 7 *Ecl.* I, 42–4; **30** Jas. 1: 3–5, 12, 17; **73** Ps. 9: 11; **92** Isa.
61: 7; **94** Rev. 7: 9; **112** John 13: 23; 19: 26–7.

ALLEN MANDELBAUM is the author of five verse volumes, of which the principal are *The Savantasse of Montparnasse* and *Chelmaxioms: The Maxims, Axioms, Maxioms of Chelm*. In addition to the *Divine Comedy* of Dante, his verse translations/editions include the *Odyssey of Homer*, the *Aeneid of Virgil*, and the *Metamorphoses of Ovid*, and volumes of Giuseppe Ungaretti, Salvatore Quasimodo, and David Maria Turoldo. He is the recipient of a National Book Award, the Order of Merit from the Republic of Italy, the Mondello Foundation Prize, the Leonardo Prize, and the Biella Prize. Both Purdue University and the University of Turin have conferred on him an honorary Doctor of Letters. He is the co-General Editor of the three-volume *California Lectura Dantis* of the U. of California Press. He is now the W. R. Kenan, Jr., Professor of Humanities at Wake Forest University.

PETER ARMOUR is Professor of Italian at Royal Holloway College, University of London. His books include *The Door of Purgatory* and *Dante's Griffin and the History of the World*.

EUGENIO MONTALE (1896–1981), one of the greatest Italian poets, was also a prolific critic and translator who introduced Italian audiences to the work of Eliot, Yeats, Hardy, Pound and Hopkins. His own work has been translated by, amongst others, Allen Mandelbaum.

This book is set in GARAMOND, the first typeface in
the ambitious programme of matrix production
undertaken by the Monotype Corporation
under the guidance of Stanley Morrison
in 1922. Although named after the
great French royal typographer,
Claude Garamond (1499–
1561), it owes much to
Jean Jannon of Sedan
(1580–1658).